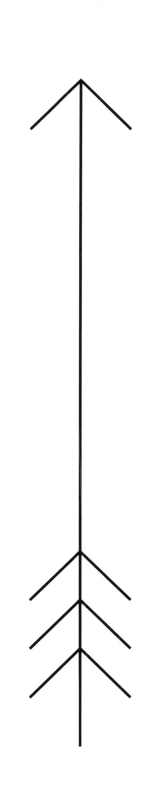

Magnus Nilsson

THE NORDIC COOK BOOK

Φ

Greenland

Iceland

Faroe Islands

North Atlantic Ocean

North

Greenland Sea

Barents Sea

Norwegian Sea

Sápmi region

Finland

Norway

Sweden

Denmark

INTRODUCTION

To write a book like this is not only impossible, it doesn't make sense, I heard myself saying to the publisher who pitched me the idea. I don't consider myself to be Nordic; I am, in fact, Swedish or possibly Jämtlandian. I think most other people living in the Nordic region feel the same. We identify ourselves with the country we are from, not with the region that place happens to be considered part of. We don't like them becoming all lumped up into one.

I might have said at some point something along the lines of: to write a book on Nordic home cooking in general is about as stupid as to write one on European cooking, lumping Estonia, France and Portugal together into one work that will never be deep enough to explain anything. Or to make one on American cooking, taking in everything between Canada and Chile, trying to describe it in one book.

I agonized for weeks over the proposal, but at the same time I realized that the publisher had already decided there was going to be a Nordic cookbook. I could, in one way, see myself doing a book of this kind, but perhaps rather about Sweden my home country, and not now, but in the future when I had more time on my hands, not while I was busy running the restaurant. However, if I were to say no, some-one else would write the book that, up until the publication of what you are now holding in your hands, hadn't existed. Whatever I would later write, it would simply not be the first one, the leader on a subject that should have been covered a long time ago. I ruminated on the structure of the possible book, why it should exist, how to make it credible. After a couple of months of self-convincing and reasoning, I decid-ed that the purpose of the book, in fact, had to be the same as the reason I was initially so put off by the idea of it.

I decided to write the book and to make its mission to explain how similar our Nordic cultures really are, but also how they differ, how everything is tied together by our mutual history and our present culture and how it can all be tracked through the food we eat. Food is an undeniable and unavoidable marker of culture and society. People have to eat, and therefore they also have to relate to food as a subject, regardless of whether they want to or not.

After deciding to make the book, the first thing I did was to buy every single other book I could find at Amazon used books on the subject of cooking, baking and entertaining in the Nordic region. I think there were about 400 of them when I added the newly acquired ones to what I already had. The oldest one in my collection is from 1755 and claims to be a 'helping hand for young women in housekeeping', the newest one was something on Scandinavian baking released just days earlier.

After spending quite a bit of time browsing through these books, skimming and looking at what was there, I realized that most of what has been published in English on Nordic and Scandinavian home cooking really sucks. Most of the time the food in them is a vague reflection of something that is a bit restauranty and central European in style, but with lingonberries added to it. I am perhaps being a bit hyperbolic but it was actually almost that bad. What these books also have in common, except for the lingonberries, is that, even though some of them surely contain correct and representative recipes, almost none of them supply context. They don't aim to explain the why and how, or even the when of things.

Published in different Nordic languages, on the other hand, are several interesting and very comprehensive books on the cooking of the different countries seen from within, written by and for people coming from the different countries. These national bibles of cooking, which are the sort of books grandmothers have a worn-down, sauce-stained copy of somewhere, obviously contain a vast number of recipes. Most of those recipes are very good and functional, however they also supply little or no context. In books like these, almost always, regardless of their qualities as cookbooks, a lot of background information is assumed. For them to make sense, you really need the kind of knowledge that you would absorb from your family and environment growing up, probably without thinking much of it.

Excluding the national bibles, out of the 400 or so books, I would say that about five had more to bring to the reader than some hopefully functional and reasonably Nordic-style recipes. Of those five, I found one in particular that I actually felt had cracked the code on telling the story of culture through food. Not exactly hot off the press, the 1968 Time-Life publication, *Cooking of Scandinavia*, is a masterpiece. It is, as far as I know, the only book printed in English about food from my home region in which someone went there, spent a lot of time, lived on-site with the perspective of an outsider, documented things and tried to tell the story to those who didn't already know it. Regardless of whether they lived in another part of the world or within the Nordic region itself that book, more than forty years later, is still a good, accurate and very amusing read.

After having assessed what was there, I started to create a plan on how to actually put *The Nordic Cookbook* together. My vision was that it was going to contain some historical references and iconic recipes but more importantly would show and explain what people eat today and why. For me, this book is about documenting and telling you how it really is, rather than trying to curate something into what I dream an ideal, nostalgic world being.

To start accumulating material we constructed a web-based poll, in which people were asked to answer a series of questions and to submit recipes that they wanted to share. The result was some very interesting dishes previously unknown to me, but mostly a vast number of instructions on how to cook generic classics like Pickled Herring (page 204). As I already had a really good recipe for Pickled Herring, that wasn't very helpful. What was, though, was that the poll told me what people thought was important. In a way it told me how they looked upon their own food culture from within. It also told me that the different countries and regions are more alike than we think. Dishes that are considered unique national treasures by one are also important in other countries, sometimes under different names or slightly different in execution but still bearing a clear kinship to one another, like the people cooking and eating them also do.

I had by now arrived at the point where I decided that the book was going to focus as much as possible on those things that we share across the different Nordic cultures. The dishes that exist in more than one country, the dishes that can be tracked through history, the story of their development to find their place in the world and the people cooking and eating them.

I found a set of local experts in each part of the Nordic region, people to act as guides, making sure that what I reported was representative and correct. I started travelling extensively, meeting people, interviewing, eating with them in their homes, photographing and photocopying recipes, sniffing around the gastro-cultural underbrush, trying to cover as much as I possibly could of a region encompassing 3,425,804 square kilometres (1,322,710 square miles). I went cooking and discovering regionally important products and techniques, some known to me and others not, but more importantly, I got to know hundreds of new people who all helped out shaping the content of this book.

After about two years of doing research and enjoying it immensely, I got a call from the publisher, who by now had begun wondering what was really happening with this book we where supposed to be doing, and why no material was coming in. I hadn't written more than a handful of recipes and the book was due to be delivered very soon. It wasn't that I hadn't been working, it was just so much to record and so much fun doing it. I had collected a vast amount of material and knew that it was going to be great at some point. I think the publisher was at times a bit less convinced.

I was told that it was now time to start delivering, that I was otherwise going to continue doing research forever, that it would never end. She was right, the total number of notes, newspaper cut-outs, search engine printouts, audio recordings, transcribed interviews, recipes from old and new books, scribbles on napkins, email conversations and data from the polls when I put an end to the research came up to just over 11,000 articles and I still felt like I was just at the beginning. On top of that came roughly 8,000 photographs taken during the various research trips. Much of this material was repetitive; hundreds of recipes were duplicates, but each was there because I had as some point deemed it important enough to keep. Starting to sift through information, prioritizing, converting recipes to English, cooking to test them and to adapt quantities at the same time as we were photographing dishes in the kitchen of my house, I began to realize just how much work that still remained. Stunned by the enormity of what was left to do, it also dawned on me how much of all the fantasticness I simply wouldn't be able to fit into the book. You might think that this is a big, fat book you are holding – I thought the same beforehand and, looking back, had I included every unique recipe, this would have become a five-volume set of big, fat books due to be released in 2022.

When I begun to get a sizable number of recipes done, I started sending them out to the local experts – some were wrong, others where ok and quite a bit was still missing. We debated and people fought bravely for things they thought should be included; sometimes they won and other times they didn't and something had to be dropped for the sake of something more important.

When most of the material was in place, I then sent it over to Richard, who has written the second introduction to *The Nordic Cookbook* (page 21). He is one of the most knowledgeable people I know on the subject of what we eat, how we do so, where and why. His task was to check the material for misinterpretations of historical events, all-round fact-checking and helping out to balance the content itself.

I have, through the journey of putting it together, realized that the book you have just purchased can never be complete, and that it is a book that a lot of people within the Nordics will consider to be flawed for that. They will feel wronged and misrepresented, simply because that very recipe or piece of information with which they identify themselves, the one that they feel is absolutely key for telling the story of their specific food culture, is not in there.

In the grand scheme of things, the important thing with this book is, in fact, not for it to be complete, as it could never be so. There is always going to be something new to learn and describe out there, and that's a good thing. I hope that this book is going to tell you something about a food culture that you wanted to know more about, that it is going to give you practical guidance and pleasure in cooking, and that you can feel who wrote it. This book is not about me and my work as a chef; I merely documented what was there already, what was created by others. However, *The Nordic Cookbook* tells the story of a big and diverse universe of food filtered through my way of looking at things and my way of telling you about them.

Going from absolutely not wanting to write it to absolutely not wanting to stop writing it, getting to produce this book has been a tremendous privilege, and a process from which I have learned so much about a food culture I thought I knew.

I really do hope that it will show how much writing it has meant to me.

Credits

This book was written by me, Magnus Nilsson, but the process of putting it together has involved many others.

The documentary and landscape images were photographed by me during the research trips and everyday life in the Nordic region, but the photos of the finished dishes, which were all shot in the kitchen of my home while we were testing recipes, were photographed by Erik Olsson.

My aunt, Birgitta Nilsson helped me with a lot of the data processing and research back home in Sweden, not to mention formatting recipes into something reasonably consistent in terms of content.

Kenneth Nars proved that he is one of the most knowledgeable people around when it comes to the cooking of Finland and Åland. So too has Andreas Viestad when it comes to Norway.

Without the help of Ann-Sofie Hardenberg, I wouldn't have had the chance to write about the food culture of Greenland, and without Claus Højby Hansen and Gudrun Einarsdottir, Denmark and Iceland would have been very difficult too.

To understand the intricacies of Faroese food, Eva and Jógvan Jón ur Stóra Dimún have been indispensable, and to explain the traditions of Sami cooking, so has Elaine Asp.

I would have loved to write down all the names here and, by doing so, thank all those who submitted recipes to the web based poll and all of you who put up with me interviewing, photographing and just generally bothering you with hundreds of questions about what you eat and what you think about it. However there were simply too many of you guys, well over 2000 actually, so that proved difficult … but thank you so much, without your input this book would never have become the record of Nordic food culture – both historical and contemporary – which it now is.

Last, but certainly not least, I would like to thank Richard Tellström, Food historian and Associate Professor of Ethnology at Örebro University, who has helped out with the correctness of events described in the book and who has very generously shared his vast knowledge on the meal in the Nordic region.

Thank you all and thank you whoever you are now holding this book, I really do hope that you will appreciate reading it.

Magnus Nilsson
Fäviken, Spring 2015

A BRIEF HISTORY OF NORDIC CUISINE

Previous page: Faroe Islands, Fjord, April 2013.

A blend of preserved and fresh flavours

The fastest way to understand the Nordic region's food culture is to eat an open sandwich topped with butter and hard cheese. Such a sandwich is usually made from fresh ingredients that have been preserved for long-term storage, such as bread, leavened, seasoned butter and dry, hard cheese that has ideally been matured for one or two years. Many northerners eat this sandwich every day; its origins can be traced back for more than a millennium and it exists in hundreds of variants. An open cheese sandwich speaks of the most fundamental aspects that make up a food culture in the Nordic region, but also demonstrates that a 'taste chord' (the harmony that comes from several flavours) can live a very long time if it's important to people and provides meaning.

The Nordic region is a large geographical area that shares a common cultural and political history, and thus it also has a partially shared food culture. The outer frame is based on a common religious belief system. These were heathen beliefs during the Viking Age, which then became a mutual Christian faith. The common religious faith also created partly shared language that even today allows northerners, when they meet, to decide whether to speak 'Scandinavian', which means speaking their own native language and simply using words they know to be understood in other Nordic countries. 'Scandinavian', however, differs from the Finnish language family so it's not as easy to speak a Scandinavian that the Finns understand. Sometimes Swedish, a minority language in Finland, is used instead. The common religious belief has also formed the basis for a common understanding of how the meals are created and also how they should be eaten in family and other gatherings. Political partnerships that created common kingdoms back in history, together with the continuous seizure of each other's lands, created a cultural affinity. But when the two remaining major powers in the Nordic area in the late 1600s, Denmark and Sweden, divided the Nordic area between them, the Scandinavian mountain range created two independent halves of a common idea and shared history which was to influence the following centuries. One can therefore describe the Nordic food culture as having west Nordic and east Nordic counterparts.

In the west Nordic part, Denmark and Danish culture were the norm. In the eastern Nordic part, Sweden and Finland shared a cultural community. The kingdom of Denmark had also comprised Norway (which left the Danish Kingdom in 1814 to be a part of Sweden until 1905 when it became an independent kingdom) and Iceland (which became a republic independent from Denmark in 1944). Even today, the Faroe Islands and Greenland are autonomous areas within the Danish Kingdom, which thus is a major north European cultural community, at least in terms of area.

The eastern part of the Nordic countries has been characterized by Sweden and the Swedish political culture. Finland was an integral part of the kingdom of Sweden–Finland from the Middle Ages to the 1800s. Sweden lost Finland to the Russians in 1809 and it ended up under Russian rule until it became an independent republic in 1917. Large parts of the Baltic region were also under Swedish rule further back in time. Both the western and eastern Nordic food cultures are characterized by an exchange of ideas throughout the history of the Holy Roman Empire but were also influenced by France, the Netherlands and the UK. Since the early 1800s, the US has been a significant culinary cultural inspiration from which the region retrieves both dishes and seasonings, but often these influences are interpreted in entirely new ways. In this cookbook are many examples of recipes the origins of which follow the Scandinavian mountain range; there are pure Danish–Norwegian dishes, such as the Danish Sugar-browned Potatoes on page 120, and Swedish–Finnish variants, such as the Browned Swede on page 113. One can sometimes determine how old a dish is in the Nordic countries by looking not only at how it is cooked, but also by the countries in which it occurs. Recipes that are found throughout the Nordic countries are usually from after the mid-1800s when industrialization introduced both new ingredients and new ways to prepare food. At this time a debate started over the idea that nations had a national food culture, while nationalism and other protective policy-making made countries favour domestic production at all costs. If, however, a recipe can only be found in two Nordic countries, it is generally older. There are also examples of unique old ways of cooking, such as salting mushrooms, found only in eastern Finland (see page 126), as until the mid-1900s the peasant population of other Nordic countries considered mushrooms inedible.

In a region that allows policy and nation building to dictate food culture, minorities are necessarily marginalised and their influence on the food culture overlooked, despite the fact that a food culture is inevitably made up of the food of people in power and those not in power. The reason the food culture is described as it is in the Nordic region is mainly because the national position of minority cuisines have not yet been researched, either in their own right or in relation to the major food cultures. Minorities vary in size; in Sweden there is a large Finnish minority made up of more than half a million people. The Sami minority is Scandinavia's oldest resident population and consists of more than 100,000 people, while the Roma people in the Nordic countries number more than 100,000. In addition to these groups, there are other ethnic and religious minority groups whose food culture constitutes an indispensable part of Nordic culture but because it is little researched, both in itself and in relation to the mainstream Nordic culinary culture, it is not yet possible to give a complete picture of the food culture that exists among the people in the Nordic countries.

The Nordic region's cuisine can also be divided according to geography and topography. It covers the lowlands of southern Denmark to the northern mountains in Norway and Sweden where cultivation and hunting take place up to 1,000–1,500 metres (3,230–4,920 feet) high. These contrasting conditions produce very different foodstuffs and after the berries have been picked and the animals hunted, they become a part of either the western or eastern Nordic cuisines. But perhaps more important than the land and the mountains are the beaches and waters, since the Nordic region's cuisine is largely a sea-and-lake-cuisine, although the ingredients found in the salty water of the areas bordering the Atlantic differ a lot from those found in the Baltic brackish water and in the lakes. The inland lake systems are also widespread, particularly in eastern Nordic countries; Sweden has over 80,000 large lakes and Finland more than 50,000. This system of lakes has allowed for extensive seasonal sea and river fishing. In winter the frozen lakes were also important as rapid transport routes which meant that food cultures from different regions travelled and mixed.

The region's northern location created a supply-management culture for the strictly seasonal food. To live in this region one had to produce a surplus from the 160 days suitable for cultivation (from May to September) and then supplement what was grown by hunting animals and birds, and the all-important fishing. A vital skill to survive in the area was to understand and take advantage of fish and animal seasonal migrations such as salmon, whitefish, eel, and different kinds of birds, whales, reindeer and deer. Food must be collected or grown during a few short months and then eked out until the next annual harvest or catch. Both the cuisine and recipe creation were characterized by a kind of rationing mentality, with cautious and controlled eating on a daily basis, with extravagant partying at the annual celebration occasions. The wild fish were more accessible to all, but the forests' wildlife was pretty strictly controlled. Right up to the end of the 1700s animals such as elk, deer and reindeer were reserved for the nobility and hunting rights belonged to royalty. In Sweden, these rights were released to those who were landowners. Thus wild game gradually became a more regular feature on the common man's table but, still today, venison and game have a higher social status than domesticated animals and are chosen often for annual celebrations and parties, at Christmas in particular. Hunting was pursued almost throughout the year, in autumn (fall) the hunting of moose and geese, in winter seals and in spring hunting migratory birds and collecting wild birds' eggs. In west Nordic countries it is still more common to eat wild waterfowl of various kinds, such as puffin and grouse. In the north east, wild birds such as ducks and eiders are hunted. Seal hunting occurs over almost the whole of the Nordic area, and was historically important, not only for meat but for the fat from the seals which was used to insulate houses and make them more water-resistant.

The key to creating an indigenous food culture that allowed survival year-round in the Nordic countries was not primarily to do with the selection of animals and edible plants.

Instead, the crucial knowledge of food culture and survival was governed by technical building skills – the ability to build secure storage buildings and houses, that were dry and insulated against the weather, with materials such as tar. Had the northerners not mastered these construction techniques, they would probably have entered the Nordic region during the summer for occasional hunting and fishing, and had to leave the area quickly when the snow and ice came in October. The basic idea of food culture was characterized by taking advantage of seasonal surpluses but not simply 'eating in season' because that would not maximise the potential use of supplies, which could instead be made to last for a long time. The basic raw material of Nordic cuisine in both historic and prehistoric times was a preserved and stored commodity that was dried (such as reindeer meat, pork, cod, and also cereals), smoked (such as haddock, moose and sausage), cured (all kinds meat and fish and, in recent times, also vegetables) or fermented in different ways (for example, meat, cheese, sour milk, sausage, beer, fish and vegetables). Sometimes several different preserving techniques are used, such as when when salting and fermentation are combined (for example, in Norwegian Fermented Trout or Char, page 175, and Sour Herring, page 198) or when meat is salted, smoked and dried, and then cooked further when it comes to be eaten. A characteristic of the Nordic 'taste chord' is to combine the flavour that comes out of preserving the raw ingredients and then adding additional seasonings and spices.

But, as in many parts of the world, the flavours in the Nordic food culture changed with industrialization and the development of electricity in the late 1800s, and then adapted further when petrol engines allowed fast food shipments during the early 1900s. The changes in what one might call a 'taste chord' were significant and it went from being influenced by preserved flavours to a mix of both fresh flavours and commercial ingredients, which are also often preserved in some way. The 'taste chord' of the traditional food culture was characterized by a lot of umami flavours, salt, acid and, to some extent, a little bitterness. This traditional heritage of preserved ingredients remains today in both festive and everyday food. During the 1800s sweetness became an important flavour because of the industrial production of sugar beet. Rapid chilled-food transportation and new freezing technology changed the raw material base in the food culture, and from the early 1900s the foundation of Nordic food culture was replaced by fresh foodstuffs that had to be consumed rather quickly. The same technology that allowed people to eat fresh food year round now also provided households with spices from around the world. Historically, the use of spices was limited in the Nordic region where preserved food tasted both very distinctive and strong. Imported spices had a highly coveted status, and from the 1500s there were regular imports of dried spices from southern Europe, Africa and Southeast Asia. The spices included allspice, cloves, both white and black pepper, cardamom and cinnamon. The food was quite highly spiced and this traditional aromatic spicy 'taste chord' is very much alive today in everyday food, from breakfast to dinner, in both hot and cold food, and especially in festive food. It stands up well against contemporary spice preferences, such as the flavours of chilli, basil and chocolate. Bread is also often highly spiced in the Nordic region, where cumin, fennel, anise and orange peel have been extensively used as bread spices since as far back as the 1600s. Since the 1800s syrup and malt have been widely used as spices for bread, particularly in celebration and festive loaves.

The Nordic food culture of the Scandinavian mainland is a sort of bread cuisine. Before the arrival of potatoes in the early 1800s, most people ate ½–1 kg (1–2 lb) of bread a day and it was the staple of their diet. In Iceland, the Faroe Islands and Greenland where grain was imported, bread was reserved for festive occasions and the everyday food was fish or mutton.

Breads are available in many different varieties and, even today, there is an historic bread map, with discernable differences in bread types, related to whether grain was added to flour (an older cereal type which existed in all Nordic countries) or rye (more common from the Middle Ages). But the most common practice was to mix cereal varieties for daily bread, porridge or gruel so it is only in the 1900s that refined flours started to occur. The differences in the breads were also related to how finely the flour was sifted; the higher the economic and social class, the finer the sieve. Both wheat and wheat flour were high-status items throughout history and became common for all only in the late 1800s.

The southern Nordic areas are still today characterized by soft rye bread that is baked frequently and eaten quite fresh. Examples of such bread are rye bread (such as the Scanian Rye Bread on page 502) or a modern, sweet flavour, such as Golden Syrup Loaf (page 496), baked from rye and wheat flour, or in its festive alternative Wort Loaf (page 498) present in both Sweden and Finland (baked from rye flour). The mid-Nordic region is characterized by a supply of dried rye bread that has been stored for the coming winter, such as Rye Crispbread in Sweden (page 516) or Finnish Rye Bread (page 504) and these are bread types that are still very popular. North and west Nordic countries still eat very thin dried bread, including Flatbread from Hardanger (page 512) and flatbread in Sweden (both baked with barley flour). In Iceland, a fried thin rye bread, Icelandic Leaf Bread (page 514), is a festive bread. Icelandic Potato Bread (page 502) is another example of the many bread varieties available in the Nordic countries, where the potatoes can sometimes be eaten boiled and sometimes used to make bread. In Iceland, as in other Nordic countries, the sandwich has, in historical times, consisted of a 'slice' of lightly pounded dried fish that is spread with butter. Pasties have been important bread variants in Finland but also on the Swedish east coast and are now found throughout the Nordic region. The dough for pasties is made of rye or wheat flour, or a mix of the two.

A distinctive feature of the sausages all over the Nordic area is that sometimes they contain so much grain that they can almost be seen as a bread. Sausage mixtures are often mixed up with some flour and semolina and then become dishes such as Cold-Smoked Fermented Barley Sausages (page 419) or Liver and Barley Casserole (page 400). Sausages can also include offal or blood, like Icelandic Liver Sausage (page 424) or Faroese Blood Sausage (page 395).

Since the open sandwich is so important, there are also many different types of fats to top it with. The choice of fats varies between hunting and fishing areas in the west and agricultural areas in central and southern Scandinavia, but includes butter, which has long been part of traditional animal husbandry, and contemporary margarine, as well as lard, fat from different whale species and also seal, duck and goose fat. Quite often in everyday cooking, blended fats are used.

There is a special daylight throughout the year in the Nordic region. In the middle of summer it is light nearly the whole day; in winter, the sun is at its peak between 9 a.m. and 3 p.m. Above the Arctic Circle, the sun doesn't climb over the horizon for a few months. Historically summer therefore was the labour-intensive period and people ate as many as six or seven meals each day. Winter was, in contrast, a rest period of indoor work and maybe two or three meals each day. The light was precious and people worked mostly by the open fire's glow. In the 1800s the Nordic food culture was changed by three important inventions: the kerosene lamp, electricity and the iron stove. The new kerosene lamp and, in some areas, electric light, made it possible to work also in the evenings during the dark season. Longer working days during the winter now became filled by more and more meals but of course not as many as in the summer when people worked in the fields from 3 o'clock in the morning till 10 at night. With the new light sources, it became possible to confine fires to the new iron stoves, which took advantage of the heat in a much more efficient way. This new stove also carried with it new cooking methods and moved the food culture away from cooking in one pot to cooking in several, maybe up to three to four, plus the ever-hot oven to bake on a daily basis. When the iron stove made its appearance in the 1800s bread went from being the centrepiece of the meal to being used just as a sandwich on the side or as a light meal. In the west Nordic countries it's still common to eat sandwiches for lunch, both in the workplace and in schools, most people bringing their own lunch sandwiches from home. The variation in sandwiches and cold cuts is also greatest in countries such as Denmark and Norway. In eastern Nordic countries people eat a hot, cooked lunch every day. Home-cooking has in recent decades become more equal, and in Sweden it is now almost as common for men to be responsible for the family's everyday cooking as women.

During the 2000s, the trend towards looking to other countries for culinary inspiration has been replaced by an urge to discover the food of the Nordic regions. Restaurant chefs have joined in a common goal to both rediscover the old kitchens' produce and preserving techniques and also to then cook the food in new ways. Particularly noticeable is the search for new types of ingredients that have not been used historically but which today have been added to the contemporary food culture using traditional cooking methods. The old Nordic flavours are reinterpreted today through a combination of preserved and fresh flavours, showing that food culture is always a living link to the people who lived in this vulnerable geographic area but also a gift to those who come after.

Richard Tellström
Food historian and Associate Professor
Örebro University, Sweden

So, if you are one of those people who will buy a book and think that you are going to be able to cook every recipe in it and that anything else doesn't make sense, put this book up for sale on Ebay asap. This book contains more than 700 recipes and the vast majority of them will be quite possible for most people to make in their homes, but not all of them. A recipe is sometimes the best way of describing the cultural reflection, which a dish always is. A book like this is as much a documentation of food culture for you to learn from and get inspired by, as it is an instruction on how to cook specific dishes.

Before we go on to more fun stuff, I am going to tell you another annoying thing right away, just to get it out of the way. If you follow the recipes to the dot as they are printed in the book, sometimes it's not going to work anyhow. Why is this you might ask? Well this book is distributed far and wide and I have tried the recipes in my kitchen back home in Sweden were the flour behaves in one way, the eggs in one way and the milk in another. The way ingredients behave in one part of the world might not be the same as how they behave where you are, for natural reasons. We have sent recipes to testers around the globe and really tried to compensate for this wherever possible, but I assure you, we have not been able to include only 100% bulletproof recipes in the book.

A good tip if you want to succeed though is to use the gram scale measurements supplied rather than the cup volume ones, which if I had been the universal decider of things would have passed, long ago to publishing's graveyard of obsolete forms of quantification because of their clear lack of accuracy. When gram measurements or millilitre measurements are supplied in the recipes, mainly in baking and pastry ones, it means that the recipe benefits from the exactness. If, on the other hand, I write 'to taste', or 'a good pinch' from time to time, it means that the exactness is less important and that the amount used is more down to your own preference.

Are you getting discouraged? Well don't, the fact is that the idea of an exact recipe which delivers every time is flawed, simply because it will never exist. Recipes are there to give you a base to start from, inspiration if you will, and also to explain the technical base on which you can then build. When you cook from this book, as with any other book, you will have to use some common sense. If it doesn't look right and doesn't taste right most likely it is not going to be right and you will have to adjust accordingly. If it does taste fantastic though, and thereby serves a purpose, does it really matter if it doesn't look exactly like the dish in that photo you saw in the book? The dish in the photo I made (admittedly in a home kitchen when testing the recipes, but still) after fifteen years of cooking professionally and also with the purpose of it looking great, as I knew it was going to be photographed. Plus, you don't know how many times I failed until it looked that way! The same goes for preparation and cooking times. They are a mere indication. Set the timer for guidance but make the final decision on whether something is done by using your senses. If the salmon turned out a little dry the first time, does it really matter? Next time you will know what it looks like when it didn't turn out perfect and you can avoid that.

As you will see, most of the recipes in this book are not for finished dishes but rather for components. They do, however, have an introduction describing how they are most commonly served and why. Please read that, it will make using the book more enjoyable.

A last piece of advice is to not be too rigid when using this book. The Nordic food culture is made up of influences from all over the world, adapted by the local circumstances and changed over time to suit our preferences. Even though it might seem so at times, Nordic cooking is not conservative, it is in fact open-minded. You should be too when cooking from it. Just because it doesn't say in a recipe that a particular vegetable garnish or sauce works really well with a particular meat or fish preparation, it doesn't mean that it won't work, only that I didn't know of it. Please go ahead and try combinations that you feel make sense, it will be much more fun that way and no less Nordic.

To tell you about where recipes are from and in which countries they are common, you will see a list of names in Nordic languages after the descriptive title in English.

EGGS

Previous page: Vast view and moody sky, about to start raining, Iceland, early May 2013.

The egg is a genius thing, a completely natural and bio-degradable outer casing filled with something very nutritious, plus it is delicious. Eggs are also fantastic because they keep for a really long time and they don't really need to be refrigerated. I have made little experiments at my restaurant and it seems like three months is not really a problem for egg storage at room temperature and that even after a longer time, like six months, more than half of the eggs are still fit to eat, albeit not enjoy.

The shelf life of an egg can be dramatically increased by submerging it in a solution of sodium silicate (also known as waterglass), sealing the porous shell to block oxygen from entering the interior of the egg. This practice was common in many farms and also in food stores up until the time where we started artificially lighting chicken stables to make chickens produce the same number of eggs all year round. With an increasingly steady egg production, need for prolonged storage to compensate for the birds' decreased egg production in winter diminished and sodium silicate became less common with eggs.

The eggs from farmed birds like chickens, ducks and geese has been eaten by northerners for as long as those birds have been kept on farms. The foraged eggs from wild birds have been eaten even longer.

Today we eat ordinary chicken eggs in much the same ways as anyone else in a western country; they are boiled, fried, scrambled, turned into omelettes and they are an integral part of many pastries.

In terms of foraged eggs from wild birds, the eggs of gulls are extensively eaten in Norway. The bright blue, avoca-

ones from the guillemot (page 51) are still collected from the steep cliffs of Iceland and are considered something of a national treasure. On Iceland another type of egg which is still harvested from the wild are those from different wild ducks. This tradition is one that I have seen most commonly around the north east Icelandic region of Lake Mývatn. The eggs, after having been collected, would be packed up in big wooden boxes filled with ash for storage (page 49). The alkalinity of the ash would act on the protein of the egg a bit like on a thousand-year-old egg in Asia, slowly curing it. At the same time the dryness of the ash would desiccate the egg still in its shell, making it possible to store the egg almost indefinitely. Eggs like these are boiled before being eaten, unlike the Asian eggs. The ash is a by-product from the traditional Icelandic smokehouse, which is fired with year old sheep's dung.

On the Faroe Islands eggs from northern fulmars (page 46–7) are collected by walking on the narrow ledges of the volcanic islands on which the birds nest. A truly exhilarating and life-affirming experience, slipping around on a narrow step of red stone a vertical drop of several hundred metres on one side and angry birds trying to vomit all over you to protect their eggs on all other sides.

Opposite: A man dangling over the edge of a cliff in Iceland to collect guillemot eggs (page 51). He is attached to a line that is, in its turn, attached to the back of a pickup truck. He will give his friends in the car a call when he wants to go upwards after which they drive forward pulling him with them.

Opposite: Guillemot eggs, Iceland, Spring 2013.

SCRAMBLED EGGS

Äggröra (Sweden)

Preparation and cooking time: 10 minutes
Serves: 1 or many

however many eggs required
50 ml/2½ fl oz (3½ tablespoons) cream per egg
salt and white pepper, to taste

Put the eggs and cream in a small bowl. Whisk them briskly, but not too much; you want the mix to be a little bit less than uniform.

Pour the mixture into a small pan over medium heat. Use a rubber spatula or wooden spoon to stir around the edges of the pan from time to time. I like my scramble to consist of ribbons of soft egg surrounded by more creamy egg, almost-liquid, but warm. I don't like the texture of scrambled eggs when people stir them too much or keep them warm for a longer duration. I think this makes them unpleasantly grainy and rubbery.

HOW TO FRY A REALLY GOOD EGG

I guess what constitutes perfection in egg frying is probably quite individual. Myself, I do not like my eggs fried in a lot of very hot butter or oil. I don't like those bubbles forming at the edges – to me they have all the pleasantness in texture of little curls of hard plastic. Neither do I like the appearance of sooty fat mingled with egg white which has hardened, that would be the grey looking stuff at the exterior thirty per cent of your average hotel breakfast egg.

I usually heat a pan with just a little bit of fat in it – butter or oil, whichever seems appropriate – then I crack the egg into the pan, which mustn't be too hot. The thing to remember here is that the fresher the egg the better it will keep together in the pan. If the egg is quite old, there will be the yolk in the middle, followed by some rather thick gelatinous white, and then, around that, a much more liquid white. In a fresher egg the liquid part is next to nonexistent. This means that in an older egg there will be three distinct thicknesses to take into

account when frying that egg. A fresh egg is easier because more or less the whole white is one uniform thickness. It will therefore cook more evenly.

I usually keep the pan just under medium heat until the white has just set. Then I keep the pan off the heat, allowing the warmth to spread through the yolk. It might take 5 minutes or so of resting. The easiest way of figuring out if the yolk is cooked is to simply by touch the top of it carefully. If it's warm, it's done; if it's cold, it's not done.

When the egg is just perfect, sprinkle a bit of salt over it, and possibly grind some pepper if you are into that – black or white – according to your preference. Serve immediately; there is to be no keeping fried eggs warm.

For image see page 403

POACHED EGGS

Pocherat ägg (Sweden)

The deeper the water in the pot, the easier it is to get a nicely shaped egg. If the eggs are very fresh – preferably laid the same day – it also makes it easier, since they keep their shape better.

Preparation and cooking time: 10 minutes
Serves: 1 or many

1 handful salt
however many eggs required

Bring 5 litres/10½ UK pints (20 cups) water to a boil in a large pot. Add the salt then turn the heat down to a very gentle simmer.

Crack 1 egg into a small cup. Using a slotted spoon, stir the water in the pot into a whirlpool. Gently slide the egg out of the cup into the middle of the swirling water. Cook for 3 minutes then lift from the water with the slotted spoon. Repeat with the remaining eggs.

You can serve your poached eggs straight away or, if you want to keep them for a bit, leave them to cool in a bowl of cold salted water.

BOILED EGGS

Kokta ägg (Sweden)

There are many ways to boil an egg. This is the least exact one, but the one I think produces the nicest result for a creamy egg, which is what I mostly eat: firm egg white and creamy centre.

Preparation and cooking time: 5–10 minutes
Serves: 1 or many

however many eggs required

Immerse the eggs in a pot of cold water. Bring to the boil over a medium heat and cook the eggs for 3 minutes and 30 seconds for soft, 5 minutes for creamy, or 8 minutes for hard-boiled.

If you want to serve the eggs warm, as soon as the time is up rinse them under cold running water for just a few minutes to stop the cooking process. If you are serving them cold, or are planning to keep them refrigerated for a while, then rinse in cold water until they are cold.

For image see page 89

COLD BOILED EGGS WITH COD'S ROE SPREAD

Kaviarägg (Sweden)

In Sweden, boiled and halved eggs are often served for a big seasonal dinner, like Christmas. They are kind of like a miniature dish themselves – very tasty on a piece of bread – but are also great as an accompaniment with salmon, herring and other fish courses.

Preparation and cooking time: 5 minutes
Serves: 4 as part of a larger meal

Cured Cod's Roe Spread (page 672), to taste
4 Hard-boiled Eggs, boiled medium
   (see above), and peeled
pickled dill, to garnish

Spoon the cod's roe spread into a piping bag.

Cut the eggs into halves and arrange them on a serving platter. Pipe some of the roe onto each half and garnish with the dill.

EGGS IN CURRY SAUCE

Æg i karrysovs (Denmark)

Preparation and cooking time: 20 minutes
Serves: 4

8 Hard-boiled Eggs (see left), freshly cooked
1 quantity Curry Cream Sauce (page 665)

Peel the eggs while still warm then cut them into halves. Arrange them on a serving platter and pour the sauce around them.

Previous page: Utensils for dairy production, north Sweden, Summer 2014.

Opposite: Cheesemaking, Myhrbodarna, Sweden, July 2014.

Previous page: Pressed cheese resting on a shelf next to a bed in a traditional north Swedish mountain farm. The cheese is kept like this and turned now and then over the course of a couple of days for them to dry out a bit on the surface, Summer 2014.

Opposite: Utensils for dairy production photographed in a north Swedish mountain farm house, Summer 2014. Do note the date on the upper handle of the milk sieve to the left (1774). These utensils are still used every day through Summer.

POTTED CHEESE

Potkes / Potkäs / Krukost (Sweden)

This recipe is an old way of making the most out of discarded cheese ends. By taking offcuts and trimmings of cheese, mixing them with butter, cream or milk and alcohol before sealing the mixture in a pot, you make these otherwise difficult to use pieces of cheese keep for a long time and remain delicious.

The one I learned to make when I started working in restaurants was made by mixing cheese, butter, cream, caraway seeds and Aquavit (page 714), but I have seen many variations in almost all of the Nordic countries using different ingredients and flavourings to the cheese itself. One old recipe from Denmark uses cheese, milk and Cognac, whilst many newer ones use things like crème fraîche, herbs and garlic. It is all optional I guess. Personally, I like my potted cheese to have quite a bit of alcohol sting to it but this can obviously be adjusted to anyone's preference.

Potted cheese is often used as a sandwich topping. It should be brought to room temperature before using, to make it spreadable.

Preparation time: 10 minutes
Maturing time: 1 week
Serves: 4

400 g/14 oz hard cheese, rinds, offcuts
  and trimmings, finely grated
200 ml/7 fl oz (¾ cup plus 1 tablespoon)
  cream
100 g/3½ oz (7 tablespoons) butter
3½ tablespoons Aquavit (page 714)
1 tablespoon caraway seeds
salt, to taste

Mix all of the ingredients together well. Spoon into a sterilized glass jar or ceramic pot, packing the mixture in really well, then seal. Refrigerate for at least 1 week before serving.

JUNKET

Tjesfil (Sweden)

In northern Sweden, fresh milk curdled with rennet is eaten either with ground cassia cinnamon, sugar and a pouring of cream, or with broken up pieces of Scanian Thick and Chewy Gingersnaps (page 562) as a dessert.

It is often served in summer, straight from the fridge, and it is one of the most refreshing things you can eat – even if it is all milk and cream.

Preparation and cooking time: 35 minutes,
* plus cooling time*
Serves: 4

1 litre/34 fl oz (4¼ cups) unpasteurized milk
1 tablespoon liquid rennet

Pour the milk into a large pot and heat to 37°C/98.6°F on a thermometer. Remove the pot from the heat. It may continue to heat up a little bit with retained heat and you need to ensure that the temperature has stabilized at a constant 37°C/98.6°F by the time you add the liquid rennet. When it reaches that temperature, add the rennet and mix well. Pour into a shallow dish, cover and leave, undisturbed, for 30 minutes to set. Transfer to the refrigerator and leave it to cool completely before serving.

FRESH WHITE CHEESES WITH EGG ADDED IN THEM

In Sweden and Finland there is a tradition of adding eggs to the milk before making certain white cheeses, which are curdled with added cultured milk or cream, and consumed fresh. In Sweden, cheeses like these were traditionally served as a sweet, as part of the savoury section of a meal (indicating that it was festive), or as a sandwich topping. Today, they are more commonly served as a dessert with whipped cream and berries or jam. In Finland a version made from skimmed (skim) milk is served as it is, whilst a full-fat (whole) version can be brushed with butter and grilled (broiled) in the oven before being eaten.

Sometimes these cheeses are pressed in a mould carved from wood (see illustration below), pressed in metal or cast in plastic, which is richly decorated and gives the cheese itself a relief often resembling a star. This is especially common in the northern parts of the Swedish west coast, around the region of Bohuslän.

These cheeses are most commonly made from cow's milk but I have seen a few recipes from the northern Swedish region of Västerbotten that also make use of goat's milk.

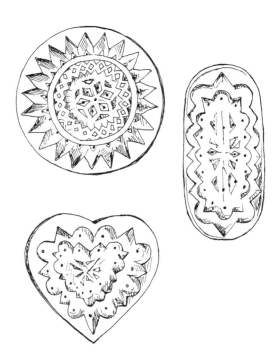

SWEDISH EGG CHEESE

Äggost / Bohuslänsk äggost (Sweden)

In the old days, cold water was added to the hot milk when the curds were ready, to stop them overcooking. Adding a few ice cubes is much more effective.

Preparation and cooking time: 30 minutes
Resting time: overnight
Serves: 8 as dessert, or more if part of
    a larger dinner party menu

8 eggs
400 ml/14 fl oz (1⅔ cups) *filmjölk* cultured
    milk or 2 tablespoons *Ättika* (24%)
    vinegar (page 656)
4 litres/7 UK pints (16½ cups) milk
200 g/7 oz (1½ cups) ice cubes
200 g /7 oz (1 cup) sugar

Line a traditional mould or a strainer with muslin (cheesecloth).

Put the eggs into a pot, which is also big enough to hold the milk, then whisk in the cultured milk (or the vinegar). Add the milk and stir slowly with a wooden spoon. Place the pot over a medium heat and slowly bring to a simmer, stirring the whole time. Remove the pot from the heat and add the ice cubes. Stir for another minute, to stop the curds from overcooking. Separate the curds from the whey in a colander, then layer them with the sugar in the prepared mould or strainer. Leave to drip overnight in a cool place.

VARIATION

Skörost (Sweden)

Instead of mixing the ingredients together while cold, heat the milk and then mix the egg with the cultured milk or *gräddfil* before adding the mixture to the hot milk. This cheese will have slightly more defined grains and it becomes a bit more crumbly than *äggost*.

FINNISH SOURED MILK CHEESE / FINNISH BUTTERMILK CHEESE

Piimäjuusto (Finland)

Use full-fat (whole) milk if you are going to grill (broil) the cheese, otherwise use skimmed (skim) milk.

Preparation and cooking time: 30 minutes
Setting time: overnight
Serves: 8 as dessert, or more if part of a larger dinner party menu

3 litres/5 UK pints (12½ cups) full-fat (whole) milk or skimmed (skim) milk
1 litre/34 fl oz (4¼ cups) buttermilk or another soured/cultured milk
5 eggs
sugar, to taste
1 teaspoon salt
butter, for brushing (optional)

Line a round 20 cm/7¾ inch cheese mould or a colander with muslin (cheesecloth).

Pour the milk into a large pan and heat to about 80°C/175°F. While it is heating, mix together the buttermilk, eggs, sugar and salt. Add the egg mixture to the hot milk, still on the stove and stir until it curdles, this could take up to 5 mintues. Remove the pan from the heat and separate the curds from the whey in a colander. Lift the curds into the prepared mould and weight down lightly with a plate. Leave overnight to set completely.

Preheat the grill (broiler) to 250°C/480°F. Place the cheese in an ovenproof dish and brush with butter before grilling (broiling) until golden. Alternatively, serve the cheese just as it is.

FINNISH SQUEAKY CHEESE / BREAD CHEESE

Leipäjuusto (Finland)
Kaffeost (Sweden)

This Finnish specialty, which is said to 'squeak' when bitten, is today also found in Sweden, especially in the northern parts that border Finland. It is either eaten in wedges, a bit like a cake, with cloudberry jam (page 690) or Sugared Cloudberries (page 692) on top, or else it can be diced and placed in a cup of strong coffee to be eaten when the coffee itself has been drunk. The Finnish name *leipäjuusto* means 'bread cheese' and the Swedish, *kaffeost* means 'coffee cheese'.

Traditionally *leipäjuusto* was made with cow's colostrum (first milk) but this practice seems more or less non-existent today and most recipes are based on regular milk.

To make squeaky cheese you will need to have a round 20 cm/7¾ inch cheese mould and a thermometer.

Preparation and cooking time: 1 hour
Setting time: 30 minutes
Makes: 1 cheese of about 300 g/11 oz

2 litres/3½ UK pints (8¼ cups) unpasteurized milk
200 ml/7 fl oz (¾ cup plus 1 tablespoon) cream
liquid rennet, use the amount indicated on your bottle

Line a round 20 cm/7¾ inch cheese mould with muslin (cheesecloth).

Combine the milk and cream in a large pot and heat to 35°C/95°F. Remove the pot from the heat. It may continue to heat up a little bit with retained heat and you need to ensure that the temperature has stabilized at a constant 37°C/98.6°F by the time you add the liquid rennet. When it reaches that temperature, add the rennet and stir it in briskly and thoroughly. Cover the pot and leave it, undisturbed, for 30 minutes to set.

Once the curds have formed, return the pot to the stove over a gentle heat. Use a slotted spoon to stir the curds carefully in towards the centre. As the mixture heats up, the curds and whey will start to separate and the curds will form a kind of lumpy ball in the middle of the pot. The whey should be fairly hot, at about 65°C/150°F, but should not be allowed to boil, or even to simmer.

After a couple of minutes at the right temperature, when the curds are cooked, use a slotted spoon to lift them into the prepared cheese mould. Cover with another layer of muslin and weight with something heavy (like a stack of plates) to press out any remaining whey.

Preheat your grill (broiler) to 250°C/480°F/Gas Mark 9.

Once cool, place the firm disc of cheese in an ovenproof dish and grill (broil) until quite darkly coloured.

REDUCED CURDS AND WHEY

Dravle / Gomme (Norway)
Sötost (Finland)
Sötost (Sweden)

Different dishes based on unpasteurized milk that is set with rennet, soured milk or other acidic additions, and is reduced until the lactose has caramelized, are common in the Nordic countries, especially in the northern regions of Norway, Sweden and Finland. Often considered festive, these preparations can either be served as desserts or as condiments to go with savoury foods and charcuterie, such as Norwegian Cured and Aged Leg of Mutton (page 348), or as toppings for flatbreads, waffles and other baked goods.

The colour of these reduced curds and whey preparations range significantly from almost white and milky to darkly caramelized and dry and spicy, depending on the cooking time and temperature. Sometimes heavy cream or butter is added towards the end and, in some recipes, starches like rye or wheat flour and/or eggs can be incorporated.

In the southern parts of Sweden these preparations are often finished in the oven to caramelize. Traditionally, the oven-baked versions (and some of the ones finished on the stovetop) often contained cow's colostrum to make them set. In most modern recipes, colostrum has been replaced by eggs, but if you happen to come across some colostrum and if you want to try using it in one of the recipes, then substitute 100 ml/3 ½ fl oz (⅓ cup plus 1 tablespoon) of colostrum for each egg and reduce the amount of cream a little bit.

Ideally, the milk used in all cheese preparations, or in recipes using rennet, should be unpasteurized, unhomogenized and full-fat (whole) in order to set properly. Some pasteurized milks will also work, but you will have to experiment yourself, since the quality and degree of pasteurization varies so much from country to country and from brand to brand.

NORWEGIAN REDUCED CURDS AND WHEY MADE WITH CULTURED MILK

Dravle (Norway)

This recipe is sometimes prepared with a cassia cinnamon stick added to the milk.

Preparation and cooking time: 4 hours
Serves: 4 as a main course with charcuterie,
*   and 8 as a dessert with cinnamon and sugar*

2 litres/3½ UK pints (8¼ cups) milk
200 ml/7 fl oz (¾ cup plus 1 tablespoon)
   cream
100 g/3½ oz (½ cup) sugar, plus extra
   for sprinkling
5 eggs
500 ml/17 fl oz (2 cups plus 1 tablespoon)
   cultured milk
ground cinnamon, for sprinkling

Pour the milk and cream into a heavy-bottomed pot, add the sugar and heat to 45°C/113°F then move it to the side of the stove. Mix the eggs well with the cultured milk then stir into the hot liquid and leave to set for about 1 hour with the lid on.

Bring to a slow boil over medium heat, stirring with a whisk now and then so that it doesn't stick to the bottom and burn. Continue cooking until the whey has started to reduce down and the desired level of caramelization has been achieved.

Transfer to a bowl and refrigerate before serving. Sprinkle with sugar and cinnamon before eating.

For image see page 71

NORWEGIAN REDUCED CURDS AND WHEY MADE WITH LIQUID RENNET

Dravle (Norway)

Preparation and cooking time: 4 hours
Serves: 4 as a main course with charcuterie
  and 8 as a dessert with cinnamon and sugar

2 litres/3½ UK pints (8¼ cups) milk
1 tablespoon liquid rennet
sugar and ground cinnamon, to serve

Pour the milk into a heavy-bottomed saucepan and heat to 37°C/98.6°F. Remove from the heat, then add the liquid rennet and stir with a spoon to mix thoroughly. Don't mix for longer than 30 seconds, as this is when the rennet starts acting on the milk and shouldn't be disturbed too much. Put the lid on and leave to set for 30 minutes.

Use a whisk to break the firm curd into smaller pieces and start heating again over a medium heat. Bring to a simmer, then cook gently for 2–3 hours, or until the desired degree of browning is achieved. Stir frequently so that it doesn't burn, but do it carefully, without crushing the grains of cheese too much. Transfer to a bowl and refrigerate before serving. Sprinkle with sugar and cinnamon before eating.

SWEDISH REDUCED CURDS, AS IN JÄMTLAND

Jämtländsk sötost (Sweden)

This dessert brings back childhood memories for me as it used to be served at my grandmother's house with cloudberries and whipped cream.

Preparation and cooking time: 3–4 hours
Serves: 4

2 litres/3½ UK pints (8¼ cups) milk
200 ml/7 fl oz (¾ cup plus 1 tablespoon) cream
2 eggs
1 tablespoon liquid rennet
1 cassia cinnamon stick
1 tablespoon golden syrup

Pour the milk and cream into a heavy-bottomed pot and heat to 37°C/98.6°F before removing it from the heat and placing it next to the stove. Whisk in the eggs and the liquid rennet, then add the cinnamon to the mixture, cover the pan and leave for 30 minutes. Use a long knife to cut the curds carefully into 3 cm/1¼ inch cubes. Slowly bring to a simmer over a low heat, then cook for 2–3 hours until the desired colour is achieved, stirring frequently. When cooked, add the syrup and refrigerate before serving.

For image see opposite page

SWEDISH REDUCED CURD FINISHED IN THE OVEN

Sötost (Sweden)

Serve warm with whipped cream and berries or jam (page 690).

Preparation and cooking time: 1 hour
Serves: 4

2 litres/3½ UK pints (8¼ cups) milk
100 ml/3½ fl oz (⅓ cup plus 1 tablespoon) cream
100 g/3½ oz (½ cup) sugar
1 cassia cinnamon stick
2 eggs
1 teaspoon liquid rennet

Combine the milk, cream, sugar and cinnamon in a heavy-bottomed pot and bring to a simmer. Cook until it has reduced in volume by half. Leave off the heat to cool until it reaches 37°C/98.6°F.

Preheat the oven to 175°C/345°F/Gas Mark 4.

Add the eggs and the rennet to the mixture in the pot and whisk briskly to combine. Don't mix for longer than 30 seconds, as this is when the liquid rennet starts acting on the milk and shouldn't be disturbed too much. Pour the mixture into an ovenproof dish, to a depth of 2–2.5 cm/¾–1 inch. Place it in the oven and cook for 40 minutes.

Clockwise from top left: Norwegian Reduced Curds and Whey made with Cultured Milk (page 69); Baked Colostrum Pudding (page 75); strawberry jam (page 690); cream; Swedish Reduced Curds, as in Jämtland (page 70); Swedish Curd Cakes (page 624)

SWEDISH REDUCED CURD FINISHED IN THE OVEN, AS IN HALLAND

Stefans halländska sötost (Sweden)

This version is from the southwest Swedish region of Halland, where it is served cold, most often with whipped cream and jam (page 690), possibly made from blackberries.

Preparation and cooking time: 5 hours
Serves: 4

2 litres/3½ UK pints (8¼ cups) milk
20 g/¾ oz (2 tablespoons) rye flour
½ tablespoon liquid rennet
120 g/4 oz (½ cup plus 1 tablespoon) sugar
½ tablespoon vanilla sugar
pinch of salt
1 egg yolk
a little potato starch, if necessary

Pour the milk into a heavy-bottomed pot and heat to 37°C/98.6°F. Add the rye flour, whisking so that no lumps form. Add the liquid rennet and remove the pot from the heat. Leave to set for about an hour.

Use a whisk to break up the curd into coarse pieces, then return the pot to a low heat. Cook gently until the mixture reduces and the desired degree of browning is achieved. Stir from time to time so that it doesn't burn, but do it carefully, without crushing the grains of cheese too much.

Once the curds have caramelized, stir in the sugar, vanilla sugar and a pinch of salt. Add the egg, and if necessary, thicken further with a little potato starch diluted in water. Refrigerate before serving.

BROWN CHEESE

Mysostur (Iceland)
Mysost (Norway)
Meesjuusto (Finland)
Myseost (Denmark)
Brunost / Mesost (Sweden)

Brown cheese is made from the whey that is left after making cheese. It is produced by reducing the whey, which is rich in milk sugars, with a bit of milk and sometimes cream for an extended period of time. The increased concentration of solids slowly thickens it at the same time as the lactose starts to caramelize giving the product its brown colour and distinctive flavour. If boiled for a shorter amount of time it will instead become soft Sweet Reduced Whey Spread (see below).

Brown cheese can be made from either cow or goat's milk or a combination of them both. I still have a hard time eating it after the traumatic childhood memories of having my ordinary yellow cheese regularly contaminated by traces of brown cheese while making myself a breakfast sandwich. The cheese knife – as I recall there was only one in the Nilsson household – was used for both.

SWEET REDUCED WHEY SPREAD

Mysingur (Iceland)
Prim (Norway)
Messmör (Sweden)

This is a reduced whey product, which in some ways resembles dulce de leche. The main difference is that it is made from the whey that is left after making cheese – much like Brown Cheese (see above).

This sweet spread is very popular on sandwiches, especially among kids. The main difference between *brunost* and this spreadable product is that the spreadable product has been cooked less. Therefore it has a higher water content and a lower concentration of dry matter.

Sweet reduced whey spread is mainly an industrial product today and few people make it on an artisanal scale. It is most often found in aluminium tubes resembling old-fashioned toothpaste tubes.

ICELANDIC CULTURED FRESH CHEESE

Skyr (Iceland)

Skyr has been made in Iceland since the island was first settled and it is mentioned several times in the Icelandic Sagas. It resembles strained yogurt but is, in fact, a fresh cheese, since it has rennet added to it in the production process. The dominant strains of lactobacillus, which give *skyr* its flavour profile, are *Streptococcus salivarius subsp. thermophilus* and *Lactobacillus delbrueckii subsp. bulgaricus.*

Skyr is made from skimmed milk and has a nutritional content of about 12% protein, 3% carbohydrate, and 0.5% fat. Traditionally made from unpasteurized milk, *skyr* today is mostly made from industrial pasteurized milk and can be bought in supermarkets much the same way as yogurt, flavoured in a multitude of ways. The whey, which is a natural by-product, is collected and drunk as a refreshing beverage called *mysa*.

Skyr is often eaten as a snack or as a dessert, with milk and sugar or with berries and it is included in recipes like Icelandic Skyr and Porridge Mix (page 469).

Preparation and cooking time: 2 days
Makes: about 2.5 litres/4¼ UK pints (10 cups)
of skyr and 2.5 litres/4¼ UK pints (10 cups)
of whey

5 litres/10½ UK pints (20 cups) skimmed (skim) milk, plus extra to serve
50 ml/2 fl oz (3½ tablespoons) *skyr*, to be used as a starter
4 teaspoons liquid rennet (or use the amount indicated on your bottle)
sugar, to serve (optional)

Pour the milk into a large heavy-bottomed pot and heat to 85°C/175°F. Maintain the heat for 10 minutes using an accurate thermometer and a timer. It's important to control this process, since both the time and temperature will affect the texture of the finished product. Basically, the higher the temperature and the longer the time you leave it, the creamier the finished *skyr* will be.

Take the pan off the heat and leave it next to the stove to slowly cool to 37°C/98.6°F before adding the *skyr* starter and the liquid rennet. Stir briskly with a whisk so that everything mixes well, but don't stir it for too long or it will impact the effectiveness of the rennet. Put a lid on the pot when you have finished stirring. The trick now is to keep the *skyr* in the pot at roughly the same temperature for 3 hours or more. This you can do either by insulating the pot with towels, or by placing it somewhere warm, but not hot.

After 3 hours, have a look and see how the curdling process is going. By now it should be firm enough to cut. Use a knife, which is long enough to reach the bottom of the pot, to cut the curds into 9 large pieces. Cover the pot again and leave in a warm place for another 3 hours. Refrigerate overnight.

The next day, tip the *skyr* and the whey into a colander lined with a sheet of muslin (cheesecloth). Leave to drip overnight somewhere cool and reserve the whey to drink if you want to use it.

When the *skyr* is ready to be served, whisk it smooth with milk and possibly some sugar. It should have the texture of creamy, strained yogurt.

COLD BUTTERMILK SOUP

Blakstampur (Faroe Islands)
Kærnemælkskoldskål (Denmark)

Koldskål is eaten in many parts of central Europe and its origin is a bit unclear. In Denmark, however, a version made from buttermilk and eggs has become one of the most iconic sweet dishes of the country. Sometimes it can be flavoured with lemon zest, and at other times with vanilla or with other sweet spices.

This dish is usually served during hot days in the summer and it is very refreshing. Little Sweet Rusks (page 574) are often served alongside, a bit like croutons in a savoury soup.

Some people also like to fold in whipped cream to the finished soup before chilling, which makes for a creamier texture and a richer flavour.

Preparation and cooking time: 10 minutes
Serves: 4

200 ml/7 fl oz (¾ cup plus 1 tablespoon)
   cream (optional)
4 egg yolks
3 tablespoons sugar
juice and/or grated zest of ½ lemon and/or
   1 teaspoon vanilla sugar
1 litre/34 fl oz (4¼ cups) cultured buttermilk

If you are using the cream, whip it to soft peaks in a bowl.

Whisk the egg yolks with the sugar until pale and creamy, making sure that all the sugar crystals dissolve. Add your choice of flavourings then add the buttermilk, stirring continuously. Fold in the whipped cream, if you are using it, and refrigerate until completely cold before serving.

MILK

Milk, most often from cows, but also from sheep and goats, is a very important part of the Nordic diet: fresh or cultured, both in cooking and as a beverage, with food or by itself. Most milk in the Nordic countries is lightly pasteurized at 72–74°C (162–165°F) for about 15 seconds and is also homogenized. It is generally available at 3%, 1.5%, 0.5% and 0.1% fat. In this book, all milk, unless otherwise specified, is full-fat (whole) at 3% fat, homogenized and lightly pasteurized. However, the milk used in all cheese preparations or recipes using rennet, and in all recipes where milk is being cultured, should be unpasteurized and unhomogenized in order to set properly. Some pasteurized milks will also work, but you will have to try with whatever milk you have, since the quality and degree of pasteurization varies so much from country to country and from brand to brand.

PIECES OF BREAD IN MILK OR CULTURED MILK

Soll | brødsoll | flatbrødsoll (Norway)
Sold (Denmark)
Sull | Brösull (Sweden)

Sull, sold or *soll* is most often some kind of liquid or creamy, cultured or fresh dairy product with pieces of dry flatbread broken into it, a bit like a combination of yogurt and cereal. In more southern parts of the Nordic region ordinary dry bread is used instead of flatbread.

Historically had as a simple meal at any time during the day, today it's seen a bit for breakfast and still quite commonly for lunch, especially in the northern parts of Sweden. Serve it with jam (page 690) or sugar – some people season it with some ground cassia cinnamon too.

Preparation time: 5 minutes
Serves: 1

300 ml/10½ fl oz (1¼ cups) cold milk or
   a Nordic cultured dairy product
1 large handful dry flatbread

Pour the milk or cultured dairy product into a serving bowl. With your hand, crush the dry bread on top. Serve with a generous spoonful of jam (page 690) or a good sprinkling of sugar and some cassia cinnamon, if you like.

LACTOFERMENTED MOUNTAIN HERB MIX

Gompa (Sami)

The Sami (page 292) have traditionally used many different indigenous herbs in their cooking, one of the more common ones being angelica. The use of angelica prevented scurvy and other nutritional diseases. Traditionally the herb components where simply barrelled with fresh reindeer milk and left to ferment. The barrels themselves were often sunk into a cold spring to keep them at a suitable temperature.

The recipe below is a slightly updated version made with cultured milk. Elaine Asp, who helped me out with the Sami recipes for this book, told me that she likes to serve it in a bowl with a bit of sugar on top and a slice of cake on the side as a sweet snack or as a dessert.

Preparation and cooking time: 10–15 minutes
Makes: about 1 litre/34 fl oz (4¼ cups)

30 g/1 oz (1¼ cups) chopped sorrel
30 g/1 oz (1¼ cups) chopped angelica stems
20 g/¾ oz (1¼ cups) chopped alpine sow-
   thistle stems
cultured milk, to cover

Blanch all of the herbs for about 30 seconds and place them in a bowl. Add enough cultured milk to cover and then mix thoroughly. Transfer to a sterilized glass jar and refrigerate until needed.

BAKED COLOSTRUM PUDDING

Ábrystir (Iceland)
Kalvdans / Kalvost / Råmjölkspannkaka
   (Sweden)

The name in Swedish refers to the immediate transformation of the temper of a calf after just having been born and had its first sip of colostrum. The calf visibly comes to life, thanks to the rich milk, and is said to dance: *kalvdans*, 'calf's dance'.

Colostrum is so rich in protein that it thickens, much like a custard containing eggs, when cooked. *Kalvdans* is often seasoned with a cassia cinnamon stick or cardamom. I prefer it to be unseasoned. Serve it cold, lukewarm or hot, straight from the oven, with whipped cream and some kind of jam like raspberry or cloudberry (page 690).

Preparation and cooking time: 40 minutes
Serves: 4

600 ml/1 pint (2½ cups) fresh cow's
   colostrum
200 ml/7 fl oz (¾ cup plus 1 tablespoon)
   cream
sugar, to taste

Preheat the oven to 225°C/435°C/Gas Mark 7.

Combine the colostrum, cream and sugar in a bowl and stir until the sugar has dissolved before pouring the mix into an ovenproof dish. It should be about 4 cm/1½ inches deep. Place in a roasting pan and pour in enough water to come about halfway up the side of the dish. Bake until set and dark golden on top.

For image see page 71

Previous page: Fields and hills close to my house, Jämtland, Sweden, June 2014.

Opposite: Resting on a very steep slope, Faroe Islands, Spring 2013.

Following page: Wood anemones, Norway, Spring 2014.

BOILED VEGETABLES

It is something special, a just-boiled, steaming-hot vegetable. Sometimes people (and by 'people' I really mean chefs) seem to think that just because it has grown from the ground it needs to be glazed and made shiny with butter and seasonings. Quite often through I think that the inherently matted surface of a cooked vegetable is nicer than that of an artificially 'polished' one (see opposite page).

Also, sometimes you just want the unadorned flavour and texture of the vegetable itself because it suits your plan for it. Imagine, for example, a big head of broccoli. You wouldn't want to glaze that. The fine buds at its top soak up an inordinate amount of butter and seasoning, making it flavourful, yes, but also sadly lacking in complexity by hiding the true virtues of the vegetable itself. No, what you would want to do would be to cook it just before serving it in all its simplicity, either boiling it or even steaming it, then perhaps giving it a good sprinkle of salt. If you desire the flavour of butter or other fats, just apply that to the top of the vegetable when you serve it, creating complexity through variation: one piece having a bit of butter and a lot of salt, the next one having less.

Boiled vegetables should be cooked until just tender and served straight away, steaming hot. If they sit for a while, they will first overcook and then they will lose colour, texture and flavour. A lukewarm, boiled vegetable will not make anyone happy.

I add quite a bit of salt to my cooking water; if you are cooking really small vegetable pieces this will have to be reduced otherwise the result will be too salty. The quantity of salt below will be good with, for example, chunky pieces of broccoli, whole Brussels sprouts, whole summer carrots or chunky florets of cauliflower.

The exact weight of vegetables to serve four people will vary slightly depending on what you choose, as will the cooking time. Refer to each vegetable section for more information on portion size and timings.

Preparation and cooking time: 15 minutes
Serves: 4

500–800 g/1 lb 2 oz–1¾ lb vegetables, cleaned and peeled where necessary
1 good handful salt

Cut your vegetables into a uniform shape and size. It doesn't really matter if they are large or small, as long as they are uniform, otherwise smaller pieces will become mushy before larger pieces are cooked.

Pour 5 litres/10½ UK pints (20 cups) water into a very large pan. Add the salt and bring to the boil. Add the vegetables to the boiling water and cook until they are just right. Times will vary, depending on the vegetable. Lift the vegetables out of the pan with a slotted spoon and into a warm serving bowl. Taste and sprinkle with salt, if you think it's really necessary, otherwise serve them immediately just as they are.

STEAMED VEGETABLES

If you have a steam oven, or another device that lets you steam in a fairly easy way in your home, it is one of the best ways of cooking vegetables. It's similar to boiling in the sense that it's really quick, with intense heat transmitted via the humidity of steam into the vegetable. This is good for the colour and vibrancy of the vegetable. The difference is that, when boiled, especially cut into small pieces, vegetables can lose quite a bit of flavour and nutrients to the cooking water itself. If you taste the cooking water after you are done using it, you can imagine all the flavour that could have been retained inside the vegetables instead. With steam there is no liquid to leak out into so that problem is taken away.

The exact weight of vegetables to serve four people will vary slightly depending on what you choose, as will the cooking time. Refer to each vegetable section for more information on portion size, preparation and timings.

Preparation and cooking time: 5–15 minutes,
depending on the vegetable
Serves: 4

500–800 g/1 lb 2 oz–1¾ lb vegetables, cleaned and peeled where necessary
salt, to taste

Cut your vegetables into a uniform shape and size. It doesn't really matter if they are large or small, as long as they are uniform, otherwise smaller pieces will become mushy before larger pieces are cooked.

If using a steam oven, set it to 100°C/200°F. Alternatively, place the vegetables in a steamer basket set over a pan of simmering water and cover. Steam the vegetables until they are just tender. The timing will vary, depending on the vegetable. Sprinkle with salt and serve immediately.

BROWNED VEGETABLES

It is essential to take your time when browning vegetables, so that they are allowed to caramelize deeply, and so that they dry out a bit during the cooking process, giving them a pleasant, chewy-firm texture.

When cutting them, it is good if the vegetables are of slightly varying shapes, with thinner and thicker parts (a wedge shape is perfect). That way, the thinner parts will be nicely browned and a bit shrivelled by the time the thicker parts are cooked through. Season well but towards the end of the browning time to provide contrast. Crystals of salt that haven't melted are very tasty with the deep sweetness of the browned vegetables.

The exact weight of vegetables to serve four people will vary slightly depending on what you choose, as will the cooking time. Refer to each vegetable section for more information on portion size and timings.

Preparation and cooking time: 15–40 minutes
Serves: 4

500–800 g/1 lb 2 oz–1¾ lb vegetables,
  cleaned and peeled where necessary
50 g/2 oz (3½ tablespoons) butter
salt and white pepper, to taste

Cut your vegetables into slightly varied shapes but make sure they are not too small otherwise you will end up with shrivelled, overly sweet 'raisins' instead of nice vegetables.

Melt the butter in a pan over a medium heat and add the vegetables. Cook until they are evenly coloured all over. This will take quite a while and you shouldn't have to stir very often to avoid them burning at the bottom. Once browned and cooked through, but still firm, increase the heat a bit so that it sizzles, season well and serve immediately.

GLAZED VEGETABLES

When I talk about glazed vegetables, what I mean most of the time is some kind of cooked vegetable coated in a thin film of melted, but still emulsified butter. In some recipes other flavourings like vinegar or citrus are added, and sometimes a little bit of sugar is sprinkled into the pot. Other fats than butter can be used with equally good results, if you desire a particular flavour.

You can reheat blanched or otherwise precooked vegetables and glaze them as you do so, but you can also cook and glaze at the same time. To me, the glazing of a precooked vegetable is very much a practise for big restaurants, establishments where a certain level of consistency is required and you have to protect yourself from failure. In a small and ambitious restaurant like my one, or in a home, I think it is silly not to cook and glaze the vegetables at the same time.

Few things are as tasty as just-cooked vegetables, glazed in butter and its own perfectly seasoned cooking juices. If you glaze precooked vegetables this will never be possible; for obvious reasons they are no longer 'just cooked' and the emulsion coating them will not be made from their own cooking liquid. If you blanch your veggies, a lot of the flavour will leak out and be discarded with the blanching water, and with the cooling water.

Simply put, I will always prefer a piping hot, 'just cooked' but slightly overcooked carrot and a fresh pea that is starting to lose some colour but that tastes like heaven over a perfectly crunchy reheated carrot and a vibrantly green blanched pea that has lost fifty per cent of its sweetness already. Be that as it may, I offer recipes for both approaches here.

TO GLAZE BLANCHED VEGETABLES

Allow about 150 g/5 oz of most vegetables (cooked weight) per person, as a side dish.

Preparation and cooking time: 5 minutes
Serves: 4

600 g/1 lb 5 oz blanched or otherwise cooked
  vegetables
50 g/2 oz (3½ tablespoons) butter
salt and pepper, to taste

Melt the butter in a frying pan or skillet just large enough to hold the vegetables in one layer. Add a splash of water and bring to the boil over a medium heat, swirling to emulsify. Add the vegetables and swirl them around the pan to evenly coat them in butter and heat them. Only add a splash more water if necessary. Remember you are only reheating the vegetables as they have already been cooked. Season well and serve immediately.

TO GLAZE RAW VEGETABLES

If you want to glaze a mixture of vegetables – with different cooking times – in the one pot, the trick is to get them all done at the same time. There are two factors influencing the result: the size of the vegetable pieces and the time they are added to the pan. For the sizing, a thinner or smaller piece will always cook faster than a bigger piece; a slice of carrot will cook in a few minutes whilst a whole one might need 15 minutes.

Vegetables that need a higher degree of cooking should be added earlier than those that don't. A potato added too late, so that the starch in it hasn't even been cooked, is as unpleasant as a fresh leaf of spinach added in the very beginning broken down by heat to a military green goo.

In the recipe below I have written down a specific list of vegetables to illustrate the method, but you can apply this technique to any vegetable you want, with great results. Remember not to add too much water during the cooking process. If you do you might end up with too much liquid, which you have to either remove (and a lot of flavour with

it) or boil down, risking overcooked vegetables. A thin layer coating the bottom of the pan at all times is enough, and you should add little and often rather than a lot in one go.

Allow about 200 g/7 oz raw vegetables per person, as a side dish. The cooking time will obviously vary with the choice of vegetables.

Preparation and cooking time: 30 minutes
Serves: 4

50 g/2 oz (3½ tablespoons) butter
8 small, firm potatoes, scrubbed clean,
  skins on
4 small winter onions (about the size of
  grapes), peeled
1 large yellow beetroot (beet), peeled and
  cut into 1 cm/½ inch wedges
1 large turnip, cleaned, skin on, cut into
  1 cm/½ inch wedges
2 carrots, peeled, sliced on a mandoline
  into 2 mm/¹⁄₁₆ inch slices
1 bunch curly kale, leaves torn into smaller
  pieces, stalks cut fine
salt and white pepper, to taste

Melt the butter in a large frying pan. Add the potatoes and onions and a little water and bring to the boil over a medium heat. You should maintain this boil throughout the entire cooking process as it will help keep the butter and vegetable juices emulsified. Cover with a cartouche and cook for about 5 minutes. Add the occasional splash of water to ensure the pan doesn't become dry. There is no need to stir (this can break up the vegetables) but swirl the pan from time to time to move things around and help the pieces cook evenly.

Add the beetroot (beet) wedges and continue for another 5 minutes or so. Season with salt, if you feel like it. Next, add the turnip wedges and continue cooking. When all these vegetables are becoming tender, adjust the seasoning and add the carrot slices. Swirl the pan and add the kale in a layer on top of the other vegetables (so they cook in the steam). Cover with the cartouche again and cook for a few minutes more, until the carrots still have a crunch and the kale has just wilted.

Swirl again to coat everything with the glaze, adjust the seasoning and serve immediately.

GRATED RAW VEGETABLE SALADS

Råkost (Sweden)

In almost every Swedish company or school canteen that serves lunch there will be a buffet of salads – many of them consisting of grated or shredded raw vegetables, sometimes dressed, sometimes plain. These sorts of salad are called *råkost*, meaning 'raw food', although they have nothing to do with raw foodism, in the contemporary sense.

The most popular versions are Grated Carrot Salad (page 110) and Cabbage and Lingonberry Salad (page 96).

BLANCHED VEGETABLES

*Preparation and cooking time: 5–10 minutes,
depending on the vegetable
Serves: 4*

500–800 g/1 lb 2 oz–1¾ lb vegetables,
  cleaned and peeled where necessary
salt, to taste

Bring a large pot of water to the boil, add the vegetables and boil until done.

While the vegetables are cooking, pour cold water into a large bowl and mix with plenty of ice. This allows you to cool the vegetables quickly, which is essential for retaining flavour and colour.

When the vegetables are ready, tip into a colander, then straight into the iced water. When the vegetables are completely cold return them to the colander and leave for the excess liquid to drain away.

CREAMED VEGETABLES

I love vegetables like sweet green peas, carrot slices or even florets of steamed cauliflower reheated in a rich, creamy Béchamel Sauce (page 666). Add a bit of finely chopped shallot if you like, and/ or finish the recipe with a handful of chopped herbs like parsley, chives or chervil. Or just season gently with some white pepper and/or freshly grated nutmeg. The key is to have perfectly cooked vegetables and a very tasty béchamel to start with.

You would think that it would be ideal to also cook the vegetables in the béchamel to lend the sweet milk the flavour of the vegetable itself. However, many vegetables in their raw state contain enzymes that break down proteins or have an unsuitable pH level and will therefore curdle the béchamel and make it grainy. Some, like green peas, will work fine, so will potatoes, but many of the other green and root vegetables do not work.

The exact weight of vegetables to serve four people will vary slightly depending on what you choose. Refer to each vegetable section for more information on portion size and timings.

*Preparation and cooking time: 5 minutes
Serves: 4*

500–800 g/1 lb 2 oz–1¾ lb cooked vegetables
½ quantity Béchamel Sauce (page 666),
  substituting half the milk with cream
aromatics, to taste
salt and white pepper. to taste

Follow the method on page 666 for preparing the béchamel sauce, then remove from the heat.

Add the cooked vegetables to the warm béchamel and heat them carefully. Stir them gently, so they don't stick to the bottom of the pan, but try to make sure they don't break up. When hot, season well with salt and white pepper and add your choice of aromatics, if using. Serve immediately.

VEGETABLE SOUPS

A vegetable soup should, in my opinion, taste mostly of whatever vegetable it is made from. This is most often not the case, mainly because people do not use good enough quality vegetables and because they put too much other stuff, like stocks (broths), dairy and spices, into their soups. Also, vegetables that are mixed or puréed to become soup are often overcooked to begin with, and an overcooked vegetable will not taste like a perfectly cooked vegetable just because you mix it into paste.

For example, when does a cauliflower taste the most of cauliflower?

My answer is, when it has just been picked and has had nothing done to it. Everything we do to it will make it a bit less of the cauliflower it once was, perhaps more tasty to us, but less of a cauliflower. There is a fine balance to do just enough to a product.

Most people who make a cauliflower soup will put the vegetables (which go sweet when cooked) into a pot with some onion (which goes really sweet when cooked), some milk and cream (which also go sweet when cooked) some chicken stock (which often is already sweet from all the overcooked vegetables in it), and they start cooking. Once the cauliflower is so soft that it falls apart when it's looked at, they mix it and start seasoning it. They taste, and then they add a bit of salt. They feel like it now has a bit more taste (which it does, but mainly because salt emphasizes sweetness), perhaps not of cauliflower but in more general terms, so they add even a bit more salt, and then finally a bit more salt and possibly some other seasoning or spices. This soup is going to be tasty, for sure. But I dare anyone to taste it blindfolded and say whether it is cauliflower, parsnip or whatever else.

I think it is better to make a simple, well thought through soup base and then add plenty of garnishes if you think it is too boring.

The soup above, for example, could instead of what I described be a plain purée, tasting of only cauliflower and a little salt, in which we fold a good spoonful of whipped cream, just before serving, to provide fluffiness, creaminess and a defined taste of dairy as it melts in swirls of the purée. Top it with some salty Crispy Fried Onions (page 108) and you have something fantastic, containing exactly the same components but actually tasting of all three.

Also, only ever use exceptionally good vegetables when making a soup like this. There is nowhere to hide when the essence of whatever vegetable you are using envelops every taste bud in your mouth. For the same reason, cook the vegetables with care before you purée them. Yes they need to be soft enough so that the mixer can turn them smooth, but they don't have to taste of poorly executed, overly long cooking.

And hold back on the salt in the soup itself. It will bring more flavour but not always those flavours that you want and expect. Instead, sprinkle some flaky salt in the bowl when you eat the soup or serve it with a salty garnish as described above.

Add any dairy towards the end so that it still tastes of dairy and not just of sweet lactose because you cooked it for too long.

Oh, and you need a very good, very strong mixer to make soups like these.

I have not specified how to cook the vegetables below, simply because the choice of cooking method reflects the choice of vegetable. Simply cook them in the way that brings the most out of each one. Some vegetables are best steamed and others are best fried. Some benefit from the addition of an onion, others don't. I have specified in the section for each individual vegetable what I think is the best way to make soup with them, but do go ahead and try any way you like. What we like is, after all, a very personal thing.

The exact weight of vegetables to make soup for four people will vary slightly depending on what you choose, and what you add to it to make a soup. Refer to each vegetable section for more information on portion size, preparation and timings.

Preparation and cooking time: 15–40 minutes,
  depending on the vegetable
Serves: 4

600–800 g/1 lb 5 oz–1¾ lb vegetables,
  cleaned and peeled where necessary

butter or oil
stock (broth), dairy or other liquids, to dilute
salt and white pepper, to taste

Refer to each particular vegetable section for preparation and cooking times. Cut into a uniform shape and size and cook until tender.

Place the cooked vegetable in a powerful blender. Add butter or oil, as specified in the recipe, and a ladleful of the hot liquid. At this stage you should add as little liquid as possible; really just enough to enable the vegetables to purée effectively. Turn on the motor and blend for about 10 minutes; it takes a lot longer than you think. If the vegetables clump together and resist blending, then add a little more liquid. If the motor seems to be getting hot, stop and let it rest for a few minutes.

Once the vegetables have turned into a smooth, thick purée, pass through a fine sieve into a pot set over a low–medium heat. Gradually add more liquid until you achieve a consistency that you like. Adjust the seasonings. If whipped cream is to be folded into the soup, do so just before serving.

SPINACH SALAD

If I am using bigger, dark green spinach leaves, I like to add the vinaigrette about 30 minutes before serving so they can wilt a bit. With young, tender leaves, dress them as late as possible.

Preparation and cooking time: 10 minutes
Serves: 4

400 g/14 oz (8 cups) spinach leaves
Vinaigrette (page 676) or Citronette
  (page 676), to taste
salt and white pepper, to taste

Put the spinach leaves in a large bowl. Add only a little dressing to the leaves – they are not tasty if they are too oily. Season well, transfer to a salad bowl and serve.

For image see page 89

STEAMED SPINACH

For steamed spinach, older, larger leaves with the stalks still attached are extra suitable. Small or very tender leaves will lose too much texture to benefit from this technique.

Preparation and cooking time: 10 minutes
Serves: 4

400 g/14 oz (8 cups) spinach leaves, stems
  attached
salt, to taste

Follow the instructions on page 82 for steaming vegetables. Sprinkle with salt and serve immediately.

CREAMED SPINACH

When steaming spinach I prefer older, larger leaves with the stems still attached. Small or too tender leaves will lose too much texture to benefit from this cooking method.

Preparation and cooking time: 10 minutes
Serves: 4

500 g/1 lb 2 oz spinach, coarse stems
  removed
½ quantity Béchamel Sauce (page 666)
freshly grated nutmeg, optional
salt and white pepper, to taste

Follow the instructions on page 85 for blanching the spinach. Drain the spinach in a colander, then squeeze out any excess water with your hands. Chop it to whatever size you prefer.

Carefully reheat the béchamel to a simmer and stir in the spinach. When hot, season well with salt and white pepper and nutmeg, if using. Serve immediately.

For image see page 89

SPINACH SOUP

Spinatsuppe (Norway)
Pinaattikeitto (Finland)
Spinat Suppe (Denmark)
Spenatsoppa (Sweden)

I like to make this soup in autumn (fall) when the spinach is dark and flavourful and can't really be eaten raw anymore. It's important to cook the spinach until tender. Spinach tends to retain a lot of oxalic acid if undercooked, so take your time. Undercooked spinach will make a soup like this feel very dry, in the same way an astringent red wine can be, but in a much less good way.

Serve it with halved Hard-boiled Eggs (page 53) and perhaps some Small Smoked Pork Sausages (page 428) called *prinskorv*.

You can also mix the soup in a blender if you want it to be more smooth and greener.

Preparation and cooking time: 20 minutes
Serves: 4

500 g/1 lb 2 oz (10 cups) spinach, preferably
   mature, dark green leaves, stems removed
2 tablespoons butter
2 tablespoons plain (all-purpose) flour
2 small shallots, finely chopped
1 litre/34 fl oz (4¼ cups) Chicken Stock
   (page 650)
250 ml/8 fl oz (1 cup) cream
salt and white pepper, to taste
freshly grated nutmeg (optional)

Bring water to the boil in a large pot, then add the spinach leaves and boil until tender. While the spinach is cooking, pour cold water into a large bowl and mix with plenty of ice. This allows you to cool the spinach quickly, which is essential for retaining flavour and colour, especially as you are cooking it until tender. When the spinach is ready, tip into a colander, then straight into the iced water. When the spinach is completely cold return it to the colander and leave for the excess liquid to drain away.

Put the butter in a pot, large enough to contain the finished soup. Place the pot on a medium heat and when it begins to stop foaming, stir in the flour.

Cook the flour for a little while, stirring, until it begins to brown lightly and it smells delicious. Add the shallots and cook them for perhaps a minute, before adding the chicken stock (broth), whisking so that no lumps form. Bring to the boil again, then leave to simmer over a medium heat for about 5 minutes before adding the cream. Season a little with salt and pepper.

Squeeze out any excess water from the spinach with your hands, then chop it finely before adding to the soup. Adjust the level of salt and pepper and finish with a bit of freshly ground nutmeg, if you like it.

For image see opposite page

SPINACH PANCAKES

Pinaattiohukaiset (Finland)

Serve with Sugared Lingonberries (page 692).

Preparation and cooking time: 20 minutes
Serves: 4

2 eggs
450 ml/15 fl oz (1¾ cups plus 2 tablespoons)
   milk
150 g/5 oz (1¼ cups) plain (all-purpose) flour
150 g/5½ oz (1½ cups) spinach, cleaned and
   very finely chopped
salt, white pepper and freshly grated nutmeg,
   to taste
butter, for frying

Mix all the ingredients together, except for the butter.

Melt a little butter in a frying pan or skillet heated to just above medium. Pour in enough batter to cover the bottom of the pan evenly and fry until just colouring on the underside. Flip the pancake over and cook the other side. Repeat until all the batter has been used.

Clockwise from top left: chopped spinach; Creamed Spinach (page 87); Spinach Salad (page 87); Spinach Soup (page 88) with a Boiled Egg (page 53)

SAUTÉED KALE

Preparation and cooking time: 10 minutes
Serves: 4

600 g/1 lb 5 oz kale (12 cups), stems removed,
  leafy parts roughly torn
50 g/2½ oz (3½ tablespoons) butter
salt and white pepper, to taste

Sauté the kale quickly in the buter in a pan over
high heat for long enough for it to just begin to
wilt, season well and serve immediately.

STEAMED KALE

If you can find young kale, then you can steam the
entire leaves (up to about 20 cm/8 inches), stems
and all.

Preparation and cooking time: 10 minutes
Serves: 4

600 g/1 lb 5 oz (12 cups) kale, stems removed,
  leafy parts coarsely torn
salt, to taste

Follow the instructions on page 82 for steaming vegetables. Sprinkle with salt and serve immediately.

KALE SALAD

I have never understood why you would make a
simple vinaigrette like this one at the bottom
of a bowl. To me, that makes sense only if you
want to emulsify your vinaigrette or when it has
thicker ingredients in it, like mustard. When I
make salads with just oil, vinegar and salt, I add
them gradually to the top of the salad instead,
until I'm satisfied with the taste.

With a vegetable like kale you can use the vinegar's
wilting properties to your advantage. If the kale
is very young and tender, dress it at the very last
minute, but if it is a little bit tougher and older,
dress it about 10 minutes before serving to tenderize it a bit.

Preparation and cooking time: 10–15 minutes
Serves: 4

400 g/14 oz (8 cups) torn curly kale, coarse
  pieces removed

For the vinaigrette
cold-pressed, nutty rapeseed (canola) oil
white vinegar
salt, to taste

Rinse the kale thoroughly, then dry in a salad spin-
ner. Put the kale in a large bowl. Drizzle with oil and
vinegar and season with salt. Toss lightly, then taste
the salad and adjust the balance until you are happy.

For image see opposite page

CREAMED KALE

When creaming a green vegetable like kale you can
do it in pure cream or with some flour. I prefer the
flour option most times because it means that you
don't have to reduce the cream that long before
it thickens, giving a slightly less heavy result and
fresher taste.

Preparation and cooking time: 20 minutes
Serves: 4

400 g/14 oz (8 cups) coarsely torn curly kale
200 ml/7 fl oz (¾ cup plus 1 tablespoon)
  cream, chilled
1 tablespoon plain (all-purpose) flour
  (optional)
salt and white pepper, to taste

Blanch the curly kale following the instructions on
page 85.

Pour the chilled cream into a pot and whisk in
the flour (if using). Add the blanched kale and
bring to the boil over a medium heat. Boil until it
is creamy enough for your taste. Season with salt
and pepper.

For image see opposite page

Clockwise from top: Kale Braised in Ham Stock with Cream and Brown Sugar (page 92);
Kale Salad (page 90); Kale Soup (page 92); Creamed Kale (page 90)

KALE SOUP

Grønkålssuppe (Denmark)
Grönkålssoppa (Sweden)

Kale soup is often served with Hard-boiled or Poached Eggs (pages 53 and 52) and with Small Smoked Pork Sausages (page 428). Some people have kale soup as part of their Christmas traditions, but for me it is just a very nice winter lunch.

Once you've added the kale to the soup, you have two options for serving it. Either leave it as it is, or transfer some of the soup to a blender and purée it, before returning it to the pan. The second option gives a bright green soup and smoother texture, the first option retains a slightly coarser texture, where the velouté keeps its light colour and the kale remains intact. I tend to prefer the first option, but a greener, smoother soup is sometimes nice too. Either way, reserve the kale blanching water as you may need it to adjust the consistency of the soup.

Preparation and cooking time: 20 minutes
Serves: 4

1 large bunch coarsely torn kale, coarse
  pieces and stems removed

1 quantity Velouté (page 652) made from:
550 ml/18 fl oz (2½ cups) Pork Stock
  (page 650)
10 white peppercorns
1 bay leaf
1 teaspoon fennel seeds
1 teaspoon aniseeds
salt and white pepper, to taste

Bring a large pot of water to the boil, add the kale leaves and boil until tender. It takes longer than you think to cook the kale, usually about 10 minutes, and it should be really tender.

While the kale is cooking, pour cold water into a large bowl and mix with plenty of ice. This allows you to cool the kale quickly, which is essential for retaining flavour and colour, especially as you are cooking it until tender.

When the kale is ready, tip into a colander, reserving some of the cooking liquid, then straight into the iced water. When the kale is completely cold return it to the colander and leave for the excess liquid to drain away. Squeeze the kale dry from any excess water and chop it finely.

Follow the instructions on page 652 to make the velouté.

When ready, strain the velouté to remove the aromatics and return to the pot. Discard the aromatics. Add the kale to the pot (or purée the kale with half of the velouté in a blender first, then add this to the pot with the remaining velouté). Adjust the seasonings to your liking and add some of the kale cooking water, if necessary.

Serve immediately once the soup is hot enough.

For image see page 91

KALE BRAISED IN HAM STOCK WITH CREAM AND BROWN SUGAR

Långkål (Sweden)

This is a classic preparation from the southern parts of Sweden and Denmark, which is often served around Christmas time with Boiled Ham (page 437) and sausages. It is important to allow enough time for the cooking; it should braise long enough that the kale is no longer green and the cream starts caramelizing a bit.

The flavour of the dish should be distinctly sweet and salty.

Preparation and cooking time: 1 hour
Serves: 4

25 g/1 oz (2 tablespoons) butter
500 g/1 lb 2 oz (10 cups) kale, thick stems
  removed, leafy parts coarsely shredded
1 tablespoon brown sugar
200 ml/7 fl oz (¾ cup plus 1 tablespoon)
  cream
300 ml/10½ fl oz (1¼ cups) ham stock
  or the cooking juices from Boiled
  Ham (page 437)
salt and white pepper, to taste

Put the butter in a large pot over a medium heat. Add the kale and the sugar and brown them together for about 10 minutes, stirring frequently, until quite soft.

Add the cream to the pot with a ladleful of the stock. Simmer for another 25–40 minutes, adding more stock every now and then. Be aware that the ham stock itself is rather salty, and as it reduces down, this will intensify. If you need to cook it longer, but feel it doesn't need any more ham stock, you can always top up with water instead. The kale is ready when it is really tender and when it tastes sweet – not only from the sugar, but also from the cooked cream. Adjust the seasoning just before serving with slices of ham and sausages.

For image see page 91

CABBAGE

Cabbage has been grown in Scandinavia since the Middle Ages and has a big part to play in food culture in most parts of the Nordic region. Cabbage is also quite special because it is so versatile. It's tasty raw and cooked, in both summer and winter. It can be harvested and eaten straight away but also kept for up to a year. In the right conditions, its layered construction will protect it from spoilage. Even though the exterior of a head of firm winter cabbage can be covered in mould, if you peel that away, just a few millimetres further down hides a pristine, light green head of cabbage, smelling of cool summer mornings.

Allow about 150 g/5 oz cabbage per person (central core part removed), as a side dish.

BOILED CABBAGE

If you cook cabbage in the summer, it cooks really quickly and you will only need to more or less dip it in the boiling water – it's a matter of perhaps 30 seconds of cooking, so there is really no point in tearing the pieces too small. Winter cabbage is denser and can withstand more cooking; it will take a little while before being done. Do not overcook them though; they should have some bite to them and not be mushy.

Preparation and cooking time: This depends on how big your pieces are and the season
Serves: 4

1 cabbage
salt, to taste (optional)

Either cut the cabbage into wedges or separate the individual leaves out and tear them into smaller pieces.

Follow the instructions on page 82 for boiling vegetables. Cook the cabbage until tender and take care not to overcook it.

Lift the cabbage out of the pan with a slotted spoon and drain briefly in a colander. Serve with a little sprinkling of salt, if you like.

STEAMED WHOLE CABBAGE

I love steaming a whole head of cabbage, its one of the most complex things you can eat, especially in winter. Because of its layered configuration and how dense it is, it takes a good while to cook. By the time the centre is just lukewarm and still crunchy, the exterior will be soft, sweet and slightly overcooked – and in between you will find every other texture imaginable in a head of cabbage.

Preparation and cooking time: 20 minutes
Serves: 4

1 cabbage
good olive oil, to drizzle
a squeeze of lemon or a dash of vinegar,
 if you like it
salt, to taste

Follow the instructions on page 82 for steaming vegetables. It will take about 20 minutes (or maybe a bit less) until it is warm all the way through. Insert a metal skewer into the centre of the cabbage, then remove it quickly and touch it to your lip to check that it is warm.

Cut the cabbage into wedges and serve it with a drizzle of oil and a squeeze of lemon juice or even a dash of vinegar. Season with plenty of salt before serving.

CREAMED CABBAGE

When creaming a vegetable like cabbage you can do it in pure cream or with some flour. I prefer the flour option most times, because it means that you don't have to reduce the cream that long before it thickens, which gives a slightly less heavy result and a fresher taste.

Preparation and cooking time: 20 minutes
Serves: 4

400 g/14 oz cabbage, coarsely chopped
200 ml/7 fl oz (¾ cup plus 1 tablespoon)
 cream, chilled
1 tablespoon plain (all-purpose) flour
 (optional)
salt and white pepper, to taste

Blanch the cabbage following the instructions on page 85.

Pour the chilled cream into a pot and whisk in the flour (if using). Add the blanched cabbage and bring to the boil over a medium heat. Boil until it is creamy enough for your taste. The longer you boil it, the thicker the consistency and the sweeter the flavour. Season with salt and pepper.

For image see opposite page

GRATIN OF CABBAGE

Preparation and cooking time: 30 minutes
Serves: 4

1 quantity Creamed Cabbage (see left)
50 g/2 oz (⅓ cup plus 2 tablespoons) grated
 mature hard cow's milk cheese
a little freshly grated nutmeg, to finish

Preheat the oven to 225°C/435°F/Gas Mark 7.

Pour the creamed cabbage into an ovenproof serving dish. Sprinkle with the grated cheese and brown in the oven for a few minutes, or until darkly golden. Season with a little bit of grated nutmeg over the top, just before serving.

Clockwise from top: Creamed Cabbage (page 94); Cabbage and Lingonberry Salad (page 96); Cabbage Casserole (page 380); Cabbage Salad (page 96); Grilled Summer Cabbage (page 96)

CABBAGE SALAD

Kål salat (Norway)
Kaalisalaatti (Finland)
Vitkålssallad / Pizzasallad (Sweden)

A simple salad of shredded cabbage, tossed in vinaigrette, sometimes served with pickled bell peppers, is always found in Swedish pizzerias (page 476). The origins of this salad are a bit unclear, but some say it came to Sweden from the Balkans. It is thought to have been served as a side to Swedish pizza since sometime in the 1960s.

It fits nicely with the Swedish habit of eating raw vegetable salads in work canteens at lunchtime (*råkost*, page 85) and it keeps for a really long time. In fact cabbage salad is almost better after a few days in the fridge, when the vinegar and salt have 'cured' the cabbage a little bit.

It should be really vinegary, so don't hold back on the vinaigrette. I like to flavour mine with caraway seeds, gently toasted in a dry pan and some finely cut shallots in addition to the original recipe. Oh, and I love making this salad with red cabbage, too.

Preparation time: 10 minutes
Resting time: at least 1 hour
Serves: 4, very generously

1 cabbage
1 quantity Vinaigrette (page 676), or to taste
shallot, finely sliced, to taste (optional)
caraway seeds, lightly toasted, to taste
   (optional)
salt and black pepper, to taste

Use a mandoline to slice the cabbage thinly. Dress the shredded cabbage really well and leave it to sit for at least an hour. Taste and adjust the seasoning, if necessary, just before serving.

For image see page 95

CABBAGE AND LINGONBERRY SALAD

Kaali-puolukkasalaatti (Finland)
Vitkål och lingonsallad (Sweden)

This theoretical insanity of a salad is often served next to black pudding (blood sausage), where it is surprisingly fantastic. It shouldn't have any salt or pepper or dressing: just the Sugared Lingonberries (page 692).

Preparation time: 10 minutes
Serves: 4, very generously

1 cabbage
200 ml/7 fl oz (¾ cup plus 1 tablespoon)
   Sugared Lingonberries (page 692)

Use a mandoline to slice the cabbage thinly. Place in a bowl with the lingonberries. Toss gently and serve straight away.

For image see page 95

GRILLED SUMMER CABBAGE

Grillad sommarkål (Sweden)

Preparation and cooking time: 20 minutes
Serves: 4

1 tender summer cabbage
cold-pressed, nutty rapeseed (canola) oil
juice of ¼ lemon
salt, to taste

Split the cabbage into suitable pieces. I like wedges, cut along the length. A small cabbage becomes quarters and a bigger one as many wedges as it takes. The natural shape of the wedge, which is thin towards the centre and thick at the outer edge, is perfect, because the thin part will roast and become really crispy and a little bitter, whilst the middle of the thicker part will remain almost raw and lukewarm – another kind of crispy.

Light a wood or charcoal grill. Place the cabbage wedges over high heat and grill until parts of the exterior are almost blackened. Transfer to a serving plate, season with salt, drizzle with rapeseed (canola) oil, and finish with a squeeze of lemon juice. Serve immediately.

For image see page 95

FINNISH CABBAGE SOUP

Kaalikeitto / Lammaskaali (Finland)

This dish resembles the Mutton or Lamb in Cabbage (*Får I kål*, page 347) a little but has an addition of carrots, onions and a bit more punch to its seasoning. The amount of liquid added to it can vary a little. Sometimes it is served very much like a soup and other times more like a stew. *Kaalikeitto* would be the most common name for the soup version and *lammaskaali* for the stew one.

The stew version is often served with Sugared Lingonberries (page 692) and Finnish Rye Bread (page 504), whereas the soup version is mostly served just with the Finnish Rye Bread.

Preparation and cooking time: 2 hours
Serves: 4

butter, for browning
500 g/1 lb 2 oz lamb or mutton suitable
   for braising, shoulder or neck is good,
   cut into 1¼ in/3 cm cubes
500 ml–1 litre/17–34 fl oz (2–4¼ cups)
   Meat Stock (page 650)
500 g/1 lb 2 oz cabbage, coarsely shredded
2 carrots, cut into 1 cm/½ inch slices
1 large onion, cut into wedges
15 black peppercorns
2 bay leaves
2 teaspoons dried marjoram
1 bunch chopped parsley, to finish
salt and black pepper, to taste

Melt a little butter in a cast iron pan over a medium heat. Add the meat and brown a bit. Add the stock (broth) and bring to a slow simmer. Cover and cook for about 1 hour or until the meat is starting to become tender.

Add the vegetables and aromatics to the pan. Some people like to wrap the aromatics in muslin (cheesecloth) but I don't mind biting into a peppercorn now and then so I usually just leave them floating freely. Adjust the level of liquid with water if necessary and continue cooking for about another 30 minutes or until the vegetables are cooked. There shouldn't be any crunchy vegetables in this dish but they shouldn't be completely boiled to mush either.

Adjust the seasoning and sprinkle with some parsley before serving.

FINNISH CREAMY CABBAGE SOUP

Maitokaali (Finland)

Some older recipes seem to contain cabbage as the only vegetable, whilst more recent versions often contain other vegetables, like carrots, celeriac (celery root) and leeks – or sometime even tomato. Newer recipes are also often seasoned with a little garlic, and herbs like thyme.

As the title of this dish consists of two words, *maito*, meaning 'milk' and *kaali*, meaning 'cabbage', I'm providing a recipe made up of just these things. Milk and cabbage are the two primary flavours, underlined with a very mild, comforting seasoning of allspice and bay leaf. If you feel like adding some other vegetables, do so. Don't cut them too big, though, or they won't cook in the same time as the cabbage.

Preparation and cooking time: 30 minutes
Serves: 4

1 tablespoon butter
1 small cabbage or ½ large cabbage,
   shredded
1 tablespoon plain (all-purpose) flour
1 litre/34 fl oz (4¼ cups) milk
1 teaspoon sugar
1 bay leaf
freshly ground allspice berries, to taste
salt, to taste

Place a pot over a medium heat and add the butter. Add the cabbage and cook without browning until it starts to become translucent. Sift the flour over the cabbage and stir. Add the milk, sugar and the bay leaf. Simmer over a low heat until the cabbage is completely tender, stirring often. Adjust the texture with water if too thick. Towards the end, season with a little allspice and salt.

SOUP OF BROWNED CABBAGE

Brynt vitkålssoppa (Sweden)

This soup is often served with Small Smoked Pork Sausages (page 428) on a side plate.

Preparation and cooking time: 1 hour
Serves: 4

2 tablespoons lard
1 winter cabbage, stem removed, finely
   shredded
2 tablespoons golden syrup
1½ litres/50 fl oz (6¼ cups) Pork Stock
   (page 650)
6–8 allspice berries
salt, to taste

Place a cast-iron pot over a medium heat and add the lard. Add the cabbage and cook until it browns slightly. Add the golden syrup and continue browning, still over a medium heat. Pour in the stock (broth) and add the allspice berries. Cover the pan and simmer until the cabbage is just tender. Adjust the level of salt.

CABBAGE AND MINCED MEAT SOUP FROM NIKKALUOKTA

Nikkaluokta soppa (Sweden)

Nikkaluokta is a small village in the very northern part of Sweden. This soup is one of my best school canteen memories from growing up. It is usually flavoured with a bit of tomato purée and a bit of mustard, but most of the flavour comes from the cabbage and minced (ground) meat itself.

Serve it with some sourdough rye crispbread with butter and cheese.

Preparation and cooking time: 35 minutes
Serves: 4, generously

½ cabbage (about 400 g/14 oz)
25 g/1 oz (1¾ tablespoons) butter
1 leek, finely sliced
400g/14 oz minced (ground) beef

2 tablespoons strong mustard
2 tablespoons tomato purée
1 litre/34 fl oz (4¼ cups) Beef Stock
   (page 650)
2 bay leaves
splash of Chinese mushroom soy sauce
salt and white pepper, to taste
1 handful parsley, chopped

Use a mandoline to slice the cabbage finely.

Heat the butter in a pot over a medium heat. Add the cabbage, leek and beef and brown until it is all quite dark. Let it take its time.

Stir in the mustard and tomato purée, followed by the beef stock. Add the bay leaves and a splash of soy sauce. Bring to a simmer and cook for about 10–15 minutes, or until the cabbage is soft. Taste and adjust the seasoning. Sprinkle with parsley and serve straight away.

SWEET-AND-SOUR BRAISED RED CABBAGE

Rödkål till jul (Sweden)

This is an indispensible part of Christmas dinner for many Nordic people. Some people braise it with blackcurrant cordial, others with red wine. I think vinegar and brown sugar are enough. It is best to prepare this dish a day or two in advance and let sit to be reheated the day of serving.

Some people (myself included) like to add diced apple to this dish. If you do, use a good firm cooking apple. There is no need to peel it but do remove the core.

Preparation and cooking time: 1 hour
Serves: 4 as a side dish, but many as part of
   a spread

1 red cabbage
100 g/3½ oz (½ cup) brown sugar
100 ml/3½ fl oz (⅓ cup plus 1 tablespoon)
   red wine vinegar
10 cloves
1 bay leaf

1 piece of cassia cinnamon
2 cooking apples, cored but not peeled, cut
  into 1 cm/½ inch dice (optional)
salt and black pepper, to taste

Shred the cabbage finely.

Place all the ingredients, except for the apple, in a large pot. Cook over a medium heat, stirring from time to time. You may need to add a bit of water if it goes too dry during the cooking process. There should be a little liquid on the bottom of the pan at all times, but it should not be too wet. Cook for about 40 minutes, or until the cabbage is tender and sweet. Add the diced apple, if using, and cook for another 10 minutes.

Increase the heat a little and reduce the liquid until it thickens to a glaze that coats all the cabbage nicely. Taste and adjust the seasoning just before serving.

For image see page 305

CARAMELIZED CABBAGE

This dish is often served as part of Christmas celebrations and it is a common garnish for ham. Make it with dripping from roasted pork or ham stock if you have it. Other broths or stocks can also be used but it is something special with the savouriness from cooked cured pork. It should be intensely sweet and salty. Some people make this in a pot on the stove and others in the oven. If you decide to make it in the oven and you happen to be roasting Pork Ribs Stuffed with Prunes (page 303), simply place the ribs on a rack above the cabbage as they cook and let the drippings season the vegetable.

I like the oven version, so that's what I have described below, but if you prefer to make it on the stove, it's the same process – just don't cook it over too high a heat though, medium is enough.

The time really depends on the type of cabbage. Older winter cabbage takes longer but it tastes the best.

Preparation and cooking time: 1–2 hours
  depending on the cabbage
Serves: 4

1 head of cabbage, cut into 1 cm/½ inch
  slices, stem removed
100 g/3½ oz (7 tablespoons) butter
140 g/4¾ oz (⅓ cup plus 2 tablespoons)
  golden syrup
400 ml/14 fl oz (1⅔ cups) liquid, pork
  dripping or pork stock
salt and white pepper, to taste

Preheat the oven to 200°C/400°F/Gas Mark 6.

Place all of the ingredients in a roasting pan but be careful with the salt as dripping or ham stock is already salty. Cook in the oven for 1–1½ hours, until deeply caramelized and until the liquid has almost reduced into the cabbage itself.

BROCCOLI

Broccoli has been grown in the Mediterranean for a very long time, but it didn't become popular elsewhere until quite late, about 1950. It is very hardy and can be grown almost everywhere in the Nordic region.

Regardless of how it is cooked, I think broccoli should have a good bit of bite to it. Overcooked broccoli is just not very nice.

Allow about 150 g/5 oz broccoli per person, as a side dish.

BOILED BROCCOLI

You can steam broccoli heads whole, or cut the florets away from the thick central stalks. Don't discard the stalks, however, instead slice them and add to the pan.

Preparation and cooking time:
  5 minutes for florets, 15 minutes
  for whole heads
Serves: 4

2 large heads broccoli, trimmed
salt, to taste

Follow the instructions on page 82 for boiling vegetables. Cook the broccoli until tender. Be careful not to overcook the delicate tips; the stalks should still have some crunch.

Lift the broccoli out of the pan with a slotted spoon and drain briefly in a colander. Serve with a little sprinkling of salt, if you like.

STEAMED WHOLE BROCCOLI TOPS

I love small broccoli tops in the spring and early summer, before the head has fully developed. I steam leaves, stems – the whole thing – and eat it with a sprinkling of salt and some good butter to dip it in. It's perfect as a starter (appetizer) or light meal.

Preparation and cooking time:
  10 minutes
Serves: 4

4 whole young, large broccoli tops
salt, to taste
soft butter, to serve

Follow the instructions on page 82 for steaming vegetables. It will take 5–8 minutes and the broccoli should still have a bit of crunch.

For image see page 133

BROCCOLI GRATIN

Serve this as a side dish with meat or as a meal in itself with some cold cuts on the side.

Preparation and cooking time: 30 minutes
Serves: 6 as a side dish, 4 as a main course

600 g/1 lb 5 oz broccoli, trimmed and cut
  into florets
½ quantity Béchamel Sauce (page 666)
  substituting half the milk with cream
100 g/3½ oz mature hard cheese, finely
  grated
1 egg yolk
freshly grated nutmeg, to taste
(optional)
salt and white pepper, to taste

Follow the instructions on page 85 for blanching or page 82 for steaming the broccoli. It should still have a bit of crunch to it.

Follow the instructions on page 666 for preparing the béchamel sauce. Take the pan off the heat and stir in the grated cheese. When it has completely melted, stir in the egg yolk and nutmeg (if using) and season well.

Preheat your grill (broiler) to 230°C/450°F.

Arrange the broccoli florets in an ovenproof dish. Pour on enough sauce to coat the top of the florets and the bottom of the dish, without drowning everything. Place under the grill until the sauce has mingled nicely with the broccoli juices and the surface is well browned.

BOILED CAULIFLOWER

It's best not to cut cauliflower florets too small or they can become too salty if you use the good handful that is specified in the base method (page 82). If you want the florets to be smaller, then reduce the amount of salt in the cooking water.

I often find it unnecessary to add more salt to cauliflower when you serve it. Sometimes I like to finish with a sprinkling of parsley.

Preparation and cooking time: 10 minutes
Serves: 4

600 g/1 lb 5 oz cauliflower, trimmed and cut
  into large florets
salt, to taste
chopped parsley, to serve (optional)

Follow the instructions on page 82 for boiling vegetables. Cook the cauliflower until tender.

Lift the florets out of the pan with a slotted spoon
and drain briefly in a colander. Serve with a little
sprinkling of salt, if you think it necessary, and
parsley, if you like the idea.

STEAMED WHOLE CAULIFLOWER

In the summer time, I love to steam a whole head
of cauliflower, straight from the garden, all the
leaves and stuff still attached, just rinsed, nothing
more. It could be a side dish, but also a shared
dish in the middle of the table. A piece of the head
itself, a couple of leaves, a lump of salty butter to
dip it in and perhaps a wedge of lemon is about as
good as it gets for me.

Preparation and cooking time: 15 minutes
Serves: 4

1 large cauliflower, leaves still attached
salt, to taste

To serve
4 lemon wedges, (optional)
salted butter (optional)

Follow the instructions on page 82 for steaming
vegetables. It will take about 15 minutes (or maybe
a bit less) to cook through. It depends on the size
of the cauliflower, whether you're using a steam
oven or basket and how soft you want it to be. Test
with a skewer to see if the thickest part of the stem
is cooked. Sprinkle with some salt before serving if
you want to.

For image see page 103

SHAVINGS OF RAW CAULIFLOWER

One of the tastiest and simplest salads I know, it is
essential to have a mandoline to make this with a
good result.

Preparation and cooking time: 5 minutes
Serves: 4

600 g/1 lb 5 oz cauliflower, trimmed and cut
  into large florets
1 quantity Vinaigrette (page 676) or
  Citronette (page 676), or to taste
1 good handful chives, finely snipped
salt and white pepper, to taste

Use a mandoline to slice the cauliflower florets
thinly, so that they look like little trees.

Put the cauliflower slices in a large mixing bowl.
Add the dressing, chives and seasonings and mix
everything together gently so as not to break up
the delicate cauliflower. Taste and adjust the
seasoning and serve immediately.

For image see page 103

BROWNED CAULIFLOWER

Preparation and cooking time: 20 minutes
Serves: 4

1 cauliflower, trimmed
1 tablespoon butter, at room temperature
salt, to taste

Cut the cauliflower into florets. If the thick stem
in the middle is tender, cut it into slices about
1 cm/½ inch thick.

Melt the butter in a non-stick pan, without browning
it. Add the cauliflower, increase the heat to medium
and cook whilst stirring every now and then until the
cauliflower has reached the desired egree of browning. I like it quite dark. Season with salt and serve.

For image see page 103

CAULIFLOWER SOUP

Blomkålsuppe (Norway)
Blomkålssoppa (Sweden)

If you like the savouriness of slowly fried cauli-flower, cook it as described in the recipe for browned cauliflower (see page 101) and use that, to make the soup as described in the method below.

I like to fold the cream into the soup, just before serving, letting it melt in white swirls of fluffiness. But if you want you can just add the cream to the soup as you make it too. Don't boil it however; it takes away the flavour of the cream itself and makes the soup a bit too sweet.

A lot of people sprinkle some pieces of fried bacon over the soup before serving it, others like it with fried Small Smoked Pork Sausages (page 428). I like bacon and a halved hard-boiled egg in there, and a little sprinkle of chives too.

Preparation and cooking time: 30 minutes
Serves: 4

800 g/1¾ lb cauliflower, trimmed and cut
    into florets
milk, to dilute
200 ml/7 fl oz (¾ cup plus 1 tablespoon) cream
    (optional)
salt and white pepper, to taste

If you have a steam oven, follow the instructions on page 82 for steaming the cauliflower. It should be quite soft, but not mushy. Retain any of the liquid that seeps out onto the tray; it is full of flavour.

If you don't have a steam oven, follow the instructions on page 82 for boiling the cauliflower. Only use enough water to barely cover the cauliflower and don't add any salt. Reserve the cooking liquid.

Place the cooked cauliflower florets in a powerful blender. Add a bit of the reserved steaming or boiling water. At this stage you should add as little liquid as possible; really just enough to enable the vegetables to purée effectively. Turn on the motor and blend for about 10 minutes; it takes a lot longer than you think. If the vegetables clump together and resist blending, then add a little more liquid, but only add milk at this stage

if it's really necessary. If the motor seems to be getting hot, stop and let it rest for a few minutes.

Once the cauliflower has turned into a smooth, thick purée, tip through a fine sieve into a pot set over a low–medium heat. Now you can gradually add milk until you achieve a consistency that you like. Be careful not to let the soup boil. There is no need to actually cook the soup any more, just to heat it until it is nice and warm to eat. Adjust the seasonings, but remember that too much salt will make it taste more of dairy than of cauliflower.

If using cream, whip it to soft peaks and fold into the soup just before serving.

For image see opposite page

CREAMED CAULIFLOWER

Preparation and cooking time: 5 minutes
Serves: 4

600 g/1 lb 5 oz cauliflower florets
½ quantity Béchamel Sauce (page 666),
    substituting half the milk with cream
salt and white pepper, to taste

Follow the instructions on page 85 for blanching the cauliflower florets.

Follow the method on page 666 for preparing the béchamel sauce.

In a small pot, bring the béchamel to a simmer, then add the cauliflower florets. Season well with salt and pepper and serve immediately.

For image see opposite page

Clockwise from top left: Steamed Whole Cauliflower (page 101); Cauliflower Soup (page 102); Cauliflower Gratin (page 104); Creamed Cauliflower (page 102); Browned Cauliflower (page 101); Shavings of Raw Cauliflower (page 101)

CAULIFLOWER GRATIN

Serve this as a side dish with a main course or as a meal in itself, with some charcuterie and a salad on the side.

Preparation and cooking time: 30 minutes
Serves: 6 as a side dish, 4 as a main course

800 g/1¾ lb cauliflower, trimmed and cut
   into florets
½ quantity Béchamel Sauce (page 666)
   substituting half the milk with cream
100 g/3½ oz mature hard cheese,
   finely grated
1 egg yolk
freshly grated nutmeg, to taste
   (optional)
salt and white pepper, to taste

Follow the instructions on page 85 for blanching or page 82 for steaming the cauliflower. It should be quite soft but not mushy.

Follow the instructions on page 666 for preparing the béchamel sauce. Take the pan off the heat and stir in the grated cheese.

When the cheese has completely melted, stir in the egg yolk and nutmeg (if using) and season well.

Preheat your grill (broiler) to 230°C/450°F.

Arrange the cauliflower florets in an ovenproof dish. Pour on enough sauce to coat the top of the florets and the bottom of the dish, without drowning everything. Place under the grill until the sauce has mingled nicely with the cauliflower juices and the surface is well browned.

For image see page 103

BRUSSELS SPROUTS

One of the most lovely autumn (fall) and winter vegetables, I just love the bitter-sweetness of a Brussels sprout. Do not overcook Brussels sprouts; they turn mushy in texture and acquire that strange sulphuric aroma that is less than pleasant.

Allow about 150 g/5 oz of sprouts per person, as a side dish.

BOILED BRUSSELS SPROUTS

Preparation and cooking time: 10–12 minutes
Serves: 4

600 g/1 lb 5 oz Brussels sprouts, cleaned
   and trimmed
salt, to taste

Pour 5 litres/10½ UK pints water into a very large pan. Add the salt and bring to the boil. Add the Brussels sprouts to the boiling water and cook for 8–10 minutes, or until just tender.

Lift them out of the pan with a slotted spoon and into warm serving bowl. Sprinkle with salt, if you think it's really necessary, and serve immediately.

BROWNED BRUSSELS SPROUTS

It is essential to let this dish take its time so that the sprouts caramelize deeply and so that they dry out a bit during the cooking process, something that gives them their pleasant, chewy, firm texture. If your sprouts are really big, cut them into halves, otherwise keep them whole.

Preparation and cooking time: 30 minutes
Serves: 4

50 g/2 oz (3½ tablespoons) butter
600 g/1 lb 5 oz Brussels sprouts, cleaned
   and trimmed
good squeeze of lemon or splash
   of vinegar
salt and black pepper, to taste

Melt the butter in a pan over a medium heat and add the Brussels sprouts. Cook over a low–medium heat until they are nicely browned and just tender, but still firm. This will take about 20 minutes and you should resist stirring them too often.

Towards the end of the cooking time, increase the heat a bit so that it sizzles, then add the lemon or vinegar and stir gently to deglaze. It should be hot enough for the liquid to evaporate in about 30 seconds, while you swirl the pan, coating the sprouts in the cooking liquid. Season well and serve immediately.

CREAMED BRUSSELS SPROUTS

Prepare this recipe with whole or halved heads of Brussels sprouts, blanched before or with the individual leaves picked, like for the salad recipe below, and added raw to the béchamel. The second version is not in any way traditional, but I love it. The sprout leaves should be just wilted but still a bit crunchy.

Preparation and cooking time: 5 minutes
Serves: 4

600 g/1 lb 5 oz Brussels sprouts, cleaned
  and trimmed
½ quantity Béchamel Sauce (page 666),
  substituting half the milk with cream
salt and white pepper, to taste

Follow the instructions on page 85 for blanching the sprouts. (Or separate the leaves and keep them raw.)

Follow the method on page 666 for preparing the béchamel sauce.

In a small pot, bring the béchamel to a simmer, then add the sprouts. If they are blanched, then heat until they warm through. For raw leaves, simply fold them through the hot sauce just before serving, letting them wilt a bit in the heat. Season well with salt and pepper and serve immediately.

GLAZED BRUSSELS SPROUTS

I like to add a little sugar when glazing Brussels sprouts; it goes really well with their slight bitterness. I also salt them at the very end, so the salt crystals don't have time to melt before I eat them.

Preparation and cooking time: 5–15 minutes
Serves: 4

600 g/1 lb 5 oz Brussels sprouts, cleaned
  and trimmed
50 g/2 oz (3½ tablespoons) cold butter, cut
  into 1 cm/½ inch dice
1 tablespoon sugar (optional)
salt and white pepper, to taste

Follow the instructions on page 85 for blanching the sprouts. (Or separate the leaves and keep them raw.)

Follow the instructions on page 83 for glazed vegetables. If using sugar, add it at the very beginning, so it cooks into the glaze. Season with salt and pepper just before serving.

For image see page 275

RAW BRUSSELS SPROUTS SALAD

This is one of my favourite winter salads. The key is to dress it and then leave it to sit for a few minutes so that the leaves wilt a little before serving. Just before you are ready to eat, sprinkle some croutons or toasted hazelnuts over it – preferably still hot from the oven or pan.

To prepare the sprouts takes a bit of time. If you are in a hurry, substitute them for kale and follow the procedure below. It's almost as delicious.

Preparation and cooking time: 30 minutes
Serves: 4 as a side dish

600 g/1 lb 5 oz Brussels sprouts
1 quantity Vinaigrette (page 676),
    substituting 1 tablespoon grain mustard
    for the Dijon
salt and black pepper, to taste
1 handful croutons or toasted hazelnuts

Use a small paring knife to separate and remove all the sprout leaves. Put them in a large mixing bowl. It looks like a large amount, but they will wilt down in the dressing.

Add the vinaigrette and season the salad well. Leave to sit for 5 minutes, then toss again. Adjust the seasoning and transfer to a serving bowl.

Top with croutons or toasted hazelnuts and serve straight away.

GRATINATED LEEKS

Serve as an accompaniment to fish or meat dishes, or by itself as a starter (appetizer).

Preparation and cooking time: 30 minutes
Serves: 4

4 leeks, trimmed and washed
6 tablespoons cream
50 g/2 oz mature hard cheese, very
    finely grated
freshly grated nutmeg, to taste
salt and white pepper, to taste

Follow the instructions on page 85 for blanching vegetables or page 82 for steaming vegetables, keeping the leeks whole.

Preheat the grill (broiler) to 230°C/450°F.

Split the cooked leeks lengthwise and place them on an ovenproof dish, cut side up.

Mix the cream and cheese together in a small bowl. Season with salt, pepper and nutmeg. Don't be shy about the seasoning here; remember that it is for the entire dish, not just the cream. Spoon onto the leeks, allowing it to sink down into all the layers. Place under the grill until the cream is nicely brown and bubbling. Finish with a sprinkling of salt and another grind of pepper just before serving.

For image see opposite page

Clockwise from top left: Gratinated Leeks (page 106); fresh leek; Onion Cream Sauce (page 663); Sweet Fried Onions (page 108)

PICKLED SMALL ONIONS

Syltede perleløg (Denmark)
Syltlök (Sweden)

You can use any aromatics you like with these pickled onions. I would normally use bay leaves, a few black peppercorns, some mustard seeds and perhaps a few slices of ginger.

You will need sterilized glass pickling jars.

Preparation and cooking time: 30 minutes
Pickling time: at least 1 week
Makes: 500 ml / 17 fl oz (2 cups)

500 ml/17 fl oz (2 cups) small pickling
  onions, cleaned, but skins left on
aromatics, to taste
1 quantity 1-2-3 Pickling Liquor (page 657)
salt, to taste

Bring a large pan of water to the boil over a medium heat. Add the onions to the pan and boil for 2 minutes. Don't overcook them; they should be cooked through but still a bit crunchy. If cooked for too long they will become overly sweet and too soft.

Drain the onions and rinse them under cold running water. When cool enough to handle, peel the onions and pack them tightly into the sterilized glass jars. Add your choice of aromatics and a pinch of salt to each jar. Pour over enough pickling liquor to cover, leaving a 1 cm/½ inch head space. Close the lids and place in a cool dark place for at least a week.

CRISPY FRIED ONIONS

Stekt løk (Norway)
Ristet løg (Denmark)
Rostad lök (Sweden)

An exceptionally important topping on Swedish hot dogs – and tasty with many other dishes too, for that matter.

Preparation and cooking time: 1 hour
Drying time: 2–3 hours
Makes: 200 g/7 oz (1 cup)

5 onions, cut into 3 mm/⅛ inch slices
2 tablespoons potato starch
1 good pinch very fine salt
neutral cooking oil, for deep-frying

Put the onions in a mixing bowl with the potato starch and salt and toss together.

Preheat the oven to 100°C/200°F/Gas Mark ½ and line a large baking sheet with paper towels.

Pour the oil into a deep pot or deep fryer and heat to 140°C/275°F.

Deep-fry the onions in batches until they are golden and quite dry. Stir from time to time, especially at the beginning, so that they don't stick together too much. Use a slotted spoon to lift them onto the prepared baking sheet to soak up excess oil. Repeat with the remaining onions. Discard the paper towels and place the sheet in the oven for 2–3 hours, or until the onions have completely dried.

SWEET FRIED ONIONS

Bløde stegte løg (Denmark)
Stekt lök (Sweden)

Sweet, soft and succulent fried slices of onion are used in dishes all over the Nordics, but it is in Denmark that they are revered. Type *bløde løg* into your browser's search engine and watch the results unfold: hundreds of tips on how to get them just right from hundreds of different sources of published media and thousands of different blogs and web forums. One of Denmark's biggest newspapers has a post on their site with tips for a fantastic fried onion; the comments field is filled with almost a hundred separate comments debating what is really the best fried onion, how it should be done and who is right.

A lot of recipes contain ingredients to help colour the onions: some contain sugar, others contain soy sauce, yet others contain a dash of coffee. I think that they colour and sweeten just fine without anything added to them but butter, and I think that what is most often missing when people do this is time. The onions should be browned and cooked slowly to acquire the right kind of deep caramelization.

Preparation and cooking time: 45 minutes
Serves: 4

50 g/2 oz (3½ tablespoons) butter
4 onions, cut into 3 mm/⅛ inch slices
salt and white pepper, to taste

Melt the butter in a frying pan over a medium heat. Season the onions lightly with salt to help them brown nicely, then fry the onions, stirring from time to time. Don't stir them too often or it will break them up too much. If you find you need to stir them to prevent them burning on the bottom of the pan, then your pan is too hot and you should lower the heat. Fry the onions until they are nice and amber. Make sure that the colour penetrates right through the onions, and is not just on the surface. Adjust the seasoning before serving.

For image see page 107

CARROTS

I love carrots, and they have been part of Nordic eating habits for a long time. They were first grown in our part of the world during the Middle Ages by monks in the monastery gardens. Winter carrots and summer carrots are so different that you can almost consider them to be two entirely separate vegetables. Winter carrots have a deep sweetness from the chemical energy stored in the root for the coming season. They are well suited for long cooking in braises and stews, or even for roasting in the oven, where the sugars can slowly caramelize. The fragrant, light and crunchy summer carrot, lighter in colour and sweetness, but powerful in aroma needs minimal treatment: perhaps just a brush or scraping to remove any dirt and then a quick glaze with butter (see right). Or why not eat them raw, as a snack?

Allow 150–180 g/5–6 oz carrots (about 2 winter carrots) per person, to serve as a side dish.

GLAZED CARROTS

Many people like their carrots in a sweet-and-sour glaze. So do I but I also enjoy them just glazed in butter. Either way, I like to season them with white pepper and sprinkle them with a bit of chopped parsley just before serving.

If you are using large carrots, clean and peel them, then cut them into slices or sticks, about 1 cm/½ inch thick. Small summer carrots can just be scrubbed clean and left whole.

Preparation and cooking time: 15 minutes
Serves: 4

8 large winter carrots or 20 small summer
   carrots
50 g/2 oz (3½ tablespoons) cold butter, cut
   into 1 cm/½ inch dice
3 tablespoons sugar (optional)
juice of ½ lemon or 1 tablespoon vinegar
   (optional)
chopped parsley, to taste
salt and white pepper, to taste

Follow the instructions on page 83 for glazed raw vegetables. If you are making a sweet-and-sour version, add the sugar and lemon juice (or vinegar) at the very beginning, so it boils into the glaze. Just before serving, adjust the seasoning and sprinkle with parsley.

BOILED CARROTS

If you are using large carrots, clean and peel them, then cut them into slices or batons, about 1 cm/½ inch thick. Small summer carrots can just be scrubbed clean and left whole.

Preparation and cooking time: 15 minutes
Serves: 4

8 large winter carrots or 20 small summer
  carrots
1 big handful salt

Bring a pot of generously salted water to the boil. Add the carrots and cook until they are cooked, but not mushy. Summer carrots are nice if they still have a bit of crunch.

Lift them out of the pan with a slotted spoon and drain briefly in a colander. Serve with a little sprinkling of salt, if you think it necessary, otherwise leave them just as they are.

For image see opposite page

GRATED CARROT SALAD

I love this salad with almost anything, even instead of pickles in a good sandwich with charcuterie. I almost always have a bowl of this sitting in the fridge at home. It keeps for more than a week and it almost gets better if it is allowed to sit for a bit.

You need to season this salad well and use quite a bit of vinegar. The trick is to have the vinegar and the salt working on the pieces of grated carrot, almost as though they were cooking it.

I don't like olive oil much in this recipe but rather make my vinaigrette for carrot salad with a neutral oil like sunflower.

Preparation and cooking time: 5 minutes
Sitting time: at least 30 minutes
Serves: 4 as a side dish

8 large carrots, peeled and finely or
  coarsely grated
1 quantity Vinaigrette (page 676) or
  Citronette (page 676), or to taste
salt and white pepper, to taste

Put the grated carrots in a bowl, add the dressing and seasonings to taste and mix everything together well. It will take more dressing than you think because a lot will be absorbed into the carrots themselves. Leave to sit for at least 30 minutes and adjust the seasoning before serving.

For image see opposite page

CREAMED CARROTS

Preparation and cooking time: 5 minutes
Serves: 4

8 large carrots, peeled, cut into 5 mm/
  ¼ inch slices
½ quantity Béchamel Sauce (page 666)
  substituting half the milk with cream
freshly grated nutmeg, to taste (optional)
chopped parsley, to taste (optional)
salt and white pepper, to taste

Follow the instructions on page 85 for blanching the carrots.

Follow the instructions on page 666 for preparing the béchamel sauce.

Reheat the blanched carrots in the béchamel over a medium heat. Stir them gently, so they don't stick to the bottom of the pan, but try to make sure they don't break up. When hot, season well with salt and white pepper, and nutmeg and/or parsley, if using. Serve immediately.

For image see opposite page

Clockwise from top left: diced carrot; Carrot Soup (page 112); Grated Carrot Salad (page 110); Boiled Carrots (page 110); Creamed Carrots (page 110)

CARROT SOUP

Gulerodssuppe (Denmark)
Morotssoppa (Sweden)

I like my carrot soup just a little bit sweet and sour. The carrots are usually sweet enough just as they are so I would usually add a dash of vinegar towards the very end. Make carrot soup with Vegetable Stock (page 650). Chicken Stock (page 650) is also tasty and gives a bit more heartiness to the soup but it tends to overpower the carrot. I almost never add dairy to carrot soup but if you want to you can add cream either to the purée or (perhaps preferably) whip it first and just fold it into the hot soup moments before serving.

I tend to like to steam my carrots when making a soup or purée.

For more information on making vegetable soup, including this one, read the general text on Vegetable Soups (page 87) before starting.

Preparation and cooking time: 30 minutes
Serves: 4

600 g/1 lb 5 oz winter carrots, peeled
   and thinly sliced (use a mandoline if you
   have one)
1 litre/34 fl oz (4¼ cups) Vegetable Stock
   (page 650), hot
a dash of vinegar (optional)
200 ml/7 fl oz (¾ cup plus 1 tablespoon),
   cream, to serve (optional)
salt and white pepper, to taste

Follow the instructions on page 82 for steamed vegetables and steam the carrots until just done, not more. Put them (still hot) into a powerful blender, add some stock (broth) and mix at full speed. Continue to add more stock until you have achieved your desired thickness. Don't add the liquid all at once, as different carrots will thicken the soup to different degrees. Season and serve immediately.

For image see page 111

ROASTED ROOT VEGETABLES

While this is not at all a traditional dish, it is one of the most popular ways of preparing root vegetables today. The exact combination of root vegetables is up to personal preference, but I think it is important to have at least some sweet vegetables (like carrots, parsnips or beetroot/beets) which acquire a soft, chewy texture and flavour, to contrast with the ones that go floury and soft (like potatoes) or sweet and succulent (like onions). Some people add a lot of seasoning to their roasted veg, but I just like some salt and possibly a bit of black pepper.

Preparation and cooking time: 30–60 minutes
Serves: 4

1 kg/2¼ lb mixed root vegetables, cleaned,
   peeled (if necessary) and cut into suitably
   sized pieces
50 g/2 oz (3½ tablespoons) butter (or a good
   dash of neutral cooking oil)
salt and black pepper, to taste

Preheat the oven to 230°C/450°F/Gas Mark 8. Line a roasting pan with baking (parchment) paper.

Pile the vegetables into the roasting pan, season them, then daub on the butter evenly or add a splash of oil over the top. Roast for about 20 minutes, or until sweet, browned and a bit shrivelled. The exact time will depend on your choice of vegetables and the size you cut them.

ROOT VEGETABLE MASH

Root vegetable mash is often served as an accompaniment to cuts of salt pork such as knuckle or shoulder, along with a good spoonful of strong mustard. The mash is usually made with the cooking liquid from the meat. I like adding a few bay leaves, allspice berries and white peppercorns while the meat is braising. If you don't have any reserved cooking liquid (or if you just don't want that flavour), cook the root vegetables in plain water with these aromatics.

The flavour balance of the mash is determined by the amount of potato you use, relative to the swede (rutabaga). The recipe below is tasty, but not overly strong; if you like the pepperiness of swede then increase the quantity and decrease the amount of potato accordingly.

This mash is best made with winter vegetables, rather than summer ones.

Preparation and cooking time: 1 hour
Serves: 4

1 large swede (rutabaga), peeled and cut into
  small pieces
2 large carrots, peeled and cut into small
  pieces
2 bay leaves (optional)
a few allspice berries (optional)
few white peppercorns (optional)
5 floury potatoes, peeled and chopped
50 g/2 oz (3½ tablespoons) butter, diced
salt and white pepper, to taste

Combine the swede and carrots in a large pot. Add enough water (or braising liquid) to cover, then add the bay, allspice and white pepper (unless these had previously been added to the pork while cooking) and bring to the boil. Cook for about 10 minutes, then add the potatoes and continue boiling until all the vegetables are completely soft. You might have to add a little more liquid, but don't overdo it as you don't want the mash to be too liquid.

Drain the vegetables (remove the aromatics if using) and mash them. For a coarser mash you can just use a stiff whisk (which is my preference) or for a smoother mash, push them through a meat mincer (grinder) with the coarse plate. Add the butter and stir until it has melted. Season the mash well before serving.

BROWNED SWEDE

This is a common accompaniment to meat dishes in Finland. I have also seen a variation of this recipe where the pieces of swede (rutabaga) were sprinkled with coarse rye flour before being browned in the pan, resulting in a crispy, chewy, soft sensation that I quite liked.

Preparation and cooking time: 25–35 minutes
Serves: 4

1 large swede (rutabaga), peeled and cut into
  rough pieces about 1.5 cm/⅝ inch
  in diameter
2 tablespoons butter
2 tablespoons brown sugar
salt and white pepper, to taste

Place the pieces of swede (rutabaga), the butter and sugar in a heavy cast-iron pan and start to cook over a medium heat. Stir frequently, especially in the beginning. Cook for 20–30 minutes. The vegetables should caramelize slowly and soften at the same time. Season with salt and pepper and serve immediately.

FINNISH VEGETABLE CASSEROLES

Laatikot (Finland)
Lådor (Sweden)

Vegetable casseroles have been a popular Christmas dish in Finland since the 1930s although they have been part of the broader Finnish menu for much longer.

This sort of casserole is baked slowly in the oven until savoury-sweet and dense. Some versions, like one made from sweet potato, use the naturally occurring amylase enzymes in flour to break down the starch in the vegetable to shorter carbohydrates, which taste sweet. Modern recipes are often sweetened with syrup or sugar instead of allowing the cooking process enough time to convert the starch into sugar naturally.

Finnish vegetable casseroles often have a sprinkling of breadcrumbs on top of them, which soak up the cooking juices from below and caramelize slowly in the heat of the oven.

FINNISH CARROT CASSEROLE (VERSION 1), GRATED

Porkkanalaatikko (Finland)
Morotslåda (Sweden)

Some recipes for *porkkanalaatikko* are made from boiled carrots and others from grated. I would have thought that grated is a more recent adaption but the majority of recipes that I have come across when surveying popular publications and the internet grate it, therefore I did in this recipe. If you want to try the one using boiled carrots, see Version 2, Boiled.

Preparation and cooking time: 1 hour 20 minutes
Serves: 4

110 g/3¾ oz (½ cup) short-grain rice
375 ml/13 fl oz (1½ cups) milk
4 large carrots, peeled and grated on the coarse side of a box grater
2 tablespoons golden syrup
½ teaspoon ground dried ginger
1 egg
3 tablespoons breadcrumbs
salt and white pepper, to taste

Preheat the oven to 175°C/345°F/Gas Mark 4.

Mix the rice with 125 ml/4 fl oz (½ cup) water in a pan. Bring to the boil, then lower the temperature so that it remains on a slow simmer. Add the milk and continue cooking until it thickens to a loose porridge. Leave it to cool down until lukewarm, then add the grated carrot, golden syrup, ginger and the egg to the porridge and stir. Season with salt and pepper, then pour into an ovenproof dish and sprinkle with the breadcrumbs. Bake in the oven for roughly 1 hour. It is done when nicely browned.

FINNISH CARROT CASSEROLE (VERSION 2), BOILED

Porkkanalaatikko (Finland)
Morotslåda (Sweden)

Preparation and cooking time: 1½ hours
Serves: 4

500 g/1 lb 2 oz carrots
90 g/3¼ oz (⅓ cup plus 2 tablespoons) short-grain rice
150 ml/5 fl oz (⅔ cup) cream
1 egg
2 tablespoons golden syrup
freshly grated nutmeg, to taste
breadcrumbs, for sprinkling
salt and white pepper, to taste

Boil the carrots in salted water, then drain, and reserve 250 ml/8 fl oz (1 cup) of the cooking water. Blend the carrots with an immersion blender until quite smooth.

Combine the rice with the reserved cooking water in a small pan. Bring to the boil, then lower the heat, cover, and cook for about 20 minutes.

Preheat the oven to 200°C/400°F/Gas Mark 6.

Drain the rice and tip it into a mixing bowl. Add the puréed carrots, the cream, egg, golden syrup, nutmeg and seasonings and mix everything together well. Tip the mixture into an ovenproof dish and sprinkle on the breadcrumbs in an even layer. Bake in the oven until the breadcrumbs are golden and the casserole is cooked through.

FINNISH SWEET POTATO CASSEROLE

Imelletty perunalaatikko (Finland)

Preparation and cooking time: 6 hours
Serves: 4, or many more if served as a part of a bigger traditional meal

1 kg/2¼ lb floury potatoes (such as King Edward)
2 tablespoons plain (all-purpose) flour
sugar, to taste (optional)
350 ml/12 fl oz (1½ cups) milk
2 teaspoons salt
1 tablespoon butter, plus extra to grease

Fill a large pan with cold water, add the potatoes in their skins and boil until tender. Drain and while still hot, peel them and push them through a ricer.

Let the riced potato cool to less than 75°C/167°F (any hotter will damage the amylase enzymes), but check with a cooking thermometer if you have been especially quick. Mix well with the flour.

Cover with clingfilm (plastic wrap) and leave somewhere warm for about 4 hours. Ideally the temperature should be maintained above 50°C/122°F for the whole duration. The oven at its lowest setting should work fine.

Preheat the oven to 150°C/300°F/Gas Mark 2.

Taste the potato and if it's not sweet enough add a little bit of sugar – or leave it longer. Mix in the milk, salt and butter, then pour the mixture into a buttered, ovenproof dish. Bake for 1–2 hours, by which time it should be nicely caramelized.

FINNISH SWEDE CASSEROLE

Lanttulaatikko (Finland)

This is often served together with a few other vegetable casseroles on the Finnish Christmas table.

Preparation and cooking time: 2 hours
Serves: 4, or many more if it is served as part
  of a bigger traditional meal

1 large or 2 small swede (rutabaga), peeled
  and coarsely cut into pieces
100 ml/3½ fl oz (⅓ plus 1 tablespoon) cream
30 g/1 oz (¼ cup) breadcrumbs
2 eggs
70 g/2½ oz (3½ tablespoons) golden syrup
freshly grated nutmeg, to taste
salt, to taste

Preheat the oven to 175°C/345°F/Gas Mark 4.

Put the pieces of swede (rutabaga) in a small pot, cover with water and cook over a medium heat until soft. Strain, reserving the cooking liquid.

Mash the swede with enough of the cooking liquid to make it nice and soft. Mix the breadcrumbs with the cream and add it to the mashed swede. Beat the golden syrup with the eggs and add that too. Season with freshly grated nutmeg and a little bit of salt.

Pour the mixture into an ovenproof dish. Make some patterns in the surface with a fork and cook for about 1 hour until a nice amber colour.

BOILED BEETROOT

Few things are tastier than young beetroot (beets). I like to keep their tender leaves raw while cooking the beetroot. I then mix the steaming-hot beetroot in a bowl, with some butter and salt, and add the leaves, letting the residual heat of the beetroot themselves wilt and just cook the leaves.

Never peel beetroot before boiling them. Instead, cook them in their skins, then rinse them under cold running water for three minutes; the skins will come away really easily by just rubbing them with your hands (wear gloves). They might initially feel cold, but after a few minutes their internal heat will reheat their surface again.

Preparation and cooking time: 1 hour
Serves: 4

800 g/1¾ lb red beetroot (beets), leaves
  trimmed and reserved (optional)
butter, to taste
salt, to taste
chopped parsley, to taste (optional)

Follow the instructions on page 82 for boiling vegetables. Cook the beetroot (beets) until just tender. Lift them out of the pan with a slotted spoon and drain briefly in a colander. Rinse under cold water and rub away the skins. Transfer to a serving bowl and mix them with butter and salt, to taste. Mix in the leaves, if using, then serve with a sprinkling of parsley, if you like.

For image see page 203

FINNISH BEETROOT SOUP

Borssikeitto (Finland)

This beetroot (beet) soup, or borscht, is clearly a testament to the Eastern European influence on Finnish food culture and its difference from Scandinavia, where dishes like this have not traditionally been prepared. More recent recipes can contain garlic, tomatoes, and thyme, but this version is more of a classic base to be adapted according to your own personal taste. Its mild seasoning of bay leaf and marjoram seems to correspond well to a majority of the older recipes I have seen and to its Russian roots. *Borssikeitto* is often served with a dollop of *smetana* as a condiment.

When making this dish I prefer to use winter beetroot and cabbage because I like their intensity of flavour and the coarser texture they provide.

Preparation and cooking time: 1 hour
Serves: 4

4 red beetroot (beets)
1 carrot
1 onion
1 small or ½ large winter cabbage
1 leek, white part only
2 tablespoons butter
1 litre/34 fl oz (4¼ cups) Beef Stock
  (page 650)
2 tablespoons *Ättika* (12%) vinegar
  (page 656)
1 tablespoon sugar
1 bay leaf
fresh marjoram, twigs and leaves separated
salt and white pepper, to taste

Shred all the vegetables, using a box grater, a mandoline or a sharp knife.

Put a large pot over a medium heat and add the butter. Add all the vegetables and cook them carefully until they are looking shiny and a bit translucent.

Add the stock (broth), vinegar, sugar, bay leaf and marjoram twigs and simmer until all the vegetables are tender. If you like, you can tie the bay leaf and marjoram twigs in a piece of muslin (cheesecloth), which makes it easier to remove them later on.

Just before serving remove the bay leaf and marjoram twigs, season with salt and pepper and add the fresh marjoram leaves.

BEETROOT SALAD

Rödbetssallad (Sweden)

Some recipes also include grated horseradish for some sting, so feel free to add that as well, if you want. I also like a good sprinkling of chopped parsley over my beetroot (beet) salad before serving.

Preparation and cooking time: 10 minutes
Resting time: overnight
Serves: 4, or more if served as part of a larger
  meal

400 g/14 oz Pickled Beetroot (page 660), cut
  into 1 cm/½ inch cubes
100 ml/3½ fl oz (⅓ cup plus 1 tablespoon)
  Mayonnaise (page 674)
100 ml/3½ fl oz (⅓ cup plus 1 tablespoon)
  cream, whipped to soft peaks
1 apple, peeled, cored and diced
grated horseradish, to taste (optional)
chopped parsley, to taste (optional)
salt and pepper, to taste

Mix all of the ingredients together in a large bowl and season well. Cover and refrigerate overnight, then mix the salad again to achieve an even colour.

For image see page 203

FINNISH BEETROOT SALAD

Sallatti (western Finland)
Rosolli (eastern Finland)

Sallatti or *rosolli* is a must for many Finns when it is time for Christmas dinner. It is often served with Boiled Eggs (page 53) and/or herring. Some recipes indicate that all the ingredients should be mixed together and that the pink, fluffy sauce should be folded into the mixture, while others state that the sauce should be left on the side. A few indicate that the components should be placed in separate piles on a serving platter, with the sauce on the side, and that everyone should be allowed to mix their own. I like the third option the most. Some recipes for this salad also contain cubes of raw apple, especially the versions where diced herring is mixed in together with the sauce, a bit like Herring and Pickled Beetroot Salad (page 202).

Preparation and cooking time: 20 minutes
Serves: 4, or many more if served as part of a
  larger festive meal

400 g/14 oz (2 cups) Pickled Beetroot (page 660), coarsely chopped into cubes, juice reserved
150 g/5 oz (1 cup) cooked carrots, cold, coarsely chopped into cubes
200 g/7 oz (1 cup) Boiled Potatoes (see right), cold, chopped into cubes
250 g/9 oz Quick Pickled Cucumber (page 658), coarsely chopped into cubes
1 large onion, finely chopped
salt, to taste

For the sauce
2 tablespoons pickling juice from the beetroot (see above)
2 teaspoons sugar
200 ml/7 fl oz (¾ cup plus 1 tablespoon) cream
Ättika (12%) vinegar (page 656), to taste
salt, to taste

To make the sauce, stir the pickling juice and the sugar into the cream and season with salt and white vinegar to taste. When you are satisfied with the flavour, carefully start whisking the mixture until soft peaks begin to form. Be careful not to start whisking before you have added all the flavourings. It is difficult to add more when the sauce has thickened because it easily curdles if you stir it around too much at this stage.

Mix all the vegetables together and season lightly with salt. Fold in the sauce and then tip onto a serving platter. If you are going to serve the sauce on the side, then arrange the vegetables on a serving platter, either mixed together or separately.

For image see page 203

BOILED POTATOES

To make *impotatis* potatoes cook them in Ham Stock (page 650) rather than water.

Preparation and cooking time: 20–35 minutes,
  depending on size
Resting time: 10 minutes
Serves: 4

1 kg/2¼ lb potatoes, skins on, but cleaned and rinsed
1 good handful salt

Put the potatoes in a large pan. Cover them with water, add the salt and bring to the boil. Reduce the heat and simmer gently until the potatoes are tender. Do not overcook the potatoes, they should be tender, but still have texture.

Drain the potatoes, then return them to the pan. Sit a sheet of paper towel on top of the potatoes, put the lid back on and leave them rest for 10 minutes before serving.

RICED POTATOES

Preparation and cooking time: 30 minutes
Serves: 6

700 g/1 lb 9 oz floury potatoes, skins on, but cleaned and rinsed
salt and white pepper, to taste

Put the potatoes in a large pan. Cover them with water and bring to the boil. Reduce the heat and simmer gently for about 20 minutes, or until the potatoes are tender.

Drain the potatoes thoroughly. Push them through a mouli or potato ricer, then season to taste.

CREAMED POTATOES
WITH DILL

Dillstuvad potatis (Sweden)

I make this mostly in the summer, with new potatoes still in their skins. It is the perfect side dish to serve with Salmon Cured in Salt (page 215) or Cold-Smoked Fermented Barley Sausages (page 419). It is also a great way of using up leftover potatoes from another day. You can use parsley instead of dill if you like.

Preparation and cooking time: 10 minutes
Serves: 4

1 quantity Béchamel Sauce (page 666),
   substituting half the milk with cream
800 g/1¾ lb Boiled Potatoes (page 117),
   cold, skins on or off, and cut into suitably
   sized pieces
1 good bunch dill, fronds picked and stalks
   finely chopped
salt and white pepper, to taste

Bring the béchamel to a simmer, then add the potatoes. Stir carefully from time to time, while heating the mixture over a low heat. Make sure the sauce doesn't burn, but also take care not to break up the potatoes too much.

Once the potatoes are hot enough, and just before serving, add the dill and season well with salt and quite a bit of white pepper.

For image see page 121

For image see page 121

MASHED POTATOES

Use an ordinary fork or potato masher for a coarser result or, for a smooth mash, use a potato ricer or mouli.

Preparation and cooking time: 35 minutes
Serves: 6

700 g/1 lb 8½ oz floury potatoes, skins on,
   but cleaned and rinsed
350 ml/12 fl oz (1½ cups) milk
100 g/3½ oz (7 tablespoons) butter
freshly grated nutmeg, to taste (optional)
salt and white pepper, to taste

Put the potatoes in a large pan. Cover them with water and bring to the boil. Reduce the heat and simmer gently for about 20 minutes, or until the potatoes are tender.

While the potatoes are cooking, combine the milk and butter in a separate pan and heat until the butter has melted.

Drain the potatoes thoroughly and peel them (yes they do have to be hot when you do it). Mash them (or push them through a mouli or potato ricer), then beat in the hot milk mixture with a wooden spoon or a stiff whisk. Season to taste.

For image see page 121

COARSE POTATO CAKES

Rårakor (Sweden)

Potato cakes like these can be served with some slices of Fried Salt Pork (page 302) and some Sugared Lingonberries (page 692), or as an excellent accompaniment to Bleak Roe (page 179).

Preparation and cooking time: 40 minutes
Serves: 4

1 kg/2¼ lb starchy potatoes
butter, for frying
salt and white pepper, to taste

Peel and grate the potatoes coarsely. Use your hands to squeeze them tightly so as to remove any excess liquid. Transfer to a bowl and season well.

Melt some butter in a frying pan (non-stick is preferable) over a medium heat. Add a thin layer of grated potatoes to the pan. It mustn't be too thick; about 8 mm/⅜ inch is ideal. Fry until the underside is deeply golden, then flip the potato cake over and fry the other side. Do not flip it back and forth. Each potato cake should be really crisp on the exterior but it is also important to make sure that the interior is cooked through; it should not taste of raw potato.

If you want, you can fry your potato cakes in multiple pans, but if you only have one pan, then you can fry the cakes one at a time, and keep them warm in a 120°C/235°F/Gas Mark ½ oven. A few grinds of white pepper just before serving is a great idea.

For image see page 121

OVEN-BAKED POTATOES HASSELBACKEN

Hasselbackspotatis (Sweden)

This fantastic potato dish was invented during the 1950s at a restaurant-turned-cooking school, aptly named Hasselbacken. There is conflicting information about how it was actually created, and by whom. Some say it was the headmaster of the school while others say it was one of the students.

The magic of this dish is that, by slicing the potatoes almost through but leaving them connected at the bottom, then covering them in butter and breadcrumbs, a perfect potato crispiness can be achieved on the exterior while the interior will be as smooth and soft as you want it to be.

Preparation and cooking time: 1 hour
Serves: 4
8–12 floury potatoes, peeled and left whole
50 g/2½ oz (3½ tablespoons) very soft butter
4 tablespoons breadcrumbs
salt, to taste

Preheat the oven to 225°C/435°F/Gas Mark 7.

Place a potato in a wooden spoon, the bowl of which is roughly the size of the potato itself. With a sharp knife, slice straight down through the potato at 6 mm/¼ inch intervals. Let the knife hit the two raised edges of the spoon, but do not let it slide into the bowl of the spoon. This prevents the knife from cutting through the potato entirely. As you finish slicing each potato, transfer it to an ovenproof, cast-iron frying pan.

When all the potatoes have been sliced, place the pan over a medium heat and add the butter. As it melts, brush it all over the potatoes to baste them generously. Season with salt, then bake for at least 30 minutes, until they are golden on the outside and soft inside. Baste them with the melted butter every 10 minutes or so. Once they are golden, baste the potatoes one final time, then sprinkle on the breadcrumbs. Return to the oven for another 5–10 minutes, or until the breadcrumbs are crisp and golden.

For image see page 121

POTATO GRATIN

Preparation and cooking time: 1½ hours
Serves: 4, with some to spare for lunch the
* following day*

1.2 kg/2½ lb starchy potatoes, peeled and cut
  into 3 cm/1¼ inch slices
1 leek, thinly sliced
500 ml/17 fl oz (2 cups plus 1 tablespoon)
  milk
400 ml/14 fl oz (1⅔ cups) cream
1 clove garlic, grated
150 g/5 oz hard cheese, grated
salt and white pepper, to taste

Preheat the oven to 175°C/345°F/Gas Mark 4.

Layer the potato and leek slices in an ovenproof dish, seasoning each layer well. Mix the milk and the cream with the garlic and season with salt and pepper. Pour in enough liquid to almost cover the potatoes, reserving any that is leftover. Use this to top up the gratin as it bakes.

Sprinkle on the cheese and bake for a good 45 minutes; the surface should be well coloured. Take the gratin out of the oven and let it rest for at least 10 minutes before serving.

For image see page 121

SCANIAN CREAMED POTATOES

Skånsk potatis (Sweden)

The difference between Scanian creamed potatoes and other creamed potatoes is that the potato is cooked from raw in the cream rather than being reheated in cream or béchamel. Some people like their Scanian potatoes boiled with some stock (broth), and others like to use a mixture of stock, cream and milk. Both are fine, but no flour should be added to thicken it.

Preparation and cooking time: 30 minutes
Serves: 4

650 g/1 lb 7 oz waxy potatoes, peeled and cut
   into 1.5 mm/¾ inch cubes
1 onion, finely chopped
20 g/¾ oz (1 heaped tablespoon) butter
150 ml/5 fl oz (⅔ cup) cream
150 ml/5 fl oz (⅔ cup) milk
dash of good strong Meat Stock (page 650),
   optional
salt and white pepper, to taste

Combine the potatoes, onions and butter in a frying pan and fry them over a medium heat for 5–10 minutes, or until golden. Colouration is essential for the flavour of the finished dish. Add the cream, milk and stock (broth), if you are using it, and leave to simmer and reduce until the potatoes are soft and the sauce coats them nicely. Add a little water, if necessary. Season with salt and pepper and serve.

For image see opposite page

DANISH SUGAR-BROWNED POTATOES

Brunede poteter (Norway)
Brunede kartofler (Denmark)

These very sweet potatoes are a must for most Danes at Christmas. They are often served with Danish roast pork or with roast birds, like goose or duck. You sometimes see them in Norway although it's not as common.

Preparation and cooking time: 20 minutes
Serves: 4

85 g/3 oz (⅓ cup plus 2 tablespoons) sugar
1 kg/2¼ lb small waxy potatoes, boiled,
   peeled and cooled
50 g/2½ oz (3½ tablespoons) butter
salt, to taste

Sprinkle the sugar in an even layer over the bottom of a cold frying pan. Place the pan over a medium heat and let the sugar melt and brown. Do not stir, or it will form lumps that don't melt. When the sugar is evenly caramelized, add the butter, increase the heat a little and add the potatoes. Turn them around very gently in the caramel to glaze them. Be careful not to break them up. Once the caramel has thickened and coated the potatoes and they are warmed through, season and serve.

For image see page 269

Clockwise from top: Creamed Potatoes with Dill (page 118); Creamy Potato Salad (page 123); Potato Gratin (page 119); Mashed Potatoes (page 118); Potato Salad (page 123); Scanian Creamed Potatoes (page 120); Coarse Potato Cakes (page 118); Oven-baked Potatoes Hasselbacken (page 119)

NORWEGIAN POTATO PORRIDGE

Potetgrøt / Jordeplegraut (Norway)

Potato porridge has historically played a tremendously important role in the Norwegian diet, although it has fallen out of favour since its last time of great popularity, during the Second World War. It has all but disappeared from the Norwegian everyday dinner table. A quick internet search reveals only 634 results on 'potetgrøt', while 'pizza' returns a good 319,000 hits from Norwegian websites alone.

Serve the potato porridge with a good knob of butter melting into it and some slices of Fried Salt Pork (page 302) – or why not with some cultured buttermilk? Sugared Lingonberries (page 692) are also often served with potato porridge.

Preparation and cooking time: 45 minutes
Serves: 4

1.2 kg/2½ lb floury potatoes, peeled but
  left whole
500 ml/17 fl oz (2 cups plus 1 tablespoon)
  milk, with extra ready if needed
100 g/3½ oz (1 cup) barley flour or
  100 g/3½ oz (¾ cup) wholegrain flour
1 good pinch salt

Place the potatoes in a large pot and cover them with water. Bring to the boil and cook for about 30 minutes, or until tender. Tip the water away.

Off the heat, pour in the milk, then add the flour and mash the hot potatoes vigorously until no lumps remain. Continue working the mixture for at least 5 minutes; it should be shiny and a bit gluey. The residual heat from the potatoes should be enough to cook the starch in the flour. If it gets too thick, add a little more milk – but warm it first, so that you don't cool the porridge down too much.

For image see page 125

POTATO SOUP

This isn't a very Nordic soup in the sense that it is rather central European in its origins. However, it came out as one of the most popular everyday soups when we asked around in our poll (page 14) at the beginning of the project of putting this book together. To distinguish it from more classic central European recipes, most Nordic potato and leek soup recipes contain no white wine. I like to fold in whipped cream just before serving but if you prefer you can add it with everything else as you cook the soup.

Preparation time: 35 minutes
Serves: 4

500 g/1 lb 2 oz floury potatoes, peeled and
  cut into pieces
1 leek, white part only, thinly sliced
1 clove garlic, crushed
1 litre/34 fl oz (4¼ cups) light
  stock, perhaps Chicken Stock
  (page 650) or Vegetable Stock
  (page 650)
1 bunch chives, finely chopped
200 ml/7 fl oz (¾ cup plus 1 tablespoon)
  cream, whipped to soft peaks
salt and white pepper, to taste

Place the potatoes, leek, garlic and stock (broth) in a pot and bring to the boil. Continue simmering over a medium heat until the potatoes are soft. Season well and mix with a handheld immersion blender or in a blender and pass through a fine mesh sieve into a new pot. Add the chives and fold in the cream just before serving.

For image see page 125

DANISH BURNING LOVE

Brændende kærlighed (Denmark)

This Danish everyday dish of mashed potato, bacon and onions is often served with Pickled Beetroot (page 660) and a slice of Danish Rye Bread (page 504) on the side.

Some versions have chives or parsley sprinkled over them, others don't.

Preparation and cooking time: 20 minutes
Serves: 4

300 g/11 oz bacon, cut into small pieces
1 quantity Mashed Potatoes (page 118)
6 onions, finely chopped
chopped parsley or snipped chives (optional)

Put the bacon in a pan over a medium heat and fry until just enough fat has rendered into the pan to make it shiny. Add the onions to the pan and continue frying over a medium heat until the onions are deeply caramelized.

Spoon one big dollop of mash onto a warm serving platter (or divide between 4 plates), top with the bacon and onion mixture and sprinkle with your choice of chopped herbs, if using.

For image see page 125

POTATO SALAD

Perunasalaatti (Finland)
Kartoffelsalat (Denmark)
Potatissallad (Sweden)

Potato salad is as common in the Nordics as it is anywhere else in the western world. Most of the time it is of poor quality, mayonnaise based and bought readymade from a supermarket. I make either that kind or one based on Vinaigrette (page 676) with plenty of herbs or leafy greens in it.

CREAMY POTATO SALAD (VERSION 1)

Preparation time: 10 minutes
Serves: 4

600 g/1 lb 5 oz Boiled Potatoes (page 117), cold, peeled and cut into suitably sized pieces
200 ml/7 fl oz (¾ cup plus 1 tablespoon)

Mayonnaise (page 674)
100 ml/3½ fl oz (⅓ cup plus 1 tablespoon) sour cream or crème fraîche
1 tablespoon strong mustard
1 good bunch herbs like chives, parsley and tarragon, coarsely chopped
salt and black pepper, to taste

Mix all of the ingredients well and season with salt and pepper. Sprinkle some herbs on top if you like.

For image see page 121

VINAIGRETTE-BASED POTATO SALAD (VERSION 2)

Preparation time: 10 minutes
Serves: 4

600 g/1 lb 5 oz Boiled Potatoes (page 117), cold, peeled and cut into suitably sized pieces
200 g/7 oz green vegetables, really whatever you have: peas, summer cabbage, collard greens or broccoli, and they can be cooked or raw depending on what you like
Vinaigrette (page 676), to taste
1 good bunch herbs like chives, parsley and tarragon, coarsely chopped
salt and black pepper, to taste

Mix all of the ingredients in a bowl and season well with salt and pepper.

COARSE POTATO PANCAKES

*Raggmunk / Lufsa / Råriven pannkaka
(Sweden)*

These pancakes can either be fried in a pan on the stove – when they are known as *raggmunk* – or baked in the oven, when they are called *lufsa* or *råriven pannkaka*. Either way, serve them with slices of Fried Salt Pork (page 302) and Sugared Lingonberries (page 692).

*Preparation and cooking time: 1 hour
Makes: 20 pancakes*

600 g/1 lb 5 oz potatoes
½ quantity Thin Pancake batter
   (page 450) made with 3 eggs
butter, for frying
salt, to taste

Peel and grate the potatoes coarsely on an ordinary box grater. Use your hands to squeeze them tightly so as to remove any excess liquid. Transfer to a bowl and stir in the pancake batter. Season with salt, to taste.

To fry them in a pan, preheat the oven to 120°C/235°F/Gas Mark ½.

Melt some butter in a frying pan over a medium heat. Add a good amount of batter to make a large pancake that covers the bottom of the pan, or dollop in spoonfuls to make several smaller ones (which I prefer). Either way, flatten the mixture with the back of your spoon so that you don't have a mound of potato sitting in a pool of batter. Fry until the underside is deeply golden, then flip over and fry the other side. Don't rush these pancakes as they have to cook all the way through to be tasty. Keep them warm in the oven while you fry the remaining pancakes.

Alternatively, to bake them in the oven, preheat the oven to 200°C/400°F/Gas Mark 6.

Melt some butter in a roasting pan. Pour in the pancake batter and return the pan to the oven. Bake until the pancake is cooked all the way through.

For image see opposite page

POTATO PATTIES

Potatisbullar (Sweden)

When I grew up, *potatisbullar* were always made from riced potatoes, or sometimes from leftover mashed potatoes. Today though, there are so many commercial varieties of *potatisbullar* around that most people think of them as being made with grated potatoes. A sort of mix between the real potato ball and a *råraka* or Coarse Potato Cake (page 118).

When I make the authentic version at home, my kids are always disappointed – not because they aren't tasty, but because from their point of view, my way (the old way), is not correct.

*Preparation and cooking time: 30 minutes
Serves: 4*

800 g/1¾ lb floury boiled potatoes, peeled,
   riced and left to cool a little
2 eggs
50 ml/2 fl oz (3½ tablespoons) milk
50 g/2½ oz (⅓ cup plus 1 tablespoon) plain
   (all-purpose) flour
butter, for frying
salt and white pepper, to taste

Combine the potatoes, eggs and milk in a bowl and sift over the flour. Mix everything together well, but not for too long (the longer you work it the firmer and denser the balls will become).

Shape the mixture into little patties. Butter a pan and fry the patties over a medium–high heat until they are golden on both sides. Don't hurry. They need to caramelize properly and heat all the way through to cook the flour.

If you want, you can fry your potato patties in multiple pans, but if you only have one pan, then you can fry them in batches and keep them warm in an oven preheated to 120°C/235°F/Gas Mark ½.

For image see opposite page

Clockwise from top left: Coarse Potato Pancakes (page 124) with Fried Salt Pork (page 302); Potato Patties (page 124); Potato Soup (page 122); Norwegian Potato Porridge (page 122); Jansson's Temptation, Swedish Potato and Sprat Casserole (page 212); Danish Burning Love (page 122)

HOW TO PREPARE MUSHROOMS
FOR DRYING

If you have been out foraging and have collected a large quantity of mushrooms, you may have too many to consume fresh. Drying mushrooms is often a very convenient and successful way of extending their lifespan, while also reducing their volume.

The key to drying mushrooms successfully is to do it quickly and to use only perfect specimens. The technique won't work with damaged or blemished mushrooms as they will spoil – as will all mushrooms if you take too long to dry them.

Thin and small mushrooms, like yellowfoot chantarelles, can be left whole, but any large or densely textured mushrooms (like the various *boletus genus*) need to be cut into slices about 1 cm/½ inch in thickness.

The most efficient way of drying mushrooms is using a special mushroom dehydrator which also heats the mushrooms a little but, more importantly, also ventilates off the excess humidity.

If you don't have a dehydrator, you can still dry mushrooms very successfully. At home, I usually spread out some sheets of newspaper on my kitchen counter and lay out my mushrooms in a single layer. Mushrooms give off a lot of moisture, so it is a good idea to have your stove's extraction fan going at the lowest speed for the first 24 hours, to ensure a good exchange of air. After this time, the mushrooms should feel dry and light, however they will not actually be as dry as they seem, so you need to leave them for another 24 hours.

After 48 hours, gather up the mushrooms and put them in a box – an ordinary cardboard box is ideal. Place the box somewhere warm and dry (but not hot): on top of a radiator, on the floor (if you have underfloor heating), on top of the stove (turned off) after a day of cooking. After another 24 hours the mushrooms will be fully dry. Transfer them to an airtight sterilized jar and they will keep almost indefinitely.

TO SALT MUSHROOMS AS IN FINLAND

Finland and the Baltic countries have a great tradition in using mushrooms that are often overlooked in other parts of Europe. One example are milk caps. Many of us have tasted saffron milk caps (*L. deliciosus*) or maybe even weeping milk caps (*L. volemus*), but most mushroom pickers leave the other members of the Lactarius family where they stand in the forest.

The Finns gladly pick the northern milk cap, the woolly milk cap, the red hot milk cap and many others. These mushrooms are sometimes very strong or flavourful, like the red hot milk cap with its chilli pepper sting.

In Finland they are commonly blanched before being preserved in salt to be used later in different preparations.

TO PRESERVE MUSHROOMS
IN SALT

Clean a suitable mixture of *Lactarius* mushrooms (not too heavy on the red hot milk caps) and blanch them (see page 85). Leave them to cool.

Weigh them, and place the cooked cold mushrooms in a bowl. Add 200 g/7 oz coarse sea salt per 1 kg/2½ lb mushrooms and stir it around. Transfer the mushrooms and salt to sterilized glass jars, seal tightly and store somewhere cool and dark until you need them. They keep almost indefinitely.

DESALTING MUSHROOMS

The evening before you are going to use the mushrooms, take a quantity of them and place in a bowl. Rinse away any visible salt and pour away any water. Add new water to the bowl – the amount should be about ten times the volume of that of the mushrooms. Leave the mushrooms in the water overnight in a cool place. Strain them and taste to make sure they are no longer too salty.

MUSHROOM SALAD

Champignonsallad (Sweden)

To toss some thin slices of raw button mushrooms with some kale and vinaigrette is one of the tastiest things I know. It's not really a Nordic classic, but it's one of the few recipes in this book I just decided to add anyway.

Preparation and cooking time: 10 minutes
Serves: 4

1 bunch kale leaves, rinsed
Vinaigrette (page 676), to taste
250 g/9 oz button mushrooms
salt and white pepper, to taste

Tear pieces off the kale leaves and discard the stems. Place the kale in a bowl, add some vinaigrette and season. Let it sit for about 5 minutes so that the vinaigrette wilts the kale just a little bit.

Meanwhile, thinly slice the mushrooms on a mandoline. Add the mushrooms to the bowl and toss very gently. You don't want too much vinaigrette and seasoning on the mushrooms as they will go soggy, but a little bit more than what's usual in a salad, as they are a bit coarser than normal salad greens. Serve immediately before the mushrooms wilt.

For image see page 129

FINNISH SALTED MUSHROOM SALAD

Sienisalaatti (Finland)
Risksallad (Sweden)

Some recipes contain dill; others don't.

Preparation and cooking time: 10 minutes
Serves: 4

200 g/7 oz salted mushrooms (see opposite)
2 cold boiled potatoes, peeled and cut into
    1 cm/½ inch cubes
1 apple, cut into 1 cm/½ inch cubes
1 egg, hard-boiled, cut into
    1 cm/½ inch cubes

1 red onion, finely chopped
1 Brined Cucumber (page 660), cut
    into 1 cm/½ inch cubes
100 ml/3½ fl oz (⅓ cup plus 1 tablespoon)
    thick, full-fat sour cream
salt and white pepper, to taste
chopped dill, to taste (optional)

Follow the instructions opposite for desalting the mushrooms, then squeeze them very dry to remove any excess water.

Place the mushrooms in a large bowl with all the other ingredients. Mix everything together well, then adjust the seasoning, and add the dill, if using.

For image see page 129

FRIED MUSHROOMS

To fry mushrooms is not as easy as people think. They should not be too dark but not light and soggy either. They should not lose too much moisture, which makes them unpleasantly strong and lacking in textural diversity from one kind to another, but they can't be too wet either as it makes them slimy. Too greasy is also horrible and overly seasoned kills the entire mushroom flavour. One of the first things to look for is perfect quality: nice, whole, clean mushrooms that can't be wet. If they are wet don't buy them, and if it was raining when you picked them, leave them uncovered on a tray in the refrigerator overnight to dry out a bit before proceeding to cook them. Every gram of water weight you don't have to fry away in the pan is a gain, up until they begin to shrivel and dry out, which means you have gone one step too far and you will lose quality. I like to fry my mushrooms in very little fat and instead add an extra tablespoon of butter at the very last second in the pan, glazing the fried mushrooms in some fresh butter, giving extra complexity to the flavour. To some, more aromatic mushrooms I don't mind adding a sprig of thyme, maybe some chopped parsley and sometimes even a clove of garlic, also added at the very last second together with the fresh butter. Just barely break the garlic though, and remove it from the pan just when it has added enough flavour to avoid something tasting of only garlic. Fried mushrooms don't keep well so fry them and serve them just when they are done, don't let them sit.

It is important to use a large enough pan when frying mushrooms, they have to all fit in one layer otherwise the water in the mushrooms won't be able to evaporate quickly enough.

Preparation time: 10 minutes
Serves: 4

800 g/1¾ lb mushrooms, cleaned and cut
  into the size of pieces you want
50 g/2 oz (3½ tablespoons) butter
salt and white pepper, to taste

Add half the butter to a large pan while it is still cold, then place over maximum heat on your stove. As soon as it has melted and is about to start browning, add the mushrooms in one layer. Now do not touch the mushrooms until you have to flip them. Let them fry and let any water coming out into the pan evaporate. Check the mushrooms here and there for colouration but do not toss them around until you are sure they are coloured enough. Toss the mushrooms around and once again spread them out into one layer, still over the highest possible heat. Cook until you have good colouration also on the side now facing downwards, this time it will go faster. When they have stopped leaking liquid into the pan it means they are cooked through. Add the remaining butter and any seasoning. Toss around to glaze and serve immediately.

For image see opposite page

CREAMED MUSHROOMS

I don't like it when my creamed mushrooms are too saucy. They should be quite stiff. What I normally do is fry the mushrooms just as described in Fried Mushrooms (see left), sometimes with the addition of a chopped shallot or onion, and then, just as they are done, instead of the remaining butter, I add 200 ml/7 fl oz (¾ cup plus 2 tablespoons) cream. Reduce the heat to medium and cook for another couple of minutes until the cream has reduced down a bit to coat the mushrooms. Add any seasoning as described above at the very end here, too.

For image see opposite page

*Clockwise from top left: Mushroom Soup (page 130); Creamed Mushrooms (page 128);
Fried Mushrooms (page 128); Mushroom Salad (page 127); Finnish Salted Mushroom
Salad (page 127); Mushroom Gratin (page 130)*

MUSHROOM GRATIN

I found this recipe in an early 1980s cookbook and I haven't seen it anywhere else. It is not very Nordic but it should be, and now maybe it might be … It's one of the most delicious things you can make with porcini (cep) mushrooms.

Preparation and cooking time: 30 minutes
Serves: 4

butter, for frying
600 g/1 lb 5 oz porcini (cep) mushrooms
100 ml/3½ fl oz (¾ cup plus 1 tablespoon)
  cream
50 g/2 oz (½ cup) grated mature hard cheese
a tiny amount of garlic, grated
freshly grated nutmeg, to taste
salt and white pepper

Start by heating a buttered pan over a medium heat.

Meanwhile with a very sharp knife cut the mushrooms into slices about 5 mm/¼ inch in thickness.

Place them in the buttered pan and fry them until golden. Flip and fry the other side and cook each batch of mushrooms until no water leaks out into the pan anymore and the mushrooms are really nicely coloured all over without being shrivelled up. Season each slice well with salt and pepper, layer them in an ovenproof dish as in the photo on page 129. It should not be too thick, no more than 1 cm/½ inch thick.

Preheat the oven to 250°C/480°F/Gas Mark 9. Mix the remaining ingredients in a bowl. Don't add too much salt here as you have salted the mushrooms quite a bit already and the cheese is also a little salty. Pour the cream mixture onto the mushrooms and place the whole thing in the oven and bake until nicely coloured on top. Leave outside of the oven to cool and set a bit before serving.

For image see page 129

MUSHROOM SOUP

Svampsoppa (Sweden)

Like most other soups I think mushroom soup tastes the best if you cook whatever mushroom you are using the way that best suits that particular mushroom. Then you make the soup with the perfectly cooked mushroom. If you want it smooth or with pieces is totally up to you and I think that it depends on the mushrooms. Sometimes you would cut them a bit before cooking them and keep them like that in the finished soup, other times you would blend the soup a little to leave some chunks in there and yet other times you would mix the soup until smooth and maybe even pass it through a fine mesh sieve. It all depends on what mushrooms you have, what you like and what you want at that moment. If it is a smooth soup, I think that it can be really nice to whip the cream part of the recipe to soft peaks and fold it into the soup just before serving, Otherwise, I prefer to add the cream earlier. For most mushrooms I think that frying them gently in a pan with a bit of onion makes a very tasty base for a soup. If you are making a smooth base, omit the beurre manie, it will be thick enough anyhow.

Preparation and cooking time: 30 minutes
Serves: 4

50 g/2 oz (3½ tablespoons) butter
1 onion or a couple of shallots, finely chopped
500 g/1 lb 2 oz mushrooms, cleaned and cut
  into suitably sized pieces
1 clove garlic, crushed
500 ml/17 fl oz (2 cups plus 1 tablespoon)
  light stock/broth (chicken, vegetable or
  why not mushroom if you have it?)
200 ml/7 fl oz (¾ cup plus 1 tablespoon)
  cream, whipped to soft peaks (optional)
1 quantity Beurre Manie (page 651)
salt and white pepper, to taste

Heat a large pot over a medium heat and add the butter and onion. When the butter is just about to start caramelizing, add the mushrooms. Cook them until cooked through and lightly golden in colour. Some mushrooms contain a lot of water, so let that reduce into the mushrooms as you fry them even if it looks like a lot. It contains a lot of flavour and should not be discarded. Add the garlic towards the end and fry it with the mushrooms for just a couple of minutes.

Add the stock (broth) to the pot and bring to the boil. Add the cream if you are going to use it and simmer for a few minutes. Thicken to the desired texture with beurre manie. Don't add it all at once, start with a spoonful, whisk it in, let simmer for a few minutes and add more until you are satisfied. Remember to not thicken the soup too much at this stage if you are going to blend it.

When the soup is perfectly seasoned and cooked, serve it. Either mix it a little bit or blend it until smooth. Adjust the seasoning one last time.

For image see page 129

NETTLE SOUP

Neslesuppe (Norway)
Nokkoskeitto (Finland)
Brændenældesuppe (Denmark)
Nässelsoppa (Sweden)

Remember to cook the nettles long enough so that they are really tender before adding them to the soup, and keep some of the cooking liquid in case you need to thin the soup later.

Serve with Boiled Eggs (page 53), halved, or Poached Eggs (page 52) and if you like some Small Smoked Pork Sausages (page 428).

Preparation and cooking time: 30 minutes
Serves: 4

2 litres/3½ UK pints (8½ cups)
    nettle leaves
salt and white pepper, to taste

1 quantity Velouté (page 652) made from:
550 ml/18 fl oz (2½ cups) Chicken Stock
    (page 650)
10 white peppercorns
1 bay leaf
1 teaspoon fennel seeds
1 teaspoon aniseeds

Bring water to the boil in a big pot, then add the nettle leaves and boil until tender. It's important to cook them until they are really tender.

While the nettles are cooking, pour cold water into a big bowl and mix with plenty of ice. This allows you to cool the leaves quickly, which is essential for retaining their flavour and colour. When the nettles are ready, tip them first into a colander, reserving some of the cooking liquid, then straight into the iced water. When the nettles are completely cold, return them to the colander and leave for the excess liquid to drain away. Squeeze the nettles dry and chop them finely.

Follow the instructions on page 652 to make the velouté.

Strain the velouté to remove the aromatics and return to the pot. Purée the nettles with half of the velouté in a blender first, then add this to the pot with the remaining velouté. Adjust the seasonings to your liking and add some of the nettle cooking water, if necessary. Serve immediately once the nettles have reached the desired temperature.

GROUND ELDER LEAF SOUP

Kirskålssoppa (Sweden)

Ground elder is a common woodland plant that is popular in Sweden. It's at its best in the spring time, before the flowers grow and the leaves become too bitter.

Serve with a couple of halves of Hard-boiled Eggs (page 53) or a Poached Egg (page 52) per person.

Preparation and cooking time: 30 minutes
Serves: 4

500 g/1 lb 2 oz (10 cups) young, tender
    ground elder leaves and stems
2 tablespoons butter
2 tablespoons plain (all-purpose) flour
2 small shallots, finely chopped
1 litre/34 fl oz (4¼ cups) Chicken Stock
    (page 650)
250 ml/8 fl oz (1 cup) cream
freshly grated nutmeg (optional)
salt and white pepper, to taste

Follow the method for Spinach Soup on page 88.

GLAZED GROUND ELDER LEAVES

Preparation and cooking time: 10 minutes
Serves: 4 as a side dish

500 g/1 lb 2 oz (10 cups) young, tender
    ground elder leaves and stems
50 g/2 oz (3½ tablespoons) butter
salt and white pepper, to taste

Follow the method for glazed green peas on page
137.

For image see opposite page

ICELANDIC MOSS (*CETARIA ISLANDICA*)

A lichen that is commonly found throughout the
northern Nordic countries. It is rich in carbohydrates and has historically been of vital importance as a source of food in the region. It contains
a lot of mildly toxic lichenic acid, which will upset
your tummy and taste very bitter. The lichen was
traditionally made digestible by soaking it before
actually cooking in potash, a potassium carbonate
solution produced by soaking wood ashes in water.
Lichen was often boiled into a porridge with some
grains, or milled into flour with grains, to bulk out
the valuable cereals. Lichen is still used to some
extent in Iceland, where you can find some breads
containing a mix of cereal and lichen. In Iceland
it can still be bought in a few places and there are
traditional recipes for soups, breads and stews
containing Icelandic moss.

ICELANDIC MOSS SOUP

Fjallagrasamjólk (Iceland)

Icelandic moss has been commonly used in the
northern Nordic regions as part of the custom of
making use of what nature has to give, but also
on a wider scale in times of hardship and famine.
This soup doesn't really seem to be cooked much in
Iceland anymore, but I think that it is both enjoyable and culturally interesting. It seems to me that it
mimics the function of many milk- and grain-based
soups that can be found in other Nordic countries,
but because cereal grains have been largely unavailable in Iceland, it makes use of a more readily
available starch, in the form of lichens.

Preparation and cooking time: 10 minutes
Serves: 4

800 ml/28 fl oz (3¼ cups) milk
1 big handful Icelandic moss, cleaned, rinsed
    and coarsely chopped
sugar, to taste
salt, to taste

Pour the milk into a large pot and bring to a slow
boil. Add the Icelandic moss and simmer for about
5 minutes. Add sugar and salt to taste.

If left simmering for any longer, the Icelandic moss
will break down more and thicken the reducing
milk, giving it a sweet, caramelized lactose flavour.

Clockwise from top left: Boiled Broccoli (page 100); Glazed Ground Elder Leaves (page 132); Glazed Cavalo Nero (page 83); Steamed Whole Broccoli Tops (page 100)

CREAMY SUMMER VEGETABLE SOUP

Kesäkeitto (Finland)
Ängamat / Snålsoppa (Sweden)

This is one of my absolute favourite dishes, made in early summer when the vegetables are young and delicate. It is often served just as it is, or with a piece of crispbread and some butter and cheese or even with fried Small Smoked Pork Sausages (page 428) on the side. In some of the Finnish recipes I have read, the *kesäkeitto* soup is served with halved hard-boiled eggs. The Finnish version sometimes also contains new potatoes. If you want to use those, add them at the beginning of the cooking process, just before the carrots, and make sure they are just done when you add all the green vegetables.

In some more recent recipes for this dish you can see that chicken stock (broth) is being used. Although it might be delicious in its own way, for me this is not right. The subtle tones of young vegetables and good quality dairy products don't benefit from the extra flavour of any kind of meat stock (broth). The whole point of this dish is that you make the most delicious vegetable stock while you are cooking the vegetables, then towards the very end, when the actual cooking is almost done, you add cream and possibly an egg yolk if you want an especially rich soup.

Sometimes I will set aside half of the cream and, just before serving, whip it, then fold it into the soup. This leaves streaks of melting unmixed raw cream that provide contrast and little fluffy bubbles of foamy air in the soup itself.

This soup is often seasoned with a commercially produced herb salt called *Herbamare®*.

Preparation and cooking time: 30 minutes
Serves: 4

knob of butter
2 tablespoons plain (all-purpose) flour
1 large onion, finely chopped
6–8 small new potatoes, washed but with
  the skins on (for the Finnish version)
4 small carrots, cut into 3 mm/⅛ inch slices
2 young parsnips, cut into 1 cm/½ inch pieces
1 stalk celery, cut into 1cm/½ inch pieces
200 ml/7 fl oz (¾ cup plus 1 tablespoon) milk
1 small cauliflower, cut into little florets
1 small broccoli, cut into little florets
60 g/2¼ oz (⅓ cup plus 2 tablespoons) fresh
  green peas
175 g/6 oz (¾ cup) young spinach
  leaves, washed
300 ml/10 fl oz (1¼ cups) cream
1–2 egg yolks (optional)
finely chopped parsley and/or snipped chives
  (optional)
salt and white pepper, to taste

Put the butter in a pot large enough to fit all the vegetables. Cook over a medium heat until it starts foaming. When it has almost stopped foaming, whisk in the flour and continue to cook over a medium heat for a few minutes until it is light amber and smells delicious.

Add the chopped onions and cook for another minute. Add 500 ml/17 fl oz (2 cups plus 1 tablespoon) water and whisk so that no lumps form. Add the potatoes first, if you are making the Finnish version, otherwise start with the carrots and parsnips. Simmer for a few minutes before adding the celery, then simmer for another few minutes before adding the milk.

At this stage the vegetables should be al dente, but if using potatoes, they should be cooked through.

Add the cauliflower and green vegetables, all at the same time (but if the broccoli is less than young and tender, add it a few minutes before the rest). At this stage, add a little salt. Finish with the cream, leaving it to cook for just a few minutes. Alternatively, add half the cream now, then whip the rest and fold it in at the very last second. This is also when the egg yolks should be added, if using.

Before serving, adjust the level of salt and grind a little white pepper straight into the casserole. Sprinkle with herbs or herb salt if you are using them.

ITALIAN SALADS IN THE NORDICS

There are two different salads in two different countries, both called 'Italian' and both considered an iconic part of that country's respective food culture. In Norway, a coleslaw-like mix of cabbage, celeriac (celery root) and carrots is creamed with *rømme* and served as part of the Norwegian *koldtbord*. In Denmark, Italian salad consists of green peas, pieces of carrot and sometimes also pieces of asparagus, all dressed with mayonnaise. Oh, and another difference is that in Denmark the Italian salad is made from cooked vegetables and in Norway from raw ones.

It is said that the Danish Italian salad, which is mostly used as a topping for Open-faced Danish Sandwiches (page 522), is so named because the colours are reminiscent of the Italian flag. This might also be the case with the Norwegian version; that is, however, less clear. And to be honest, if someone asked me which flags the colours of those salads reminded me of, I would rather go with Ireland or the Ivory Coast than Italy. I mean, have you ever seen a red carrot in an Italian salad?

It is not entirely unlikely that the salad originated in Denmark and was brought to Norway in the early 1930s by a Danish carpenter, Mr Jensen, who later opened Delikat, a big Norwegian producer of readymade, mayonnaise-based salads. If it was indeed Mr Jensen that made the first Italian salad in Norway, it is fascinating how quickly it has adapted to the local produce and taste preferences in just over 80 years, and become just as iconic and authentically Norwegian as the Danish version is for the Danes.

ITALIAN SALAD IN NORWAY

Italiensk salat (Norway)

Sometimes the recipes for Italian salad in Norway include grated celeriac (celery root) and grated or diced apple. On occasion they also contain pieces of smoked ham. The recipe below seems to be the most authentic one I've found, and contains none of these things. But feel free to add a handful of any one of them, at will. If you do, then you might need to increase the mayonnaise and cream.

Preparation and cooking time: 10 minutes
Resting time: 1 hour
Serves: 4

2 carrots, peeled and coarsely grated
200 g/7 oz cabbage, shredded
60 g/2¼ oz Quick Pickled Cucumber
    (page 658), coarsely chopped
1 tablespoon sugar
3 tablespoons Mayonnaise (page 674)
100 ml/3½ fl oz (⅓ cup plus 1 tablespoon)
    rømme
dash of white vinegar
salt and white pepper, to taste

Mix all of the ingredients together and season well. Leave the salad in the refrigerator for about an hour to rest before serving.

ITALIAN SALAD IN DENMARK

Italiensk salat (Denmark)

Enjoy as a topping on open-faced sandwiches (*smørebrød*, page 522), or as a side dish with cold cuts and bread for a light meal.

Preparation and cooking time: 10 minutes
Serves: 4

2 carrots, peeled and cut into
    1 cm/½ inch pieces
130 g/4½ oz (¾ cup plus 2 tablespoons)
    green peas
4 green asparagus spears (optional)
2–3 tablespoons Mayonnaise (page 674)
1 teaspoon strong mustard
squeeze of lemon juice or a dash
    of white vinegar
salt and white pepper, to taste

Follow the instructions on page 85 for blanching the vegetables. If you are using asparagus, cut the spears into similar sized pieces to the carrots. Leave them all to cool completely.

Mix the vegetables with the mayonnaise, then add mustard, lemon/white vinegar, salt and pepper to your liking.

RUSSIAN SALAD AS IN DENMARK

Russisk salat (Denmark)

Preparation and cooking time: 1½ hours
Chilling time: overnight
Serves: 4

100 ml/3½ fl oz (⅓ cup plus 1 tablespoon)
  cream
400 g/14 oz Pickled Beetroot (page 660), cut
  into 1 cm/½ inch cubes
1 Brined Cucumber (page 660), diced
2 cold Boiled Potatoes (page 117), peeled
  and diced
2 tablespoons capers, finely chopped
1 red apple, cored and diced
1 red onion, finely chopped
100 ml/3½ fl oz (⅓ cup plus 1 tablespoon)
  Mayonnaise (page 674)
grated horseradish, to taste
salt and white pepper, to taste

Whip the cream to soft peaks.

Mix all of the ingredients together in a large bowl
and season well. Cover and refrigerate overnight,
then mix the salad again to achieve an even colour.
It should have a good sting of horseradish.

GREEN PEAS

Few things are as delicious as green peas fresh
from the pod, whether just cooked or even raw.
But they are also one of the few vegetables that
freeze really well, making them widely accessible
all year around. The funny thing is that if you
can't get them very fresh and pop them from the
pod more or less the same day as you cook and
eat them, peas that have been frozen straight after
being picked are most likely going to be sweeter
and tastier.

You could pop the individual cooked peas out of
their little membrane, a bit like with broad beans
(page 138), but I have always felt like that was a
really unnecessary restaurant way of displaying
unnecessary waste of manpower.

To prepare fresh green peas, remove the peas from
their pods and blanch them in boiling water for a
minute, or even less (page 85).

If you buy peas in the pod, you'll need to allow
for half of the weight being wasted. Allow about
250 g/9 oz unpodded peas per person, for a good-
sized portion as a side dish.

For image see page 667

PEAS IN THE POD, DIPPED IN BUTTER

Apposet (Finland)
Släpärter (Sweden)

This is a classic seasonal delicacy in Sweden. Some
peas are kept back from the main crop and left a
little longer in the field. They are harvested a bit
later on, but still before they mature fully, turn
yellow and start to dry for winter storage.

To eat *släpärter*, pick a steaming hot pod up with
your fingers and dip in melted butter. Put the
whole pod in your mouth and pull it out between
your teeth, so that only the peas and all the soft,
edible parts remain inside.

Släpärter is a communal dish: put a big plate of
peas and a bowl of butter in the middle of the
table for everyone to share.

Some people like to grate some horseradish into
their butter; I prefer it without.

Preparation and cooking time: 30 minutes
Serves: 4 as a starter (appetizer)

1 good handful salt
1 kg/2¼ lb fresh peas in their pods (make
  sure they are almost mature, but have not
  started to yellow)
100 g/3½ oz (7 tablespoons) butter, melted

Bring a pot of salted water to the boil. Add the
peas and cook until they are sweet and soft.

Drain the peas and serve them immediately with a
bowl of melted butter for dipping.

CREAMED GREEN PEAS

Preparation and cooking time: 20 minutes
Serves: 4 as a side dish

1 kg/2¼ lb fresh peas in their pods
½ quantity Béchamel Sauce (page 666),
   substituting half the milk with cream
salt and white pepper, to taste
chopped chervil, to taste (optional)
freshly grated nutmeg, to taste (optional)

Follow the method on page 666 for preparing the béchamel sauce.

Follow the instructions on the opposite page for podding the peas. Blanch briefly, if necessary. Taste one before to judge. If they taste sweet and tender glaze them raw and if they taste starchy blanch them first.

Reheat the peas in the béchamel. Season well with salt and pepper and add chervil or nutmeg, if using.

GLAZED GREEN PEAS

If you are using really young and fresh peas, which have no bitterness and a very delicate texture when raw, the peas should be glazed without being blanched first. Just pop them out of the pod and follow the recipe below as if they were cooked.

If you want to, some finely chopped shallot is a nice seasoning but other times the flavour of peas and butter is enough.

Don't use less butter than is called for in the recipe. The butter, emulsifying with the pea-infused cooking water, is the best sauce you can imagine for whatever you are serving the peas with.

Preparation and cooking time: 5 minutes
Serves: 4 as a side dish

1 kg/2¼ lb fresh peas in their pods
50 g/2 oz (3½ tablespoons) cold butter, cut
   into 1 cm/½ inch dice
1 shallot, finely chopped (optional)
salt and white pepper, to taste

Follow the instructions on the opposite page for podding the peas. Blanch briefly, if necessary.

Follow the instructions on page 83 for glazed vegetables using a tablespoon of the pea cooking water as your liquid. (Use plain water if this isn't available.) Adjust the seasoning and serve immediately.

NORWEGIAN MASHED PEAS

Ertestuing (Norway)

Traditionally, *ertestuing* was made from dried green peas, but today, with frozen green peas accessible all year round, many people use these to make it. It is served alongside many savoury dishes in Norway, among others *Kjöttekaker* or Norwegian Beef Patties (page 376) and Lutefisk (page 230). Below are recipes for each method.

For image see page 667

MASHED DRIED PEAS (VERSION 1)

Preparation and cooking time: 2 hours
Soaking time: overnight
Serves: 4

200 g/7 oz dried green peas, soaked
   overnight in plenty of cold water
50 g/2 oz (3½ tablespoons) butter
2 teaspoons sugar
salt and white pepper, to taste

Drain the peas and discard the soaking water. Place the peas in a pot, cover with water and bring to the boil. Simmer for at least 30 minutes, or until tender. When ready the water should barely cover the peas. If it doesn't, add more until it does. Add the butter and sugar and stir briskly so that the peas start breaking up and thickening the cooking liquid a little. Season well with salt and pepper.

MASHED FROZEN PEAS (VERSION 2)

Preparation and cooking time: 10 minutes
Serves: 4

50 g/2 oz (3½ tablespoons) butter
1 tablespoon plain (all-purpose) flour
400 g/14 oz frozen green peas, defrosted
salt and white pepper, to taste

Melt the butter in a saucepan, then add the flour and whisk until no lumps remain. Add the peas to the pan and cook them for a few minutes, stirring all the time. When they begin to break up and turn into a kind of porridge, they are ready. Season well before serving.

BROAD BEANS

Broad (fava) beans are not really beans at all, but are, botanically, closer to peas. They have been grown in Scandinavia since the thirteenth century, or earlier, and used to be a very important staple. They were often grown in kitchen gardens together with other climbing vegetables, like peas and some other legumes, which could use the sturdy broad bean plant as a kind of natural trellis. Traditionally, broad beans were grown until fully mature and then dried and stored, but I think they should be eaten in the summer, when they are fresh and tasty. The following recipes can all be made from either dried or fresh beans.

TO PREPARE FRESH BROAD BEANS

Remove the beans from their outer pods, blanch them quickly in boiling water (page 85), then drain and refresh them in iced water. For really young beans, this is all you need to do. After draining, serve them with a knob of melting butter and a sprinkling of good salt.

For older, more mature beans, you will need to remove the tough membrane that surrounds each individual bean. After draining, refresh the beans in iced water. Once refreshed, tear a small opening in the membrane and squeeze the other end gently to pop out the bright green bean. To judge if the membrane should stay or go just pop a bean in your mouth and do what seems right.

If you buy your broad beans whole, in the pod, you'll need to allow for two-thirds of the weight being wasted. Allow about 500 g/1 lb 2 oz unpodded beans per person, for a good-sized portion as a side dish.

TO PREPARE DRIED BROAD BEANS

Before cooking dried beans you need to soak them overnight in plenty of cold water. Discard the soaking water, then cook the beans in fresh boiling water until they are soft enough for your preference. The actual cooking time will depend on the age of the beans themselves, so you will need to check them. Once soft enough, drain the beans and cook them in iced water, then pop them out of their skins, as described above. Or keep the skins on, if you prefer. Allow 75 g/2¾ oz dried beans per person.

CREAMED BROAD BEANS

I like serving creamed broad (fava) beans with braised salted meats like pork knuckle or braised salted shoulder of pork. On the other hand, in the late summer, some creamed broad beans with a good piece of poached white fish next to them, is about as good as it gets, too.

If you are going with braised meat, follow the method described below, which is based on a creamy Velouté (page 652) made from the cooking liquid of the meat itself. If there is no suitable braising liquid – or you don't want to have the meat flavour in there – make the recipe below with a half quantity of Béchamel Sauce (page 666) in which you have substituted half of the milk with cream.

It's nice to add boiled slices of carrot (page 110) to this dish. If you do, substitute half the beans with carrots and proceed with the recipe, as described.

Preparation and cooking time: 10 minutes
Soaking time if using dried beans: overnight
Serves: 4 as a side dish

2 kg/4½ lb fresh broad (fava) beans in their
  pods or 300 g/11 oz dried broad beans
½ quantity creamy Velouté (page 652)
1 good handful herbs, coarsely chopped
  (parsley, chives and chervil are all good)
salt and white pepper, to taste

Follow the instructions for preparing your choice
of fresh or dried beans.

Follow the instructions on page 652 for preparing
the creamy velouté, using the cooking liquid from
your accompanying meat.

Reheat the broad (fava) beans in the velouté. Season well and add the herbs. Serve immediately, so
that all the green ingredients stay nice and vibrant.

SALAD OF BROAD BEANS
AND SPINACH

Spenat och bondbönssallad (Sweden)

This is in no way a classic Swedish dish, but it's a
very nice little end-of-summer salad.

Preparation and cooking time: 15 minutes
Serves: 4

2 kg/4½ lb fresh broad (fava) beans in their
  pods or 300 g/11 oz dried broad beans
500 g/1 lb 2 oz spinach leaves
1 shallot, finely chopped
1 good bunch parsley, leaves coarsely
  chopped, stems finely chopped
Vinaigrette (page 676), to taste
salt and black pepper, to taste

Follow the instructions on the opposite page
for preparing your choice of fresh or dried beans.
Allow them to cool.

Follow the method on page 85 for blanching the
spinach. After refreshing in iced water, squeeze out
any excess water and chop the spinach finely.

Combine the beans, spinach, shallot and herbs in a
salad bowl. Dress with vinaigrette and season well
with salt and pepper.

BROAD BEAN AND CARROT SOUP

Bonbönsvälling / Bondbönssoppa (Sweden)

In older recipes this soup is often accompanied
with Plain Salted Herring (page 201) that's been
desalted (page 200), or with cured ham. If you
want to make it a bit richer, incorporate a couple
of egg yolks into the hot soup just before serving.
Garnish and season with parsley if you like it.

Preparation and cooking time: 20 minutes
Serves: 4

butter, for frying
2 carrots, peeled and sliced into thin circles
1 onion, finely chopped
800 ml/28 fl oz (3¼ cups) Chicken Stock
  (page 650)
2 tablespoons Beurre Manié (page 651)
500 g/1 lb 2 oz fresh broad (fava) beans,
  trimmed, blanched and peeled
200 ml/7 fl oz (¾ cup plus 1 tablespoon) milk
100 ml/3½ fl oz (⅓ cup plus 1 tablespoon)
  cream
1–2 egg yolks (optional)
chopped parsley (optional)
salt and white pepper, to taste

Heat the butter in a pan over a medium heat. Add
the carrots and onion and fry for a few minutes
until the onion becomes translucent.

Add the stock (broth) to the pan and bring to a
simmer. Add the beurre manié and continue cooking for a few more minutes. Add the broad (fava)
beans to the pan, then the milk and cream, and
simmer for a bit longer. Stir in the egg yolks, if
using. Season with salt and pepper, sprinkle with
parsley, if using, and serve.

SPLIT PEA SOUP

This hearty and warming soup has been a staple in the Nordic region for a very long time. Historically, the protein-rich dried peas were a reliable source of nutrition through winter and they have been eaten in the Scandinavian countries since the Bronze Age, if not before.

The base of the soup is the peas themselves, boiled with vegetables and, usually, with salted meat. The kinds of meat, vegetables and seasonings used differ a bit from country to country. Yellow dried split peas are used everywhere, except in Finland, where green dried split peas are used. In Sweden and Finland pea soup is traditionally eaten on Thursdays, with Thin Pancakes (page 450) for dessert. This tradition dates back to before the Reformation and was a way of preparing for fasting on Fridays. Thursday as 'pea soup day' is a tradition that has been kept alive – especially within the military community of Sweden and Finland where it is still very common.

Sometimes the meat used for the soup, which is always boiled in one whole piece, is cut into smaller pieces before serving and then added back to the soup. I am not a huge fan of this. I think it turns this fantastic dish into sloppy canteen food. I prefer to cut the pieces of meat and serve them separately to the soup. This way everyone can add what meat they want to the soup and you can serve it in nice slices as opposed to tiny chopped up pieces. For the same reason I think that the table should be set with a knife and fork as well as a spoon, not just a spoon.

SPLIT PEA SOUP BASE RECIPE

Use the quantities and method from this base recipe as a guide for the regional versions, varying the meat, vegetables and aromatics, as specified.

Preparation and cooking time: 1½ hours
Soaking time: overnight
Serves: 6

450 g/1 lb (2¼ cups) yellow split peas
1 onion, finely chopped
400 g/14 oz boned salted meat, or
  800 g/1¾ lb meat on the bone

vegetables, as specified in the recipes below
  and overleaf
aromatics, as specified in the recipes below
  and overleaf
salt and white pepper, to taste

Soak the split peas overnight in plenty of cold water. They will swell significantly as they absorb water, so make sure you use a large enough container.

Skim away any free-floating pea skins from the surface of the soaking water, then drain the peas and put them in a large pot with 1½ litres/50 fl oz (6¼ cups) fresh water. Add your choice of vegetables, meat and aromatics and season lightly with salt and pepper. (Remember that the salty meat will add to the saltiness of the soup itself, so it's best to salt more at the end than too much in the beginning.) Bring to the boil and skim carefully during the first 10 minutes of cooking. Continue to simmer over gentle heat until the meat is fully cooked, then remove it from the soup and reserve for later. Continue cooking the peas if they are not completely soft. The whole cooking process should take about 1½ hours.

Before serving, slice the meats and serve them separately (or cut into small pieces and add them back to the soup). Adjust the seasoning before serving.

SPLIT PEA SOUP IN NORWAY

Ertesuppe (Norway)

Use salted shoulder or belly (side) of pork, Norwegian Cured Ham (page 439) or Norwegian Cured and Aged Leg of Mutton (page 348).

Season the Norwegian version of split pea soup with fresh thyme in addition to the salt and pepper of the basic recipe. Sometimes the potatoes are not cooked in the soup, but boiled separately and served on the side for people to put in their soup themselves.

Serve Norwegian split pea soup with Norwegian Crisp Flatbread (page 513).

Preparation and cooking time: 1½ hours
Soaking time: overnight
Serves: 6

450 g/1 lb (2¼ cups) yellow split peas
400 g/14 oz salted shoulder or belly (side)
  of pork
few sprigs thyme, to taste
1 onion, finely chopped
4 potatoes, cut into 1.5 cm/¾ inch dice
2 carrots, cut into 1.5 cm/¾ inch dice
¼ celeriac (celery root), cut into 1.5 cm/
  ¾ inch dice
¼ swede (rutabaga), cut into 1.5 cm/
  ¾ inch dice
salt and white pepper, to taste

Follow the method for the base recipe but add the
vegetables halfway through the cooking process of
the meat, after perhaps 30–40 minutes of simmering.

For image see page 349

Soak the dried beans overnight in plenty of cold
water. They will swell significantly as they absorb water, so make sure you use a large enough
container.

Drain the beans and put them in a large pot with
650 ml/22½ fl oz (2¾ cups) fresh water. Add the
golden syrup and bring to the boil. Cover the pot
and simmer until the beans are soft. Top up with
more water, if necessary.

Once the beans are done, thicken the cooking
water with some potato starch. Add vinegar, salt
and pepper to taste. It should add a nice fresh
acidity, to balance the rich sweetness of the beans.

SWEET-AND-SOUR BROWN BEANS

Bruna bönor i sirapssås (Sweden)

Brown beans are commonly grown on the Swedish island of Öland in the Baltic and they used to
be a very important staple. This recipe, consisting
of brown beans cooked until tender in a sweet-
and-sour gravy, is not quite as common as it used
to be, but can definitely still be found in traditional canteens for lunch. The beans are usually
served with slices of Fried Salt Pork (page 302)
or fried Falu Sausage (page 417) and some Boiled
Potatoes (page 117) and/or Boiled Carrot slices
(page 110).

Preparation and cooking time: 1 hour
Soaking time: overnight
Serves: 4

250 g/9 oz dried brown beans
3 tablespoons golden syrup
a bit of potato starch, to thicken
Ättika (12%) vinegar (page 656), to taste
salt and white pepper, to taste

SPLIT PEA SOUP IN DENMARK

Gule ærter (Denmark)

Split pea soup in Denmark is prepared in a slightly different way. It is generally seasoned with thyme and contains more vegetables than in other countries. Also, the order in which the soup is produced is quite different, and in my opinion preferable. The meat is first cooked in water until done. The cooking liquid from the meat is then used to cook the split peas, as opposed to the one-pot solution in the basic recipe (page 140). This way it is easier to control the texture of the peas and the soup is often a little bit more brothy, instead of being thickened by a pea mush, as in other countries.

Use salted shoulder or back of pork, and in addition to the pork serve the soup with some Medister Pork Sausages (page 430) cooked in broth or salted water. Accompany with slices of Danish Rye Bread (page 504) and strong mustard on the side.

Preparation and cooking time: 2–3 hours
Soaking time: overnight
Serves: 6

450 g/1 lb (2¼ cups) yellow split peas
400 g/14 oz salted shoulder or back
  of pork
few sprigs thyme
2 onions, finely chopped
1 leek, cut into 1.5 cm/¾ inch dice
2 carrots, cut into 1.5 cm/¾ inch dice
1 small celeriac (celery root), cut into
  1.5 cm/¾ inch dice
1 parsnip, cut into 1.5 cm/
  ¾ inch dice
salt and white pepper, to taste

Soak the split peas overnight in plenty of cold water. They will swell significantly as they absorb water, so make sure you use a large enough container.

Put the meat in a pot and cover with 1½ litres/50 fl oz (6¼ cups) fresh water. Bring to the boil, then lower the heat and simmer for about 1–2 hours or until it is tender. Remove from the pot and set aside, reserving the cooking liquid.

Drain the split peas and add them together with the thyme to the pot and season lightly with salt and pepper. (Remember that the cooking liquid from the meat will itself be salty.) Bring to the boil and skim carefully during the first 10 minutes of cooking.

After about an hour, add the vegetables. Continue to simmer over gentle heat until the vegetables are cooked and split peas are completely tender. It should take about 1½ hours.

Before serving, slice the pork and sausage, if using, and serve them separately (or cut them into small pieces and add them to the soup). Adjust the seasoning just before serving.

SPLIT PEA SOUP IN SWEDEN

Ärtor med fläsk / Ärtsoppa (Sweden)

The choice between thyme and marjoram tends to divide Swedes into two groups. I am pro marjoram and I like quite a lot of it, too. Some recipes contain a sad little carrot, bobbing around in there somewhere. I never really liked that: either have plenty of vegetables, like the Danes do, or none at all.

In addition to the pork, serve the soup with some cooked Medister Pork Sausages (page 430) and a strong unsweetened mustard. Pea soup is often accompanied by a cup of warm Arrack Flavoured Liqueur (page 717).

Preparation and cooking time: 1½ hours
Soaking time: overnight
Serves: 6

450 g/1 lb (2¼ cups) yellow split peas
400 g/14 oz salted shoulder, belly (side)
  or knuckle of pork (or a combination
  of these)
few sprigs thyme or marjoram
  (or both)
a few cloves
2 bay leaves
piece of dried ginger, to taste
salt and white pepper, to taste

Follow the method for the base recipe (page 140).

SPLIT PEA SOUP IN FINLAND

Ärtsoppa / Hernekeitto (Finland)

Replace the yellow split peas with green ones, but aside of that follow the procedure in the base recipe. Use salt pork or salted and smoked pork. Serve the soup with mustard on the side.

Preparation and cooking time: 1½ hours
Serves: 6

450 g/1 lb (2¼ cups) green split peas
400 g/14 oz salted shoulder, knuckle or belly
  (side) of pork
1 onion, finely chopped
salt and white pepper, to taste

Follow the method for the base recipe on page 140.

Soak the peas overnight, then drain them and put in a large pot with 1½ litres/50 fl oz (6¼ cups) fresh water. Add the meat and thyme and season lightly with salt and pepper. (Remember that the salty meat will add to the saltiness of the soup itself, so it's best to salt more at the end than too much in the beginning.) Bring to the boil and skim carefully during the first 10 minutes of cooking.

After 30–40 minutes, add the vegetables. Continue to simmer over gentle heat until the meat is fully cooked, then remove it from the soup and reserve for later. If the split peas are not completely soft, then continue cooking. The whole cooking process should take about 1½ hours.

Before serving, slice the lamb and serve separately with boiled potatoes. Adjust the seasoning just before serving.

SPLIT PEA SOUP IN THE FAROE ISLANDS AND ICELAND

Saltkjøt og baunir (Faroe Islands)
Saltkjöt og baunir (Iceland)

Split pea soup in the Faroe Islands and Iceland is generally prepared with salt mutton or lamb, instead of pork, and it often has quite a lot of vegetables in it, a bit like the Danish version. It is often served with the meat and Boiled Potatoes (page 117) on the side.

Preparation and cooking time: 1½ hours
Soaking time: overnight
Serves: 6

400 g/14 oz (2 cups) yellow split peas
400 g/14 oz salted mutton or lamb
few sprigs thyme
2 onions, finely chopped
1 leek, cut into 1.5 cm/¾ inch dice
2 carrots, cut into 1.5 cm/¾ inch dice
1 small celeriac (celery root), cut into
  1.5 cm/¾ inch dice
1 parsnip, cut into 1.5 cm/¾ inch dice
salt and white pepper, to taste

FRESHWATER FISH

Previous page: A house next to a West Finnish Highway, Autumn (Fall) 2013. Inside the house lampreys are being grilled and sold.

Opposite: Man flipping lampreys grilled over alder wood, west Finland, October 2013.

HOW TO GUT A ROUND FISH

Hold the fish so that the belly is facing upwards. Insert your knife into the anus near the tail of the fish and cut all the way along the length of the fish towards the head.

Spread the abdominal cavity open with your fingers and scrape out the insides.

Once the abdominal cavity is empty, rinse it thoroughly under cold running water and pat dry. For illustrations see opposite page.

HOW TO FILLET AND SKIN A ROUND FISH

Make diagonal cuts into the back on both sides of the fish head to form a 'v-shaped cut. Snap the head off by bending it back away from the body.

Keep the knife flat and then cut into the skin of the top fillet above the dorsal fin and along the back. Use long sweeping cuts from head to tail to reveal the backbone. Insert the tip of the knife at the tail end and cut down to the tail to release the underside of the fillet. Repeat with the remaining fillet.

To remove the skin, use a flexible knife and start at the tail end or thinnest part of the fish fillet. Using the middle of the blade, cut into the fillet as far as the skin. Slide the knife up towards the other end to free the fillet. For illustrations see opposite page.

WHOLE FISH, FRIED IN A PAN

This is a fantastic way of cooking smaller fish, weighing 400–600 g/14–21 oz, as each is a perfect serving for one person. Also, filleting fish of this size creates an unnecessary large amount of waste, relative to the size of the fish. This method can also be used for pieces of larger fish, like trout or sole, that are still on the bone. For

fish fried on the bone, a good way of checking whether they are done is to pull the dorsal fin. If it just comes out with the bones attached to it, the fish is perfect. If it sticks, keep cooking it for a bit longer.

Fish with scales need to have them very carefully removed, or even be skinned, while flat fish should be thoroughly scraped. Keep the heads on smaller fish that fit in your frying pan. For larger fish, that wouldn't otherwise fit, you can remove both the heads and tails. If you do keep the heads on, then at least remove the gills as they can easily discolour the flesh of the fish while cooking.

The four techniques on the next few pages are referred to in many of the recipes in the fish chapters of this book. The flavourings and presentation will vary slightly with each particular recipe. In the first technique, the fish is only salted before cooking, while the other two include additions to make the skin crisper. Which technique you choose all depends on the recipe you're using and the desired result.

A bigger fish needs to be cooked at lower temperature than a small one, otherwise the outside will be burnt before the fish is cooked through. For the opposite reason a small fish needs to be cooked at higher temperature, because otherwise the flesh will be overcooked before you have sufficient colouration of the exterior.

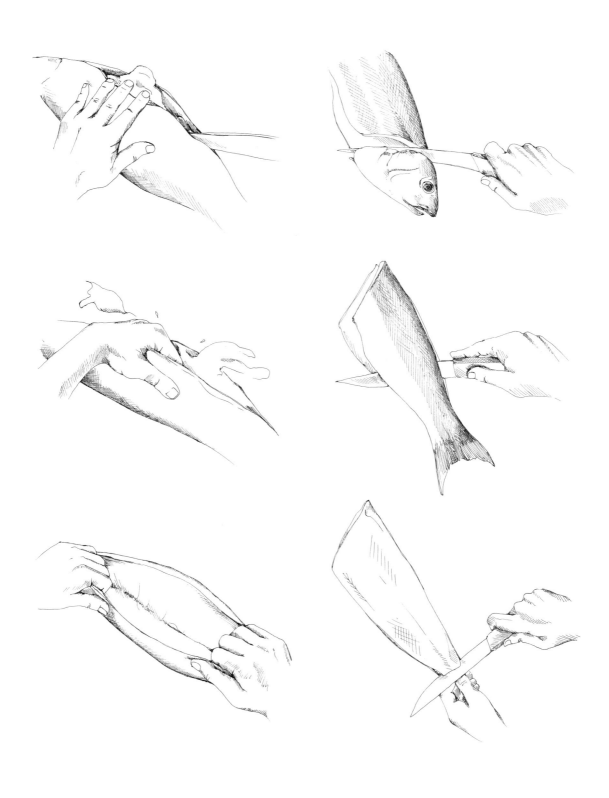

FRIED IN BUTTER (VERSION 1)

I like this technique for lean white fish, such as perch, where you want to be able to closely monitor the cooking process, I also prefer this method for dishes where the fish is going to be served with a warm sauce and where a breaded surface might feel a little too rich and will quickly become soggy.

Preparation and cooking time: 20–30
minutes, depending on the variety and size
of the fish
Serves: 4

4 x 400–600-g/14–21-oz whole fish, cleaned,
  gutted and scaled
butter or neutral-flavoured cooking oil,
  for frying
salt and white pepper, to taste

Salt the fish inside and out, then leave them for a few minutes to let the salt dissolve a bit. This will help them to get a nice colour when they are being cooked.

To fry the fish, heat a frying pan over a medium–high heat. Add butter, or equal parts of butter and a neutral-flavoured cooking oil, depending on what you prefer. The amount you use depends on the size of your pan and the number of fish you are frying, but it is important to have enough fat to avoid uneven distribution of heat to the fish, which can result in uneven browning. About 5 mm/¼ inch of melted fat over the bottom of the pan should be sufficient.

Wait until the butter just stops foaming and starts to brown and to smell beautifully of caramelizing milk-sugars. Add the fish to the pan, one by one. When you lift a fish to place it in a pan, pick it up by the tail and first touch the head onto the part of the pan closest to you, then lower the rest of the fish away from you in one fluent motion. By paying a little extra attention here and working carefully, instead of just lifting the fish in with a spatula, you will avoid splattering hot fat everywhere – and if it does splatter, at least it will be directed away from you. Don't put more than 2 fish into each pan, as that will lower the temperature too much. Your fish will then take too long to brown and may become soggy or overcooked on the inside by the time they are crisp enough on the outside.

Leave the fish in the pan without moving them until they are deeply golden-brown, but not burning, and only then flip them over. Try to only turn the fish once, and don't flip them back and forth, as this will only break the fish and impact on both their look and flavour.

To ensure a perfect result, it is crucial to maintain a good temperature in the pan throughout the cooking process. If the pan cools down too much, be quick to crank up the heat, and if the fish darken too quickly, then pull the pan off the heat for a moment to cool a bit. During the last minute of cooking, season both the fish and the butter with a little bit of freshly ground white pepper; any earlier, and it will burn and lose its aroma and flavour.

When the fish is ready, lift it up with a spatula that is large enough to carry it without breaking, and place it on a clean cloth or paper towels for a minute or two before serving. This allows the skin to crisp up a bit more and helps distribute the heat more evenly within the fish.

Tip: When you take the fish out of the pan, make sure you immediately remove the pan from the heat so that the butter doesn't burn while you are fiddling with the fish. If properly executed, the butter should be deeply caramelized, but not burnt, and should taste cleanly of fish combined with the aroma of toasty bread or rye. Add a little lemon juice and some chopped herbs as a quick sauce with the fish, if you like.

DUSTED WITH FLOUR (VERSION 2)

Preparation and cooking time: 20–30
minutes, depending on the variety
and size of the fish
Serves: 4

4 x 400–600-g/14–21-oz whole fish, cleaned,
  gutted and scaled
plain (all-purpose) flour, to dust
salt and white pepper, to taste

Salt the fish inside and out, then leave them for a few minutes to let the salt dissolve a bit. This will help them to get a nice colour when they are being cooked.

Put a good layer of flour onto a plate and turn the piece of fish in it, carefully coating all sides. For small pieces of fish like the fillets of a small perch, put flour into a plastic bag, add the seasoned fillets to it before shaking the bag around for a few seconds. This coats the fish very evenly and quickly. Don't coat the fish in flour too early but rather wait until the very last minute and pop them straight in the pan after they have been coated. This way you will get a nicer surface.

Follow the instructions in version 1 (see opposite page) to fry the fish.

BREADED (VERSION 3)

A classic thick coating of breadcrumbs is perfect for gelatinous fish, such as flatfish, or for cod and other fish that don't dry out easily. It is important that the crust is really cooked through and golden-brown, so that it stays crisp long enough for you to eat. I like to serve thickly-coated fish like this, with a slice of lemon, some *matättika* (page 657) or other vinegar or perhaps a cold sauce of some kind.

Preparation and cooking time: 20–30
* minutes, depending on the variety*
* and size of the fish*
Serves: 4

4 x 400–600-g/14–21-oz whole fish, cleaned,
  gutted and scaled
plain (all-purpose) flour, to coat
1 egg, lightly beaten
breadcrumbs, to coat
salt and white pepper, to taste

Salt the fish inside and out.

Place the flour, beaten egg and breadcrumbs into 3 separate wide, shallow bowls.

Press the fish gently into the bowl of flour, then turn and coat the other side. Make sure the entire surface is completely covered in flour before proceeding to the next step. Continue by dipping the fish into the egg, making sure it is completely coated. Finish by pressing it into the breadcrumbs, once again making sure the fish is completely coated before cooking. Repeat with the remaining fish.

Follow the instructions in version 1 (see opposite page) to fry the fish.

WITH A RYE FLOUR CRUST (VERSION 4)

This produces a slightly thinner crust, which I like for succulent oily fish, like herring or mackerel, which are sensitive to over-cooking. This crust crisps up quickly, thanks to its thinness, and colours quickly, thanks to the milk.

Preparation and cooking time: 20–30
* minutes, depending on the variety*
* and size of the fish*
Serves: 4

4 x 400–600-g/14–21-oz whole fish, cleaned,
  gutted and scaled
milk, to dip
coarse rye flour, to coat
salt and white pepper, to taste

Salt the fish inside and out.

Pour some milk into a wide, shallow bowl and place some flour into another. Dip the fish quickly in the milk before pressing it gently into the flour. Turn and coat the other side. Make sure the fish is completely covered before cooking. Repeat with the remaining fish.

Follow the instructions in version 1 (see opposite page) to fry the fish.

HOW TO BREAD AND FRY FISH

It is quite simple to bread and fry fillets of fish and yet, how many bad ones have you been served over the years? From crooked curls of plaice, overcooked, yet still not properly browned, to herring in a thick clotted crust of bread and egg, as stiff as a suit of armour or chunks of pike, cremated to a strange kind of charcoal on the outside but still raw inside.

The key is to master every step of the process: you need to apply an even and just-thick-enough layer of breadcrumbs, you need to do it swiftly and then you need to fry it at the correct temperature so that all parts of the fish are ready at roughly the same time. In other words, the exterior needs to be browned at the same time that the centre of the fish is done.

You shouldn't crumb your fish in advance. For a crisper and more uniform result, do it just before frying.

And remember that you can't season fish through a coating, so you need to do it before you crumb them. On the other hand you also have to season the breadcrumbs after the frying, and seasoning the fish alone won't be sufficient.

You can choose to deep-fry your fish in oil in a large saucepan or shallow-fry it in a frying pan. The basic technique is the same, but remember that deep-frying is always faster that shallow-frying as the oil will come in contact with a larger surface area at any given time, transporting more energy into the fish.

Finally, it might seem obvious, but I'll say it anyway: the thinner the fillet of fish, the higher the temperature the butter or oil should be. And vice versa. So a thin fillet of a small perch should probably be fried at 190°C/375°F for just a few minutes, while a compact chunk of turbot in a 5 x 5 cm/ 2 x 2 inch cube should fry at 160°C/315°F for about 8–10 minutes.

Preparation and cooking time: 30 minutes
Serves: 4

80 g/3 oz (⅔ cup) plain (all-purpose) flour
100 g/3½ oz (1 cup) breadcrumbs

2 eggs
50 ml/2 fl oz (3½ tablespoons) milk
650 g/1 lb 7 oz fish fillet, cut into 4 equal
  pieces
salt and white pepper, to taste
butter or oil, for frying

Put the flour and the breadcrumbs in 2 separate 5 litre/10½ UK pint plastic bags. Whisk the eggs and milk together in a bowl.

Arrange the fish fillets on a tray and season them well on all sides with salt and pepper. Place the fish fillets in the bag of flour. Blow into the bag to inflate it, then twist the opening a few times to seal it. Shake the bag briskly to coat the fish pieces with flour, then remove them from the bag and place them back on the tray.

Working one at a time, dip the fish into the egg-milk mixture, making sure it covers the surface entirely. Shake off any excess, then return it to the tray. When all of the fish have been egged, transfer them to the bag of breadcrumbs, inflate the bag, twist to seal it and shake. Now return the crumbed fillets to the tray and start cooking them as quickly as you can.

HOW TO SHALLOW-FRY FISH

Start by preheating your oven to 150°C/300°F/ Gas Mark 2 and line a baking pan with paper towels.

Place a good-quality, rather large frying pan on the stove and add a knob of butter. Heat to melt it. There's an old saying that it will be hot enough when the butter goes silent and stops foaming – in other words, when all the water has evaporated – and this is pretty accurate.

The temperature settings obviously vary from stove to stove but, in my experience, people either turn the heat up full, which is generally too high for frying, or they turn it down too low, because they are frightened of burning the food. We can establish immediately that a normal domestic stove is unlikely to burn your food because it gets too hot but, rather, because you are too slow. If you pay close attention and work in a concentrated fashion, then that won't happen. On the other hand, what is likely to happen at full power is that the oil itself will get too hot and may burn. This doesn't taste good, and it isn't very good for your health either. On my stove at home, 80% of full power is pretty much perfect for frying: it is hot enough to both colour and cook the product, but not so hot that the fat itself burns.

Once the pan and the fat are hot, the next thing to remember is not to put too many items in at any one time, as this will inevitably cool everything down; aim to cover no more than half of the surface area of the bottom of the pan. It's much better to fry the fish in two batches, and let them rest somewhere warm, than to overload the pan by trying to cook everything at once.

Fry the fish pieces on one side until you are satisfied with the colour before flipping them over. Do not flip them back and forth as this will tend to overcook the fish and not achieve enough colourization. A good thing to do while browning the first side, is to move the pieces around in the pan a bit. That way, nothing stays in one spot too long, which cools that particular part of the pan down while another empty part gets too hot. Once you are happy with the colour, flip the fish over and cook the other side in the same way. You can add a bit more butter to the pan at this stage if it looks dry.

When the fish is nicely browned on both sides, remove it from the pan. If it is a really thick piece of fish, it won't be cooked all the way through yet, so transfer it to the preheated baking pan and place in the oven until cooked through. If you've crumbed it properly, it won't go soggy. If you're cooking the fish in batches, then you should also keep it warm in the oven in this way; don't worry, it won't go dry.

Just before serving, season the fish all over with salt and a little white pepper. You can do this when they are still in the pan, if you prefer.

As long as you haven't burned the butter, one of the most delicious things you can serve with a piece of crumbed fish is that frying butter, which is like a sauce that's been infused with fishy and breadcrumby goodness. I like to arrange the fish on a warm plate, along with any accompaniments, and then add a small knob of butter (per person) to the still-hot pan – sometimes I add a squeeze of lemon, too. Just as it begins to caramelize, I spoon the hot butter over the fish, along with any lingering bits of fish, crumbs and juices that are still in the pan.

TO DEEP-FRY FISH

Start by preheating your oven to 150°C/300°F/ Gas Mark 2 and line a baking pan with paper towels.

Irrespective of whether you own a proper deep-fat fryer or whether you use a saucepan on top of your stove, the most important part of deep-frying is temperature control. You need to know the temperature of your fat, you need to be able to maintain that temperature when you add items to it and then also maintain it for the duration of the cooking time.

I understand that many people have safety concerns about deep-frying and temperature control, and even I've been asked on occasion whether the old trick of testing temperature with a cube of bread isn't better and safer. In my opinion, not only does this method not work, but I think that it can actually be dangerous. The problem with the bread cube method is that it is not very accurate; all bread is different, and so will brown differently. To be honest, I think that the best you can say with this rule of thumb approach, is that the oil is hot!

I firmly believe that with the bread-cube method, the best-case scenario is that your food may be soggy or will burn. The worst-case scenario is that you risk setting your kitchen alight with a greasy ball of fire from burning oil. While I understand that not everyone has a thermometer in their kitchen drawer, you will never ever see a professional cook attempt to fry without one. I strongly urge everyone who wants to fry to buy an ordinary digital kitchen thermometer; ideally one with at least 1 metre/40 inch steel (not plastic) cable attached. I purchased one myself the other week at my local supermarket and it cost the same as coffee and sandwich in a no-frills café. Plus, it has a built-in timer!

And it couldn't be simpler to use a digital thermometer: all you do is submerge the sensor in the oil and you will have perfect control of the temperature all the time – and you can even leave it there until the oil has cooled down, if you want to.

You should never let the oil rise above 200°C/400°F. The reason for this is that most cooking oils have

a smoking point of just above that temperature and, from then on, they will start to decompose into toxic substances. Additionally, if you have a powerful stove and are not properly in control of the temperature, it takes a very short time for the oil to increase to 300°C/570°F, at which point it can start to burn.

As for the actual frying, once the fat has reached a suitable temperature, this is the time to add your pieces of fish. As with shallow-frying, it is better to cook in several batches than to overcrowd the pan. Don't stir the items around too much, but do make sure that they don't stick to each other and ensure that any which don't move around in the oil by themselves are evenly coloured, by turning them from time to time.

Once they are nicely browned, transfer to the preheated baking pan and place in the oven to keep warm while you fry the remaining pieces of fish. Season the fish all over with salt and a little white pepper just before serving.

BURBOT *(LOTA LOTA)*

Burbot is the only fish of the cod family to live in freshwater. It has firm white flesh and a mild but very distinctive flavour. Cusk or ling are suitable substitutes for burbot.

BURBOT STEW

Mademuhennos (Finlad)
Stuvad lake (Sweden)

Serve with Boiled Potatoes (page 117) and possibly a slice of lemon or a little *Matättika* vinegar (page 657) on the side, for freshness.

Preparation and cooking time: 35 minutes
Serves: 4 as a main course

1 x 1.5–2-kg/3¼–4½ lb whole burbot
ground mace, to taste
4 allspice berries

1 bay leaf
1 small onion, finely chopped
200 ml/7 fl oz (¾ cup plus 1 tablespoon)
   dry white wine
200 ml/7 fl oz (¾ cup plus 1 tablespoon) cream
1 quantity Beurre Manié (page 651)
salt, to taste

Skin, clean and rinse the burbot well under cold running water before patting it dry with paper towels or a clean cloth. Slice off and keep the head. Use a heavy knife to cut the fish straight through the spine and the flesh into slices about 4 cm/1½ inches thick.

Place the slices, together with the burbot's head, in a pot, which should be just large enough to fit them all snugly in one layer. Sprinkle on the seasonings, the finely chopped onion and a little bit of salt before pouring in the wine and 200 ml/7 fl oz (¾ cup plus 1 tablespoon) water.

Place the pot on a stove over a medium heat and bring to a simmer. Let the fish cook until firm to the touch, which usually takes about 10 minutes. When done, carefully transfer the fish to a warm serving plate and cover while finishing the sauce.

Keep the cooking liquid in the pot and bring to the boil. Add the cream and sufficient beurre manié for the liquid to thicken enough to coat a spoon. Simmer for about 5 minutes, then season with salt to taste, before straining the sauce through a fine sieve directly onto the fish on the serving plate. Make sure you glaze all the fish with sauce.

Tip: If the burbot contains roe and has a big liver, poach these in a pan of salted water for a few minutes until they firm up. Slice and serve on buttered toast on the side of the dish or without toast next to the fish.

For image see page 169

FRESH EEL COOKED ON STRAW

Halmad färsk ål (Sweden)

This is an old speciality from Skåne, the southernmost region of Sweden. It is served as part of an *Ålagille* (eel) feast (page 160) in the autumn (fall) and the best way to describe it, is as something in between roasted and smoked eel. The smoke comes from a bed of moist rye straw beneath the eel as it roasts. During the cooking process, there will be a fair bit of smoke coming from the straw and the rendering eel fat. It may stink up your house a bit, but this is what gives the dish its special character.

If you serve this as a dish on its own, and not as part of a bigger meal, like the *Ålagille* feast, it is often accompanied by Mashed Potatoes (page 118) and possibly a lemon wedge or some *Ättika* (6%) vinegar (page 656), for acidity.

You will also need rye straw, cut into 10 cm/4 inch lengths.

Preparation and cooking time: 30 minutes
Serves: 4–8 people depending on how
   hungry you are and how much you
   like eel

1 large eel, gutted, skinned and cut through
   the bone into chunks
10 white peppercorns, crushed
10 allspice berries, crushed
salt, to taste

Preheat the oven to 225°C/435°F/Gas Mark 7. Arrange the rye straw in a roasting pan.

Season the pieces of eel inside and out with the spices and salt. Place them on the straw, with the back facing upwards. Roast until cooked through and golden. It does take a little bit of time, since the eel needs to be properly cooked through so that it comes off the bone easily.

SMOKED EEL

Røkt ål (Norway)
Røget ål (Denmark)
Rökt ål (Sweden)

Smoked eel in the Nordics has been most widely consumed in the southern parts of Scandinavia – especially in the southern Swedish region of Skåne and in Denmark. If not eaten at a Scanian *Ålagille* (a traditional eel party), smoked eel is often served around Christmas or on a slice of Danish rye bread with Scrambled Eggs (page 52) as an Open-faced Danish Sandwich (page 522).

An eel is either flat-smoked or round-smoked. The former means that the eel has been cut open along its full length and has had the bones removed from inside, before being forced open and flattened a bit before being smoked. Round-smoked eel is when it is just gutted and then smoked, the shape kept as if it were whole. Flat-smoked eel can just be skinned and sliced, whilst round-smoked eel needs to be skinned and filleted before being eaten. I prefer round-smoked eel as it is creamier and a bit milder on smoke, since less of it has been exposed to the smoke itself.

Smoked eel of great quality is very firm to the touch when cold and it has a bright grey, pink and white colour to its flesh.

Never try to work with eel that isn't cold, as it gets soft when the fat heats up, but always let it warm up to almost room temperature before eating it, as it tastes better then.

If you want to smoke your own eel, see the section on page 416 for more information. Most people would probably buy their eel smoked, as you rarely need more than one and it seems an awful lot of trouble to smoke only one single eel.

TO PREPARE SMOKED EEL

To prepare a flat-smoked eel, place it flesh-side down on a cutting board and make a small incision behind the head with a pair of scissors, with- out damaging the flesh. The skin can be pulled back in one piece, from the head towards the tail (see illustrations, opposite).

For the round-smoked eel there are more options. If you are serving the eel as a part of a buffet, then keep it intact and let people lift pieces off the bone themselves. If you want to make things easier for people then you can skin it first, as described above for flat-smoked eel.

If you are going to serve a round-smoked eel as part of a dish, then you need to skin, gut (see illustrations, opposite) and and fillet it first. Place it on a chopping (cutting) board and use a very sharp knife to carefully slice away one fillet, as if you were filleting a raw fish. You should then have one bone-free length of eel and one that is still attached to the spine. Use fish tweezers or pliers to pull out the pin bones from the fillet, then turn it over and pull the skin off, working from the head end towards the tail. Be careful not to tear the flesh. The secret to success is to pull the skin off backwards and not upwards.

To remove the spine from the other piece of eel, use your hands (and the help of a small paring knife where necessary) to lift all of the bones off the fillet and then discard them. Remove any remaining pin bones, then skin this fillet in the same way as the first. You should now have two skinned fillets of eel on the work counter, skin-side facing upwards. Cut them into the desired lengths and continue with your recipe.

EEL BAKED OVER SMOULDERING BEECH OR JUNIPER TWIGS

Luad ål (Sweden)

This is a very old dish, which predates domestic ovens by a hundred years or more. The traditional way of preparing it was to suspend the eels on sticks in the chimney; they would then roast and smoke over a fire set below them.

Today *luad ål* is mainly baked in a very hot oven using twigs of beech (and sometimes juniper) which smoulder in the heat, thereby smoking the fish at the same time as it roasts.

Serve with Boiled Potatoes (page 117) or Riced Potatoes (page 117) and with Hard-boiled Egg and Cream Sauce (page 676), a wedge of lemon or a dash of white vinegar.

You will also need some juniper twigs and some beech twigs and shavings.

Preparation and cooking time: 1 hour
Salting time: overnight
Serves: 4

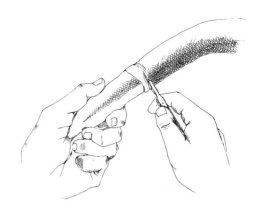

1 eel, gutted and cleaned
1 handful coarse salt

Rub the eel, inside and out, with the salt. Place in a large dish and refrigerate overnight.

The next day, rinse the eel under cold running water, then pat it dry with paper towel or a clean dish cloth.

Preheat your oven to its highest temperature – as hot as it will go. If it can do 300°C/570°F/Gas Mark 10, that's perfect. Line a roasting pan with aluminium foil, then cover with a thick layer of the wood shavings and twigs.

Arrange the eel on a wire rack and sit it on top of the twigs. Bake in the oven for a good 15 minutes, turning it once halfway through the cooking time. There will be a lot of smoke coming from the oven so keep your extraction fan on at maximum strength throughout the whole cooking process.

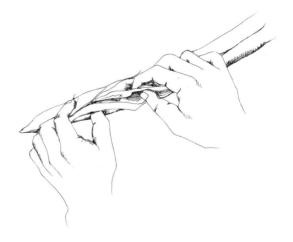

Let the eel rest for a couple of minutes before you serve it.

BOILED SALTED EEL

Saltet kogt ål (Denmark)
Kokt rimmad ål (Sweden)

Serve with Boiled Potatoes (page 117) and Hard-boiled Egg and Cream Sauce (page 676).

Preparation and cooking time: 20–30 minutes
Serves: 4

1 x 1-kg/2¼-lb whole salted eel, cut
   crosswise into 4 pieces
1 onion, sliced
1 carrot, sliced
1 bay leaf
1 sprig thyme
12 white peppercorns

Place all of the ingredients in a pot and cover with water. Bring to a simmer and cook for 10–20 minutes, or until done. The timing will depend on the thickness of the eel. The meat should come off the bone if you pull it.

BREADED EEL

Stegt ål (Denmark)
Griljerad ål (Sweden)

In traditional recipes, it seems that the eel meat was left on the bone and whole chunks were coated in breadcrumbs and fried. I prefer to take the meat off the bone before crumbing and frying it.

Griljerad ål is served with tangy condiments like Tartar Sauce (page 675) or Hard-boiled Egg and Cream Sauce (page 676).

Preparation and cooking time: 20 minutes
Serves: 4

500 g/1lb 2 oz eel
plain (all-purpose) flour, to coat
1 egg
breadcrumbs, to coat
salt and white pepper, to taste

Place the eel in a pan of boiling water and boil for 10–20 minutes, or until done. The timing will depend on the thickness of the eel.

Drain and let the eel cool, before skinning it (see illustration, page 161) and taking the meat off the bone in as big pieces as possible.

Preheat the oven to 220°C/425°F/Gas Mark 7 and line a baking sheet with baking (parchment) paper.

Place the flour, beaten egg and breadcrumbs into 3 separate wide, shallow bowls. Coat the fish pieces all over with flour, dip them into the beaten egg and then into the breadcrumbs.

Arrange the pieces of eel on the prepared sheet and bake in the oven until golden and crisp. Season with salt and pepper.

ROASTED EEL

Ovnstegt ål (Denmark)
Ål stekt i ugn (Sweden)

Serve with Hard-boiled Egg and Cream Sauce (page 676) and Boiled Potatoes (page 117), some Rye Crispbread (page 516), mature cheese and Aquavit (page 714). Some people also like Scrambled Eggs (page 52) and snipped chives with their roasted eel.

Preparation and cooking time: 40 minutes
Serve: 4

1 large eel, gutted, rinsed and patted dry
soft butter, for brushing
salt and white pepper, to taste

Preheat the oven to 275°C/525°F/Gas Mark 9.

Working from inside the chest cavity, cut out and remove the backbone from the eel, but avoid piercing the skin.

With the backbone removed, you should now be able to fold the eel open and lay it out flat. Rub both sides of the eel with liberal amounts of salt and pepper before placing it, skin side down, on a cooking grid set in a roasting pan.

Roast until the eel is cooked through and golden. After the first couple of minutes it can be a good idea to brush some soft butter over the eel to help it colour nicely. When the eel is done, cut it in thin slices and serve immediately.

POACHED FISH, SERVED COLD

Almost any fish can be used in this recipe, but pike, salmon or flat fish are the most common ones.

Allow about 1.5 litres/50 fl oz (6¼ cups) poaching liquid for each kg/2 lb 4 oz fish. Fillets cook faster than whole fish and it is important that the cooking liquid is very hot when you add the fish, since this cooks the skin and makes it easier to remove later on.

The seasoning of this recipe is mild and basic. If a recipe in this book calls for use of this technique and gives a seasoning of its own it should replace the seasoning below (including salt).

Serve the fish without the cooking liquid, together with Boiled Potatoes (page 117) and a cold sauce like Dill Mayonnaise (674), or Horseradish Sauce (page 675).

Preparation and cooking time: 1–3 hours
  depending on the fish, plus cooling time
Serves: 4

1 pike, salmon or a flat fish, whole or filleted

For the poaching liquid
50 ml/2 fl oz (3½ tablespoons) *Ättika* (12%)
  vinegar (page 656)
20 g/¾ oz (1 tablespoon) salt
4 white peppercorns
4 allspice berries
1 bay leaf
4 cloves

For the poaching liquid, pour 950 ml/30 fl oz (3¾ cups) water into a large pan or fish kettle and add all the remaining ingredients. Bring to a strong boil and then put in the fish.

Move the pan to the side of the stove and allow the residual heat of the liquid to slowly cook the fish. If you are cooking a whole fish, or if the fillet is very thick, you might have to move the pan back on the stove for a while to add more heat. Different fish have different degrees to which they should be cooked, but a rule of thumb is that fish on the bone needs to be cooked so that the flesh just begins to lift away from the bone. This can be tested by pulling at the dorsal fin. If it comes away from the back of the fish, with all bones intact, the fish is done. I prefer to cook oily fish like mackerel or salmon in fillets, because it is best eaten barely cooked (sort of medium-rare) and the flesh wouldn't come away from the bones if it was kept whole.

When the fish is done, transfer it to a new container and chill both the fish and the poaching liquid separately in the fridge. Once cold, pour the poaching liquid through a sieve, onto the fish. Fish cooked like this keeps for at least 4 days in your refrigerator and I think it is best after a day or so of resting in the liquid.

POACHED PIKE, THREE VERSIONS

POACHED PIKE, SERVED COLD
(VERSION 1)

Pocheret gedde (Denmark)
Inkokt gädda (Sweden)

Serve with Boiled Potatoes (page 117), Quick Pickled Cucumber (page 658), and a sauce like Dill Mayonnaise (page 674), Horseradish Sauce (page 675) or Hard-boiled Egg and Cream Sauce (page 676). I think it is also nice to serve the mildly pickle-tasting leeks and carrots used in the cooking liquid with the fish.

Preparation and cooking time: 40 minutes,
  plus cooling time
Resting time: just under 24 hours
Serves: 4–6 as a main course

1 x 1–2-kg/2¼ lb–4½-lb whole pike,
  gutted, cleaned and scaled, head left on
2 litres/3½ UK pints (8¼ cups) cooking
  liquid from Poached Fish, Served Cold
  (page 163)
1 carrot, cut into 3 mm/⅛ inch slices
1 small leek, cut into 5 mm/¼ inch
  slices
60 g/2¼ oz (2½ tablespoons) salt
few parsley stalks
10 white peppercorns
1 lemon, halved

Place the fish in a large pan or fish kettle.

Mix the vinegar and water from the base recipe on page 163 and substitute the seasonings in the base recipe with those listed above. Pour over the fish and proceed to cook according to the method described in the base recipe until the flesh at the back bone of the fish is white and the dorsal fin pulls out easily from the meat of the fish.

When the fish is done, transfer it to a new container and chill both the fish and the poaching liquid separately in the refrigerator. Once cold, pour the poaching liquid through a sieve, onto the fish. Fish cooked like this keeps for at least 4 days in your refrigerator and I think it is best after a day or so of resting in the liquid.

POACHED PIKE, SERVED
WARM WITH HORSERADISH
(VERSION 2)

Pocheret gedde med peberrod (Denmark)
Pepparrotsgädda (Sweden)

Preparation and cooking time: 40 minutes
Serves: 4–6 as a main course

Follow the recipe from version 1 (see left), but instead of chilling the fish when it has finished cooking, serve it straight away, with Boiled Potatoes (page 117), the vegetables from the cooking liquid, melted or browned butter, plenty of grated horseradish and a finely chopped Hard-boiled Egg (page 53) for each person.

CROOKED PIKE (VERSION 3)

Krumgädda (Sweden)

Preparation and cooking time: 40 minutes
Serves: 4–6 as a main course

This dish is often found in very old Swedish recipe books and the name refers to the way the fish is cooked, with its tail stuck in its mouth so that it looks like it is biting its own tail.

Stick the tail into the mouth of the fish and fix with a toothpick or cooking needle. Place the fish carefully in a large pan. Follow the method for version 1 (see left), but instead of chilling the fish when it has finished cooking, serve it straight away, with Boiled Potatoes (page 117), the vegetables from the cooking liquid and the Basic Fish Sauce (page 662) seasoned with plenty of chopped dill or parsley and salt, to taste.

PIKE WITH EGG SAUCE

Hauki kera muna kastike (Finland)

For this recipe it's best to use fillets or cutlets from a large pike; allow 150–200 g/5–7 oz per person.

Pike has a lot of bones in it and it can be quite hard to remove them all before cooking. If you use portions cut from a large fish, however, and if you cook it well, it is easy to pull out any missed ones as you eat it.

Serve the pike with Egg Sauce for Fish (page 676) with chives, and with Riced Potatoes (page 117) and lemon wedges.

Preparation and cooking time: 30 minutes
Serves: 4

4 x 150–200 g/5–7 oz pike fillets or cutlets
salt and white pepper, to taste

Follow the instructions on page 163 for poaching fish.

Season the pike with salt and pepper and serve, steaming hot.

PIKE BALLS

Gjeddeboller (Norway)
Fiskefrikadeller med gedde (Denmark)
Gäddfärsbullar (Sweden)

Reheat the pike balls in the sauce and garnish with plenty of fresh dill just before serving with Boiled Potatoes (page 117), Riced Potatoes (page 117) and/or steamed vegetables, lettuce and a slice of lemon.

Preparation and cooking time: 1 hour
Serves: 4 as a main course

1 quantity Fish Balls (page 224), made
   from pike
chopped dill, to garnish
1 quantity creamy Velouté (page 652),
   made from 550 ml/18 fl oz (2½ cups) Fish
   Stock, made from the pike bones

Make one quantity of fish balls using pike and poach the balls in fish stock made from the pike bones. Reduce, strain and use the pike stock to make a creamy veloute (page 652).

Reheat the pike balls in the velouté and garnish with plenty of fresh dill just before serving with Boiled Potatoes (page 117), Riced Potatoes (page 117) and/or steamed vegetables, lettuce and lemon slices.

PIKE STEW

Stuvet gedde (Denmark)
Stuvad gädda (Sweden)

Serve with Boiled Potatoes (page 117) and lemon wedges.

Preparation and cooking time: 35 minutes
Serves: 4–6 as a main course

1 x 1–2-kg/2¼–4½-lb whole pike, gutted,
  cleaned and scaled
ground mace, to taste
4 allspice berries
1 bay leaf
1 small onion, finely chopped
200 ml/7 fl oz (¾ cup plus 1 tablespoon) dry
  white wine
200 ml/7 fl oz (¾ cup plus 1 tablespoon)
  cream
1 quantity Beurre Manié (page 651)
1 bunch parsley, leaves finely chopped
salt, to taste

Use a heavy knife to cut the fish straight through the spine and the flesh into slices about 4 cm/1½ inches thick.

Place the slices in a pot, which should be just large enough to fit all of the fish snugly in one layer. Sprinkle on the seasonings, the chopped onion and a little bit of salt before pouring in the wine and 200 ml/7 fl oz (¾ cup plus 1 tablespoon) water.

Place the pot on a stove over a medium heat and bring to a simmer. Let the fish cook until firm to the touch, usually about 10 minutes.

When done, carefully transfer the fish to a warm serving plate and cover while finishing the sauce.

Keep the cooking liquid in the pot and bring to the boil. Add the cream and enough beurre manié for it to thicken enough to coat a spoon. Simmer for about 5 minutes, then season with salt, to taste. Strain the sauce through a fine mesh sieve, directly onto the fish on the serving plate. Make sure you glaze all the fish with sauce. Sprinkle generously wuth parsley before serving.

OVEN-BAKED WHOLE PIKE

Uunissa paistettu kokonainen hauki
  (Finland)
Ovnbagt gedde (Denmark)
Ugnsbakad hel gädda (Sweden)

Serve with Boiled Potatoes (page 117) or Mashed Potatoes (page 118) and some green vegetables, like Steamed Broccoli (page 82) or Steamed Spinach (page 87).

Preparation and cooking time: 1 hour
Serves: 4

1 x 1.5-kg/3 ¼-lb whole pike, gutted,
  cleaned and scaled, gills removed but
  head left on
1 lemon
butter, for greasing
breadcrumbs, to sprinkle
500 ml/17 fl oz (2 cups plus 1 tablespoon)
  cream
salt and white pepper, to taste

Make parallel incisions through the skin of the fish, straight across its body. Rub the whole fish, inside and out, with lemon and plenty of salt and white pepper.

Preheat the oven to 225°C/425°F/Gas Mark 7. Lightly butter an ovenproof dish. Arrange the fish in the prepared dish in the position it swims when alive. Sprinkle the fish with breadcrumbs and pour the cream into the dish.

Bake the pike for 15–20 minutes. When on the bone, pike needs to be cooked right through to be tasty. The fish is done when a fin comes away easily when gently pulled. If you want, you can also baste it with the cream halfway through the cooking time. This will give the exterior a darker, more caramelized flavour and appearance as the cream soaks into the hot breadcrumbs. Serve the fish straight from the oven, together with the cream, which is now gently infused with cooking juices from the fish, as a sauce.

For image see page 169

STEWED PERCH

Ahvenmuhennos (Finland)
Stuvet aborre (Denmark)
Stuvad aborre (Sweden)

Preparation and cooking time: 40 minutes
Serves: 4 as a main course

4 x 400–600-g/14–21-oz whole perch,
    gutted, cleaned and scaled, heads
    left on
ground mace, to taste
10 white peppercorns
1 bay leaf
1 small onion, finely chopped
200 ml/7 fl oz (¾ cup plus 1 tablespoon) dry
    white wine
200 ml/7 fl oz (¾ cup plus 1 tablespoon)
    cream
1 quantity Beurre Manié (page 651)
few sprigs thyme
salt and white pepper, to taste

Place the perch in a pot, which should be just large enough to fit them all snugly in a single layer. Sprinkle on the seasonings, the onion and a little bit of salt before pouring in the wine and 200 ml/7 fl oz (¾ cup plus 1 tablespoon) water.

Place the pot on the stove over a medium heat and bring to a simmer. Let the fish cook for about 5 minutes, or until barely done. The flesh near the backbone should be white and the dorsal fin should pull away easily. Be careful not to over-cook the perch, as it easily becomes dry. When done, carefully transfer the fish to a warm serving plate and cover while finishing the sauce.

Keep the cooking liquid in the pot and bring to the boil. Add the cream and enough beurre manié for it to thicken enough to coat a spoon. Simmer for about 5 minutes, then season with salt, to taste. Strain the sauce through a fine sieve directly onto the fish on the serving plate. Make sure you glaze all the fish with sauce.

Finish the dish by sprinkling with thyme and freshly ground white pepper just before serving.

Tip: If any of the perch contain roe, leave it inside. It will be cooked perfectly medium-rare by the time the fish is done.

PERCH, FRIED WHOLE

Helstegt aborre (Denmark)
Helstekt aborre (Sweden)

Serve with Riced Potatoes (page 117) or Boiled Potatoes (117) and the frying butter mixed with some lemon, parsley or horseradish.

Preparation and cooking time: 30 minutes
Serves: 4

4 x 400–600-g/14–21-oz whole perch,
    or 2 larger ones, up to 1 kg/2¼ lb, gutted,
    cleaned and scaled, heads left on
butter, for frying
juice of 1 lemon
1 bunch parsley, leaves and stalks
    finely chopped, or finely grated
    horseradish root

Follow the method for whole fish, fried in a pan (page 152), version 1.

Remember that smaller fish will need shorter cooking time and a hotter pan, whilst bigger fish will need a slightly cooler pan and a somewhat longer cooking time.

After cooking the fish, remove them from the pan and place on a serving platter.

Season the butter that is left in the pan with the lemon juice and add the chopped parsley or grated horseradish. Pour it over the fish on the serving platter.

BREADED AND FRIED FILLETS
OF PERCH

Stekt abborfilet (Norway)
Stegt aborre (Denmark)
Panerad aborrfilé (Sweden)

I have fond memories of my grandma frying
little fillets of perch after my childhood summer
fishing adventures. Serve them with lemon wedges, boiled new potatoes, if they are in season, and
a dollop of butter, which is tasty with both the
potatoes and the fish. If you prefer, serve with
Mashed Potatoes (page 118) or Riced Potatoes
(page 117). Browned Butter (page 662) is also
good, preferably made with the fish cooking
butter itself or perhaps a Hard-boiled Egg and
Cream Sauce (page 676).

Preparation and cooking time: 30 minutes
Serves: 4

650 g/1 lb 7 oz perch fillets
80 g/3 oz (½ cup) plain (all-purpose) flour
2 eggs
50 ml/2 fl oz (3½ tablespoons) milk
100 g/3 ½ oz (1 cup) breadcrumbs
salt and white pepper, to taste
butter, for frying

Follow the instructions on page 156 for how to
bread and fry fish in a pan.

For image see opposite page

PIKE-PERCH, FRIED WHOLE

Helstekt gjørs (Norway)
Helstegt aborre (Denmark)
Helstekt gös (Sweden)

Serve with Riced Potatoes (page 117) or Boiled
Potatoes (117) and the frying butter mixed with
some lemon, parsley or horseradish.

Preparation and cooking time: 30 minutes
Serves: 4

4 x 400–600-g/14–21-oz whole pike-perch,
   or 2 larger ones, up to 1 kg/2¼ lb, gutted,
   cleaned and scaled, heads left on
butter, for frying
juice of 1 lemon
1 bunch parsley, leaves and stalks finely
   chopped or finely grated horseradish root

Follow the method for whole fish, fried in a pan
(page 152), version 1.

Remember that smaller fish will need shorter
cooking time and a hotter pan, whilst bigger fish
will need a slightly cooler pan and a somewhat
longer cooking time.

After cooking the fish, remove them from
the pan and place it on a serving platter. Season the butter that is left in the pan with
the lemon juice and the chopped parsley or
grated horseradish. Pour over the fish on the serving platter.

Clockwise from top left: Burbot Stew (page 158); Breaded and Fried Fillets of Perch (page 168); Poached Whitefish (page 172); pieces of pike-perch fried in butter (page 154); Oven-baked Whole Pike (page 166)

POACHED WHOLE PIKE-PERCH

Kokt gjørs (Norway)
Kogt sandart (Denmark)
Kokt hel gös (Sweden)

Serve with Boiled Potatoes (page 117) or Riced Potatoes (page 117) and garnishes like chopped Hard-boiled Eggs (page 53), Egg Roll (page 654), grated horseradish or parsley and melted or Browned Butter (page 662).

I've also seen some older recipes for a classic sauce to serve with poached pike-perch and some other fish, which used the poaching liquid from the fish, thickened with roux with a lot of butter (equal parts by volume), a good spoonful of strong mustard and chopped hard-boiled eggs. If I choose a buttery garnish I like to have a wedge of lemon or some *Ättika* (6%) vinegar (page 656) on the side.

Preparation and cooking time: 20–30 minutes
Serves: 4

1 x 2-kg/4½-lb whole pike-perch
  (sander) gutted, cleaned and scaled
2 bay leaves
10 allspice berries
salt, to taste

Place the fish and the aromatics in a large pan and cover with cold, generously salted water. Bring to the boil over a medium heat and then remove the pan from the stove. Leave the fish in the hot water until the dorsal fin pulls away without much resistance, which means the fish is done.

Carefully lift the fish out of the poaching liquid and place on a serving platter to serve.

PIKE-PERCH WITH HORSERADISH AND CREAMED MUSHROOMS

Kuhaa Mannerheimin tapaan (Finland)
Gös à la Mannerheim (Sweden)

Serve with Boiled Potatoes (page 117) and a wedge of lemon.

Preparation and cooking time: 30 minutes
Serves: 4

500 g/1 lb 2 oz fillet of pike-perch
150 g/5 oz (1 stick plus 2 tablespoons)
  butter
50 g/2 oz horseradish
1 quantity Creamed Mushrooms (page 128),
  prepared with button mushrooms
salt and white pepper, to taste

Melt the butter in a small saucepan, over low heat. Grate the horseradish and add it to the butter. Place the pan next to the stove, cover with a lid and leave the horseradish to soften a bit in the hot butter.

As the horseradish butter sits, prepare and fry the fish according to the instructions for whole fish, fried in a pan (page 155), version 3, breaded. Only turn it in the breadcrumbs though, not the egg and flour.

Place a portion of creamed mushrooms on a plate and place a piece of fish – straight from the pan – on top of the mushrooms. Spoon some of the warm horseradish and butter over the fish just before serving.

WHITEFISH (*COREGONUS LAVARETUS*)

A fish belonging to the salmon family, common in the northern parts of the Nordic region where it is found in rivers, lakes and the brackish parts of the Baltic sea. There are several different varieties of whitefish, ranging in size from 10–60 cm (4–24 inches) and in weight from 100 g–8 kg (3½ oz–17½ lb). Whitefish are especially popular in northern Finland and Sweden, where they have always been caught in large quantities. Sometimes whitefish are fished with hand nets from large, semi-permanent wooden structures called pata, which are built in rivers like the Torneälven. The fish has a white, delicate flesh and is slightly less fatty than salmon. It could possibly be replaced in a recipe by trout or char, but the colour will be different.

CURED WHITEFISH

Gravet sik (Norway)
Graavisiika (Finland)
Gravad sik (Sweden)

Serve as part of a *smörgåsbord* or as a starter (appetizer) with Sweet-and-Strong Mustard Sauce for Cured Fish (page 664) and Boiled Potatoes (page 117).

Preparation time: 30 minutes
Curing time: 5–12 hours
Serves: 8 as a starter (appetizer) and 20 as part of a smörgåsbord

1 x 1-kg/2¼-lb fillet (or fillets) whitefish, scaled
35 g/1¼ oz sugar
35 g/1¼ oz coarse salt
1 bunch dill or 10 juniper berries

Follow the method for curing fish with salt and sugar (page 190).

If you choose to flavour with dill, chop the stalks and use them in the cure while reserving the tips to use for garnishing the fish, just before serving. If you use juniper berries, crush them coarsely before mixing them with the curing mix.

If you cure more than one fillet of fish, place them resting flesh side against flesh side and skin side against skin side with some cure and seasoning in between.

For a light cure and very tender result, leave the fish in the cure for about 5 hours, for a firmer result, leave overnight.

WHITEFISH IN CHIVE SAUCE

Sik i gräslökssås (Sweden)

Preparation and cooking time: 30 minutes
Serves: 4 as a main course

1 x 1 kg/2¼ lb whitefish, gutted, cleaned and scaled, gills removed, head left on

1 large carrot, coarsely chopped
1 onion, coarsely chopped
5 white peppercorns
1 bay leaf
2 tablespoons *Ättika* (12%) vinegar (page 656)
salt, to taste

For the chive sauce
1 quantity Basic Fish Sauce (page 662), made from the fish cooking liquid (above)
20 g/¾ oz (⅓ cup plus 2 tablespoons) finely snipped chives
1 egg yolk

Place the fish in a large pan or fish kettle and add all the remaining ingredients. Pour on enough water to barely cover the fish and season lightly with salt.

Bring to a simmer over a medium heat and poach the fish until just about done. The dorsal fin should come away easily from the back of the fish when pulled. Carefully lift the fish onto a warm serving plate and cover while making the sauce.

Strain the cooking liquid and measure out 200 ml/ 7 fl oz (¾ cup plus 1 tablespoon). Follow the instructions on page 662 to make a basic fish sauce and finish by adding the chives and egg yolk. Stir until the egg is completely incorporated before salting to taste. Once the egg has been added the sauce should not be heated further, but served immediately.

I like to pour the sauce directly onto the fish on the serving platter, but if it seems too complicated to fillet the cooked fish in a pool of sauce, then it is also fine to serve it on the side in a sauce boat.

POACHED WHITEFISH

Kokt sik (Sweden)

Preparation and cooking time: 35 minutes
Serves: 4 as a main course

1 x 1 kg/2¼ lb whitefish, gutted, cleaned
    and scaled, gills removed, head left on
1 large carrot, coarsely chopped
1 onion, coarsely chopped
5 white peppercorns
1 bay leaf
2 tablespoons Ättika (12%) vinegar
    (page 656)
salt, to taste

Place the fish in a large pan or fish kettle and add all the remaining ingredients. Pour on enough water to barely cover the fish and season lightly with salt. Bring to a simmer over a medium heat and poach the fish until just about done. The dorsal fin should come away easily from the back of the fish when pulled. Carefully lift the fish onto a warm serving plate and serve.

HOT-SMOKED WHITEFISH

Varmrøkt sik (Norway)
Lämminsavustettu siika (Finland)
Varmrökt sik (Sweden)

Gut and clean the fish and leave the head(s) on. Cure, using about 25 g/1 oz of salt per 1 kg/ 2¼ lb of fish, distributing it evenly on both sides and inside the fish. Put the fish into a plastic bag and leave overnight in the fridge.

Before smoking, rinse the fish under cold, running water and hang them to dry for half a day, or until dry to the touch. Smoke them in a smoker over juniper branches or alder wood.

The slight drying of the fish before smoking it prevents soot from the fire sticking to its surface.

The temperature in a hot smoker suitable for fish should be about 80°C/175°F. The fish are ready when the dorsal fins come out easily when pulled

away from the back of the fish – 15–35 minutes depending on the size of the fish.

Smoked whitefish is either enjoyed as part of a *smörgåsbord*, as a starter (appetizer) or on a piece of Rye Crispbread (page 516).

COMMON ROACH (*RUTILUS RUTILUS*)

A silvery fish with red eyes that can reach a length of up to 45 cm/17¾ inches. Most of the time though it is considerably smaller, weighing around 500 g/1 lb 2 oz on average when seen at fish markets. Because it has a complicated bone structure, making it difficult to turn into boneless fillets, roach has fallen slightly out of fashion. But it is still used in some more old-fashioned preparations like the central Swedish fermented roach dish called *surmört*, see below.

SOUR ROACH

Surmört (Sweden)

Fish has been salted and fermented all over the world and still is in many parts. People have used what they had at hand in terms of fish. Where I live, close to the mountains and the Norwegian border, the Norwegian classic fermented trout, *rakfisk* (page 175) has always been made while along the Baltic coast, people were preparing Sour Herring (page 198), long before today's popular canned version, *surströmming* (page 198), was available.

When canned sour herring was invented and popularized, and modern refrigeration became available to most people, the need for sour roach to survive diminished. *Surströmming*, distributed in its practical can, filled that space. Most people also stopped preparing sour trout in my region, whilst in Norway, where *surströmming* never really caught on, *rakfisk* is still popular and available almost everywhere.

Sour roach was quite widely made in pre-industrial times, especially in poorer parts of Scandinavia, where the coast wasn't close enough to provide access to fish. The only guy I know who still makes sour roach is a Swedish musician named Stefan Sundström. It is quite delicious; stronger than Norwegian fermented trout, but a million times more elegant than sour herring.

If you want to make sour roach, follow the instructions on page 175 for Norwegian Fermented Trout (*rakfisk*).

The instruction on how to eat and enjoy *surströmming* on page 198, will give you good guidance on how to eat your sour roach.

POACHED WHOLE TROUT

Avkokt ørret (Norway)
Kogt ørred (Denmark)
Kokt öring (Sweden)

Preparation and cooking time: 30 minutes
Serves: 4

1 x 1.5-kg/3¼-lb whole trout, gutted, cleaned and scaled

For the stock (broth)
75 ml/2½ fl oz (⅓ cup) *Ättika* (12%) vinegar (page 656)
1 carrot, sliced
1 small onion, studded with 2 cloves
1 small fennel bulb, cut into pieces
1 celery stick, chopped
1 sprig thyme
1 bay leaf
1 handful parsley stalks

For the stock (broth), combine all the vegetables and aromatics in a pan, which is large enough to fit the fish as well. Add enough water to cover and bring to the boil. Leave the stock to cool down a bit before adding the fish to the pan. Add more water until the fish is just covered. Bring to a slow simmer and then remove the pan from the heat and leave it to sit until the fish is cooked.

I like oily fish like trout to be a little bit underdone and to barely come off the bone. But that is a matter of personal taste. Carefully lift the fish out of the poaching liquid and place on a serving platter to serve.

SMOKED TROUT

Røkt ørret (Norway)
Røget ørred (Denmark)
Rökt Öring (Sweden)

Wherever trout is found in the Nordic region, it will be smoked. It can be hot-smoked (page 416) or cold-smoked (page 416) and in Iceland it can even be smoked over sheep's dung (see below).

What used to be a widespread and important way of preserving food is now something that people do because they like the flavour of it.

Hot-smoked trout is often eaten as a part of a larger meal, like Christmas or Easter dinner, or else it is taken off the bone and eaten on a sandwich.

The same applies for cold-smoked trout, which is often served with a Sweet-and-Strong Mustard Sauce for Cured Fish (page 664).

TROUT SMOKED OVER SHEEPS DUNG

Taðreykta silungur (Iceland)

In Iceland, trout is traditionally cold-smoked (page 416) over burning sheep's dung, much like with mutton (page 358). It is carried out simply by hanging the cured fillets of fish from the rafters of a traditional Icelandic smokehouse and lighting a small fire on the floor from time to time. The dung is aged for one year before being collected and used for fuel so that it is no longer chemically active, i.e. so that most of the ammonium smell in it will have disappeared. Trout in Iceland is sometimes also smoked over birch twigs and is then called *birkireyktan silungur*. This type of smoking gives a slightly milder result than the sheep's dung one.

TROUT LIKE IN JÄMTLAND

Öring på jämtvis (Sweden)

This recipe comes from Jämtland, the region where I grew up and still live now. I'm not sure if it actually originated in Jämtland, or whether it was invented by someone wanting to create the feeling of being there. Either way, it is a popular dish up here, and involves a creamy sauce which has a distinctive flavour from using the Sweet Reduced Whey Spread (page 72).

Serve Jämtland trout with Boiled Potatoes (page 117) or Riced Potatoes (page 117).

Preparation and cooking time: 30 minutes
Serves: 4

4 x 400-g/14-oz trout, gutted, cleaned,
  scaled and heads still on
1 onion, finely chopped
100 ml/3½ fl oz (⅓ cup plus 1 tablespoon)
  white wine
300 ml/10½ fl oz (1¼ cups) cream
100 g/3½ oz (⅓ cup) Sweet Reduced
  Whey Spread (page 72)
salt and pepper, to taste

Salt all the trout inside and out, then leave them for a few minutes to let the salt dissolve a bit. This will help them to get a nice colour when cooked.

Follow the instructions on page 154 for frying fish.

Towards the end of the frying process, after you have flipped the fish over, but before they are ready, add the onion to the pan and fry for a few more minutes, still over rather high heat. Add the wine and cook for a few minutes before adding the cream and the *Messmör*. Continue cooking until the fish is ready and the sauce is thick enough to just coat a spoon. Adjust the seasoning of the sauce and serve immediately.

FRIED TROUT

Small fried trout are for me a great treat in late spring and early summer – going out in the wild, fishing for brown trout in the smallest of creeks, dwarfed in size, but not in flavour, by the confines of their habitat. When I was growing up, the old and wise people always said that it was time to catch trout when the leaves of the birch had grown to a size resembling the ear of a mouse. They were right.

Enjoy your fried brown trout as a midnight snack after a successful session of fishing: warm flesh taken off the bone, melting the butter on a piece of Rye Crispbread (page 516).

Or serve them as part of a meal, with the first new potatoes of the season – or, if later in the year, with Mashed Potatoes (page 118) or Riced Potatoes (page 117) – and a wedge of lemon.

Preparation and cooking time: 30 minutes
Serves: 4

butter, for frying
1 x 1.2 kg/2½ lb whole trout, gutted,
  cleaned and scaled
salt and pepper, to taste

Salt the trout inside and out, then leave it for a few minutes to let the salt dissolve a bit. This will help it to get a nice colour when cooked.

Follow the instructions on page 154 for frying fish. Don't be shy about the amount of fat you use; more butter won't make your fish any fattier, but it will help you get great colour and crispy fins.

The trout is cooked when the dorsal fin can be pulled out from the back of the fish with very little resistance.

NORWEGIAN FERMENTED TROUT OR CHAR

Rakfisk (Norway)

Fermented trout or *rakfisk*, is yet another recipe in which *lactobacillus* bacteria, our favourite pet microbe, plays the leading role in preserving a perishable product. It is one of the most iconic

Norwegian recipes and as culturally important there as Sour Herring (page 198) is in Sweden.

Sour herring and *rakfisk* are enjoyed in much the same way, on a soft flatbread with some sour cream and red onions or perhaps some chives, and usually potatoes on the side.

When producing fermented trout it is very important to avoid soil contamination because of the risk of *Clostridium botulinum* bacteria growing during the largely anaerobic fermentation process. Apart from that, it is quite a straightforward procedure that works in much the same way as any other lacto-fermentation process.

Preparation and cooking time: 1 hour
Maturing time: at least 6 months
Makes 8 kg/18 lb, enough for a big party

10 kg/22 lb very fresh trout or char, gutted and cleaned
500 g/1 lb 2 oz (50 cups) salt
100 g/3½ oz (½ cup) sugar

The first step is to decide how strongly flavoured you want the fish to be. Is its aroma going to meet you at the door of the room where it is served? If you want it strong, leave the gills on and leave the blood that accumulates next to the spine. These contain plenty of bacteria and nutrition for them to live on. If you want a milder flavour (which I personally prefer), remove these parts and rinse the fish carefully.

Put a small handful of salt and sugar in the cavity of each fish. Place them on their sides in a very clean bucket or container. Continue to layer the fish until they all fit snugly. Place a lid that fits inside the bucket on top of the fish and weigh it down with something heavy and very clean. Leave at 6–8°C/43–46°F for a couple of days.

After no more than 3 days, a brine should have accumulated to cover the fish. If not, make and chill a brine with 5% salt and top up the bucket until the fish are completely covered. Place in the fridge at a temperature no higher than 3.3°C/38°F to minimize the risk from *Clostridium botulinum*. Check and control the pH levels so that it drops quickly to below 4.46°C/40°F.

Leave to mature for a minimum of 6 months. If the pH level isn't low enough after 1 week you need to discard it and start again. It is also a good idea to send a sample to be analysed by a professional before you eat it, so you know it is safe.

POACHED WHOLE CHAR

Kokt röding (Sweden)

Preparation and cooking time: 30 minutes
Serves: 4

1 x 1.5-kg/3¼-lb whole char, gutted, cleaned and scaled

For the stock (broth)
75 ml/2½ fl oz (⅓ cup) *Ättika* (12%) vinegar (page 656)
1 carrot, sliced
1 small onion, studded with 2 cloves
1 small fennel bulb, cut into pieces
1 celery stick, chopped
1 sprig thyme
1 bay leaf
1 handful parsley stalks

For the stock (broth), combine all the vegetables and aromatics in a pan large enough to fit the fish as well. Add enough water to cover and bring to the boil. Leave the stock to cool down a bit before adding the fish to the pan. Add more water until the fish is just covered. Bring to a slow simmer, remove from the heat and leave it to sit until the fish is cooked.

I like fatty fish like char to be a little bit underdone and to barely come off the bone, but that is a matter of personal taste. Carefully lift the fish out of the poaching liquid and place on a serving platter to serve.

LAMPREY

Nahkiainen (Finland)
Nejonöga / Nätting (Sweden)

Lampreys are a primitive kind of jawless fish that live in both the sea and fresh water. They are parasites, which attach to their prey, pierce the skin and suck blood and other body fluids out. Only the fresh water variants – river lamprey (*nätting*) and brook lamprey – are suitable for cooking. The river lamprey can be 45 cm/18 inches long and the brook lamprey up to 25 cm/10 inches. Lampreys are best in December and thinnest and less good during the summer months.

Lampreys are often bought smoked or grilled, or smoked and marinated in vinegar. You do not often find fresh lampreys in the shop, but if you do, keep in mind that the skin mucous and the blood of this fish are all poisonous, so take care not to expose open wounds on your hands to them.

The tradition of eating lampreys today is strongest in Finland but is still also practised in some parts along the northern Swedish Baltic coast. In Finland, the little shops where lampreys are grilled over a burning elder wood fire and sold by the *kerppu* – which is an old measuring unit, meaning 30, plus one laid across the bunch to mark the correct number – can be a real destination.

I was standing outside a place like this, smelling the fat of the fish mingling with aromatic smoke, and enjoying the late autumn (fall) afternoon sun on my face, when a very large Mercedes with a very large man in it pulls to a screeching halt right in front of me – almost too close for comfort. The man gruntingly leaves the car, his face red and harried, as he pushes past me, muttering something in Finnish, a language I do not understand.

Once he's clear of me, he almost runs into the little shop and comes back, not a full minute later, one grilled lamprey already on the way down his throat, first half eaten, the other half hanging at the corner of his mouth like a shiny, unlit fish-cigar. As he opens the car door – lamprey hanging from his mouth, more lampreys squeezed into a paper package under his arm, a can of Jaffa in his hand – his phone rings.

I guess it is his wife waiting somewhere as I hear a high-pitched voice talking loudly in Finnish with the energy of the annoyed. The large man looks apologetic as he speaks to the woman on the phone. He gets hung up on and stands there with the phone in one hand, the pack of lamprey in the other, one half still in his mouth. But the Jaffa has, as a consequence of the impossible juggling of objects and only one free hand, fallen to the ground.

The man exhales deeply, making a noise that reminds me of the sound produced by an angry hippopotamus. He hurls the packet of lampreys onto the passenger seat. I can see that they leave a skid-mark of fish fat as the greasy packet comes to a halt on the tanned leather upholstery. The door slams and the car starts off with a jump. Some gravel, hurled away by the action of the car's tires, strums the corrugated-iron roof of the house that contains the little fish shop.

Left in the parking area am I, one unopened can of Jaffa and the front end of a lamprey, now lightly coated in dust. I walk into the shop and do like the very large man, I buy myself a *kerppu* of lampreys and one can of Jaffa. When I ask the man behind the counter how he likes his lampreys, he looks pensive, for quite some time – a bit longer than is quite comfortable – then he says, 'With a bottle of *Koskenkorva*.'

HOW TO EAT SMOKED OR GRILLED LAMPREY

Pick the fish up by the head and start eating it as if it was a hot-dog sausage. You start by eating the tail and work you way towards the head, which is used a bit like a handle and then discarded. Lampreys are not gutted before being cooked. You eat their filled intestines. Also their skeleton is all cartilage – no bones – so you eat that too. A little splash of white vinegar can be advisable to mediate the sensation of eating pure fat.

CREAMED LAMPREYS

Stuvat nejonöga (Sweden)

Enjoy with Boiled Potatoes (page 117) and possibly a dash of white vinegar.

Preparation and cooking time: 15 minutes
Serves: 4

20 smoked or grilled lampreys
2 onions, cut into 3 mm/⅛ inch slices
200 ml/7 fl oz (¾ cup plus 1 tablespoon) cream
salt and black pepper, to taste

Cut the lampreys into 5 cm/2 inch lengths and put them in a pan with the onion. Place the pan over a medium heat and cook until some of the fat has rendered out of the lampreys and the onions have softened. Add the cream and continue cooking until it thickens and lightly coats the lampreys. Adjust the seasoning but be careful with the salt, as the lampreys themselves are often a bit on the salty side.

VENDACE (*COREGONUS ALBULA*)

A small freshwater white fish belonging to the salmon family, it is found in the northern Baltic area (the exact area is defined by the salinity of the brackish sea) and in quite a few of the bigger lakes in northern Scandinavia. In Sweden vendace is called *siklöja*, and is mostly caught to produce Bleak Roe (page 179) but in Finland (where it is called *muikku*) also to eat. In Finland, vendace is available in many versions – fresh, hot-smoked and even canned – and it is an integral part of dishes like *Kalakukko* (page 178), a fish and rye pie from the eastern Finnish region of Savo.

SEARED VENDACE

Hiillostetut muikut (Finland)

Serve with Dill Butter (page 655), a wedge of lemon or a few drops of *Ättika* (6%) vinegar

(page 656). I also like it with Kale Salad (page 90) but a more traditional accompaniment would be Boiled Potatoes (page 117) and Creamed Spinach (page 87).

Preparation and cooking time: 15 minutes
Serves: 4

1 kg/2¼ lb vendace, gutted, cleaned and scaled, heads left on
2 tablespoons salt

Place the fish in a bowl and sprinkle inside and out with salt. Leave for the salt to dissolve while you preheat the oven to 200°C/400°F/Gas Mark 6. At the same time, heat a cast-iron pan as hot as your stove can make it.

Sear the fish a few at a time so that the pan doesn't cool down too much. Give them 30–40 seconds on each side; they should be very darkly coloured in places. Transfer each batch of cooked fish to a warm serving platter and continue cooking the rest of them. The heat from the outer surface of the fish themselves should cook the interiors just enough, if you leave them to rest for a few minutes somewhere not too cool. If the fins don't come out when you pull them, place them in the preheated oven for a few minutes to give them a little more heat.

SMALL FISH (VENDACE OR PERCH) BAKED IN RYE, AS IN SAVO

Kalakukko (Finland)

The first half of *kalakukko*, '*kala*', means 'fish'; and '*kukko*', the second half (that in today's Finnish means 'rooster'), is originally derived from '*kukkaro*' meaning 'purse' or 'pouch'.

Kalakukko is sometimes referred to as the world's oldest preserve – which is probably incorrect, since it needs an oven to exist. And those haven't been common for quite as long as many of the foodstuffs preserved by *lactobacillus* fermentation and/or drying, like olives or cured meats.

The idea is that a stew of fish and pork is encased in a dense rye dough, and baked for a long time in the oven, essentially pasteurizing the filling at the same time as it cooks it. The surrounding bread acts as a sort of edible barrier, protecting the filling from oxidisation or from contamination by microbes.

When doing the research for this book, we sent batches of *kalakukko* to a food laboratory to see how efficient the ancient technique really was at preserving the interior. We sent a number of these pasties – baked on the same day – and had one tested every 5 days. After 7 weeks we ran out and the fish inside was still not showing any significant microbiological activity. They were kept at room temperature the whole time.

Bones are left in the fish, since they become tender during the lengthy cooking process. The crust is often cut open from above, then buttered and eaten with the filling and buttermilk or other cultured milks as a condiment. *Kalakukko* can be eaten cold or reheated.

Preparation and cooking time: 10 hours
Serves: 4 for dinner, with a bit to spare
for lunch

1 kg/2¼ lb vendace or perch, cut and scaled
450 g/1 lb pork belly (side), sliced
rye flour, to sprinkle
salt, to taste

For the dough
600 g/1 lb 5 oz (5 cups) plain (all-purpose) flour

1.2 kg/2½ lb (9¼ cups) rye flour, plus extra
for sprinkling
1 tablespoon salt
250 g/9 oz (2¼ sticks) butter, melted

Preheat the oven to 275°C/525°F/Gas Mark 9 and line a baking sheet with baking (parchment) paper.

Combine all the ingredients for the dough in a large bowl and pour in 750 ml/25 fl oz (3 cups) water. Work to a stiff dough.

Roll it out on a work counter to an oval about 2 cm/¾ inch thick. Sprinkle a little rye flour over the centre of the dough and start layering on the fish and pork. Season each layer with a little bit of salt, sprinkle with a little rye flour and finish with a layer of pork. It is very important that no filling spills onto the edge of the dough that is going to create the seam, because if that happens it will not hold securely through the cooking process. Fold the edges of the dough over the filling so that they meet in the middle. Use a wet hand or brush to dampen the edges with water and pinch them tightly to seal. Smooth the surface of the pasty with a wet hand, sprinkle some more rye flour on top and continue smoothing it out with your hand until it looks nice and silky smooth.

Place the pasty on the baking sheet and bake for about 45 minutes. Lower the temperature to 125°C/240°F/Gas Mark 1, cover the pasty in aluminium foil and continue cooking for 8 hours.

Transfer to a wire rack and leave to cool. The *kalakukko* should now be stored for a few days somewhere cool, before being eaten.

FINNISH VENDACE SOUP

Muikkukeitto (Finland)

This traditional Finnish soup is made from a whole vendace, which is gutted and the head removed, but otherwise left intact. Its tiny bones are very tender, so there is not much point in trying to pick them out of the fish.

Some recipes for *muikkukeitto* contain cream (like this one) while others don't. If you prefer to omit it, then you can thicken the soup with 3 tablespoons of rye flour, that's probably more historically correct, but it doesn't seem so common today. If you do use flour, then add it to the pan with the butter at the very beginning and make sure no lumps form.

You could garnish the soup with dill fronds just before serving it with some Finnish Rye Bread (page 504), butter and hard cheese on the side.

Preparation and cooking time: 1 hour
Serves: 4

50 g/2 oz (3½ tablespoons) butter
8 waxy potatoes, cut into pieces
2 carrots, cut into 5 mm/¼ inch slices
2 onions, cut into wedges
300 ml/10½ fl oz (1¼ cups) cream
1 x 500 g/1 lb 2 oz vendace, gutted, cleaned and head removed
salt, to taste

Melt the butter in a large pot over a medium heat. Add the vegetables and cook until the onions soften. They shouldn't colour. Add 1½ litres/50 fl oz (6¼ cups) water and bring to the boil. After a few minutes, add the cream, then cook for another 15 minutes, or until all the vegetables are beginning to soften. Season the soup well before adding the vendace and return the soup to a very slow simmer. You shouldn't stir the soup any more after adding the vendace, so just leave it for about 10 minutes, until the fish are cooked through.

of *gräddfil*. Sometimes you see *löjrom* served with crème fraîche, but I think this is a bad idea as crème fraîche is much too heavy and rich in both flavour and texture for the delicate roe – especially if whipped thick before serving.

A starchy little something to carry the roe from plate to mouth is always nice. It can be a piece of toast, a Potato Pancake (page 124) or a slice of bread, fried in butter.

Allow 50 g/2 oz bleak roe per person, for
   a good starter (appetizer)
black pepper and white pepper, to taste

I prefer my bleak roe to be taken out of the fridge a little bit of time in advance of eating it, so that it is not cold but just cool. This tends to enhance the roe's inherent nuttiness.

In addition to the above accompaniments, serve bleak roe with a pepper grinder close by. A few turns of white pepper is nice to have, especially if it is a big serving.

Drink a hoppy, bitter pilsner and Aquavit (page 712) with your roe.

HOW TO SERVE AND EAT BLEAK ROE

Muikunmäti (Finland)
Löjrom (Sweden)

Bleak roe is the eggs from the vendace (page 177) and it is commonly eaten in the northern Baltic region as well as in Norway.

Löjrom is often served with finely snipped chives and red onions, a lemon wedge and/or a dollop

SALTWATER FISH

Previous page: Fishing village, Lofoten, Norway, Spring 2014.

Opposite: Lady frying fish cakes in her summer home, Vega Archipelago, Norway, Spring 2014.

SALT AND SUGAR CURING METHOD

Remove the pin bones from a clean and even-ly thick piece of fish fillet. Rub it all over with a mixture of salt, sugar and aromatics. I like to store the fish and the curing mix in a plastic bag, which makes it easy to keep the whole surface of the fish in contact with the cure, ensuring an even result. When the fish is thoroughly coated, place it in its bag on a tray and set a few plates on top to weight it down a little (or use something else flat and suit-ably heavy). Transfer it to the refrigerator to cure for the required length of time.

To stop the cure, take the fish out of the bag and either rinse it quickly under cold running water or scrape the cure and seasonings off it. Transfer the fish to a new plastic bag, place it back on the tray and return it to the refrigerator. This allows the cure to even out within the fish. Leave it for about the same length of time as it was in the curing mix.

The fish can be served straight away or after only a short rest, but it will appear more cured on the surface than in the middle. Fish prepared this way is either cut straight down, at a 90-degree angle rel-ative to the chopping (cutting) board, in slightly thicker slices of 4–5 mm (⅛–¼ inch) or else it is cut at a 45-degree angle into very thin and much larger slices.

CURING FISH WITH SALT AND SUGAR

There are many cured fish preparations around the Nordic region using different varieties of fish, different amounts of salt and sugar (or no salt), different seasonings and different curing times. There are wet cures, dry cures and many in-be-tween cures.

The purpose of curing fish is to lessen the amount of water available in the flesh of the fish to prevent harmful microorganisms from reproducing and, by doing so, prolonging the shelf life of the fish. An-other factor to take into account when curing fish, especially when using longer curing times and sweet cures, is that the presence and growth of beneficial lactobacillus will lower the pH level in the fish, further adding to both its preservation and flavour.

The length of a salt-and-sugar cure can last from anything between 3 hours to several days, depend-ing on the desired result. The longer the fish stays in its cure, the more water will migrate out of the fish and dissolve into the salt-and-sugar mixture, making the flesh more dense and firm.

The more sugar the cure contains, the creamier the result will be. In a short cure, where lactobacillus hasn't had much time to grow, a higher sugar cure will result in a sweeter taste, whilst in a long cure, where the sugar is largely consumed by the lacto-bacillus, a high sugar content will result in a more acidic taste.

Saltier cures produce firmer products and so does the lower pH level from the lactic acid. Longer cures mean more breakdown of proteins into ami-no acids, which in turn means a more savoury and mouth-filling result.

Looking at literature spanning the last 100 years or so, sweet cures (like for gravlax) have become even sweeter and the not-so-sweet cures have be-come less sweet. It seems like almost all cures are stored for less time before being eaten today than what used to be the case, sometimes verging more on a kind of borderline sashimi product.

FERMENTED SALTED FISH

Fermented whole fish or other fermented products made from salted fish are today, and have histori-cally been, popular all over the world. Whether it be an ancient Roman garum fish sauce or a spicy Korean freshwater skate fermented a few months ago, not only do they rely on the same basic pro-cesses, but they also seem to share the same um-ami-rich appeal and the same provocative aroma of death and decay.

The idea is to take fish, salt it to keep available wa-ter to a minimum and by doing so prevent most bacteria from growing. Lactobacillus, who don't mind a little salt, can reproduce rapidly in this en-vironment, where they have an unfair advantage over most other bacteria. And while enjoying this advantage, they create lactic acid, lowering the pH level of the product; this further protects the fish from spoilage. The mass of proteins, fat and other nutrients is now stable and can be stored for a long time without significant danger.

During storage, enzymes, which are pretty much unaffected by these bacterial processes, continue to break down the proteins to amino acids and the fat to fatty acids. These are the components that make fermented stuff taste savoury. The longer the fermentation and the higher the initial protein content, the more savoury the end result will be. The aroma of similar products – for some delicious, but for most appalling – comes from hydrogen sulphide and acetic, propionic and butyric acids.

The two most notable fermented products made from salted fish that are still commonly found today in the Nordic region are Swedish *surströmming* or Sour Herring (page 198) and Norwegian *rakfisk* or Fermented Trout (page 175). Historically, many other freshwater fish, such as roach (page 172), were fermented the same way, and a really old-fashioned Gravlax (page 216) was probably more like a Norwegian *rakfisk* (page 175) than the mildly cured, dill-flavoured fish we know today.

HERRING (*CLUPEA HARENGUS*)

Herring has been, and is still today, one of the most widely consumed fishes in the Nordic region. It figures in a multitude of different recipes, and historically was important not only as food. In the eighteenth century, the streetlights of Paris and many other European cities were fuelled by train oil, boiled from herring along the Scandinavian Atlantic coast and many European hands were washed in soap made from the same substance.

The herring has always been easy to catch, thanks to its behaviour of approaching the coastline in enormous shoals. Stories are told of shoals so dense that herring could be plucked from the water at the shoreline, as if it was already caught and was being picked from barrels. In years when the shoals were plentiful, people moved to the coasts in a sort of gold-fever herring frenzy, and in years when no, or only a few, shoals approached the shore, starvation and misery followed.

Today most Atlantic herring is fished further out from the coast and it's available to consumers either fresh or salted in barrels, graded by the estimated number of fish per kilogram. Large northern Atlantic herring caught in the late autumn (fall) are considered superior in quality because of their high fat content.

Grade 1: 1–4 per kg/2¼ lb
Grade 2: 5–8 per kg/2¼ lb
Grade 3: 9–11 per kg/2¼ lb
Grade 4: 12–20 per kg/2¼ lb

BALTIC HERRING (*CLUPEA HARENGUS MEMBRAS*)

A subspecies of the Atlantic herring, found only in the Baltic Sea. It is generally smaller, and has a lower fat content, than Atlantic herring.

HOW TO CLEAN A BALTIC HERRING

Using the back of a knife or scissors, scrape away the scales from tail to head.

To gut the Baltic herring, support the back of the fish with your free hand. Insert the tip of the knife at the vent end and run it up the belly in one single action.

Remove the guts and discard. Pull away the gills and briefly rinse the fish to remove the blood line (a dark line of blood that runs along the spine).

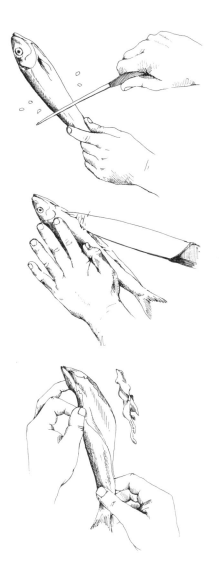

SEARED BALTIC HERRINGS

Sotare (Sweden)

The Swedish name of this dish – *sotare* – means 'chimney sweep', which tells you something about how hot the stove should be and how darkly seared the herrings should be.

A word of warning: I would never ever try to cook this dish in my kitchen at home, as it will make it smell like burnt herring fat to the ends of time. Borrow a restaurant, do it in an outside kitchen, do it wherever you can, except in a room where you plan to make your coffee the next morning.

Sotare is usually seared directly on the flat iron plate on top of an old-fashioned stove or in a glowing-hot cast-iron pan. Some people like to salt the pan or the stove top liberally, before putting the fish on to cook, while others prefer to splash the surface of the fish itself during cooking with very salty water, using a small branch with leaves on it dipped in brine. I like the brine method.

Sotare is served with Parsley Butter (page 655) and Boiled Potatoes (page 117). I also like a few drops of *Ättika* (6%) vinegar (page 656) sprinkled over the fish.

Herrings prepared this way are also delicious on some buttered Rye Crispbread (page 516) with a little bit of mature hard cheese.

Preparation and cooking time: 10 minutes
Serves: 4

800 g/1¾ lb fresh Baltic herrings, gutted and
    cleaned with heads still on
coarse salt for sprinkling in the pan or a jug
    (pitcher) of brine (10% salt solution) and a
    branch for splashing

Heat a cast-iron pan or the flat iron plate on top of your stove until it is as hot as you can possibly make it.

If you are using salt, then sprinkle it over the cooking surface now and then place the herrings directly onto the hot salted surface. If you are using brine, place the herrings on the cooking surface without the salt and splash them with the brine just after turning them over. The herrings should cook long enough on each side to blacken and char them deeply.

BALTIC HERRING MARINATED IN SPRATS CURED IN SANDALWOOD

Mannerströmming (Sweden)

The name of this version of fried, floundered Baltic herring is an amalgamation of the Swedish word for Baltic herring, *strömming*, and the name of the person who invented it, Leif Mannerström, one of the foremost defenders of traditional Swedish gastronomy.

In some recipes the herrings are coated in breadcrumbs. I remember being told a long time ago that it was supposed to be coarse rye flour. Some other recipes contain a mixture of the two. Do as you prefer.

Preparation and cooking time: 30 minutes
Marinating time: overnight
Serves: 4

800 g/1¾ lb fresh Baltic herrings, floundered
 (see page 195)
1 egg, lightly beaten with a little milk
coarse rye flour, for coating the fish
butter, for frying
salt and white pepper, to taste

For the marinade
50 ml/2 fl oz (3½ tablespoons) Mayonnaise
 (page 674)
100 ml/3½ fl oz (⅓ cup plus 1 tablespoon)
 sour cream
55 g/2 oz Sprats Cured in Sandalwood
 (page 212), plus the curing juice
1 good bunch dill, chopped
1 tablespoon Cured Cod's Roe Spread
 (page 672), an un-smoked variety

Mix all the ingredients for the marinade in a large bowl. Add the herring and continue mixing so they are well coated. Cover with clingfilm (plastic wrap) and set aside in a cool place overnight.

When ready to cook, place the beaten egg mixture and rye flour into 2 separate wide, shallow bowls.

Press the flesh sides of 2 herrings together. Dip the pressed herrings into the egg and then the flour.

Heat a generous amount of butter in a pan over a medium–high heat and fry on both sides until they are cooked through and golden-brown. Season with salt and pepper

---

PICKLED FRESH BALTIC HERRING, BASE RECIPE

Graavisilakka (Finland)
Gravet sild (Denmark)
Gravad Strömming (Sweden)

This is probably my favourite herring preparation. Small and delicate fillets of Baltic herring, pickled just enough to set in a mild vinegar solution, are marinated in a delicious sauce like mustard, some herbs or smoked cod's roe.

This pickle is eaten fresh and unlike pickles made from salted herring it won't keep for more than perhaps a week in the refrigerator.

Preparation time: 20 minutes, plus time to sit
Curing time: 6 hours
Serves: 4

400 g/14 oz skinless fillets of Baltic herring, rinsed and patted dry with paper towels
100 ml/3½ fl oz (⅓ cup plus 1 tablespoon) *Ättika* (12%) vinegar (page 656)
20 g/¾ oz salt
20 g/¾ oz sugar

Mix 400 ml/14 fl oz (1⅔ cups) cold water with the vinegar, sugar and salt in a bowl and stir until the salt and sugar have both dissolved. Drop in the fish fillets and leave in the fridge for about 6 hours. Every 2 hours, go there and carefully stir around a bit so that the fish cures evenly.

The fish is ready when it has firmed up and looks like it has been cooked almost all the way through when broken. This is the acidity of the pickling liquid working on the proteins of the fish and it is important not to leave it in there longer than necessary otherwise the fish will turn mushy or, if left for a really long time, dissolve.

Remove the fish from the pickling liquid, leave to drain in a colander and continue with any of the steps below.

If you are making plain pickled fresh herring, do the first pickle for a slightly shorter time, perhaps 3 hours instead of 6, because the second pickle will continue curing the fish.

PLAIN, FRESH PICKLED BALTIC HERRING

Klargravad strömming (Sweden)

Preparation time: 20 minutes
Marinating time: 24 hours
Serves: 4

1 quantity Pickled Fresh Baltic Herring, Base Recipe (page 194)
1 carrot, cut into 2 mm/¾ inch slices
1 red onion, sliced
10 allspice berries
10 white peppercorns
1 bay leaf
500 ml/17 fl oz (2 cups plus 1 tablespoon) 1-2-3 Pickling Liquor (page 657)

Layer all of the ingredients and seasonings in a large sterilized glass jar, top with the pickling liquor and replace the lid. Leave to marinate in the fridge for 24 hours before eating.

PICKLED FRESH BALTIC HERRING IN MUSTARD SAUCE

Senapsströmming (Sweden)

Preparation time: 10 minutes
Marinating time: 24 hours
Serves: 4

1 quantity Pickled, Fresh Baltic Herring, Base Recipe (see left)
1 quantity Sweet-and-Strong Mustard Sauce for Cured Fish (page 664)

Layer fillets of herring and mustard sauce in a large sterilized glass jar or bowl and leave to marinate for 24 hours before eating.

PICKLED FRESH, BALTIC HERRING IN DILL MAYONNAISE

Dillströmming (Sweden)

You can make this recipe with any herb you want, by substituting the dill for it in the mayonnaise recipe.

Preparation time: 10 minutes
Marinating time: 24 hours
Serves: 4

1 quantity Pickled, Fresh Baltic Herring, Base Recipe (see opposite page)
1 quantity Dill Mayonnaise (page 674)

Layer fillets of herring and dill mayonnaise in a jar or bowl, leave to marinate for 24 hours before eating.

FRIED FLOUNDERED BALTIC HERRING

Stekta strömmingflundror (Sweden)

In this dish, floundered fillets of Baltic herring are seasoned and then arranged in pairs, flesh sides pressed together. 'Floundered' simply means that the fillets are still attached to the skin and the backbone has been removed, making it look a bit like a flounder. They are then dipped in egg and floured before frying in butter. The seasonings can be very diverse, and include things like tomato purée (paste), mustard, grated cheese or Sprats Cured in Sandalwood (page 212). The most common seasoning is simply chopped parsley or dill, or sometimes the fish are served with a herb butter.

Stekta strömmingsflundror is often served with Mashed Potatoes (page 118) or Boiled Potatoes (page 117), some of the frying butter, and a wedge of lemon – or perhaps some Sugared Lingonberries (page 692). Other accompaniments with this kind of herring dish are likely to be some kind of boiled vegetable, like carrots, cauliflower, green peas or possibly some spinach.

Leftover fried herring can be marinated in vinegar (see the recipe on page 212) and stored for a few days in the refrigerator. They make a wonderful little snack, served on a piece of crispbread with some mature hard cheese.

Preparation and cooking time: 30 minutes
Resting time: 30 minutes
Serves: 4

800 g/1¾ lb fresh Baltic herrings, floundered
your choice of seasonings (chopped parsley or dill, tomato purée (paste), mustard, grated cheese or Sprats cured in sandalwood, page 212)
1 egg, lightly beaten with a little milk
coarse rye flour, for coating the fish
butter, for frying
salt and white pepper, to taste

Lay out the floundered herrings, flesh side up, on a baking sheet lined with baking (parchment) paper. Sprinkle them all over with a little salt and leave for about 30 minutes at room temperature.

Spread the flesh side of half of the fillets with your choice of seasoning and top with the unseasoned fillets. Press them together gently with the palm of your hand so they stick together.

Place the beaten egg mixture and rye flour into 2 separate wide, shallow bowls. Dip the pairs of herrings into the egg and then the flour.

Melt a generous amount of butter in a pan over a medium–high heat. Season the herrings with salt and pepper and fry until they are cooked through and golden-brown on both sides. Be careful not to burn the butter as you want to serve it as a simple sauce to go with the fish.

FRIED BALTIC HERRING IN VINEGAR

Etikkasilakat (Finland)
Stekt inlagd strömming (Sweden)

These are prepared in the same way as ordinary herring. However, Baltic herrings are almost always 'floundered'. This means that the fillets are still attached to the skin and the backbone has been removed, making it look a bit like a flounder.

Fried Baltic herring in vinegar keeps for a week or so in the refrigerator, covered with pickling liquor.

You will need 1 clean, lidded sterilized glass jar, big enough to fit the ingredients.

Preparation and cooking time: 30 minutes
Marinating time: overnight
Serves: 4

16 fresh Baltic herrings, floundered
strong, unsweetened mustard, to taste
 (optional)
chopped dill and/or parsley, to taste (optional)
coarse rye flour, for coating
butter, for frying
salt and white pepper, to taste

For the pickling liquor
2 red onions, sliced
2 carrots, thinly sliced
10 allspice berries
10 black peppercorns
10 white peppercorns
2 bay leaves
800 ml/28 fl oz (3¼ cups) 1-2-3 Pickling
 Liquor (page 657)
salt, to taste

Lay out the floundered herrings on your work counter, flesh side up. Spread them with a little mustard, if using, then sprinkle with herbs, if using, and season with salt and pepper.

Arrange the floundered herrings in pairs, with the seasoned sides pressed together. Season the skin sides with salt and white pepper before rolling each in coarse rye flour.

Melt plenty of butter in a pan over a medium heat. Fry the herrings on each side until lightly browned.

Drain briefly on paper towels.

Place the herrings, vegetables and aromatics in a sterilized glass jar, then pour in the 1-2-3 pickling liquor, leaving a 1 cm (½ inch) head space. Cover and seal. Leave to marinate in the refrigerator at least overnight. Store in the refrigerator for up to a week.

For image see page 209

PAN-FRIED WHOLE BALTIC HERRING

Paistetut silakat (Finland)
Helstegt sild (Denmark)
Stekt hel strömming (Sweden)

Enjoy with some Boiled Potatoes (page 117), Riced Potatoes (page 117) or Mashed Potatoes (page 118), some Dill or Parsley Butter (page 655), some Sweet Fried Onions (page 108) and perhaps some Sugared Lingonberries (page 692)

Preparation and cooking time: 30 minutes
Serves: 4

800 g/1¾ lb fresh herrings, gutted
 and cleaned

Follow the instructions on page 152 for frying whole fish in a pan, choosing any of the three versions that you like.

POACHED BALTIC HERRING,
SERVED COLD

Pocheret hel sild (Denmark)
Inkokt strömming (Sweden)

Serve the herrings cold, with either the pickling vegetables and some Boiled Potatoes (page 117) and a lump of salted butter, or in their pickling juice, sprinkled with plenty of chopped hard-boiled egg to soak up the delicious liquid. Or perhaps just serve them with a dollop of cultured dairy like *gräddfil*.

Preparation and cooking time: 30 minutes
Marinating time: 24 hours
Serves: 4

1 kg/2¼ lb Baltic herrings, floundered
 (see page 195)
For the marinade
150 ml/5 fl oz (⅔ cup) *Ättika* (12%) vinegar
 (page 656)
2 carrots, cut into 5 mm/¼ inch slices
1 onion, sliced
1 bay leaf
10 white peppercorns
8 allspice berries
2 tablespoons sugar
1 good bunch dill, stalks finely chopped,
 tips reserved
salt, to taste

Pat the herrings thoroughly dry with paper towels. Roll them, skin side out, into little rolls and place them in a deep tray. They should fit snugly, with no gaps, and the marinade needs to be able to cover them completely. (If they are not snug they might unroll when you pour the hot liquid over them.)

Combine all the marinade ingredients in a large pan and pour in 400 ml/14 fl oz (1⅔ cups) water. Bring to the boil. Adjust the seasonings – it should be quite salty – then pour over the herrings. Allow to cool, then leave for 24 hours to marinate. Sprinkle with the dill tips just before serving.

finely chopped
10 small fresh herrings or Baltic herrings,
 gutted and cleaned, head, tail and fins
 removed
2 tablespoons breadcrumbs
mature hard cheese made from cow's milk,
 to grate over the dish
50 ml/2 fl oz (3½ tablespoons) cream
50 ml/2 fl oz (3½ tablespoons) curing juice
 from the sprats
salt and white pepper, to taste

Preheat the oven to 250°C/480°F/Gas Mark 9. Lightly butter an ovenproof dish that is just large enough to fit the herrings snugly.

Heat a little butter in a frying pan and sauté the onion, garlic and sprats over a medium heat until soft, but not coloured.

Spoon some of the mixture into the belly of each herring and season well with white pepper. Be a little cautious about adding salt as the sprats are salty already.

Arrange the herrings in the prepared dish with their backs up, as though they are swimming. Sprinkle with breadcrumbs and grated cheese and pour in the cream and curing juice. Cook for 10–15 minutes, or until the fish just comes away from the bone and the top is nicely browned – the exact time will depend a bit on the size of the fish.

FRESH HERRING OR BALTIC
HERRING CASSEROLE

Sillåda / Strömmingslåda (Sweden)

Serve with Boiled Potatoes (page 117). I also like a wedge of lemon on the side too, but this is not really traditional.

Preparation and cooking time: 30 minutes
Serves: 8

butter, for frying
1 onion, finely chopped
1 clove garlic, finely grated
10 Sprats Cured in Sandalwood (page 212),

SOUR HERRING

Surströmming (Sweden)

Surströmming is a small fermented Baltic herring that is sold in cans. It is widely recognized as the world's most smelly food and has a huge following – especially in northern Sweden where 'sour herring' parties are common after the annual sour herring 'premiere', which takes place on the third Thursday of August.

The Baltic herring used for producing *surströmming* are caught just before their mating season in April or May, when they are in their prime: fatty and filled with roe.

The fish are fermented in large barrels where the wood itself, after many years of use, inoculates the fish (salted to approximately 12% salinity) with the right strains of salt-hardy lactobacillus. These, together with enzymes already present in the fish's spines, produce both a microbiological fermentation and an autolytic one that account for much of the product's particular flavour.

The fish is usually canned in July and left to ferment in the can, where Haloanaerobium bacteria further ripen the herring into a product vastly different from all other fermented fish products that are not in-can ripened.

A real connoisseur of *surströmming* will get especially exited over either female herrings that are filled with roe or last year's vintage of herring, where the in-can fermentation will have built up enough pressure for the initially flat can to bulge into a pressurized sphere. These should be considered nothing less than a time bomb of olfactory destruction.

Surströmming is often considered to be an ancient historical food, and it's certain that herring and many other fish have been fermented in Sweden for hundreds of years. But the product we know today as *surströmming* relies so heavily on the can itself to acquire its characteristic perfume. Because of this, *surströmming* must, by logical conclusion, be considered a product younger than the popular use of the tin can, which itself was invented in 1810, but hardly available before 1875 when mechanized manufacture of the vessel was invented.

HOW TO EAT AND ENJOY SOUR HERRING

Surströmming is only ever eaten by serious people after the third Thursday of August – anything else would be considered sacrilegious. This is true, whether the can be a mature one from a previous vintage or an under-ripe 'black-market' can from the current year's production, somehow acquired before the proper release date.

Here are a few of my own rules of thumb for achieving a successful herring party:

It should take place outside, regardless of the weather and the level of mosquito activity in the area.

There should be generous amounts of Aquavit (page 714) to hand, kept at your preferred temperature. Myself, I like it frozen to the point of the alcohol becoming viscous. It should feel like a tasteless, frozen lead pellet hurtling past your larynx when swallowed. A teardrop of ice that, seconds later, heated by the warmth of your body, blossoms into an aromatic fire that roars up the throat with aromas of caraway, aniseed and perhaps bitter wormwood.

There should be beer, preferably a clean, crisp and well-hopped lager to quench the thirst that is induced by the salty herring.

The herrings are best eaten on a Tunnbröd flatbread with slices of boiled new potatoes, butter, onion and *gräddfil*.

There should be Västerbotten cheese (page 67), available in large chunks to nibble on.

There should be no damned dessert! The aroma of *surströmming* has a tendency to contaminate any mild and fatty foodstuffs within a radius of 100 metres/110 yards from where the can is opened and I have never been particularly fond of *surströmming* and strawberry layer cake.

Tip: How to open the can

Place the *surströmming* can in a big bucket filled with cold water. Pierce the can with an ordinary can opener and don't keep your face too close to the surface of the water as the pressure within the can will release a bubble of smelly gaseous odours that hurtle upwards towards you. The whole point of submerging the can itself is because if it is opened above the surface of the water, the gas will force the liquid out through the hole, spraying everything and everyone in the vicinity from top to toe.

Once the can is open you can choose to rinse the fish under cold water or eat them as they are. I prefer to rinse them, since it makes them a little less salty and makes the aroma a bit subtler than if they are left un-rinsed.

Surströmming is available either as fillets or as whole fish. Most people would consider the fillets inferior in flavour to their whole counterpart, but others will choose the fillets as they are very convenient to eat.

2 tablespoons butter
2 red onions, finely chopped
500 g/1 lb 2 oz sour herrings (page 198), well rinsed, filleted and patted dry with paper towels
3 eggs
300 ml/10½ fl oz (1¼ cups) milk
salt and white pepper, to taste

Preheat the oven to 200°C/400°F/Gas Mark 6.

Heat the butter in an ovenproof cast-iron pan over a medium heat. Fry the onions until soft but not coloured. Arrange the herring fillets on top of the onions.

Whisk the eggs with the milk in a bowl and season with salt and pepper. Pour over the fish and bake until the egg mixture is just set and has turned a light golden colour on the surface.

SOUR HERRING CASSEROLE

Surströmmingslåda (Sweden)

This is one of those dishes that you never see today. During my life I have had it perhaps once or twice. I think though that it is a really important recipe, because it shows the significance of the *surströmming* or Sour Herring (page 198) as food.

Today *surströmming* is something we eat perhaps once a year, as part of summer festivities, however it was not that long ago, before the days of modern refrigeration and imported foods, that it was an everyday staple – especially in central Sweden which is further away from the coast.

This recipe has all the hallmarks of an everyday dish. It uses a cheap and readily available ingredient, is easy to make and has no added cream. It is also a way of preparing a product that many people probably ate quite often in a different way.

Serve with Boiled Potatoes (page 117) and a glass of milk on the side.

Preparation and cooking time: 45 minutes
Serves: 4

HOW TO DESALT A SALTED HERRING

If the herring is whole, place it in cold water for 24 hours. You will need 3 litres/5 UK pints (12½ cups) water for 2 whole herrings. If it is in fillets, place them in cold water for 8 hours. You will need 3 litres/5 UK pints (12½ cups) water for 4 fillets.

Taste the herring to verify that it is done. It should be firm and pleasant in texture and a little bit salty. If it is too salty leave it in the water for a bit longer. However, if left soaking for too long the herring will go soft and boring in texture.

SALTED HERRING DRIZZLED WITH BROWNED BUTTER

Lertallrikssill (Sweden)

Traditionally, this dish was cooked and served on a clay plate. Its name is a combination of the Swedish word for the clay plate, which is *lertallrik*, and herring, which is *sill*. This recipe comes from the southern Swedish region of Skåne. Serve with Boiled Potatoes (page 117). In more recent recipes I have seen people adding little things that are acidic, like a lemon wedge or *gräddfil*.

Preparation and cooking time: 20 minutes
Serves: 4 as a starter (appetizer), 2 as a
*   light meal*

4 large salted herring fillets, desalted
    (page 200)
2 tablespoons cream
100 g/3½ oz (7 tablespoons) butter
1 red onion, finely chopped
1 bunch parsley, stalks finely chopped, leaves
    coarsely chopped
1 bunch dill, stalks finely chopped, fronds
    coarsely chopped

Preheat the oven to 250°C/480°F/Gas Mark 9.

Place the herring fillets in a roasting pan and drizzle on the cream. Bake until it is just beginning to colour.

While the herrings are in the oven, follow the instructions on page 662 for browning the butter.

Take the herrings out of the oven and sprinkle with the onion and herbs. Drizzle on the browned butter and serve.

HERRING BALLS

Sildboller (Norway)
Sildeboller (Denmark)
Sillbullar (Sweden)

Herring balls, which if you look at old menus from canteens and in old cookbooks seem to have been as common as any other thing prepared with herring, have dropped out of fashion and are very rarely prepared as far as I can understand.

In Sweden and Denmark, herring balls include leftover cooked meat and are served with a Sweet-and-Sour Currant Sauce (page 669), and Boiled Potatoes (page 117).

In Norway, they are made from herring alone and are served with boiled swede (rutabaga) and/or Boiled Carrots (page 110) and Boiled Potatoes (page 117) and a few slices of Fried Salt Pork (page 302).

HERRING BALLS WITH MEAT

Preparation and cooking time: 35 minutes
Serves: 4

butter, for frying
1 onion, finely chopped
250 g/9 oz salted herring fillets, desalted
    (page 200)
200 g/7 oz cold meat leftovers (anything
    you like), cut into pieces
200 g/7 oz cold Boiled Potatoes
    (page 117), peeled
1 egg
2 tablespoons potato flour
50 g/2 oz (½ cup) breadcrumbs
salt and white pepper, to taste

Melt some butter in a pan over a medium heat. Add the onions and fry until soft, but not coloured.

Tip into a mixing bowl and leave to cool.

Cut the herring fillets into pieces and add them to the bowl along with all the remaining ingredients, except for the breadcrumbs. Mix together well, then pass through a meat mincer (grinder) on the fine plate.

Season the mixture well, then shape into 5 cm/2 inch patties, about 2 cm/¾ inch thick. Turn the patties around in the breadcrumbs to coat.

Heat some more butter in a large frying pan over a medium heat. Fry the patties for about 10 minutes until golden and crisp.

HERRING BALLS MADE ONLY WITH HERRING

Enjoy still warm with butter, marmalade and mature hard cheese.

Preparation and cooking time: 1½ hours
Serves: 4

250 g/9 oz salted herring fillets, desalted
 (page 200)
250 g/9 oz potatoes, peeled and coarsely
 chopped
250 g/9 oz cold Boiled Potatoes
 (page 117)
1 onion, finely chopped
5 tablespoons barley flour
salt and white pepper, to taste

Combine all the ingredients in a mixing bowl. Mix together well, then pass through a meat mincer (grinder) on the fine plate. Season well.

Bring a large pot of water to a simmer. You probably won't need to add any salt as the herring itself is already quite salty.

Shape the mixture into 3 cm/1¼ inch balls with clean, wet hands. Drop the herring balls into the water as you make them. Cook for about an hour, or until the raw potato is completely cooked.

PAN-FRIED SALTED HERRING

Stekt sild (Norway)
Saltet stegte sild (Denmark)
Stekt salt sill (Sweden)

In Sweden fillets of fried salted herring are most often enjoyed with Boiled Potatoes (page 117) and Onion Cream Sauce (page 663) or a spoonful of Sugared Lingonberries (page 692).

Preparation and cooking time: 20 minutes
Serves: 4

8 small or 4 large salted herring fillets,
 desalted (page 200)

Prepare and cook the fillets according to the instructions on page 152 for Whole Fish, Fried in a Pan, Breaded if you like thick breading or version 4 if you prefer a lighter crust made from rye flour.

PAN-FRIED SALTED BALTIC HERRING

Stekt saltströmming (Sweden)

Follow the instructions for Pan-fried Salted Herring (see above) and serve with an Onion Cream Sauce (page 663) and Boiled Potatoes (page 117) or with a wedge of lemon, some of the frying butter and Mashed Potatoes (page 118).

For image see page 209

PLAIN SALTED HERRING

Spekesild (Norway)
Saltet sild (Denmark)
Spicken sill (Sweden)

This dish is rarely eaten these days, which is a pity as it makes a great, simple everyday lunch or a light meal. Fillets of salted herring that have been desalted (page 200) are patted dry, cut into pieces about 2.5 cm/1 inch wide, and served with *gräddfil*, chives and warm Boiled Potatoes (page 117).

HERRING AND PICKLED BEETROOT SALAD

Sildesalat med rødbeter (Norway)
Sildesalat med rødbeder (Denmark)
Sillsallad med rödbetor (Sweden)

In most older recipes you use salted herring fillets, desalted and cubed as the base of this recipe. This is delicious, but most of the time I use Pickled Herring (page 204) instead. I find it more tasty, plus most times when I am preparing this dish, which is part of the traditional Swedish festive meal, I am also preparing pickled herring, so there might be trimmings perfectly suited to be chopped up.

In older Danish recipes, and in some Swedish ones too, the list of ingredients can include cubes of cold braised meat and cubes of cold boiled potato.

Prepare it with either a coating of whipped cream or mayonnaise, or as I do, a 50/50 mix of both. Use pickling juice from the beetroot (beets) to add some acidity towards the end, if necessary.

If you want to garnish with parsley, as some people do, use a lot of it, coarsely chopped. Almost like a little salad on top – it is delicious. A few whole leaves arranged over the dish is just pointless.

Preparation time: 10 minutes
Resting time: overnight
Serves: 8 as part of a large meal, 4 as
  a standalone starter (appetizer) or as
  a light lunch with bread and cheese

2 fillets Pickled Herring (page 204) or salted
  and desalted herring (page 200)
2 Boiled Potatoes (page 117), peeled and cut
  into 1 cm/½ inch cubes
1 acidic red apple, skin on, cored and cut
  into 1 cm/½ inch cubes
2 Pickled Beetroot (page 660), cut into
  1 cm/½ inch cubes
1 onion, finely chopped
1 Hard-boiled Egg (page 53), chopped
150 ml/5 fl oz (⅔ cup) Mayonnaise (page 674)
  and/or double (heavy) cream, whipped
chopped parsley, to garnish (optional)
salt and white pepper, to taste

Cut the herring fillets into 1 cm/½ inch cubes. Place in a large mixing bowl with all the other cubed and chopped ingredients and season with salt and pepper. Mix in the mayonnaise then taste and adjust the seasonings. Cover the bowl and refrigerate overnight.

Fold in the cream, if using, just before serving.

HERRING AND POTATO PUDDING

Sildepudding (Denmark)
Sillpudding (Sweden)

Sillpudding is served with melted butter, in the same way as is *laxpudding* (page 219). I also like to serve it with some Sautéed Kale (page 90).

Often a generous amount of dill is added between each layer, but I prefer instead to sprinkle my dill on top of the cooked dish just before it is eaten.

Preparation and cooking time: 1–1¼ hours
Serves: 4

200 g/7 oz salted herring fillets, desalted
800 g/1¾ lb Boiled Potatoes (page 117),
  peeled and cut into 5 mm/
  ¼ inch slices
2 eggs
500 ml/17 fl oz (2 cups plus 1 tablespoon)
  milk
1 good bunch dill, fronds finely chopped
salt and white pepper, to taste

Preheat the oven to 225°C/435°F/Gas Mark 7.

Cut the herring fillets into strips or thin slices. Layer them with the potato in an ovenproof dish, starting with the potato. Season each layer with salt and pepper (and dill, if you like), but be careful with the salt as the herring is usually quite salty already.

Mix the eggs into the milk and season with salt and pepper before pouring it over the potatoes and fish. Make sure it covers them completely. Finish with a sprinkling of dill, then bake for 45–60 minutes, or until it has set and is a golden colour.

Clockwise from top left: Finnish Beetroot Salad (page 116); Pickled Beetroot (page 660); Beetroot Salad (page 116); Boiled Beetroot (page 115)

STUFFED, BREADED HERRING

Fyldte stegte sild (Denmark)
Fylld sill (Sweden)

Serve straight from the oven with the cooking juices and oil from the fish itself and accompany with a Spinach Salad (page 87).

Preparation and cooking time: 45 minutes
Makes: 2 large or 4 smaller portions

2 big, fat salted herrings
breadcrumbs, to coat
butter, for cooking

For the stuffing
2 Hard-boiled Eggs (page 53), coarsely
  chopped
2 tablespoons breadcrumbs
100 ml/3½ fl oz (⅓ cup plus 1 tablespoon) cream
freshly grated nutmeg, to taste (optional)
salt and white pepper, to taste

Follow the instructions on page 200 for soaking the herrings to remove excess salt. Preheat the oven to 250°C/480°F/Gas Mark 9.

Very carefully remove the backbones from the herrings. Do this from the belly-side and be sure you don't pierce the skin.

In a bowl, mix together the stuffing ingredients, seasoning with salt, pepper and nutmeg, to taste. Spoon the stuffing into the empty cavity of the herring. Shape it with your hand to look as natural as possible before rolling the fish in more breadcrumbs.

Place the prepared herrings in an ovenproof dish and top each one with a knob of butter. Bake until they are golden.

TOMATO MARINATED HERRING

Tomatsild (Norway)
Tomatsild (Denmark)
Tomatsill (Sweden)

As with other types of pickled herring, enjoy these as a light meal or as part of a bigger selection of herring for a more festive meal. These are not pickled herring in the true sense, and they don't keep as long, but if you do have any leftovers they easily keep for a week in the refrigerator.

As with pickled herring, you can choose to cut the fillets into pieces before putting them in the marinade, or cut them after. Before is easier and less sticky, and gives them a nicer, cleaner cut. I generally do it after, at the time of serving, but if you are cooking for many people the other option can be very convenient.

Preparation and cooking time: 30 minutes
Marinating time: overnight
Serves: 4, as a light meal

4 salted herring fillets, desalted (page 200)
1 red onion, finely chopped
5 tablespoons neutral/flavourless oil
1 tablespoon white vinegar
100 ml/3½ fl oz (⅓ cup plus 1 tablespoon)
  tomato purée (paste)
salt and white pepper, to taste
1 good bunch parsley, finely chopped

Dab the herring fillets dry with a clean cloth, trim them so that they look nice and then cut them into pieces (or leave them whole, if you prefer).

Put them into a glass or stainless steel bowl and sprinkle on the chopped onion. Mix the oil with the vinegar and tomato purée and season well. If it looks too thick, dilute with a little bit of water. Pour the sauce over the herring and refrigerate overnight.

Sprinkle on a generous amount of chopped parsley just before serving.

PICKLED HERRING, BASE RECIPE

Súrsuðum síld (Iceland)
Sursild (Norway)
Silliä (Finland)
Syltede sild (Denmark)
Inlagd sill (Sweden)

Salted herring fillets, desalted in water before being pickled in a mild and slightly spicy, sweet-and-sour liquor, are common all over the Nordic region. Usually eaten as a starter (appetizer) with Boiled Potatoes (page 117), sour cream and chives or chopped red onions, this recipe can also be the base for other herring dishes like Creamy Pickled Mustard Herring (page 206) or Tomato Marinated Herring (see opposite page).

The fillets can be pickled whole and cut into smaller pieces just before serving or they can be cut into pieces before they are pickled. I prefer the first way as it produces a slightly prettier looking result with a freshly cut surface on each piece of fish. Pickling herring that has already been cut into pieces can be convenient if you are cooking for many and want to minimize the amount of work on the day you are serving them. Even if you are cooking for less than eight people, prepare the full recipe and keep the rest for another day. Pickled herring will keep for several months, as long as it is kept refrigerated.

You will need 1 clean, lidded glass jar, big enough to fit all the ingredients.

Preparation time: 30 minutes
Pickling time: overnight
Serves: 8 as a starter (appetizer)

1 large carrot
1 red onion
8 salted herring fillets, desalted (page 200)
15 allspice berries
15 white peppercorns
2 bay leaves
1 litre/34 fl oz (4¼ cups) cold 1-2-3 Pickling
  Liquor (page 657)

Peel the carrot and onion then slice them to a thickness of about 2 mm/¹⁄₁₆ inch with a knife or a mandoline. Reserve the prepared vegetables on your chopping (cutting) board. Dab the herring fillets dry with a clean cloth, trim them so that they look nice and then cut them into pieces if you are not intending to pickle them whole.

Place a few fillets or pieces of herring at the bottom of a glass jar, sprinkle some of the prepared vegetables on top of the fish and season with some of the spices. Continue to layer the herring, vegetables and spices in the jar until they are all used up. Pour on enough pickling liquor to cover completely; the amount you use will vary a little depending on the shape of the jar you are using. Seal the jar and refrigerate overnight before eating.

Tip: When serving pickled herring, garnish with the pickled vegetables from the jar. They look beautiful and add a welcome crunch to the texture of the fish.

For image see page 209

GLASSBLOWER'S HERRING

Glassmestersild (Norway)
Lasimestarin silli (Finland)
Glarmestersild (Denmark)
Glasmästarsill (Sweden)

This is a variation of Pickled Herring, Base Recipe (see left) in which the gutted and desalted herrings are not filleted, but cut into pieces across the fish, backbone still in, fins and heads still on. In addition to the ordinary seasoning of a batch of pickled herring, add 2 teaspoons of brown mustard seeds and a piece each of fresh horseradish and fresh ginger into the jar, and use thinly sliced red onion, no white onion.

Glasmästarsill is served straight from the glass jar, with a generous handful of chopped parsley mixed into the pickling liquor just before serving. Proper Glassblower's Herring is very rare today and most people don't know that it should be made with whole pieces of fish, as opposed to fillets. I think this is because the industry makes their version with fillets and that's what most people use today in their homes. It is a bit more difficult to eat real Glassblower's Herring since it has bones in it, but fantastic things shouldn't be so user-friendly all the time; it makes us lazy.

CREAMY PICKLED MUSTARD HERRING

Sennepssild (Norway)
Sinappisilli (Finland)
Sennepssild (Denmark)
Senapssill (Sweden)

This dish can be made using fresh herring or herring that is already pickled. The first recipe below, using pickled herring, will turn out a little stronger and more sweet-and-sour in flavour; it also keeps a bit longer than the fresh version. The second recipe, using fresh herring, is lighter and fresher and should be consumed within a week or so after being made.Myself, I usually prefer to make a big batch of Pickled Herring (page 204), and use it as a base, turning it into many different variations by adding different sauces and seasonings.

However, if I were to serve this dish as a main course, I would probably choose version two, since the version with pickled herring can be a little too strong to eat a big portion. Serve as a part of the *smörgåsbord/kolde bord* or, if served by itself, with Boiled Potatoes (page 117), a Hard-boiled Egg (page 53), Rye Crispbread (page 516) and mature cheese. In Denmark you will sometimes find the herring layered with cold slices of boiled potato and slices of raw onion before serving.

For image see page 209

USING PICKLED HERRING (VERSION 1)

Preparation time: 20 minutes
Curing time: 2–3 days, depending on whether you already have pickled herring or not
Serves: 8 as a starter (appetizer) and 4 as a main meal

1 quantity Pickled Herring, Base Recipe (page 204) or 8 fillets store-bought pickled herring
1 quantity Sweet-and-Strong Mustard Sauce for Cured Fish (page 664)

Dab any excess pickling liquor off the fish with a paper towel or clean cloth. If the herring wasn't already cut into suitable pieces before pickling, do

so, unless you want to serve whole fillets, which works just as well.

Spoon about a quarter of the mustard sauce into the bottom of a sterilized glass jar and place some of the herring pieces on top. Cover with more mustard sauce and then continue layering until you run out of both sauce and herring. Make sure that the fish is well covered in sauce. Cover with a lid and refrigerate for at least 48 hours before serving.

It is quite common to decorate this herring with a generous amount of chopped dill, but I prefer it served straight from a glass jar without any added decoration than the beautiful golden brown sauce, through which silvery slivers of fish can be glimpsed.

USING FRESH HERRING (VERSION 2)

Serve with Boiled Potatoes (page 117), Hard-boiled Eggs (page 53), Rye Crispbread (page 516) and some mature cheese.

Preparation time: 20 minutes
Curing time: 2 days
Serves: 8 as a starter (appetizer) and 4 as a main meal

45 g/1¾ oz (3 tablespoons) sugar
60 g/2¼ oz (3½ tablespoons) salt
200 ml/7 fl oz (¾ cup plus 1 tablespoon) *Ättika* (12%) vinegar (page 656)
4 large, fatty fresh herrings, gutted, cleaned and filleted

For the creamy mustard sauce
1½ tablespoons *Ättika* (12%) vinegar (page 656)
100 ml/3½ fl oz (⅓ cup plus 1 tablespoon) cream
4 tablespoons mustard
180 ml/6 fl oz (¾ cup) cooking oil
salt and white pepper, to taste
1 big handful dill fronds, to serve

Pour 400 ml/14 fl oz (1⅔ cups) water into a large ppt and stir in the sugar and salt. Bring to the boil and stir until the sugar has completely dissolved. Add the *Ättika* vinegar then chill before using.

Prepare the herrings while the pickling liquor is cooling. Cut them into smaller pieces and drop them into the pan with the chilled pickling liquor. Let the fish marinate for about 2 hours in the liquid before picking the pieces out and patting them dry with a paper towel or a clean cloth.

While the fish is marinating, prepare the creamy mustard sauce. Mix together the *Ättika* vinegar, cream and mustard in a bowl, then whisk in the oil, little by little, as if you were making a mayonnaise. It should thicken slightly and become homogenous when it is ready. Season with salt and white pepper to taste.

Place the pieces of herring in a bowl and cover with the sauce. Sprinkle generously with dill and serve.

FRIED HERRING IN VINEGAR

Stegt sild i eddike (Denmark)
Stekt inlags sill (Sweden)

Eat these lukewarm or cold as a meal with Boiled Potatoes (page 117) or on a slice of rye bread or as a snack with Rye Crispbread (page 516). Always serve the fish with the vegetables from the pickle – they are delicious.

If the herrings are big, then fillet them. Roll them up after seasoning and secure with a cocktail stick (toothpick) before cooking them. If they are smaller, pull the backbone out from inside the chest cavity and fill it with seasoning to leave it looking like a whole fish. Some people fill the herring with mustard and chopped herbs like parsley and dill, while others just season with a bit of salt and pepper. I like to stuff my herrings with plenty of aromatics.

Fried herring in vinegar keeps for about a week or so in the refrigerator, covered with pickling liquor.

You will need 1 clean, lidded sterilized glass jar, big enough to fit the ingredients.

Preparation and cooking time: 30 minutes
Marinating time: at least overnight
Serves: 4

8 large fresh herring fillets or 8 small whole
  herrings, gutted, cleaned and backbones
  removed
strong unsweetened mustard, to taste
  (optional)
chopped dill and/or parsley, to taste
  (optional)
coarse rye flour, for coating
butter, for frying
salt and white pepper, to taste

For the pickling liquor
2 red onions, sliced
2 carrots, thinly sliced
10 allspice berries
10 black peppercorns
10 white peppercorns
2 bay leaves
800 ml/28 fl oz (3¼ cups) 1-2-3 Pickling
  Liquor (page 657)
salt, to taste

Lay the fish out on your work counter, flesh side up. Spread with a little mustard, if using, then sprinkle with herbs and season with salt and pepper.

If using fillets, then roll them up and secure with a toothpick. If using whole herrings, press the sides together, to close them. Either way, season the exterior with salt and white pepper before rolling the fish in coarse rye flour.

Melt plenty of butter in a pan over a medium heat. Fry the herrings on each side until lightly browned. Drain briefly on paper towels.

Place the herrings, vegetables and aromatics in a sterilized glass jar, then pour in the 1-2-3 pickling liquor leaving a 1 cm (½ inch) head space, cover and seal. Leave to marinate in the fridge at least overnight. Store in the refrigerator for up to a week.

CURRY HERRING

Karrisild (Norway)
Karrysild (Denmark)
Currysill (Sweden)

Preparation time: 10 minutes
Marinating time: 24 hours
Serves: 8 as a starter (appetizer) and 4 as a
  main meal

1 quantity Pickled Herring, Base Recipe
  (page 204) or 8 store-bought pickled
  herring fillets
1 quantity Mayonnaise (page 674)
1 tablespoon yellow curry powder
salt and pepper, to taste

Dab any excess pickling liquor off the fish with a paper towel or clean dish cloth. If the herring wasn't already cut into suitable pieces before pickling, do so, unless you want to serve whole fillets, which works just as well.

Mix the mayo with the curry powder and season well.

Layer the herring and mayonnaise in a jar or bowl and leave to marinate in the fridge overnight.

SPICED HERRING

Kryddersild (Norway)
Maustesilli (Finland)
Kryddersild (Denmark)
Kryddsill / Matjessill (Sweden)

This Scandinavian speciality is made by curing large fatty herrings in 8–13% salt and about 20–25% sugar by weight, together with different aromatics. Spiced herring is often aged in barrels for about a year before being consumed and one of the main seasonings used is sandalwood. Its fragrant sawdust adds a special pinkish colour, as well as flavour, to the finished product – very much like the cured sprats, known as *ansjovis* (page 212).

Today in Sweden the commercially available product is known as 'matjes herring' and in the other Scandinavian countries as 'spiced herring'. The Swedish name comes from *maatjesharing*, which refers to a Dutch speciality made from a young, not yet sexually mature herring, between May and July and then stored in a mild preserving liquid.

The word 'matjes' herring has been used in Sweden since the mid eighteenth century but probably meant something more closely related to the Dutch original at that time. The renaming of spiced herring probably occurred during the expansion of the canning industry in the nineteenth century as a way of motivating a higher price for a canned product, simply by giving it a fancy name.

In their homes people continued making this herring and calling it spiced herring. The use of this name in Sweden didn't die out until industrialized herring production completely took over and those keeping this tradition alive got too old and stopped doing it.

Nowadays the words for 'spiced' in all the Scandinavian countries are sometimes used to describe an ordinary pickled herring (page 204) with spices, which is completely wrong.

Kryddsill recipes from old books, presumably made mainly by people in their own homes, share the same salt and sugar ratios, but the gutted herring are additionally dipped in a vinegar solution before being layered with the curing mix. From a technical standpoint the vinegar dipping could make up for some lack in hygiene during the production process, since it lowers the pH level before the fish are actually laid down. This is something that happens naturally with time anyhow, as lactobacillus feed on the sugars in the barrel. By dipping the herring in vinegar, the time when they are at risk of spoiling is greatly shortened. However at the end of the curing process, the difference between properly laid down *kryddsill* and a matjes herring is undetectable.

Most people would buy their matjes herring already prepared but I have included a recipe for those who would like to try to make a version at home.

For image see opposite page

Clockwise from top left: Spiced Herring (page 208); Sprats Cured in Sandalwood (page 213); Herring and Pickled Beetroot Salad (page 202); Curry Herring (page 208); Fried Baltic Herring in Vinegar (page 196); Pan-fried Salted Baltic Herring (page 201); Salad of Sprats Cured in Sandalwood (page 214); Creamy Pickled Mustard Herring (page 206); Pickled Herring (page 204)

HOW TO MAKE SPICED HERRING

It might still seem like a large amount, but do not reduce the quantities of this recipe as it is very difficult to make it work properly. If you can't eat this amount of herring within a year – or give it to friends and family – then you should buy your herring instead.

If you can't get hold of saltpetre, substitute part of the salt with a nitrite product according to the instructions on the bag of the particular brand. (See also page 434.) This is a precautionary measure to avoid the growth of *Clostridium botulinum,* which can cause botulism.

Preparation time: 1 hour
Maturing time: at least 6 months
Makes: 5 kg/11 lb herring fillets

10 kg/22 lb large fresh herrings, gutted, cleaned and filleted, heads left on, gills removed
150 ml/5 fl oz (⅔ cup) *Ättika* (24%) vinegar (page 656)

For the curing mixture
750 g/1 lb 10 oz (2¾ cups) coarse, iodine-free sea salt
2 kg/4½ lb (10 cups) sugar
100 g/3½ oz fresh ginger, sliced
50 g/2 oz allspice berries, crushed
50 g/2 oz black peppercorns, crushed
50 g/2 oz sandalwood dust
50 g/2 oz dried oregano
50 g/2 oz dried bitter orange peel
35 g/1¼ oz saltpetre
25 g/1 oz fennel seed
25 g/1 oz cloves, crushed
10 bay leaves

For the extra brine
1 litre/34 fl oz (4¼ cups) water
100 g/3½ oz (⅓ cup) salt
200 g/7 oz (1 cup) sugar

Place the herrings in a large, clean stainless-steel bucket (or some other suitable container). Stir the vinegar into 1.5 litres/2½ UK pints (6¼ cups) water then pour it over the herrings. Shake the bucket a bit so that the marinade really reaches all the herrings properly. Leave in a cold place overnight.

Combine the curing mixture ingredients in a large bowl. Spread a 1 cm/1½ inch layer of the mixture on the bottom of a clean stainless-steel, glazed ceramic or glass container. It should be large enough to contain all the herrings fairly snugly. It's better to use a tall narrow container (rather than a shallow wide one) since there will be less oxidation and evaporation from a smaller surface area. Something similar in shape to a wine barrel or bucket is about right.

Take the herrings out of the vinegar solution, one by one, and arrange them in a layer on top of the curing mixture in the container. They should be packed together tightly, with the open chest cavities facing upwards, to decrease the risk of air pockets and spoilage. Sprinkle more of the curing mixture onto the first layer of herrings. Continue layering herring and curing mixture until all the herring are packed in tightly. Finally, sprinkle a good layer of the curing mixture on top.

Weight the herring down with something clean, flat and heavy. Leave at room temperature for 24 hours to encourage some lactobacillus fermentation. During the first 24 hours enough moisture should have been drawn out of the fish to form a liquid brine that covers them completely. If this is not the case, then make the extra brine to top it up. Combine the ingredients in a large pan and bring to the boil. Remove from the heat and leave to cool completely. Pour on enough to cover the herring completely. Cover before leaving the herring to mature.

Leave the *kryddsill* in a cool place to mature for at least 6 months.

For image see page 209

HOW TO SERVE COLD SPICED HERRING

When handling homemade *kryddsill* always use scrupulously clean utensils and be careful not to put your hands into the barrel where you're storing the herrings, as this will make them spoil quicker.

Allow 1 fillet per person for a light meal or a starter (appetizer) and ⅓ fillet per person if it is part of a bigger meal or a traditional *smörgåsbord* buffet (page 522).

Trim the fillets and either keep them whole or cut them into smaller pieces. (If you have purchased matjes herrings and they are whole, rather than fillets, then follow the method on page 152 for filleting round fish.)

Serve at room temperature, or slightly chilled, with Boiled Potatoes (page 117), Hard-boiled Eggs (page 53), *gräddfil*, snipped chives and/or chopped red onions.

HOW TO PREPARE AND SERVE WARM SPICED HERRING

Preparation and cooking time: 15 minutes
Serves: 4 as a light meal or a starter
  (appetizer)

4 trimmed fillets of spiced herring
  (or purchased matjes herring)
150 g/5 oz (11 tablespoons) butter
4 Hard-boiled Eggs (page 53),
  chopped
1 red onion, finely chopped
fresh dill, fronds picked
50 ml/2 fl oz (¼ cup) curing juice from
  the herring

Preheat the oven to 130°C/200°F/Gas Mark ½.

Arrange the herring fillets on a small ovenproof serving platter and heat in the oven for 3–4 minutes. This should just warm them up to about body temperature. Another way of achieving this is to preheat the serving platter in the oven to about 50°C/120°F and then place the fish on the platter a couple of minutes before serving it.

Follow the instructions on page 662 for browning the butter.

While the butter is browning, scatter the chopped eggs onto the herring fillets, followed by the onion and the dill, and pour on the curing juice.

Pour the foaming browned butter onto the fish – it should be sizzling hot – and serve straight away. The butter and curing liquid should meld with the other garnishes to create a delicious sauce.

ANN-CHARLOTTE'S KIPPER CASSEROLE

Ann-Charlottes böcklinglåda (Sweden)

This is a recipe I got from Ann-Charlotte Brummer, my boss at Fäviken. It is commonly served for Christmas and one of the most fantastic things you can do with it is to enjoy it straight from the fridge on a piece of Rye Crispbread (page 516) with an ice cold hoppy lager next to it.

Preparation and cooking time: 10 minutes
Serves: 4

3 kippers, skinned, gutted, cleaned and
  filleted
150 ml/5 fl oz (⅔ cup) cream
1 tablespoon Cured Cod's Roe Spread
  (page 672), preferably un-smoked

Preheat the oven to 250°C/480°F/Gas Mark 9.

Place the kipper fillets in a single layer in a small ovenproof dish. They should fit in snugly without much space between them.

Mix the cream with the cured cod's roe spread in a mixing bowl then pour it over the kippers.

Bake for a couple of minutes, or until golden on the surface.

MARINATED SMOKED HERRING

Marinerad böckling (Sweden)

These are very nice on a piece of buttered Rye Crispbread (page 516) with some mature hard cheese on the side.

Preparation time: 10 minutes
Marinating time: at least 2 hours
Serves: 4 as a starter (appetizer), or many
 more if it is part of a bigger menu

2 whole smoked Atlantic herrings or
 4 whole smoked Baltic herrings
2 tablespoons *Ättika* (12%) vinegar (page 656)
2 tablespoons neutral/flavourless oil
1 small red onion, finely chopped
1 teaspoon coarse, unsweetened mustard
1 tablespoon capers, finely chopped
1 handful parsley leaves, finely chopped

Fillet the herrings carefully, making sure you remove all of the bones. Arrange the herrings in a single layer on a serving platter or tray.

Mix all the remaining ingredients together to make a sauce and spoon it over the herring. Leave to marinate for at least a couple of hours.

JANSSON'S TEMPTATION, SWEDISH POTATO AND SPRAT CASSEROLE

Janssonin kiusaua (Finland)
Janssons frestelse (Sweden)

There are conflicting stories in Sweden about the origins of this dish. Some think that it was named after a Swedish opera singer named Pelle Janzon, and others that it was named after a 1928 Swedish film called *Janssons Frestelse*. Regardless, this salty-sweet and fantastic dish is probably the greatest thing you could ever eat, together with a well-hopped, ice-cold pilsner and a side of Aquavit (page 714). Jansson's Temptation is often served as a late-night snack towards the end of a party or as a part of a traditional festive meal. It is probably one of my top five traditional Swedish dishes.

I like to use filleted sprats and their pickling juice in the dish itself and finish it by garnishing it with whole sprats after the cooking. Many recipes suggest placing knobs of butter on top of the whole thing to melt into the breadcrumbs. I don't like this as those crumbs get soaked enough in butterfat from the cream, and the additional butter just makes the whole dish greasier than it should be.

Preparation and cooking time: 1 hour
Serves: 4

4–6 waxy potatoes, cut into thin strips
2 onions, thinly sliced
10 sprat fillets, cured in sandalwood
 (see right), rinsed and dried
 (reserve the pickling liquid)
300–400 ml/10½–14 fl oz (1¼–1⅔ cups)
 cream
breadcrumbs, for sprinkling
6 whole sprats, to garnish
white pepper, to taste

Preheat the oven to 180°C/350°F/Gas Mark 4.

Combine the potato, onion and sprat fillets (whole or chopped, whichever you prefer) in an ovenproof dish and season with pepper. Mix in the reserved pickling liquid, the quantity depends on how strong a flavour you want, and flatten the surface. (The liquid is quite salty, so you probably won't need to add any salt.) Pour in cream until the surface is almost covered, then sprinkle on a generous layer of breadcrumbs.

Bake until the potatoes are soft and the crumbs are golden. If it looks dry towards the end of the cooking time, you can always add a little more cream during the last 5 minutes in the oven. Garnish with the whole sprats before serving.

For image see page 125

SPRATS CURED IN SANDALWOOD

Swedish Ansjovis (Sweden)

If you can't get hold of saltpetre, substitute part of the salt with a nitrite product according to the instructions on the bag of the particular brand. (See also page 434.) This is a precautionary measure to avoid the growth of *Clostridium botulinum,* which can cause botulism.

Preparation and cooking time: 1 hour
Maturing time: at least 6 months
Makes: 5 kg/11 lb sprat fillets

10 kg/22 lb sprats, gutted, cleaned and
  filleted, head left on, gills removed
150 ml/5 fl oz (⅔ cup) *Ättika* (24%) vinegar
  (page 656)

For the curing mixture
750 g/1 lb 10 oz coarse, iodine-free sea salt
2 kg/4½ lb (10 cups) sugar
100 g/3½ oz fresh ginger, sliced
50 g/2 oz allspice berries, crushed
50 g/2 oz black peppercorns, crushed
50 g/2 oz sandalwood dust
50 g/2 oz dried oregano
50 g/2 oz dried bitter orange peel
35 g/1¼ oz saltpetre
25 g/1 oz fennel seed
25 g/1 oz cloves, crushed
10 bay leaves

For the extra brine
1 litre/34 fl oz (4¼ cups) water
100 g/3½ oz (⅓ cup) salt
200 g/7 oz (1 cup) sugar

Place the sprats in a clean, large stainless-steel bucket (or some other suitable container). Stir the vinegar into 1.5 litres/2½ UK pints (6¼ cups) water then pour it over the sprats. Shake the bucket a bit so that the marinade really reaches all the sprats properly. Leave in a cold place overnight.

Combine the curing mixture ingredients in a large bowl. Spread a 1 cm/1½ inch layer of the mixture on the bottom of a clean stainless-steel, glazed ceramic or glass container. It should be large enough to contain all the sprats fairly snugly. It's better to use a tall narrow container (rather than a shallow wide one) since there will be less oxidation and evaporation from a smaller surface area. Something similar in shape to a wine barrel or bucket is about right.

Take the sprats out of the vinegar solution, one by one, and arrange them in a layer on top of the curing mixture in the container. They should be packed together tightly, with the open chest cavities facing upwards, to decrease the risk of air pockets and spoilage. Sprinkle more of the curing mixture onto the first layer of sprats. Continue layering sprats and curing mixture until all the sprats are packed in tightly. Finally, sprinkle a good layer of the curing mixture on top.

Weight the sprats down with something clean, flat and heavy. Leave at room temperature for 24 hours to encourage some lactobacillus fermentation. During the first 24 hours enough moisture should have been drawn out of the fish to form a liquid brine that covers them completely. If this is not the case, then make the extra brine to top it up. Combine the ingredients in a large pan and bring to the boil. Remove from the heat and leave to cool completely. Pour on enough to cover the sprats completely.

Leave the sprats in a cool place to mature for at least 6 months.

SALAD OF SPRATS CURED IN SANDALWOOD, AND EGG

Gubbröra (Sweden)

The name means 'old man's mess' or 'mix' and I have actually not been able to find out why it is called what it is called. It is a dish that suits an old man though; and in a good way. It's salty, sweet and subtly creamy – excellent with a well-hopped pilsner and a glass of Aquavit (page 714). I have decided to stick to this as an explanation for the strange name until evidence can be found that contradicts me.

In many recent recipes for *gubbröra* you can find the addition of things like crème fraîche or mayonnaise. This is probably delicious for those greedy people who aren't satisfied with the subtle, ascetic creaminess of raw egg yolks and who want more from life. That's fine for them, but to call it *gubbröra* is not fine. I have even seen a few recipes lately that contain boiled potatoes; I am not even going to get started on my feelings about that.

I like to eat *gubbröra* on hard rye sourdough or on dark Scanian Rye Bread (page 502), but I have seen it on menus now and then, served with toast.

Preparation and cooking time: 20 minutes
Serves: 4 as a starter (appetizer) or light
*   meal, possibly after midnight, when you*
*   have had a few beers*

4 Hard-boiled Eggs (page 53),
   chopped
2 egg yolks
2 tablespoons salted (not smoked) Cured
   Cod's Roe Spread (page 672)
6 Sprats Cured in Sandalwood
   (page 212)
finely chopped parsley, dill
   and chives, to taste

Place all the ingredients in a bowl. Mix everything together carefully, and in a loving way, without breaking up the egg yolks too much. It is good if there are some pieces of unseasoned egg and some streaks of salty cod's roe to provide contrast to the salad.

SALAD OF SPRATS CURED IN SANDALWOOD

Solöga / Fågelbo (Sweden)

This salad of sprats cured in sandalwood (*ansjovis*, page 212) is mostly served in Sweden as a starter (appetizer) or as a light course for lunch. I like it with Rye Crispbread (page 516) and perhaps some mature hard cheese on the side. Some people prefer it with bread fried in butter. It is a dish that is also very suitable as a late night-time snack after drinking a few beers.

The names for this dish mean 'eye of the sun' (*solöga*) and 'bird's nest' (*fågelbo*), and refer to the shape, which should be plated in widening circles, starting with the egg yolk in the middle, and finishing with the chopped beetroot (beets) as the outer layer of the nest. Imagine a circled target at a shooting range; in this case the egg yolk will be the bull's eye. It is not traditionally part of the recipe, but I also like to include a smaller ring of finely snipped chives.

Preparation time: 15 minutes
Serves: 4

4 egg yolks
125 g/4½ oz Sprats cured in sandalwood
   (page 212), chopped
1 bunch chives, finely snipped with a very
   sharp knife or scissors
2 onions, finely chopped
6 tablespoons capers, chopped
2 Pickled Beetroot (page 660), cut into
   small dice
black pepper, to taste (optional)

Start by making 4 fairly flat round mounds of the sprats on 4 separate plates. Make a small pit in the middle of each mound where an egg yolk can rest later. Continue to arrange the other garnishes in rings around the sprats, finishing with the beetroot (beets). Place the yolk in the centre and season with a little black pepper, if you like it.

For image see page 209

SALMON CURED IN SALT

Speket laks (Norway)
Saltet laks (Denmark)
Rimmad lax (Sweden)

This is prepared in a similar way to Gravlax (page 216), but contains less sugar than gravlax (or none at all) and it is not flavoured with dill or white pepper during the cure.

Salmon cured in salt considered typical summertime food, delicious when served on a warm summer day in thin slices with lemon wedges, and accompanied by creamed potatoes that are flavoured with a generous amount of dill. A twist of white pepper over the salmon as you serve it is a good idea.

Include the sugar if you want a softer cure and use salt on its own if you want a firmer, denser cure.

Preparation time: 30 minutes
Curing time: 2 days
Serves: 4 as a main course and more
 if it is part of a larger meal

1 kg/2¼ lb salmon fillet, skin on, scales
 removed, pin bones removed
120 g/4 oz (⅓ cup plus 1 tablespoon) salt
40 g/1½ oz (2½ tablespoons) sugar (optional)
white pepper, to taste

Follow the instructions on page 190 for curing fish with salt and sugar.

I like to cure the salmon for about 24 hours before washing off the curing mix. I then like to leave it for another 24 hours before eating, so that the cure can even out a bit in the fish itself.

If I don't serve this in the traditional way, then I like to accompany the fish with a sauce made from the cooking butter with a bit of lemon juice added at the end and then serve it with some kind of green vegetable, perhaps Steamed Broccoli (page 82).

Preparation and cooking time: 10 minutes
Soaking time: overnight
Serves: 4

500 g/1 lb 2 oz Salmon Cured in Salt
 (see left)
plain (all-purpose) flour, to coat
1 egg, beaten lightly
breadcrumbs, to coat
butter, for frying
salt and white pepper, to taste

Cut the fillet into 4 pieces, then pat them dry with a clean cloth.

Place the flour, beaten egg and breadcrumbs into 3 separate wide, shallow bowls. Coat the fish pieces all over with flour, dip them into the beaten egg and then into the breadcrumbs.

Heat a generous amount of butter in a pan over a medium–high heat. Fry the fish pieces until they are a good golden-brown before turning and cooking on the other side. Lower the heat when the colour is good to allow the salmon to cook through without becoming dark brown.

Finish by seasoning with white pepper while the fish is still in the pan. Salt is usually unnecessary as the fish itself is salty, however this is a matter of personal preference.

BREADED AND FRIED SALT SALMON

Griljerad rimmad laxrygg (Sweden)

For this recipe, Salmon Cured in Salt (see left) is used. It is often served with Boiled Potatoes (page 117) and a Sweet-and-Sour Currant Sauce (page 669).

GRAVLAX

Gravlaks (Norway)
Graavilohi (Finland)
Gravad laks (Denmark)
Gravlax (Sweden)

Few things – except the Swedish chef from *The Muppets Show* and the *smörgåsbord*, of which this dish is an indispensible part – are so associated with Sweden and Swedish cooking as gravlax. It's enjoyed in many ways, but the favourites are either as a standalone dish, with lemon wedges and a warm side like Creamed Potatoes with Dill (page 118), or in very thin slices as part of a festive buffet, such as the Julbord Christmas dinner, with Sweet-and-Strong Mustard Sauce for Cured Fish (page 664). Leftover gravlax is excellent in Salmon and Potato Pudding (page 219).

The name of the dish itself comes from the Swedish word meaning 'to bury'. This refers back to the original gravlax, which was just salted and buried in the ground to ferment before being eaten, a technique similar to Norwegian *rakfisk* (page 175).

The use of white pepper and dill as aromatics, which is completely dominating gravlax recipes today, started in the eighteenth century, but before that the fish was probably not seasoned at all, except by the cure itself.

Preparation time: 20 minutes
Curing time: 2 days
Serves: 4 as a stand-alone dish,

1 x 1-kg/2¼-lb salmon fillet, skin on, pin
    bones removed and patted dry
4 tablespoons salt
4 tablespoons sugar
20 white peppercorns, coarsely crushed
1 bunch dill, stalks and fronds separated

Cure according to the method on page 190, curing fish with salt and sugar.

I like to cure the salmon for about 24 hours before washing off the cure mix. I then like to leave it for another 24 hours after the cure is washed off, before eating, so that the cure can even out in the fish.

For image see opposite page

SEARED GRAVLAX

Stegt gravad laks (Denmark)
Bräckt gravlax (Sweden)

The skin of cured salmon (if descaled before the curing process) can be cut into thick slices and fried crisp in some butter and used as a garnish.

Serve seared gravlax with Sweet-and-Strong Mustard Sauce (page 664) and Boiled Potatoes (page 117) or with eggs, scrambled, boiled or cooked in whatever way you prefer them (pages 52–53). These days it isn't uncommon to see seared gravlax with a wedge of lemon as an additional garnish. This is not traditional but it is very tasty.

Preparation and cooking time: 15 minutes
Serves: 4

600 g/1 lb 5 oz Gravlax (see left) cut into 2
    cm-/¾ inch-thick slices, skin removed and
    cut into strips (optional)
butter, for frying the skin (optional)

Heat a cast-iron pan until extremely hot and sear the gravlax slices for a couple of seconds on each side and serve immediately.

If you want the crispy skin to go with the gravlax, then remove the pan from the heat when you are done cooking the salmon and add the strips of skin along with a couple of tablespoons of butter. The residual heat will cook the skin until crisp and golden, then rest the strips for a few seconds on paper towels to soak up any excess fat before serving.

Cockwise from top left: cold-smoked salmon; Gravlax (page 216); Poached Trout, Served Cold (page 163); Dill Mayonnaise (page 674); Sweet-and-Strong Mustard Sauce for Cured Fish (page 664)

HOT-SMOKED SALMON FINS

Rökta laxfenor (Sweden)

Hot-smoked salmon fins are quite commonly found at fish counters in the Scandinavian countries. You do not eat the actual fin but, rather, the fleshy and fatty parts by which it is attached to the body of the fish.

The fins can be eaten as a snack with a beer – perhaps outside a sauna – or even as part of a meal. I like to warm them briefly in the oven so that the fat begins to melt a bit. If I serve them as part of a meal I like them with Mashed Potatoes (page 118), something green, like Spinach Salad (page 87) and a wedge of lemon or white vinegar.

POACHED AND PICKLED SALMON, SERVED COLD

Pocheret syltet laks (Denmark)
Kall inkokt lax (Sweden)

This is a real summer dish, often served with Boiled Potatoes (page 117), Dill Mayonnaise (page 674) and Quick Pickled Cucumber (page 658). The pickled vegetables are delicious and should also be served with the fish. The salmon is not pickled in the sense that herrings are pickled and won't keep for very long but should be eaten within a week if stored in the refrigerator.

In a restaurant, where you would fillet a whole salmon to make this dish, it's a good idea to cook the salmon bones and head together with the pickling liquor. If you do so, it will produce a light and very delicious jelly when it cools down. If you decide to try this at home, then add the bones, head and any salmon scraps you have to the pickling liquor, but leave out the vegetables. Bring it slowly to a simmer, then let it sit for 5 minutes before proceeding as described below. If you like the idea of the jelly, but you have no fish bones, then add 2 leaves of gelatine per 1 litre/34 fl oz (4¼ cups) of finished pickling syrup.

Preparation and cooking time: 30 minutes
Pickling time: overnight
Serves: 4

800 g/1¾ lb salmon fillet, cut into
  4 pieces
50 g/2 oz (¼ cup) sugar
2 tablespoons salt
100 ml/3½ fl oz (⅓ cup plus 1 tablespoon)
  red wine vinegar
100 ml/3½ fl oz (⅓ cup plus 1 tablespoon)
  Ättika (12%) vinegar (page 656)
2 carrots, cut into 5 mm/¼ inch slices
1 red onion, thinly sliced
1 small fennel bulb, sliced
1 celery stalk, chopped
1 sprig thyme
2 bay leaves
12 white peppercorns
1 handful parsley stalks

Place the salmon pieces in a pot and keep at room temperature to warm up slightly.

Pour 2 litres/3½ UK pints (8¼ cups) water into another pot and add the sugar, salt and vinegars. (Remember that it needs to be saltier than you would think because it is supposed to season the salmon. 2 tablespoons fine salt could be a starting point point but you will have to taste your way forward.) Bring to the boil, then add the vegetables and aromatics and continue boiling for 1 minute. Pour the pickling liquor over the pieces of salmon in the other pot and leave to cool to room temperature.

Refrigerate the salmon in the pickling liquor overnight. Serve the salmon cold.

SALMON POACHED ON THE BONE

Kokt laks (Norway)
Kogt laks (Denmark)
Kokt lax (Sweden)

Serve with Boiled Potatoes (page 117) and Hollandaise sauce or melted butter and a perhaps a wedge of lemon. I also like to serve spinach with oily fish like salmon, either steamed (page 87) or perhaps in a salad (page 87).

Preparation and cooking time: 30 minutes
Sitting time: 20–30 minutes
Serves: 4

1 x 1.5-kg/3¼-lb piece salmon, cut straight
   across the fish, still on the bone
For the stock (broth)
75 ml/2½ fl oz (⅓ cup) *Ättika* (12%) vinegar
   (page 656)
1 carrot, sliced
1 small onion, studded with 2 cloves
1 small fennel bulb, cut into pieces
1 celery stick, chopped
1 sprig thyme
1 bay leaf
1 handful parsley stalks

For the stock (broth), combine all the vegetables and aromatics in a pot, which is also large enough to fit the fish. Add enough water to later cover the fish and bring to the boil. Leave the stock to cool down a bit before adding the fish to the pot. Add more water until the fish is just covered. Bring to a slow simmer and then remove the pot from the stove and leave it to sit for 20–30 minutes, or until the fish is cooked, before transferring it to a serving platter. I like oily fish like salmon to be a little bit underdone and to barely come off the bone. But that is a matter of personal taste.

Carefully lift the fish out of the poaching liquid and place on a serving platter to serve.

SALMON AND POTATO PUDDING

Lohilaatikko (Finland)
Laksepudding (Denmark)
Laxpudding (Sweden)

This dish makes excellent use of leftover cured salmon and leftover Boiled Potatoes (page 117). It is delicious served with melted butter and lemon wedges.

If you don't have any leftover potatoes, then you can also use raw potatoes. After peeling, just cut them a bit thinner and then leave the bake in the oven until they are cooked tender – perhaps 15 minutes longer than the version using cooked potatoes.

Often a generous amount of dill is added between the layers of salmon, but I prefer to add my dill on top of the cooked dish just before it is eaten instead.

Preparation and cooking time: 1¼ hours
Serves: 4

200 g/7 oz Gravlax (page 217), thinly sliced
   or cut into pieces
800 g/1¾ lb Boiled Potatoes (page 117),
   peeled and cut into 5 mm/
   ¼ inch slices
2 eggs
500 ml/17 fl oz (2 cups plus 1 tablespoon)
   milk
1 good bunch dill, fronds finely chopped
salt and white pepper, to taste

Preheat the oven to 225°C/435°F/Gas Mark 7.

Layer the salmon and potato in an ovenproof dish, starting and finishing with potato. Season each layer with salt and pepper (and dill, if you want to), but be careful with the salt as the salmon is usually quite salty already.

Mix the eggs and the milk and season with salt and pepper before pouring it over the potatoes and fish. Make sure it covers them completely. Finish with a sprinkling of dill, then bake in the oven until it has set and is a golden colour.

Serve with a sprinkling of dill on top.

SALMON GRILLED OVER JUNIPER BRANCHES

Lax på enrisbädd (Sweden)

We sat down for dinner at my grandparents' house on the farm and my aunt Märit was cooking. It was 1989 and my family was just about to eat our first salmon cooked on a bed of charred, still smouldering juniper branches. The twigs and their needles were all still intact, but jet black as opposed to forest green, contrasting brightly with the orange flesh of the fish.

I remember it so vividly. It was the first time I realized that food was more than just the obvious, more than just the smells and flavours we are used to. I realized that food was not just about being edible: it was about stimulating all the senses, smell, flavour and aesthetics and so much more. It was about evoking emotions.

I could feel already from my seat by the table that there was something going on, something new and unexpected. Grandpa, a conservative man when it came to what he ate, twisted anxiously in his chair. Grandma looked a bit nervous – I think she might have gone out for a smoke on the patio to cope. Märit opened the oven door and a cloud of blue smoke billowed out into the room. The air tingled with the smell of the forest – but not damp forest, warm, coniferous forest in the autumn (fall) – and the smell of my dad making a fire to boil some coffee. Strangely enough, it also smelled of cooking fish. It brought up so many memories; happy memories.

We ate the salmon with Boiled Potatoes (page 117), lemon wedges and a sauce made with sour cream and lumpfish roe (page 226). It was delicious.

See *Luad ål* (page 160), for a cultural analysis as to where this mystery dish might have originated.

To make this dish at home, you will need enough fresh juniper branches to thickly cover the bottom of a roasting pan so you can't see it any more.

Preparation and cooking time: 30 minutes
Serves: 4

1 kg/2¼ lb salmon fillet, skin on, scales
  removed, pin bones removed
salt, to taste

Preheat the oven to 220°C/425°F/Gas Mark 7 and spread the juniper branches in a thick layer on the bottom of a roasting pan.

Place the salmon on top of the branches and season the flesh side with salt. You'll probably need more than you think, as it is a big piece of fish. Let the salt dissolve for a few minutes then put the salmon in the oven.

Roast the salmon until the branches are completely blackened. I like my salmon medium-rare, which will take about 10 minutes, but if you want it cooked more, cook it for 15 minutes instead. Remove it from the oven and leave it to rest for a bit before serving.

SALMON SOUP

Laksesuppe (Norway)
Lohikeitto (Finland)
Laksesuppe (Denmark)
Laxsoppa (Sweden)

This is a preparation eaten in many of the Nordic countries. However, it is in Finland where the soup is most common and cherished.

There is an on-going, sometimes rather heated, debate as to whether the soup should contain cream or not; about half the recipes I have collected do and the other half don't. The recipe below uses some cream but, if you want to be more ascetic, it can be omitted – although you might then have to add more water.

Serve with slices of Finnish Rye Bread (page 504) and butter.

Preparation and cooking time: 30 minutes
Serves: 4

8 firm potatoes, cut into 5 mm/¼ inch slices
  or 2 cm/¾ inch cubes
2 carrots, cut into 5 mm/¼ inch slices

2 onions, cut into wedges
2 bay leaves
10 allspice berries or black peppercorns
   (your choice), ground
300 ml/10½ fl oz (1¼ cups) cream
500 g/1 lb 2 oz salmon fillet, cut into
   2.5 cm/1 inch cubes
salt, to taste
1 bunch dill, fronds picked and stalks
   finely cut, for sprinkling

Put all the vegetables and aromatics into a large pot and add enough water to cover them completely. Bring to the boil, then simmer for 10 minutes. Add the cream and adjust the level of salt. Continue simmering until the potatoes are almost done, then add the salmon to the pot. Taste and adjust the seasoning one last time, then remove the pot from the heat and leave the salmon to sit in the hot liquid for a few minutes until just done. You mustn't stir the soup any more after adding the salmon.

Sprinkle the dill over the soup just before serving.

SEARED FRESH SALMON

Stekt laks (Norway)
Stegt laks (Denmark)
Bräckt lax (Sweden)

Serve with Riced Potatoes (page 117) and perhaps some of your favourite green vegetables and a lemon wedge. The frying butter will become infused with flavour from the salmon, pepper and browned flour, making a fantastic sauce. Some people add chopped capers and a bit more butter to the pan once the fish is cooked.

Traditionally butter is added to the pan for frying, but I prefer to gently brush each slice of salmon all over with a very small amount of soft butter instead. This is a good way of making sure that the butter ends up where you want it – in contact with the fish itself, and not flowing around in the pan and burning.

Preparation and cooking time: 20 minutes
Serves: 4

1 x 600-g/1 lb 5-oz salmon, cut into 2 cm/
   ¾ inch thick slices
plain (all-purpose flour), to coat
4 tablespoons butter, very soft
juice of ½ lemon
capers, chopped (optional)
salt and black pepper, to taste

Pat the salmon pieces thoroughly dry. Season with salt and pepper then turn them in flour to coat evenly. Brush the fish pieces on both sides with just a little of the softened butter. Reserve the rest for later.

Heat a pan until really hot. If you have brushed the butter onto the salmon, then it isn't necessary to add more to the pan. But if you prefer the more traditional approach, then instead of buttering the fish itself, add just enough butter to lightly cover the bottom of the pan.

Sear the salmon slices for a few seconds on each side then transfer them to a warm serving platter. They should be gently browned and still raw in the middle. Remove the pan from the heat and add the rest of the butter, whisking as it browns. As it stops foaming, add the lemon juice and the capers, if using. Wait for a few seconds then pour the foaming sauce over the salmon on the serving platter.

FINNISH SALMON PIE

Lohipiirakka (Finland)

Any cooked salmon can be used in this recipe, but I advise against using any sort of smoked salmon because I find they are often a bit too salty and strongly flavoured. However, many recipes that can be found on the internet and in modern recipe books are based on hot-smoked salmon. I would assume this is because it is readily available and more convenient than cooking a piece of raw salmon yourself, just for this dish. *Lohipiirakka* is an excellent thing to make from other oily fish, such as trout, char, or even mackerel. But then of course it stops being a *lohipiirakka* – lohi means 'salmon' – and turns into something else.

You can make this fish pie using leftovers from a meal of salmon or another oily fish. Aside from the fish, the filling most often contains hard-boiled eggs and rice, although sometimes the rice is omitted. Dill is a common and traditional seasoning, but more recent recipes can also contain things like sundried tomatoes, cheese and garlic. Modern recipes sometimes also substitute the traditional pastry containing potato with readymade, frozen puff pastry.

Sometimes the *lohipiirakka* is baked in the shape of a fish, but most often in a rectangle.

Preparation and cooking time: 1 hour
Resting time: 1–2 hours
Serves: 4

For the pastry
250 g/9 oz potatoes, boiled, cooled and
  pushed through a ricer
250 g/9 oz (2¼ cups) plain (all-purpose) flour
250 g/9 oz (18 tablespoons) butter, softened
pinch of salt

For the egg wash
1 egg
50 ml/2 fl oz (3½ tablespoons) milk

For the filling
220 g/7¾ oz (1 cup) short-grain rice
600 g/1 lb 5 oz cooked salmon
4 Hard-boiled Eggs (page 53), chopped
1 onion, chopped

1 bunch dill, fronds picked and coarsely
  chopped
salt and white pepper, to taste

Cook the rice following the instructions on the packet. Once cooked, leave to cool to room temperature.

To make the pastry, combine the potato, flour, butter and 1 tablespoon cold water in a food processor and pulse until just combined. Wrap in clingfilm (plastic wrap) and leave to rest in the fridge for 1–2 hours.

Preheat the oven to 180°C/350°F/Gas Mark 4. Line a baking sheet with baking (parchment) paper.

Divide the pastry into 2 pieces and roll each one into a rectangular sheet, about 3 mm/⅛ inch thick. Place the first sheet on the prepared baking sheet. Spread half the cooled rice over the pastry, leaving a border of about 3 cm/1¼ inches around the edge, so you can seal it with the top piece later on. Arrange pieces of salmon and egg over the rice, then add the onion and dill and season with salt and pepper. Top with the rest of the rice, then place the second sheet of pastry on top and pinch the edges together with your fingers.

Whisk the egg and milk together. Brush the surface of the *lohipiirakka* lightly with the egg wash. Cook until golden brown.

HOW TO FILLET AND SKIN A FLAT FISH

When filleting or skinning fish, keep the knife clean and sharp for a much cleaner and safer cut. Use long sweeping strokes. Flat fish are generally easier to fillet than round fish and are a good fish to practise your filleting technique.

Trim the fish by removing the fins with sharp scissors. Cut around the head with a knife and discard.

Place the fish on a chopping (cutting) board with the dark side facing up. Slip the tip of your knife into the fillet just above the main bone and close to the central backbone, sliding the knife out to the side to release the fillet at the fin.

Turn the fish so that the bones are facing towards you. Cutting away from you, run the tip of the knife over the backbone and along the bones on the other side to release the fillet.

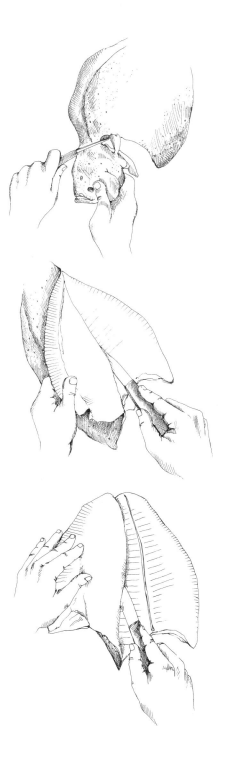

FRIED, BREADED PLAICE

Skarkol i (Iceland)
Stekt/panert rødspette (Norway)
Stegt Rødspættefilet (Denmark)
Stekt rödspättafilet (Sweden)

Serve with Mashed Potatoes (page 118) or Boiled Potatoes (page 117), with a wedge of lemon or some remoulade sauce. Or serve it on top of a Danish open-faced sandwich, *Stjerneskud* (page 522).

Preparation and cooking time: 20 minutes
Serves: 4

500 g/1 lb 2 oz fillet of plaice
butter, for frying
salt and white pepper, to taste

Follow the method for Whole Fish, Fried in a Pan (page 155), version 3, Breaded.

FISH BALLS

Fiskeboller (Norway)
Fiskeboller (Denmark)
Fiskbullar (Sweden)

Serve with a fish Velouté (page 652), Curry Cream Sauce (page 665) or just as they are. I like this childhood favourite with Boiled Potatoes (page 117) and some Green Peas (page 136) or Boiled Carrots (page 110).

If you are making a velouté and you have some fish stock prepared for that, you might as well cook the fish balls in the stock also. If you don't have fish stock, cook them in lightly salted water and add that to the sauce instead of stock.

Preparation and cooking time: 45 minutes
Serves: 4

500 g/1 lb 2 oz white fish, such as cod, saithe, pollock or something similar
1 tablespoon potato starch
1 egg white
50 ml/2 fl oz (3½ tablespoons) milk
salt and white pepper, to taste
some freshly grated nutmeg, if you like that

Mince (grind) your chosen fish on the fine plate of your mincer (grinder), twice.

Mix the minced (ground) fish and quite a bit of salt in the bowl of a stand mixer for a couple of minutes on medium speed. Add the remaining ingredients and season well. Stir for another couple of minutes to make sure everything is well mixed.

Bring your chosen cooking liquid to a simmer in a pot and cook a small piece of fish mixture. Taste it and adjust the seasoning if necessary.

Shape the fish mixture with clean, wet hands into balls the size of a walnut and as you finish them, drop them straight into the simmering liquid. Let them cook for about 20 minutes, then lift them out with a slotted spoon.

If you are using the cooking liquid to make a sauce, keep the balls warm in an ovenproof dish covered with a lid. If not, serve them straight away.

FAROESE BOILED FISH BALLS

Knetti (Faroe Islands)

Knetti can be served in Faroese Fish Ball Soup (see below) or with Boiled Potatoes (page 117).

Preparation and cooking time: 40 minutes
Serves: 4

1 kg/2¼ lb white fish, such as cod, haddock, saithe or pollock (use fillet, trimmings or scraps of clean white flesh)
1 onion, finely chopped
1 tablespoon potato starch
1 teaspoon sugar
200 g/7 oz sheep's suet, cut into small dice
salt and white pepper, to taste

Push the fish through a meat mincer (grinder) twice. Place in a bowl with the onion, potato starch, and sugar and add 125 ml/4 fl oz (½ cup) water. Season with salt and pepper and mix everything together well. Mix in the suet thoroughly, but without breaking the pieces too much. Shape into fairly large balls with clean, wet hands.

Bring 1.2 litres/40 fl oz (5 cups) water to a simmer in a large pot. Salt the water, then carefully drop in the fish balls and cook until they are cooked all the way through.

FAROESE FISH BALL SOUP

Knettnasupan (Faroe Islands)

This soup is usually slightly sweet and sour from the prunes and vinegar. Sometimes it is thickened with a little flour or potato starch, and sometimes not.

Preparation and cooking time: 20 minutes
Serves: 4

1 quantity Faroese Boiled Fish Balls (see above) together with the poaching liquid from the fish balls
1 quantity Beurre Manié (page 651), to thicken (optional)

2 carrots, thinly sliced
100 g/3½ oz (¾ cup) green peas
10 pitted prunes
sugar, white vinegar and salt, to taste

Follow the recipe on the opposite page to prepare and cook the fish balls. Once cooked, remove the fish balls from the poaching liquid and keep them on a warm plate.

Bring the poaching liquid back to a simmer. Add the beurre manie if you want a thicker soup.

Once the soup is of the desired consistency, add the carrot and prunes and season to your liking with sugar, vinegar and salt. Simmer until the carrots are just tender. Return the fish balls to the soup and simmer for another minute or so before serving.

NORWEGIAN FISH CAKES

Fiskekaker (Norway)

One of the most iconic Norwegian everyday dishes, this very finely minced (ground), fluffy patty of fish is often served with Brown Gravy (page 671), Boiled Potatoes (page 117) and some slices of Fried Salt Pork (page 302).

Fiskekaker can be made from almost any kind of fish and its name is just added in front. A cake made from saithe, is a 'saithecake', one from cod is a 'codcake' and so on.

I have come across more than one recipe that uses a bit of baking powder in the batter for extra fluffiness. If you want to try this in the recipe below, add 1 tablespoon together with the potato starch.

Fishcakes can also contain onion. If you want that, finely chop and sauté one onion in a little butter (without colouration) for the quantity below. Let it cool completely before adding it to the mix.

It is very important that the fish is really cold before you start working on this recipe, otherwise the batter might split. It might even be a good idea to chill the bowl of the food processor too, because a lot of friction heat tends to develop when making preparations like this in a food processor.

Preparation and cooking time: 45 minutes
Serves: 4

600 g/1 lb 5 oz fillet of fish, like saithe or cod
2 teaspoons salt
2 tablespoons potato starch
200 ml/7 fl oz (¾ cups plus 1 tablespoon) cream
butter, for frying
salt and white pepper, to taste

Mince (grind) the fish on the fine plate of a mincer (grinder), twice. Place the minced (ground) fish in the bowl of a food processor with the salt, potato starch and some pepper. Blitz for about 30 seconds on full speed, then pour in the cream with the motor still at full speed in a steady stream for about another 30 seconds. Turn the mixer off.

Fry a bit of the fish mixture in a buttered pan over a medium heat, and taste it to check the seasoning and adjust if necessary. Spoon patties of the fish mixture into the pan and fry on both sides until golden and cooked through.

DANISH FISH CAKES

Fiskefrikadeller (Denmark)

In Denmark fishcakes are often a little bit coarser than in Norway and they are often served with remoulade sauce and some Danish Rye Bread (page 504), or with Boiled Potatoes (page 117).

Fiskefrikadeller has historically always been made from white fish like cod or pollock but today salmon is also quite a popular choice.

Preparation and cooking time: 45 minutes
Serves: 4

500 g/1 lb 2 oz minced (ground) fillet
   of fish, like cod, pollock or salmon
2 tablespoons plain (all-purpose) flour,
   potato starch or breadcrumbs
150 ml/5 fl oz (⅔ cup) cream
1 egg
1 onion, finely chopped
salt and white pepper, to taste

Mix all of the ingredients in the bowl of a stand mixer and work it until it has come together and started to firm up. It is important to add as much of the intended salt as you dare from the start to achieve a good firm texture. I would add 2 teaspoons at the start.

Fry a little piece of the mixture in a buttered pan over a medium heat, taste it and adjust the seasoning if necessary.

Shape the rest of the mixture into patties with a big spoon and fry them in the buttered pan until golden on both sides.

LUMPFISH
(*CYCLOPTERUS LUMPUS*)

The female lumpfish, which during spawning season in winter and early spring can carry up to 350,000 eggs, is mainly fished to harvest those eggs. The male though is used in cooking for its firmer flesh. A large lumpfish can exceed 50 cm (20 inches) in length and weigh up to 7.5 kg/ 16 lb 8 oz. Lumpfish and lumpfish roe is eaten in all of the Scandinavian countries but is an especially cherished seasonal delicacy in Denmark. Stenbiderrogn, which is the Danish name for the eggs, is often served as a topping on a slice of bread as an open-faced *smørebrød* sandwich (page 522) or as a part of other dishes.

POACHED TURBOT

Pocheret pighvar (Denmark)
Piggvar kokt i bit (Sweden)

Few things are as tasty as a thick piece of turbot, poached still on the bone, served simply with a big stack of grated horseradish, some melted butter and a couple of Boiled Potatoes (page 117). I like it with Steamed Broccoli (page 82) on the side too, and maybe a wedge of lemon or a drizzle of *Ättika* (12 %) vinegar (page 656).

The portion size below might look large but flat fish on the bone is not something you eat in small portions. It doesn't cook as well as a big piece and you have to remember that 50% of the raw weight will disappear before you have it in your mouth. This is partially from the cooking but mostly from the bones and skin, which you have to remove on the plate.

The amount of salt stated below might also seem excessive but for a big piece like this, on the bone, it is simply delicious and not too much at all.

The amount of water required is entirely dependent on the size of your pot. There needs to be enough water to later cover the fish.

Preparation and cooking time: 40 minutes
Serves: 4

1.2 kg/2½ lb turbot, cut into 4 thick pieces
50 g/2 oz (¼ cup) salt per 1 litre/34 fl oz
   (4¼ cups) water used for the cooking

Bring water and salt to the boil in a big pot, take it off the heat and put in the pieces of fish. Cover with a lid and wait for about 10 minutes. With a slotted spoon, carefully lift a piece up to the surface and touch it with your hand. Is it firm or still a bit wobbly? If it is wobbly it can go back and you might have to heat the pot a bit more to finish cooking it. If it is firm, take a pallete knife and slide it along the bones of the fish. If the flesh just lets go of the bone, it is done and you should serve it immediately. If it sticks to the bone, put it back into the water again and place over a medium heat for a couple of minutes before checking it again.

Lift the pieces of fish out of the cooking liquid and place them on a serving platter. Pull off the skin to reveal the beautiful flesh or let every person eating do it themselves.

POACHED HALIBUT

Pocheret helleflynder / hellefisk (Denmark)
Kokt kveite (Norway)

In Norway, halibut is cooked much like cod in very salty and lightly vinegary water. Serve with Boiled Potatoes (page 117) or riced potatoes, Quick Pickled Cucumbers (page 658) and some Sandefjord Sauce (page 662)

Preparation and cooking time: 30 minutes
Serves: 4

800 g/1¾ lb halibut fillet, cut into 4 thick
   pieces, or 1.2 kg/2½ lb if your fish is
   cooked on the bone

For the cooking liquid
50 g/2 oz (3½ tablespoons) salt and
   1 tablespoon vinegar for each 1 litre/
   34 fl oz (4¼ cups) water used

Fill a large pot with water and add the salt and vinegar before bringing to a hard boil. When the water is boiling, pull the pot to the side of the stove, off the heat, and put the pieces of halibut in the pot. Cover with a lid and leave for about 10 minutes.

If cooked on the bone it should just about come off the bone clean if the palette knife is slid along the bone itself. Halibut is very lean and not as gelatinous as, for example, turbot, so be really careful not to overcook it, which will make it dry.

SMOKED HALIBUT

Røget hellefisk (Denmark)

Cold-smoked Halibut called *røget hellefisk* is very popular in Denmark, where it is served much like cold-smoked salmon or Gravlax (page 216), in large thin slices. It is often used as a topping for Danish *smørebrød*, open-faced sandwiches.

SMELT (*OSMERUS EPERLANUS*)

A small fish that is found in both fresh and salt water. Smelts are most commonly seen at about 6–10 cm (2½–4 inches) in length but can grow up to 25 cm (10 inches) in rare conditions. Smelt has a particular smell, reminiscent of fresh cucumber.

DEEP-FRIED SMELTS

friturestegt smelt (Denmark)
Friterad nors (Sweden)

These fish are so small that even their little bones are edible. I like them to be fried really golden and very crisp. Serve with a wedge of lemon or Hard-boiled Egg and Cream Sauce (page 676), to dip in.

Preparation and cooking time: 20 minutes
Serves: 4 as a light meal or starter
  (appetizer)

vegetable oil, for deep-frying
plain (all-purpose) or coarse rye flour, to coat
100 g/3½ oz smelts, gutted, cleaned and
  heads left on, gills removed
milk, to cover
salt and white pepper, to taste

Heat the oil for deep frying in a deep pan or deep fryer to 190°C/375°F.

Place the flour into a wide, shallow bowl.

Place the smelts in a bowl and pour on milk to cover. Roll them in the flour, one at a time, to coat.

Deep-fry the smelts until golden and crisp. Remove them from the oil with a slotted spoon and leave for a second or two on paper towels, to soak up any excess oil. Season with salt and pepper.

GRILLED MACKEREL

Grillet makrell (Norway)
Grillet makrel (Denmark)
Halstrad makrill (Sweden)

Serve with something green from the vegetable section of this book or, if you want to be more traditional, with some Mashed Potatoes (page 118) and a wedge of lemon or a few drops of *Ättika* (6%) vinegar (page 656).

A dollop of Dill Butter (page 655) melting over the warm fish is also delicious and is included in many traditional recipes for this dish.

Preparation and cooking time: 10 minutes
Serves: 4

4 mackerel fillets, at room temperature
salt

Heat a cast-iron pan as hot as your stove can possibly make it. Before you put in the fish, carefully wipe the hot pan with a thick wad of dry paper towels.

Place the mackerel fillets in the pan, skin-side down. It will smoke as the fat renders out into the pan and the skin sears, so keep your extractor fan on high.

Season the flesh side of the fish while the skin side is cooking. Once the skin is cooked – it should be really dark in places – turn the fillets over and cook for another 30 seconds or so. They should still have a little bit of an inner core that isn't fully cooked. Lift the mackerel onto a warm serving platter. Season a bit on the skin side too, and serve.

For image see opposite page

Clockwise from top left: Turbot piece fried in butter (page 154); Boiled Cod (page 234); Grilled Mackerel (page 228); Haddock and Lumpfish (page 226); Open-Faced Danish Sandwich, Stjerneskud (page 522)

LUTEFISK

Lutefisk (Norway)
Lipeäkala (Finland)
Lutfisk (Sweden)

Lutefisk is a fillet of white fish, such as cod, ling or saithe, which is wind-dried, or salted and dried (*klippfisk*, see opposite page) and soaked in a solution of lye (sodium hydroxide, page 731), slaked lime (calcium hydroxide, page 734) and water.

This practice probably originates from the Netherlands or northern Germany and has been common in most of the Nordic region since the Middle Ages. Today *lutefisk* is mostly eaten in Norway, Sweden and Finland, where it is part of the traditional Christmas preparations. The process of producing *lutefisk* for Christmas is traditionally started on the 9th December.

The caustic effects of the highly alkaline solution on the proteins of the fish is very pronounced, and the firm flesh breaks down into a gelatinous texture and acquires a particular savoury-sulphur kind of flavour.

I imagine that this technique was conceived to provide some variation in a diet that, for many people, consisted of a lot of dried fish, which was rehydrated in water and boiled into soups and savoury porridges. Today, with modern refrigeration and a constant supply of fresh or frozen fish, the need for this technique for any reasons other than satisfying those who acquired the taste for it is probably pretty minimal.

In Norway, *lutefisk* is often enjoyed with grated horseradish, melted or cold butter, crispy bacon and sometimes bacon fat. Split pea purée is also common, as is Brown Cheese (page 72), which is often made from goat's milk. Boiled Potatoes (page 117) seem to be part of almost every recipe.

In most of Sweden, *lutefisk* is also served with potatoes but in the region of Jämtland it is sometimes served on a barley flatbread with reduced whey cheese. Most Swedes serve their *lutefisk* with Béchamel Sauce (page 666) on the side, except the southern Swedish Scanians, who prefer Mustard Cream Sauce (page 664). Accompaniments like fried bacon and green peas are common and some

freshly ground allspice is often seen close to the fish too.

An old classic recipe is to mix some leftover béchamel with pieces of leftover *lutefisk* and to reheat it as a kind of stew for lunch on Christmas day. This could be served with some fried potatoes and perhaps a dollop of coarse-grain mustard.

For image see page 667

TO PREPARE LUTEFISK

It is difficult to give an exact recipe for the actual preparation of the *lutefisk* itself, since the amount of time and the exact quantities of lye and quicklime depend a bit on the fish. Most people would probably buy their *lutefisk* already soaked and ready to cook. It's vital to follow proper safety procedures and to be very careful indeed preparing *lutefisk* yourself, as the ingredients are highly corrosive in concentrated form. Anyhow, here follows a broad description of the technique.

Take some nice looking pieces of stockfish or *klippfisk* (see opposite page) prepared from cod, ling or saithe. Put them in a big tub of cold water and leave them to soak for about 6 days, changing the water daily. The fish will soak up the water and swell to almost its original size.

Wearing gloves, sprinkle a good layer of slaked lime (page 734) into a new tub and then transfer the fish to this new tub. Sprinkle more slaked lime between each layer of fish. Cover with ice-cold water and add lye (approved for foodstuffs, page 731), following the instructions on the packet. The soaking solution should have a pH level of 11–12. To check this, use litmus paper or a digital pH meter. It is important that the temperature never rises above 10°C/50°F, as this would impact on the quality of the lutefisk. As the chemicals themselves create heat, be sure you use really cold water, and perhaps even add some ice to the tub.

Leave the fish in the lye solution for another 2 days, until the texture of the fish has changed, becoming uniformly soft. You should be able to poke a spoon or a gloved finger through the flesh with a little bit of force. It is completely normal for the fish to swell quite a bit during the lye-soaking process.

Next, the fish should be transferred to another tub of cold water and left to soak for 6–7 days, changing the water daily. You can check to see if it is ready from the third day onwards. Do this by cutting off a very small piece of fish and boiling it. If it dissolves into gelatinous goo it still has too much lye left in it. If it becomes too hard, it has too little lye in it and you have to start over. If the texture is just right, the fish is done and you can remove it from the water and store it ready for cooking.

TO COOK LUTEFISK

No other metal than stainless steel should come into contact with *lutefisk* because of its alkalinity, so that means no aluminium or copper pots and no aluminium foil.

If you don't make it yourself, then I recommend always buying *lutefisk* from a skilled lye master. If you bought your *lutefisk*, make sure that there is not too much residual lye in it by soaking it for 24 hours in cold water before cooking.

Preparation and cooking time: 30–45 minutes
Soaking time: 24 hours (for store-bought lutefisk)
Serves: 4

50 g/2 oz (3½ tablespoons) butter
1 kg/2¼ lb lutefisk, rinsed
salt, to taste

Melt the butter in a pot over a medium heat. Add the lutefisk and sprinkle it with some salt. Cover it with a sheet of baking (parchment) paper and a lid and cook over a low heat for 20 minutes or so, or until the fish is done. Discard the cooking liquid before serving the fish.

An alternative way of cooking *lutefisk* is in the oven. Preheat the oven to 175°C/345°F/Gas Mark 4. Cover as described above, then bake for 35 minutes, or until the fish is done.

SALTED, DRIED COD

Klippfisk (Norway)
Klipfisk (Denmark)

Klippfisk is a Norwegian salted and dried cod. It was named after the traditional production process in which whole cod, split along the spine and salted, were spread out on cliffs (*klippor*) to dry. The sun and the wind were allowed to dry the fish during the day and at night, or during rainy days, they were stacked in a shingled pile and covered with a wooden roof for protection. Today most of the salt cod in Norway is produced indoors in big processing plants, and a lot of it is exported outside of the Nordic region. Traditionally the salt cod was graded according to a five-step scale: superior extra, superior, imperial, universal and popular. Today this grading system is scarcely used, but especially fine quality *klippfisk* is still sometimes graded. *Klippfisk* is eaten in many traditional Norwegian dishes like bacalao.

Before eating *klippfisk*, it first needs to be soaked in water to remove the salt and rehydrate it. Place the whole piece of fish in a bucket of water and leave it to soak, changing the water 3–4 times every 24 hours until the fish has inflated to look almost as if it was fresh and until the water doesn't taste overly salty any more. For normal size pieces it is usually enough to desalt them for about 24 hours but for big pieces longer can be necessary.

NORWEGIAN SALT COD CASSEROLE

Klassisk bacalao (Norway)

It might seem strange that a dish which feels as distinctly Spanish or Portuguese as this, is one of the greatest Norwegian classics. Sometimes, in to-day's fast-moving world, we forget that travelling is something people have been doing for a long time. Salt cod has been produced for at least 500 years and has been traded for as long as the Nordic populations have been able to sail the seas and for as long as they have been aware of its market potential. Salt cod travelled south in the holds of Norwegian ships; the idea of stewing it with tomatoes, peppers and olives then travelled north in the minds of those returning after a successful trade.

Preparation and cooking time: 1½ hours
Soaking time: overnight, or longer if very big
Serves: 4

600 g/1 lb 5 oz salted cod, desalted
    (page 231)
50 ml/2 fl oz (⅓ cup plus 1 tablespoon)
    olive oil
2 large onions, cut into 4 mm/¼ inch slices
500 g/1 lb 2 oz firm waxy potatoes, cut into
    4 mm/¼ inch slices
2 sweet red bell peppers, cut into
    4 mm/¼ inch slices
1 red chilli pepper, finely chopped
1 x 400 g/14 oz can whole tomatoes, cut into
    large chunks
50 g/2 oz (3½ tablespoons) tomato purée
salt and black pepper, to taste

Skin and rinse the salted cod, then cut it into 3 cm/1¼ inch cubes.

Pour the oil into a heavy pot. Add a layer of onions, then continue by layering, fish, potatoes, tomato purée (paste), more onions and peppers until the pot is almost full. Add the chilli and tomatoes and pour in 350 ml/12 fl oz (1½ cups) water.

Carefully bring to a slow boil over a medium heat, then lower the heat, cover with a lid and leave to simmer for about an hour until the potatoes are soft. Stir from time to time to prevent the stew burning at the bottom. But do it carefully, and preferably with a wooden spoon, so that you don't crush the pieces too much and turn the whole dish into orange mashed potatoes with fish in it.

Finish by seasoning with black pepper and perhaps a little bit of salt.

For image see opposite page

STOCKFISH

Turrur fiskur (Iceland)
Tørrfisk (Norway)

Stockfish are unsalted wind-dried fish commonly produced in the whole of the north Atlantic coastal region, perhaps most notably in Norway but also in Iceland and the Faroe Islands. Stockfish has been and is still one of Norway's biggest export commodities, and has been historically very important. It has been documented in the Icelandic Sagas than cod was exported from Norway to Britain during the ninth century. It is still consumed in vast quantities by many of the Mediterranean countries, especially Italy. It is sometimes confusingly referred to as '*baccalao*', which would actually be *klippfisk*, salted dried cod (page 231).

Fillets of dried fish are either rolled between heavy rollers or pounded with a mallet and become flaky. It is a popular snack in Norway, Iceland and the Faroe Islands, where it is often served with a lump of salty butter in which you dip strands or flakes of cod broken from the processed fillet. Cod, saithe or ling are most commonly dried for export, but lumpsucker, halibut and wolfish are also dried for snacks.

Before being hung up to dry, heads and innards are removed and the fish is either hung up like this on wooded frames, or further processed by removing the backbone before being dried. The fish is hung up in winter when the weather is still cold and no insects are active. Like this, when summer comes and the weather grows warm the fish is already dried and microbiologically stable. The drying itself takes about three months and before the fish is sold it will be allowed to further age indoors in a warehouse for a couple of months. Stockfish can also be processed into *lutefisk* (page 230).

From top: black olives; Norwegian Salt Cod Casserole (page 232)

SALTED, AGED STOCKFISH

Boknafisk (Norway)

This is an old fashioned Norwegian variation of Stockfish (page 232) produced much in the same way but lightly salted before being hung on the wooden frames. It is not dried for quite as long as stockfish but rather for just a couple of weeks so that it matures a bit and acquires a slightly stronger flavour.

In addition to the fish commonly used for stockfish, herring can also be used for *boknafisk*.

Desalt *boknafisk* overnight in cold water, skin it and place pieces of it on top of potatoes boiling in a pot of water. It should be good to add the fish towards the second half of the estimated cooking time for the potatoes. Serve with some fried bacon, and maybe some Creamed Carrots (page 110).

FAROESE AGED FISH

Ræstur fiskur (Faroe Islands)

This is the practise of aging fish like saithe, pollock and cod according to the same principles as with Faroese Aged Mutton (page 350). The aged fish is often served boiled with potatoes on the side.

HOW TO COOK FAROESE AGED FISH

The whale blubber, if it is fresh, can be diced and dropped into the water with the fish itself for the second half of the cooking. If it is salted it can be served just as it is, in pieces. If aged suet is served with the fish, melt it carefully on the stove before serving it like a sauce with the fish and blubber.

Preparation and cooking time: 40 minutes
Serves: 4

1 kg/2¼ lb Faroese Aged Fish (see above)
pilot whale blubber or Faroese Aged
  Intestinal Fat (page 358), cut into

1 cm/½ inch dice, to serve (optional)
salt, to taste

Trim, clean and cut the aged fish into suitable pieces. Bring a large pot of salted water to a simmer over a medium heat. Drop in the pieces of fish and simmer until cooked through. The cooking time will vary depending on the thickness of the fish but will take about 15–25 minutes.

If you are also cooking whale blubber, add it after a couple of minutes of cooking the fish. Once the fish and blubber are cooked, remove them from the cooking liquid with a slotted spoon and drain them in a colander.

BOILED COD

Kokt torsk med lever og rogn (Norway)

Often a smaller cod is used for this festive dinner dish and it is common to serve it with either the liver or roe or with both of them. Boiled cod is often served with Boiled Potatoes (page 117), boiled vegetables and some kind of condiment, like salted butter, a lemon wedge, Sandefjord Sauce (page 662) or hollandaise sauce.

Don't neglect the head; after being prepared this way both the cheeks and other bits of this gelatinous part of the fish are delicious.

In many older recipe books the liver is cooked together with the fish, whilst in newer ones it is suggested that it is cooked separately, so as not to taint the cooking water with liver flavour. I like to cook the liver separately in a small ovenproof dish, chopped up in rough pieces with some finely cut onion, a little bit of black pepper, a chunk of butter and salt to taste.

Preparation and cooking time: 30 minutes
Soaking time: 2 hours
Serves: 4

1 x 2-kg/4½-lb whole cod, head and innards
  intact

For the cooking liquid
50 g/2 oz (3½ tablespoons) salt and
  1 tablespoon *Ättika* (6%) vinegar
  (page 656) for each 1 litre/34 fl oz
  (4¼ cups) water used

Gut and clean the fish, reserving the liver for later. If you want to use the roe, follow the cooking method on page 236.

Chop the fish into suitable portion sized pieces, then place in a bowl and soak in cold water for at least 2 hours, changing the water a few times, before cooking.

Fill a large pot with water and add 60 g/2¼ oz (3½ tablespoons) salt and 1 tablespoon vinegar for each 1 litre/34 fl oz (4¼ cups) water used. Bring to a hard boil. When the water is boiling, move the pot to the side of the stove and add the pieces of cod and cook in the residual heat. The cooking time will depend on the size of the pieces, but count on about 10 minutes for a fish of this weight. The flesh should just about come off the bone cleanly when done. If it doesn't seem to cook enough from the residual heat, you can put it back over the heat again. Be careful not to heat it too much though.

If you are cooking the liver together with the cod, add it to the cooking liquid about halfway through the cooking of the fish itself. Serve immediately.

For image see page 229

FAROESE BOILED COD OR SAITHE

*Kókaður feskur seiður og livur
  (Faroe Islands)*

On the Faroe Islands, white fish like cod or saithe is often boiled in salted water, together with its liver, and served with Boiled Potatoes (page 117).

Carefully drop the liver into the pan with the fish for the last 10 minutes of cooking. Season the liver well with white pepper and salt before serving. Sometimes, the potatoes are also cooked together with the fish and liver to absorb their flavour.

FRIED TONGUES AND CHEEKS OF COD

Lippur og kjálkar (Faroe Islands)

Serve with Boiled Potatoes (page 117), melted butter and perhaps a wedge of lemon.

Preparation and cooking time: 30 minutes
Serves: 4

1.5 kg/2½ lb cod tongues and cheeks,
  cleaned, rinsed and trimmed
flour, for dusting
salt, to taste
butter, for frying

Pat the fish pieces thoroughly dry. Dust them all over with flour and season lightly with salt.

Melt a little butter in a pan over a medium heat. Add the fish pieces and fry them on both sides until golden.

POACHED COD'S ROE

Kokt torskerogn (Norway)
Kogt torskerogn (Denmark)
Kokt torskrom (Sweden)

Poached cod's roe can be served either as a dish of its own with Boiled Potatoes (page 117) and a Basic Fish Sauce (page 662) or as a condiment to dishes like Fried Cod (page 150) or Boiled Cod (page 234). Poached cod's roe can also be chilled, sliced, dusted with a little flour and fried in butter.

Preparation and cooking time: 25–45 minutes
Serves: 4

800 g/1 lb 12 oz cod's roe, with unbroken
    and undamaged membranes
salt, to taste
freshly ground white pepper, to taste

Clean and rinse the roe carefully under cold running water. Wrap the roe in baking (parchment) paper or in muslin (cheesecloth). Place in a pot, cover with cold water and add 2 tablespoons sea salt for each l litre/34 fl oz (4¼ cups) water used.

Slowly bring the water to the boil over a medium heat, then lower the temperature and keep it at a simmer. Cook for 20–40 minutes, or until the roe is cooked through and firm to the touch. The cooking time depends on the size of the pieces of roe. Serve steaming hot, possibly seasoned with a little freshly ground white pepper.

FAROESE COD'S ROE BALLS

Rognaknetti (Faroe Islands)

Preparation and cooking time: 40 minutes
Serves: 4

1 kg/2¼ lb cod's roe, rinsed and pushed
    through a coarse sieve (strainer) to
    separate the membranes from the roe
220 g/7 oz (1 cup plus 2 tablespoons)
    sugar
100 g/3½ oz (¾ cup) raisins

500 g/1 lb 2 oz (4 cups) plain (all-purpose)
    flour
4 teaspoons baking powder
salt, to taste

Combine the cod's roe with the sugar and raisins in a large bowl. Mix together well, then sift over the flour and baking powder. Season with salt and mix until fully incorporated. Leave to rest, while you bring a large pot of salted water to a simmer.

Shape the mixture into balls with clean, wet hands. Drop the fish balls straight into the simmering water and simmer until they are cooked through.

The balls can be served straight from the pot or else they can be chilled and then reheated, either in a little bit of water or by frying them in butter until golden.

FAROESE COD'S ROE PATTIES

Rognafrikadellur (Faroe Islands)

Serve with Boiled Potatoes (page 117)

Preparation and cooking time: 40–60 minutes,
    plus cooling time
Serves: 4

400 g/14 oz cod's roe
400 g/14 oz cod (use fillet or clean scraps or
    trimmings)
1 onion, finely chopped
2 eggs
2 tablespoons plain (all-purpose) flour
salt and white pepper, to taste
butter, for frying

Follow the recipe for poached cod's roe (see left). Once cooked, allow to cool down completely.

Combine the cooled roe and the fish and push them through a meat mincer (grinder) twice. Place in a bowl with the onion, eggs, flour and 100 ml/3½ fl oz (⅓ cup plus 1 tablespoon) water. Season with salt and pepper and mix everything together until fully combined. Shape into patties with clean, wet hands.

Melt a little butter in a pan over a medium heat. Cook the patties on each side, or until cooked through and nicely browned on each side.

FISH SOUP FROM BERGEN

Bergensk fiskesuppe (Norway)

Bergensk fiskesuppe is one of the world's great fish soups, perfectly mirroring its place in the world in ingredients and flavours. Unfortunately, it is rare to find this soup prepared properly, even in south-western Norway, where it comes from.

Bergensk fiskesuppe exists in many variations, but in my opinion what distinguishes it from other fish soups is, firstly, the broth (which is traditionally made from a type of small saithe fish called *pale* and a selection of root vegetables); the lack of any seasoning other than the fish itself and a very light sweet-and-sourness from vinegar; and lastly, the flavour of *rømme*.

Sometimes a couple of pieces of smoked bacon are added to the soup to give more body and depth. In modern versions, the bacon is sometimes chopped small and fried crisp, before being sprinkled on top of the soup just before serving.

Traditionally, *Bergensk fiskesuppe* is served with Quick Pickled Purslane Stalks (page 661) on the side, but today it is often served sprinkled with chives or parsley. I rather feel that this turns it into any old fish soup, instead of *Bergensk fiskesuppe*. However it is also tasty, so go ahead if it seems appropriate. The soup is also often made with Norwegian Fish Balls (page 225).

Preparation and cooking time: 1 hour
Serves: 4

500 g/1 lb 2 oz white fish fillets (preferably a mix of cod, saithe and halibut)
1.5 litres/50 fl oz (6¼ cups) good strong Fish Stock (page 650), made from the bones of small saithe
4 carrots
1 leek
300 g/11 oz celeriac (celery root)

2 tablespoons *Ättika* (12%) vinegar (page 657), or more to taste
2 tablespoons sugar, or more to taste
2 tablespoons plain (all-purpose) flour
300 ml/10½ fl oz (1¼ cups) double (heavy) cream
1 quantity Norwegian Fish Balls (page 225) or some slices of smoked bacon (optional)
300 ml/10 fl oz (1¼ cups) *rømme* or sour cream
3 egg yolks
salt and white pepper, to taste
slices smoked bacon (optional)

Cut the fish fillets into about 3 cm/1¼ inch long pieces. Place them on a tray and let them come to room temperature outside of the refrigerator before you cook them.

Pour the stock (broth) into a large pot and bring to a simmer.

While the stock is heating, peel and julienne the vegetables, then add them to the simmering broth. Add the vinegar and sugar and simmer for a few minutes.

Stir the flour into the cream until no lumps remain. Add it to the pot and continue to simmer for a few more minutes. Add the fish pieces and the fish balls (if you are using them) and cook for about 10 minutes or until perfect.

While the fish is cooking, mix the sour cream with the egg yolks and keep them to one side.

When the fish is perfectly poached, adjust the seasoning if necessary, using a little salt, white pepper and perhaps some more sugar or vinegar. You have to stir very carefully at this stage so as not to break up the fish.

Just before serving, add the sour cream-egg mixture to the soup and stir a little. I prefer not to blend it in completely, but instead leave streaks of unmixed cream and egg in the soup. Once the sour cream and egg has been added the soup cannot be reheated.

ICELANDIC FISH AND POTATO MASH

Plokkfiskur (Iceland)
Plukkfisk (Norway)
Plukfisk (Denmark)

This is an ancient dish, which exists today in many variations. In the old days I imagine that it was made from salted and dried fish (*klippfisk* page 231) or just dried fish and the connection to central European dishes, like for example *brandade,* is quite apparent. Today, *plokkfiskur* is mostly made from fresh cod or haddock, which is boiled specifically for the dish, or else from leftovers from another recipe. Most older recipes contain some onion and pepper as the only flavourings, but recent recipes contain things like curry powder, Dijon mustard, grated cheese – or pretty much anything that seems fitting and delicious.

Plokkfiskur is often served with slices of Icelandic Rye Bread (page 503) and it is often seen with a lump of butter melting on top of each serving or sitting in a little mound on the mash. The texture of the finished dish depends on how much you stir everything together. More stirring results in a finer structure and denser texture. I prefer to stir just a little so that there are still some chunks of fish and potato left.

In Norway this dish may also contain finely cut leeks, and it is often served with fried bacon or Fried Salt Pork (page 302), or a dollop of salty butter. In Denmark a good spoonful of coarse grain mustard is often added to the sauce.

Preparation and cooking time: 20 minutes
Serves: 4

2 tablespoons butter
1 onion, finely chopped
1 tablespoon plain (all-purpose) flour
600 ml/1 UK pint (2½ cups) milk
600 g/1 lb 5 oz cooked white fish, like cod or haddock, skin and bones removed, broken up into flakes
300 g/11 oz floury potatoes, boiled, peeled and coarsely cut into cubes
salt and white pepper, to taste

Melt the butter in a pan over a medium heat. Add the onion to the pan and cook until translucent, but do not allow them to brown. Sift the flour over the onions and stir into a sort of roux, then add the milk, whisking until no lumps remain. Bring to the boil, then reduce the heat and simmer for a few minutes. When the sauce has thickened, add the fish and whisk so that the flakes break up. Add the potatoes and season with salt and white pepper. Leave the pan on the stove over a low heat until the potato is warmed through. Finish by stirring the mixture until the fish and potatoes are just broken up enough for your taste.

FISH AND RICE CASSEROLE

Fiskpudding med ris (Sweden)

The leftover meat from any cooked fish can be used in this dish. Serve with melted butter and possibly a lemon wedge.

Preparation and cooking time: 30 minutes
Serves: 4

300 g/11 oz cooked fish pieces, all skin and bones removed
310 g/11¼ oz (1⅔ cups) Boiled Rice (page 654)
2 eggs
300 ml/10½ fl oz (1¼ cups) milk
200 ml/7 fl oz (¾ cup plus 1 tablespoon) cream
freshly grated nutmeg, to taste
breadcrumbs, for sprinkling
salt and white pepper, to taste

Preheat the oven to 250°C/480°F/Gas Mark 9.

Mix the fish with the rice in an ovenproof dish.

Beat the eggs, milk and cream together in a bowl and season with salt, pepper and possibly some nutmeg. Pour the egg mixture over the rice and the fish, then sprinkle with a layer of breadcrumbs. Bake until golden brown.

SAITHE WITH CARAMELIZED ONION

Seibiff med løk (Norway)

Seibiff med løk is an iconic dish in Norway. It is one of those everyday dishes that the processed food industry has turned into something you can get in a packet from the shelf of a supermarket freezer. It's probably a great sale as it is such a tasty dish if you make it right. The rather fatty and rich saithe with the sweet browned onion is simply delicious. Traditionally it is served with Boiled Potatoes (page 117) or Mashed Potatoes (page 118) and some Boiled Carrots (page 110). If you look at some blogs and Instagram accounts depicting what people eat today, the Norwegians seems to have added also some greens to their *Seibiff*. I would go for a Kale Salad (page 90) myself. A wedge of lemon can also be a good idea.

Preparation and cooking time: 20 minutes
Serves: 4

1 quantity Sweet Fried Onions (page 108)
1 x 600 g/1 lb 5 oz saithe fillet, cut into
    4 pieces
butter, for frying
salt and white pepper, to taste

Fry according to the instructions on page 152 for Whole Fish, Fried in a Pan, Version 1. Finish by placing the pieces of fish on a serving platter and cover them with the hot onions.

NORWEGIAN BARREL-AGED SAITHE

Gammelsei/Gammelsatet Sei/Røsei (Norway)

This saithe preparation is a very old fashioned Norwegian way of preserving this fatty and abundant fish during the warm months of the year when turning it into stockfish (page 232) was not an option. The fish was caught during summer and salted in barrels without being bled out before being laid down. The head and guts where kept on the fish for at least a couple of hours for the blood to coagulate before it was cut into. The blood is kept in the saithe to promote the correct flavour of the subsequent fermentation.

The fish should be aged for at least 6 months before being eaten but can last for many years in the barrel. It was and is eaten raw. Sometimes it is desalted a bit like salted herring (page 200), boiled or even turned into *Lutefisk* (page 230).

FAROESE SAITHE PATTIES

Seiðaknetti (Faroe Islands)

See recipe for Faroese Cod's Roe Patties on page 236, but substitute the cod with saithe.

ICELANDIC ROTTEN SHARK

Kæstur Hákarl (Iceland)

The cool ocean breeze keeps blowing a lock of hair in front of my face, the director has repeatedly asked me to put the stray tuft behind my ear. Each time the wind dies away for a brief moment and I pull the hair back again, the strange feeling in my nose comes back. Not quite a smell, but rather the sensation of inhaling something containing more than just clean air, the air itself stinging the inside of my nose. It feels like when scrubbing the inside of a bathtub with some strong detergent and inhaling at the wrong moment. There is smell too, but much more faint than I expected it to be, just a little fishy, a little rancid, a little bit like old cheese and fish oil and dark harbour water, but not really in a very bad way.

On a wooden table, piled on a paper plate and pierced with cocktail sticks (toothpicks), rests cubes of skin-coloured firm flesh, the piece it was carved from lying on a chopping (cutting) board with the knife next to it.

Next to me, and next to the rotted Icelandic shark, too, for that matter, a man is seated. He is very cheery, he is joking and smiling and he appears to be having the time of his life in front of the camera recording my discovery of this ancient and odd delicacy.

After each bite of shark, I feel a little bit queasier, and after each bite the director asks for another take and with that another piece of strangeness.

After each bite the cheery man pours me a swig of something very alcoholic in a plastic cup. He proudly and loudly proclaims it to be the result of ancient traditions and craftsmanship coming together, the perfect pairing with *Hákarl*. Its pale red colour and excellent flavour, the cheery man says, are derived from a very special, very secret berry, picked high up on the volcanic slopes of the island, plus of course very good homemade booze. I am absolutely certain that he is not lying about the booze being possibly eye-disabling moonshine. The red colour and flavour, though, definitely come from no secret berry. I suspect it comes from a diet cordial called Fun Light, the taste of artificial sweetener and fake raspberry is hard to mask even with the alcohol content, which rests safely around 75% alcohol by volume.

The strange physical sensation of ammonia is even more pronounced when eating the pieces of shark. It burns as the alkaline chemicals attack the fragile mucus membranes inside of my mouth – not hot like chilli, if anything it is rather mild and nothing compared to many other fermented foods when it comes to the aroma. It is just that strange burning that makes the shark so thoroughly unpleasant to eat for the uneducated, like myself.

The sharks – the Greenland shark and the Basking shark – used to produce this pungent and completely singular type of food are predators. They eat a lot of meat and thereby a lot of protein all through their rather long lives. Most other animals would pee and get rid of excess nitrates from the digestion of all that meat. But not these sharks, no, they can live for up to 200 years and they will not take a piss one single time. Instead they will accumulate all the nitrate in their muscle tissue. To balance the nitrate-rich urea the muscles of the shark also contain a metabolic product called trimethylamine oxide, making it wildly toxic to eat for humans. To ingest Greenland shark supposedly leads to a state similar to that of extreme drunkenness as the chemical breaks down in the human body. Drunkenness so severe that you would risk dying even from a rather small amount.

To make the shark edible for humans, it is dug down into the beach or sealed up in huge crates to ferment, or as some say, rot. Then after a designated number of months to achieve perfect putrefaction, the pieces of shark are hung to dry for another bit of time. The fermentation process and the wind drying together turn a lot of the nitrates into ammonia, some of which is vented off by the air and it destroys the trimethylamine oxide, making the meat safer to eat.

Who came up with the idea to do this and who perfected the process is obviously a bit of an enigma and there is more than one impossible-to-verify story about how it might have gone down.

ICELANDIC FERMENTED SKATE

Kæstur skata (Iceland)

Skate is fermented in a saltless fermentation much like the more well know outside of Iceland, Icelandic Rotten Shark (see opposite), *Kæstur Hákarl*. The skate was traditionally also hung up to wind dry, just like the shark, but today it is consumed when it has done fermenting or it is frozen until later if it isn't all eaten at once. Fermented skate is eaten all year round in Iceland but predominately on St Thorlak's day, *þorláksmessa*, which takes place on the 23rd December. Historically most common in the West fiord part of Iceland, the practice of having skate on the 23rd has now spread over the entire island and has become a cherished national dish. Serve your skate with Boiled Potatoes (page 117) and *Hnoðmör* or *Hamsatólg*, both aged sheep's tallow products that you would allow to melt over your skate just before serving. Icelandic rye bread is also a common side with *Kæstur skata*.

Sometimes skate like this is boiled in the cooking water from *hangilæri* (page 345), which is often served on Christmas Day itself.

As you can probably imagine, the fish stinks quite a bit when cooked so it might be good to do so on a portable stove outside of the house.

Preparation and cooking time: 25 minutes
Serves: 4

800 g/1¾ lb fermented skate, rinsed

Bring a large pot of water to the boil and add the fish. Let it simmer for at least 15 minutes, until cooked through. Remove from the water with a slotted spoon and place on a serving platter. Remove the skin and cartilage before serving.

MARINE MAMMALS AND SEAFOOD

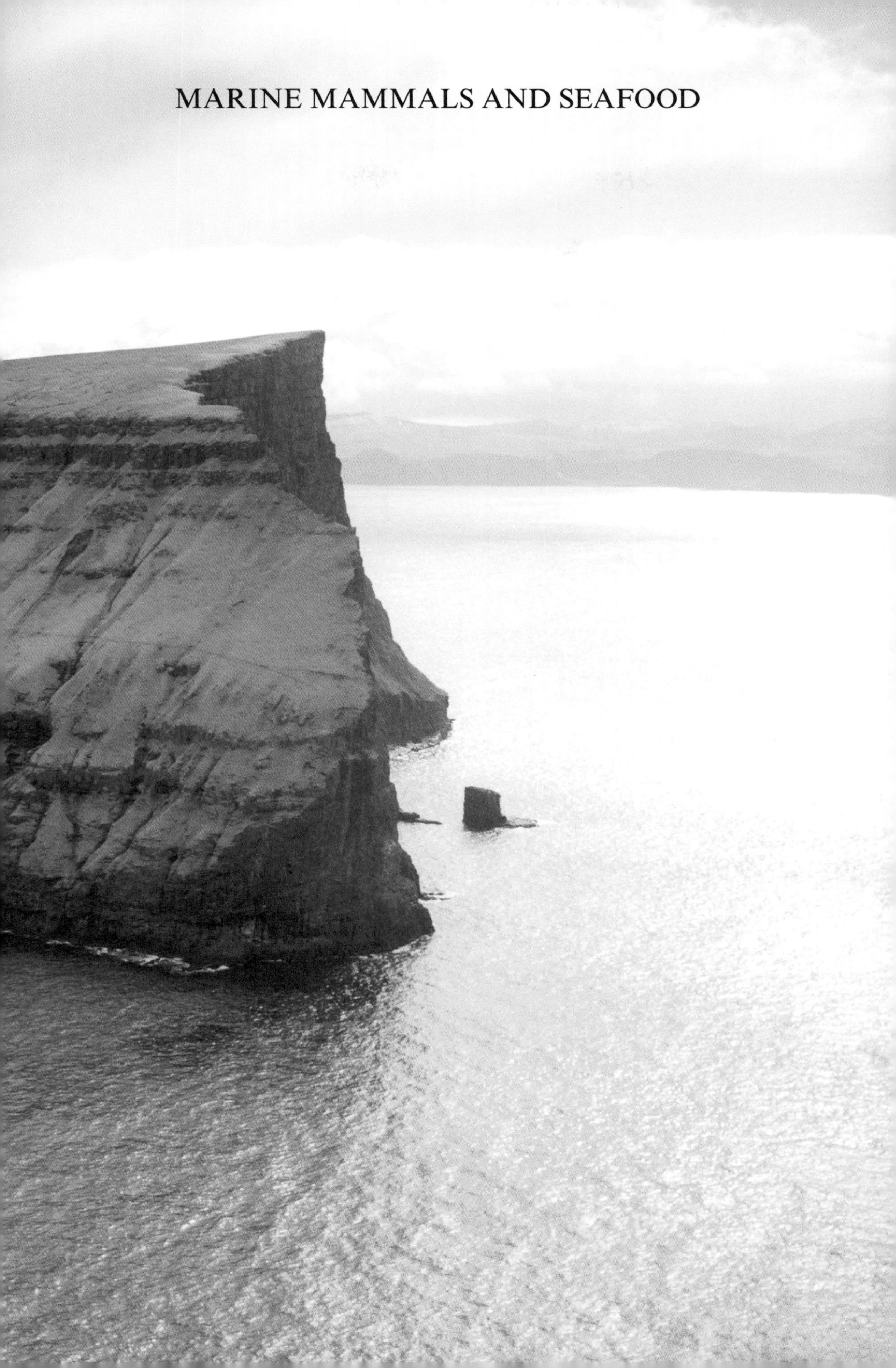

Faroese whale hunt

I am sitting on a bench coated by the fine drops of morning mist, surface tension keeping them almost perfectly round. Not that it would be seen of course; for someone sitting on the bench the little globes of evaporated sea water condensed onto the cold, dark planks of wood simply look like a thin layer of grey, iridescent velvet. I listen to the silence of the film team, they are recording something they call 'room tone'. A minute of silent nothing that can be used when editing for something technical that I don't understand. The thing with recording room tone is that everyone on site has to be quiet, really quiet, everyone holds their breath and concentrates so much so that it almost stops the movement of earth itself.

About thirty seconds in, the thunderous silence is broken by the door of a van slamming shut and by excited voices from the direction of the car park (parking lot) followed by a loud and annoyed exhale from the direction of the sound-man and his microphone. I stand up and leave behind me a butt-shaped mark where the fabric of my pants has absorbed the drops of watery velvet on the bench.

The Faroese part of our documentary film team are chatting excitedly but in hushed tones.

Not three minutes later I find myself in the passenger seat of a van racing across the islands at break-neck speed. The last words I heard before leaving were the admonishing words of the American director, realizing that not only were half of the crew leaving but so was the person being filmed. 'You better be back no later than 12, the helicopter leaves at 12 and it is the only helicopter for days,' he said, slightly red-faced, but with the look of someone who knows that it doesn't quite matter what he says right now.

The Faroe Islands is a very close-knit community, a large part of the islands' population know each other and there is a strong sense of affinity.

When someone spots a pod of pilot whales at sea, they will call in to shore and the word of a coming hunt spreads like wildfire. Everyone drops what he or she has at hand to rush to wherever the hunt is taking place and help out.

Anyone who has an available boat will go out to help herd or drive the whales closer to shore. There are particular whaling bays, chosen hundreds if not thousands of years ago, as being suitable for the purpose of beaching the whales to kill them. This type of hunting, primarily for pilot whale, is called *grindadráp* in Faroese.

When beached, the whales are met by hundreds of people on shore helping out handling them. They are killed with a tool called *mønustingari*, which is inserted through the back of the animal, severing its spinal cord. Anyone is allowed to participate in the hunt and help out, but to handle the killing tool you need to be trained and licensed. After the whale is dead a special long-bladed *grindaknívur* knife is used to sever its arteries, draining the carcass of blood.

What is unique about this ancient custom is that it is a communal activity, everyone participates and there is a strict system, supported by the Faroese legal structure, by which the meat is then shared among the citizens, none of it is sold. The person who first spotted the whales will get a whole whale for his family, those who are not participating, the ones who might be at sea fishing, or ill in the hospital, will also get a share. In the old days, the *grindadráp* was vital for people to survive in this remote group of islands and the meat was an important source of fat and proteins.

Today it is still an active culture and the Faroese people do still eat a lot of whale meat. Even though it is not vital to survival any more, it is an integral part of Faroese social culture, a bit like moose hunting is in large parts of Sweden, something that brings people together with a common sense of purpose.

The fairly small number of pilot whales killed by the Faroese each year comes from a rather large population in the north Atlantic, and it is non-commercial. Therefore it is not directly comparable to the large scale, commercial whale hunting conducted by many countries of the world in the past, the kind of industrial killing leading to the collapse of many whale populations around the globe.

Whether it is right or not to kill these animals in this particular way is a question for every person's own moral compass. However, in comparison to much other horribleness subjected to animals by people, I think that the Faroese whale drive has gotten a slightly unfair treatment by the media and by animal rights groups like Greenpeace.

I do, however, understand why the sea covered in a thick layer of warm blood and people carving up the whales so close to shore, where they are visible to every spectator, makes for powerful and sometimes disturbing photos.

What I do know from having seen it with my own eyes is that the way it is done is not any worse or any better than any other form of recreational hunting. We will always be putting animals at the risk of suffering when we decide to kill them, that is an unavoidable fact.

In the Faroes, the number of pilot whales killed over the past 10 years has ranged between zero and about 1,100 per year. As a comparison, in Sweden, 80,000–100,000 moose are shot every year and no veterinarian is present on site, which is the case on the Faroe Islands.

Seals

Different species of seal have historically been eaten around pretty much all of the Nordic coastal regions but perhaps a bit less during modern times and lately almost not at all around the central Scandinavian parts.

Today seal is most commonly hunted and eaten in Greenland, where it is a cherished and important everyday food. Historically it was harpooned but today it is hunted with a rifle like many other animals on land.

In the old days, the Inuit, who are the indigenous inhabitants of Greenland, could subsist almost entirely from eating seal for long periods of time. I have been told by Anne Sofie Hardenberg, who helped me out with all of the queries on the food culture of Greenland, that the seal was and is still considered a very convenient meat because it is there all the time. A luxury to the old Inuit populations because many of their other foods sources like capelin and whales are migratory and therefore only available at certain times of the year. The seal, with its high level of omega 3 fatty acids, vitamin B12, iron and zinc is highly nutritious.

In Greenland, every part of the seal is used and nothing is wasted. The hides become the skins of kayaks or clothing, while the blubber is eaten fresh or fermented in the seal's stomach but can also be rendered into oil for lighting or heat. The meat and offal are either consumed fresh or dried before being eaten. Even the guts will be used: simply by washing them and cooking them together with the meat or on their own. The stomach was historically stretched out and dried to be used as a kind of window, and the blood pored into a length of intestine and hung up to wind dry before being cut in strips. It's is an excellent snack to chew called *kukkarnaat*.

One of the most important historical dishes made from seal in Greenland is a seal soup called suaasat. It was traditionally prepared in a soap stone vessel over a stove fuelled with rendered seal fat and it was left to simmer there for a long time. It gave its heat to the people cooking it and the house in which it was cooked in a country where food containing a lot of energy and warmth is necessary due to its climate.

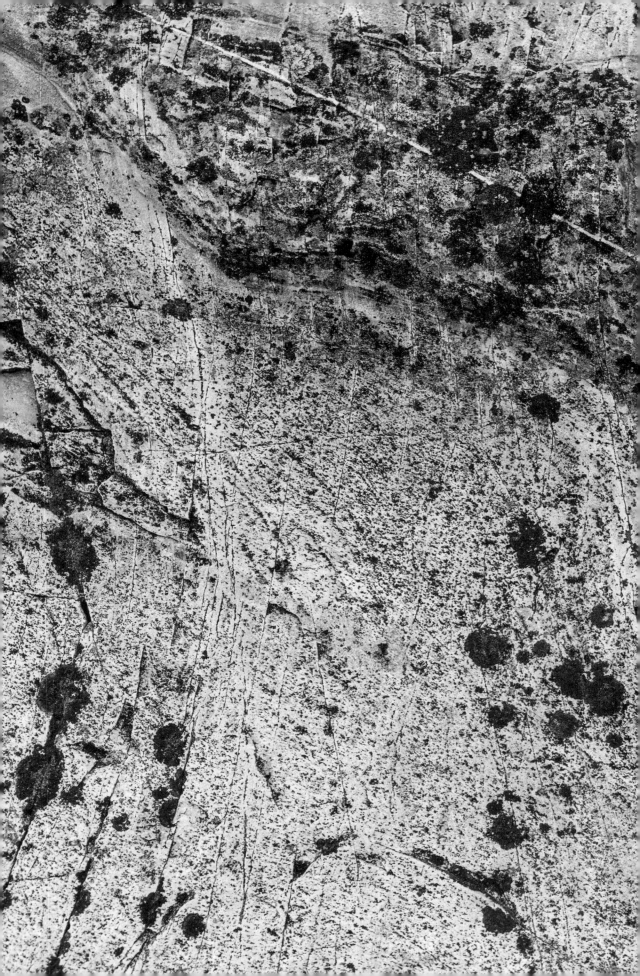

SKAGEN SALAD

Skagenröra (Sweden)

This mix of shrimp (baby shrimp) and mayo was invented by Swedish chef Tore Wretman in the 1950s and it was named after the northern Danish city of Skagen. Skagen salad is funnily enough almost completely unknown in Denmark, whereas in Sweden it has remained one of the most popular starters (appetizers) altogether. Often served on slices of white bread fried in butter and topped with Bleak Roe (page 179) in a dish called Toast Skagen. Today *skagenröra* loosely refers to any creamy salad made from something that could possibly be red shellfish. Some of these salads are great and others are awful. The original contains shrimp, mayonnaise and dill (according to some accounts with the addition of a bit of grated horseradish). The worst more recent addition is onion – red or any other kind. It makes the delicate dilly mix smell to me like standing in a dirty second-hand clothes store, a bit like sweat aged on synthetic fibres from the 1960s. Don't add onion to your Skagen salad. Also it contains absolutely no dairy products. Many modern recipes contain crème fraîche and they are wrong. It will only result in a sour taste and a too liquid salad.

If you have made a great mayo it will be acidic enough and you won't feel that the salad lacks in acidity. This is important as adding liquids like vinegar or lemon will make it too wet. Serve the salad with a wedge of lemon on the side.

Preparation time: 10 minutes
Sitting time: at least 10 minutes
Serves: 4 as a starter (appetizer)

400 g/14 oz boiled shrimp (baby shrimp)
 tails, shelled
100–200 ml/3½–7 fl oz (½–¾ cup plus
 1 tablespoon) homemade Mayonnaise
 (page 674), it needs to be very thick
1 good bunch dill, leaves picked fine
 and stems cut fine
salt and white pepper, to taste
grated horseradish, to taste

Coarsely chop half the shrimp (baby shrimp) tails and place them in a bowl with the remaining whole shrimp tails. Add enough mayo to properly coat all of the shrimp and make the mix creamy. Be careful though not to add too much as this will turn everything into more of a sauce, which is not the idea. Add the dill, salt and pepper and some grated horseradish if you like it. Let the salad sit for 10 minutes or so in the fridge. Stir again, adjust the texture with more mayo if necessary and once again adjust the seasoning.

For image see opposite page

ICELANDIC SHRIMP SALAD

Rækjusalat (Iceland)

This dish is not, from an historical perspective, very old in Iceland but it is indeed very popular. It is often served with Ritz brand crackers as an appetizer at parties or on a slice of Icelandic rye bread as a light meal. To distinguish it from the Swedish Skagen Salad (see left), Icelandic shrimp salad contains Hard-boiled Eggs (page 53) and, as far as I have seen, rarely any dill. There seems to be a huge variety of seasonings but common ones are a bit of paprika or some curry powder.

Preparation time: 10 minutes
Sitting time: at least 10 minutes
Serves: 4 as a starter (appetizer)

400 g/14 oz boiled shrimp (baby shrimp)
 tails, shelled
100–200 ml/3½–7 fl oz (½–¾ cup plus
 1 tablespoon) homemade Mayonnaise
 (page 674), it needs to be very thick
4 Hard-boiled Eggs (page 53), shelled and
 coarsely chopped into pieces
powdered paprika or curry powder,
 to taste
salt and white pepper, to taste

Coarsely chop half the shrimp (baby shrimp) tails and place them in a bowl with the remaining whole shrimp tails and the egg. Add enough mayo to properly coat all of the shrimp and make the mix creamy. Season and let the salad sit for 10 minutes or so in the refrigerator. Before stirring again, adjust the texture with more mayo if necessary and once again adjust the seasoning.

Clockwise from top left: Skagen Salad (page 256); Crab; Langoustine; Crayfish; Shrimp; Lobster

WEST COAST SALAD

Västkustsallad (Sweden)

This salad was popular in Sweden during the 1960s and it is most often seen today as more of a shellfish-in-mayonnaise kind of salad – a bit like Skagen Salad (page 256), but using a mixed selection of shellfish, not seldom bought in a jar from a supermarket shelf.

The original salad is topped with lobster, shrimp (baby shrimp), mussels, tomatoes, sliced raw mushrooms and, in some recipes, green peas. In most older recipes, the dressing is a simple Vinaigrette (page 676) but sometimes it's Rhode Island sauce or different mixes of Mayonnaise (page 674) and cultured dairy products, like *grädfil* or crème fraîche.

Preparation and cooking time: 15 minutes
Serves: 4 as a starter (appetizer) or light
  meal

1 iceberg lettuce, leaves separated
1 cooked lobster, meat only, coarsely cut
  into pieces
50 mussels cooked, cooled and
  shells discarded
2 large handfuls cooked shrimp (baby
  shrimp), cooled and peeled
8 large button mushrooms, thinly sliced
2 tomatoes, cut into wedges
200 g/7 oz (1½ cups) cooked green peas

Spread the lettuce leaves out on a serving platter and top with all the remaining ingredients. Finish with vinaigrette or Rhode Island sauce.

PILOT WHALE
(*GLOBICEPHALA MELAS*)

A small whale belonging to the oceanic dolphin family, traditionally hunted on the Faroe Islands. The hunts, known as *grindadráp*, are non-commercial and the meat is divided up within the community. Pilot whale meat used to be an important source of food in the Faroe Islands and most Faroese consume quite a bit of its meat and blubber each year. Aside from the obvious conflict with organisations working for preservation of the sea, concerns about eating the meat of these whales have been raised because of the high levels of mercury and other toxins like PCBs (polychlorinated biphenyls) and dioxin, which accumulate in the flesh. This situation, which is not uncommon with predators in the sea, is made more problematic because the whales live considerably longer than most predatory fish and therefore accumulate more toxins over their lifespan.

The meat and blubber can be eaten fresh but is traditionally most often preserved, in different ways. Today, freezing the fresh meat is one of those methods. It can also be salted dry (*turrsaltað*) or in brine (*lakasaltað*) or it can be cut in slices called *grindalikkja* and hung up to dry.

I find that the meat itself is a little bit like lean beef with a subtle hint of sea and that the cured blubber tastes much like toasted hazelnuts, in a strange animal way.

BOILED PILOT WHALE WITH BLUBBER
AND POTATOES

Kókað fesk grind (Faroe Islands)

Preparation and cooking time: 1¾ hours
Serves: 4

1 kg/2¼ lb pilot whale, coarsely cut
  into cubes
250 g/9 oz pilot whale blubber, cut into
  cubes of about 2 cm/¾ inch
800 g/1¾ lb potatoes
salt, to taste

Place the whale meat and blubber in a pot large enough to also fit the potatoes. Cover the meat with cold water and quickly bring to the boil over a medium heat. Strain and discard the water. Return the meat to the pot and cover with fresh water. Add salt and bring to a simmer. Cover the pot and cook the meat until tender, which will take at least an hour. Skim away excess fat.

When the meat is almost tender, add the potatoes to the pot and add more water to cover, if necessary. Cover the pot and cook for 30 minutes, or until the potatoes are tender. Strain well, then arrange the meat, blubber and potatoes on a platter.

BRAISED PILOT WHALE

Grindabúffur (Faroe Islands)

Serve with Boiled Potatoes (page 117) and Braised Red Cabbage (page 98).

Preparation and cooking time: 1 hour
Soaking time: overnight
Serves: 4

1 kg/2¼ lb pilot whale meat, soaked
  overnight in cold milk
butter, for frying
2 onions, thinly sliced
1 tablespoon plain (all-purpose) flour
Meat Stock (page 650), to cover
Chinese mushroom soy sauce, to taste
salt and white pepper, to taste

Drain the soaked whale meat, pat it dry with a clean cloth, then cut it into 2-cm/¾-inch thick strips.

Melt some butter in a pan over a medium heat. Add the strips of whale meat and the onions and fry until brown. Towards the end of the browning process, sift over the flour and add enough stock (broth) to cover. Cover the pan and simmer for about 40 minutes, or until the meat is tender. Season to taste with soy sauce, salt and pepper.

SEAL SOUP

Suaasat (Greenland)
Sælsuppe (Denmark)

Serve the meat on a platter with strong mustard on the side next to a bowl containing the soup.

Preparation and cooking time: 1 hour
Serves: 4

100 g/3½ oz (½ cup) pearl barley, rolled
  oats or short-grain rice
1 onion, finely chopped
1 kg/2¼ lb mixed seal meat, blubber
  and innards
salt, to taste

Mix the grains and onion with 1 litre/34 fl oz (4¼ cups) water in a pot and bring to a boil. Lower the heat to a simmer and cook for about 15 minutes. Add the seal and some salt and keep simmering for another 20–30 minutes or until the meat is tender. Season to taste. Lift the meat out of the pot with a slotted spoon and place it on a serving platter, serve the soup from the pot.

BOILED SEAL INTESTINES WITH BLUBBER AND CROWBERRIES

*Kogte sæltarme med sælspæk og sortebær
  (Greenland)*

Crowberries are very rich in vitamin C and are popularly eaten both in sweet and in savory preparations like this one from Greenland. This recipe is not a dish in itself but one which is served as a side with dried seal meat or dried fish.

Preparation and cooking time: 40 minutes
Serves: 4

1 tablespoon salt
300 g/11 oz seal intestines, cut
  into 2 cm/¾ inch slices
500 g/1 lb 2 oz seal blubber
200 g/7 oz crowberries
2 handfuls roseroot leaves

Bring 2 litres/3½ UK pints (8½ cups) water and the salt to a boil in a pot. Add the intestines and lower the heat to a simmer. Cook for 20 minutes before removing the intestines with a slotted spoon and allow them to cool.

Cut the blubber into 1 cm/½ inch dice, and mix with the intestines, crowberries and roseroot leaves.

POULTRY

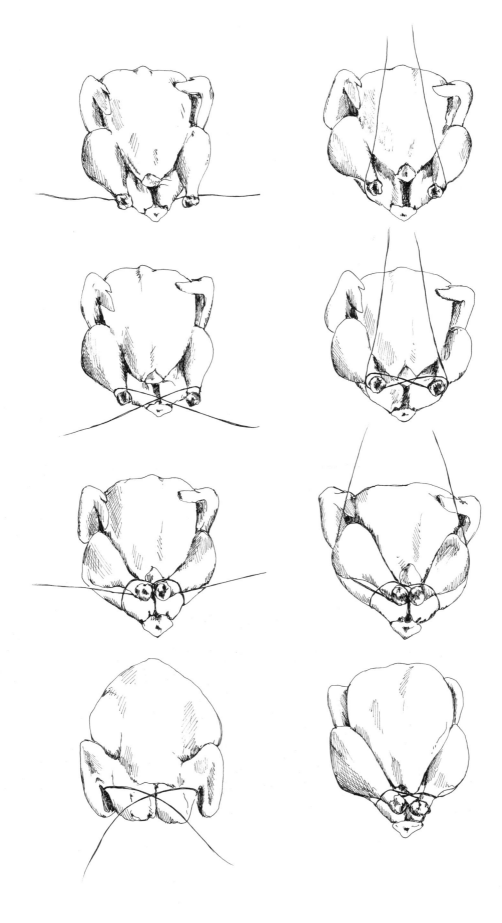

CHICKEN IN CURRY SAUCE

Kylling i karry (Denmark)
Kyckling i curry sås (Sweden)

Curry powder was introduced into Danish kitchens in 1828, through a cookbook written by Maria Hemmingsen, which included a recipe for duck in curry. How long chicken curry has been prepared in Denmark is less clear, but I would assume for almost as long, considering the rather small step between one bird and another in the mind of a cook who can't get a hold of all the ingredients for a recipe.

Chicken in curry is eaten in most of the Nordic region as it is in most parts of the western world, but it is not regarded quite as highly as it is in Denmark, therefore I have chosen a Danish recipe for this dish. The one my mum cooked at home was quite similar to this though, but she would have gone a bit lighter on the curry powder than most Danes seem to do.

Looking in Danish cookery books, magazines and on the internet, you will find some very serious and elaborate recipes where the curry powder is made spice by spice, and which resembles something actually cooked in India or sometimes perhaps Southeast Asia. Truth be told though, I think that most Danes use the yellow turmeric-, cardamom- and ginger-heavy stuff you buy in a supermarket. To me that is also what tastes right; possibly not the pinnacle of curry flavour in general, but that kind of curry kind of belongs in a dish like this. Similarly, while the recipe below calls for homemade chicken stock (broth), most people would probably use stock (bouillon).

If you feel like you really want to walk all over the identity of Indian food, add the contents of a small can of diced pineapple towards the end of the cooking time. However wrong this might feel, I reckon it is still, in some way, true to the Danish spirit of the dish.

Kyllin i karry is most often served with Boiled Rice (page 654).

Preparation and cooking time: 45 minutes
Serves: 4

650–800 g/1½–1¾ lb meat from a whole
   chicken, cut into pieces
butter, for frying
2 onions, finely chopped
2 tablespoons yellow curry powder (or more,
   depending on its strength)
2 large carrots, cut into 5 mm/¼ inch slices
200 ml/7 fl oz (¾ cup plus 1 tablespoon)
   Chicken Stock (page 650)
300 ml/10½ fl oz (1¼ cups) cream
1 clove garlic, crushed
salt, to taste

Melt a knob of butter in a pot over a medium heat. Add the chicken, onion and curry powder and fry for about 10 minutes or so. Take your time with this step so that it doesn't all stick to the bottom of the pan and burn.

Add the carrots and stock (broth) to the pan and bring to the boil. Boil for a few minutes, then add the cream. Lower the heat and simmer until the chicken is tender and the sauce has thickened to coat it a little. If the curry flavour is not strong enough for your liking, then add a little more as it is cooking. Finish by adjusting the level of salt.

POT-ROASTED CHICKEN

Grydestegt kylling (Denmark)
Grytstekt kyckling (Sweden)

Pot-roasted chicken is a dish with a very old history. It would seem logical that this was a practical way of cooking a whole bird until juicy and tender, without the use of an oven, the pot in itself creating a little miniature oven when placed on top of a heat source. The wood-fired cast iron stove which offered the first really usable oven available to most modest homes that couldn't afford or fit a brick oven was popularized during the mid-nineteenth century and it is easy to imagine this technique being way older than that.

The funny thing, today, is that most of the more recent recipes for pot-roasted chicken place the pot in the oven for the actual cooking as opposed to the stove top. This is obviously very convenient, but also makes you question if it wouldn't be better to just roast the bird without the lid to get some crispness on the skin and just skipping the pot altogether and using an ordinary roasting pan... Anyhow, I often make pot-roasted chicken in the oven and, even if it doesn't make sense, it feels good somehow.

Chicken like this is, in Denmark, often served with Boiled Potatoes (page 117), Brown Gravy (page 671) and Quick Pickled Cucumber (page 658). In Sweden the gravy is most often substituted with a Basic Cream Sauce (page 663). Both the gravy and sauce most of the time are seasoned with liberal amounts of Chinese mushroom soy sauce. Most Swedes would also want some Black-current Jelly (page 691) and some, including myself, like some Browned Brussels Sprouts (page 104) with their chicken.

Preparation and cooking time: 2 hours
Serves: 4

1 chicken, liver, heart and gizzard reserved
butter, for browning
cooking oil, for browning
2 carrots, cut into medium pieces
8 small shallots
6–12 button mushrooms, depending on size,
　　whole, halved or quartered, according
　　to their size and your preference
2 cloves garlic, crushed with the side
　　of a knife
1 bay leaf
2 sprigs thyme
200 ml/7 fl oz (¾ cup plus 1 tablespoon)
　　white wine
salt and white pepper, to taste

Follow the illustrations on page 266 for trussing the chicken. Season it well with salt and pepper, both inside and out.

Melt some butter with a little oil in a heavy cast iron pot or ovenproof dish over a medium–high heat and brown the bird all over. Take the pot off the heat and sit the bird breast-side up. Add the liver, heart, gizzard, vegetables, garlic and herbs, then pour in the wine. Cover with a lid and bring to a simmer over a low heat. (Or place it in an oven, preheated to 150°C/300°F/Gas Mark 2.) Cook the bird for 30–40 minutes, which makes it just cooked and juicy, or longer if you like it more well-done.

When the chicken is ready, strain off the cooking liquid and use it to make gravy or cream sauce, as you prefer.

Follow the illustrations on page 271 for carving the chicken and arrange on a serving platter with the vegetables from the pot. Serve the sauce in a sauce boat on the side.

For image see opposite page

Clockwise from top left: Sweet-and-Sour Braised Red Cabbage (page 98); Roast Pork and Crackling (page 300); Quick Pickled Cucumbers (page 658); Danish Sugar-browned Potatoes (page 120); Basic Cream Sauce (page 663); Pot-Roasted Chicken (page 268)

CHILLI CREAMED CHICKEN AND BANANA CASSEROLE

Flygande jakob (Sweden)

This dish is one that every Swede who grew up after 1980 has a relationship with, and most of those growing up before too for that matter. Few dishes are as emblematic and unique to the contemporary food culture of Sweden as this. The recipe was first published in Swedish magazine *Allt om Mat* in 1976. The inventor of the dish was Ove Jacobsson, a man working in air-freight, hence the name in Swedish, *flygande Jakob* or Flying Jacob in English. The combination of chicken, cream, Heinz chilli sauce, salted peanuts and one of Sweden's most cherished fruits, the banana, is truly spectacular and one of the strongest lasting cultural expressions of the early eighties, at least in my opinion. Oh, it is also seasoned with readymade Italian salad dressing mix.

If you search the internet, flygande jakob gives you 109,000 hits, not bad for a dish which only exists in one country with not even ten million inhabitants.

Serve *flygande jakob* with white rice, shredded iceberg lettuce and cucumber (no vinegar, please), then lean back, close your eyes, and pretend you are me eating in 1989 and enjoy yourself.

Preparation and cooking time: 1 hour
Serves: 4

1 large chicken, roasted (page 268) and
    cooled down
store-bought dry, Italian salad dressing mix,
    to taste
2 bananas, cut lengthwise and then halved
300 ml/10½ fl oz (1¼ cups) cream
100 ml/3½ fl oz (⅓ cup plus 1 tablespoon)
    Heinz chilli sauce
150 g/5 oz bacon, cut into small pieces
80 g/3 oz (½ cup) salted peanuts

Preheat the oven to 225°C/435°F/Gas Mark 7.

Pull the meat off the chicken carcass and tear it into rough pieces. Spread the meat out in an ovenproof dish and sprinkle generously with the Italian seasoning. Arrange the banana pieces on top of the chicken, cut surface facing upwards.

Whip the cream to soft peaks, then fold in the chilli sauce. Spread over the chicken and banana and bake in the oven until the surface is nicely caramelized.

Meanwhile, fry the bacon in a pan over a medium heat until it is crisp. Drain on paper towels.

Remove the casserole from the oven and leave it to sit for at least 10 minutes (otherwise you risk burning your mouth on the lethally-hot banana). Sprinkle on the bacon and peanuts and serve.

DANISH CHICKEN SALAD

Hønsesalat (Denmark)

This creamy salad is made using cooked chicken, vegetables, mayonnaise and sometimes crème fraîche. It is usually eaten on Danish Rye Bread (page 504) as an open sandwich (page 522).

Popular vegetables for *hønsesalat* are celery, celeriac (celery root), peas, cooked mushrooms and asparagus or peas. I have even come across recipes that include fruit – usually apple, pineapple or grapes.

Many recipes also contain herbs, like chives, parsley or tarragon. It is also quite common to have a little curry powder added, although not every recipe includes this. I remember one Danish chef, of a previous generation, once made *hønsesalat* in a restaurant I worked at when I was watching, and she explained how important Maggi Seasoning sauce was for a 'proper' Danish chicken salad.

Preparation and cooking time: 10 minutes
Serves: 4 for a lunchtime sandwich

200 g/7 oz button mushrooms
150 g/5 oz (1 cup) green peas
500 g/1 lb 2 oz cooked chicken, coarsely
    chopped
2 celery stalks, cut into 5 mm/¼ inch slices
100 ml/3½ fl oz (⅓ cup plus 1 tablespoon)
    Mayonnaise (page 674)
100 ml/3½ fl oz (⅓ cup plus 1 tablespoon)
    crème fraîche

Worcestershire sauce, to taste
curry powder, to taste
chives, parsley or tarragon, to taste
    (optional)
salt and white pepper, to taste

Follow the instructions on page 85 for blanching
the mushrooms and the peas. Cut the mushrooms
into 5 mm/¼ inch slices.

Put the mushrooms and peas in a large mixing bowl
with all the other ingredients and mix everything
together. Season generously – Danish chicken
salad should be very flavourful.

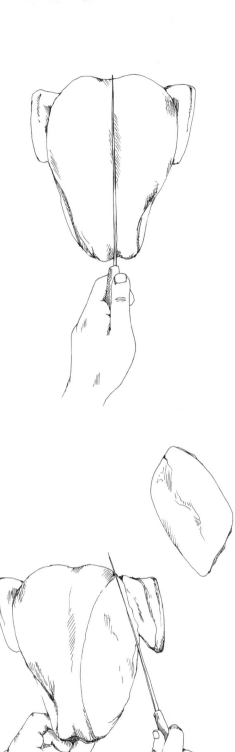

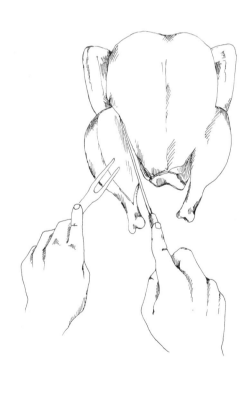

FRICASSÉE OF HEN

Hønsefrikasse (Norway)

Hønsefrikassé is a loved Norwegian comfort food and despite its French-sounding name and its French roots, it is considered very Norwegian. It was in fact one of the dishes that Andreas Viestad, who helped me with Norway, pointed out for me as a crucial dish missing from the first draft of this book's recipe list. Serve your fricassée of hen with Boiled Potatoes (page 117).

The older recipes for this dish are very bland and contain little but bird and carrots. Most more recent recipes are a little bit more central European in style, containing a bit of garlic, some herbs and more vegetables. This is one of those recipes.

Green peas are also a commonly added. If you want to use them add a couple of handfuls of blanched peas to the hot fricassée just before serving.

Preparation and cooking time: 1½ hours
Serves: 4 with a bit to spare for lunch the
*   day after*

1 hen, cleaned and ready to cook
10 white peppercorns
1 bay leaf
1 clove garlic, crushed
1 sprig thyme
1 quantity Beurre Manié (page 651)
2 carrots, cut into 1 cm/½ inch slices
1 onion, cut into wedges
1 piece of celeriac, cut into pieces
1 leek, the white part cut into 1 cm/½ inch
    slices, the green part kept for the cooking
    of the bird
200 ml/7 fl oz (¾ cup plus 1 tablespoon)
    cream
salt and white pepper, to taste

Place the hen in a large pot with the peppercorns, bay leaf, garlic and thyme. Cover with water and bring to the boil, then lower the heat to a simmer and skim the surface of the cooking liquid. Continue cooking until tender, it should take about 45–60 minutes or so.

Lift the bird out of the broth and place it on a baking sheet next to the stove. Strain the broth

into a new pot and continue simmering until about 1 litre/1¾ pints (4¼ cups) remains. Add the beurre manié and again bring to a simmer. Add the vegetables and continue cooking them until they are done – perhaps 15 minutes or so. Add the cream after the first 5 minutes have passed.

While the vegetables are cooking, pull the meat off the bird and into suitable pieces. Discard the skin, cartilage and bones. Just before serving add the meat to the pot with the vegetables and the sauce and adjust the seasoning with salt and pepper.

SCANIAN SPICED GOOSE BLOOD SOUP

Svartsoppa (Sweden)

This soup is mainly enjoyed as part of the traditional St Martin's goose feast (see opposite page) in the southern Swedish province of Scania.

In its most traditional form a basic meat broth (sometimes including cooking juices from goose giblets), is thickened with flour and goose blood. Most versions of this soup are, to some extent, sweet-and-sour. This is generally achieved by adding prunes, apples, Redcurrant Jelly (page 691), golden syrup, Ättika vinegar (page 656) and/or red wine to the broth.

Svartsoppa is seasoned with plenty of sweet spices like cinnamon, ginger, cloves or allspice as well as white pepper. A good dash of strong alcohol like Cognac or Calvados is often added just before serving, so that the soup has the bite of raw alcohol.

A simple way of making this soup is to make a batch of Velouté (page 652) from light veal or Chicken Stock (page 650), combined with goose cooking juices or goose broth, if you have it.

Preparation and cooking time: 40 minutes
Serves: 4 if you are a huge fan of blood soup,
*   many more if you just want a taste of it*
*   as part of a goose feast menu*

2 litres/3½ UK pints (8½ cups) light veal or
    Chicken Stock (page 650)
6 pitted prunes

1 apple
200 ml/7 fl oz (¾ cup plus 1 tablespoon)
   red wine
1 tablespoon Ättika (12%) vinegar
   (page 656)
cinnamon, ginger, cloves or allspice, and
   white pepper, to taste
4 quantities Roux (page 651)
200 ml/7 fl oz (¾ cup plus 1 tablespoon)
   goose blood
good dash Cognac or Calvados

To make the velouté, heat the liquid, prunes, apple, red wine, vinegar and the spices in a pot until simmering. Keep the roux in the pot in which it was made. The pot used to make the roux needs to be large enough to eventually hold all of the liquid.

Pour the liquid and fruit into the pot with the roux while whisking briskly so that no lumps form. Place the pot on the stove over medium heat and bring to a simmer stirring once in a while. Cook for 10 minutes or until the liquid has thickened and no longer tastes of flour.

Strain the finished velouté to get rid of all the aromatics and add 200 ml/7 fl oz (¾ cup plus 1 tablespoon) goose blood for each 2 litres/3½ UK pints (8½ cups) of finished velouté. When you have added the blood the soup can never boil. Heat it slowly until it darkens and serve immediately after adding the alcohol, if using.

For image see page 275

ST MARTIN'S GOOSE

Mortensgås (Norway)
Gåsamiddag (Sweden)

The region of Skåne, or Scania, the southernmost Swedish region, is a part of the country which doesn't feel quite Swedish, and as a matter of fact, since it became part of the kingdom of Sweden as late as 1658, it has been Danish a lot longer than it has been Swedish.

The connection to Denmark is felt both culturally when looking at the traditions of food and eating, and in the way people speak and express themselves in the region – there are many common denominators to their southern neighbours. Obviously over three hundred years of Swedification, and with plenty of people moving around the whole country, the edges have been rounded off a bit. To me it becomes obvious though each time I go to Denmark with my wife, who is Scanian. She understands Danish with no effort whilst I, who comes from much further north, have to speak English.

On the eve of 10 November, the day before St Martin's Day, a vast number of Scanians and Danes alike will cook a goose or a duck. I read somewhere, possibly not on official records, that based on the number of sold birds, at least a third of the Danish households will take part in this old tradition.

In Scania it is probably more common to have goose dinner in a restaurant sometime in early November as a goose easily serves fifteen people and is quite impractical in that sense. This could also be a reason why the Danes, who more often eat it in their home, have shifted to duck, a bird of more convenient size.

There are several stories on why goose is eaten on the 10th, one having to do with St Martin himself being exposed by the sound of a flock of excitable geese when in hiding from the villagers of Tours, who wanted to make him bishop against his will. A more easy-to-confirm theory is that St Martin's Day marks the start of Lent before Christmas and goose is nice, fatty and festive.

Most Danes will cook a duck whilst most Scanians will cook a goose. In Denmark the duck is typically roasted and served with caramelized potatoes called *brunede poteter* (page 120), Brown Gravy (page 671) and dessert is often, Danish Almond Rice Pudding (page 626).

In Sweden the goose is usually roasted and served with Roast Potatoes (page 112), some vegetables like Braised Red Cabbage (page 98) and/or some green vegetables like Brussels sprouts or green beans. A spiced soup thickened with the goose blood, called *svartsoppa* (see opposite page), or 'black soup' is often served alongside the giblets and a Scanian apple cake is customary for dessert.

ROAST GOOSE OR DUCK WITH
PRUNES AND APPLES

Steikt Dunna (Faroe Islands)
Stegt and med svesker og æbler (Denmark)

In a Danish home for Christmas, if the family doesn't eat roasted pork with crackling (*flæsk-esteg,* page 300) they will most likely have a roast duck. It would be served with Danish Sugar-browned Potatoes (page 120), Sweet and sour braised Red Cabbage (page 98) and some Brown Gravy (page 671) or cream gravy. The technique below works just as fine with goose as it does with duck. Use the roasting juices to make the sauce. Myself I like to serve a roast bird like this with cream gravy, some Apple Compote (page 700), Kale Salad (page 90) or Brussels Sprouts (page 104) and some small potatoes still in their skins, roasted together with the bird in the oven.

I didn't really like roast duck and goose before, I always thought it was a pity to not break it down into breast and leg and cook them separately to en-sure perfect cooking of both pieces. This was until I realized that I was always scared of overcooking it, a fact that lead to me tending to undercook it. In my opinion a roast goose or duck needs to be well done, it simply needs to roast long enough to first go tough and then to pretty much braise tender in its own fat. These days I always brine it lightly as this helps to make the bird both more tender and more juicy. Place the bird for 24 hours in a cold 2% salt brine (page 434). Rinse it before cooking if you want to do this. It helps to start with a dry skin if you want a crispy bird. What I do is I usually leave the uncovered bird on a rack in the refrigerator for 24 hours before starting to cook it. This means that if you are going to brine it as well (which I recommend you do) you need to start preparations 48 hours before you intend to start cooking it.

Preparation and cooking time: 3–7 hours,
 allow at least 45 minutes of cooking per
 1 kg/2¼ lb of bird
Brining time: 24 hours (optional)
Drying time: 24 hours (optional)
Resting time: 20 minutes
Serves: a small duck will be enough for
 4 but a large goose can feed 12

1 goose or duck, brined as explained
 above, or fresh
salt, to rub (if you haven't already
 brined the bird)
equal parts of whole pitted prunes and
 quartered pitted apples, enough to fill
 the cavity of the bird

Preheat the oven to 250°C/480°F/Gas Mark 9.

If you haven't already brined the bird, rub it inside and out with a generous amount of salt. Fill the cavity withe prunes and apple quarters. Place the brined or salted bird, breast down on a roasting pan, in the oven. Make sure to colour both breasts equally by shifting the bird once or twice so that they both come in contact with the pan itself. It should take about 15 minutes.

Flip the bird so that it's breast side up and low-er the temperature of the oven to 140°C/275°F/Gas Mark 1 and pour enough water into the pan to cover the entire bottom. Continue roasting until the bird is done. It is important that the bottom is always covered with liquid to ensure that the gravy won't taste burned afterwards. It is rather difficult to assess whether a bird like this is done but if you insert a pairing knife into the thick part of the breast and pull it straight out it should come out with very little resistance.

If you are roasting potatoes with the bird, add them to the tray when about 1 hour remains of the cooking time.

When done, the bird should rest for a good 20 minutes on a wire rack outside of the oven while you make the gravy and finish the garnishes.

For image see opposite page

Clockwise from top left: Sweet-and-Sour Braised Red Cabbage (page 98); Glazed Brussels Sprouts (page 105); Roast Goose or Duck with Prunes and Apples (page 274); Scanian Spiced Goose Blood Soup (page 272); Brown Gravy (page 671)

GAME

Previous page: Some reindeer grazing on the last dry grass after winter, north Norway, May 2014.

Game has been a part of people's diet all over the Nordic region since Neolithic times, at first as a free source of food necessary for survival and later increasingly as a recreational occupation, however still contributing with large quantities of food feeding a lot of people. Myself, for example, I grew up in northern Swedish middle-class suburbia and my parents didn't need to hunt to feed the family. Yet, each autumn (fall) in September, alongside 270,000 other people, my dad went back to where he grew up to hunt for moose, like his father before him and like people had done since prehistoric times, except for a few hundred years when large game was the property of the crown and nobility.

When I left home to go to high school I had probably not eaten beef more than a handful of times in my life, simply because we had moose. The word *kött*, meat in Swedish, was to me until I started cooking school, pretty much synonymous with moose meat.

I have met people in every Nordic country except Denmark who even today live their life largely from harvesting wild meat, and even though the vast majority of hunting carried out is recreational, it is still interesting to see these remains of something which was once such a vital part of people's subsistence, especially in the more remote central and northern parts of Sweden and Denmark, northern and eastern Finland and the island regions of the Atlantic.

What game people have hunted and still hunt is, like in any other part of the world, directly related to what's there. In Sweden, with its vast coniferous forests and abundant moose, that's common, while the Faroese hunt puffin and on Greenland Inuits kill the occasional narwhal for food.

Opposite: Man smoking and waiting for a puffin to come close enough for him to net it, Stóra Dímun, Faroe Islands, end of July 2013.

ICELANDIC GROUSE SOUP

Rjúpusúpa (Iceland)

The different recipes I have found for this soup either use the leftover carcasses from another grouse recipe, and no actual meat in the soup itself, or they use whole grouse, from which the breasts are separated and cooked separately, to be added back to the soup just before serving. It seems the versions that include meat in the soup are more recent than the ones using the leftover carcasses.

The type of grouse found in Iceland is rock ptarmigan (*Lagopus muta*). Different recipes are flavoured in different ways; some contain fortified wine, like Madeira or Sherry, some contain blue cheese (like the sauce for Icelandic Christmas Grouse, see right) or juniper berries and most seem to contain Currant Jelly (page 691). This is a relatively basic recipe, to which you can add any of the above-mentioned flavourings, if you feel like it.

Preparation and cooking time: 2 hours
Serves: 4

2 whole grouse, breasts reserved, carcasses
   cleaned and coarsely chopped (or use
   4 leftover carcasses, coarsely chopped)
butter, for browning and frying
1 handful dried wild mushrooms
1 small onion, finely chopped
1 carrot, coarsely chopped
1 celery stalk, coarsely chopped
250 ml/8 fl oz (1 cup) cream
2 tablespoons redcurrant jam or
   jelly (page 690, page 691)
your choice of juniper berries, fortified wine
   or blue cheese, to taste
salt and white pepper, to taste

Heat a pot over a medium heat and carefully brown the chopped carcasses in some butter. Add the dried mushrooms and the vegetables and continue cooking for a few more minutes before adding enough water to cover. Bring to a slow boil, then simmer, uncovered, for about an hour.

Strain the stock (broth) through a fine-mesh sieve, into another pot. Bring back to a slow boil then add the cream. Continue to simmer, uncovered, until the soup is reduced to the desired texture and intensity of flavour. Finish by adding the currant jam or jelly and any other flavourings of your choice. Season to taste with salt and pepper.

Heat some butter in a frying pan over a high heat. Fry the grouse breasts quickly, 1–2 minutes on each side, then season with salt and pepper. Remove the breasts from the pan, cut anyway you want and serve immediately with the soup. Grouse meat doesn't respond well to over-cooking or to resting too long because it is very lean and finely textured; it tends to go mushy if treated poorly.

ICELANDIC CHRISTMAS GROUSE

Steiktar rjúpur / Jólarjúpa (Iceland)

Once upon a time this dish was only for those so poor that they couldn't afford any other food for Christmas. Today that's hardly the case, and it is the second most popular Christmas Day dinner after Icelandic Leg of Lamb, Cold-Smoked and Boiled (page 345). Christmas grouse is served with caramelized potatoes – a bit like Danish Sugar-browned Potatoes (page 120) – Braised Sweet-and-Sour Red Cabbage (page 82) and marrowfat peas. The variety of grouse found in Iceland is rock ptarmigan (*Lagopus muta*).

In older recipes, the grouse is essentially a braised dish where the birds are browned and then simmered until tender, before the cream sauce, seasoned with currant jelly and cheese, is prepared from the broth. In older recipes, brown cheese was used, rather than blue cheese, as this wasn't used in Iceland historically. I have also seen recipes that have an addition of cultured whey or *mysa*, to give freshness and acidity.

Today, recipes are found making use of the carcasses only for the preparation of the sauce, leaving the breasts to be quickly fried in a pan instead. It results in two distinctly different dishes. I think it is a great example of the evolution of a traditional dish, fuelled by the changing taste preferences of those cooking it. Today more people would prefer their meat cooked pink than was the case historically.

In this recipe the grouse is braised. If you want to try the more modern approach to this classic dish, the preparation of the sauce is still done in the same way, the only difference is that you cut out the breasts and cook them in a pan with a little butter, just before serving, a bit like in the recipe for Icelandic Grouse Soup (opposite page).

Preparation and cooking time: 2 hours
Serves: 4

4 whole grouse, plucked, gutted
  and cleaned
butter, for frying
1 carrot, chopped
1 onion, finely chopped
1 bay leaf
1 sprig thyme
1 tablespoon Beurre Manié (page 651)
2 tablespoons Blackcurrant Jelly
  (page 691)
1 tablespoon crumbled blue cheese
salt and white pepper, to taste

Remove the breastbone from the grouse, with the breasts attached. Reserve the breasts on the bone for later. Coarsely chop the remaining parts of the carcasses.

Heat some butter in a pot over a medium heat and brown the chopped carcasses. Add the vegetables, bay leaf and thyme, barely cover with water and bring to a simmer. Cover with a lid and simmer for about 1 hour, then strain the stock (broth) through a fine-mesh sieve into a bowl.

In a separate pot, lightly brown the breast meat, still attached to the breastbone, in some butter over a medium heat, before pouring on the stock. Leave to simmer for about 45 minutes, or until the meat is tender.

When ready, lift the breasts onto a serving platter and add the remaining ingredients to the stock to make the sauce. Start with the beurre manié and currant jelly, which both need to boil a little bit. Next, add the blue cheese, which should just melt and be stirred into the warm sauce. Finish by seasoning with salt and pepper to taste. Serve the sauce over the grouse breasts or in a separate sauce bowl.

ROASTED OR BRAISED GUILLEMOT

Lomviga (Faroe Islands)

Guillemot is most often roasted or braised until tender and served with Boiled Potatoes (page 117) and gravy, and sometimes also with Poached Apples Stuffed with Jam (page 678).

Preparation and cooking time: 2–3 hours
Serves: 4

2 guillemots, plucked, gutted and cleaned,
  ready for cooking
butter, for frying
Brown Gravy (page 671)
Chinese mushroom soy sauce
salt and white pepper, to taste

If you are going to braise the birds, place them in a large pot, cover them with water and add plenty of salt. Bring to a simmer over a medium heat and cook until tender, which will take 1–2 hours, depending on the age of the bird.

To roast your guillemots, first preheat the oven to 150°C/300°F/Gas Mark 2.

Season the birds well with salt and pepper. Melt some butter in a casserole (Dutch oven) over a medium heat. Brown the birds, turning them so they colour evenly. When they are nicely browned, deglaze by adding 200 ml/7 fl oz (¾ cup plus 1 tablespoon) water and stirring the bottom of the casserole to scrape up any dark flavoursome bits. Cover the casserole with a lid and roast the birds for 1–2 hours, or until tender. Check every now and again to see that the water doesn't all evaporate; if it does, add some more.

When the birds are cooked to your liking, tip the cooking liquid from the casserole and use it to make a brown gravy, flavoured with Chinese mushroom soy sauce.

Increase the oven temperature to 220°C/425°F/ Gas Mark 7. Put the birds back in the oven, without the lid, for another 15 minutes, to give them a bit of colour.

ROASTED WOODCOCK

Stekt morkulla (Sweden)

Serve this classic preparation with very little garnish – possibly some Blackcurrant Jelly (page 691) on the side.

If you are squeamish about preparing these little birds, then ask your butcher or game dealer to pluck and gut them and to reserve the offal for you. He will also skin the heads of the birds and remove the eyes.

Preparation and cooking time: 2 hours
Serves: 4–8, depending on the size and
  condition of the birds and how hungry
  you and your guests are

4 woodcock, plucked and gutted, heads
  skinned and eyes removed; livers, hearts
  and gizzards cleaned, coarsely chopped
  and reserved for the sauce
butter, for frying
1 dash Cognac
200 ml/7 fl oz (¾ cup plus 1 tablespoon)
  Meat Stock (page 650)
200 ml/7 fl oz (¾ cup plus 1 tablespoon)
  cream
8 slices white bread
salt and white pepper, to taste

Preheat the oven to 100°C/200°F/Gas Mark ½.

Instead of trussing each bird, as you normally would for roasting, bend the head around the body and pierce the thighs with the long beak (see illustration right). Season with salt and pepper.

Heat a large frying pan over a fairly high heat. Melt some butter, then brown the birds, basting continuously so that the hot butter also flows into the cavity and it starts to cook from within. Be sure to baste the parts that can be difficult to get in direct contact with the pan, such as the head and the bottoms of the legs.

Once the birds are properly browned, transfer them to an ovenproof platter and put them in the oven to rest while you prepare the sauce and the toast. But work quickly, as they shouldn't stay in the oven for more than about 10 minutes.

Tip off any excess fat from the frying pan and wipe it carefully with a wad of paper towels (this is just to remove any unwanted fat). Return to a medium heat and add the reserved innards to the pan. Fry until lightly browned, then add a splash of Cognac to the pan and stir. Flambé to burn off the alcohol, then add the meat stock (broth) to the pan. Simmer for a few minutes, then strain the stock into a small pot and discard the innards.

Stir the cream into the stock, season with salt and pepper, then bring to the boil and simmer until just thickened.

While the sauce is simmering, heat a little more butter in a clean frying pan and fry the slices of bread. Season with salt and pepper and set aside.

Take the birds out of the oven and carefully remove the beak from the thigh. Use a meat cleaver or heavy knife to cut the birds in half along the length of the spine, neck and head. Give them a quick final fry on both sides over a medium heat. Check the seasoning just before serving.

Serve half a bird on a piece of fried bread and serve the sauce separately in a warm sauce boat.

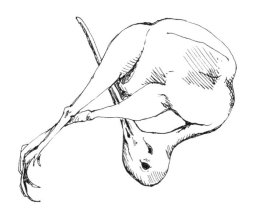

PUFFIN STUFFED WITH CAKE

Fyltur lundi (Faroe Islands)

Puffins on the Faroe Islands are most often filled with a sort of cake batter mixed with raisins, sewn shut and braised, or just braised without the cake. The batter can also be wrapped in little pouches of aluminium foil and braised together with the birds rather than inside them.

Leave the plucked, gutted and cleaned puffins to soak in cold water overnight before cooking them. They have a peculiar but tasty, fresh-ocean flavour to them, which can grow very strong and a bit heady for my taste if they are not handled well.

Serve with Boiled Potatoes (page 117), butter and Faroese rye bread. Sometimes when I have been served this, the cake batter has been prepared with the eggs of northern fulmar, which brings the fishy dimension to the stuffing as well.

Preparation and cooking time: 2 hours
Soaking time: overnight
Serves: 4

4 puffins, plucked, gutted, cleaned and
   soaked overnight in cold water

For the cake batter
200 g/7 oz (1¾ tablespoons) butter, soft
200 g/7 oz (1 cup) sugar
4 eggs
250 g/9 oz (2¼ cups) plain (all-purpose)
   flour
½ teaspoon baking powder
180 g/6½ oz (½ cup) raisins
pinch of salt

To make the cake batter, beat the butter and sugar in a mixing bowl until pale and fluffy. Add the eggs, one by one, and mix until fully combined. Sift the flour, baking powder and salt together onto the batter and mix again until fully combined. Fold the raisins into the batter.

Tie the neck of each bird with string so that the batter cannot escape that way and then fill the cavity of each one with a good amount of batter. Sew the other end shut with string. Wrap any remaining batter in packages of aluminium foil to cook alongside the birds, or pour it into a buttered and breaded cake pan to cook in the oven for dessert.

Place the birds and any aluminium foil packages in a large pot. Cover with water and a bit of salt. Bring to a slow boil and braise for about 1½ hours, or until the birds are tender.

NORTHERN FULMAR

Northern fulmar (*Fulmarus glacialis*) is a species of seabird highly abundant in the Nordic region. Its eggs and meat have surely been harvested wherever they were available in older times. Today, as far as I have seen, the only place where this bird is hunted and its eggs collected is the Faroe Islands. In spring, foragers will go out on the narrow cliff ledges of the windswept islands to collect the just-laid eggs of the fulmar. It used to be a common and important trade commodity for many islanders as well as a source of food. Today, probably due to the risk of falling down when picking the eggs and also the declining seabird populations of the world, foraging for northern fulmar eggs is less common.

Fulmar eggs are often boiled and enjoyed with a mild Curry Cream Sauce (page 665). If kept for a longer time, the eggs are often preserved in sodium silicate and can then be kept for as long as a year. If preserved, the fulmar eggs are more often used for baking cakes and similar.

The fatty chicks of the northern fulmar are considered a great delicacy and in spring, just after they have left their nest to tumble into the seas, people often go out in small boats to catch some before they learn how to properly fly. Sometimes they are collected before even leaving their nests.

Fulmar chicks are either eaten fresh or preserved in barrels filled with coarse sea salt. If salted they can easily keep for a year, but the fishiness of the fat will become more pronounced over time because of the ongoing rancidification. I rather like this mackerel-like flavour of northern fulmar. If cooked from fresh, rather than salted, quite a few people I have spoken to seem to like to brine their fulmar chicks before cooking them.

ROASTED OR BRAISED NORTHERN FULMAR CHICKS

Steiktir havhestaungar (Faroe Islands)

Fulmar chicks, braised or roasted, are often served with Boiled Potatoes (page 117) and Faroese rye bread or *rugbreyð*. Each person is presented with a whole bird and a sharp knife to take the meat off the bone. No sauce is necessary, thanks to the rich layer of fat under the young fulmar's skin, but sometimes you see seabirds like these served with Poached Apples Stuffed with Jam (page 678).

I recommend that you braise or roast them until well-done and tender. If they are fresh you could also choose to roast them pink. This, however, is not traditional or even very common on the islands today.

Preparation and cooking time: 1–3 hours
Brining time for a fresh bird: overnight
  in 2% brine (page 434)
Soaking time for salted birds: overnight
  in cold water
Serves: 4

4 northern fulmar chicks, fresh
  or preserved

To prepare fresh fulmar chicks, first follow the instructions for brining meat on page 434.

Salted fulmar chicks should be left overnight in cool water to remove excess salt, with the water changed several times.

To slow-roast fresh or preserved fulmar, first preheat the oven to 150°C/300°F/Gas Mark 2. Place the birds in a roasting pan and roast for about 2 hours, or until they are tender.

To quickly roast fresh fulmar, increase the oven temperature to about 230°C/450°F/Gas Mark 8 and roast them for 20–30 minutes, until the leg meat is cooked, with the breast meat still pink.

To braise the birds, put them in a big pot and cover with water. Simmer, covered, over a low heat for about 2 hours, or until the meat is very tender.

NORTHERN FULMAR EGGS IN CURRY CREAM SAUCE

The humid air of the small farmhouse kitchen condenses into pearls of water on the window panes separating the warm stillness inside from the harsh cold and howling wind outside. As Eva pours the boiling water from a big pot into the sink, a puff of noticeably warm steam flows through the kitchen, almost like I am seated in a sauna, only marginally cooler and with me being dressed rather than naked. We are cooking the just-picked eggs from northern fulmar, eggs that I have been collecting with Eva's husband Jógvan Jón and her brother Janus earlier the same day. Together we have been climbing around the edges of the little North Atlantic island, I paralyzed from fright of falling to a premature death at the bottom of the steep surrounding cliffs, them surefootedly jumping from ledge to slippery ledge in loose-fitting wellies, looking like this is everyday stuff, which it actually is to them.

The fulmar will naturally do its best to stop those trying to steal its eggs and even if it won't attack you physically and try to claw your eyes out, it will scream loudly and then projectile vomit a red and stinky ooze of semi-digested sea creatures in your direction. From my own experiences I can tell you two things: first, that the accuracy with which the birds release this spray of stuff, which if you weren't there would have stayed where it belongs, inside of the bird, is spot on. Second, there is surely no detergent yet discovered by mankind, which will make the smell go away from your clothes.

To trick the birds into depleting their stocks of ammunition prematurely when they are still out of range, the Faroese will repeatedly throw little tufts of grass towards them to trigger the vomiting reflex. This practice however is no guarantee of not becoming a casualty to a spray of vomit. You might have overlooked a bird hiding somewhere in the grass not protecting the particular egg you are after but still not really minding some collateral damage.

This dish is often served in spring, when the eggs are fresh. Some people like eggs that have been lying in the nests for a couple of days incubating, but most seem to want them collected and cooked on the same day they were laid.

Preparation and cooking time: 30 minutes
Serves: 4

8 northern fulmar eggs
1 quantity Curry Cream Sauce (page 665)

Hard-boil the fulmar eggs. See page 53 for method and boiling times.

Shell the eggs and cut them in half while still warm. Arrange them on a serving platter and pour the sauce around them.

STEW OF SHAVED REINDEER MEAT

Finnbiff (Norway)
Poronkäristys (Finland)
Renskav (Sweden)

This dish, which consists of braised thin shavings of reindeer carved from a frozen piece of meat, is a traditional Sami preparation, which has (in a slightly bastardized version) gained great popularity in Norway, Sweden and Finland. I doubt that historically Sami populations of the Nordics used much cream from cows, but that's usually how you see it today, so that's the recipe you will find below: the shavings and mushrooms braised in cream.

I imagine that this dish would have originated after slaughtering a reindeer late in the season, when it would have been possible to store it for as long as temperatures stayed below freezing. This would have made it possible to enjoy the 'fresh' meat of the animal over a longer period of time. The carving of frozen meat is not only an excellent way of not having to defrost a whole piece (but rather just use what you must of it), it is also a way of using the less tender cuts of the animal without having to cook them for a long time to make them palatable, as you can easily slice them very thin.

A stew like this would usually be served with Mashed Potatoes (page 118) and Sugared Lingonberries (page 692).

Preparation and cooking time: 45 minutes
Serves: 4

butter, for frying
300 g/11 oz girolles (golden chanterelles), cleaned
500 g/1 lb 2 oz frozen reindeer (secondary cuts, like shoulder, are preferable)
1 onion, finely chopped
400 ml/14 fl oz (1⅔ cups) cream
salt and white pepper, to taste

Melt some butter in a frying pan over medium heat. Fry the mushrooms until they are quite dry; you don't want to dilute the stew too much with the liquid they release. Once cooked, transfer the mushrooms to a pot.

As the mushrooms are cooking, take a knife of which you are not too fond, and slice thin shavings of the frozen reindeer. Allow to defrost a bit on a platter.

Add some more butter to the frying pan. Add the meat and onion and cook over a rather high heat until everything is well browned and cooked through. Add to the pot with the mushrooms.

Add a splash of water to the frying pan and stir over a high heat to deglaze. Pour into the pot and bring to the boil. Add the cream and simmer for about 20 minutes, or until the meat is tender and the sauce has thickened a little.

Taste and adjust the seasoning to your liking, then serve immediately.

SLOW-COOKED FROZEN MEAT, BRINED AFTER THE COOKING AND SERVED COLD

Tjälaknul / Tjälknöl (Sweden)

This iconic Northern Swedish way of preparing tougher cuts of mainly moose was invented in the early 1980s by a woman named Ragnhild Nilsson from the village of Torpshammar. The history goes that she phoned her husband and asked him to defrost a piece of moose meat in the oven at a very low temperature. He subsequently forgot the meat was in there and it was cooked overnight. Ragnhild then tried to salvage the dry piece of meat by soaking it in a marinade and found that it produced a very tender and tasty result.

The idea is that you take a tougher cut of meat, like shoulder, still frozen, and you wrap it in aluminium foil so that it doesn't dry out during the lengthy cooking process. The low temperature and the lengthy time of cooking break down a lot of connective tissue in the meat – much like when you are braising things – thereby tenderizing it. The soaking in a seasoned brine then makes the meat juicy and adds flavour to it.

Serve *tjälaknul* cold, in thin slices, with a good salad – perhaps made from kale (page 90) – some Boiled Potatoes (page 117), Currant Jelly (page 691) and Brown Gravy (page 671); Potato Gratin (page 119) is also popular. Or serve as a sandwich toppings or part of a picnic as charcuterie.

Preparation and cooking time:
  8–12 hours depending on size and shape
  of the cut of meat you are using
Marinating time: at least overnight
Serves: 4

1 kg/2¼ lb moose shoulder (beef works
  well too), frozen

For the brine

45 g/2 oz (⅓ cup) salt
2 tablespoons sugar
10 juniper berries
2 bay leaves
10 black peppercorns
1 onion, cut into wedges

Preheat the oven to 75°C/167°F/Gas Mark ¼.

Wrap the frozen meat tightly in aluminium foil, place it in the oven and cook for 8–10 hours, or until it reaches a core temperature of 62°C/145°F. The exact timing will depend on your oven and the shape of the meat.

While the meat is cooking, prepare the brine by mixing all of the ingredients in a pot with 1 litre/ 34 fl oz (4¼ cups) water. Bring to the boil, then immediately remove the pot from the heat. Leave the brine to cool down completely.

Once the meat is cooked, remove it from the oven and place in the cold brine, making sure it is completely covered. One easy way of achieving this is to put the meat in a plastic bag with the brine, tying the bag to seal it, then sitting it in a bowl. This ensures the liquid will surround the meat completely. Leave the meat to marinate at least overnight.

When ready to serve, discard the brine, pat the meat dry and slice the meat thinly.

REINDEER AND THE SAMI CULTURE OF THE NORDIC REGION

The Sami people are an indigenous population in the Nordic region inhabiting an area called Sápmi which stretches over large parts of northern Norway, Sweden and into Russia.

Historically many Sami families have led a semi-nomadic lifestyle herding reindeer. Today only about 10% of Sami people are actually engaged in reindeer herding but even so the reindeer has remained hugely important for the cultural identity of this group of people.

When the reindeer was slaughtered, everything was put to good use. Not just the meat itself, which was often simply dried or both smoked and dried to keep, but the furs where used for bedding and clothes, the antlers and bones became tools and utensils, and the blood was turned into blood pancakes (page 392) that were consumed fresh as was the offal. The intestines where stuffed with meat and turned into sausages and the stomach was cleaned and turned into a bag for storage. Even semi-digested stomach content, usually consisting of lichens, was sometimes consumed as a source of carbohydrates. The animals that weren't slaughtered provided milk that was either drunk, turned into cheese or cultured, and the live animal pulled sleds to move both people and objects.

People lived from and together with their herds of reindeer.

The year starts when all of the calves are born, high up in the mountains during spring. At this time the herders have to stand guard and protect the flocks every hour of every day otherwise predators would kill and eat most of the new born calves. The female reindeer called *vaja*, returns to and gives birth in the same place every year.

During Summer, when the mountain meadows are at their most productive in giving plenty of food to the animals, they are moved into large paddocks and the young ones are branded by their human family by having a sign cut into their ears. The work of handling the animals is carried out at night because it is much cooler, which is better for the animals but also because there are far fewer mosquitos around, which is good for those people who are working. As the northern Nordic summer night is not really dark at all, working all through the night is no problem.

During summer the herders will try to keep the animals from decending from the mountains to make the most out of the high altitude grazing which won't be accessible later in the season, this is sometimes very difficult, especially in mushroom season when the reindeer can walk long stretches to eat bollets, a type of mushroom they love.

In mid-September, when autumn (fall) has arrived any male reindeer, called *sarv*, that is going to be sold as meat will be slaughtered. This is done before the start of the mating season and this is when the reindeer meat will be the best quality.

In October, after the mating season has finished, calves and females will be slaughtered. This is done in batches and can continue until just before Christmas. When the herds have gotten a suitable size and composition for winter they will be herded to the more sheltered valleys and forests below the mountains where they will stay until spring.

SALTED, DRIED AND SOMETIMES SMOKED REINDEER MEAT

Goike bearkoe / Goike suovas (Sami)

After the slaughter season in autumn (fall) and early winter, reindeer meat is cut into flattish pieces about 10 x 30 cm/4 x 12 inches in size and 3 cm/1¼ inch in thickness. The meat is layered with salt in barrels and left through most of winter to cure. Sometimes it is lowered into a natural spring which keeps it a at a steady and low temperature regardless of the weather and ambient temperatures. A slow lactofermentation will occur during the curing process as *lactobacillus* will consume whatever carbohydrates there still are in the meat itself. This will lower the pH value a little at the same time as the slow and controlled decomposition, much like in the production of charcuterie will give a lot of the savouriness to the finished product.

In late winter, before the snow is gone, the meat will be stretched over birch twigs to remain flat and either hung up in the roof of the goahti, the traditional Sami hut, or in a latticed hut on stilts to keep food away from wild animals. Keeping them in the goahti will produce a smoked result as the building itself, which people will live in, is heated simply with an open fire on the floor in the middle of the hut. This meat is called *goike souvas*. If the meat is hung in the dedicated storage house it won't acquire any smoke and will simply become dried meat and be called *goike bearkoe*. It is important that the meat has finished drying when the snow melts away in spring and the flies wake up again after winter, otherwise it will easily spoil.

Meat like this weighs very little and is extremely nutritious. It was, and is still, one of the dry foods a reindeer herder can carry during the work day in the mountains. It is either eaten as it is in thin slices, a bit like charcuterie, or boiled in stews and broths. The salted meat, before being dried, is also eaten but is then desalted in running water before being boiled.

PORK

ROAST PORK AND CRACKLING IN THE NORDIC REGION

Ribbenstek (Norway)
Flæskesteg (Denmark)

A piece of pork with all the fat and skin still attached, roasted until unbelievably crisp is enjoyed on occasion in many parts of the world. This is also the case in the Nordic region but most importantly in Denmark and Norway. In Denmark *flæskesteg* can be found on lunch menus in hundreds of restaurants and it is available under three names depending on which cut is being used. *Svinekam* is the loin, *ribbensteg* is made from the side and *nakkekam* from the front end of the back, towards the neck. It can be served with Braised Red Cabbage (page 99), Danish Sugar-browned Potatoes (page 120), Boiled Potatoes (page 117), Brown Gravy (page 671) and Quick Pickled Cucumber (page 658). The latter is often referred to as *sødt og surt*, meaning 'sweet-and-sour' in Danish. If a Danish family is not having a roast duck for Christmas dinner, the chances are they are having a piece of pork like the kind described above.

In Norway, roast pork with crackling is referred to as *ribbenstek* and is almost always made from the side. If served around Christmas it can also be called *juleribbe*. The roast pork in Norway is served a bit like it is in Denmark with the addition of a couple of other side dishes, for example, meat patties, Small Smoked Pork Sausages (page 428), or fried apple wedges. Sometimes it's served with Brown Gravy prepared with the cooking juices from the roast and finished with a good handful of Brown Cheese (page 72). Sugared Lingonberries (page 692) are also commonly seen next to a *ribbenstek*.

One big difference between the Norwegian and Danish roast is that the crackling is most often cut differently. In Denmark it will be cut straight across in thin strips as shown on the *ribbensteg* on page 269, while in Norway it will be cut into 3–4 cm/1¼–1½ inch squares. As you cut the skin before roasting it, the shape in which you cut it will determine how you can later carve the finished roast. If you make strips, it will be sliced the same width as the strips and if you cut squares that will be the format dictating your cut. This is simply because it is very difficult to cut through a proper crackling with a normal knife and you do best to place the cut between the strips instead.

To make perfect crackling you have to understand what happens to the pork when it cooks and why it fluffs up and becomes crispy. No one wants crackling that has simply dried down into chewy and inedible shoestrings.

The function of the puffing up part is simply that of minute amounts of water getting caught between layers of connective tissue in the pig's skin, turning into water vapour as they heat up and thereby creating little bubbles that, if the conditions are just right, will harden and create that fluffy, crisp texture. One thing to remember is that every excess water molecule that is still in the rind when you cook it is an enemy, which will make your crackling less crunchy if you don't get rid of it. Whatever water necessary for puffing it up will always be there even in a rind that is completely dry and hard to the touch, simply because the amount needing to be trapped within the layers of connective tissue is so minute. I like to score the skin of my pork just after buying it and then to keep it in the fridge for a day or two with no cover for the skin to dry out as much as possible.

Also let us just establish before you go on cooking this that some sad, lean fatless modern breed of pig won't work for this recipe. It needs to have a good layer of fat on it, like 3 cm/1¼ inches in thickness.

Preparation and cooking time: 2–3 hours
Resting time: 15 minutes
Serves: 8–10

2 kg/4½ lb pork suitable for roasting,
  with the skin still on
coarse sea salt
bay leaves (optional)
1 quantity Brown Gravy
  (page 671)

Preheat the oven to 200°C/400°F/Gas Mark 6.

Score the skin of the pork as described above depending on whether you go Danish or Norwegian. I like to use a very sharp carpet knife for this. The cut should go through the skin and into the fat but not quite all the way down to the meat.

Rub the whole piece of pork with plenty of salt and make sure some of it makes it down into the cuts you created though the skin and into the fat. Place it on a rack resting in a roasting pan. Pour in enough water to cover the bottom of the pan with 2.5 cm/1 inch depth. Stick some bay leaves in between the cuts if you like.

Place the pork in the oven and roast until cooked. Its internal temperature should go up to about 60°C/140°F when ready. If, when the thermometer hits 55°C/130°F you still aren't satisfied with the pork skin's level of crispness, simply increase the temperature a bit to 250°C/480°F/Gas Mark 9 for the remainder of the time but pay close attention so that you do not burn the crackling. Make sure that the bottom of the roasting pan does not dry out at any point during the whole cooking process. Replace the water if necessary.

Remove the roasted pork from the oven and leave to rest for a good 15 minutes before carving it. Use this time to make some gravy using the roasting juices collected in the pan.

For image see page 269

PORK TENDERLOIN WITH SWEET FRIED ONIONS

Mørbradbøf med bløde løg (Denmark)

This Danish favourite is served either with some Danish Rye Bread (page 504) almost like a deconstructed Open-faced Danish Sandwich (page 522) or as a main course with Boiled Potatoes (page 117), Brown Gravy (page 671), and Quick Pickled Cucumber (page 658).

Preparation and cooking time: 30 minutes
Restions time: 10 minutes
Serves: 4

800 g/1¾ lb pork tenderloin cut into
　3 cm/1¼ inch slices
butter, for frying
salt and white pepper, to taste
1 quantity Sweet Fried Onions (page 108),
　to serve

Preheat the oven to 80°C/175°F/Gas Mark 4.

Season the slices of meat on all sides. Fry them in some butter in a frying pan or skillet over a medium–high heat on both sides until golden. It should take about 3 minutes for each side. Place in the oven or somewhere warm to rest for 10 minutes. They should be pink inside when done. Spoon the hot onions over the slices of tenderloin just before serving.

For image see page 305

PORK TENDERLOIN WITH BANANAS AND CURRY

Fläskfile med banan (Sweden)

Recipes like this one and other sweet and salty meat and fruit combinations, like Chilli Creamed Chicken and Banana Casserole (page 270) started to become really popular during the 1970s. When reading old food magazines and cookbooks from the time, each issue seems to feature exotic combinations of food that most people wouldn't have tried – and probably didn't ever really feel much like trying either. However, some of the recipes, like the one mentioned above, survived the passing of time and became part of our food culture. Even today they are often mentioned in articles and blogs and the recipes are routinely shared. They are served in institutions like schools and hospitals and in many people's homes. Personally, I have never been a huge fan of kassler with pineapple but I definitely appreciate a good *flygande jakob* or a slice of pork tenderloin with a perfectly caramelized banana and a mild, yellow curry-cream sauce.

For this recipe you need nothing authentic from India or Southeast Asia. It needs to be the kind of generic yellow curry powder you find in a supermarket, which smells of sweet spices and turmeric.

Preparation and cooking time: 45 minutes
Serves: 4

butter, for frying
800 g/1¾ lb pork tenderloin, trimmed and
   cut into 2.5 cm/1 inch slices
3 bananas, halved lengthwise
300 ml/10½ fl oz (1¼ cups) cream
1 tablespoon yellow curry powder
salt and white pepper, to taste

Preheat the oven to 250°C/480°F/Gas Mark 9.

Melt a little butter in a frying pan or skillet over a medium heat. Season the meat with salt and pepper and fry until evenly browned all over. Transfer it to a roasting pan.

Add another generous amount of butter to the pan and fry the bananas on both sides until golden. Place them on top of the pork. Add the cream to the frying pan and stir the bottom of the pan to deglaze it, then add the curry powder. Season the cream to taste with salt, then pour it over the meat and bananas. Bake until the pork is cooked, but still pink in the centre, and the surface is golden.

FRIED SALT PORK

Stekt flesk (Norway)
Stegt flæsk (Denmark)
Stekt rimmat fläsk (Sweden)

Slices of salt pork belly are often enjoyed fried until quite crisp and served alongside Boiled Potatoes (page 117). In Norway, a sauce called *duppe* (page 666), prepared with the fat from the pork, is commonly served as an accompaniment, as is Root Vegetable Mash (page 112) or Creamed Cabbage (page 94). In Sweden, an Onion Cream Sauce (page 663) and Sugared Lingonberries (page 692) are common, and in Denmark, Parsley Sauce (page 671) is the classic accompaniment.

Salt pork can be fried in a pan or baked in the oven. The oven will give a more crisp and dry result, and the pan version will be a bit softer, but still nicely caramelized. I prefer the pan.

Some people like the rind of the pork still on for this preparation; I don't. It never turns into crispy crackling because the process is too short, and the rind is inevitably damp. The rind if left on will only turn into a chewy shoestring of pig's hide; at least it has every time I have tried it.

For image see page 125 or 403

SALT PORK FRIED IN THE PAN

Preparation and cooking time: 20 minutes
Serves: 4

600 g/1 lb 5 oz salt pork, rind removed, cut
   into 4 mm/⅛ inch slices
butter, for frying (depending on how fatty
   the pork is)

Arrange the slices of pork in a large, cold pan over a medium heat. Slowly fry until they are nicely coloured on both sides. If they don't render enough fat to fry properly, then add a small knob of butter to the pan. Serve as soon as they are nicely coloured.

SALT PORK BAKED IN THE OVEN

Preparation and cooking time: 20 minutes
Serves: 4

600 g/1 lb 5 oz salt pork, rind removed, cut
   into 4 mm/⅛ inch slices

Preheat the oven to 200°C/400°F/Gas Mark 6 and line a roasting pan with baking (parchment) paper (so it is easier to clean).

Spread the pork slices out in a single layer. Bake until they are golden brown and as crisp and crunchy as you want. Serve immediately.

FRIED FRESH PORK

Stekt färskt fläsk (Sweden)

Follow the recipe for Fried Salt Pork on the opposite page but season the fresh pork belly (side) generously with salt and white pepper before cooking.

PORK RIBS STUFFED WITH PRUNES AND ROASTED

Plommonspäckat revbensspjäll (Sweden)

Serve cold or warm as part of a festive meal like Swedish Christmas or Easter, or just as a main course with some nice green vegetables like Brussels sprouts (pages 104–6) or kale (pages 90–2). Use the cooking liquid from the pan as a sauce.

For this recipe ask your butcher to leave the bone in a cut of belly pork from the thicker side, just below the back. Ask for the skin to be removed, but the fat left on.

Preparation and cooking time: 3 hours
Soaking time: 20 minutes
Serves: 4

200 g/7 oz (1½ cups) pitted prunes
butter, for frying
1 onion, finely chopped
1 kg/2¼ lb bone-in pork belly (side), skin
   removed, fat left on
10 cm/4 inch piece fresh ginger, peeled
   and finely grated
salt and white pepper, to taste

Soak the prunes in water for 20 minutes, then set them aside and keep the soaking liquid for later.

Preheat the oven to 200°C/400°F/Gas Mark 6.

Melt a little butter in a pan over a medium heat. Add the onion and fry it quickly until it starts to soften. Set aside.

Push a long, thin knife through the pork belly in a direction perpendicular to the ribs themselves. Stuff the incisions with a mixture of the prunes, onion and grated ginger. Rub the meat all over with salt and pepper. Place the pork in a roasting pan, bones down. Pour the soaking liquid from the prunes into the pan and cook for 2–3 hours, or until the meat is very tender. The ribs should be pulling away from the meat.

Once the meat has coloured a little, baste regularly with the soaking liquid, mixing in the pan with the cooking juices. You can add water to the pan if necessary for it not to dry out during the cooking, but add no more water about 30 minutes before the end of the cooking time. That way the cooking liquid can reduce and thicken a bit to nicely coat the meat's exterior and, if there's enough, to make a nice sauce.

PORK AND BLACK PUDDING STEW

Rössypottu (Finland)

This is a very traditional regional speciality from the northern Finnish region of Oulu/Uleåborg. It is essentially a stew based on Black Pudding (page 392). In its simplest form only potatoes are added but most recipes include some other vegetables and diced smoked side of pork.

Preparation and cooking time: 1 hour
Serves: 4

600 g/1 lb 5 oz potatoes, cut into wedges
2 carrots, peeled, and cut into 1 cm/
   ½ inch slices
1 onion, cut into wedges
200 g/7 oz smoked side of pork, rind
   removed, meat and fat cut into 2 cm/
   ¾ inch pieces
300 g/11 oz Black Pudding (page 392),
   cut into 2 cm/¾ inch cubes
salt and white pepper, to taste

Put the potatoes, carrots, onion and pork into a large pot, cover with water and bring to the boil. Lower the heat to a simmer and cook until the potatoes are done. When about 10 minutes of cooking time remains, add the black pudding to heat it through in the soup. Adjust the seasoning before serving.

For image see opposite page

MEDISTERDEIG

Medisterdeig is a finely minced (ground) fatty pork common in Norway, normally containing 23% fat. It is commonly used in Norwegian Pork Patties (see right) and Medister Pork Sausages (page 430).

NORWEGIAN PORK PATTIES

Medisterkaker (Norway)

Finely minced (ground), tender and delicately seasoned with ginger and nutmeg, *medisterkaker* are served with Boiled Potatoes (page 117) or Mashed Potatoes (page 118) and Brown Gravy (page 671). This is also a very common side dish with the classic roast rib of pork for Norwegian Christmas celebrations.

Preparation and cooking time: 40 minutes
Serves: 4

500 g/1 lb 2 oz fatty minced (ground) pork
2 teaspoons potato starch
1 teaspoon ground ginger
freshly grated nutmeg, to taste
200 ml/7 fl oz (¾ cup plus 1 tablespoon) milk
butter, for frying
salt and white pepper, to taste

Start by mixing together the pork and all the dry ingredients (including salt, which is important for the firm texture). Work the paste for a while, until it becomes homogenous. Add the milk, little by little, until you achieve a good texture. It should be fairly loose and very sticky. Check the levels of salt and seasoning by making a small patty and frying it. Taste and adjust the seasoning if necessary.

Shape into round patties with a wet, clean hand or into egg-shaped ones with a wet spoon. Melt a little butter in a pan over a medium heat. Place the patties straight into the pan as you are making them. Cook until nicely browned on each side, then continue to cook them in the pan or in an oven preheated to 150°C/300°F/Gas Mark 2 until the patties are cooked through.

For image see opposite page

*Clockwise from top left: Danish Boiled Meatballs in Curry Cream Sauce (page 372);
creamy Brown Gravy (page 671); Norwegian Pork Patties (page 304); Pork and Black
Pudding Stew (page 304); Danish Pork Tenderloin with Sweet Fried Onions (page 301);
Sweet-and-Sour Braised Red Cabbage (page 98)*

SALTED PORK BELLY WITH BROWNED APPLES AND ONIONS

Æbleflæsk (Denmark)
Äppelfläsk (Sweden)

Serve with Boiled Potatoes (page 117) or Mashed Potatoes (page 118).

Preparation and cooking time: 30 minutes
Serves: 4

800 g/1¾ lb lightly salted pork belly (side),
    rind removed, thinly sliced
3 onions, sliced
3 apples, cored and cut into wedges
    (choose a nice eating variety which doesn't
    explode when you cook it)

Preheat the oven to 120°C/250°F/Gas Mark ½.

Place a pan over a medium heat. Fry the pork slices just until the fat starts to render out and they begin to brown. Transfer them to a serving platter and keep warm in the oven.

Add the onions and apples to the pan and fry in the pork fat until deeply golden. Spoon the soft apples and onions over the pork before serving.

––––––––––––––––––––––––––––––

TROTTERS

Syltelabb (Norway)
Kogte svinefødder (Denmark)
Kokta grisfötter (Sweden)

The trotters can be served cold or they can be reheated, depending on what you like. Serve them cold in jellied stock (broth) as part of the Swedish Christmas table or as a course on their own, with some Pickled Beetroot (page 660), some Brined Cucumbers (page 660) and perhaps some mustard (page 652).

Another nice option is to bread the trotters and then grill (broil) them in the oven until crisp. Use the technique for breading Swedish Christmas Ham (page 438) if you want to try this.

Preparation and cooking time: 3¼–5 hours,
    plus cooling time
Serves: 4

4 pig's trotters
1 handful salt

The butcher should supply the pig's trotters well rinsed and scraped. There should be no hair or dirty looking skin anywhere. If there is, you need to blanch them quickly in boiling water, then scrape them again with a sharp kitchen knife.

Place the trotters in a large pot, cover with cold water and add quite a bit of salt. Slowly bring to a simmer and then cook until they are completely tender. This should take at least 3 hours, but can take longer, depending on the size of the trotter.

When the trotters are tender, leave them in the cooking liquid to cool down. Transfer them to a container, together with the jellied stock (broth) and store them in the refrigerator until ready to eat.

––––––––––––––––––––––––––––––

*Clockwise from top: Pork Mince and Rice Cabbage Rolls (page 308); Sugared
Lingonberries (page 692); Golden Syrup Gravy (page 672)*

PORK MINCE AND RICE CABBAGE ROLLS

Kaalikääryleet (Finland)
Kåldolmer (Denmark)
Kåldolme (Sweden)

This dish is very interesting. If you ask a Swede to name an iconic dish from his or her country, there is a good chance the answer is going to be *Kåldolme*. What makes this sweet-and-salty roll of pork and rice wrapped in the leaf of a cabbage so intriguing is that it is an adaptation of another regional speciality where both name and basic method are still clearly linked to the original. Between 1709 and 1713 King Charles XII of Sweden, following a non-successful war campaign against Russia, camped outside a town called Bender located in present day Moldova. Historically that region was part of the Ottoman Empire and it is thought (but not confirmed) that the Swedes themselves, or some of the Turks who followed the Swedes back north, brought with them the practice of making vine-leaf dolmas. We know for sure that the original dish was being made in Sweden at the time, and in Cajsa Warg's 1765 cookery book, the first reference in print to the use of cabbage instead of vine leaves can be found. The Turkish vine-leaf dolma adapted to its new surroundings and the produce available there. The filling still has rice in it but also pork, which is probably not very common in its Muslim country of origin. The vine leaf was later permanently exchanged for a boiled cabbage leaf – much easier to get in Sweden than a vine leaf, as vines don't really grow here. The shape stayed much the same, as did the name, *kåldolme*, *kål* being the Swedish word for cabbage and *dolme* describing both the shape and technique used.

Serve with Golden Syrup Gravy (page 672), Sugared Lingonberries (page 692) and Boiled (page 117) or Mashed Potatoes (page 118).

You might as well make a double quantity of the recipe below while you are at it, as they freeze really well and it is a lot of work to make just four portions.

Preparation and cooking time: 2 hours
Serves: 4

¼ quantity Rice Porridge (page 466)
1 head of cabbage, preferably winter cabbage, in the summer the leaves are usually too thin
4 tablespoons golden syrup
25 g/1 oz (1½ tablespoons) butter

For the filling
1 onion, finely chopped
butter, for frying
300 g/11 oz minced (ground) pork or
   150 g/5 oz minced pork mixed with
   150 g/5 oz minced beef
2 eggs
salt and white pepper, to taste

Start by making the porridge and allow it to cool completely.

In a frying pan over medium heat, lightly fry the onion in butter then set aside to cool down.

Meanwhile, bring a large pot of water to the boil. To make it easier to take the leaves off the head of cabbage we are going to boil it first and take the leaves off one by one as they are perfectly cooked. This is a restaurant trick but very efficient. Be careful though not to drop the head of cabbage into the boiling water, scalding yourself on the splash. Stick a very sturdy meat fork into the base of the stem of the cabbage itself and dip it into the water. Hold it submerged for perhaps a minute to cook and soften a layer of cabbage leaf. Lift the cabbage up and, with a sharp knife, cut through the base of the leaf. Peel it off and put it straight into a large bowl of cold water. Return the head of cabbage to the boiling water and repeat until you have 20 leaves of cooked and cold cabbage. Reserve the cooking liquid and make something else with the remaining cabbage another day. If the base of the leaf has a very thick stalk, trim that down a bit.

Preheat the oven to 220°C/425°F/Gas Mark 7.

Mix the cooled fried onions with all of the ingredients for the filling in a bowl and season well.

Take a cabbage leaf and place it onto your chopping (cutting) board. Place a spoonful of the filling in the middle of the leaf. Fold the edges of the leaf in and roll into a nice dolma shape. Place seam-side down in an ovenproof dish, so they fit snugly in one layer.

When all of the cabbage leaves and filling have been used, drizzle the golden syrup over the top of the rolls and add the butter. Place in the oven and cook for about 10 minutes. Pour 500 ml/ 17 fl oz (2 cups plus 1 tablespoon) of the reserved cooking liquid from boiling the cabbage into the dish containing the rolls and continue cooking them for another 10–15 minutes or until deeply coloured on top and cooked through. Use the cooking liquid from the dish in which the rolls have cooked to make the sauce.

For image see page 307

SWEDISH POT

Svensk panna (Sweden)

Serve with a generous amount of grated horseradish or coarse-grain mustard on the side. Myself, I don't mind a Grated Carrot Salad (page 110) too.

Preparation and cooking time: 1 hour
Serves: 4

200 g/7 oz calves' kidney, fat attached
　(1 small kidney is about right)
200 g/7 oz pork tenderloin
200 g/7 oz veal tenderloin
800 g/1¾ lb potatoes, cut into 5 mm/
　¼ inch slices
3 onions, cut into 5 mm/¼ inch slices
1 bay leaf
250 ml/8 fl oz (1 cup) hoppy lager
100 ml/3½ fl oz (⅓ cup plus 1 tablespoon)
　Meat Stock (page 650)
salt and white pepper, to taste

Preheat the oven to 200°C/400°F/Gas Mark 6.

Cut the meat into 1.5 cm/¾ inch slices, making sure you include the fat with the kidney. Layer the meat slices with the potatoes and onions in a roasting pan. Season each layer as you go and slip the bay leaf somewhere in the middle. Finish with a layer of potatoes.

Pour on the lager and the stock (broth). It should almost cover the top layer of potatoes, so add

a little more stock if it doesn't. Bake in the oven until the potatoes are soft and the surface is nicely coloured. Serve steaming hot from the oven.

PORK, KIDNEY AND POTATO CASSEROLE

Hökarepanna av fläsk (Sweden)

Serve it with mustard, Sugared Lingonberries (page 692) and Cabbage Salad (page 96).

Preparation and cooking time: 50 minutes
Soaking time: overnight
Serves: 4

2 pig kidneys, halved, soaked in iced water
　overnight, water changed 1–2 times
300 g/11 oz lean pork (from the leg or
　the back)
butter or lard, for browning
6 waxy potatoes, cut into 5 mm/¼ inch
　thick slices
2 onions, thinly sliced
1 sprig thyme
1 bay leaf
500 ml/17 fl oz (2 cups plus 1 tablespoon)
　good hoppy lager
salt and pepper, to taste

Preheat the oven to 150°C/300°F/Gas Mark 2.

Cut the kidneys and the meat into slices about 1 cm/½ inch thick and season with salt and pepper. Melt the butter or lard in a pan over a medium–high heat. Add the meat and brown it quickly.

Layer the meat and kidneys with the potatoes and onions in an ovenproof dish. Season the layers with salt and pepper and add the sprig of thyme and the bay leaf somewhere in the middle. Pour in the beer and bring it to the boil over a medium heat. Cover with a tight-fitting lid and bake in the oven for 30 minutes.

BEEF AND VEAL

Previous page: Iceland, Spring 2013.

Opposite: Lichen on a stone wall, Faroe Islands, Spring 2012.

ROYAL SWEDISH POT ROAST

Slottsstek (Sweden)

Most older recipes for this dish are made with various lean parts of the back end of beef, like rump and such. Personally I don't much like this, as they have a tendency of going really dry. I prefer to use shoulder of beef, or even chuck, which both lend themselves to braising in this way.

Serve the beef in slices with Boiled Potatoes (page 117) or Riced Potatoes (page 117), Redcurrant Jelly (page 691) or Sugared Lingonberries (page 692) and maybe some glazed vegetables or why not Steamed Broccoli (page 82). When I was growing up, a meal like this was also served with a plain iceberg lettuce salad on the side, but I prefer the Kale Salad on page 90.

Preparation and cooking time: 4 hours
Serves: 8

2 kg/4½ lb beef chuck or shoulder, trimmed
  and tied up for roasting
butter, for frying
500 ml/17 fl oz (2 cups plus 1 tablespoon)
  Beef Stock (page 650)
1 onion, cut into wedges
2 Sprats Cured in Sandalwood
  (page 212)
1 bay leaf
10 allspice berries, crushed
50 ml/1¾ fl oz (3½ tablespoons) Ättika
  (12%) vinegar (page 656)
50 ml/1¾ fl oz (3½ tablespoons) golden
  syrup
salt and white pepper, to taste

For the sauce
reserved braising juices (above)
300 ml/10½ fl oz (1¼ cups) cream
1 tablespoon of curing juice from the sprats
  (above)
Beurre Manié (page 651), enough to thicken
  the sauce
Chinese mushroom soy sauce, to taste
salt and white pepper, to taste

Season the beef with salt and pepper. Heat some butter in a pot. Brown the beef on all sides over a medium heat.

Add the beef stock (broth), onion, aromatics, vinegar and golden syrup and bring to a simmer. Cook for about 3½ hours, or until the meat is very tender. Turn the meat in the braising liquid from time to time. You could also cook the roast in a covered pot in an oven preheated to 130°C/265°F/ Gas Mark ½.

When ready, remove the meat from the pot and keep it warm. Strain the braising juices into a smaller pot and add the cream and the curing juice from the sprats. Bring to a simmer over low heat and add enough beurre manié to thicken it to a sauce. Add the soy sauce and season to taste with salt and pepper.

Slice the meat and serve with the sauce in a sauce boat.

SALTED BEEF BRISKET, BOILED

Sprængt oksebryst (Denmark)
Kokt rimmad oxbringa (Sweden)

Serve the brisket thinly sliced in some of its cooking liquid with Mashed Root Vegetables (page 112) cooked in the salty brisket stock (broth), or with *impotatis* Boiled Potatoes (page 117) also cooked in the stock. I like to have some strong mustard with my cured brisket too.

Preparation and cooking time: 2–4 hours
Resting time: overnight
Serves: 4

1.5 kg/3¼ lb salted beef brisket,
  thoroughly rinsed
1 carrot, chopped
1 onion, quartered
1 sprig thyme
1 bay leaf
10 white peppercorns

Place the rinsed brisket in a pot, together with the vegetables and aromatics. Cover with cold water and bring to a simmer. Cover the pan and cook until the brisket is tender, which can take from 2–4 hours. Skim from time to time.

To test if the meat is done, pierce it with a paring knife and lift it straight up. If the meat releases the knife straight away it is done, if it doesn't fall from the knife, then cook it for a bit longer. Once the brisket is done to your liking, slice it thinly and serve in its cooking liquid.

Tip: Instead of eating the brisket straight away, you can allow it to cool in the cooking broth, then cover it with baking (parchment) paper and weight it overnight in the refrigerator (or longer if you wish). This makes it really easy to slice. Reheat the slices in some of the cooking liquid to serve.

SWEET-AND-SOUR MARINATED BEEF POT ROAST

Surstek (Sweden)

This very old dish is served with Roasted Potatoes (page 112) or Boiled Potatoes (page 117) and boiled vegetables like carrots, Brussels sprouts, green peas or perhaps broccoli. Some Redcurrant Jelly (page 691) on the side and perhaps some Quick Pickled Cucumber (page 658) is nice, too.

Preparation and cooking time: 3 hours
Marinating time: 10 days
Serves: 8

2 tablespoons mustard powder
2 kg/4½ lb beef silverside
butter, for frying
1 quantity Basic Cream Sauce (page 663), made with the cooking juices from the meat

For the marinade
1.5 litres/50 fl oz (6¼ cups) good hoppy lager
100 ml/3½ fl oz (⅓ cup plus 1 tablespoon) Ättika (12%) vinegar (page 656)
1 red onion, sliced
2 bay leaves
10 cloves
10 allspice berries
10 white peppercorns
10 juniper berries

100 g/3½ oz (½ cup) sugar
2 teaspoons salt
white pepper, to taste

Combine all the ingredients for the marinade in a pot large enough to also fit the meat, and bring to a quick boil. Leave to cool down completely.

Rub the mustard powder into the meat and place it in the pot. It should fit snugly and the marinade should cover the meat completely. Weight the meat with something heavy to keep it submerged. Leave to marinate in the refrigerator for 10 days.

Remove the meat from the marinade and pat it dry with paper towels. Strain the marinade back into the cleaned-out pot.

Heat some butter in a frying pan over a medium heat and brown the beef until it is a dark golden brown all over. Lift it into the pot with the strained marinade. Bring to a simmer, then braise the beef for about 2 hours, or until the meat is tender. To test if the meat is done, pierce it with a paring knife and lift it straight up. If the meat releases the knife straight away it is done, if it doesn't fall from the knife, then cook it for a bit longer.

Remove the meat from the pot and keep warm while making the cream sauce. Follow the recipe on page 663, using the beef cooking juices.

Carve the meat into 1 cm/½ inch slices. Glaze with the cream sauce or serve it separately in a sauce boat.

SEARED BRISKET WITH ONIONS

Bräckt färsk oxbringa med lök (Sweden)

This dish does not use salted brisket, but fresh meat that is braised, cooled down and then thinly sliced. It is traditionally served with Boiled Potatoes (page 117) or Mashed Potatoes (page 118). I like to offer some grated carrots or why not a Kale Salad (page 90). Condiments like Brined Cucumbers (page 660) and Mustard (page 652) are welcome.

Preparation and cooking time: 20 minutes
Serves: 4

600 g/1 lb 5 oz Braised Beef Brisket
  (see below), cooled and cut into thin slices
butter, for frying
4 small onions, thinly sliced
salt and white pepper, to taste

Heat a pan until very hot. Sear the slices of brisket until nicely coloured, which shouldn't take more than a few seconds on each side. Place onto a serving platter and season with salt and pepper.

When you've finished cooking the meat, remove the pan from the heat and add butter to the fat that is still in the hot pan. Add the onions and fry over a medium heat until they are soft and browned. Spread the onions over the meat.

BOILED BEEF BRISKET

Kokt färsk oxbringa (Sweden)

Brisket prepared this way is usually served warm in thin slices with Horseradish Sauce (page 668). These days I see too often in restaurants Boiled Salted Beef Brisket (page 316) with horseradish sauce. I think it is as much a pity to serve that dish with anything other than its deliciously salty and sweet cooking juices, as it is to serve this braised fresh brisket without the deliciously rich horseradish sauce and its eye-watering sting. Boiled Potatoes (page 117) and perhaps some Glazed Carrots (page 109) should be on the side.

An old trick is to cook the brisket at least a day before eating it. On the first day, cook it until tender before sprinkling it with a bit of salt and leaving it with a little bit of pressure on top to cool down in the refrigerator. Store the cooking liquid separately. The second day – or whenever it is time to serve it – cut it into thin slices and reheat them in some of the cooking liquid from the braise.

Preparation and cooking time: 2–3 hours
Serves: 4

1.5 kg/3¼ lb fresh beef brisket on
  the bone, rinsed
1 large carrot, chopped
1 leek, chopped
1 onion, quartered
2 celery sticks, chopped
10 white peppercorns
1 sprig thyme
1 bay leaf
1 clove garlic, crushed with the side
  of a knife
salt, to taste

Place all of the ingredients in a large pot and salt quite liberally. They should fit snugly, as too much space will create a diluted braise. Barely cover with water and bring to a simmer over a medium heat, skimming regularly.

Cook, covered, for about 2 hours, or until the brisket is tender. Skim from time to time. When ready, it should be possible to pull the meat off the bone, but it should not fall into pieces. Either serve right away in slices or cool it in the refrigerator, as described above, to serve another day.

For image see opposite page

Clockwise from top left: Danish Skipper's Potato and Meat Stew (page 322); Beef and Vegetable Soup (page 326); Boiled Beef Brisket (with horseradish) (page 318); Swedish Beef Stew with Allspice (page 324)

BEEF ROULADES

Okseroulader (Denmark)
Oxrulader (Sweden)

Serve with Boiled Potatoes (page 117) and/or greens, like Steamed Kale (page 90). Some extra mustard on the side and perhaps a Brined Cucumber (page 660) is always nice.

Preparation and cooking time: 1 hour
Serves: 4

butter, for frying
1 onion, finely chopped
500 g/1 lb 2 oz beef topside, cut
   into 12 thin slices, pounded flat
strong, unsweetened mustard,
   for spreading
12 strips salted belly pork, about
   10 cm/4 inches long and
   1 cm/½ inch in diameter
3 Brined Cucumbers (page 660),
   quartered lengthwise
2 carrots, cut lengthwise into thin
   sticks about 10 cm/4 inches long
1 tablespoon plain (all-purpose) flour
500 ml/17 fl oz (2 cups plus 1 tablespoon)
   light lager
2 bay leaves
1 sprig thyme
200 ml /7 fl oz (¾ cup plus 1 tablespoon)
   cream
salt and white pepper, to taste

Melt some butter in a pan over a medium heat. Add the onion and fry until soft but not coloured. Remove from the pan and leave to cool down.

Spread all the slices of beef out on a flat clean work counter. Spread them with a thin layer of mustard, sprinkle with the cooked onion and season well with salt and pepper. Place a piece of pork, a piece of cucumber and a piece of carrot in a little stack towards the edge of each slice of beef (see illustrations right). Roll each slice into a tight roll and tie both ends with string to secure.

Add a bit more butter to the pan. Add the roulades and brown them all over. Sift over the flour, then pour on the beer and tuck in the bay leaves

and thyme. You might need to add a little bit of water, so that the roulades are more or less covered by liquid. Cover the pan and simmer over a medium heat for about 30 minutes until the roulades are tender. They should not be tender to the point of falling apart.

When the roulades are ready, remove them with a slotted spoon and transfer them to a serving platter. Strain the cooking liquid into a pot, bring it to the boil over a medium heat and pour in the cream. Leave to simmer for a few minutes, then adjust the seasoning and pour the sauce over the roulades before serving.

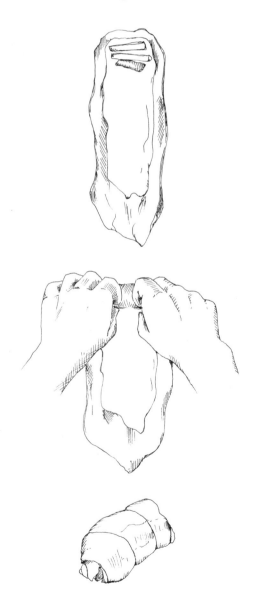

MASHED POTATOES AND CURED BRISKET

Lapskoussi (Finland)
Lappskojs / Lapskojs / Lappsko (Sweden)

This dish, which basically consists of mashed potato and shredded braised meat, exists in this form in Finland and Sweden. But other dishes of meat and potatoes, such as *skipperlabskovs* (page 322) in Denmark, and *Lapskaus* in Norway, all the names come from the same source, if not necessarily from the same origin in terms of content. The names come from the old German word *Labskaus* or the English Lobscouse, but where they came from and how it all ties into these Nordic dishes is quite uncertain.

Lappskojs in Sweden is often served with Pickled Beetroot (page 660) and/or Brined Cucumbers (page 660) and/or a fried egg, sunny side up. In Finland, a dollop of butter to melt in the middle of each portion is not uncommon.

Some people use cured knuckle or shoulder of pork or brined brisket and braise it tender themselves. Myself, I kind of like a version prepared with a brand of canned corned beef called *Salta Biten*. It just tastes right to me, like in my school canteen. If you do use canned corned beef, it can't be the Spam kind of product. It needs to have fibres and whole pieces of meat in it.

Preparation and cooking time: 30 minutes
Serves: 4

350 g/12 oz cured and braised beef brisket
  (or use canned cured beef brisket)
800 g/1¾ lb floury potatoes, peeled
300 ml/10½ fl oz (1¼ cups) cooking liquid
  from the brisket (or use the liquid from
  the can)
1 bay leaf
8 allspice berries, ground
60 g/2¼ oz (4 tablespoons) butter
salt and pepper, to taste

Cut the beef into 3 cm/1¼ inch pieces.

Put the potatoes in a large pot and add the cooking liquid and enough water to just cover them. Add the aromatics, season with salt and pepper, then bring to the boil. Add the beef after about 5 minutes. Cook for another 15 minutes or so, or until the potatoes are soft and the beef has warmed through.

Add the butter and use a masher to crush and mix everything together. Taste and adjust the seasoning, then serve immediately.

DANISH SKIPPER'S POTATO AND MEAT STEW

Skipperlabskovs (Denmark)

This dish, which is a Danish classic, shares a similarity in its name with both the Swedish dish *Lappskojs* and Norwegian *Labskaus* (page 321). Name aside, however, the Swedish dish has little in common with the Danish recipe and there is in fact another dish – Sailor's Beef Stew with Beer and Potatoes (see right) – which is much more similar. It shares some similarities with the Norwegian stew, but not enough to say they are the same.

The name itself comes from the old German word *Labskaus,* or English Lobscouse, but where they came from and how it all ties in with these Nordic dishes is quite uncertain.

Danish Skipper's Stew sometimes contains a mixture of lamb and beef, but is usually just made with beef. If you like, you can replace 250 g/9 oz of the beef with lamb shoulder.

It is often served with Pickled Beetroot (page 660) and some Danish Rye Bread (page 504).

Preparation and cooking time: 1½ hours
Serves: 4

butter, for frying
750 g/1 lb 10 oz braising beef (shoulder
  or breast work well) cut into 3 cm/
  1¼ inch cubes
5 onions, cut into 5 mm/¼ inch slices
3 bay leaves
800 g/1¾ lb firm potatoes, peeled and cut
  into 2 cm/¾ inch dice
60 g/2¼ oz (¼ cup) cold butter, diced small
1 good bunch chives, finely snipped, to serve
salt and white pepper, to taste

Melt some butter in a heavy-bottomed pan over a medium heat and brown the meat all over. Add the onions and continue cooking until soft.

Pour in enough water to cover everything, then add the bay leaves and season with salt and pepper. Bring to a simmer, then cook, covered, for about 1 hour, or until the meat starts to become tender.

Add the potatoes to the pan and cook until the meat is tender and potatoes are cooked. Taste and adjust the seasonings, then stir in the cold butter so that it emulsifies the sauce. As you stir, the potato particles that come off from the friction will also help to thicken the sauce.

Sprinkle with chives as you serve.

For image see page 319

A SAILOR'S BEEF STEW WITH BEER AND POTATOES

Sjömansbiff (Sweden)

Serve this with a couple of Brined Cucumbers (page 660) on the side. I like to sprinkle my *sjömansbiff* with plenty of coarsely chopped parsley just before serving, although this is probably restaurant practice rather than something people have done in their homes traditionally.

Preparation and cooking time: 1½ hours
Serves: 4

800 g/1¾ lb beef topside, cut into
  12 slices, pounded flat
plain (all-purpose) flour, for dusting
butter, for frying
4 onions, finely sliced
10 large waxy potatoes, cut into 1 cm/
  ½ inch slices
2 bay leaves
2 sprigs thyme
200 ml/7 fl oz (¾ cup plus 1 tablespoon)
  Beef Stock (page 650)
500 ml/17 fl oz (2 cups plus 1 tablespoon)
  pilsner beer
coarsely chopped parsley, to serve
  (optional)
salt and white pepper, to taste

Cover a plate with a generous amount of flour, then turn each slice of beef in the flour.

Melt some butter in a pan over a medium heat and fry the beef slices so they are browned on both sides. Remove them from the pan and set them aside. Add a bit more butter to the pan, if needed, and brown the onions, then set them aside too. Next, brown the potatoes, then set them aside.

Once everything is browned, layer the beef, onions and potatoes back in the pan, seasoning generously with salt and pepper, and tucking in the herbs as you go. Pour in the beef stock (broth) and beer so that everything is just covered. Cover the pan and bring to a low simmer. (Alternatively, place in an oven preheated to 150°C/300°F/Gas Mark 2.) Cook for about 1 hour, or until the meat is tender. Sprinkle with chopped parsley, if using, just before you serve.

Once ready, tip the onions into a dish, set aside and keep warm.

Wipe out the pan with paper towels and return to a relatively high heat. Add just a little bit of butter and while it is melting, quickly season the beef slices with salt and pepper on both sides. Fry them until coloured on both sides. Towards the end of the cooking time, take the pan off the heat.

Return the onions to the pan and add a couple of tablespoons of butter. When the butter has just browned, immediately transfer everything to plates and serve straight away.

STEAK AND ONIONS

Sipulipihvi (Finland)
Biff med lök (Sweden)

This Swedish classic is a bit like the French minute steak: a thin slice of sirloin seared over high heat, served with a generous stack of sliced onion fried amber. Sometimes a little reduced beef stock (broth) or Brown Gravy (page 671) is poured over the steak, along with plenty of browned frying butter from the cooking of the meat itself and the onions.

Serve with Boiled Potatoes (page 117) and a green vegetable, like Steamed Broccoli (page 82) or perhaps a Kale Salad (page 90).

Preparation and cooking time: 30 minutes
Serves: 4

butter, for frying and serving with
  the meat
2 large onions, thinly sliced
4 slices beef sirloin, about 12–15 mm/
  ½–¾ inch thick
salt and white pepper, to taste

Melt some butter in a large frying pan or skillet over a medium heat. Fry the onions quite slowly, until they are soft, amber-coloured and sweet. It should take 10–15 minutes, so don't rush it.

SWEDISH BEEF STEW WITH ALLSPICE

Kalops / Skånsk kalops (Sweden)

Kalops is a simple, traditional and very popular Swedish stew, consisting of beef and onions, some bay leaf and a bit of allspice. If you add carrots it turns into *Scanian kalops*, which is probably the version most Swedes actually mean when they talk about *kalops*.

Personally, I like to add a good dash of Ättika (12%) vinegar (page 656) and some brown sugar (*brun farin*), because I like this dish to be a bit sweet-and-sour. This is really wrong, but very tasty.

Kalops is usually served with Boiled Potatoes (page 117) and Pickled Beetroot (page 660).

Preparation and cooking time: 2 hours
Serves: 4

butter, for frying
1kg/2¼ lb beef chuck, cut into 4 cm/ 1½ inch pieces
1 tablespoon plain (all-purpose) flour
1 bay leaf
12 allspice berries
2–3 onions, quartered
3 carrots, cut into 1 cm/½ inch slices (optional)
3 tablespoons Ättika (12%) vinegar (page 656), optional
3 tablespoons brown sugar (optional)
salt and white pepper, to taste

Melt a little butter in a heavy-bottomed pot. Add the beef to the pan and sift over the flour while it is frying. Brown the beef fairly well, and just before it gets too dark, and as the meat proteins and flour stuck to the bottom of the pot get too dark, pour in enough water to cover. Bring to a simmer, then add the bay leaf and allspice and season well. Add the sugar and vinegar, if using.

Cover the pot and cook for about an 1 hour or so, or until the meat is becoming tender. Add the onion to the pot, along with the carrots, if you are using them. Cover again and cook until the vegetables are tender. Taste and adjust the seasoning.

For image see page 319

OVEN-BAKED SWEDISH MEAT PATTIES WITH PARSLEY

Persiljejärpar (Sweden)

I like to eat *persiljejärpar* with Boiled Potatoes (page 117) and Brined Cucumbers (page 660).

Preparation and cooking time: 40 minutes
Serves: 4

For the meat patties
250 g/9 oz finely minced (ground) beef
250 g/9 oz finely minced (ground) pork
100 g/3½ oz (1¼ cups) breadcrumbs
200 ml/7 fl oz (¾ cup plus 1 tablespoon) cream
2 eggs
1 bunch parsley, finely chopped
1 tablespoon strong mustard
salt and white pepper, to taste
butter, for greasing
1 quantity Basic Cream Sauce (page 663), made from the meat cooking liquid

Combine the meat, breadcrumbs, cream and eggs in a mixing bowl and work them together well. Season with salt and pepper, then leave it for about 10 minutes for the bread to swell.

Preheat the oven to 225°C/435°F/Gas Mark 7 and butter a roasting pan.

With a clean, wet hand and a wet spoon, shape the mixture into oval balls, the size and shape of a large egg. Place them in the prepared pan and bake until the patties are lightly golden in colour.

Transfer the meat patties to a pan with a lid. Strain the cooking juices from the roasting pan into a pot and prepare the cream sauce, following the method on page 663.

Pour the cream sauce into the pan with the patties. Simmer over a low heat until the patties are cooked through.

FAROESE BEEF AND FISH PATTIES

Mørfrikadellur (Faroe Islands)

Serve with Brown Gravy (page 671), Boiled Potatoes (page 117) and Braised Red Cabbage (page 98).

Preparation and cooking time: 40 minutes
Serves: 4

500 g/1 lb 2 oz white fish fillet, such as cod, saithe or pollock
500 g/1 lb 2 oz minced (ground) lean beef
1 onion, finely chopped
2 eggs
1 tablespoon plain (all-purpose) flour
butter or oil, for frying
salt and white pepper, to taste

Push the fish through a meat mincer (grinder) twice. Place in a large bowl with the beef, onion and eggs and add 200 ml/7 fl oz (¾ cup plus 1 tablespoon) water. Season with salt and pepper and mix everything together thoroughly. Shape into patties with clean, wet hands.

Melt a little butter or heat some oil in a pan over a medium heat. Cook the patties in batches until cooked right through and nicely browned on each side.

STEAK AND MASHED POTATOES WITH BACON AND LEEKS

Skomakarlåda (Sweden)

Skomakarlåda means 'shoemaker's box', and it is thought to refer to the shape of the steak, vaguely resembling that of the sole of a shoe. The finely cut bacon could possibly also be the old-fashioned nails in the shoemaker's box.

This dish is most likely to be found on the menus of very traditional Stockholm restaurants.

Serve it with some Mashed Potatoes (page 118) and Brown Gravy (page 671).

Preparation and cooking time: 20 minutes
Serves: 4

butter, for frying
650 g/1 lb 7 oz sirloin steak, cut into 4 slices
125 g/4½ oz bacon, cut into (nail-like) strips
1 leek, finely diced
salt and white pepper, to taste

Melt a little butter in a large frying pan over a medium–high heat. While it is melting, quickly season the beef slices on both sides with salt and pepper. Fry them for a couple of minutes on each side. Transfer to a warm platter to rest.

Quickly wipe out the pan with paper towels, then add the bacon and leeks. Add a small knob of butter and cook over a medium heat until the bacon is quite crisp.

Meanwhile divide the mashed potato between 4 plates and spread it out roughly. Top each pile of mash with a slice of steak, then top with the bacon and leeks, straight from the pan. Serve the gravy on the side.

BEEF AND VEGETABLE SOUP SOMETIMES WITH DUMPLINGS

Köttsoppa, ibland med klimp (Sweden)

This soup is a real classic and Soup Dumplings (page 457) can be added if you like them. Most classic recipes contain carrot, parsnip and leeks for vegetables, but I like to add some swede (rutabaga) as well, for its pepperiness. In some recipes, celeriac (celery root) is also included.

Today, the meat is served almost as part of the soup, but up until about thirty years ago, that was not the case, judging from how the recipes of the soup have changed through the chronological sequence of publication of books and magazines. Traditionally it was far more common to serve the vegetables cooked in the meat broth with soup dumplings as one meal and then serve the meat itself some other time, reheated in slices with, for example, Horseradish Sauce (page 668) and potatoes. That particular dish is called *pepparrotskött* and is today usually prepared not in relation to meat soup but as a standalone dish.

Serve the soup dumplings – if you are making them – either in the soup or on a separate plate, so that people can help themselves.

Preparation and cooking time: 3–5 hours
Serves: 4

1 kg/2¼ lb beef and bones (shoulder,
  brisket, chuck or tail are all suitable)
1 onion, peeled
10 cloves
2 bay leaves
10 white peppercorns
2 carrots, peeled and cut into 5 mm/
  ¼ inch slices
1 parsnip, peeled and cut into 5 mm/
  ¼ inch slices
1 fist-sized piece of celeriac (celery root),
  peeled and cut into 1.5 cm/¾ inch
  pieces
1 fist-sized piece of swede (rutabaga),
  peeled and cut into 1.5 cm/¾ inch pieces
1 leek, cut into 5 mm/¼ inch slices
salt, to taste
1 quantity Soup Dumplings (page 457), to
  serve (optional)

Place the meat and bones in a large pot – it doesn't matter whether the meat is on or off the bone. Cover with water and bring to the boil, then pour away the boiling water. This saves a lot of skimming away fat later on.

Add fresh water to the pot and bring to a simmer. Stud the onion with the cloves and add it to the pot, along with the bay leaves and peppercorns. Simmer for a good 2–4 hours (depending on the cut of meat), or until the meat is tender. You might have to top up the water every now and then and you should skim away the fat occasionally.

Once the meat is tender, lift it out of the soup onto a tray. Strain the soup into a clean pot and return it to a simmer. Add the vegetables and season with salt. Cook until the vegetables just begin to soften.

While the vegetables are cooking, separate the meat from the bones and cut it into 1.5 cm/¾ inch pieces. Just before serving, adjust the seasoning and add the meat back to the soup. Serve with the dumplings, if you like.

For image see page 319

FINNISH FLOUR DUMPLING SOUP

Klimppisoppa (Finland)

You can either serve the meat separately as another meal or leave it in the soup.

Preparation and cooking time: 3–5 hours
Serves: 4

1 quantity Beef and Vegetable Soup
  (see left)
4 potatoes, peeled and cut into 1.5 cm/
  ¾ inch dice
1 quantity Soup Dumplings (page 457)

Follow the instructions on the left for the beef and vegetable soup, adding the potatoes at the same time as the other vegetables.

Follow the instructions on page 457 for the soup dumplings cooked in broth or soup.

Once the soup is ready, separate the meat from the bones and cut it into 1.5 cm/¾ inch pieces. Set aside for another meal, or return the meat to the soup.

Form the dumpling mixture into egg-shaped dumplings and drop them into the simmering soup. Cook until they are cooked all the way through (it will depend on their size).

Put all the ingredients in a pot or ceramic vessel with a tight-fitting lid. Pour in 1 litre/34 fl oz (4¼ cups) water, then place in the oven and leave to braise for about 5 hours, or until very tender. Stir only once or twice, and not at all during the second half of the cooking process as that would break up the pieces of meat.

KARELIAN STEW

Karjalanpaisti (Finland)

Karjalanpaisti, from the eastern Finnish and Russian region of Karelia, is traditionally a mix of beef, lamb and pork, seasoned simply with black pepper and salt and braised in a ceramic vessel in a cooling oven after bread has been baked. Today it is often seasoned with onion, bay leaf and allspice, in addition to the black pepper. Carrots, turnips and other similar root vegetables are also often added in more recent recipes. *Karjalanpaisti* is often enjoyed with Boiled Potatoes (page 117) and Finnish Rye Bread (page 504).

Preparation and cooking time: 6 hours
Serves: 4 for dinner, with some to spare for
  a light lunch the day after, perhaps served
  with Kale Salad (page 90)

500 g/1 lb 2 oz chuck beef, cut into
  rough cubes
500 g/1 lb 2 oz lamb or mutton shoulder,
  cut into rough cubes
500 g/1 lb 2 oz pork shoulder, cut into
  rough cubes
1 large onion, cut into wedges
15 allspice berries
15 black peppercorns
1 bay leaf
salt, to taste

Preheat the oven to 175°C/345°F/Gas Mark 4.

OXTAIL STEW

Oksehaleragout (Denmark)
Oxsvansragu (Sweden)

I like my oxtail with a steamed head of broccoli (page 82) and a good dollop of mustard.

Preparation and cooking time: 4½–5½ hours
Serves: 4

For the braise
1.5 kg/3¼ lb oxtail, cut into thick slices
2 tablespoons plain (all-purpose) flour
butter, for frying
500 ml/17 fl oz (2 cups plus 1 tablespoon)
    light lager
2 carrots, chopped
1 onion, quartered
1 clove garlic, crushed with the side
    of a knife
2 celery sticks, chopped
2 bay leaves
1 sprig thyme
12 black peppercorns
6 cloves

To finish
200 g/7 oz salted belly pork, cut into
    2 cm/¾ inch cubes
2 carrots, thickly sliced
20 Pickled Small Onions (page 108)
20 button mushrooms
salt and black pepper, to taste

Dust the oxtail slices generously with the flour and season them well with salt and pepper.

Melt some butter in a pan over a medium heat. Brown the oxtail slices on both sides until they are quite dark. Pour in the beer and stir well to deglaze the bottom of the pan. Add the vegetables and the aromatics, then pour in enough water to just cover the meat.

Bring to a simmer and cook, covered, for 4–5 hours, or until tender to the point that the meat is falling off the bone. Transfer the oxtail to a new pot and strain the cooking juices over it, discarding the aromatics and spent vegetables.

To finish, add the salted pork, carrots, pickled onions and mushrooms to the pan. Bring back to a simmer and cook until the carrots are perfectly done. Adjust the seasoning and serve.

TACO QUICHE

Tacopaj (Sweden)

It is a Friday around 7 p.m. and you are for some reason standing outside of a suburban Stockholm villa. It is a nice suburb, upper middle class, German SUVs are parked on each driveway and on the deserted lawns automatic mowers roam like robotic sheep, manicuring the green turf into perfection, zigzagging between abandoned toys. As your breath condenses on a cold windowpane the tip of your nose leaves a round mark where it touched the glass. A scent of cumin reaches your nostrils. The family of five seated around a table, just a couple of metres away from you, are passing little bowls and plates around. You can see flatbreads, salad, tomatoes, diced cheese and a glass jar marked 'salsa, mi'. The family is about to enjoy one of the most common Friday night meals of Norway or Sweden: a taco. Not a taco as it would be thought of in the part of the world where it originated but another kind, let's call it a 'Scandinavian' kind. The taco passed through a corporate filter when it was introduced to Sweden around the mid 1980s by spice companies. The idea of it further softened around the edges by the passing of time and adaptation to suit the produce available and the flavour preferences of those cooking and eating it. The Scandinavian taco is here to stay and I sometimes wonder what will become of it in the future. Will it change further and merge even more with our own food culture? Will we start to look upon the taco as traditional? It might seem far fetched but it has happened before, just look at the Pork Mince and Rice Cabbage Rolls (page 308), one of the most genuinely Swedish dishes according to most, imported from Turkey not more than a few hundred years ago, vine leaves exchanged over time with cabbage, and mutton for pork.

The concept of the taco has been established in Scandinavia for about as long as I have lived.

During that time people have found several ways of merging the fake, Tex-Mex industrial products sold to them with beloved local classics. One of those is the taco quiche or as it is locally known, *tacopaj*. I imagine the reasoning behind it began something like this: we like pie and we like pie with minced meat in, why not season it with pre-mixed taco seasoning and serve it with some salsa (also bought ready and of crap industrial standard) and some tortilla chips on the side?

If you wonder why this recipe has a place in a book like this, simply type *tacopaj* into your internet search engine and marvel over the 175,000 hits you will get from Sweden alone, a country with just over 9 million people in it. In just a few years the taco quiche has become an institution and a unique part of Swedish food culture. It's a national dish, which as far as I know, doesn't exist anywhere else.

Preparation and cooking time: 1 hour
Serves: 4–6

For the pastry
50 g/2 oz (3½ tablespoons) butter, soft
200 g/7 oz (1¾ cups) weak (soft) wheat flour
1 teaspoon baking powder
1 good pinch salt
100 ml/3½ fl oz (⅓ cup plus 1 tablespoon) milk

For the meat
500 g/1 lb 2 oz minced (ground) meat, most commonly beef, although I have also seen recipes using moose
taco spice mix, follow the packet instructions and add enough for the above mentioned amount of meat
1 tablespoon butter, for frying

For the topping
300 ml/10½ fl oz (1¼ cups) crème fraîche
1 egg
100 g/3½ oz (¾ cup) grated cheese
2 tablespoons industrial mayonnaise

Preheat the oven to 175°C/345°F/Gas Mark 4.

Add all of the ingredients for the pastry, except the milk, to the bowl of a food processor. Mix for a couple of seconds until everything is almost mixed together, then add the milk and mix a bit more until just combined. Transfer the dough to a 24 cm/9½ inch springform mould and press it out in an even but rather thick layer, almost all the way up to the edge of the mould. Refrigerate for a bit.

Meanwhile, brown the minced (ground) meat in a pan over a medium heat and when cooked through and nicely coloured, add the seasoning and some water (for the amount, follow the instructions on the back of your particular spice bag). Let it simmer for a couple of minutes until the water has almost reduced into the meat again.

As the meat is cooking, mix all of the ingredients for the topping together in a separate bowl. (Do not use homemade mayonnaise as this recipe needs all the stabilizer in the processed one. Without it the topping will separate in the oven.)

Transfer the cooked meat to the uncooked pastry shell and spread it out in an even layer. Continue by spreading a layer of topping over the meat. Place the pie in the oven for 35–45 minutes or until golden and crisp around the edges. Let it sit for a bit and cool before serving.

For image see page 331

BRAISED VEAL, SERVED IN A SWEET-AND-SOUR DILL SAUCE

Kokt kalv med dillsås (Sweden)

Serve with Boiled Potatoes (page 117) or Riced Potatoes (page 117).

Preparation and cooking time: 3–4 hours
Serves: 4

For the braise
1.5 kg/3¼ lb veal breast on the bone, or
   brisket, cleaned and ready to cook
1 leek, chopped
1 carrot, chopped
1 sprig thyme
1 bay leaf
10 white peppercorns
2 tablespoons Ättika (12%) vinegar
   (page 656)
salt, to taste

To finish the stew
butter, for frying
2 tablespoons plain (all-purpose) flour
2 tablespoons sugar
200 ml/7 fl oz (¾ cup plus 1 tablespoon)
   cream
Ättika (12%) vinegar (page 656), to taste
2 egg yolks
1 bunch dill, stalks finely chopped, fronds
   coarsely chopped
salt and white pepper, to taste

Place the meat and the other braise ingredients in a large pot and cover with cold water. Bring to a slow simmer, then cook over a medium–low heat for about 2 hours, or until the meat is just tender. Skim the surface of the broth from time to time.

To test if the meat is done, pierce it with a paring knife and lift it straight up. If the meat releases the knife straight away it is done, if it doesn't fall from the knife, then cook it for a bit longer. Once the meat is cooked, remove it from the pot and set aside.

Strain the cooking liquid into a clean pot and discard the solids. Bring to the boil, then simmer until it has reduced to about 400 ml/14 fl oz (1⅔ cups).

Once the veal is cool enough to handle, pull the meat away from the bone and cut it into cubes of about 3 cm/1¼ inches. Heat some butter in a pan over a medium heat. Add the cubed veal and fry until it is very lightly coloured. Sift over the flour, then pour in the reduced cooking liquid, together with the sugar and cream. Cook for a few minutes, then adjust the flavour balance to your liking with vinegar, salt and white pepper.

Just before serving, stir in the egg yolks and dill.

Clockwise from top centre: tortilla chips; Taco Quiche (page 329); store-bought salsa

FRICASSÉE OF VEAL

Kalvefrikasse (Norway)
Kalvefrikasse (Denmark)
Kalvfrikasse (Sweden)

This is one of those French dishes that reached the rich homes of the northern parts of Europe a couple of hundred years ago and stayed to become part of our own food culture. Serve with Boiled Potatoes (page 117) and a nice vegetable side dish like Steamed Kale (page 90) or Green Peas (page 136) or perhaps a Grated Carrot Salad (page 110).

Preparation and cooking time: 1½ hours
Serves: 4

butter, for frying
1.5 kg/3¼ lb veal, breast or brisket,
   trimmed and cut into 4 cm/1½ inch cubes
1 tablespoon plain (all-purpose) flour
1 litre/34 fl oz (4¼ cups) light Veal Stock
   (page 650)
1 bay leaf
1 sprig thyme
1 onion, finely chopped
1 large carrot, sliced
2 tablespoons vinegar or lemon juice
100 ml/3½ fl oz (⅓ cup plus 1 tablespoon)
   cream
2 egg yolks, lightly beaten
salt and white pepper, to taste

Heat a little butter in a cast-iron pan over a medium heat. Add the veal and brown it very lightly. Dust the flour over the meat in the pan, then pour in the veal stock (broth). Add the aromatics, the vegetables and the vinegar or lemon juice. Cover the pan with a lid, reduce the heat and simmer until the meat is just tender. I don't think veal should be braised until it falls apart, as it is not pleasant to eat. Add the cream and continue to simmer, uncovered, for another couple of minutes. Adjust the seasoning and stir in the egg yolks just before serving.

VEAL, KIDNEY AND POTATO CASSEROLE

Hökarepanna av kalv (Sweden)

The name for this dish in Swedish comes from the old word for a retailer of food products, *hökare*. It can be made either with veal and veal kidneys or with pork and pig's kidneys – or with a mix of both. Most people I have asked who actually cook or eat this dish like to serve it with mustard. I like that too, but I also like Sugared Lingonberries (page 692) with it and maybe a Cabbage Salad (page 96).

Preparation and cooking time: 50 minutes
Soaking time for the kidneys: overnight
Serves: 4

2 veal kidneys, halved, soaked in iced water
   overnight, water changed 2–3 times
300 g/11 oz lean veal (from the leg
   or the back)
butter or lard, for frying
6 potatoes, cut into 5 mm/¼ inch slices
2 onions, thinly sliced
1 sprig thyme
1 bay leaf
500 ml/17 fl oz (2 cups plus 1 tablespoon)
   good hoppy lager
salt and pepper, to taste

Preheat the oven to 150°C/300°F/Gas Mark 2.

Cut the kidneys and the meat into slices about 1 cm/½ inch thick and season with salt and pepper. Melt the butter or lard in a pan over a medium–high heat. Add the meat and brown it quickly.

Layer the meat and kidneys with the potatoes and onions in an ovenproof dish. Season the layers with salt and pepper and add the sprig of thyme and the bay leaf somewhere in the middle. Pour in the beer and bring it to the boil over a medium heat. Cover with a tight-fitting lid and bake in the oven for 30 minutes.

OVEN-BAKED SWEDISH VEAL PATTIES

Kalvjärpe (Sweden)

The name of this dish in Swedish refers to the word for veal, which is *kalv* and the word for the small game bird, known as a hazel hen, which is *järpe*. The patties are shaped into the form of a large egg, and resemble the shape of a roasted hazel hen carcass. In older recipes I have also seen the patties rolled in salted pork, much as you would do when roasting a small game bird.

Kalvjärpe is often served with Boiled Potatoes (page 117) or Mashed Potatoes (page 118) and Quick Pickled Cucumber (page 658). In late autumn (fall) I like to eat *kalvjärpe* with Freshly Brined, Unfermented Cucumber Pickles (page 659).

Preparation and cooking time: 40 minutes
Serves: 4

For the veal patties
500 g/1 lb 2 oz finely minced (ground) veal
100 g/3½ oz (1¼ cups) breadcrumbs
200 ml/7 fl oz (¾ cup plus 1 tablespoon)
  cream
2 eggs
butter, for greasing
1 quantity Basic Cream Sauce (page 663),
  made from the veal cooking liquid
salt and white pepper, to taste

Combine the veal, breadcrumbs, cream and eggs in a mixing bowl and work them together well. Season with salt and pepper, then leave it for about 10 minutes for the bread to swell.

Preheat the oven to 225°C/435°F/Gas Mark 7 and butter a roasting pan.

With a clean, wet hand and a wet spoon, shape the mixture into oval balls, the size and shape of a large egg. Place them in the prepared pan and bake until the patties are lightly golden in colour.

Transfer the veal patties to a pan with lid. Strain the cooking juices from the roasting pan into a pot and prepare the cream sauce, following the method on page 663.

Pour the cream sauce into the pan with the patties. Simmer covered over a low heat until the patties are cooked through.

VEAL ROULADES FILLED WITH PARSLEY BUTTER

Kalvkyckling (Sweden)

The name of this dish in Swedish translates to 'veal-chicken'. I have tried to figure out why, but not succeeded. This veal-chicken is a roulade of veal, filled with Parsley Butter (page 655) before being braised tender and served with cream sauce. These roulades are often served with Boiled Potatoes (page 117) and Quick Pickled Cucumber (page 658). Sometimes a jar of Blackcurrant Jelly (page 691) or Rowanberry Jelly (page 691) can also accompany the dish.

Preparation and cooking time: 1 hour
Serves: 4

1 kg/2¼ lb topside of veal, boned, cut into
   12–14 even slices, pounded flat
1 quantity Parsley Butter (page 655)
200 ml/7 fl oz (¾ cup plus 1 tablespoon)
   Veal Stock (page 650)
70 g/2¾ oz (5 tablespoons) butter, plus
   extra for browning
1 quantity Basic Cream Sauce (page 663),
   made from the veal cooking liquid
salt and white pepper, to taste

Lay the slices of veal out on your work counter and season them with salt and pepper. Place a small knob of the butter on each slice before rolling them up tightly. Tie each roulade with string at both ends to secure its shape. See illustrations on page 320.

Melt some butter in a pan over a medium heat. Add the roulades to the pan and brown them all over. Pour in the veal stock (broth) and bring to a simmer. Cover the pan and cook until the roulades are just tender.

When done, reserve the cooking liquid and transfer the roulades to a serving platter and keep warm while you make a cream sauce.

Prepare the cream sauce with the cooking liquid from the roulades, following the method on page 663.

To serve, either pour the sauce over the roulades on the platter just before serving or serve it in a sauce boat on the side.

LAMB AND MUTTON

Previous page: Farmland becoming beach and then fiord, Norway, Spring 2014.

Opposite: Mutton hanging to age in a hjallur, the traditional Faroese storage house, Stóra Dímun, April 2013.

Previous page: View of mountains and a small lake crossed by a power line, north Norway, May 2014.

Opposite: Lunch in a Faroese home, April 2013. The man is cutting himself a piece of Aged Mutton (page 350).

LAMB BRAISED IN A SWEET-AND-SOUR DILL SAUCE

Lam i dildsovs (Denmark)
Kokt lamm i dillsås (Sweden)

The preparation of this dish can be split over two days if you want. Cook the meat and reduce the cooking liquid on day one and finish the dish on day two. Serve with Boiled Potatoes (page 117) or Riced Potatoes (page 117).

Preparation and cooking time: 2 hours
Serves: 4

butter, for frying
2 tablespoons plain (all-purpose) flour
2 tablespoons sugar
200 ml/7 fl oz (¾ cup plus 1 tablespoon) cream
Ättika (12%) vinegar (page 656), to taste
2 egg yolks
1 bunch dill, stalks finely chopped, fronds coarsely chopped
salt and white pepper, to taste

For the braise
1.5 kg/3¼ lb lamb breast on the bone, cleaned and ready to cook
1 leek, chopped
1 carrot, chopped
1 sprig thyme
1 bay leaf
10 white peppercorns
2 tablespoons Ättika (12%) vinegar (page 656)
salt, to taste

Place the meat and the other braise ingredients in a large pot and cover with cold water. Bring to a slow simmer over medium–low heat, then cook for about 1 hour, or until the meat is just tender. Skim from time to time.

To test if the meat is done, pierce it with a paring knife and lift it straight up. If the meat releases the knife straight away it is done, if it doesn't fall from the knife, then cook it for a bit longer. Once the meat is cooked, remove it from the pot and set aside.

Strain the cooking liquid into a clean pot and dis-card the remaining solids. Bring to the boil, then simmer until it has reduced to about 400 ml/14 fl oz (1⅔ cups).

Once the lamb is cool enough to handle, pull the meat away from the bone and cut it into cubes of about 3 cm/1¼ inches. Heat a little butter in a large frying pan or skillet over a medium heat. Add the cubed lamb and fry until it is very lightly coloured. Sift over the flour, then pour in the reduced cooking liquid, together with the sugar and cream. Cook for a few minutes, then taste and adjust the flavour balance to your liking with vinegar, salt and white pepper.

Just before serving, stir in the egg yolks and dill.

For image see page 353

SALTED BREAST OF LAMB, BOILED

Sprengt lammebryst (Norway)
Kokt rimmat lamm (Sweden)

I like to sprinkle the lamb slices liberally with chopped parsley or snipped chives before serving.

Preparation and cooking time: 2–4 hours
Resting time: overnight
Serves: 4

1.5 kg/3¼ lb salted breast of lamb, thoroughly rinsed
1 carrot, chopped
1 onion, quartered
1 sprig thyme
1 bay leaf
10 white peppercorns
chopped parsley or snipped chives, to serve

Place the rinsed lamb in a pot, together with the vegetables and aromatics. Cover with cold water and bring to a simmer. Cover the pot and cook until the lamb is tender, which can take from 2–4 hours. Skim from time to time.

To test if the meat is done, pierce it with a paring knife and lift it straight up. If the meat releases the knife straight away it is done, if it doesn't fall from the knife, then cook it for a bit longer. Once the lamb is done to your liking, slice it thinly and serve in the cooking liquid sprinkled with chopped parsley or snipped chives.

Tip: Instead of eating the lamb straight away, you can allow it to cool in the cooking liquid, then cover it with baking (parchment) paper and weight it overnight in the refrigerator (or longer if you wish). This makes it really easy to slice. Reheat the slices in some of the cooking liquid to serve, and sprinkle with chopped parsley or snipped chives.

ICELANDIC LEG OF LAMB, COLD-SMOKED AND BOILED

Hangilæri (Iceland)

This is the most common way of cooking *hangikjöt*, Icelandic cold-smoked lamb or mutton, and it is an essential part of most people's traditional Christmas meal. Usually, *Hangilæri* is served with browned potatoes, a bit similar to Danish Sugar-browned Potatoes (page 120), as well as canned marrowfat peas, boiled, Braised Sweet-and-Sour Red Cabbage (page 82) and *Uppstúf* (page 666), essentially a béchamel seasoned with nutmeg and sometimes a spoon or two of sugar. At Christmas, Icelandic Leaf Bread (page 514) is also often part of the meal.

Preparation and cooking time: 1 hour
Cooling time: at least overnight
Serves: 4–6

1 whole leg cold-smoked Icelandic *hangikjöt* lamb or mutton

Place the leg of lamb or mutton in a pot large enough to fit it. Cover with water and slowly bring to the boil. This will take about 45 minutes, depending on the strength of your stove.

Once boiling, lower the heat and simmer for about 15 minutes, then remove the pot from the heat and leave the lamb to cool down in the cooking liquid.

Remove the lamb from the liquid and place on a serving platter. Cover and leave to rest in the refrigerator, for at least a night, before using.

LEG OF LAMB COOKED IN THE GROUND

Holugrillað lambalæri (Iceland)

This is a summertime classic in Iceland. A leg of lamb or mutton is wrapped in aromatics and aluminium foil before being buried in a fire pit in the ground for slow cooking. Many Icelandic homes and vacation houses have a fire pit in their back yard. This technique bears a clear resemblance to that of a Mexican or Caribbean *barbacoa,* where whole pieces of meat suitable for extended roasting, like shoulder of mutton or lamb, are wrapped in something, then cooked by the steam of their own juices, which is trapped in by the wrapping.

ICELANDIC MEAT SOUP

Kjötsúpa (Iceland)

One of their most important dishes, if you ask many Icelandic citizens, *Kjötsúpa* bears a clear cultural connection to the national meat soups of other Nordic countries. Based on whatever meat is predominantly available – in this case lamb or mutton – and root vegetables that store well in winter, this brothy soup is often but not always thickened with something starchy like rice, pearl barley or rolled oats. Sometimes the meat is served on a separate plate next to the actual soup and sometimes it is served in the broth itself.

The vegetables in this soup should preferably be winter ones, coarse and sweet. In more recent recipes, other flavourings, like thyme, garlic and bay leaves are used, which is probably very tasty, but reduces the soup to any other meat soup from anywhere.

Stock (broth) should not be added to this recipe, whether homemade or from cubes. It will create an overly savoury soup that lacks the desired balance between vegetables and meat.

Preparation and cooking time: 2 hours
Serves: 4

1 kg/2¼ lb mutton or lamb from the front
 quarter of the animal (shoulder, neck or
 similar is perfect), cut into rough pieces,
 not too small
1 large swede (rutabaga), cut into rough
 pieces
4 large carrots, cut into rough pieces
6 waxy potatoes, cut into wedges
1 onion, cut into wedges
3 tablespoons *súpujurtir* (dried vegetables
 and herbs)
salt and black pepper, to taste

Optional
50 g/2 oz (½ cup plus 1 tablespoon) rolled
 oats
50 g/2 oz (¼ cup) short-grain rice
100 g/3½ oz (¼ cup) pearl barley

Place the meat in a large pot and cover with cold water. Slowly bring to the boil, then lower the heat and leave to simmer for 45–60 minutes until the meat starts to tenderize. Skim away excess fat and scum now and then, if necessary. Add the prepared vegetables and seasonings and cook until the vegetables are tender. Adjust the seasoning again and serve immediately.

FÅRFIOL

Fårfiol is a traditional cured, dried, and in some cases also lightly cold-smoked, leg of mutton from Sweden. The name refers to the shape of the mutton leg, and basically means 'sheep's fiddle'. *Fårfiol* has a clear historical connection to Norwegian *fenalår* (page 348), Icelandic *hangikjot* (page 358) and, to some extent, Faroese *skjerpikjott,* although the Icelandic and Faroese versions are unsalted. Today, commercially produced hot-smoked leg of lamb – or sometimes even lamb shoulder – can be referred to as *fårfiol*. This is completely wrong and bordering on sacrilegious. These traditional ways of preserving meat arose out of necessity, and are still practised today, but because we like the taste of them, rather than needing them for survival, they should in my opinion be respected for what they are and left untouched in terms of techniques used. *Fårfiol* is most often served in thin slices, like the cured hams of central Europe, on occasion with Scrambled Eggs (page 52) or with creamed potatoes with parsley (page 120). *Fårfiol* can also be served warm in *glödhoppor* (see below).

CURED FÅRFIOL LEG OF MUTTON,
SEARED AND SERVED WARM

Glödhoppor (Sweden)

The name *glödhoppor* refers to the way the pieces of meat sizzle and jump off the glowing hot surface of a stove or cast-iron pan.

Glödhoppor has become very rare, since real fårfiol, or cured mutton (see above), isn't so common in Sweden any more and is mostly hot-smoked leg of lamb, which doesn't work in this dish.

Serve the just-cooked shavings of salty meat with Scrambled Eggs (page 52), Creamed Potatoes (page 120) or on a slice of *rågsiktskaka*, a round wheat loaf, with butter.

Preparation and cooking time: 10 minutes
Serves: 4

200 g/7 oz thin slices of *Fårfiol*
  (see left)

Heat a cast-iron pan as hot as your stove can possibly make it. Sear the slices of mutton for a couple of seconds on each side and serve immediately.

MUTTON OR LAMB IN CABBAGE

Fårikål (Norway)
Lammaskaali (Finland)
Får I Kål (Sweden)

The name of this dish in Norwegian literally translates to 'sheep in cabbage', which is sort of what it is. The Norwegian national dish traditionally tastes only of mutton, summer cabbage and whole black peppercorns, which might sound simple, but correctly prepared it is a marvel of balanced umami and cabbagy bitter-sweetness. Today you can find recipes making use of both rosemary and garlic, and other recipes that even encourage browning the meat before adding it to the braise are not uncommon. These new recipes are surely delicious dishes too, but they are not quite right. In Norway, *fårikål* is most often enjoyed with Boiled Potatoes (page 117), Norwegian Crisp Flatbread (page 513) and Sugared Lingonberries (page 692).

A common autumn (fall) dish, *fårikål* is most often prepared from either that year's fully-grown lamb or from mutton. However, today you can find, in Norway, special *fårikål* meat available all year around. It is often made from younger, unwanted male lambs and even though quite often very tender, it can be lacking in flavour.

Some people like to tie the peppercorns in a gauze spice bag and others like to have them loose in the finished dish to brighten it with sudden flashes of peppery spiciness when you bite into them. Do as you prefer.

Fårikål is occasionally thickened a little, and this is done by dusting some flour onto the raw pieces of meat before cooking them.

Preparation and cooking time: 2 hours
Serves: 4

1 kg/2¼ lb braising cut of mutton, hogget
  or lamb (shoulder, neck or shank are most
  commonly used)
1 kg/2¼ lb green cabbage, cut into wedges,
  roughly the same size as the pieces
  of meat
30 black peppercorns
salt, to taste

Use a band saw (or ask your butcher) to cut the meat through the bone into slices about 3 cm/1¼ inches thick.

Layer the cabbage wedges and meat snugly in a large pot. Add the peppercorns and barely cover with water. Season a little with salt, cover the pot and bring to a simmer over a medium heat. Cook for 45–90 minutes, or until the meat is tender, which will depend on which kind of meat you use. It may be less for young animals and more for older. Add more water if necessary during the cooking process, but don't stir. Just spin the pan a little from time to time to make sure the food doesn't stick to the bottom. When the meat is tender, adjust the level of salt and serve immediately.

For image see page 353

FRICASSÉE OF LAMB OR MUTTON

Lammefrikasse (Denmark)
Lamm i fårfrikasse (Sweden)

Preparation and cooking time: 1½ hours
Serves: 4

butter, for frying
1.5 kg/3¼ lb lamb or mutton, shoulder
    or breast, trimmed and cut into 4 cm/
    1½ inch cubes
1 tablespoon plain (all-purpose) flour
1 litre/34 fl oz (4¼ cups) Lamb Stock
    (page 650)
1 bay leaf
1 sprig thyme
1 onion, finely chopped
1 large carrot, sliced
2 tablespoons vinegar or lemon juice
100 ml/3½ fl oz (⅓ cup plus 1 tablespoon)
    cream
2 egg yolks, lightly beaten
salt and white pepper, to taste

Heat a little butter in a cast-iron pan over a medium heat. Add the lamb or mutton and brown it very lightly. Dust the flour over the meat in the pan, then pour in the stock (broth). Add the aromatics, the vegetables and the vinegar or lemon juice. Cover the pan with a lid, reduce the heat and simmer for about 1 hour, or until the meat is just tender.

Add the cream and continue to simmer, uncovered, for another couple of minutes. Adjust the seasoning and stir in the egg yolks just before serving.

NORWEGIAN CURED AND AGED LEG OF MUTTON

Fenalår (Norway)

Fenalår is most often a salted and dried leg of mutton, but it can, rarely, also be produced from goat. It is dry-salted and aged for at least three months and although it was produced historically as a means to preserve meats for survival, today it is considered a great delicacy. The dry-salting and aging of meat, which is in Norway called *speking*, has been going on for at least a thousand years in the region. A great *fenalår* will be at least 2 years old and can be as many as 6 years old.

In the old days, every farm made its own *spekemat*, but today the process has been largely industrialized and specimens of outstanding quality can be very hard to come by. It is funny to see, though, that the tradition of curing meat today is carried on not so much by farmers in the countryside, but rather by a new group of people in the cities, people who think it is important to keep the old ways alive. Something that was once done for survival in places where it made sense is now being done by those living in the places where it makes the least practical sense, by those who least need to do it to have food through the winter.

There is a cultural connection to other aged mutton meats like Swedish *fårfiol*, Faroese *raest*, and Icelandic *hangikjott*.

Norwegian cured mutton is often eaten, thinly sliced, like charcuterie, by itself, but can also be served with Split Pea Soup (page 140) and with Norwegian Sour Cream Porridge (page 468).

For image see opposite page

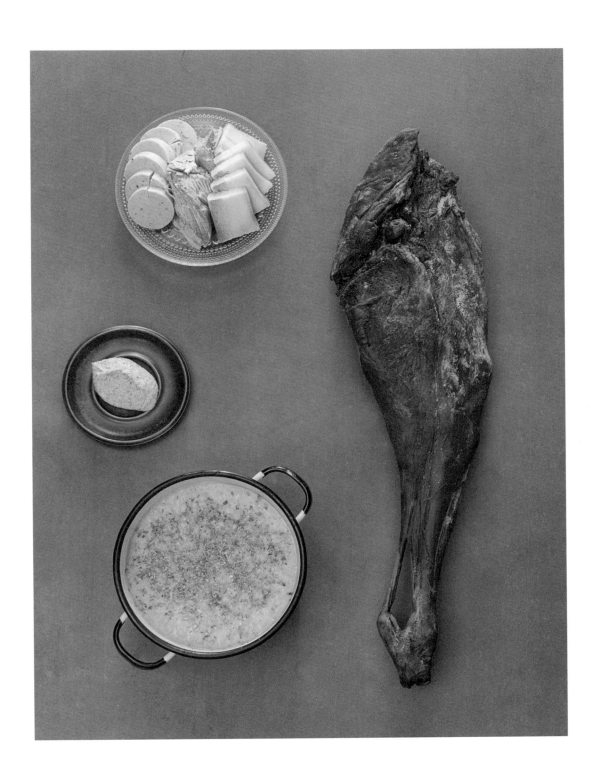

Clockwise from top left: Medister Pork Sausages (page 430); salt ham hock; salt pork belly; Norwegian Cured and Aged Leg of Mutton (page 348); Split Pea Soup (page 140); Scanian Mustard (page 653)

DRIED RIB OF LAMB STEAMED OVER BIRCH TWIGS

Pinnekjøtt (Norway)

This dish, consisting of salted and dried, or salted and cold-smoked rack of mutton or lamb, traditionally comes from the western parts of Norway but is today widespread in the country and one of the most popular dishes for Christmas Eve.

There are different opinions on where the name *pinnekjøtt* comes from: if it refers to the birch twigs, *pinnar*, or to the old Norse name for rib, which is *pinni*.

Serve *pinnekjøtt* with Mashed Swede (rutabaga) and Boiled Potatoes (page 117). In some families lingonberry jam (page 690) or coarse mustard is offered as a condiment. It is not entirely uncommon to see this dish served with pieces of Vossa Sausage (page 431) either. If the sausage is used, it is added to the steaming meat for just the last 15 minutes of cooking. Another variation of this dish is to grill (broil) the braised meat in the oven at a very high temperature for 10 minutes or so, just before serving, to crisp the fat.

You will need enough fresh birch twigs (with the bark peeled off) to cover the bottom of a pot which is large enough to accommodate all the meat, raising it 3.5–5 cm/1½–2 inches from the bottom of the pot itself.

Preparation and cooking time: 3 hours
Soaking time: overnight
Serves: 4

1.5 kg/3¼–lb dried or salted and cold-smoked
    rack of lamb or mutton (*pinnekjøtt*)
plain (all-purpose) flour, to thicken
    the cooking juices (optional)

Cut the ribcage into strips following the length of the individual ribs, then cut each rib in half with a sturdy pair of scissors. Place the rib pieces in a bowl with plenty of cold water and leave them to soak overnight.

Spread the birch twigs over the bottom of a large pot to form a rack on which the meat can rest.

Pour in just enough water to cover the bottom of the pot, then stack the ribs in even layers on top of the twigs.

Bring to a simmer, then cover the pot and leave to steam for 2–4 hours, or until tender. The cooking time will depend on the age of the animal. Be sure to add fresh water from time to time so that the pot doesn't boil dry.

When the meat is done, transfer it to a serving platter. Strain the cooking liquid and either serve it as it is with the meat or thicken it slightly with a little flour.

FAROESE AGED MUTTON

Skerpikjøt (Faroe Islands)

Skerpikjøt is the traditional preserved meat (or perhaps, it's better to say 'kept' meat) from places where salt hasn't been affordable – or even available – until the last few hundred years. The Faroese climate is too cool to evaporate seawater in salterns and there are no naturally growing trees on the islands to fuel saltpans. This situation, combined with the Islands' remoteness, especially during the era of sailing ships, has historically made salt a rare and expensive commodity.

The Faroese method of producing *skerpikjøt* is basically to hang pieces of raw, unsalted mutton in a drying shed called *hjallur*. The meat is left until it has either reached the desired maturity, or until it is required. The country's location in the middle of the Gulfstream makes the climate quite humid, and so completely drying a piece of meat is a very lengthy process, often taking more than one full year.

There are three stages of maturation in *skerpikjøt* production, known as *hjaldane*. The first stage is called *visnadur*, which is reached after a few days. The Faroese name for this stage literally means 'wilting,' and it is what most would refer to as 'dry-aged meat'. If it is eaten at all, it must be cooked. The next stage, *raestur*, depends on atmospheric factors like humidity and temperature. It can be challenging for those who are not used to it as it is, essentially, decaying meat. Covered in a thick crust of mould and smelling intensely of putrefaction, *raestur* is consumed raw, or else it is cooked and eaten warm as a meal, or cold on bread. The third and final stage of maturation is *turrur*, which means 'dry.' *Turrur* is reached when enough water has evaporated and the meat has become firm, like a sort of unsalted charcuterie. Surprisingly, *turrur* has a much milder flavour than *raestur* and it is sliced thinly and eaten raw on bread.

FAROESE AGED MUTTON WITH SOUP

Raest kjöt og supan (Faroe Islands)

This is one popular way of cooking and eating Faroese aged mutton, which used to be a widely eaten, everyday food, that was essential for survival, but these days it is seen as more of a festive, and cherished dish.

Historically, vegetables weren't commonly eaten on the Faroe Islands, so most likely this soup didn't contain any. Today, most people use carrots and quite a few add onion or leeks and cabbage or turnips too – a bit depending on what's available I guess.

The meat is often served on one big platter for the table and the soup is served on the side in separate cups. Faroese rye bread and butter is also common.

Short-grain rice or rolled oats are commonly added to the soup during cooking, and a version with yellow split peas, making the soup a little thicker, is also prepared. If you use any of these, add them when about 30 minutes of cooking remains. The peas will have to be soaked in water overnight.

Preparation and cooking time: 2 hours
Serves: 4

1.2 kg/2½ lb Faroese aged mutton (*raest*), on the bone

For the soup
5 large carrots, cut into 1 cm/½ inch slices

1 leek, white part only, cut into 5 mm/ ¼ inch slices (reserve the green part for another recipe)
salt, to taste

Clean the meat under cold running water and use a stiff brush to scrub away any remaining mould. Place the meat in a big pot and cover it with water.

Bring the meat to a slow simmer and cook for a good hour or so, or until tender. The exact timing will depend on the meat.

Transfer the meat to a serving platter and leave it to rest somewhere warm until ready to serve.

Strain the broth and return it to a clean pan. Bring it back to a simmer, then skim. Simmer until everything is quite soft. Season quite lightly with salt.

LAMB CHOPS AS IN KALMAR

Kalmarlåda (Sweden)

Whether this dish was actually invented in the Swedish east coast city of Kalmar is a bit unclear. However it has been a popular and slightly festive restaurant lunch dish throughout the twentieth century. I have found it on plenty of old menus from iconic Stockholm restaurants. *Kalmarlåda* should be served with either Brined Cucumbers (page 660) or slices of fresh cucumber. A dollop of strong mustard on the side is always nice too.

Preparation and cooking time: 30 minutes
Serves: 4

8 lamb chops
butter, for frying
4 slices smoked ham, about 3 mm/
  ⅛ inch thick
1 bunch parsley, chopped
salt and white pepper, to taste
Scanian Potatoes, to serve

While the Scanian Potatoes are cooking, season the lamb chops all over with salt and pepper.

Heat a little butter in a large frying pan over a medium–high heat. Fry the chops on both sides until they are well-coloured on the outside, but still pink and juicy inside. Take the chops out of the pan and quickly wipe them with paper towels to remove any excess fat and burnt solids. Set them aside on a warm serving platter.

Add the ham slices to the same pan and sear them on both sides. They should colour just a bit and curl up a little.

Transfer the ham slices to the platter, along with the Scanian potatoes and sprinkle with lots of chopped parsley as you serve.

For image see opposite page

SHEEP'S HEAD

Seydarhövd (Faroe Islands)
Svið (Iceland)
Smalahove (Norway)

In a time when man could not afford the excessive wasting of food to which we have grown accustomed today, every part of an animal was eaten by someone. Originally considered a poor man's cut, the head of the sheep has grown into an appreciated delicacy in those parts of the Nordics where sheep are most common: the Faroe Islands, Iceland and Norway.

It is eaten in a similar fashion in all three countries, where it is actually rather common. The head is singed clean of any wool and in some cases smoked and dried a bit for storage. When the time has come to serve the sheep's head, which can be either whole or halved along its length, the head is boiled until tender. The brain, which in a whole head can still be inside the skull, is then cooked inside the head; for halved heads the brain is often cooked separately.

Sheep's head is often served with Root Vegetable Mash (page 112) and potatoes.

In Iceland, the head can be pickled (*surmatur*) in whey before being prepared and there is also a difference in how it is eaten in Norway and Iceland. In Norway the ears are considered one of the nicest parts, whereas in Iceland, since they carry the mark of the sheep's owner, they are always taken off the head before serving, out of superstition.

At the Reykjavik bus terminal food joint, called *fljótt og gott*, a fast food version of *svið* is offered and is also very popular.

For image see opposite page

Clockwise from top left: Norwegian Broth with Soaked Flatbread (page 354); Mutton or Lamb in Cabbage (page 347); Sheep's Head (page 352); Lamb Braised in Sweet-and-Sour Dill Sauce (page 344); Lamb Chops as in Kalmar (page 352)

353   *Recipes   /   Lamb and mutton*

NORWEGIAN MUTTON AND MEATBALL SOUP FROM TRØNDELAG

Trøndersodd (Norway)

Sodd is not really a soup, nor a stew. If you ask a Norwegian, it is simply *sodd*, which means 'to simmer'. Most of the time mutton is used, but in some parts of Norway beef is more common. It contains both pieces of braised meat and little meatballs. It is commonly eaten in most parts of the country but most notably in the central Norwegian region of Trøndelag.

Sodd is often served with Norwegian Thin Crispbread Baked from Potato and Oatmeal called *skjenning* (page 515) and sometimes with Boiled Potatoes (page 117) on the side, or sliced raw and added to the broth towards the end of cooking.

The basis behind *sodd* is that all the different ingredients are cooked separately and then combined just before serving. This makes for a very elegant broth with no vegetable sweetness as would have been the case if all the vegetables were cooked in the broth itself, as is most often the case with this kind of dish.

Sodd is generally quite mild in seasoning, but can also have a bit of bite from ginger and some subtle spiciness from nutmeg.

Preparation and cooking time: 2–4 hours
Serves: 4

1 kg/2¼ lb mutton or lamb on the bone
   (shoulder or neck are both good)
5 large carrots, peeled and cut into sticks
freshly grated nutmeg, to taste (optional)
ground ginger, to taste (optional)
salt and white pepper, to taste

For the meatballs
300 g/11 oz minced (ground) lamb
2 teaspoons potato flour
1 teaspoon ground ginger
50 ml/2 fl oz (3½ tablespoons) cream
freshly grated nutmeg, to taste
salt and white pepper, to taste

Put the mutton or lamb into a big pot and cover it with water. Bring to a simmer and cook for 1½–3 hours, or until the meat falls off the bone. The timing will depend a bit on the cut and which meat you use.

While the meat is braising, prepare the meatballs. Combine all the ingredients in the bowl of a stand mixer and mix them together thoroughly. It's important to work the mixture well; the texture should be very dense and firm, otherwise the meatballs can fall apart when they are added to the broth later.

To check the seasoning, make a small meatball and add it to the pan with the braising meat for a few minutes. When cooked, taste and adjust the balance, if necessary. Set the mixture aside.

When the mutton or lamb is very tender, remove it from the braising liquid and pull the meat off the bone. Cut it into 3 cm/1¼ inch pieces and set aside. Strain the braising liquid through a chinois (conical strainer) or a fine sieve into a clean pot and return it to a simmer.

With clean, wet hands, form 2.5 cm/1 inch meatballs and drop each one into the simmering broth as you finish it. Once the last meatball has been added, simmer for 7 minutes.

Once the meatballs are cooked, add the braised meat back into the broth.

While the meat is reheating, boil the carrots, following the instructions on page 82.

Just before serving, taste the broth and adjust the seasoning. Add nutmeg and ginger to taste, if using. Add the carrots to the broth and serve.

NORWEGIAN BROTH WITH SOAKED FLATBREAD

Flotmylje (Norway)

This is a very old, but historically important, dish that was everyday food throughout the country. It has been especially popular in the south, where it can also be known as *flatbraudsoll* – literally 'flatbread mix'.

To make *flotmylje*, pieces of Norwegian Crisp Flatbread (page 513) are placed in a bowl with a good lump of cultured butter on top and a hot meat broth – either mutton, lamb or beef – is then poured on top.

For image see page 353

not to mash the potatoes as they are cooking, since that will give a muddy appearance to the *lapskaus*, which is not desirable.

Season with white pepper and possibly some salt, if necessary. Sprinkle plenty of parsley over the steaming hot stew before serving.

NORWEGIAN LIGHT STEW OF SALTED MUTTON

Lys lapskaus (Norway)

The name *lapskaus* refers to many different dishes in the Nordic countries, but the Norwegian version is a simple meat stew – in this case a light one, made from salted lamb or mutton. It is generally served with Norwegian Crisp Flatbread (page 513) and lingonberry jam (page 690).

Preparation and cooking time: 2 hours
Soaking time: overnight
Serves: 4

700 g/1 lb 8½ oz salted mutton on
  the bone, soaked overnight in plenty
  of cold water
6 firm potatoes
3 carrots
1 swede (rutabaga)
1 onion
½ celeriac (celery root)
coarsely chopped parsley
salt and white pepper, to taste

Bone the desalted mutton and cut it into 2–3 cm/¾–1¼ inch cubes. Place both the meat and bones in a big pot and cover with cold water. Bring to the boil over a medium heat and then lower the temperature. Simmer, covered, for 45–60 minutes, or until the meat is almost tender. Skim from time to time.

While the meat is braising, peel and clean the vegetables, then cut them into cubes, a little smaller than the meat. Add the vegetables to the pot and continue to simmer until they are cooked through. Stir from time to time, but be careful

FINNISH MUTTON AND HERRING CASEROLE

Vorschmack (Finland)

There are several dishes around the world that bear the same (or similar) name to this, from the Jewish *vorschmack*, based on herring and sometimes eggs, to the Polish chicken stew called *forszmak*. This Finnish speciality didn't originate in Finland but has an unknown origin in the eastern parts of Europe. It is not established exactly when it came to Finland, but Marshall Mannerheim, Finnish war hero and later President, popularized it as his favourite dish.

This warm mix of lamb or mutton, minced (ground) after the cooking with herring and Sprats Cured in Sandalwood (page 212), is often served with Pickled Beetroot (page 660), Brined Cucumbers (page 660), *smetana* and baked potatoes. A glass of iced vodka or Aqavit (page 714) is recommended: Marshall Mannerheim had his own flavoured aquavit named *Marskin ryyppy* (page 714).

Preparation and cooking time: 40 minutes
Soaking time: overnight
Serves: 4

500 g/1 lb 2 oz lamb or mutton leg or
  shoulder, coarsely cut into cubes
150 g/5 oz chuck beef, coarsely cut
  into cubes
1 large onion, cut into wedges
½ tablespoon tomato purée (paste)
1 clove garlic, grated
1 fillet salted herring, desalted (page 200)
80 g/3 oz Sprats Cured in Sandalwood
  (page 212), drained
salt and white pepper, to taste

Preheat the oven to 225°C/435°F/Gas Mark 7.

Place the meat, onion, tomato purée (paste) and garlic in a roasting pan and roast until everything is nicely browned and cooked through. Add a splash of water during the last couple of minutes, and stir to deglaze the pan.

Push the roasted mixture through the coarse plate of a meat mincer (grinder), together with the herring and the drained sprats. Season with salt, if necessary, and a little bit of white pepper.

For image see opposite page

A serving of Finnish Mutton and Herring Casserole (page 356)

FAROESE AGED INTESTINAL FAT

Garnatálg (Faroe Islands)

This traditional condiment is often enjoyed with aged fish (page 234). It is produced a little bit differently from island to island, and from cook to cook, on the Faroe Islands.

The preparation of *garnatálg* starts in the autumn (fall), when sheep are normally slaughtered and when the weather is growing cooler.

Preparation and drying time: at least
  6 months
Makes: about 1 kg/2¼ lb

6 sheep large intestines, the last third or
  so removed
3 sheets of sheep caul fat (plus/minus 1,
  depending on how fatty they are)

First, rinse the intestines under cold running water, both inside and out until the water is completely clear.

Fold them up, in pairs, into loaf-shapes and wrap each loaf tightly in caul fat. The wrapping mustn't have any holes in it and it needs to be airtight.

Place these 'envelopes' on a platter somewhere cool to firm up overnight. Next, transfer them to a traditional Faroese drying house called a *hjallur*.

Garnatálg is aged for a few months and most people on the Faroe Islands will continue processing them around Christmas time, when they are passed through a meat mincer (grinder) or chopped really fine with a knife and kneaded before consuming.

ÞORRAMATUR

This is a buffet selection of traditional Icelandic foods that are consumed as part of the midwinter *Þorrablót* festivals, held by many student associations, and connected to the fourth winter month in the Icelandic calendar (mid-January to mid-February). *Þorramatur* comprises very old-fashioned recipes, such as Icelandic Rotten Shark (page 240) and Sheep's Head (page 352).

Contrary to what many believe, *Þorramatur* was only popularized during the period of intense urbanisation that followed the Second World War. It was first connected to *Þorri* in 1958 by a restaurant in Reykjavik named *Naustið*. Today the serving of *Þorramatur* dishes alone is enough for an event to be called *Þorrablót*, and these can be anything, from the large festivals of old days to small family gatherings.

ICELANDIC SMOKED LAMB
OR MUTTON

Hangikjöt (Iceland)

Hangikjöt literally means 'hung meat' and it is one of the traditional Icelandic ways of preparing meat for storage. In the old days, as in other remote parts of the Nordic Atlantic region, salt was a very expensive and rare commodity. It had to be imported, because in a place like Iceland, a country with no trees to produce firewood for fuelling salt-pans, and too humid and cool to evaporate seawater in salterns, it was difficult to produce. A lot of the traditional food preservation techniques from Iceland are, because of this, saltless or use very little salt, as opposed to mainland Europe, where salt was, and still is, the base for microbiological control in everything from charcuterie to pickles.

Hangikjöt is essentially a piece of leg or shoulder of lamb or mutton, very lightly salted and then hung up in the rafters of a small windowless shack. In the middle of the room there is a small fireplace, often fuelled with dried pieces of sheep dung. The fire is not constantly fuelled, but rather lit and relit a few times, until the desired amount of smokiness in the meat is achieved. The cold-smoked meat is left to hang for storage in the smokehouse until needed.

This technique of cold smoking over sheep dung is often used for fish – especially fillets of trout and char. These are usually salted a bit more than mutton and not hung for storage but, rather, removed from the smokehouse when the actual smoking is done after a couple of days. The dung-smoked fish is often enjoyed in thin slices with some Icelandic Rye Bread (page 503) baked in the ground in geothermal areas.

Hangikjöt is often boiled in dishes like Icelandic Leg of Lamb, Cold-smoked and Boiled (page 345) or boiled and served on sandwiches. I have been served thinly sliced raw *hangikjöt* a few times, almost like a central European charcuterie, but I am told that this is a relatively new occurrence. *hangikjöt* bears a resemblance to *raest,* Faroese Aged Mutton (page 350), which is not smoked and is a bit more pungent, but aside from that, is treated in much the same way. The ashes from Icelandic smokehouses are used to preserve wild birds eggs.

FAROESE BRINED MEAT

Saltkjøt (Faroe Islands)

Saltkjöt on the Faroe Islands is either mutton or beef cured in brine and stored. *Saltkjöt* should be soaked in cold water overnight to remove excess salt, with the water changed from time to time. *Saltkjöt* is either braised and served with Boiled Potatoes (page 117) and Béchamel Sauce (page 666) or used in Split Pea Soup (page 140), much like in the other Nordic countries.

NORWEGIAN MUTTON PRESERVED IN A JELLY OF ITS OWN COOKING LIQUID

Pottekjøtt (Norway)

This is an ancient Norwegian dish in which the tough neck parts of mutton are braised until tender and then left to cool in the cooking liquid, which jellifies around the meat as it cools down. This allows the mutton to keep for weeks – if it is untouched and properly refrigerated. This recipe comes from Andreas Viestad who helped me out with the Norwegian parts of this book and he has updated the original eighteenth-century version slightly. It still uses the same spices but in a slightly larger quantity and it has had a little bit of malt vinegar added to it for acidity.

If prepared and stored properly, *pottekjøtt* keeps for several weeks as it is pasteurized in a very rudimentary way.

Preparation time: 30 minutes, plus cooling time
Cooking time: 12¼–15¼ hours
Resting time: overnight
Serves: 4

800 g/1¾ lb neck of lamb or mutton, cut into slices about 3 cm/1¼ inch thick
2 bay leaves
4 allspice berries
20 white peppercorns
1 clove
1 teaspoon mustard seeds
2 teaspoons salt
1 tablespoon malt vinegar

Preheat the oven to 90°C/195°F/Gas Mark ½.

Place the meat in layers with seasoning in between in an ovenproof glazed ceramic or sterilized glass jar. Add enough water to just cover the meat and put on the lid. Place in the oven. Cook the lamb for 12 hours or the mutton for 15 hours.

Take the jar out of the oven without opening it. Let it cool and then refrigerate until needed but at least overnight. When you want to eat the meat, take it out of the jar and transfer to a pot. Heat it and simmer for at least 10 minutes before serving.

MUTTON AND POTATO STEW OVEN-BAKED IN A BIRCH TROUGH

Särä (Finland)

Särä is a Finnish mutton dish, which is named after the vessel in which it is cooked, a trough constructed from birch wood. It originates in the southern region of Carelia and the tradition of making *särä* is especially strong around the town of Lemi.

Traditionally the trough is soaked before cooking in 2% brine, filled with meat and potatoes and placed in a wood-fired oven on top of branches of fresh alder. The alder wood separates the trough itself from the hot stones at the bottom of the oven, protecting it from burning. At the same time it slowly gives off smoke, which then flavours the meat.

The recipe below is made with 1 kg/2¼ lb meat, which is enough for four people. This is about a tenth of the amount in the original recipes I have found. *Särä* is considered a festive dish and one that you cook for many on a special occasion.

You will need 4–6 pieces of fresh alder wood, 30 cm/12 inches long and 4 cm/1¾ inch in diameter.

Serve with Finnish Semisweet Fermented Rye Malt Beverage (page 723) and Finnish flatbread.

Preparation and cooking time: 7–8 hours
Curing time: 4 days
Serves: 4

1 kg/2¼ lb mutton, suitable for braising, cut
  into large chunks
100 g/3½ oz (⅓ cup) coarse sea salt
1 kg/2¼ lb waxy potatoes

Rub the meat with the salt and leave it in the fridge for 4 days to cure.

On the day the meat is going to be cooked, rinse thoroughly with water.

Place the meat in the soaked trough and place the alder wood at the bottom of a wood-fired bread oven, which shouldn't be burning on full flame but rather smouldering. Pour about 200 ml/7 fl oz (¾ cup plus 2 tablespoons) water into the trough together with the meat and place it on top of the alder branches in the oven. Cook the meat for 4–5 hours and turn it every 30 minutes or so. If it dries out, replace the water.

While the meat is cooking, peel the potatoes and boil them for 10 minutes. They should not be done but just half cooked.

When the mutton is tender and well browned, remove the trough from the oven and the meat from the trough. Keep all of the fat and cooking juices from the meat in the trough and add the half cooked potatoes to them. Replace the meat on top of the potatoes and return everything to the oven for another 1–2 hours.

HOTCHPOTCH OF MUTTON

Hotchpotch (Sweden)

There seem to be many dishes named something like *hotchpotch* all over the world, and most of them are stews of some kind. In Sweden, as in many other European countries, a *hotchpotch* is a stew made of mutton or lamb with vegetables. I have found recipes in Swedish books from the end of the nineteenth century and, between then and now, every recipe actually looks fairly similar, with one great exception: in this recipe for *hotchpotch* by Tore Wretman, he adds pearl barley.

Normally, a single recipe diverging from the norm in my research for this book would make me disregard that particular feature. In this case, the oddity is added by Tore, the grandmaster of Swedish cooking, and a person who carefully adjusted many old-fashioned recipes to fit the contemporary ways of his time – most often without people even noticing. He might have included pearl barley in his version because he found evidence of this while doing his own research like myself or simply because he felt that it would improve the dish. I don't know. However, I like pearl barley myself, so here it is, the *hotchpotch* recipe with barley! If you want to follow a more Swedish conformist style, omit the barley.

Wretman also puts green peas in this otherwise very wintery dish. This is another addition by him, which probably relates to the mentality early in the second half of the twentieth century, when deep-frozen vegetables were a fantastic novelty. To be honest, I like this addition to the older recipes; the stew really benefits from the popping freshness of the peas. Don't let them cook for too long though, just long enough to defrost.

Oh, and Wretman, and many cooks with him from the old times, preferred a soup or stew like this to be served with the meat on a side plate. I don't like that, so I have changed the method in a way that keeps it all in one soup bowl, which is more delicious and more convenient, although a slight, respectful alteration to the grand-master's recipe.

Preparation and cooking time: 3 hours
Serves: 4

For the soup
1 kg/2¼ lb mutton soup bones (I prefer shoulder or leg), cut into pieces by your butcher on his band saw
1 leek, chopped
1 bay leaf
1 bunch parsley, stalks only
1 sprig thyme

For the stew
1 x 500-g/1 lb 2-oz piece mutton breast
butter, for frying
2 onions, sliced
2 tablespoons pearl barley
2 teaspoons plain (all-purpose) flour
1 celeriac (celery root), diced
2 carrots, sliced in circles
1 parsnip, sliced in circles
1 small cauliflower, trimmed to florets
200 g/7 oz (1½ cups) frozen peas
1 bunch parsley, leaves only, chopped
1 good dash dry sherry (optional)
salt and white pepper, to taste

Place the soup bones in a large pot and pour in 2.5 litres/4¼ UK pints (10 cups) water. Bring to a gentle boil, then skim once before adding the leek, bay leaf, parsley stalks and thyme. Cover the pot and let the stock (broth) simmer gently for about 1½ hours.

Add the mutton breast to the stock and simmer for about 1 hour, or until the meat is just cooked through, but not tender. When done, remove the meat from the stock and cut it into 1.5 cm/¾ inch pieces.

Melt some butter in another pot over a medium heat and brown the meat pieces and the onion. Sprinkle in the pearl barley and the flour, then ladle in 150–200 ml/5–7 fl oz (⅔–¾ cup plus 1 tablespoon) of the stock from the other pot. Cover, and cook the meat over a low heat until just tender. Add more liquid during the cooking process if necessary; the mixture should be thick but not dry. Stir occasionally, but not too violently, so that the pieces of meat remain intact.

While the meat is cooking, strain the remaining stock through a fine sieve into a third pot. Bring it to a simmer, then add the root vegetables. Simmer for about 15 minutes, or until they tender, then add the cauliflower and peas a few minutes before serving. Add the parsley and a dash of dry sherry in the last few seconds.

It is important to time things so that the vegetables in the soup are ready at the same time as the meat. I think it is better to add the vegetables too late, rather than too early. Not much happens if the meat has to remain warm for a bit longer while waiting for the vegetables, but if the reverse happens your vegetables will be really sad.

When serving, ladle the soup and vegetables into bowls, then add a big spoonful of the barley and meat mixture to the same bowls and let it trickle down among the vegetables in front of your eyes.

HASH AND MINCED MEAT

Previous page: Vega archipelago with de syv søstre (The Severn Sisters) mountain range visible in the background, Spring 2014.

Opposite: Interior of Kosmos Restaurant, Helsinki, Autumn 2013.

Following page: Traditional Icelandic smoke house beside Lake Mývatn, May 2013.

NORDIC HASH

Pytt i panne (Norway)
Pyttipannu (Finland)
Biksemad (Denmark)
Pytt i panna (Sweden)

This 'leftovers' dish is prepared and served quite similarly all over the Nordics, perhaps with slightly different ingredients from region to region, depending on what meat is most often used. Hash is often served with a fried egg, sunny side up (page 52) and with Pickled Beetroot (page 660) or Brined Cucumbers (page 660).

In the Nordics, hash is sometimes seasoned with Worcestershire sauce, HP sauce or Chinese mushroom soy sauce, but can also be seasoned simply with salt and black or white pepper. You can also make the hash with raw, diced potatoes but it will take a bit longer. Cut them smaller (1 cm/½ inch dice are good) and count on frying the potatoes alone for at least 15 minutes.

Preparation and cooking time: 15 minutes
Serves: 4

50 g/2 oz (3½ tablespoons) butter
650 g/1lb 7 oz cold boiled potatoes,
   peeled and cut into 2 cm/¾ inch dice
500 g/1 lb 2 oz meat leftovers
   (anything from steak to sausages
   or bacon), diced
2 onions, finely chopped
Worcestershire sauce, to taste
   (optional)
HP sauce, to taste (optional)
Chinese mushroom soy sauce, to taste
   (optional)
1 bunch parsley, chopped
salt and pepper, to taste

Melt all of the butter in a large frying pan over a medium heat (don't use less, or it will just disappear into the cold potatoes). Add the potatoes, meat and onion and season to taste, then fry, making sure you don't move the mixture around too much in the pan, which will break up the potatoes. Only stir when the bottom of the hash is properly browned.

When everything is nicely browned and hot,

season and add any other flavourings of your choice. Sprinkle with parsley and serve.

For image see page 403

CREAMED HASH

Pytt Bellman (Sweden)

In Sweden a creamed version of hash is called *Pytt Bellman* after Carl Michael Bellman (1740–1795), who was a Swedish poet, songwriter and composer.

Preparation and cooking time: 15 minutes
Serves: 4

1 quantity Nordic Hash (see left)
200 ml/7 fl oz (¾ cup plus 1 tablespoon)
   cream
½ tablespoon Chinese mushroom
   soy sauce
salt and white pepper, to taste

Once the hash is ready, add the cream and soy sauce to the hot pan, toss everything around a few times and, when the liquid starts to thicken, adjust the seasoning and serve immediately.

BEEF TENDERLOIN AND POTATO HASH

Biff Rydberg (Sweden)

This variation on hash was named after the Rydberg Hotel in Stockholm, where it was allegedly first served, sometime early in the twentieth century.

The ingredients for *Biff Rydberg* are normally served plated separately and not mixed together as in most hashes. It should be served with a raw egg yolk in its shell, resting on the side of the plate. A sprinkle of chopped parsley over the finished dish is also quite common. I like to serve my *Biff Rydberg* with a dollop of Mustard Cream Sauce (page 664) too, as that was how it was done

at Pontus in the Green House, one of the first restaurants I ever worked in.

Most of the time – and traditionally – all the
ingredients are cut into cubes of the same rather
small size, about 1–1.5 cm/½–¾ inch. Myself, I
prefer to cut the potato and onion to that size,
while leaving the meat a bit larger – perhaps
3 cm/1¼ inches – so that it is actually possible
to brown it, without overcooking it completely.
You can cook this either in one pan starting with
potato and continuing with onions to finish with
the meat, or you can cook it in three pans so that
it is all ready at the same time.

Preparation and cooking time: 30 minutes
Serves: 4

butter, for frying
8 potatoes, cut into neat 1–1.5 cm/
  ½–¾ inch cubes
2 large onions, cut into neat 1–1.5 cm/
  ½–¾ inch dice
800 g/1 lb 12 oz beef tenderloin, cut into
  3 cm/1¼ inch cubes
1 bunch parsley, chopped
4 egg yolks, put back into their
  half shells
salt and white pepper

Melt some butter in a frying pan. Add the potatoes
and cook them slowly over a low–medium heat
until they are soft inside, but well browned on the
outside. Set them aside and keep warm.

Melt more butter in the same pan (or cook them
simultaneously, in a separate pan) and fry the
onions slowly until they are sweet and translucent, with just a little caramelization. Keep warm
until ready to serve.

Melt more butter and fry the beef over a high
heat until it is brown on the outside and medium-rare inside.

Season the potatoes, onions and beef with salt
and pepper. Arrange them on a serving platter,
and sprinkle with parsley. Place the egg yolks in
their shells on the plate and serve straight away
with some mustard cream sauce.

NORWEGIAN STEW

Lapskaus (Norway)

Lapskaus in Norway, pretty much means stew,
and exactly how it is prepared and served can
vary quite a bit. Different meats can be used,
ranging from beef and pork to mutton and game,
and they are usually boiled with any of – or a mix
of – carrots, turnips, onions and potatoes.

There are three different basic types of Norwegian Stew: light (based on pork), brown (most
often made from browned beef and beef stock),
and soup (where quite a bit more of the broth
is used).

Buttered crispbreads are often served alongside
lapskaus.

NORWEGIAN STEW, BROWN VERSION

This version is made with beef, but I have also seen it made with mutton, in which case use neck or shoulder.

Preparation and cooking time: 1½ hours
Serves: 4

butter, for frying
800 g/1¾ lb braising beef (shoulder, breast or chuck are all good), cut into 2.5 cm/1 inch dice
600 ml/1 pint (2½ cups) Beef Stock (page 650)
2 onions, cut into wedges
4 carrots, cut into 5 mm/¼ inch slices
500 g/1 lb 2 oz potatoes, cut into pieces
1 parsnip or parsley root, cut into 5 mm/¼ inch slices
salt and white or black pepper, to taste
chopped parsley, to serve (optional)

Melt a good knob of butter in a heavy-bottomed pan over medium heat and brown the meat thoroughly all over.

Add the stock (broth) to the pan and bring to a simmer. Cook for about an hour, skimming from time to time, until the meat is almost tender. Add the vegetables to the pan and cook until they are tender. Stir from time to time.

Season with salt and your choice of pepper, then sprinkle with chopped parsley, if you like, and serve.

NORWEGIAN STEW, LIGHT VERSION

Lys lapskaus (Norway)

This is almost a little like a French *pot-au-feu*, but made from salted pork shoulder. The potatoes should fall apart just enough to make the broth slightly viscous. Serve with buttered Norwegian Thin Crispbreads (page 515).

Preparation and cooking time: 1½ hours
Serves: 4

600 g/1 lb 5 oz salted pork shoulder, skin removed, thoroughly rinsed and cut into 2.5 cm/1 inch cubes
800 g/1¾ lb floury potatoes, diced
1 swede (rutabaga), diced
3 large carrots, sliced
½ celeriac (celery root), diced
1 leek, cut into 5 mm/¼ inch slices
salt and white pepper, to taste

Place the pork in a large pot and cover with water. Bring to a simmer, then cook for about an hour, skimming from time to time, until the meat is almost tender. Add the vegetables to the pot and cook until they are tender. The potatoes should be starting to fall apart a little, to thicken the stew.

Season well with pepper, but be cautious with the salt as the pork will already have made the cooking liquid quite salty.

NORWEGIAN STEW, SOUP VERSION

Suppelapskaus (Norway)

The soup version of Norwegian stew is, it seems to me, a more modern invention, at least when it is defined as a dish on its own with a name of its own. The other versions of *lapskaus* are, owing to the way they are prepared, difficult to judge as to whether they are stews or soups; it's just a matter of how much broth you like in them and how much you boil the potatoes.

There are many recipes for *suppelapskaus* on the internet and most of them are based on commercially available frozen *lapskaus* vegetable mix. The way I see it, you can use either of the recipes above and add some extra liquid to it to obtain *suppelapskaus*. You can also substitute the salted pork/beef for some lean and tender pork (like loin), if you want it to be a quicker recipe. If you do use fresh pork, then slice it more finely than the salted pork/beef: 1 x 10 cm/½ x 4 inch strips would be about right.

MEATBALLS IN THE NORDIC REGION

Kjötbollar (Faroe Islands)
Kjøttboller (Norway)
Lihapullat (Finland)
Frikadeller(Denmark)
Köttbullar (Sweden)

There is a huge variety to meatballs in the Nordic region. As with most other preparations that have been in existence longer than modern transportation, refrigeration and eating habits, they are, even today, greatly influenced by what was available and preferred in a specific place a long time ago, when people didn't have as much choice as we have today.

As an example, as a Swede I would never make meatballs from just minced (ground) pork, something commonly done in both Denmark and Norway. This is not because I think it tastes bad, or because I can't get enough pork, but because that's not what meatballs are to me. The other way round, you will also have to try hard to find a Dane using moose meat in his or her meatballs, like I grew up with.

That said, there is also a huge influence from other parts of the world and in all the Nordic countries, Italian meatballs, Asian meatballs, Greek meatballs and Spanish meatballs are being made – served with everything from jasmine rice to pasta, as well as the more historically common potato.

As much as history has influenced the way we eat today – not because we have to eat this way anymore, but because it just feels right to do things in a particular way – it will be interesting to see how eating habits today influence the future of eating. Maybe what we consider to be a meatball with a distinctly Italian seasoning will become the prevalent norm in the Nordics and will therefore be considered a thoroughly Nordic meatball.

BASIC MEATBALLS

Preparation and cooking time: 45 minutes
Serves: 4

butter, for frying
1 onion, chopped
200 ml/7 fl oz (¾ cup plus 1 tablespoon) milk or cream
2 eggs
50 g/2 oz (½ cup) breadcrumbs
300 g/11 oz minced (ground) pork
300 g/11 oz minced (ground) beef
salt and white pepper, to taste

Melt some butter in a frying pan or skillet, add the onion and fry it gently without colouration until soft. Remove from the heat, set aside and allow to cool.

Pour the milk or cream into a bowl, add the eggs and some salt and pepper. (The salt is good for the texture of the meatball.) Whisk the breadcrumbs into the cream and make sure no lumps remain. Leave the dairy and bread mixture to swell for 5 minutes before adding the remaining ingredients. Work well until completely smooth and dense in texture.

To check the seasoning, melt some butter in a frying pan, add a little piece of the meat mixture and fry. Taste and adjust the seasoning if necessary.

Shape the rest of the meat mixture into balls with the help of a spoon and your clean, wet hand.

Melt a knob of butter in a large frying pan or skillet over a medium heat. Fry the meatballs until nicely coloured and cooked through if you cut one open. It should take about 10 minutes.

MY GRANDMOTHER'S MEATBALLS

Mormors köttbullar (Sweden)

My grandmother made her meatballs really big. I remember them being almost the size of my fist as a child. They could have been slightly smaller in the real world as many things tend to turn out being when you grow up... She didn't work the meat much, making the balls really tender and almost a little crumbly soft in texture. They were always served with Boiled Potatoes (page 117), creamy Brown Gravy (page 671), Sugared Lingonberries (page 692) and, in summer, Quick Pickled Cucumber (page 658).

Preparation and cooking time: 50 minutes
Serves: 4

100 ml/3½ fl oz (⅓ cup plus 1 tablespoon milk
100 ml/3½ fl oz (⅓ cup plus 1 tablespoon)
  cream
1 egg
8 allspice berries, ground
1 large floury potato, boiled, cooled, peeled
  and riced
300 g/11 oz minced (ground) pork
300 g/11 oz minced (ground) beef
30 g/1¼ oz (¾ cup plus 2 tablespoons)
  breadcrumbs
1 onion, finely chopped
salt and white pepper, to taste

Pour the milk and cream into a bowl, add the egg, allspice and some salt and pepper. Whisk the breadcrumbs into the cream mixture and make sure no lumps remain. Add the riced potato and leave the mixture to swell for 5 minutes before adding the remaining ingredients. Work well until smooth but not longer.

To check the seasoning, melt some butter in a frying pan, add a little piece of the meat mixture and fry. Taste and adjust the seasoning if necessary.

Shape the mixture into large, loose balls with the help of a spoon and your clean, wet hand.

Melt a knob of butter in a large frying pan or skillet over a medium heat. Fry the meatballs until nicely coloured and cooked through if you cut one open. It should take about 15 minutes.

DANISH BOILED MEATBALLS

Boller (Denmark)

This is classic Danish comfort food. The two most common versions are served with a Curry Cream Sauce (page 665) or with celeriac in a sauce made from the cooking liquid. Regardless of the sauce, the dish is often served simply with white rice. The minced (ground) meat is used for danish meat patties as well.

Preparation and cooking time: 45 minutes
Serves: 4

500 g/1 lb 2 oz minced (ground) pork
  or veal
1 onion, grated, or finely chopped
30 g/1¼ oz (3 tablespoons) plain
  (all-purpose) flour
100 ml/3½ fl oz (⅓ cup plus 1 tablespoon)
  milk
1 egg
salt and white pepper, to taste

Mix all of the ingredients in the bowl of a stand mixer and work until dense and homogenous. You need to add quite a bit of salt from the start to facilitate this.

Bring a pot of water to the boil and start shaping the mince into suitably sized meatballs, dropping them into the water one by one as you finish shaping them. Simmer the meatballs until done. Lift them out of the water with a slotted spoon and place them on a serving platter.

DANISH BOILED MEATBALLS IN CURRY CREAM SAUCE (VERSION 1)

Boller i Karry (Denmark)

Preparation and cooking time: 1 hour
Serves: 4

1 quantity Curry Cream Sauce
  (page 665)
1 quantity Danish Boiled Meatballs (see
  above)

Pour the hot sauce over the hot meatballs just before serving them.

For image see page 305

DANISH BOILED MEATBALLS WITH CELERIAC (VERSION 2)

Boller i Selleri (Denmark)

Preparation and cooking time: 1 hour
Serves: 4

400 ml/14 fl oz (1⅔ cups) cooking liquid
   from the meatballs
1 quantity Danish Boiled Meatballs
   (see opposite)
1 celeriac (celery root), cut into 1 cm/½ inch
   dice
1 quantity Beurre Manié (page 651)
150 ml/5 fl oz (⅔ cup) cream
salt and white pepper, to taste
1 handful chopped parsley

Bring the meatball cooking water to the boil in a pot over medium heat, add the celeriac and simmer until the vegetable is just done. Remove the celeriac with a slotted spoon and place it with the meatballs on the serving platter.

Add the beurre manié and cream to the pot and bring to a simmer. Cook for 5 minutes and season well with salt and pepper. Add the parsley to the sauce and pour it over the meatballs and celeriac.

FAROESE MEATBALLS IN SAUCE

Kjøtbollar í sós (Faroe Islands)

These Faroese meatballs are usually quite big, using something like a small handful of meat for each ball. Some recipes are seasoned with just a little salt and pepper, while others contain spices like ginger, allspice or nutmeg.

Most recipes I have read use bouillon cubes for the sauce and I don't think that before the invention of the cube, people made a dedicated stock for sauce like I have done here. I image that they just used water that was seasoned and thickened in the end. Do as you please. Serve with Boiled Potatoes (page 117).

Preparation and cooking time: 1 hour
Serves: 4

Beef Stock (page 650), to cover
1 quantity Brown Gravy (page 671)
   seasoned with Chinese mushroom
   soy and made with the cooking
   liquid from the meatballs

For the meatballs
1 kg/2¼ lb minced (ground) beef
1 tablespoon plain (all-purpose) flour
   or potato starch
1 egg
100 ml/3½ fl oz (⅓ cup plus 1 tablespoon)
   cream
salt, to taste
white pepper and/or ground ginger, allspice
   or nutmeg, to taste
butter, for frying

If you want to cook the meatballs in the oven, preheat it to 150°C/300°F/Gas Mark 2.

Combine all the ingredients for the meatballs in a bowl and mix together well. Leave to rest for a couple of minutes while heating a pan. Shape into large balls and fry in a little butter until nicely browned. Transfer to an ovenproof dish if you want to cook them in the oven or to a pot if you are going to cook them on the stove.

Cover the meatballs with beef stock (broth) and transfer to the oven. Bake for 20 minutes, or until cooked through. Alternatively, simmer over a medium heat until cooked through.

Once the meatballs are cooked through, lift them out of the stock with a slotted spoon and keep warm while you finish the sauce.

Add the roux to the stock and bring to a simmer, season with the soy sauce, salt and pepper. Once the sauce has thickened, return the meatballs to the pot so that they are nicely glazed with sauce.

TORE WRETMAN'S MEATBALLS

Tore Wretman's köttbullar (Sweden)

The recipe for these mild and delicate meatballs comes from the grandfather of Swedish traditional cooking, Tore Wretman. I usually prepare them when I want meatballs to be part of the menu of a bigger meal, like Swedish Christmas dinner, rather than serving them as a dish on their own. For meatballs as a meal, I prefer my grandma's coarser, leaner and more well-seasoned meatballs (page 372).

Preparation and cooking time: 45 minutes
Serves: 4

butter, for frying
1 onion, finely chopped
30 g/1 oz (¾ cup plus 2 tablespoons) fresh
　white breadcrumbs
200 ml/7 fl oz (¾ cup plus 1 tablespoon)
　cream
1 egg
200 g/7 oz minced (ground) beef
100 g/3½ oz minced (ground) veal
100 g/3½ oz minced (ground) pork
salt and white pepper, to taste

Melt a knob of butter in a pan over a medium heat. Add the onions and fry until soft and golden. Tip them out of the pan and leave them to cool down.

Combine the breadcrumbs with the cream in a large mixing bowl and leave for a little while to swell. Add the cool onion and the egg, and mix everything together well.

In a separate bowl, mix the beef, veal and pork so they are thoroughly combined. Add them to the bread and cream, season well, then mix everything together.

Shape the mixture into balls the size of a small walnut.

Melt a knob of butter in a large frying pan or skillet over a medium heat. Fry the meatballs until brown all over.

For image see opposite page

DANISH MINCED BEEF PATTIES WITH ONIONS

Hakkebøf med bløde løg (Denmark)

These seared beef patties with Sweet Fried Onions (page 108) are often served with a fried egg, sunny side up. If so, they are called *hakkebøf med bløde løg og spejlæg*. Other common accompaniments are Pickled Beetroot (page 660) or Quick Pickled Cucumbers (page 658), fried potatoes and sometimes also Brown Gravy (page 671).

Preparation and cooking time: 20 minutes
Serves: 4

600 g/1 lb 5 oz minced (ground) beef
butter, for frying
salt and black pepper, to taste

Shape the beef into 4 round and rather thick patties and season them. Heat some butter in a frying pan over a medium heat. Brown the patties well on both sides; it should take about 10 minutes in total. They shouldn't be raw in the centre, but should definitely not be cooked right through either.

Serve one beef patty per person with a big stack of onions sitting on top. If you are serving them with fried eggs, then place them on top of the onions. Serve with your choice of extra accompaniments.

Clockwise from top: Mashed Potatoes (page 118); Basic Cream Sauce (page 663);
Tore Wretman's Meatballs (page 374); Quick Pickled Fresh Cucumber (page 658);
Sugared Lingonberries (page 692)

BEEF PATTIES À LA LINDSTRÖM

Bøf lindstrøm (Denmark)
Biff à la Lindström / Lindströmmare
  (Sweden)

Allegedly introduced to Sweden from Russia by Captain Henrik Lindström in 1862, this beef patty seasoned with onion, beetroot (beet) and capers is a very common lunch classic.

It is most often served with Boiled Potatoes (page 117) or Mashed Potatoes (page 118) and some Brown Gravy (page 671). I like my *Biff à la Lindström* with a fried egg, sunny side up. I don't think this is classic, but you do see it sometimes. I also like a couple of Brined Cucumbers (page 660) on the side of my *Lindströmmare* and I have seen recipes in which people add chopped pickled cucumbers into the actual mince as well.

Preparation and cooking time: 30 minutes
Serves: 4

600 g/1 lb 5 oz lean minced (ground)
  beef
4 egg yolks
100 ml/3½ fl oz (⅓ cup plus 1 tablespoon)
  cream
1 large boiled potato, cooled, peeled and
  finely diced
1 large Pickled Beetroot (page 660), finely
  chopped, plus pickling liquid, if needed
1 onion, finely chopped
1 tablespoon capers, finely chopped
salt and white pepper, to taste
butter, for frying

Combine all the ingredients, except the butter, in a mixing bowl and work them together well until nice and smooth. Adjust the texture with some beetroot (beet) pickling liquid if it seems too dry. Shape into about 12 patties with wet hands.

Fry the meat patties in butter in a pan over a medium heat until golden on both sides. They should be cooked through, but still juicy, so don't overcook them or cook them too far ahead of when you want to eat them. And remember that they contain no starch to help stop them drying out if they are poorly cooked.

NORWEGIAN BEEF PATTIES

Kjøttekaker (Norway)

These rather mildly seasoned beef patties are a real favourite in Norway. What makes them a bit different from many similar recipes in other countries is the Norwegian insistence of mincing (grinding) the meat finely, working it quite a bit afterwards and adding potato starch – factors that all contribute to the firm, almost dense, texture.

Sure, there are recipes for *kjøttekaker* that contain breadcrumbs, eggs and cream – as do similar dishes in, for example, Sweden. There are also recipes made from meat other than beef – or a mix of other meats – but the majority of *kjøttekaker* recipes, both in other books and on the internet, look a bit like the recipe below. In addition to the spices in this recipe, some also include cloves and/or allspice.

Kjøttekaker are often served with Boiled Potatoes (page 117), Brown Gravy (page 671), some Sugared Lingonberries (page 692), and creamed vegetables (like cabbage, page 94), Mashed Peas (page 137) or simply some Boiled Carrots (page 110).

Preparation and cooking time: 45 minutes
Serves: 4

600 g/1 lb 5 oz finely minced (ground)
  beef
3 tablespoons potato starch
2 teaspoons salt
1 teaspoon ground ginger
freshly grated nutmeg, to taste
ground cloves (optional)
ground allspice (optional)
150 ml/5 fl oz (⅔ cup) milk
butter, for frying
freshly ground white pepper, to taste

Place all the ingredients, except for the milk and butter, in the bowl of a stand mixer. Mix well until smooth, then add the milk and mix until combined.

To check the seasoning, make a small patty and fry it in a frying pan with a little butter. Taste and adjust the balance if necessary.

Shape into 12 patties with clean, wet hands. Heat some more butter in the frying pan over a medium heat. Fry the patties until cooked right through and browned on both sides.

TOMATO AND MINCED MEAT SAUCE

Jauhelihakastike (Finland)
Köttfärssås (Sweden)

As is the case everywhere else in the world, bastardized versions of Bolognese sauce are commonly served in the Nordic region. Most of them are tomato based and most are based on beef – although where I grew up, it was mainly moose. I have also seen plenty of recipes from Norway, Iceland and the Faroe Islands that use mutton or lamb.

I remember growing up, my dad used to grate a carrot or two, which he subsequently fried a little with the onions before adding the meat and later the tomatoes. I was never a fan of that practice, but today I have come to understand that it was in fact a kind of misunderstood or perhaps rather Swedified *soffritto* – a true manifestation of Italian culture filtered through decades of Swedes cooking minced meat sauce with spaghetti. It is fantastic how quickly food culture adapts to where it is practised.

Most often the tomato and meat sauce is served with spaghetti or macaroni, not like in Italy, where a Bolognese sauce would normally be served with flat, broad kinds of pasta or with shorter tube-shaped pasta.

Preparation and cooking time: 45 minutes
Serves: 4

butter, for frying
2 carrots, coarsely grated
2 onions, finely chopped
1 clove garlic, finely grated
600 g/1 lb 5 oz minced (ground) meat
1 tablespoon plain (all-purpose)
    flour
300 ml/10½ fl oz (1¼ cups)
    Meat Stock (page 650)
400 g/14 oz canned tomatoes

salt and black pepper, to taste
your choice of cooked pasta, to serve

Start by melting a knob of butter in a large frying pan over a low–medium heat. Add the carrot, onion and garlic, and fry the vegetables without colouring them for about 5 minutes, or until they become soft and sweet.

Add the minced (ground) meat and increase the heat a bit to brown it. Once the meat has cooked through and everything has coloured, sift over the flour and mix it in thoroughly. Add the stock (broth) and the tomatoes and bring everything to a simmer. Cook until the sauce has thickened nicely. Taste and adjust the seasoning before serving.

MEATLOAF

Forloren hare (Denmark)
Köttfärslimpa (Sweden)

Meatloaf is an everyday dish all over the Nordic region and there is endless variation on the theme, with meats used and seasonings added. I would say that only in Denmark is there a consensus strong enough on how it should be prepared and served, to talk about meatloaf as one dish, rather than a theme or a basic technique for a number of dishes.

Meatloaf in Denmark has a slightly peculiar name, *Forloren hare*. *Forloren* comes from the old Danish word for 'false' and *hare* means 'hare'. Ergo, meatloaf is, in this part of the world, known as 'mock roast hare'.

Forloren hare is usually made from a mixture of minced (ground) pork and veal. It can be studded with lardons and is often wrapped in slices of bacon before being baked in the oven.

In other parts of the Nordic region, whatever meat is most common is used most frequently. In most parts of Sweden a mix of beef and pork would be used – myself, I mostly had moose meatloaf when growing up – and I have seen recipes in both Iceland and the Faroe Islands that use mutton or lamb.

Meatloaf like this, in both Denmark and other parts of the Nordics, is often served with Sugared Lingonberries (page 692), Basic Cream Sauce (page 663) in which the cooking juices from the roasting pan are added, or a simple Brown Gravy (page 671). Boiled (page 117) or Mashed Potatoes (page 118) are commonly served alongside the meat and I don't mind some Steamed Broccoli (page 82), Green Peas (page 136) or a Grated Carrot Salad (page 110) on the side.

The recipe below is a kind of Danish *Forloren hare* base. You can exchange the veal part for another minced (ground) meat. This exact recipe, with veal exchanged for moose, and a bit of allspice added, would be, for example, the meatloaf that I was served at my grandmother's house. As for the dry component, flour is a bit more Danish, while most other countries use breadcrumbs.

Preparation and cooking time: 1 hour
Serves: 4, plus a bit to spare for lunch
the next day

400 g/14 oz minced (ground) fatty pork
400 g/14 oz minced (ground) veal, or other
 meat as specified above
4 tablespoons breadcrumbs or plain
 (all-purpose) flour
2 onions, finely chopped
2 eggs
200 ml/7 fl oz (¾ cup plus 1 tablespoon)
 cream
salt and white pepper, to taste
lardons, to stud the loaf (optional)
250 g/9 oz long thin bacon slices,
 for wrapping
200 ml/7 fl oz (¾ cup plus 1 tablespoon)
 milk or stock (broth)

Preheat the oven to 225°C/435°F/Gas Mark 8.

Combine the minced (ground) meat with the breadcrumbs or flour, the onion, eggs, cream, salt and pepper and mix everything together well. Make sure that no lumps of breadcrumbs or flour remain. I usually add them to the meat first and add the liquid ingredients last.

To check the flavour, make a small patty and fry it in a frying pan with a little butter. Taste and adjust the balance if necessary.

Form the meat into a smooth loaf-shape. If you are using lardons, push them down into the meat with your finger. Wrap the slices of bacon around the loaf, and then place it in a roasting pan. Make sure it is not too big otherwise your cooking juices will burn. There should only be a little bit of space around the loaf itself.

Place in the oven and bake until nicely browned. Lower the temperature, pour in the milk or stock (broth) – or even 200 ml/7 fl oz (¾ cup plus 1 tablespoon) water – and roast for another 15–20 minutes, or until the meatloaf is cooked all the way through.

The accumulated juices in the pan can be served with the meatloaf just as they are, or they can be added to a cream sauce or gravy that you make to serve with it.

STEAK TARTARE SEARED ON TOAST

Pariserbøf (Denmark)
Parisersmörgås (Sweden)

Pariserbøf is mainly a Danish dish, which consists of a patty of minced (ground) beef, with a piece of white bread attached to one side of it. Both sides are seared in butter in a frying pan, and the patty is most often cooked pink. It is commonly found in restaurants all over the country, but it is also often prepared in people's homes, too. *Pariserbøf* also exists in other parts of the Nordic region, but it is not as widespread or culturally significant.

There is a huge variety of chopped garnishes to serve with *pariserbøf,* but the most common ones are raw onion, red or yellow peppers (capsicum), capers, Pickled Beetroot (page 660), gherkins or other pickled vegetables (page 656), grated horseradish and raw egg yolks.

Sometimes, the ground beef is seasoned by mixing it with some of the condiments but most often it is just a plain beef patty, with some salt and black pepper sprinkled on the surface, and the garnishes are served in little piles surrounding the beef or else scattered on top of it.

Worth mentioning (to avoid the possibility of linguistic confusion) is that there is a Swedish roadside fast-food dish called *parisare,* consisting of a fried slice of smooth pork sausage (like a larger version of *falukorv,* page 416), which is served in a burger bun (with no sesame seeds). A man named Tore Strand allegedly invented this dish in the northern Swedish city of Umeå. However, I have not been able to confirm this as a fact.

Preparation and cooking time: 30 minutes
Serves: 4

800 g/1¾ lb minced (ground) beef
4 slices white bread, crusts cut off
butter, for frying
salt and black pepper, to taste

Shape the meat into 4 thick patties, then leave them for at least 20 minutes to come to room temperature. Place a slice of bread on top of each patty and press it down a bit so that it attaches to the meat. Season well on both sides.

Heat some butter in a large frying pan and fry the patties on both sides. Both the meat and bread should be well-coloured. Leave to rest for a few minutes before serving, so that the heat inside can even out a bit.

DANISH MINCED MEAT STEW

Millionbøf (Denmark)

The name of this dish in Danish translates roughly to 'million steaks', referring, I guess, to the little pieces of minced (ground) meat. *Millionbøf* is a very popular everyday dish in Denmark and there are endless variations of the recipe. However most contain minced (ground) beef, onion, beef stock, gravy browning to make it dark, and a bit of flour to thicken it.

Many different ingredients may then be added to this base recipe: among the most popular are ground paprika, tomato purée (paste), mushrooms, sliced red peppers (capsicum) and Chinese mushroom soy sauce.

The recipe below uses Beef Stock (page 650) but, honestly, almost every recipe I've ever come across uses stock (bouillon) cubes and water and it almost seems as if their unique and strangely savoury flavour has become a key part of the flavour profile of this kind of everyday dish – not just in the Nordic countries, but the world over.

Serve your *millionbøf* with pasta, Boiled Rice (page 654), Boiled Potatoes (page 117) or Mashed Potatoes (page 118).

Preparation and cooking time: 30 minutes
Serves: 4

butter, for frying
3 onions, finely chopped
500 g/1 lb 2 oz minced (ground) beef
2 tablespoons plain (all-purpose) flour
350 ml/12 fl oz (1½ cups) Beef Stock
  (page 650)
gravy browning, enough to colour
  the sauce to your liking
salt and pepper, to taste

Heat some butter in a large heavy-bottomed pot. Add the onions (yes, there are a lot of them) and fry over a medium heat. After a couple of minutes, add the beef and continue frying until it has browned and is cooked through.

Sift over the flour and stir it in. Pour in the stock (broth), gravy browning and your choice of additions. Bring to the boil and simmer for about 10 minutes. Taste and adjust the seasoning and colour before serving. It should be quite a dark shade of brown.

CABBAGE CASSEROLE

Kålpudding (Sweden)

The sweetness of caramelized golden syrup and the bitter, savoury richness of almost burnt cabbage in this dish is one of the tastiest things I know. It can be seen as a less labour-intensive version of the Pork Mince and Rice Cabbage Rolls on page 308, which share much of the same flavour. In different parts of Sweden *kålpudding* contains different kinds of starch. In southern regions it usually contains either rice (like the cabbage rolls), or breadcrumbs (as in this recipe). Further north it can be made with pearl barley.

If you want to make this dish with barley or rice, instead of breadcrumbs, then substitute the meat section below with that from Pork Mince and Rice Cabbage Rolls (page 308), using either barley or rice depending on what you like.

Serve with Boiled Potatoes (page 117), Sugared Lingonberries (page 692) and possibly some grated raw vegetables (page 85). Sometimes, *kålpudding* is served with melted butter, Basic Cream Sauce (page 663) or Brown Gravy (page 671).

Preparation and cooking time: 1½ hours
Serves: 4

For the cabbage
1 x 1-kg/2¼-lb cabbage
butter, for frying
5 tablespoons golden syrup
salt and white pepper, to taste

For the meat
250 g/9 oz minced (ground) beef
250 g/9 oz minced (ground) pork
1 onion, finely chopped
200 ml/7 fl oz (¾ cup plus 1 tablespoon)
  cream
3 tablespoons breadcrumbs

salt and white pepper, to taste
100 ml/3½ fl oz (⅓ cup plus 1 tablespoon)
  Meat Stock (page 650) or water
2 tablespoons Chinese mushroom
  soy sauce

Preheat the oven to 180°C/350°F/Gas Mark 4.

Split the cabbage in half and cut out the core.
Shred the cabbage finely or cut it into 2 cm/
¾ inch dice, which create cabbage 'flakes' as the
layers fall apart.

Heat a large pan and add a good spoonful of
butter, the cabbage and the golden syrup. Cook
slowly, allowing the cabbage to wilt and colour
deeply as it slowly dehydrates in the pan. This
stage should take a good 15–20 minutes and is
crucial for enabling the right flavour to develop.
Season well with salt and pepper.

While the cabbage is cooking, thoroughly combine the beef and pork with the onion, cream,
breadcrumbs and seasoning; there should be no
lumps. Mix the meat with a third of the warm
cabbage and quickly transfer it to an ovenproof
dish. Press the mixture down to cover the entire
dish to a depth of about 4 cm/1½ inches. For the
recipe to succeed, it is important that the dish not
be too large. Spread the remaining cabbage over
the meat and pour in the stock (broth) or water
and the soy sauce.

Bake for about 45 minutes. The cabbage should
be deeply caramelized and chewy-dry.

Let the casserole sit for about 10 minutes before
you serve it with your choice of accompaniments.

For image see page 95

BLOOD AND OFFAL

Previous page: Woods and path, Jämtland, Sweden, Summer 2012.

Opposite: Interior of Icelandic home, May 2013. Súrmatur (page 352), black pudding, head of mutton and testicles pickled in whey.

BREAD BAKED WITH BLOOD AND DRIED

Paltbröd (Sweden)

This is one of those preparations that used to fill a very important function in the days before refrigeration and industrialized food production. On a farm when a beast was slaughtered the whole animal needed to be prepared in different ways to keep, or be consumed more or less immediately. This is why we have charcuterie among many other things.

The blood – which is extremely perishable – was either eaten straight away in the form of, for example, Blood Pancakes (page 392), baked into Black Pudding (page 392), or turned into Blood Sausages (page 394). All of these keep for a little while. If people wanted to keep it for a longer duration, pretty much the only option was to bake it into bread, which was then dried.

When eaten, the bread is soaked and subsequently cooked in a broth. It is very tasty and not as uncommon as some other techniques that were invented a long time ago out of necessity and for which there is now not really any practical motivation.

Commonly served with the bread are Boiled Potatoes (page 117), Béchamel Sauce (page 666), slices of Fried Salt Pork (page 302) and Sugared Lingonberries (page 692).

Preparation and cooking time: 1½ hours
Drying time: depends on the humidity
Makes: 20 pieces

200 ml/7 fl oz (¾ cup plus 1 tablespoon)
   blood (either pig or cow), strained
140 g/4¾ oz (⅓ cup plus 1 tablespoon)
   golden syrup
50 g/2 oz (¼ cup) lard
25 g/1 oz yeast
2 tablespoons dried marjoram
1 tablespoon fennel seeds, crushed
1 tablespoon ground ginger
2 teaspoons salt
300 g/10½ oz (2 cups plus 3 tablespoons)
   strong bread flour
300 g/10½ oz (2¼ cups) rye flour
150 ml/5 fl oz (⅔ cup) dark beer

Combine the blood, lard and golden syrup in a pot and warm it slowly and carefully to body temperature (37°C/98.6°F). Dissolve the yeast in some of the warmed liquid then return it to the pot.

Tip the warm liquid into the bowl of a stand mixer. Add the herbs, spices, salt and both flours. Knead at a medium speed until it is smooth, shiny and elastic.

Cover the bowl and leave the dough to rise until doubled in size. It should take about 30 minutes.

Line baking sheets with baking (parchment) paper. Tip the dough onto a lightly floured work counter and divide it into 20 equal pieces. Roll them into smooth, flat buns and transfer to the prepared baking sheets. Cover with a clean dish cloth and leave at room temperature for another 30 minutes.

Meanwhile, preheat the oven to 225°C/435°F/ Gas Mark 7.

Bake the buns until golden brown. Transfer to wire racks and leave to cool.

Leave the baked buns in the open air until completely dry, it might take several days depending on the humidity where you live, before storing them in an airtight container.

To serve the bread, see page 392.

For image see opposite page

Bread Baked with Blood and Dried (page 390) served with Boiled Potatoes (page 117) and Béchamel Sauce (page 666)

HOW TO SERVE BREAD BAKED WITH BLOOD

It's best to soak this bread in a really good, well-seasoned beef or pork stock (broth) or, even better, the cooking liquid from a ham or other brined meat, but otherwise, use 1 litre/34 fl oz (4¼ cups) water with 15 g/½ oz (1 tablespoon) salt added.

Preparation and cooking time:
15 minutes
Soaking time: at least 2 hours
Serves: 4

1 quantity Bread Baked with Blood
   and Dried (or 500 g/1 lb 2 oz purchased
   equivalent)
1 litre/34 fl oz (4¼ cups) good,
   tasty stock
1 quantity Béchamel Sauce (page 666)
1 quantity Fried Salt Pork (page 302)

Either break the bread into pieces or keep them intact, if you prefer. Put them in a large pot and pour on the stock (broth) which should be warm enough to be liquid and not gelatinous. Leave them to soak for at least 2 hours, although if the bread is left whole it usually takes a bit longer. The bread must be completely soaked through before being cooked. You may have to turn them over a couple of times for an even soak.

Put the pot onto a low–medium heat and slowly bring to a simmer. Cook for about 10 minutes, then serve with or without the cooking liquid. If using broth, I like to serve it with the breads, but if it is salted water, perhaps not.

BLACK PUDDING

Blodpudding (Norway)
Rössy (Finland)
Blodpudding (Denmark)
Blodpudding (Sweden)

To serve black pudding, don't slice it too thin; about 2.5 cm/1 inch slices are good. Fry them crisp in some butter and serve them with bacon or slices

of Fried Salt Pork (page 302) and some Sugared Lingonberries (page 692). Historically this dish was served hot from the oven and spooned on a plate rather than fried like we do today.

Preparation and cooking time: 1½ hours
Chilling time: overnight
Makes: 1 loaf pan, enough for 4 people

600 ml/20 fl oz (2½ cups) pig or cow's blood,
   strained
80 g/3 oz (¼ cup) golden syrup
15 g/½ oz (1 tablespoon) salt
1 tablespoon dried marjoram
200 g/7 oz (1¾ cups) fine rye flour
100 ml/3½ fl oz (⅓ cup plus 1 tablespoon)
   beer
200 g/7 oz pork back fat, cut into 1.5 cm/
   ¾ inch cubes

Preheat the oven to 175°C/345°F/Gas Mark 4 and line a loaf pan with baking (parchment) paper.

Strain the blood into a mixing bowl, then add the golden syrup, salt and marjoram and mix together well. Sift over the flour and whisk it in to make sure no lumps remain. Stir in the beer and the pork back fat, then pour the batter into the loaf pan.

Sit the loaf pan in a roasting pan and pour in boiling water from the kettle, to reach halfway up the sides. Bake until the pudding reaches a core temperature of 72°C/162°F.

Lift the pudding out of the water bath, still in the loaf pan, and leave to cool down. Once the pudding is cold, refrigerate it overnight before slicing and frying it.

For image see page 397

BLOOD PANCAKES

Blodpannekake (Norway)
Veriohukaiset (Finland)
Blodpannkaka (Sweden)

Some recipes contain onion, and if you want to try this then adding one onion, finely chopped, is enough for this recipe and I think it is a good idea to fry it soft in some butter before adding it; this might be a little less authentic, but is very tasty.

There is also a difference in the types of flour used between different recipes. Some have a mix of rye and wheat flour, and others are all wheat or all rye. The Finnish recipes definitely contain a larger proportion of rye flour than those from the Scandinavian countries.

Blood pancakes in Finland also do not contain eggs, as opposed to the ones in, for example, Sweden. The recipe below is more Finnish in style but works just as well with the addition of two eggs. The pancakes will then become a little more tender and you can fry them slightly thinner in the pan.

Some recipes for blood pancake contain no real seasoning except salt, while others contain sweet spices like cloves, allspice and pepper. Others contain dried marjoram, like many other dishes containing blood.

Serve blood pancakes with Sugared Lingonberries (page 692) and some fried slices of Fried Salt Pork (page 302).

Preparation and cooking time: 1 hour
Serves: 4

1 onion, finely chopped (optional)
butter, for frying
500 ml/17 fl oz (2 cups plus 1 tablespoon)
  blood, strained
250 ml/8 fl oz (1 cup) *Svagdricka* or beer
200 g/7 oz (1¾ cups) flour (use rye, wheat
  or a mixture of both)
70 g/2½ oz (3½ tablespoons) golden syrup
good pinch of salt
your choice of flavourings, to taste (cloves,
  allspice, pepper, dried marjoram)
2 eggs (optional)

If using onion, then fry in butter over a medium heat until soft and translucent. Transfer to a large mixing bowl and leave to cool.

Add all the remaining ingredients to the cooled onions (including the eggs, if using) and whisk until there are no lumps.

Let the batter sit at room temperature for at least 30 minutes before frying.

Use an ordinary frying pan, skillet or a special small pancake pan called a *plättjärn* to fry the blood pancakes. (The batter is liquid and it fills the whole pan in one thin layer.) Add a generous spoonful of batter to the pan. Fry on a medium heat until the underside is golden and the pancake is starting to set. Turn it over carefully and fry the other side until golden. Remove the pancake from the pan and keep warm while you continue with the rest of the batter.

For image see page 453

ELAINE'S SAMI BLOOD PANCAKES WITH SMOKED REINDEER FAT

Gampasuelje (Sami)

This recipe came from Elaine Asp, who helped me out with the Sami recipes for this book. Serve it with Sugared Lingonberries (page 692).

Preparation and cooking time: 30 minutes, plus cooling time
Serves: 4

For the pancakes
3 onions, finely chopped
butter for frying
300 ml/10 fl oz (1¼ cups) reindeer blood, strained
300 ml/10 fl oz (1¼ cups) reindeer stock or water
325 g/11½ oz (2¾ cups) plain (all-purpose) flour
70 g/2¾ oz (3½ tablespoons) golden syrup
2 tablespoons salt
1 tablespoon allspice, ground

For the sauce
200 g/7 oz lightly smoked reindeer back fat, cut into 1 cm/½ inch dice
100 ml/3½ fl oz (⅓ cup plus 1½ tablespoons) cream
100 ml/3½ fl oz (⅓ cup plus 1½ tablespoons) Sweet Reduced Whey Spread (page 72)

Melt some butter in a frying pan or skillet over a medium heat and fry the onion until soft but not coloured. Remove from the heat and leave to cool.

Combine all the remaining ingredients for the pancakes in a bowl, adding the cooled onions last, and mix well with a whisk. Leave the batter to sit for 10 minutes while you make the sauce.

In a saucepan over medium heat, fry the reindeer fat for a couple of minutes until it is just beginning to colour. Add the cream and the reduced whey spread. Simmer until slightly thickened, then set aside and keep warm.

Heat another frying pan to just over a medium heat. Brush the pan with a little melted butter then ladle in some batter. Tilt the pan so that it coats the bottom of the pan evenly. Cook until the batter has set completely and the pancake has a nice golden colour, then flip it over with a fish slice (spatula) and cook the other side. Transfer the cooked pancake to a warm plate. Repeat with the rest of the batter, stacking the cooked pancakes as you go so that they remain warm.

Serve immediately with the sauce.

BLOOD SAUSAGES IN THE NORDIC REGION

Blood sausages have been and are still being made in most parts of the world, the Nordic region being no exception. Historically, using every part of the animal was important for survival, and making blood sausage or Bread Baked with Blood (page 391) was an excellent way of making the very perishable blood keep longer.

There are similarities but also many differences between the various Nordic blood sausages, so I have included a few recipes from a few different places to illustrate this. As in most cases when it comes to traditional cooking, the recipes are perfectly adapted to where they are being made; a Danish recipe using pig's blood, a Faroese sheep's and a Sami one using reindeer. Seasonings vary with the flavour preferences of those making and eating them.

SWEDISH BLOOD SAUSAGE

Blodkorv (Sweden)

A Swedish *blodkorv* is most often served in the southern parts of the country, especially in the region of Skåne. Further north, Black Pudding (page 392) is a more common blood-based food than blood sausage. To differentiate it from black pudding, blood sausage often contains a bit of apple compote and, almost always, quite a lot of raisins.

Fry the sausages whole or in slices and serve them with some fried potatoes, Coarse Potato Pancakes (page 124) or Potato Patties (page 124). Sugared

Lingonberries (page 692) are a common condiment. Some people like to serve bacon or slices of Fried Salt Pork (page 302) with their blood sausages; others don't. Unlike blood sausage, black pudding is never served with a potato garnish.

You will need 2 metres/6½ feet pork casing, soaked and rinsed.

Preparation and cooking time: 1½ hours
Serves: 4

4 tablespoons Apple Compote (page 700)
80 g/3 oz (⅔ cup) raisins
1 quantity Black Pudding (page 392) mixture

Mix the apple compote and the raisins into the prepared black pudding mixture and let it sit for 30 minutes before starting to fill the casing.

Tie off the casing to seal it at one end. Using the sausage-making attachment of your mincer (grinder), stuff the mixture into the lengths of casing. Fill it slowly and steadily, making sure there are no pockets of air. Don't fill it too tight, or it may burst when you cook it. Knot it at the open end then tie into 20 cm/8 inch lengths.

Carefully lift the blood sausage links to a large pot and pour in enough water to just cover. Place over a low–medium heat and slowly bring to a slow simmer. Simmer gently or until the sausages reach a core temperature of 68°C/154°F and are firm.

Lift the sausages out of the water and leave them to cool down completely. If you want to store them, they will keep for a week or so in the refrigerator and for a very long time in the freezer.

FAROESE BLOOD SAUSAGE

Blodpylsa (Faroe Islands)

This recipe for blood sausage freezes well, so it is worth making the whole thing even though it might seem a lot.

Preparation and cooking time: 1½ hours
Makes: 4 blood sausages, each serving about 4

1 sheep's stomach, cleaned
1 litre/34 fl oz (4¼ cups) sheep's blood, strained
400 g/14 oz (2 cups) sugar
3 teaspoons ground cassia cinnamon
1 teaspoon ground allspice
1 teaspoon ground black pepper
500 g/1 lb 2 oz (3¾ cups) rye flour
250 g /9 oz (1⅔ cups) raisins
1 kg/2¼ lb lamb or mutton suet, cut into 1 cm/½ inch dice
salt, to taste

Lay the sheep's stomach out on a chopping (cutting) board and slice it straight across in 4 places. This will produce ring-like tubes of the intestine. Stitch up each tube at one end with string and leave the other end open so that you can then fill it.

Mix all of the remaining ingredients together in a large bowl then divide the mixture evenly among the sausage casings, making sure there are no pockets of air. Stitch the casings to seal. It is important that they are neither overfilled nor too tight because the stuffing will swell a little when you cook it, which could make the skin burst. It is a good idea to prick each sausage a few times with a sharp needle to further guard against them bursting.

Place the sausages in a large pot and cover them with plenty of salted water (it should taste quite salty). Bring to a slow simmer, then cover the pan and cook until the sausages are firm to the touch and until a larding needle or small knife can be inserted into the centre and no blood comes out.

DANISH BLOOD SAUSAGE

Blodpølse (Denmark)

A Danish blood sausage has quite a bit of pearl barley or rolled oats in it and is therefore more granular in texture. It is also different from the Swedish version in that the added fat is kidney fat, cut quite finely, instead of coarsely diced pork back fat; back fat is firmer in texture. It is also commonly seasoned with cardamom, too.

The biggest difference between *blodpølse* in Denmark and other Nordic blood sausages is that the batter is lightly cooked, to thicken it, before it is stuffed, warm, into the casing.

Danish blood sausage is almost always served fried in slices and quite often with fried wedges of apple, or Apple Compote (page 700) on the side.

You will need 2 metres/6½ feet pork casing, soaked and rinsed.

Preparation and cooking time: 1½ hours
Resting time: overnight
Serves: 4

500 ml/17 fl oz (2 cups plus 1 tablespoon)
  pig's blood, strained
80 g/3 oz (½ cup plus 2 tablespoons)
  rye flour
150 g/5 oz (¾ cup) pearl barley
100 g/3½ oz (⅓ cup plus 2 tablespoons)
  brown sugar
100 g/3½ oz (⅓ cup) raisins
2 teaspoons salt
1 teaspoon ground cinnamon
1 teaspoon ground cardamom
200 g/7 oz pig kidney fat, cut into
  5 mm/¼ inch dice

Place all the ingredients, except for the kidney fat, in a large mixing bowl. Mix together well then leave in the refrigerator overnight to rest and swell.

Pour 250 ml/8 fl oz (1 cup) water into a pot large enough to contain all the blood mixture. Bring it to a boil, then add the diced kidney fat and stir well. Remove the pan from the heat and pour in the cold blood mixture, stirring briskly. Return to the stove and heat gently, stirring frequently so that no lumps form and it doesn't stick to the bottom of the pan. Once it starts to thicken and change colour, remove from the heat and tip into a mixing bowl. Leave to cool for about 10 minutes, stirring frequently, until just higher than body temperature (37°C/98.6°F).

Tie off the casing to seal it at one end. Using the sausage-making attachment of your mincer (grinder), stuff the mixture into the casing. Fill it slowly and steadily, making sure there are no pockets of air. Don't fill it too tight, or it may burst when you cook it. Tie it with string at the open end. You can keep it as one long sausage, or tie it into shorter lengths.

Carefully lift the sausage into a large pan and pour in enough water to just cover. Place over a low–medium heat and slowly bring to a simmer. Simmer gently until the sausage reaches a core temperature of 68°C/154°F.

Lift the sausage out of the water and leave to cool down completely. Store in the refrigerator for up to two days. Freeze them if you would like to keep them for longer.

From top: Sugared Lingonberries (page 692); Black Pudding (page 392)

BLOOD SAUSAGE FROM TAMPERE

Mustamakkara (Finland)

Mustamakkara is interesting because it has been produced and eaten for hundreds of years, largely unchanged. It is still part of people's everyday life and you can buy it from street food stalls in the city of Tampere and elsewhere. It is commonly served hot with a side of Sugared Lingonberries (page 692) and possibly a small carton of milk to drink.

Most of the *mustamakkara* consumed today is not made from scratch but is bought homemade.

You will need about 2 metres/6½ feet pork or beef casing, soaked and rinsed.

Preparation and cooking time:
   1½ hours
Soaking time: overnight
Makes: 1 kg/2¼ lb

75 g/2¾ oz (¼ cup plus 1 tablespoon)
   pearl barley
300 ml/10½ fl oz (1¼ cups) Meat Stock
   (page 650)
500 ml/17 fl oz (2 cups plus 1 tablespoon) pig
   or cow blood, strained
180 g/6½ oz (1⅓ cups) coarse rye flour
200 g/7 oz pork back fat, cut into
   1 cm/½ inch dice
1 onion, finely chopped
2 teaspoons sugar
2 teaspoons marjoram
1 tablespoon salt
1 teaspoon freshly ground white pepper
butter, for frying

Mix the pearl barley with the stock (broth) then refrigerate and leave to soak overnight.

Transfer to the bowl of a stand mixer and add all the remaining ingredients. Mix thoroughly so that no lumps of flour remain. To check the flavour (it should be well-seasoned), make a small patty and fry it in a bit of butter. Taste and adjust the balance if necessary.

Preheat the oven to 180°C/350°F/Gas Mark 4.

Tie off the casing to seal it at one end. Using the sausage-making attachment of your mincer (grinder), stuff the mixture into the casing. Fill it slowly and steadily – ensuring there are no pockets of air – and make one long sausage. Tie it at the open end.

Roll the sausage into a coil and place on a buttered roasting tray. Cook for 15–25 minutes, until the sausage is firm to the touch and the core temperature is 68–70°C/154–158°F.

If you plan to store the sausage for serving later then remove from the oven and leave to cool completely. Otherwise turn the sausage over and cook for another 10 minutes to crisp and brown.

Once cold the *mustamakkara* should be stored in the fridge for up to a week. Cut into pieces and reheat in a 200°C/400°F/Gas Mark 6 oven for about 10 minutes.

NORWEGIAN BLOOD SAUSAGE

Blodpølse (Norway)

Norwegian blood sausage recipes tend to be the sweetest ones of all the recipes I have read through in my research for this chapter. They are often seasoned with sweet spices like cloves, cinnamon and allspice, and they almost always contain a good amount of raisins.

In Norway, blood sausage seems to be exclusively eaten fried in slices, often with a sprinkling of sugar or a drizzle of golden syrup as their only accompaniment. Some recipes also suggest serving with boiled potatoes and with fried bacon or salt pork.

Worth mentioning is that I found one recipe for blood sausage in Norway which was leavened with baker's ammonia. I tried it and it was quite interesting – it definitely fluffed up a bit and the slices turned noticeably crisper when fried. If you want to try it, add 1 teaspoon of baker's ammonia along with the flour and stuff the casing less tightly to avoid them bursting, as they will swell more than other sausages.

You will need 2 metres/6½ feet pork casing, soaked and rinsed.

Preparation and cooking time: 1½ hours
Serves: 4

500 ml/17 fl oz (2 cups plus 1 tablespoon)
  pig, cow or sheep's blood, strained
100 g/3½ oz (½ cup) pearl barley or
  short-grain rice, boiled, strained and
  cooled down (page 654)
100 g/3½ oz (⅔ cup) plain (all-purpose) flour
200 g/7 oz pig kidney fat, cut into
  5 mm/¼ inch dice
100 g/3½ oz (½ cup) brown sugar
100 g/3½ oz (¼ cup plus 1 tablespoon)
  golden syrup
80 g/3 oz (½ cup) raisins
1 teaspoon ground allspice
1 teaspoon ground cloves
1 teaspoon ground cinnamon
2 teaspoons salt

Combine all the ingredients in a large mixing bowl and work together until the lumps are all gone. You might need to add a splash of water if the mixture seems too stiff; it should be like runny yogurt in texture.

Tie off the casing to seal it at one end. Using the sausage-making attachment of your mincer (grinder), stuff the mixture into the casing. Fill it slowly and steadily, making sure there are no pockets of air. Don't fill it too tight, or it may burst when you cook it. Tie it with string at the open end. You can keep it as one long sausage, or tie it into shorter lengths.

Carefully lift the sausage into a large pan and pour in enough water to just cover. Place over a low–medium heat and slowly bring to a simmer. Simmer gently, until the sausage is firm to the touch and has reached a core temperature of 68°C/154°F.

Lift the sausage out of the water and leave to cool down completely. Store in the refrigerator for up to two days. Freeze them if you would like to keep them for longer.

FINNISH LIVER CASSEROLE

Maksalaatikko (Finland)

This sweet and salty liver casserole is often served with Sugared Lingonberries (page 692).

Preparation and cooking time: 1½ hours
Serves: 4

120 g/4 oz (½ cup plus 2 tablespoons)
  short-grain rice
800 ml/28 fl oz (3¼ cups) milk
butter, for greasing and frying
2 onions, finely chopped
250 ml/8 fl oz (1 cup) cream
300 g/11 oz minced (ground) pork
  or beef liver
60 g/2¼ oz (½ cup) raisins
1 egg
70 g/2¾ oz (3½ tablespoons) golden syrup
1 teaspoon ground ginger
2 teaspoons marjoram
salt and white pepper, to taste

Put the rice and milk in a large pot and bring to a simmer over medium heat. Lower the heat and simmer gently, until the rice is soft. Remove from the heat and leave to cool completely. Tip into a mixing bowl.

Preheat the oven to 175°C/345°F/Gas Mark 4 and butter an ovenproof dish.

Heat some butter in a frying pan or skillet and cook the onions until soft and translucent. Add them to the cooked rice, along with the remaining ingredients and mix well. To check the seasoning, make a small patty and fry it. Taste and adjust the balance if necessary.

Tip the mixture into the prepared dish and bake for about 1 hour, or until set and deeply coloured on the surface.

LIVER AND BARLEY CASSEROLE

Maksalaatikko (Finland)
Korvkaka / leverlåda (Sweden)

The Swedish name of this dish translates to 'sausage cake'. It has very little to do with sausages, but I imagine that it has its origins in the fact that it is a bit like a liver sausage without a casing and it is cooked in a tray, a bit like a cake. In the Swedish speaking parts of Finland this dish goes under the name *leverlåda*.

Liver and barley casserole is usually served with Boiled Potatoes (page 117) and Sugared Lingonberries (page 692). Incidentally, this is one of the few dishes that my father, a great lover of food – traditional or not – hates with a passion from being forced to eat it in his elementary school cafeteria.

Preparation and cooking time: 1–1½ hours
Serves: 4

130 g/4½ oz (⅔ cup) pearl barley or short-
   grain rice
1 litre/34 fl oz (4¼ cups) milk
butter, for frying
1 onion, finely chopped
300 g/11 oz calves' liver (pork is also fine,
   but can have a strong flavour if the
   animal is mature)
100 g/3½ oz pork shoulder or belly
   (side)
3 tablespoons golden syrup
2 eggs
marjoram, to taste
thyme, to taste
large handful of raisins
salt and white pepper, to taste

Put the barley or rice in a pot with 200 ml/7 fl oz (¾ cup plus 1 tablespoon) water. Bring to the boil, then pour in the milk. Return to the boil, cover and simmer until done. Remove from the heat and leave to cool.

Melt a little butter in a frying pan or skillet and fry the onion until soft, golden and sweet. Leave to cool.

Preheat the oven to 225°C/435°F/Gas Mark 7.

Push the liver and pork through a meat mincer (grinder). Add it to the cooled barley or rice, then add the onion and all the remaining ingredients. Mix together well. It should be sweet and salty and quite well seasoned.

Transfer the mixture to an ovenproof dish and bake for 40–60 minutes until cooked through and nicely golden.

LIVER PATTIES

Leverbiff (Sweden)

My aunt on my mother's side used to make liver patties when I was growing up; I have fond memories of them. They are usually served with Sugared Lingonberries (page 692), Boiled Potatoes (page 117), creamy Brown Gravy (page 671) and possibly green vegetables, like broccoli or peas.

Preparation and cooking time: 30 minutes
Serves: 4

300 g/11 oz liver (your choice of beef, veal,
   pork, lamb, chicken), diced small
250 g/9 oz pork shoulder with some fat,
   cut into pieces small enough for
   your meat mincer (grinder)
1 onion, finely chopped
2 tablespoons breadcrumbs
100 ml/3½ fl oz (⅓ cup plus 1 tablespoon)
   cream
2 teaspoons dried marjoram
salt and pepper, to taste
butter, for frying

Preheat the oven to 120°C/235°F/Gas Mark ½.

Place all the ingredients in a bowl, except for the butter, and use your hands to mix together well. Pass through a meat mincer (grinder) on the finest setting. To check the flavour, make a small patty and fry it. Taste and adjust the balance if necessary.

Heat some butter in a frying pan or skillet over a medium heat. Dollop spoonfuls of the rather loose mixture into the pan and fry until browned on one side. Flip the patties over and fry them on the other side. Transfer the cooked patties to an oven-proof dish and keep them warm in the oven while you fry the rest of the mixture.

DANISH 'SCRATCHINGS'

Fedtegrever (Denmark)

When fat from the body cavity of animals, like kidney fat, is rendered down into other purer products, pieces of connective tissue remain. These can be fried until crisp and are used as toppings on savoury dishes such as Danish Ground Offal Stew (below) or on open-faced sandwiches (page 522).

For this recipe you will need to get solid raw suet from the butcher, and not the ready-shredded version, which is commercially available from the supermarket.

Preparation and cooking time: 1 hour
Serves: 4

2 kg/4½ lb pig or cow kidney fat, cut into
    3 cm/1¼ inch chunks
salt, to taste

Put the chunks of kidney fat into a pot and heat gently until they start to melt. Once the fat is translucent, increase the heat to medium and cook until the fat renders out to a liquid, leaving behind the shrivelled pieces of connective tissue. These should become nice and golden and crisp. Strain the fat, cool it completely and keep it for deep-frying – it keeps very well in the freezer.

Season the scratchings generously with salt and serve them warm.

DANISH GROUND OFFAL STEW

Finker (Denmark)

This Danish classic has something of a resemblance to Swedish *pölsa* (page 402) but it is served a bit differently. *Finker* always has Danish Rye Bread

(page 504) on the side, is often sprinkled with Danish 'Scratchings' (see left) and is sometimes served with Beetroot Salad (page 116).

Some *finker* recipes contain prunes and apples; others don't. I found one recipe containing the tongue also, so I have included that as an option. If you add the tongue you will have a bit more than 4 portions.

Preparation and cooking time: 1½ hours
Serves: 4

1 pig's liver
1 pig's heart
2 pig's kidneys
1 pig's tongue (optional)
2 bay leaves
1 sprig thyme
10 white peppercorns
1 leek, coarsely chopped
1 quantity Danish 'Scratchings' (see left),
    and some of the rendered fat
1 onion, finely chopped
1 apple, peeled and cut into 1 cm/½ inch dice
    (optional)
8 pitted prunes, diced (optional)
White vinegar, to taste
salt and pepper, to taste

Clean and rinse all the offal, then place in a large pot with the herbs, peppercorn and leek and add enough water to cover. Bring to a simmer over a medium heat then cook for 45 minutes, skimming frequently to remove any scum from the surface.

Remove the offal from the cooking liquid and peel the skin off the tongue. Coarsely chop it and pass it through a meat mincer (grinder) on the coarse setting.

Strain the cooking liquid into a clean pot and keep warm. Discard all the spent aromatics.

Pour a little of the rendered fat into a large pan. Add the onion and sweat gently over a low–medium heat for a couple of minutes, they should be soft but not coloured. Add the diced apple and prunes, if using, followed by the ground offal. Add a generous ladle of the strained cooking liquid, a splash of vinegar and salt and pepper to taste. Simmer for 10 minutes before serving.

MASHED PLUCK AND PEARL BARLEY HASH

Lungmos / Pölsa (Sweden)

Cooked meats of some kind, often containing offal (organ meats), are coarsely ground and mixed in a cooking liquid thickened with pearl barley. The dish is often served with Pickled Beetroot (page 660), Brined Cucumbers (page 660) and a fried egg (page 52).

There is a great deal of overlap between the two dishes in the title, *lungmos* and *pölsa*, and to me they are really just the same thing with different names. Some previous accounts call a hash made with pork and barley *pölsa* and one made with pluck (which is the heart, lungs and liver, joined together) *lungmos*. Others call the pluck version *pölsa* and make no mention of the one made just from meat. Some hash recipes contain pearl barley while others are thickened with just a bit of flour.

Below is a recipe that I like and that, to me, is either *lungmos* or *pölsa*. If you want to make a pure meat one, just substitute the pluck with 1.5 kg/3¼ lb of meat on the bone – knuckle, shoulder or something like that.

Preparation and cooking time: 2½ hours
Serves: 4, with plenty leftover to make fried
 pölsa (page 404) the next day

For the braise
1 pig's pluck, rinsed thoroughly, windpipe
 and oesophagus removed
2 carrots
1 leek
2 celery stalks
1 bay leaf
6 cloves
1 piece dried ginger
10 white peppercorns

To finish
50 g/2 oz (3½ tablespoons) butter
1 onion, finely chopped
2 tablespoons plain (all-purpose) flour
120 g/4 oz (½ cup plus 2 tablespoons)
 pearl barley
dried marjoram, to taste
salt and white pepper, to taste

Place the pluck in a large pot with the other ingredients for the braise – it should all fit quite snugly. Add enough water to cover. Bring to a boil over medium heat and cook for about 2 hours, or until the organ meats are very nearly tender. Skim frequently to remove any scum from the surface.

Remove the pluck from the cooking liquid. Coarsely chop it and pass it through a meat mincer (grinder) on the coarse setting.

Strain the cooking liquid into a clean pan and keep warm. Discard all the spent aromatics.

To finish the dish, melt the butter in a small pan set over a medium heat. Add the onion and fry until lightly browned. Add the flour, stirring well, then add the pearl barley. Add a generous ladle of the strained cooking liquid, stirring well to ensure no lumps form. Continue adding the warm liquid, a little at a time, stirring continuously, until the barley is soft.

Add the ground offal to the pan and adjust the consistency with a little more cooking liquid, if you want. Add salt, pepper and marjoram, to taste; it should be well seasoned, so don't be stingy.

For image see opposite page

Clockwise from top left: Fried Salt Pork (page 302) and Fried Falu Sausage (page 417) on Plain Wheat Loaf (page 498); quartered Brined Cucumbers (page 660); How to Fry a Really Good Egg (page 52); Nordic Hash (page 368); Pickled Beetroot (page 660); Mashed Pluck and Pearl Barley Hash (page 402)

FRIED MASHED PLUCK AND PEARL BARLEY

Stekt pölsa (Sweden)

This is one of my favourite ways of eating *pölsa* (page 402). Do it either because you like it or because you have some *pölsa* left over from the day before and want to make yourself a nice lunch. Fry an egg sunny side up and bring out some of your Brined Cucumbers (page 660) to serve with it.

You don't have to make the full recipe for four portions, it works just as well for one if that's the quantity of *pölsa* you have available.

Preparation and cooking time: 10 minutes
Serves: 4 generously

butter, for frying
1 quantity Mashed Pluck and Pearl Barley
  Hash (page 402)
4 fried eggs, sunny side up, to serve
brined cucumbers (page 660), to serve

Melt a little butter in a large frying pan over a medium heat (a non-stick pan is useful here). Add the cold hash and fry, without stirring, until it has warmed through and the bottom of the hash is deeply caramelized. Serve immediately.

For image see page 403

SAMI REINDEER HEART STEW

Bidos / Bidus (Sami)

Serve with Sami Soft Flatbread (page 524) and diced reindeer back fat.

Preparation and cooking time: 1–1¼ hours
Serves: 4

800 g/1¾ lb reindeer heart, cut into small
  dice, about 1 cm/½ inch
reindeer broth, to cover
6 potatoes, cut into 3 cm/1¼ inch pieces
salt and white pepper, to taste

Place the diced heart in a pot and just cover with broth. Bring to a simmer over medium heat, cover and cook for about 45–60 minutes or until just tender. After 30 minutes add the potatoes. Season with salt and pepper towards the end.

TONGUE

Kieli (Finland)
Tunge (Denmark)
Tunga (Sweden)

Almost all mammal tongues are great food. I like them best braised until just tender, cooled down and then either sliced thin as charcuterie or a sandwich topping, or cut into pieces and seared in a hot pan to serve with a simple vegetable side dish. Some steamed green peas, some grated carrots, a salad and a fried egg (page 52) all make good accompaniments, and a spoonful of mustard and/or a Brined Cucumber (page 660) on the side is never wrong.

One of my favourite open-faced Danish *smørebrød* sandwiches (page 522) includes cold boiled tongue and something called Italian Salad (page 134).

The tongues that I use most often are beef, veal, moose, pork and lamb. The cooking times obviously vary widely with the size and age of the beast: a large beef tongue might take up to 3 hours of simmering, whilst a bunch of lamb tongues will be done in just over 1 hour. You can cook the tongue just in some salted water or add some vegetables and aromatics to it if you want to.

Tongue should not be cooked until too tender; it is unpleasant to eat because it becomes mushy. It is done when a paring knife inserted into the meat can be pulled out with ease, but not without resistance. The meat should follow the knife about halfway out of the cooking liquid before it falls back.

Tongues are covered in a thick and chewy skin. This peels away really easily on a just-cooked, still-warm tongue, so don't let them wait when they are perfectly cooked but rather skin them immediately.

Tongues can be bought both fresh and brined. If your tongue is fresh you can salt the braise a little, whilst if it is brined you have to watch out that the whole thing doesn't turn too salty.

If you want to brine a fresh tongue yourself to make some charcuterie, then follow the instructions for brining meat on page 434.

SAUSAGE AND CHARCUTERIE

Previous page: Clear cut forest, north Sweden, late Summer 2013.

Charcuterie

Before the time of modern refrigeration, industrialized production and motorized transportation, charcuteries were an absolute must to spread the meat harvested from one single animal over a large enough time, giving the members of a family running the farm where the animal lived a chance to consume its meat before it went bad. In every part of the world, those who lived there have, through cultural transfer and in some cases natural selection, developed an affinity for the flavours of the foods available locally which were historically safe to eat.

In Europe and Scandinavia, with access to salt and plenty of meat from its farmlands, we have developed a taste for the savouriness of cured meats. Which animal being used is subject to local supply and demand but the principle is always the same. Our minds tell us that this here is something that won't kill you.

In other parts of the Nordics other flavours have become more appreciated for the same reason. Two good examples are Icelandic *surmatur* and Faroese *raest*, two methods of preservation that have developed parallel to those in Central Europe and for the same reasons, but which have turned out completely different because of the local circumstances.

Both Iceland and the Faroes are very remote places, so cheap salt in large quantities is not older than commercial shipping. On Iceland the low pH level of cultured whey is used to more or less pickle pieces of meat, whilst on the Faroe Islands legs of mutton are simply hung up unsalted and can, due to the very particular climate of the small archipelago, hang for a very long time without becoming dangerous to eat.

Opposite: Traditional Norwegian charcuteries, fenalår (page 348) and pinnekjøtt (page 350) curing in an Oslo apartment, Norway, Spring 2014. The artisanal ways of producing these charcuteries, which where once vital to those living on Norwegian farms, have all but been forgotten and are kept alive by enthusiasts preparing it their homes, not because they have to but because they want to.

Next page: A piece of fenalår (page 348) having been nibbled on, photographed on a desk in an Oslo home, Norway, Spring 2014.

NORDIC HOT DOGS

We love hot dogs in the Nordics and I would say that they could be considered the only prevalent form of street food that has been available in the Nordic region long enough to have developed an expression unique enough to be considered a regional speciality.

The most distinctive dog in itself is probably the Danish one, coloured bright red, originally with Erythrosine, also known as Red No. 3 or E 127. After having found out that the synthetic compound Erythrosine is probably not very good for you, it was substituted for Carmine. Historically, substandard or old sausages were dyed red to differentiate them from the good ones. Over time though the Danes grew to appreciate the red colour more and subsequently all of them where coloured, good and bad. The Danish dogs are commonly known as *røde pølser* and they are most often heated in water and served on a paper tray with mustard, ketchup and crispy onions. They are never grilled. The bread in Denmark is not cut to hold the sausage but is rather dipped in the condiments to be eaten separately. Danish hot dogs are often served and eaten on the streets, but have also grown increasingly common in other simple restaurants.

In Norway, the best expression of regional hot dog culture is *pølse i lompe*, which consists of a small potato flatbread (*potetlefse*) in which a sausage and some condiments are rolled up. The sausage is traditionally of frankfurter type but increasingly often of some other kind. Different grilled sausages are popular, some rolled in slices of bacon before being cooked.

Common Norwegian hot dog garnishes are mustard, ketchup, crispy onions or onion griddled soft and sweet on site together with the dog itself. Grated cheese, Potato Salad (page 123) or shrimp salad, are not uncommon but must be regarded as being rather new additions to the *pølse* repertoire. The practice of serving dogs and shrimp salad seems to have been adopted from Sweden.

In Sweden hot dog culture has developed into rather a gastronomy of its own since the first dog was served in Stockholm in 1897. Originally hot dogs were offered from portable hot boxes in the streets of the city and served simply with bread and possibly mustard. As time passed, because of hygiene regulations and the popularization of the car, little restaurants called Gatukök, literally meaning 'street kitchens', started to become popular. I imagine that this is also climate related; the harsh winters are not really suitable for selling hot dogs in the street or for eating them there.

When the Swedish *varmkorv* moved indoors, probably thanks to the increased storage and cooking capacity of the fixed location, the real development of its unique expression suddenly took off. Today, boiled hot dogs and grilled sausages are widely available, either in buns, with mashed potatoes or wrapped in flatbreads with mashed potatoes, or with fries. Common condiments are mustard (strong, sweet or coarse), ketchup, onions (raw or crispy), shrimp salad, cucumber mayonnaise, pickled cucumber mix (incidentally, called Boston cucumber) salad and, especially further north, Sugared Lingonberries (page 692).

A special nomenclature has also developed over the years and I thought it would be good to explain this system and include the names of some legendary combinations as the menus are often rather extensive.

You are expected to first say which hot dog you want: a boiled (*en kokt*), grilled (*en grillad*) or really big griddled one (*en bamse*).

Then you communicate how you want to enjoy it:

I papper, tack: No bread, please, just in sandwich paper.

Med bröd, tack: In bread, please.

Med strips, tack: With fries, please.

Mosbricka, tack: With mash, please.

I tunnbrödsrulle, tack: With mash wrapped in a flatbread, please.

Then you will be asked what condiments and garnishes you want. The vendor will actively ask you if you want certain things whilst others you are expected to ask for if you want them. Depending on which sausage you have asked for served how, different things are standard. For example, you will always be asked if you want mustard and/or ketchup, however you will not always be asked which kind of mustard even though there is always a choice of at least two. Shrimp salad on the other hand will always be proposed if you ask for one with mash in a flatbread, whilst never if you have chosen another serving option. If you want it with your fries you have to ask for it (the obscenity). Salad will be proposed with anything that contains mash and never otherwise. You will almost always be asked if you want onions. If it is for a hot dog in bread or one with mash it is assumed that they are crisp, if you do not ask for raw. For one with mash you will be asked if you want raw or crisp onion and no one eats onion with fries.

There are also some popular classics named for convenience:

Kioskvältare: One in bread, with shrimp salad and onion.

Halv special: One in bread with mash and shrimp salad on top.

Hel special: Two dogs in one bread with mash and shrimp salad on top.

Parisare: A thick slice of falu sausage (page 416) in a burger bun.

Mosbricka med extra allt: One with mash and all the garnishes.

Tunnbrödsrulle med extra allt: One with mash rolled up in a flatbread, with all the garnishes.

Most Swedish hot dog places will serve a range of soft drinks but also chocolate milk. This would be the appropriate choice if you have ordered one with mash in a flatbread with shrimp salad.

In Finland one of the most fantastic and unique street food dishes is the Blood Sausage from Tampere. You can read more about that one on page 398.

SMOKING

Smoking is one of our oldest methods for preserving foodstuffs. It can be used on fish and meat, dairy and even malted barley for making beer. As with most preservation techniques, smoking gives a distinctive character to the food. In this case it mainly comes from the aroma and flavour of the smoke itself.

The smoke and the substances left behind on the surface of the product are not enough on their own to completely preserve any foods, they have to be used in combination with others, often salt-based cures. The smoke, though, has some antimicrobial properties and acts as an antioxidant, an effect especially noticeable with fatty fish like salmon or herring, which if smoked keep for a lot longer without going rancid.

There are two kinds of smoking: hot smoking and cold smoking. They work in slightly different ways.

Hot smoking is essentially a cooking process in which the product is cooked in an enclosed smoky space where a temperature of 80–120°C/175–250°F is maintained long enough for the product to cook through and become flavoured with smoke. The preserving effect from hot smoking is mostly due to the fact that the heat kills many microbes during the cooking process. The same results could pretty much be reached by cooking the product in an ordinary oven. If this hot-smoked product, now mostly free from microbes, is enclosed in an atmosphere where new microbes can't get to it, it will keep really well. An example of such a place could be a vacuum bag. If, on the other hand, the hot-smoked product is left at room temperature, the fact that most microbes – good or bad – are dead, would be a bad thing as that leaves the field wide open to invading microbes, which will quickly spoil the food.

Cold smoking is carried out at a temperature of 15–30°C/59–86°F over a much longer period of time. Meat or fish cured with salt and sugar, and in that sense already preserved, are hung up in the cool smoke and will further dry making microbial spoilage less likely. As the smoking process lasts a lot longer than with hot smoking, more of those antimicrobial and antioxidative substances will adhere to the surface of the product itself.

LACTO-FERMENTED, HIGH STARCH CONTENT SAUSAGES

In parts of the Nordic region and particularly the southern parts of Sweden, coarse sausages with a very high content of starch are common. They usually have an addition of cooked barley, oats or rye, which during the curing process, feeds the lactobacillus in the sausage meat, producing a high level of lactic acid. This preserves the sausages by lowering their pH level. It gives them a particularly firm texture because it acts on the proteins of the meat, and it gives them a very marked, acidic flavour.

Examples like Cold-smoked, Fermented Barley Sausages (page 419), will almost certainly have 25% by weight of cooked barley and sometimes as much as 50%.

The more starch you add to the sausage, the more acidic it will become in the end.

Fermented sausages should smell very fresh when opened. They should be pink and healthy looking and they should have a marked yogurty kind of acidic flavour to them.

The Norwegian *surpølse* or Soured Sausage (page 421) is a very interesting variation in which all of the meat is cooked before being stuffed into the casing.

FALU SAUSAGES, HOT-SMOKED SMOOTH MOUSSELINE SAUSAGES FROM FALUN

Lenkkimakkara (Finland)
Falukorv (Sweden)

This very old type of smooth sausage made from beef and pork is a sort of Swedish baloney. Its origins date back to the sixteenth century, when ropes made from ox hide were used in great quantities in the central Swedish Falu copper mines and something had to be done with all the meat from the animals. Germans working in and around the mines taught the Swedes the techniques for making sausages like *falukorv*. Originally they were stuffed into circles of beef casings, but today they are mostly sold in a bright orange cellulose tube.

It is very important that all of the ingredients and equipment are as cold as possible when you start making this recipe for the fats to emulsify properly. Everything should be as close to frozen as possible, without actually being frozen.

If you choose to use some kind of nitrate, then reduce the salt according to the instructions on the packet.

You will need 2 metres/6½ feet beef round casings, soaked and rinsed.

Preparation and cooking time: 3–4 hours
Resting time: overnight
Makes: 2.5 kg/5½ lb

950 g/2 lb 2 oz lean beef, cut into pieces
    and chilled
625 g/1 lb 6 oz pork shoulder, cut into cubes
    and chilled
150 g/5 oz pork back fat, cut into pieces
    and chilled
150 g/5 oz lard, chilled
40 g/1½ oz potato starch
50 g/2 oz (3½ tablespoons) salt
1 clove garlic, finely grated
12 white peppercorns, ground
1 teaspoon mustard powder
a little freshly grated nutmeg

Combine the chilled beef, pork, back fat and lard in a mixing bowl and stir in the potato starch. Pass through a meat mincer (grinder) on the fine plate, then transfer to the chilled bowl of a stand mixer.

Add the remaining ingredients along with 650 ml/22 fl oz (2¾ cups) ice-cold water. Work until the mixture is very smooth.

Tie off the casings to seal them at one end. Using the sausage-making attachment of your mincer, stuff the mixture into the lengths of casings. Knot at the open end, then tie into 30 cm/12 inch lengths. Refrigerate overnight.

Follow the instructions on page 416 for hot-smoking the sausages at 100°C/212°F for 3–4 hours.

The sausages are ready when they reach a core temperature of around 68°C/155°F.

Leave the sausages to cool completely before refrigerating. If you want to keep them for more than about a week you should freeze them. Frozen they will keep for several months.

FRIED FALU SAUSAGE

Paistettu lenkkimakkara (Finland)
Stekt falukorv (Sweden)

Enjoy with Creamed Macaroni (page 465) and Green Peas (page 136), or with Creamed Vegetables like carrots, peas, broccoli or cauliflower (page 85) and some Boiled Potatoes (page 117). Some mustard, sweet or strong, on the side is always nice. I also like ketchup, but that is almost socially unacceptable.

Preparation and cooking time: 10 minutes
Serves: 4

1 x 500 g/1 lb 2 oz *falu* sausage, skinned
    and cut into 1 cm/½ inch slices
butter, for frying

Heat some butter in a large frying pan or skillet over a medium heat. Fry the sausage slices on both sides until golden. They will tend to buckle and look a bit like little hats, and the remedy for this is to make an incision in each slice, which allows the sausage to expand evenly as it cooks. Best practice is to do this when you are actually skinning the sausage by making a 1.5 cm/¾ inch deep slash along the entire length of the sausage. This also makes it easier to skin them.

For image see page 403

FALU SAUSAGE STROGANOFF

Makkarastroganoff (Finland)
Korv stroganoff (Sweden)

An internet search on *korv stroganoff* returns about 150,000 hits, which makes it one of Sweden's most popular contemporary dishes. This slight oddity of a recipe has its roots in the classic beef stroganoff, but using *falu* sausages (page 416) instead of beef. In Finland, this dish is also quite popular, but can contain other sausages than *falukorv*.

Through recent history, the recipe has changed in other parts, too. Where a classic stroganoff always contains mushrooms, the *Falu* Sausage Stroganoff does not, and while this sausage stroganoff always contains some type of tomato, the classic stroganoff does not, at least not in most versions.

Serve your *Falu* Sausage Stroganoff with Boiled Rice (page 654). Some people pour it over pasta or couscous, but I could never do that; too many fond childhood memories of parboiled, long-grain rice would get in the way. I can accept and appreciate Green Peas (page 136) on the side.

Below is my wife Tove's recipe. The sambal oelek is not to be considered traditional, but it does bring something special to the dish.

Preparation and cooking time: 30 minutes
Serves: 4

1 x 500 g/1 lb 2 oz *falu* sausage, skinned
butter, for frying
2 onions, finely chopped
3 tablespoons tomato purée (paste)
1 teaspoon strong mustard
1 teaspoon sambal oelek
300 ml/10½ fl oz (1¼ cups)
   crème fraîche
salt and white pepper, to taste

Cut the skinned sausage into slices and then into 1 cm/½ inch sticks.

Heat the butter in a large frying pan or skillet over a medium heat. Fry the sausage pieces for a few moments, then add the onion and continue frying until the sausage and onion are both starting to colour.

Add the tomato purée, mustard, sambal oelek and the crème fraîche, then bring to a simmer and cook until the sauce has thickened a bit. Season with salt and pepper to taste.

For image see page 429

FALU SAUSAGE GRATIN

Gratinerad falukorv (Sweden)

This is one of my school canteen favourites. Serve it with Mashed Potatoes (page 118), Green Peas (page 136), and sweet mustard.

Falu sausage can be stuffed with different things; I like slices of onion and apple – and I like to keep the skin on the apple, but that's a matter of personal preference. I don't like slices of tomato as they get hotter than lava when cooked, plus most tomatoes available in the Nordics aren't very tasty.

The trick for perfection is letting the sausage take its time in the oven so that whatever it is stuffed with has a chance to cook properly. I often see recipes for this dish in which the temperature is set to 230°C/450°F/Gas Mark 8 and the cooking time is about 20 minutes. No less than 35 minutes in the oven is acceptable in my opinion, and for this to work out a temperature of around 200°C/400°F/Gas Mark 6 is usually fine.

Preparation and cooking time: 45 minutes
Serves: 4

1 x 600 g/1 lb 5 oz *falu* sausage, skinned
2 tablespoons strong mustard
   (not sweet here)
3 tablespoons tomato purée (paste)
1 onion, thinly sliced
1 apple, halved, cored and thinly sliced
   (peeled if you like)
50 g/2 oz well-aged hard cheese, grated

Preheat the oven to 200°C/400°F/Gas Mark 6.

Cut the sausage straight acorss at 1 cm/½ inch intervals. You don't want to cut all the way through, but leave 1.5 m/¾ at the base so that it creates a row of connected slices

Place the sausage in a baking pan and smear it with the mustard and tomato purée (paste). Insert pieces of onion and apple into the slits along each sausage and scatter the cheese over the top. Bake until the surface is crusted and golden brown and the sausage is hot at the centre. Leave to rest for about 10 minutes before biting into it.

For image see page 429

COLD-SMOKED, FERMENTED BARLEY SAUSAGES

Isterband (Sweden)

Isterband sausages can be either fried in a pan or baked in the oven. I prefer the oven; 200°C/400°F/ Gas Mark 6 is a good temperature and they will take about 10 minutes.

Serve them with creamed potatoes: some like Scanian Creamed Potatoes (page 120), some like plain, others with parsley. I like Creamed Potatoes with Dill (page 118). Some mustard and a Pickled Beetroot or two (page 660) on the side is not bad either.

If you choose to use some kind of nitrate, then reduce the salt according to the instructions on the packet.

You will need 2 metres/6½ feet pork casings, soaked and rinsed.

Preparation and cooking time: 2 hours plus time to dry and smoke them
Makes: 2 kg/4½ lb

125 g/4½ oz (½ cup plus 1 tablespoon) pearl barley
2 onions, finely chopped
625 g/1 lb 6 oz lean beef, cut into pieces and chilled
625 g/1 lb 6 oz lean pork, cut into pieces and chilled
625 g/1 lb 6 oz pork back fat, cut into pieces and chilled
60 g/2¼ oz (¼ cup) salt
20 white peppercorns, ground
10 allspice berries, ground
625 g/1 lb 6 oz boiled barley porridge (cooked weight)

Put the pearl barley and onions in a large pan with 800 ml/28 fl oz (3¼ cups) water. Bring to a simmer and cook until the grains are completely soft. Remove from the heat and leave the porridge to cool down.

Combine the beef, pork and back fat in a mixing bowl, then pass through a meat mincer (grinder) on the coarsest setting. Add the salt, spices and cold barley porridge and work by hand until just combined.

Tie off the casings to seal them at one end. Using the sausage-making attachment of your mincer, stuff the mixture into the lengths of casings fairly tightly as they will shrink a bit as they dry. Knot them at the open end then tie into suitable lengths.

Hang the sausages somewhere warm (around 20–25°C/70–77°F) for about 24 hours so that the lacto-fermentation to get off to a good start.

Follow the instructions on page 416 for cold-smoking the sausages. It will take about 3 days to achieve the correct level of smokiness.

Isterband keeps for a really long time but they will eventually dry out and turn into more of a cured preparation, which is also tasty in thin slices, a bit like salami. Store them in the refrigerator for up to a month. Freeze them if you want to keep them for longer and prevent them from drying out.

For image see page 429

FERMENTED AND DRIED 'POLE' SAUSAGES

Stångkorv (Sweden)

These sausages get their name from the Swedish word for 'pole', referring to the wooden poles on which they were historically dried. Quite similar to Cold-smoked, Fermented Barley Sausages (page 419) – but never smoked – *stångkorv* is often served with fried potatoes, some Pickled Beetroot (page 660) and a fried egg, sunny side up. It is also used to make *Stångkorv Hash* (see right).

Stångkorv is most often made from pork alone, but can sometimes also contain some beef and offal (organ meat).

You will need about 4 metres/13 feet pork or beef casings, soaked and rinsed.

The drying time will take a different amount of time depending on the levels of humidity where you live. Anything between three and seven days though would be a good guideline.

Preparation and cooking time: 2 hours, plus
  drying time
Makes: 2 kg/4½ lb

1 litre/34 fl oz (4¼ cups) Ham Stock
  (page 650) or water
250 g/9 oz (2¼ cups) pearl barley
2 kg/4½ lb pork shoulder or neck, nice and
  fatty, cut into 3 cm/1¼ inch cubes
2 onions, finely chopped
10 allspice berries, ground
10 black peppercorns, ground
10 white peppercorns, ground
8 cloves, ground
40 g/1½ oz (2½ tablespoons) salt
butter, for frying

Combine the stock (broth) or water with the barley and bring to the boil. Lower the heat and simmer until the barley is soft. Remove from the heat and leave to cool completely. Transfer the barley and its cooking liquid to a large bowl.

Pass the meat through a meat mincer (grinder) on the coarsest setting. Add to the barley, together with all the remaining ingredients. If you cooked the barley in stock, rather than water, and the liquid tastes quite salty, then reduce the amount of salt you add to the sausage mixture by half.

Tie off the casings to seal them at one end. Using the sausage-making attachment of your mincer, stuff the mixture into the lengths of casings as tightly as you can, without them bursting. Remember that the sausages are going to dry for a while and so the mixture will shrink a little.

Twist the casings to create 20 cm/8 inch sausages and hang the links on wooden poles. Take care to separate the sausages so that they do not touch each other any more than necessary.

Place the poles somewhere warm (around 20°C/70°F) for 24 hours to get the fermentation started and then move them somewhere cool and well-ventilated for the rest of the drying process, which should take 10–14 days. The humidity should not be less than 70% as you don't want them to dry out too quickly.

The sausages will be ready when they have lost just over 20% of their initial weight. To measure this, weigh one sausage at the start as a reference, and note the weight, then check the weight every two days from then on.

The dried sausages should be firm to the touch, should smell fresh and spicy and should taste freshly of lactic acid. Once dried, they can be stored for a very long time sealed so that they don't dry more and refrigerated.

To cook *stångkorv*, fry them in some butter in a medium pan for a few minutes on each side. I like them cooked medium, which is a core temperature of about 60°C/140°F.

STÅNGKORV HASH

This is a preparation in which a *stångkorv* sausage has its casing removed before being chopped into small pieces to be fried and served with diced potato and onion.

The dish is commonly seasoned with white pepper and/or dried marjoram, or with allspice. Brined Cucumber (page 660) or Pickled Beetroots (page 660) and a fried egg are often served as accompaniments. Coarse mustard is a suitable condiment.

NORWEGIAN SOURED SAUSAGE

Surpølse (Norway)

This traditional Norwegian sausage is made much like Swedish Cold-Smoked, Fermented Barley Sausages (page 419), except that the meats and all of the other components are cooked before being stuffed into the casing. According to some, these sausages were, much like their Swedish counterparts, left to hang in the chimney to ferment for at least a week and there received a bit of smoke flavour. However, most recipes I have found that are used today do not smoke this sausage but rather leave them hanging somewhere warm for the required amount of time. As in most cases with food that was never industrialized, it is impossible to say what is correct, nor is it necessary. There is, and should always be allowed to be, a lot of local variation to recipes like this. To serve it, *surpølse* is fried in a pan over a medium heat in no other fat than what comes out naturally from the sausage itself. The traditional side dish is simply Boiled Potatoes (page 117) and Norwegian Crisp Flatbread (page 513). Some recipes suggest some boiled swede (rutabaga) as a side in combination with the potatoes or on its own.

The meat used in *surpølse* differs with each recipe but most of the recipes contain a good portion of mutton and sheep's tallow. Reindeer and beef are also used however to differentiate them from similar Swedish products. I have not come across any recipes containing pork.

Some recipes use an addition of vinegar to quickly lower the pH level and others use some cultured milk. The latter will add strains of lactobacillus present in the milk to the sausage meat. However, what makes sausage like this acidic is the conversion of starch into lactic acid by the action of lactobacillus. There will be more than enough lac-

tobacillus present anyhow, without the addition of anything. If you want you can add 2 tablespoons vinegar or 50 ml/2 fl oz (3 tablespoons) cultured milk to try anyway.

You will need 2.5 metres/8 feet pork casings, soaked and rinsed.

Preparation and cooking time: 2 hours
Maturing time: 4–7 days
Makes: about 2 kg/4½ lb

200 g/7 oz (1 cup) pearl barley
1 onion, finely chopped
1 litre/34 fl oz (4¼ cups) Meat Stock
 (preferably from mutton), page 650,
 or water
2 kg/4½ lb meat of which up to 50% can
 be offal, diced
350 g/12 oz sheep's tallow
40 g/1½ oz (2½ tablespoons) salt

Place the barley and onion in a pot and add the stock (broth) or water. Bring to the boil and simmer until the barley has softened. It might take 15 minutes or so. Add some more water if the mixture, at some point during the cooking process, becomes too dry. Remove the pot from the heat and add the meat to the mixture. Let everything cool down a bit.

Pass the mixture once through a meat mincer (grinder) on the coarse plate.

Tie off the casings to seal them at one end. Using the sausage-making attachment of your mincer, stuff the mixture into the length of casings fairly tightly as they will shrink a bit as they dry. Knot at the open end, then tie into suitable portion-sized lengths.

Bring a large pot of water to a simmer and add the sausages to it. Cook the sausages very carefully. It will take about 10 minutes or a bit longer and they should be firm to the touch. Drain the sausages, then hang them up somewhere warm and airy to let them ferment and dry for 4–7 days.

HOT-SMOKED SAUSAGE OF BEEF AND PORK WITH COGNAC

Cognacsmedwurst (Sweden)

Cognacsmedwurst is a true classic when it comes to Swedish sandwich toppings. Most versions are bought in a supermarket and of horrible quality. This sausage has quite a bit of starch in it from the potato and because it undergoes lacto-fermentation (page 416), so it has quite a fresh acidity to it.

You will need 4–7 metres/13–22 feet of beef casings, either circles or middles, depending on your preference, soaked and rinsed.

Preparation time: 2 hours
Fermenting, drying and smoking: 3 days
Makes: 3 kg/6 lb 6 oz sausages

500 g/1 lb 2 oz potatoes, coarsely cut
    into cubes
1 kg/2¼ lb lean beef, coarsely cut
    into pieces
2 kg/4½ lb pork shoulder, coarsely cut
    into cubes
750 g/1 lb 10 oz pork back fat, coarsely
    cut into cubes
75 g/3¾ oz (¼ cup) salt
4 teaspoons ground sandalwood
3 teaspoons ground ginger
4 teaspoons finely ground white
    peppercorns
1 teaspoon freshly grated nutmeg
1 large clove garlic, finely grated
2½ tablespoons Cognac

Day 1: Place the potatoes in a blender and add 100 ml/3½ fl oz (⅓ cup plus 1 tablespoon) cold water. Blend until as smooth as raw potatoes go, then transfer to a mixing bowl.

Add all of the remaining ingredients to the bowl, then pass the mixture through a meat mincer (grinder) on the coarse setting. Transfer to the bowl of a stand mixer and beat for 3 minutes. You can also do this by hand, which will take 10–15 minutes.

Tie off the casings to seal them at one end. Using the sausage-making attachment of your mincer, stuff the mixture into the lengths of casings. Fill them slowly and steadily, making sure there are no pockets of air. Knot them at the open end then tie them at suitable lengths.

Arrange the sausages on a tray or in a big bowl and cover with clingfilm (plastic wrap). Leave overnight somewhere not too cold (15–20°C/60–68°F) so that the lacto-fermentation really kicks off.

Day 2: Rinse the sausages well under cold running water, then pat them dry and hang them up in a warm place for 24 hours so the surfaces of the sausages dry out a bit. A temperature in the room of 20–25°C/68–77°F is perfect.

Day 3: Smoke the sausages in a smoker. The smoker temperature should be around 120°C/250°F and the sausages should be smoked until a core temperature of 68°C/155°F is reached. It will take 2–3 hours.

Leave the sausages to cool and refrigerate before eating.

POTATO SAUSAGE

Värmlandskorv / Potatiskorv (Sweden)

Värmlandskorv is an unsmoked sausage made from pork, beef and potato. It has a relatively low meat content – only around 30% in most recipes – and should be rather grey and have a coarse texture and flavour from the potato content.

In the central Swedish region of Värmland this sausage is known simply as potato sausage or *potatiskorv*, whilst in the rest of the country it is known as *värmlandskorv*, sausage from Värmland. And to confusing things further, there is yet another sausage from the region of Småland sharing the name *potatiskorv* but which uses a different recipe.

Värmlandskorv is for many an important part of the traditional Swedish Christmas dinner and it is often served with Boiled Potatoes (page 117), Mashed Potatoes (page 118), Root Vegetable Mash (page 112) and a good dollop of Scanian Mustard (page 653).

Traditionally sausages like these were rubbed with a form of nitrite called saltpetre and left on for a day and a night before they were cooked, pasteurized or fermented in brine. I don't do that because it is pointless in terms of preservation, since it works just as well to freeze sausages like this fresh, and boil them on the day you want to eat them instead. The saltpetre doesn't give any significant pinkness to the colour either, as the sausage consists of so much potato.

The casing to this sausage is beef rounds. They are often peeled off before the sausage is eaten since they can be a little chewy. Many of the potato sausages commercially available today have plastic skins that are obviously even less edible and much less attractive to look at.

You will need 4–7 metres/13–22 feet of beef casing, preferably circles, soaked and rinsed.

Preparation and cooking time: 2 hours
Drying time: overnight
Makes: about 5 kg/ 11 lb

1 kg/2¼ lb lean beef, coarsely cut into
    pieces
1.5 kg/3¼ lb fatty pork, coarsely cut into
    cubes
3 kg/6 lb 6 oz potatoes, coarsely cut into
    cubes
2 large onions, cut into cubes
1 tablespoon allspice berries, crushed
1 tablespoon white peppercorns, crushed
80 g/3 oz (⅔ cup) salt

Combine all the ingredients in a large bowl and mix together well. Push it through a meat mincer (grinder) on a fine setting. However, if your grinder is not really good and sharp, then push it through twice.

If the mixture seems very stiff, then add a splash of water, which makes it easier to fill the casings and to do so more evenly. Imagine a thick, grainy mayonnaise-like texture.

Tie off the casings to seal them at one end. Using the sausage-making attachment of your mincer, stuff the mixture into the lengths of casings. Fill them slowly and steadily, making sure there are no pockets of air. Knot them at the open end,

then tie them at suitable lengths. Leave the sausages overnight somewhere cool (or cold) to firm up a little.

When ready to use the sausages, poach them in salted water for 10–15 minutes, until they are cooked through and firm to the touch. The core temperature in the sausage should be about 68°C/155°F.

LIVER SAUSAGES

Maksamakkara (Finland)
Leverkorv (Sweden)

These liver sausages are most often served cold in slices as a sandwich topping, but they can also be served warm as part of a meal and have traditionally been an important part of the Christmas meal in the south Swedish region of Skåne. If you want to serve *leverkorv* as part of a meal, do so with Boiled Potatoes (page 117) and Pickled Beetroot (page 660).

You will need about 5 metres/16 feet pork or beef casings, soaked and rinsed.

Preparation and cooking time: 2 hours
Makes: about 3 kg/6 lb 6 oz

For the porridge
120 g/4 oz (½ cup plus 2 tablespoons)
   short-grain rice
700 ml/24 fl oz (3 cups) milk

For the sausage meat
1 kg/2¼ lb pork liver, cut into 3 cm/
   1¼ inch pieces
1 kg/2¼ lb fatty pork belly, cut into
   3 cm/1¼ inch pieces
500 g/1 lb 2 oz pork back fat, cut into
   3 cm/1¼ inch pieces
3 onions, finely chopped
8 teaspoons potato starch
50 g/2 oz (3 tablespoons) salt
2 teaspoons sugar
4 teaspoons dried marjoram
10 allspice berries, finely ground
15 black peppercorns, finely ground
freshly grated nutmeg (optional)

Put the rice in a large pot and add 300 ml/10½ fl oz (1¼ cups) water. Bring to the boil over a medium heat, stirring constantly. Lower the heat and stir in the milk. Continue simmering for a further 35 minutes, stirring every now and then. You don't want to break up the grains of rice too much. Remove from the heat and leave to cool completely before proceeding.

Transfer the cold rice porridge to a large mixing bowl and add all the sausage meat ingredients.

Mix together thoroughly, then pass through a meat mincer (grinder) on the finest setting.

Tie off the casings to seal them at one end. Using the sausage-making attachment of your mincer (grinder), stuff the mixture into the lengths of casings. Fill them slowly and steadily, making sure there are no pockets of air. Don't fill them too tightly as they will expand during the cooking. Knot them at the open end, then tie them into lengths. (For pork casings, 20 cm/8 inch lengths are about right; beef casings have a wider diameter, so slightly shorter lengths are better.)

Place the sausages in a large pot and pour in enough cold water to just cover. Bring to a bare simmer and cook until a core temperature of 68°C/155°F is reached. Do not rush the cooking process or the sausages will burst.

ICELANDIC LIVER SAUSAGE

Lifrarpylsa (Iceland)

This sausage stuffed in lamb's stomach is either eaten warm or in cold slices and is served with accompaniments like Mashed Potatoes (page 118), mashed swede or porridge. It is sometimes also used for sandwich topping. *Lifrarpylsa* is considered part of *Þorramatur* (page 358) and is sometimes also pickled in whey. If kidneys are used in the recipe, count 2 kidneys per liver and mince (grind) together with the liver.

Preparation time: 30 minutes
Cooking time: 2–2½ hours
Serves: 4

500 g/1 lb 2 oz lamb's liver, membranes and
   veins removed, coarsely minced (ground)
300 ml/10½ fl oz (1¼ cups) milk
100 g/3½ oz (¾ cup) rolled oats
75 g/2¾ oz (½ cup) multigrain flour
200 g/7 oz (1½ cups) rye flour
250 g/9 oz sheep's suet, chopped into
   1 cm/½ inch pieces
1 whole lamb's stomach, washed, cleaned
   and ready to use
salt, to taste

Mix the liver with the milk, then add the oats and multigrain flour and mix well. Add enough of the rye flour to produce a fairly stiff mix, then add the suet and salt to taste.

Fry a small piece of the stuffing mix in a pan, then taste and adjust the seasoning, if necessary, before proceeding.

Lay the stomach out on a cutting board and cut it straight across in 4 places. This will produce ring-like tubes of the intestine. Stitch each tube up at one end with cooking yarn and leave the other end open so that you can fill it.

Spoon the stuffing into the tubes, making sure there are no pockets of air. Stich the casings to seal. It is important that the tubes are not over-filled and that they are not too tight because the stuffing will swell a little when you cook it, which could make the skin burst. It is a good idea to prick each sausage a few times with a sharp needle to further insure against them bursting.

Bring plenty of salted water to boil in a pan. Put the sausages in the water, then lower the heat and simmer, covered, for 2–2½ hours, or until the sausages are firm to the touch and cooked through.

NORWEGIAN CURED SAUSAGES

Morrpølse | Mårpølse | Mørpölse | Morr | Mòr (Norway)

Originally *morrpølse* were made from offal (organ meats) and blood and they date back to the Viking times. In old recipes (and a few more current ones) the majority of the sausage is made up from liver, kidneys, lungs and blood.

Today, most of the commercially available *morrpølse* are made mainly with one of the following meats or a mix of these meats: mutton, beef, pork and game (for example, moose). Some brands use offal with muscle tissue (like hearts), and others a bit of blood.

The name itself can indicate which kind of meat has been used, for example, *svinemør*, in which

the Norwegian word for 'pig' is added before the name of the sausage itself.

Traditionally *morrpølse* were probably seasoned with caraway; today a multitude of spices and other seasonings are used, including garlic and sometimes even chilli pepper.

These sausages, which are cured for anything from a couple of weeks to many months, are sometimes served raw in 5 mm/¼ inch slices as a snack. Sometimes they are steamed, boiled or fried. If they are to be cooked and served as the main part of a meal, they need to be soaked in cold water overnight to make them less salty and a bit less dense in texture.

Morrpølse are not uncommonly served with Dried Rib of Lamb Steamed Over Birch Twigs (page 350). They are first soaked in water, then cut into pieces and added to the pot in which the meat is steaming for the last 10 minutes or so of cooking.

SWEDISH CHRISTMAS PORK SAUSAGES

Julkorv (Sweden)

These raw pork sausages are often served around Christmas time – or as part of the Swedish Christmas meal itself – with Mashed Potato (page 118) or Root Vegetable Mash (page 112) and some coarse-grain mustard.

You will need around 3 metres/10 feet beef casing, preferably runners, soaked and rinsed.

Preparation and cooking time: 1½ hours
Makes: about 1 kg/2¼ lb, enough for 4 as a
  meal or many as part of a bigger menu

For the sausages
1 kg/2¼ lb fatty minced (ground) pork
20 g/¾ oz salt
40 g/1½ oz (5½ tablespoons) potato
  starch
10 white peppercorns, ground
10 cloves, ground
10 allspice berries, ground

To cook
3 tablespoons salt
2 bay leaves

Combine all the sausage ingredients in a large bowl and mix together with your hands. Add around 500 ml/17 fl oz (2 cups plus 1 tablespoon) water, a little at a time, mixing it until you achieve a nice, loose and homogenous texture.

Tie off the runners to seal them at one end. Using the sausage-making attachment of your mincer, stuff the mixture into the runners. Fill them slowly and steadily, making sure there are no pockets of air. Don't fill them too tightly as they will expand during the cooking. Knot them at the open end then tie them into 15 cm/6 inch lengths.

Place the sausages in a large pot with the salt, bay leaves and 5 litres/10½ UK pints (20 cups) cold water. Bring to a bare simmer and cook until a core temperature of 68°C/155°F is reached. It is a good idea to prick each sausage a few times with a needle as they are poaching so that any trapped air can find a way out rather than bursting the casing open.

You can either cook them as a whole string of sausages and cut them apart after cooking or, tie them off with string in between every 2–3 sausages and cut them apart before cooking.

NORWEGIAN SOFT PORK SAUSAGE

Fleskepølse (Norway)

Fleskepølse is a very smooth and very fatty spreadable pork sausage that is used as a sandwich topping. It is another of those things that people really only buy in stores today; almost no one seems to make them at home. *Fleskepølse* is often seasoned with cloves and/or nutmeg. There is a smoked version of the sausage, but it is most commonly boiled; the industrial version most often in a plastic tube.

Some recipes have half of the lean pork meat substituted with veal or beef. So do try that if you feel like it.

You will need around 1 metre/3 feet beef casings, soaked and rinsed.

Preparation and cooking time: 1½ hours
Makes: 1 kg/2¼ lb

400 g/14 oz lean pork
300 g/11 oz fatty pork belly
300 g/11 oz lard
20 g/¾ oz salt
15 white peppercorns, finely ground
½ onion, grated on the fine side of
  a box grater
freshly grated nutmeg and/or ground cloves,
  to taste

Mix all the ingredients together, then pass 3 times through a meat mincer (grinder) on the finest setting.

Tie off the casings to seal them at one end. Using the sausage-making attachment of your mincer (grinder), stuff the mixture into the lengths of casings fairly tightly. Knot at the open end, then tie into 25 cm/10 inch lengths.

Place the sausages in a pan with salted water and gradually bring to a slow simmer. Poach until the sausages reach a core temperature of 68°C/155°F. Place the pan in the sink under cold running water until the sausages have completely cooled down.

Refrigerate and keep in the fridge for up to a week. If you want to keep it for longer, it freezes very well for up to 3 months.

FAROESE MEAT SAUSAGES

Kløtpylsa (Faroe Islands)

After an initial fermentation and brining, these sausages can be cooked and served warm or else they can be hung up to air-dry, similar to a central European salami.

Like the Swedish *spickekorv* these Faroese sausages are soaked in a very salty brine. It doesn't make the sausage itself saltier than if it had the salt added into the meat, but it leaves a layer of white crystalized salt on the exterior of the casing. This becomes more visible as it dries, if the sausages are allowed to age for a bit longer.

The sugar in this rather old-fashioned recipe is vital for a quick enough growth of the lactobacillus (page 190), so don't cut back or it might risk ruining the whole batch. Remember that the sugar will be consumed by bacteria, so it won't be there when the sausage is actually ready to eat. Even if it tastes a bit sweet in the beginning it won't when the sausage is done.

Most Faroese meat sausage is made from mutton but it can also contain beef.

You will need several metres/feet of beef middle casings, soaked and rinsed.

Fermentation and brining time: 11 days
Drying time (optional): another 10 days
Cooking time: 40 minutes
Serves: 4

1 quantity strong brine for charcuterie
   (page 434)

For the sausages
1 kg/2¼ lb meat (use mutton or beef) finely
   minced (ground)
250 g/9 oz suet, cut into small dice
4 tablespoons salt
3 tablespoons sugar
2 teaspoons ground allspice
2 teaspoons ground ginger
500 ml/17 fl oz (2 cups plus 1 tablespoon)
   Meat Stock (page 650), milk or water

Day 1: Combine all of the ingredients for the sausages in a large bowl and mix them together well. The more you work the mixture, the better the sausages will hold together later on.

Tie off the casings to seal them at one end. Using the sausage-making attachment of your mincer (grinder), stuff the mixture into the lengths of casings. Fill them slowly and steadily, making sure there are no pockets of air. Knot them at the open end, then tie them at suitable lengths.

Hang the sausages overnight in a warm spot. It should be at least 20°C/68°F for the lactobacillus fermentation to start.

Day 2: In the evening of the second day, place the sausages in a large container and cover with the brine. Weigh them down with a plate or something else clean and a bit heavy. Leave them somewhere cooler (10–15°C/50–60°F) to ferment for about 10 days. After the fermentation, the brine can have a sort of cheesy, yogurty kind of aroma to it – almost a bit animal-like. While it can smell quite strongly, it should not smell bad, as this would mean that something has gone wrong with the fermentation and the sausages should be discarded.

Day 12: Rinse the sausages very well under cold running water and pat them dry. At this stage the sausages are ready to be cooked and eaten warm, or else they can be dried to make a kind of charcuterie.

To cook the sausages, bring a large pan of water to a simmer, then cook them for 40 minutes.

To air-dry the sausages, wrap them in greaseproof paper and hang them in the same warm spot as for the initial overnight drying. Leave them for a further 10 days or so before eating.

SMALL SMOKED PORK SAUSAGES / PRINCE SAUSAGES

Prinskorvar / Prinskorv (Sweden)

These little 'prince' sausages are very popular at Swedish festive meals, like Christmas or Easter dinner, but also for an everyday lunch with, for example, Boiled Potatoes (page 117) and Creamed Spinach (page 87). They are always fried before eating and sometimes also served as a side dish with Poached or Boiled Eggs (page 53), or with Spinach Soup (page 88) or Kale Soup (page 92).

If you cut a cross in both ends of the sausages, when you fry them the ends will curl up and look a bit like a pig. This is often done for Christmas dinner.

As this is an emulsion sausage it is crucial that all of the ingredients and tools used are as close to 0°C/32°F as possible when starting.

If you want to substitute nitrates for salt, do so according to the instructions for your particular brand. You will need 5 metres/16½ feet of sheep casings, soaked and rinsed.

Preparation and cooking time: 2 hours
Makes: 100 sausages

625 g/1 lb 6 oz minced (ground) beef
625 g/1 lb 6 oz minced (ground) pork
313 g/11¼ oz minced (ground) back fat
250 ml/8 fl oz (1 cup) cream
60 g/2¼ oz salt
1 onion, finely chopped
1 g/0.03 oz nutmeg, grated
1 small clove of garlic, grated fine
10 white peppercorns, ground
4 g/⅛ oz mustard powder
40 g potato starch

Place all of the ingredients together in the bowl of a powerful foodprocessor. Add 685 ml/23 fl oz (2¾ cups) very cold water and blitz until fully combined. It will take 3–4 minutes.

Using the sausage stuffing attachement on your mincer (grinder) fill the whole length of casing in one go. Tie one end off and leave one open. Create little sausages, starting at the sealed end sim-ply by pinching the stuffed casing between your thumb and index finger about 5 cm/¼ inch from the end knot. Twist the small sausage you have just created 2 turns so that the casing spins and seals the meat in. Repeat until you reach the end of the casing and twist in a different direction for each step towards the end you take, one towards you and the next away form you, otherwise they-sausages will easily unwind.

To braid the prince sausages and fix them before proceeding to cook, do the following. Hold the first sausage in your hand and fold the second sausage so that they rest side by side. Holding the first end knot of the casing against the link between the second and the third sausage, twist the first and the second sausage together twice, then fold the third sausage against the first twoso that it rests parallel with them. Make sure that the link between the third and the fourth sausage rests on top of the link between the first and the second one, then push the third one in between the first and the second 1 to fix the ends of all 3. This will keep the first 3 sausages together in a bunch. Proceed in the same way until you have braided the whole casing into 1 long braid, each step of it containing 3 sausages in a bunch. It is a lot more difficult than it sounds – you can always tie them off with string, even if it isn't quite right.

Proceed by hot smoking (page 416) the sausages at 100°C/210°F for 30–40 minutes or until they have a core temperature of about 70°C/160°F.

Leave to cool down and then refrigerate or freeze if you want to keep them for a long time.

Clockwise from top left: Danish Sausage and Potato Casserole (page 430); Falu Sausage Gratin (page 418); Falu Sausage Stroganoff (page 418); Cold-smoked, Fermented Barley Sausages (page 419)

DANISH SAUSAGE AND POTATO CASSEROLE

Svensk pølseret (Denmark)

This creamy Danish potato and sausage casserole is a pinkish colour from the tomato and paprika. Bizarrely, it is named *Svensk pølseret* – 'Swedish sausage dish' – although, as far as I am aware, it does not exist in Sweden. The sausage part does, though, have a resemblance to Swedish Falu Sausage Stroganoff (page 418). It is claimed that Danish kids were served this dish at a summer camp somewhere in Sweden and brought the recipe back home with them.

Preparation and cooking time: 30 minutes
Serves: 4

25 g/1 oz (2 tablespoons) butter
1 onion, finely chopped
500 g/1 lb 2 oz mildly smoked sausages (like hot dogs), sliced
3 teaspoons ground paprika
3 tablespoons concentrated tomato purée (paste)
200 ml/7 fl oz (¾ cup plus 1 tablespoon) cream
800 g/1¾ lb cold boiled potatoes, peeled and cut into 1 cm/½ inch slices
salt and white pepper, to taste
snipped chives, to garnish (optional)

Melt the butter in a pan over a medium heat. Add the onions, and fry until soft and sweet, but without colour. Add the sausages and paprika and cook for a minute or two. Add the remaining ingredients and simmer gently until the potatoes have warmed through and the cream has thickened slightly. Adjust the seasoning before serving, but don't stir too much or you risk breaking up the potatoes.

For image see page 429

MEDISTER PORK SAUSAGES

Medisterpølse (Norway)
Medisterpølse (Denmark)
Fläskkorv (Sweden)

These sausages, whose name comes from the German word *met* for 'pork' and the Swedish word *ister* for 'lard', have been prepared at least since the sixteenth century. The recipe has evolved quite a bit since then. In Sweden *medister* sausages are hardly ever seen any more and if so are rather like a smoked sausage – a bit like *Falu* Sausages (page 416), but made solely with pork. In Norway and Denmark *medister* sausages have remained truer to their historical roots and they are also more popular. In both countries *medisterpølse* is understood to be a coarsely-ground raw pork sausage which may be poached, roasted or fried before serving. It is commonly seasoned with allspice, cloves and black pepper. Some Danish recipes occasionally include marjoram, sage and mace.

In Norway *medister* sausages are often served with the *Juleribbe* (page 300) as part of the Christmas meal. In Denmark they are usually fried and served with Boiled Potatoes (page 117), and some boiled vegetables and mustard on the side.

You will need around 2 metres/6½ feet pork casings, soaked and rinsed.

Preparation and cooking time: 1 hour
Makes: 1 kg/2¼ lb

1 kg/2¼ lb fatty minced (ground) pork
4 teaspoons potato starch
10 allspice berries
8 cloves
10 black peppercorns
marjoram, sage and mace, to taste (optional)
20 g/¾ oz (1 tablespoon) salt
400 ml/14 fl oz (1⅔ cups) milk
butter, for frying

Start by mixing the pork with all the dry ingredients (including salt, which is important for the texture), by hand or in a standmixer. Work the paste for a while, until it becomes firm and homogenous. Add the milk, little by little, until you achieve a good texture. It should be fairly loose and very sticky. To check the flavour (it should be well seasoned), make a small patty and fry. Taste and adjust the balance if necessary.

Tie off the casings to seal them at one end. Using the sausage-making attachment of your mincer (grinder), stuff the mixture into the casings. Fill them slowly and steadily, making sure there are no pockets of air. Knot them at the open end, then tie them at suitable lengths.

Roll the sausages into coils and cook immediately or refrigerate for cooking later (but no later than the following day). To cook, poach the sausages in simmering salted water for about 20 minutes, or until cooked through. Alternatively, you can fry them in butter over a medium heat for about 20 minutes, until they are browned all over and cooked through.

For image see page 349

VOSSA SAUSAGES

Vossakorv (Norway)

These coarse, smoked and fairly well-seasoned sausages are often served as a part of the *Pinnek-jøtt* meal (page 350) or on their own with Root Vegetable Mash (page 112) and/or Boiled Potatoes (page 117). They can also be sliced cold and used as a sandwich topping.

When serving, fry the sausages in a little butter until golden on all sides and warm all the way through.

You will need 4 metres/13 feet beef runners – or use pork casings if you want to eat the skins as well.

Preparation and cooking time: 4 hours
Maturing time: 24 hours
Makes: 3 kg/6 lb 6 oz

2.5 kg/5½ lb mutton (preferably neck
  or shoulder), coarsely chopped
500 g/1 lb 2 oz belly or fatty shoulder
  of pork, coarsely chopped

150 g/5 oz (¾ cup) potato starch
75 g/2¾ oz (¼ cup plus ½ tablespoon) salt
50 g/2 oz (¼ cup) sugar
1½ teaspoons ground ginger
2 teaspoons white peppercorns, ground
1 teaspoon freshly grated nutmeg
800 ml/28 fl oz (3¼ cups) Meat Stock
  (page 650)

Combine the mutton and pork in a mixing bowl, then pass through a meat mincer (grinder) on the coarsest setting. Mix in the potato starch, salt, pepper, sugar and spices and refrigerate for at least 12 hours.

Transfer to the bowl of a stand mixer and start working at low speed. With the motor running, add the stock (broth), little by little, and work for at least 10 minutes. The resulting sausage mixture should be quite loose in texture.

Tie off the runners or casings to seal them at one end. Using the sausage-making attachment of your mincer, stuff the mixture into the lengths of casings fairly tightly. Knot at the open end then tie into 20 cm/8 inch lengths.

Hang the sausages somewhere warm (around 20°C/70°F) for 24 hours.

Follow the instructions on page 416 for hot-smoking the sausages at 100°C/212°F for 3–4 hours. The sausages are ready when they reach a core temperature of around 68°C/155°F.

Leave the sausages to cool completely before storing

PRESSED HEADCHEESE

Hodesylte (Norway)
Painesyltty (Finland)
Sylte (Denmark)
Pressylta (Sweden)

Different cold cuts, made by pressing cooked brined meats, are common all over Scandinavia and exactly what's in them will differ from country to country and region to region. Most commonly some amount of pork with skin on is used, as this will give the cooking liquid the required amount of gelatine for everything to stick together nicely. For a firmer headcheese, you can always add some gelatine leaves. Mostly I find this superfluous. Most of the headcheese you will find is, in fact, not made from head but rather from shoulder of pork, which works just as fine. It's a pity though, as the origin of headcheese was to make something enjoyable out of a portion of the animal that was otherwise difficult to use. A shoulder can be used to make so many things, whereas the dishes for which a head is suitable are quite few.

If you brine your pig's head yourself (page 434) make sure to shave any bristles off with a disposable razor or singe them off with a blowtorch before placing it into the brine. If you buy it ready brined, make sure that the butcher has done a satisfactory job de-hairing it for you.

Preparation and cooking time: 3 hours
Sitting time: overnight
Makes: about 2 kg/4½ lb

1 large pig's head, split in two, brined,
  rinsed and clean
10 allspice berries
10 white peppercorns
10 cloves
2 bay leaves
10 black peppercorns
1 piece dried ginger
3 large carrots, cut into pieces
3 onions, cut into quarters
10 soaked gelatine leaves (optional)

Place the 2 halves of pig's head in a large pot and add everything else apart from the gelatine. Add enough water to just cover the contents of the pot and then bring everything to the boil. Skim

and continue simmering the pig's head for about 2 hours or until done. It should be just coming off the bone but not more. If you overcook the meat so that it becomes overly tender the head won't slice nicely in the end.

Remove the head from the pot and place the parts on a large tray. Reserve the cooking liquid. Take a clean dish cloth, rinse it with water and line the interior of a large bowl with it. With a fish slice (spatula) and your hands, remove layers of skin and fat from the pig's head and place in the bowl. Cover the sides and bottom of it in one layer of skin and fat, about 2 cm/¾ inch thick. Continue to lift pieces of meat from the head halves and place them at the bottom of the bowl to create a layer of meat about 3 cm/1¼ inch in thickness. Place another layer of fat and skin on top of the meat and continue layering like this until all the meat and fat is taken off the head. If you are using gelatine, place 2 sheets between each layer of meat and fat.

When all of the meat and fat is laid down into the bowl, fold the edges of the dish cloth over the top to close it into a sort of 'bag', then seal it tightly with string.

Strain the reserved cooking liquid into a new large pot and place the cloth containing the meat and fat in the pot with the liquid. Bring everything to the boil and maintain the boil for a couple of minutes. Remove the cloth 'bag' from the liquid and place it between two flat objects like chopping (cutting) boards. Place something heavy on top of the second chopping board and refrigerate at least overnight before unwrapping and slicing.

SPICED MEAT ROLL

Rullupylsa (Faroe Islands)
Rullupylsa (Iceland)
Rullepølse (Norway)
Rullasyltty / Kääresyltty (Finland)
Rullepølse (Denmark)
Rullsylta (Sweden)

There are many different versions of cooked, rolled meats served as charcuterie in the Nordic region. They are all made in roughly the same way, but the choice of meat and the seasonings used can vary quite a bit. As with most traditional recipes with a long history, this dish was created when there was little choice of ingredients. People developed their recipes around what was there, rather than trying to procure what they thought they needed but which wasn't there.

In the south of Sweden and Denmark, with their rich agricultural history, this kind of charcuterie product is commonly made from pork, in Iceland or the Faroe Islands almost always mutton and in Norway, a bit of both. There is some variation – you will find lamb recipes in Denmark, beef ones in Sweden and so forth – but as an overall principle, whichever meat was historically prevalent in any region has also shaped the historical repertoire of charcuterie.

These spiced meat rolls are often seasoned themselves, or else they are boiled in a broth that is seasoned with spices like pepper, allspice, bay leaves and cloves.

In Denmark, the Faroe Islands and Iceland, after rolling, the meat is often placed in a specific kind of wooden press, creating a flattened, almost square roll.

The recipe below is for a basic pork roll. You can use almost any cut of any animal, as long as it is suitable for braising and can be cut in such a way that a fairly large and even rectangle can be created to roll up into a log.

The only consequence of using a meat other than pork is that the cooking juices won't jellify into aspic. This isn't essential, but if you want them to and you are using, for example, a shoulder of lamb, add 10 soaked gelatine leaves to each litre/34 fl oz (4¼ cups) of cooking liquid used.

If you are using meat that has not been pre-brined, measure out 2% salt to the weight of the meat itself, and season the meat with it. If you are doing this, after rolling up and tying the meat, and before you cook it, you need to wrap it tightly in clingfilm (plastic wrap) and refrigerate it for about three days so that the salt can properly penetrate the meat.

Preparation and cooking time: 2 hours
Resting time: at least 24 hours
Makes: 2 kg/4½ lb

2 kg/4½ lb pork belly, skin on
1 onion, finely chopped
10 black peppercorns, crushed
10 allspice berries, crushed

Place the meat, skin side up, on a chopping (cutting) board and slice it horizontally through the centre. Start from the side closest to you, slicing away. Don't cut all the way through to the other edge, but stop around 2 cm/¾ inch from that edge to create a sort of hinge. Fold the upper half (with the skin) away from you, forming a rectangle that is twice as long and half as thick. Trim the edges so that they are as straight as possible, which will make the rolling up easier.

Season the surface of the meat evenly with the onion and spices, then roll it up tightly, a bit like a Swiss roll, starting with the edge closest to you. At the halfway mark you will reach the skin-on part of meat and you will know that you are on the last lap. Keep rolling and, once the skin wraps around the log completely, cut away any excess so that the skin doesn't overlap anywhere. Secure the roll tightly with string.

Place the meat roll in a large pan, cover it with water and bring to a slow simmer. Cook gently for about 2 hours, or until the core temperature reaches 70°C/160°F.

Remove the meat roll from the pan and place it on a large sheet of muslin (cheesecloth) or on a clean dish cloth. Roll it up tightly in the cloth and secure it with string on the outside. This ensures a very nice, tight round shape. Return the meat to the cooking liquid and leave it to cool. Refrigerate for at least 24 hours.

Alternatively, if you like the Danish/Icelandic/Faroese method, then after cooking the meat, instead of wrapping it in cloth, transfer it while warm to a suitable press to create the special squared off and flattened shape. Refrigerate for at least 24 hours.

VEAL HEADCHEESE

Kalvsylta (Sweden)

Eat on a piece of Rye Crispbread (page 516) with some pickles, as part of a buffet dinner or as a meal with Boiled Potatoes (page 117) and Pickled Beetroot (page 660) or Brined Cucumbers (page 660).

You will need 2 23 x 13 x 8 cm/9 x 5 x 3 inch loaf pan.

Preparation and cooking time: 5 hours, plus
  cooling time
Setting time: overnight
Makes: 2 loaf pans of headcheese

2 kg/4½ lb veal shanks
2 kg/4½ lb veal neck or 1 calf's head
4 carrots, coarsely chopped
2 onions, quartered
4 celery stalks, coarsely chopped
2 tablespoons white peppercorns
2 tablespoons allspice berries
2 bay leaves
salt, to taste

Place all the ingredients, except for the salt, in a large pot and cover with water. Bring to a slow simmer, then cook until the meat falls off the bone. You might have to add more water from time to time.

Remove the meat from the pot and transfer it to a tray. Strain the broth and discard the solids. Return it to the cleaned-out pot and simmer until reduced to 1 litre/34 fl oz (4¼ cups).

Remove the meat and skin from the bones and push it through a meat mincer (grinder) on a coarse setting. Mix the minced (ground) meat into the broth and bring to the boil. Season with salt, to taste. Remember that when it is warm it will seem saltier than when it is eaten cold, so don't be shy on the salt.

Pour the mixture into the loaf pans or terrine moulds. Once cool, transfer to the refrigerator and leave overnight to set.

BRINING MEAT

We brine meat (soak it in a salt solution) mainly for two reasons, one is that it makes the meat more moist after being cooked and the other one is that the increased level of salt helps preserve it from spoilage.

When meat is placed in brine, because the brine has a higher concentration of salt than the meat, salt ions start migrating from the brine into the cells of the meat to equalize the levels. These salt ions denature some of the meat proteins, causing them to unwind and collapse. As a result, the cells draw in and retain more water. And when the meat is cooked, the heated proteins then tighten, trapping some of the water in and making the meat juicier.

A general principle of preserving foods is that the more water you remove from a product the more stable it becomes from a microbiological standpoint. In this case, it would seem contradictory that brined meat keeps longer than fresh, since a lot of water is absorbed into it in the process. However, since the water in the cells contains quite a bit of salt, it is unavailable for microbes to use.

In brining there can also be other factors contributing to longer shelf life as much as to a change in the products original flavour profile.

One very important process, especially for larger cuts of meat (like whole hams) that need to be brined for a long time, is that of lactobacillus fermentation. Fresh meat contains glucose, which provides food for bacteria (not just the benevolent ones). The lactobacillus won't mind the salinity of the brined meat and one can say that by salting food we give them an advantage over other, dangerous microbes. The lactobacillus consume the glucose so that no other bacteria will flourish and, at the same time, they produce lactic acid which lowers the pH level of the meat and the brine, making it even less likely for other microbes to thrive. Sometimes, when an even sourer result is desired, some sugar can be added to the brine, which encourages the lactobacillus to produce even more lactic acid.

There are many traditional ways of judging how long something should brine by looking at size, weight and the shape of the cut. The truth is that they are all kind of wrong because it is almost impossible to generalize how long it takes for the level of salinity to even out in a big cut of meat, since each piece is different. If you want to brine something just to make it juicier (like a chicken or turkey for roasting), then you really don't need to bother about calculations and I recommend that you just brine the poultry overnight.

However if you are brining for other reasons – as when you make charcuterie, for instance – when the salt has a preserving function as well as adding flavour and moisture, then it is good to be a little more careful. First you need to weigh the meat, make a note of the weight and then place it in a very clean container. Next, measure out the amount of water you need to completely cover the meat and weigh it as well. Add the two weights together (1ml water = 1g) and calculate 2% of the total. Weigh out this quantity of salt and place it in a pot. Add the water and bring to the boil. Leave this brine to cool completely and then pour it over the meat in the container.

If a piece of meat is not too big (like lamb tongues, for instance) or if it is big but not very thick (like a side of pork), it can be left just as it is. If the cut is larger or thicker, then it is a good idea to inject some of the brine directly into the meat as it makes for a more even result and shortens the brining time a little. Use some type of brine injector and make sure not to pump air into the meat, which will make it spoil. Now place a very clean weight of some sort on top of the meat to keep it submerged and place it in a refrigerator. Every few days take the container out and, wearing rubber gloves, stir around the meat, and massage it a bit to help the salt move around within the muscle tissue.

The exact time it takes for meat to brine properly is, as I mentioned earlier, very difficult to judge but the good thing with using the method above, as opposed to a fixed recipe for brine that doesn't take into account the amount of meat, is that it can never become too salty. When it has brined all the way through, the level of salt in the brine will be the same as in the meat. As a very general guideline I would say smaller pieces should brine for a week, most other larger things will take about two weeks, and a whole ham will take three weeks.

For brining endeavours that are longer than one week the pH level of the brine needs to be lowered and I often add about 3% sugar to the brine when I boil it. After adding meat to a sugary brine I like to leave it out of the refrigerator for a good 24 hours to give the lactobacillus a head start. The lactobacillus is already present on the surface of the meat so there is no real need to add more. However there are specific strains of lactobacillus that you can buy online or from charcuterie suppliers, and these will give a better flavour, better colour and a much higher success rate in most cases.

If you want to add some form of nitrate, then do so when you boil the brine and follow the instructions on the particular product you are using. Nitrates give a more uniformly pink result and, more importantly, they protect your meat from the growth of *Clostridium botulinum*, a very nasty microbe that is fatally toxic even in very small doses. It is a good idea to use nitrates when making certain charcuterie products, especially those with quite high pH levels, cooked charcuterie, and charcuterie that you store in vacuum bags. However for brined meats that are used in warm food – such as a brined tongue that you are going to braise and eat straight away, or salt pork which is going to be fried crisp – the nitrates only affect the colour since the *Clostridium botulinum* toxins are sensitive to heat.

Once meat has been brined, it should be rinsed and then thoroughly scrubbed under plenty of cold running water. Check the meat all over; it should have a nice healthy-looking colour and should smell fresh. Sometimes the brine itself can smell a bit strange without it meaning that the meat has gone bad. Once the meat has been thoroughly rinsed and scrubbed then inspect it carefully. If it doesn't feel right, it probably isn't. Trust your instincts on this one and throw away any dodgy looking bits.

BRINED AND BOILED EYE OF ROUND AS CHARCUTERIE

Saltkød (Denmark)
Kokt saltrulle (Sweden)

This is quite a common sandwich topping in both Sweden and Denmark, featuring, for example, in Danish open-faced sandwich classics like *Dyrlægens natmad* (page 522). *Saltrulle* is generally speaking always cut in very thin slices, something it is well suited to because of its dense texture.

In this recipe the beef should be boiled until is cooked through and firm, not braised until tender.

Preparation and cooking time: 1½ hours,
  plus cooling time
Marinating time: overnight
Makes: enough for many sandwiches

1 x 1.5–3 g/3¾– 6 lb 6 oz whole eye of
  round, brined (page 434)
2 carrots, peeled, and cut into pieces
2 onions, cut into wedges
2 celery stalks, cut into pieces
1 bay leaf
few sprigs thyme
10 cloves
1 good chunk ginger, sliced
10 black peppercorns

Rinse the brined meat very well.

Place the meat in a pot big enough to fit it and the vegetables. Cover with water and bring to a boil. Reduce the temperature to a simmer and cook until done. It should take about 1 hour in total. Add the vegetables and aromatics when about 30 minutes remain of the cooking time. The beef should be boiled until it reaches about 60°C/140°F in the centre and then left to cool down in its cooking liquid in the pot. As it cools, the pot should sit where the air can circulate under it, i.e. not directly on the work counter. After turning off the heat, the temperature in the meat will continue to rise for a bit longer before it finally starts to drop, along with the cooling cooking liquid.

Once it has cooled, store in the refrigerator overnight before removing the meat from the cooking liquid. To serve, slice the beef very thinly.

HAM BROTH FOR DIPPING BREAD

Dopp i grytan (Sweden)

In traditional recipes, this was made from a mixture of meat juices from dishes prepared as part of the Swedish Christmas dinner. Today, the only charcuterie that most people actually do prepare in their homes is their Ham (page 438), so that's the stock (broth) most commonly used. The danger with using ham stock alone is that it can be a bit salty, since the ham is cured before being cooked. I like to add some other meat stock, if I have some, and I am not picky about it being only from pork, which is traditional.

Dopp i grytan meaning 'dip in the pot', is usually served as part of the Swedish Christmas meal (*Julbord*), and the idea is that you take pieces of Wort Loaf (page 498) – lightly sweet and spicy – and dip them into the warm salty broth before you eat them.

Preparation and cooking time: 20 minutes

cooking liquid from Boiled Ham (see
  opposite) or other charcuterie
pieces fresh ginger
allspice berries
black peppercorns
1 bay leaf

Pour the cooking stock (broth) into a large pot and bring it to the boil. Cook until reduced to the desired intensity and saltiness, skimming away excess fat from time to time. Add the aromatics of your choice and leave to infuse for a little while before straining and serving hot.

BRINED HAM

Rimmad skinka (Sweden)

This ham is usually cured and baked, boiled or smoked, then served cold as a sandwich topping. In many Nordic homes, especially Swedish ones, a ham is often prepared as part of the traditional Christmas dinner (*Julskinka*).

If you want to brine your own ham, follow the instructions for brining meat on page 434.

Before continuing with any of the recipes below, rinse the brined ham thoroughly under running water and then place in a bowl and soak in cold water for at least 1 hour, changing the water a few times, before cooking it.

Cooking times for brined ham:

2–4 kg/4–8½ lb = 2–3 hours
4–6 kg/8½–13 lb = 3–4 hours
6–8 kg/13–17½ lb = 4–5 hours

BOILED HAM

Kokt skinke (Norway)
Keittokinkku (Finland)
Kogt skinke (Denmark)
Kokt skinka (Sweden)

I like to pour a couple of bottles of beer into the cooking liquid, but this is probably more because it smells really good when it heats up than because the beer actually flavours the ham.

1 x brined ham, rinsed and soaked
2 onions, quartered
4 cloves
½ tablespoon white peppercorns
2–3 bay leaves
2 x 330 ml/12 fl oz bottles beer (optional)

Place the rinsed ham in a pot that is just large enough to fit it snugly. Stud the onions with the cloves and add them to the pot with the peppercorns, bay leaves and beer, if using. Add enough water to cover and bring to a slow boil over a medium heat.

Make sure the ham is always covered with liquid and skim from time to time. I tend to use a cartouche to cover the ham, rather than using too much water, which can dilute its flavour.

Follow the cooking times above, depending on the weight of the ham, or until the centre reaches 60°C/149°F on a probe thermometer. Transfer

the ham to a wire rack and leave to cool. Otherwise you can leave the ham to cool in the cooking liquid; take the pot off the heat and add 500 g/1 lb 2 oz ice to the pot to stop the cooking.

When the ham has cooled down completely, use a sharp knife to remove the rind.

If you are making Christmas Ham, follow the instructions on page 438 and reserve the salty ham cooking liquid for Ham Broth for Dipping Bread (see opposite).

BAKED HAM

Bakt skinke (Norway)
Uunikinkku (Finland)
Ovnstegt skinke (Denmark)
Ugnsbakad skinka (Sweden)

A lot of old recipes tell you to bake ham to a much higher core temperature than I have done here, and sometimes a lower oven setting, which will almost guarantee a poorly textured, dry and mealy ham. If you take the ham out of the oven and leave the thermometer for an hour you will see how much the temperature continues to climb, even when it is no longer in the oven.

1 x brined ham (see opposite), rinsed and
  soaked

Preheat the oven to 150°C/300°F/Gas Mark 2.

Pat the rinsed ham dry, wrap it in aluminium foil and place in a roasting pan. If you pour some water into the pan and refill it from time to time during the baking process, it will be a lot easier to clean the pan afterwards.

Follow the cooking times on the oppsite page, depending on the weight of the ham, or until the centre reaches 60°C/149°F on a probe thermometer. Remove from the oven and leave to cool down completely, then use a sharp knife to remove the rind. If you are making Christmas Ham, continue as described on page 438.

HOT-SMOKED HAM

Savukinkku / Palvikinkku (Finland)
Varmrøget skinke (Denmark)
Rökt skinka (Sweden)

One of the most common and delicious sandwich toppings is smoked ham. A key point to remember about producing great smoked ham is that it can't be as hot in the smoker as it would be in an ordinary oven, because then there won't be enough time for the meat to absorb the smoke. On the other hand, it can't be too cold either, because the longer the ham takes to reach the desired core temperature and level of smokiness, the longer it remains microbiologically active, which changes the pH level of the meat.

Another key factor is that many of the enzymes in ham (which break down proteins), become hyper-efficient at elevated, but not hot, temperatures. This means that the texture will become mealy if the ham takes too long to climb past the temperatures where the enzymes work the fastest – typically up to 45°C/113°F. To get a perfectly textured, juicy, firm and smoky tasting ham takes a lot of practice.

I prefer ham that is smoked over alder wood, which I think gives a nice clean smoke that is not too heavy and creates a great dark-amber colour.

Aim for a temperature in the smoker of about 120°C/234°F and a cooking time of no more than 10 hours. Core temperature is likely to be good at 65°C/150°F, considering the lower temperature in the smoker as opposed to the oven.

SWEDISH CHRISTMAS HAM

Juleskinke (Norway)
Joulukinkku (Finland)
Julskinka (Sweden)

Each year, on the 23rd December, myself and many other Swedes will cook their ham either in the oven or by boiling it. Then we will bread it, roast it a bit more in the oven, and finally, with great anticipation, we cut the first slice of succu-lent pink perfection and sample the pièce de ré-sistance of the traditional Christmas dinner.

In the north of Sweden, we eat our *julskinka* on soft flatbread, and in the south on Wort Loaf (page 498). Most people will spread it with mustard, some with Apple Compote (page 700) and a very few, like my mum, with Sugared Lingonberries (page 692).

The ham sits there all through Christmas, and at every meal it gets sliced down, layer after layer. In most homes, including mine, just before New Year's Eve, the motivation to eat a lot of ham drastically declines and the ham just sits there. Some years, as a token of consumer guilt, I might cut some of it down and make a Christmas ham 'carbonara'; other years, come St Knut's Day, Krut my dog gets his fill of ham.

Preparation and cooking time: 10 minutes
Serves: 4

1 brined ham, cooked (boil or bake it, as
  you prefer)
1 egg
3 tablespoons string mustard
3 tablespoons breadcrumbs

Preheat the oven to 220°C/425°F/Gas Mark 7.

Carefully slice away the skin from the ham, but leave an even layer of fat.

Whisk the egg and the mustard together and spread the mixture all over the ham. Sprinkle it with an even layer of breadcrumbs and bake in the oven until nicely coloured.

BOILED HAM HOCK

Fläsklägg (Sweden)

Often served with Root Vegetable Mash (page 112), cooked in the briny broth from the braising of the hock itself, or Mashed Potatoes (page 118). A good dollop of coarse-grain mustard and some Brined Cucumbers (page 660) are never wrong as condiments.

Preparation and cooking time: 3–4 hours
Serves: 4, with some to spare for lunch the next day

1 x 2-kg/4½-lb brined ham hock, trimmed
   and rinsed (page 434)
1 bay leaf
1 sprig thyme
1 onion, cut into wedges
10 white peppercorns
8 allspice berries

Leave the ham hock whole, or use a band saw to cut it through the bone into pieces that easily fit in your pot.

Place the meat and the aromatics in a large pot and cover with cold water. Bring to a slow simmer, then cook until the meat is tender. Skim the stock (broth) from time to time.

To test if the meat is done, pierce it with a paring knife and lift it straight up. If the meat releases the knife straight away it is done, if it doesn't fall from the knife, then cook it for a bit longer.

Once the meat is cooked, strain and reserve the stock. Use it for making the mashed root vegetables, otherwise, it is always good to have in the freezer.

CURED AND BRAISED HAM HOCK

Rimmat fläsklägg (Sweden)

Ham hock prepared in this way is often served with Root Vegetable Mash (page 112), prepared from vegetables boiled in the juices of the hock.

Serve it with some strong mustard on the side.

Preparation and cooking time: 3 hours
Serves: 4

1 x 1-kg/2¼-lb brined ham hock, trimmed
   and rinsed (page 434)
2 bay leaves
10 allspice berries
10 cloves

10 white peppercorns
1 piece dried ginger

Place the meat and the aromatics in a large pot and cover with cold water. Bring to the boil, skim, then lower to a simmer and cook for about 2 hours, or until the meat is tender enough to pull off the bone.

When the meat is ready, lift the hock into another pot and cover. Set over a very low heat to keep warm while you make the root vegetable mash.

Strain the broth and use for making the mash. Serve the meat on a platter in the middle of the table, with the mash in a bowl alongside, so that everyone can share.

NORWEGIAN CURED HAM

Spekeskinke (Norway)

In Norway, meat has been cured for more than one thousand years. *Spekeskinke* is much like other Norwegian *speke* products (see *Fenalår,* page 348), dry-salted and then hung to mature. A ham will salt for up to 8 weeks and mature for at least a year before being served, much like a ham would be served in central Europe, as charcuterie.

Historically, when salting meat was all about protecting it from spoilage and the aging and drying was just part of a storage process, ham like this was more likely reconstituted in water and cooked much like other meats, rather than being eaten raw in thin slices.

LIVER PÂTÉ

Leverpostei (Norway)
Maksapasteija (Finland)
Leverpostej (Denmark)
Leverpastej (Sweden)

Liver pâté of different kinds are very commonly served in the Nordic countries and even though they are quite similar in many ways, seasonings do vary. In Denmark, where liver pâté is a very important part of traditional open-faced sandwiches, it is often flavoured with a little allspice and nutmeg and the pâté is baked in a loaf pan lined with slices of bacon. In Sweden, almost every recipe contains marjoram and some also include the pickling juice from Sprats Cured in Sandalwood (page 212). The sprat juice is also found in the occasional Norwegian recipe but not, as far I have seen, in a Danish one.

The recipe below has my preferred seasonings, but feel free to vary them as much as you want. If you choose to use some kind of nitrate, then reduce the salt according to the instructions on the packet.

You can use any kind of liver, they will all impart their characteristic flavour to the final dish. I have seen beef, calf, lamb, mutton, pig and even seal liver pâté in Greenland (see right).

Preparation and cooking time: 2 hours
Makes: about 2.2 kg/5 lb, or 2 loaf pans

long thin bacon slices, for lining the
 loaf pan (optional)
25 g/1 oz (2 tablespoons) butter
2 onions, finely chopped
1.5 kg/3¼ lb liver, from whatever animal
 you happen to have access to
500 g/1 lb 2 oz pork back fat or another
 firm pork fat, cut into pieces
10 eggs
50 ml/2 fl oz (3½ tablespoons) cream
150 g/5 oz (1¼ cups) plain (all-purpose)
 flour, sifted
3 tablespoons salt
2 tablespoons dried marjoram
generous amount freshly ground
 black pepper
1 dash Cognac

Preheat the oven to 175°C/345°F/Gas Mark 4. Line 2 loaf pans with baking (parchment) paper or bacon slices, if using.

Heat a frying pan over a medium heat, then add the butter and the onions. Fry until the onions are soft, but not coloured. Tip into the bowl of a stand mixer and leave to cool.

Pass the liver and back fat through a meat mincer (grinder) on the finest plate. Add to the onions, together with all the remaining ingredients, and mix everything together very well.

Divide the mixture between the prepared loaf pans. Bake until the core temperature reaches 70°C/160°F. The pâtés should be really nice and brown on top.

Cool down, cover and refrigerate.

ANNSO'S SEAL LIVER PÂTÉ

Annso's grove sælleverpostej (Greenland)

This recipe is a truly excellent example of Danish influence having mingled with the deeply rooted food culture of Greenland and the products available there. Seal (page 248) has always been the most important food for the Greenland Inuit population. Here it is crossed with a distinctly Danish recipe for liver pâté. This recipe was given to me by Anne Sofie Hardenberg, who helped me out with much of my queries on the food culture of Greenland.

Preparation and cooking time: 2 hours
Makes: about 1.4 kg/3 lb or 1 loaf

1 kg/2¼ lb seal liver, any coarse
 veins or membranes removed
250 g/9 oz reindeer or lamb suet
2 onions, finely chopped
4 eggs
65 g/2½ oz rolled oats
5 teaspoons salt
1 teaspoon white pepper
20 juniper berries, crushed
550 ml/18 fl oz (2½ cups) milk or cream

Preheat the oven to 175°C/345°F/Gas Mark 4. Butter a 23 x 13 x 8 cm/9 x 5 x 3 inch loaf pan.

Pass the liver, suet and onion through a meat mincer (grinder) on the coarse plate. Place the minced (ground) mixture in a bowl and incorporate all the remaining ingredients. Work with a large wooden spoon for about 5 minutes until well mixed.

Pour the mixture into the prepared loaf pan and place it in turn in a roasting pan. Pour boiling water from a kettle into the roasting pan so that it reaches about three quarters of the way up the loaf pan.

Place everything in the oven and bake for about 1 hour or until the core temperature in the pâté is 70°C/158°F.

Cool down and refrigerate for up to a week.

GRAINS AND CEREALS

When I look at Nordic food culture of the last one hundred years and Scandinavian food culture for a lot longer than that, I see food cultures which have grains and dairy as their common denominators and whatever products we all consume besides them – whatever is available locally in all the different corners of this geographically vast region – as those components separating them culturally from each other.

For example, in every country and part of the region one or several versions of rye bread is produced. Exactly what it contains, how it is prepared and baked, and with what we serve it differs hugely. In Sweden and many parts of Finland the loaf would traditionally be baked on the residual heat from a big stone oven also used for baking many other things while it is hot, whilst on Iceland bread would have been, and still is for that matter, steamed in areas of geothermal activity simply by putting a container filled with dough in a cavity dug out straight into the hot ground.

In Denmark, its continental culture and rich agricultural history is reflected in a wide variety of sometimes very elaborate toppings for *smørrebrød*, the Danish open-faced sandwich, one of the country's most emblematic dishes.

At the same time, in Norway, you would be far more likely to find a simple sandwich with one single topping. Probably something dairy based, like Brown Cheese (page 72), a thick layer of salty butter or a chunk of aged cheese, reflecting that country's history and culture through the flavour preference of those living today.

Opposite: Krinalefse photographed on a bench covered in rag rugs just before I ate it with some coffee on the side, north Norway, late afternoon, May 2014.

THIN PANCAKES

Pannukakur (Faroe Islands)
Pannekake (Norway)
Lettuja/räiskäleitä (Finland)
Pandekage (Denmark)
Tunnpannkaka / Plättar (Sweden)

These thin, delicate and eggy pancakes are enjoyed in many parts of the Nordic region. They are served with a huge variety of toppings but the most common ones would be some kind of jam (page 690) or fruit compote (pages 700–1) and a dollop of cream. Or just a sprinkling of sugar.

Nordic pancakes are cooked quite thin and the batter is therefore very liquid. They contain more eggs than their Central European relatives and are therefore a bit more fragile to work with. The technique for cooking them is to have your pan quite hot and lightly buttered, then you pour in the amount of batter required and tilt the pan in all different directions until the batter has completely coated the bottom of the pan. Do not attempt to turn your pancakes over until they have cooked all the way through. If you have a good pan, you can easily flip them from the pan into the air, avoiding the use of tools, which can easily pierce them. If this fails, or if you don't want to sacrifice a few practise ones, just use a fish slice (spatula) to flip them.

Thin pancakes can be made in many different sizes, the most common being simply the diameter of a normal frying pan. There are also pans with up to 7 circular indentations producing very small pancakes, on average 8 cm/3¼ inches in diameter. In Sweden these small pancakes, especially suitable for dessert, are called *plättar*. This word can be a bit deceptive though because in Finland all pancakes cooked on the stove top will be referred to as *plättar* by Swedish-speaking Finns.

Preparation and cooking time: 30 minutes
Makes: 12–15 pancakes, depending on the size of the pan

150 g/5 oz (1¼ cups) weak (soft) wheat flour
2 tablespoons sugar
5 eggs
600 ml/20 fl oz (2½ cups) milk
good pinch of salt
melted butter, for frying

Mix all the ingredients in a bowl, mixing the milk in last, little by little, until you have a smooth batter and no lumps remain.

Heat a frying pan to just over a medium heat, butter it lightly and ladle some batter into it. Tilt the pan so that it coats the bottom of the pan evenly. Cook until the batter has set completely and the pancake has a nice golden colour, then flip it over with a fish slice (spatula) and cook the other side. Transfer the cooked pancake to a warm plate. Repeat with the rest of the batter, stacking the cooked pancakes as you go, so that they remain warm.

ICELANDIC OATMEAL PANCAKES

Lummur (Iceland)

These thick pancakes, often made with leftover oatmeal or pearl barley porridge, are served either with sugar or jam, or with savoury toppings, like cheese, lamb or trout smoked over sheep's dung (page 173).

The recipe below has the oats added straight to the batter; I guess that most people don't have cold oat porridge lying around much.

You can fry these pancakes in a heavy-bottomed frying pan or skillet, two or three at a time, or use a special pan for small pancakes called a *plättjärn*.

Preparation and cooking time: 30 minutes
Makes: 10 pancakes

150 g/5 oz (1¼ cups) weak (soft) wheat flour
75 g/2¾ oz (¾ cup plus 2 tablespoons) rolled oats
1 teaspoon baking powder
1 tablespoon sugar
250 ml/8 fl oz (1 cup) milk
1 egg
good pinch of salt
butter, for frying

Combine all of the ingredients for the batter in a mixing bowl and stir together, making sure no lumps remain.

Heat some butter in a frying pan, skillet or *plät-tjärn* over a medium heat. Spoon batter into the pan, until the bottom is almost covered. Fry over a medium heat until the underside is golden and the *lummur* is starting to set. Turn it over carefully and fry the other side until golden.

Remove the *lummur* from the pan and keep warm while you continue with the rest of the batter.

THICK OVEN-BAKED PANCAKE

Uunipannukakku (Finland)
Tjockpannkaka / Ugnspannkaka (Sweden)

My dad is the true master of *tjockpannkaka*. When he makes them, they are light, fluffy, bubbly and crisp – a bit like a fried Danish pastry.

Serve with jam (page 690), Sugared Lingonberries (page 692) and cream, or with a sprinkling of sugar.

Preparation and cooking time: 1 hour
Serves: 4

250 g/8 oz (2 cups plus 1 tablespoon) weak
  (soft) wheat flour
4 eggs
good pinch of salt
1 litre/34 fl oz (4¼ cups) milk
50 g/2 oz (3½ tablespoons) butter

Preheat the oven to 225°C/435°C/Gas Mark 7.

Combine the flour, eggs, salt and half the milk in a mixing bowl and whisk until no lumps remain. Add the rest of the milk, whisking continuously.

Put the butter into a 30 x 40 cm/12 x 16 inch roasting pan and heat in the oven until the butter has completely melted.

Pour the batter into the hot pan and bake for 25–30 minutes until it is dark golden and completely set.

Remove from the oven and leave to sit for 5 minutes, which will make it much easier to remove from the pan.

Serve with your preferred combination of accompaniments.

For image see page 453

THICK OVEN-BAKED SALT-PORK PANCAKE

Fläskpannkaka (Sweden)

Follow the recipe as described above, but add 300 g/11 oz salt pork, cut into sticks, to the roasting pan and bake in the oven for 5 minutes or so until starting to colour before you pour in the batter.

Serve with sugared lingonberries.

OVEN-BAKED SCANIAN EGG CAKE

Äggakaka (Sweden)

This is an eggy version of the Thick Oven-Baked Pancake (page 451). It is a traditional dish from the southern Swedish region of Skåne. Serve with Sugared Lingonberries (page 692) and slices of Fried Salt Pork (page 302).

To make this dish properly you need a frying pan that can go into the oven, preferably a cast-iron one.

Preparation and cooking time: 45 minutes
Serves: 4

400 g/14 oz Salt Pork Fried in the Pan
  (page 302)

For the batter
120 g/4 oz (1 cup) weak (soft) wheat flour
10 eggs
3 tablespoons sugar
good pinch of salt
650 ml/22 fl oz (2¾ cups) milk

Preheat the oven to 225°C/435°F/Gas Mark 7.

When you fry the pork, leave the cooking fat in the ovenproof frying pan or skillet to fry the egg cake in, just remove the pork itself and set aside.

To make the batter, combine the flour, eggs, sugar, salt and half the milk in a mixing bowl and whisk until no lumps remain. Add the rest of the milk, whisking continuously.

Heat the greased frying pan over a medium heat. Pour in the batter and fry until it starts to firm up a bit around the edges and is a good golden colour on the underside. Turn the egg cake over carefully, which will be difficult as it will be fragile and still runny inside. I recommend using a plate or a pot lid for support when doing the actual flip.

Transfer the pan to the oven and bake for 10 minutes. Arrange the pork on top of the egg cake and return to the oven for a final 5 minutes, which will help it crisp up a bit.

NORWEGIAN THICK SALT-PORK PANCAKES

Fleskepannekaker (Norway)

In Norway, a salt pork or bacon pancake can be made in various ways. It can be pan fried, as here, or it can be a thick oven-baked pancake, like the Swedish *fläskpannkaka* on page 451.

This version is often served with finely snipped chives, and sometimes a bit of *rømme*, or even grated cheese. I have also seen a recipe or two that suggest fried apple wedges as an accompaniment. The Swedish version of this dish is usually served with Sugared Lingonberries (page 692).

Preparation and cooking time: 35 minutes
Makes: 4–6 pancakes

100 g/3½ oz (¾ cup plus 1 tablespoon) weak
  (soft) wheat flour
5 eggs
good pinch of salt
550 ml/20 fl oz (2 cups plus 1 tablespoon)
  milk
butter, for frying
300 g/11 oz salt pork or bacon, sliced or cut
  into sticks

Combine the flour, eggs, salt and half the milk in a mixing bowl and whisk until no lumps remain. Add the rest of the milk, whisking continuously.

Heat a little butter in a frying pan or skillet and add a generous amount of the pork or bacon batons. Fry until they start to brown a little, then ladle in some batter. You are aiming to get 4–6 pancakes in total, so divide the pork and batter accordingly. Fry the pancake until the underside is golden, then turn and fry on the other side.

Keep warm while you fry the remaining pancakes and serve with your choice of accompaniments.

For image see opposite page

Clockwise from top left: Sugared Cloudberries (page 692); Norwegian Thick Salt-Pork Pancakes (page 452); Waffles (page 455); Thick Oven-baked Pancake (page 451); Blood Pancakes (page 392); Pancake Torte (page 603)

SUGARED PANCAKES LEAVENED WITH BAKING POWDER

Amerikanske pandekager (Denmark)
Krabbelurer / Pösplättar (Sweden)

These thick pancakes are a bit like something in between actual pancakes and sponge cake, a bit like an American pancake perhaps. They are turned in sugar after they are fried and either eaten straight away with jam (page 690) and some whipped cream, or left to cool down and eaten later like a pastry.

To get them nice and round, fry them in a small pancake iron known as a *plättjärn*. If you don't have a *plättjärn* pan, use an ordinary frying pan or skillet and live with them not being perfectly round but equally delicious.

Sometimes *krabbelurer* are flavoured with vanilla, and other times with lemon zest or cardamom. I tend to like them with vanilla, or else just as they are.

Preparation and cooking time: 30 minutes
Makes: 20 pancakes

1 egg
75 g/2¾ oz (⅓ cup) sugar
350 ml/12 fl oz (1½ cups) milk
good pinch of salt
vanilla, lemon zest or ground cardamom,
  to taste (optional)
150 g/5 oz (1¼ cups) weak (soft) wheat flour
1 teaspoon baking powder
butter, for frying

To serve
plenty of sugar
jam (page 690) or fruit compote
  (pages 700-1)
whipped cream

Whisk the egg and sugar together until pale and creamy. Add the milk, salt and flavouring, if using. Sift the flour and baking powder together into the bowl and mix in gently until just combined.

Melt a knob of butter in a frying pan, skillet or *plättjärn* pan. Add generous spoonfuls of batter to the pan, as neatly as you can. You will need to fry them in batches and don't overcrowd the pan. Fry over a medium heat until the undersides are golden and the *krabbelurer* are starting to set. Turn them over carefully and fry the other sides until golden. Continue with the rest of the batter.

Sprinkle a good layer of sugar on a plate. As the *krabbelurer* are cooked, turn them in the sugar. Eat them straight away, or transfer them to a wire rack to cool.

DANISH THICK CREAM PANCAKES

Flødepandekager (Denmark)

Enjoy piping hot, sprinkled with sugar and perhaps with some tart jam on the side.

Preparation and cooking time: 35 minutes
Makes: 20 small pancakes

300 ml/10½ fl oz (1¼ cups) cream
100 ml/3½ fl oz (⅓ cup plus 1 tablespoon)
  Danish *ymer*, cultured milk or yogurt
2 eggs
1 tablespoon sugar
220 g/7¾ oz (1¾ cups plus 1 tablespoon)
  weak (soft) wheat flour
good pinch of salt
melted butter, for frying

Whip the cream to stiff peaks, then fold in the cultured dairy product.

In a separate bowl, beat the eggs with the sugar, then add to the whipped cream. Sift the flour and salt together into the bowl and mix the batter gently until just combined.

Melt a knob of butter in a frying pan or skillet. Add generous spoonfuls of batter to the pan; you will need to fry them in batches and don't overcrowd the pan. Fry the *flødelapper* over a medium heat until the undersides are golden. They should puff up quite a bit and it isn't always easy to turn them. Once they are cooked on both sides, eat them hot from the pan, with sugar and jam.

WAFFLES

Waffles are served all over the Nordic region and each country has got a multitude of recipes. Some have eggs in them and others don't. In general terms a waffle with eggs will be less crisp and more rich than one without. Some versions are leavened with yeast or chemical leavening agents and others are not. If leavened with yeast or not at all, the recipe will produce a pancake-like texture and if leavened with chemical leavening agents, a shorter texture. Waffles are often served as lunch, a snack in the afternoon or as a dessert. In Norway, waffles can also be found with Brown Cheese (page 72) for breakfast. In the whole Nordic region, waffles are most commonly cooked in the classic Scandinavian waffle iron, which produces heart-shaped pieces (see illustration below).

180 g/6½ oz (1¼ cups) weak (soft) wheat flour
good pinch of salt
good pinch of sugar
300 ml/10½ fl oz (1¼ cups) cream
melted butter, for brushing

Pour 200 ml/7 fl oz (¾ cup plus 1 tablespoon) of water into a mixing bowl. Stir in the flour, salt and sugar to form a batter.

Whip the cream to soft peaks and fold it into the batter gently. It should be fully combined, but not overmixed.

Heat your waffle iron to proper working temperature and brush it very lightly with melted butter. Pour in a suitable amount of batter and cook until nice and golden. Repeat with the rest of the batter.

CRISP WAFFLES

Vohveleita (Finland)
Sprøde vafler (Denmark)
Frasvåfflor (Sweden)

My favourite kind of waffle, crisp and delicate in an almost unreal way. Enjoy them hot off the iron with whipped cream and jam (page 690).

Preparation and cooking time: 25 minutes
Makes: 10 waffles

EGG WAFFLES

Äggvåfflor (Sweden)

Waffles containing egg get a soft texture and taste a bit like good pancakes. Enjoy them hot off the iron with whipped cream and jam (page 690).

Preparation and cooking time: 25 minutes
Makes: 10 waffles

500 ml/17 fl oz (2 cups plus 1 tablespoon) milk
150 g/5 oz (1½ sticks) butter
2 eggs
good pinch of salt
250 g/9 oz (2 cups plus 1 tablespoon) weak
  (soft) wheat flour
melted butter, for brushing

Combine the milk and butter in a pan and heat until the butter has melted. Remove from the heat, tip into a mixing bowl, and leave to cool a bit.

Add the eggs and salt to the cooled milk mixture and mix in well. Sift over the flour and stir the batter until no lumps remain.

Heat your waffle iron to proper working temperature and brush it very lightly with melted butter. Pour in a suitable amount of batter and cook until nice and golden. Repeat with the rest of the batter.

NORWEGIAN WAFFLES

Vaffel (Norway)

Norwegian waffles almost always contain eggs and sometimes cardamom or vanilla sugar. They are generally served with jam and whipped cream or *rømme* or with Brown Cheese (page 72), or sometimes with savoury condiments like sausage and cured meats.

Preparation and cooking time: 40 minutes
Resting time: at least 1 hour
Makes: 10 waffles

250 g/9 oz (2 cups plus 1 tablespoon) plain
  (all-purpose) flour

5 tablespoons sugar
1 teaspoon baking powder
ground cardamom or vanilla sugar, to taste
pinch of salt
400 ml/14 fl oz (1⅔ cups) milk
5 eggs, lightly beaten
100 g/3½ oz (7 tablespoons) butter, melted
  and cooled, plus extra for brushing

Mix all of the dry ingredients in a bowl, including the cardamom or vanilla sugar and a pinch of salt. Pour in the milk, little by little, mixing all the time so that no lumps form.

Add the eggs and the melted butter, mix well and leave the batter to sit for at least an hour to swell.

Heat your waffle iron to proper working temperature and brush it very lightly with melted butter. Pour in a suitable amount of batter and cook until nice and golden. Continue with the remaining batter. Serve warm or cold.

FAROESE WAFFLES

Vaflur (Faroe Islands)

Faroese waffles are rich and sweet, and are mostly eaten for dessert or as a sweet snack between meals.

Preparation and cooking time: 30 minutes
Serves: 4

75 g/2½ oz (5 tablespoons) butter
150 g/5 oz (¾ cup) sugar
pinch of salt
3 eggs
275 g/9¾ oz (2¼ cups) plain (all-purpose)
  flour
2 teaspoons baking powder
1 teaspoon vanilla sugar
100 ml/3½ fl oz (⅓ cup plus 1 tablespoon)
  milk
melted butter, for brushing

Combine the butter, sugar and salt in a mixing bowl and beat together well. Beat in the eggs, one by one. Sift the flour, baking powder and vanilla sugar together into the mixture and beat well.

Pour in the milk, little by little, beating all the time so that no lumps form.

Heat your waffle iron to proper working temperature and brush it very lightly with melted butter. Pour in a suitable amount of batter and cook until nice and golden. Serve warm or cold.

ICELANDIC WAFFLES

Vöfflur (Iceland)

Icelandic waffles are usually rich egg waffles, often leavened, in traditional recipes with yeast and in more recent ones with baking powder. The batter is commonly flavoured with vanilla, ground cinnamon, cardamom or grated lemon zest.

In Iceland, waffles are eaten as a treat in the afternoon or sometimes as dessert, often with whipped cream and berries or jam. Waffles in Iceland are most often cooked in the Scandinavian-style waffle iron (see illustration, page 455), producing heart-shaped pieces of waffle.

Preparation and cooking time: 30 minutes
Makes: 8 waffles

2 eggs
250 ml/8 fl oz (1 cup) milk
400 g/14 oz (3½ cups plus 1 tablespoon)
  weak (soft) wheat flour
1 teaspoon baking powder
3 tablespoons sugar
salt, to taste
vanilla, ground cinnamon, cardamom or
  grated lemon zest, to taste (optional)
120 g/4 oz (8 tablespoons) butter, melted

Whisk the eggs and milk together in a large bowl. Sift the flour, baking powder, sugar and salt into the egg mixture and incorporate with the help of a whisk to avoid lumps forming. Add flavourings, if you are using any.

Heat your waffle iron to proper working temperature and brush it very lightly with melted butter. Pour the rest of the butter into the batter and mix in well. Pour a suitable amount of batter into the waffle iron and cook until nice and golden. Serve immediately.

SOUP DUMPLINGS

Mjølbollar til súpan (Faroe Islands)
Klot/Melbollar (Norway)
Melboller (Denmark)
Klimp (Sweden)

There are many types of soup dumplings in the Nordic region. They are either cooked in the soup itself or separately, in broth or water, to be added to the soup when serving it. Another way of making soup dumplings is where the batter is cooked into a very thick stew or sauce which is then left to cool, before being cut into cubes and added back into the soup just before serving. I prefer the ones that you cook in the soup.

Soup dumplings all over the Nordics can be served plain or seasoned with nutmeg. Soup dumplings in Norway and Sweden are sometimes a bit sweet and flavoured with cardamom, and in Sweden sometimes with grated bitter almond. On occasion I have also come across dumplings into which some grated mature cheese has been added – I quite like these.

Soup dumplings can go into pretty much any clear stock or broth based on soups like köttsoppa (page 326).

PRECOOKED SOUP DUMPLINGS

Preparation and cooking time: 15 minutes
Setting time: overnight
Serves: 4

50 g/2 oz (3½ tablespoons) butter
3 tablespoons plain (all-purpose) flour
500 ml/17 fl oz (2 cups plus 1 tablespoon)
   milk
sugar, to taste
freshly grated nutmeg, ground cardamom or
   grated bitter almond, to taste
50 g/2 oz (½ cup) grated mature cheese
   (optional)
2 egg yolks
salt and white pepper, to taste

Melt the butter in a saucepan over a medium heat. Add the flour, whisking constantly until no lumps remain. Add the milk, stirring constantly, and bring to a simmer. Simmer for at least 5 minutes and then season with salt, sugar and pepper and add your choice of flavourings. Finish by taking the pan off the heat and stirring in the egg yolks. Pour the batter into a shallow tray and leave it to cool down and set overnight.

When ready to use, cut the set dumpling batter into 2 cm/¾ inch cubes or simply just spoon it into your choice of soup as it is heating.

For image see opposite page

SOUP DUMPLINGS COOKED IN
BROTH OR SOUP

These dumplings are either cooked in the soup it-self, or separately, in broth or water, and then added to the soup when serving. I like them cooked in the soup itself because I think it is tastier, but you do run the risk of clouding the broth when you do it that way.

Preparation and cooking time: 20 minutes
Serves: 4

2 eggs
100 ml/3½ fl oz (⅓ cup plus 1 tablespoon) milk

250 g/9 oz (2¼ cups) plain (all-purpose) flour
sugar, to taste
freshly grated nutmeg, ground cardamom or
   grated bitter almond, to taste
50 g/2 oz (½ cup) grated mature cheese
   (optional)
2 litres/3 UK pints (8½ cups) broth (soup)
   (optional)
salt and white pepper, to taste

Combine all of the ingredients for the batter in a mixing bowl, including your choice of flavourings or grated cheese, if using. Stir everything together well until no lumps remain. The finished batter should be like very stiff pancake batter.

Pour the broth into a large pot (or just use salted water, if cooking the dumplings separately) and bring to the boil. Use 2 tablespoons to shape the batter into egg-shaped dumplings, dropping them carefully into the boiling liquid. Cook the dumplings for about 5 minutes, or until they are cooked all the way through (it will depend on their size). The dumplings will float to the surface when cooked all the way through.

Clockwise from top left: Soup Dumplings (page 458); Öland style Potato and Wheat Dumplings (page 460); Swedish Raw Potato Dumplings with bacon (page 463) and Sugared Lingonberries (page 692); Pitepalt Raw Potato and Wheat Dumplings (page 463); Norwegian Pancake Dumplings in Milk (page 461)

SMÅLAND-STYLE POTATO AND WHEAT DUMPLINGS

Småländska kroppkakor (Sweden)

These soft, tender dumplings come from the central Swedish region of Småland. They are made with a mixture of mashed potato and flour and are filled with salt pork (page 302). They are often served with butter – either melted or at room temperature – and some Sugared Lingonberries (page 692).

With these dumplings it is very important not to work the dough too much. If you do they will not have the desired tender consistency, but will be rather chewy.

Preparation and cooking time: 2 hours
Serves: 4

For the filling
250 g/8 oz salt pork, cut into small dice
1 onion, finely chopped
white pepper and allspice, to taste

For the dough
1 kg/2¼ lb floury potatoes, boiled, peeled, pushed through a ricer and cooled to room temperature
2 eggs, lightly beaten
200 g/7 oz (1⅔ cups) weak (soft) wheat flour, plus extra to dust
pinch of sugar
pinch of salt

Fry the salt pork in a frying pan or skillet over medium heat. Add the onion and sauté for a few minutes until it starts to soften. Season to taste with pepper and allspice, then remove from the heat and let cool to room temperature.

Put all the ingredients for the dough in a large bowl. Work with your hands until everything is fully combined, but don't overwork it. Transfer the dough to a floured work counter and divide it into 12–20 pieces, depending on what size dumplings you want. With lightly floured hands, shape each piece of dough into a ball and create a cavity. Don't make the cavity too small.

Divide the filling according to the number of dumplings. Fill each cavity about two thirds full,

then squeeze the edges of it tight to seal the dumplings completely. Roll them a bit more in your floured hand so that they become really round.

Combine 5 litres/10½ UK pints (20 cups) water and a handful of salt in a very large pan and bring to the boil. Use a large spoon to lower the dumplings carefully into the boiling water. With the spoon, keep the water moving all the time in the beginning so that the dumplings keep tumbling around a bit in the hot water rather than settling in a big pile at the bottom of the pan. Keep simmering for 10–20 minutes, depending on the size of the dumplings. They will float to the surface of the water when they are almost ready. Once all the dumplings are floating, simmer for a few more minutes, then lift them out of the water with a slotted spoon.

ÖLAND-STYLE, POTATO AND WHEAT DUMPLINGS

Öländska kroppkakor (Sweden)

These dumplings from the Baltic island of Öland use both raw and cooked potato. They are a bit denser in texture and have a more pronounced potato flavour than those made only from cooked potato. Sometimes a little cream is spooned over them just as they are served, and they are often accompanied by butter – either melted or at room temperature – and some Sugared Lingonberries (page 692).

Because these dumplings contain raw potato they will take quite a bit longer to cook than other ones made from just cooked potato.

Preparation and cooking time: 2½ hours
Serves: 4

For the filling
1 onion, finely chopped
250 g/9 oz salt pork, cut into small dice
white pepper and allspice, to taste

For the dough
800 g/1¾ lb floury potatoes, peeled and finely grated

200 g/7 oz floury potatoes, boiled, peeled,
    pushed through a ricer and cooled to
    room temperature
60 g/2¼ oz (½ cup) weak (soft) wheat flour,
    plus extra to dust
pinch of salt

Fry the salt pork in a frying pan or skillet over a
medium heat. Add the onion and sauté for a few
minutes until it starts to soften. Season to taste
with pepper and allspice, then remove from the
heat and leave to cool down.

Wrap the grated potato in a clean dish cloth and
squeeze out as much water as you can. Place the
grated potato in a large bowl with the remaining
dough ingredients. Work with your hands until
everything is fully combined, but don't overwork.

Transfer the dough to a floured work counter and
divide it into 12–20 pieces, depending on what size
dumplings you want. With lightly floured hands,
shape each piece of dough into a ball and create a
cavity. Don't make the cavity too small.

Divide the filling according to the number of
dumplings. Fill each cavity about two thirds full,
then squeeze the edges of it tight to seal the dumplings completely. Roll them a bit more in your
floured hand so that they become really round.

Combine 5 litres/10½ UK pints (20 cups) water
and a handful of salt in a large pan and bring to the
boil. Use a large spoon to lower the dumplings
carefully into the boiling water, one by one as you
finish rolling them. With the help of the spoon,
keep the water moving all the time in the beginning so that the dumplings keep tumbling around
a bit in the hot water rather than settling in a big
pile on the bottom of the pot. It will take about
35 minutes to cook them, depending on the size
of the dumplings. They will float to the surface of
the water when they are almost ready. Once all the
dumplings are floating, simmer for a few minutes
more, then lift them out with a slotted spoon and
serve them immediately.

For image see page 459

NORWEGIAN PANCAKE DUMPLINGS
IN MILK

Kleppmelk / Bollemelk / Kleppesuppe
(Norway)

These dumplings consist of a thick, pancake-
batter-like base, spooned into simmering milk and
boiled until done. The dumplings are served in a
deep bowl with some of the cooking milk, which
thickens lightly, and a lot of sugar.

Preparation and cooking time: 1 hour
Serves: 4

2 litres/3½ UK pints (8¼ cups) milk
sugar, to serve

For the batter
2 eggs
50 g/2 oz (¼ cup) sugar
200 ml/7 fl oz (¾ cup plus 1 tablespoon) milk
200 g/7 oz (1⅔ cups) weak (soft) wheat flour
pinch of salt

Combine all the batter ingredients in a medium
bowl and mix together well. The batter should be
thick enough to form into spoonfuls, but not as
stiff as a bread dough.

Bring the milk to the boil in a large pot over medium heat, then lower to a simmer. Form the dumplings using 2 spoons, the first to scoop up and
shape the batter into dumplings and the second to
slide the dumpling off the first spoon and carefully
into the simmering milk. The amount of dumplings will depend on the size of your spoon but aim
for 20–30. It will get a bit crowded in the pot but
that is fine and how it should be. Cook the dumplings slowly, moving the milk around occasionally
to ensure the dumplings don't stick to the bottom
of the pot and burn. It will take about 20 minutes,
and they will become more buoyant as they cook.

For image see page 459

BLOOD DUMPLINGS

Blodpalt (Sweden)

Blodpalt is a dumpling made with an addition of blood in the batter. It can be made with just wheat flour, or a mixture of wheat, barley and/or rye. Blodpalt doesn't necessarily have to have potatoes in it, but if it does, they are most often boiled. This breaks the system of how Swedish dumplings are named, since dumplings containing cooked potatoes would normally be called *kroppkakor* and those based on raw potatoes would be known as *palt*.

Do not mistake *blodpalt* for *Paltbröd* (page 390), which is another blood-based Swedish dish.

Preparation and cooking time: 2 hours
Serves: 4

500 g/1 lb 2 oz floury potatoes, boiled, peeled, pushed through a ricer and cooled to room temperature
250 ml/8 fl oz (1 cup) pig's or cow's blood
200 g/7 oz (1⅔ cups) weak (soft) wheat flour, plus extra to dust
200 g/7 oz (1½ cups) coarse rye flour
good pinch of salt

Put all the ingredients in a large bowl. Work with your hands until everything is fully combined, but don't overwork.

Transfer the dough to a floured work counter and divide it into 12–20 pieces, depending on what size dumplings you want. With lightly floured hands, shape each piece of dough into a ball until they are really round.

Combine 5 litres/10½ UK pints (20 cups) water and a handful of salt in a large pan and bring to the boil. Use a large spoon to carefully lower the dumplings into the boiling water. With the spoon, keep the water moving all the time in the beginning so that the dumplings keep tumbling around a bit in the hot water rather than settling in a big pile at the bottom of the pan. Keep simmering for 10–20 minutes, depending on the size of the dumplings. They will float to the surface of the water when they are almost ready. Once all the dumplings are floating, simmer for a few minutes, then lift them out of the water with a slotted spoon.

NORWEGIAN POTATO DUMPLINGS WITH SALTED MUTTON

Komle / Kompe (Norway)

This recipe contains both boiled and raw potatoes, which makes it medium-light as Nordic dumplings go. If you put chopped pieces of the meat inside the dumplings, it is called *komle med dott I*, the meat could also be served sliced next to the dumplings. Serve with mashed swede, soft salted butter to dip in and Sugared Lingonberries (page 692) on the side.

Preparation and cooking time: 2 hours
Soaking time: overnight
Serves: 4

550 g/1 lb 4 oz salted mutton, soaked overnight in plenty of cold water
350 g/12 oz smoked bacon
600 g/1 lb 5 oz floury potatoes, peeled and grated
200 g/7 oz floury potatoes, boiled, peeled and pushed through a ricer
75–120 g/2¾–4 oz (½–¾ cup) barley flour
30–55 g/1–2 oz (¼–½ cup) weak (soft) wheat flour
salt, to taste

Place the mutton and bacon in a big pot and cover with water. Bring to the boil, then lower the heat and simmer until tender.

While the meat is cooking, prepare the potatoes. Combine them in a bowl and add a little salt and some of each of the flours. Mix and continue to add flour until the right texture is achieved. The mixture should be firm, but still nice and pliable.

Preheat the oven to 180°C/350°F/Gas Mark 4.

Remove the meat from the stock (broth), place on a serving tray and keep warm in the oven. Keep the stock simmering. Wet a spoon in the hot liquid and use it to shape the dumplings. Carefully drop them straight into the simmering liquid and cook until they all float at the surface, which should take about 30 minutes. You should be able to make 12–16 dumplings from this recipe.

To make *komle med dott I*, either braise the meats until tender, then chill before dicing and stuffing into the dumplings or use the soaked but uncooked meat. If you use raw meat in the dumplings, you won't have the braising liquid for cooking the dumplings, so you will have to use another stock.

SWEDISH RAW POTATO DUMPLINGS

Palt / Kams (Sweden)

Dumplings based on raw potatoes and flour (wheat, barley, rye or a mix of them), are most commonly produced in the more northern parts of Sweden. They are called different things in different parts, but all refer to roughly the same dish. In the northernmost part, a dumpling made from raw potato and flour is called *palt*, whilst in the southern part of northern Sweden, where I grew up, they are called *kams*.

All these recipes exist in a flat version with no filling, a bit like a very dense pancake. If this is the case, the name has the old Swedish word for 'flat' in front: *flatkams* or *flatpalt*. This style of flat dumpling is served with Fried Salt Pork (page 302) plus the fat from the frying pan and some Sugared Lingonberries (page 692).

The Swedish word *paltkoma* – palt 'coma' – refers to a stage of extreme drowsiness after having eaten too many *palt*, a very heavy food.

Filling for dumplings
butter, for frying
1 onion, finely chopped
250 g/9 oz salt pork, cut into small dice

Heat some butter in a frying pan and sauté the onion for a few minutes until it starts to soften. Remove from the heat and let cool. Add the salt pork to the cooled onion and mix well.

PITEPALT RAW POTATO AND WHEAT DUMPLINGS

Pitepalt (Sweden)

Pitepalt are named after the northern Swedish town of Piteå. They should, as far as I can understand, be made with wheat flour. However a lot of people who live in Piteå make their *pitepalt* with an addition of barley flour, which would make them *gråpalt* (page 464) regardless of whether they are made in Piteå or elsewhere.

Preparation and cooking time: 2 hours
Serves: 4

1 kg/2¼ lb floury potatoes, peeled
    and finely grated
200 g/7 oz (1⅔ cups) weak (soft) wheat
    flour, plus extra to dust
pinch of salt
1 portion of filling for dumplings (see left)

Place the grated potato and any liquid that came out of it in a large bowl with the flour and salt. Work with your hands until everything is fully combined. Continue working the dough to develop the gluten; you want it to be firm but pliable and very sticky.

Transfer the dough to a floured work counter and divide it into 12–20 pieces, depending on what size dumplings you want. With lightly floured hands, shape each piece of dough into a ball and create a cavity. Don't make the cavity too small.

Divide the filling according to the number of dumplings. Fill each cavity then squeeze the edges together around it to seal completely. Roll them a bit more in your hands until really round.

Combine 5 litres/10½ UK pints (20 cups) water and a handful of salt in a very large pan and bring to the boil. Use a large spoon to lower the dumplings carefully into the boiling water. With the spoon, keep the water moving all the time in the beginning so that the dumplings keep tumbling around a bit in the hot water rather than settling in a big pile at the bottom of the pot. Keep simmering for 10–20 minutes, depending on the size of the dumplings. They will float to the surface of the water when they are almost ready. Once all the dumplings are floating, simmer for a few minutes, then lift them out with a slotted spoon.

For image see page 459

RAW POTATO AND BARLEY DUMPLINGS

Kams / Gråpalt (Sweden)

In most parts of northern Sweden, barley or rye makes up a part of the traditional dumpling batter. Sometimes they are all that is used, and other times it is mixed with some quantity of wheat flour. When I was growing up and we made *kams* in my family, we usually used one-third of barley to two-thirds of wheat flour. The word *grå* (in *gråpalt*) means 'grey', and refers to the colour of a dumpling which has barley or rye added to it.

Preparation and cooking time: 2 hours
Serves: 4

For the dough
1 kg/2¼ lb floury potatoes, peeled and
  finely grated
200 g/7 oz (1⅔ cups) flour (barley, rye or
  plain [all-purpose], or a mixture), plus
  extra to dust
pinch of salt
1 portion of the Filling for Dumplings (page
  463)

Heat some butter in a frying pan and sauté the onion for a few minutes until it starts to soften. Remove from the heat and let cool.

Place the grated potato and any liquid that came out in a large bowl with the flour and salt. Work with your hands until everything is fully combined. Continue working the dough to develop the gluten; you want it to be firm but pliable and very sticky.

Transfer the dough to a floured work counter and divide it into 12–20 pieces, depending on what size dumplings you want. With lightly floured hands, shape each piece of dough into a ball and create a cavity. Don't make the cavity too small.

Divide the filling according to the number of dumplings. Fill each cavity around two-thirds full, then squeeze the edges together around it to seal the dumplings completely. Roll them a bit more in your hands so that they become really round.

Combine 5 litres/10½ UK pints (20 cups) water and a handful of salt in a very large pan and bring to the boil. Use a large spoon to lower the dumplings carefully into the boiling water. With the spoon, keep the water moving all the time in the beginning so that the dumplings keep tumbling around a bit in the hot water rather than settling in a big pile at the bottom of the pan. Keep simmering for 35–45 minutes, depending on the size of the dumplings. They will float to the surface of the water when they are almost ready. Once all the dumplings are floating, simmer for a few minutes, then lift them out of the water with a slotted spoon.

MACARONI CASSEROLE

Makaronipudding (Norway)
Makaronilaatikko (Finland)
Makaronipudding / Makaronibudding
  (Denmark)
Makaronipudding (Sweden)

In most Nordic countries this dish has a meat component baked into the casserole itself, as opposed to the rest of Europe where it is more often served as a side dish to something. In Finland, the meat is often minced (ground) beef and in the other countries, diced, cured and smoked meats like ham, salt pork or different sausages that are used.

In some recipes the casserole is flavoured with nutmeg, in others, not.

Preparation and cooking time: 1 hour
Serves: 4

250 g/8¾ oz macaroni
butter, for frying
1 onion, chopped
500 g/1 lb 2 oz minced (ground) beef,
  or, 250 g/9 oz cured or smoked meat,
  sausages or leftover meat, cut into
  1 cm/½ inch pieces
3 eggs
250 ml/8 fl oz (1 cup) cream
250 ml/8 fl oz (1 cup) milk
freshly grated nutmeg (optional)
150 g/5 oz mature hard cheese,
  grated
salt and white pepper, to taste

Preheat the oven to 225°C/435°F /Gas Mark 7.

Cook the macaroni, following the instructions on the packet. Drain it well and leave to cool.

Meanwhile, heat some butter in a frying pan or skillet and sauté the onion for a few minutes until it starts to soften. Add your choice of meat and fry for another minute or long enough to brown the minced (ground) meat, if using. Season to taste with salt and pepper, then remove from the heat.

Combine the macaroni and sautéed meat in a large ovenproof dish.

In a separate bowl, mix together the eggs, cream and milk. Season to taste with salt and pepper and nutmeg, if using. Pour onto the macaroni mixture. Sprinkle on the grated cheese in an even layer and bake until the top is golden but the macaroni is still nice and creamy.

CREAMED MACARONI

Stuvade makaroner (Sweden)

A must with slices of Fried Falu Sausage (page 417). Flavour with a little grated nutmeg if you like.

Preparation and cooking time: 30 minutes
Serves: 4

1 litre/34 fl oz (4¼ cups) milk
500 g/1 lb 2 oz macaroni
salt and white pepper, to taste
freshly grated nutmeg (optional)

Pour the milk into a large pot and add a pinch of salt. Bring to the boil over a medium heat, then add the macaroni. Lower the heat and simmer for about 25 minutes, or until the macaroni has softened and the milk has thickened. Adjust the seasoning and finish by grating on a bit of nutmeg, if you like.

RICE PORRIDGE

Jólagrautu (Iceland)
Riisipuuro (Finland)
Risengrød (Denmark)
Risgrynsgröt / Tomtegröt (Sweden)

Rice porridge is eaten all year round in most Nordic countries, although sparingly. On or around Christmas, however, most families will eat it – either as it is warm, or as part of a Rice Pudding (page 626). It was – and is still – common to hide an almond in the Christmas porridge. The person finding it will, in Denmark, Norway, Iceland and southern Sweden, receive a gift called an 'almond gift', often a sweet (candy). In most parts of Sweden and in Finland, according to folklore, the person finding the almond will get married during the coming year.

Rice porridge is most often eaten warm with cold milk and a sprinkling of sugar and ground cassia cinnamon. Sometimes a knob of butter is added to the bowl and some people will have their porridge with Cordial Soup (page 694) in the bowl and a glass of milk on the side.

I like to cook my porridge with a stick of cassia cinnamon bobbing around in it for the whole process.

Preparation and cooking time: 1 hour
Serves: 4

180 g/6½ oz (¾ cup plus 2 tablespoons)
  short-grain rice
good pinch of salt
800 ml/28 fl oz (3¼ cups) milk
1 cassia cinnamon stick (optional)

Put the rice and salt in a pot and add 400 ml/ 14 fl oz (1⅔ cups) water. Bring to the boil over a medium heat, stirring constantly. Lower the heat and stir in the milk. Continue simmering for another 35 minutes, stirring every now and then. You don't want to break up the grains of rice too much.

If the porridge becomes too thick before the rice has softened, adjust the consistency with more milk.

For image see page 471

WHEAT SEMOLINA AND MILK PORRIDGE

Semuliegrøt (Norway)
Mannapuuro (Finland)
Mannagrynsgröt (Sweden)

Serve hot with cold milk, garnish with sugar and ground cassia cinnamon or some jam (page 690). Some people also like a dollop of salty butter melting in a mound in the middle of their porridge.

Preparation and cooking time: 15 minutes
Serves: 4

1 litre/34 fl oz (4¼ cups) milk
good pinch of salt
8 tablespoons fine semolina

Combine the milk and salt in a pot and bring to the boil over a medium heat. Add the semolina, whisking hard to prevent lumps forming. It is extremely important to whisk the semolina in, rather than stirring it, as any lumps that form now will remain in the porridge until you eat it.

Simmer for about 5 minutes, stirring all the time, until the porridge has thickened.

COLD SEMOLINA AND RED BERRY PORRIDGE

Vispipuuro / Vispgröt (Finland)
Klappgröt / Trollgröt (Sweden)

This children's favourite is most often served as a dessert. I have fond pre-school memories of its fluffy, pink deliciousness. You can prepare it from fresh or frozen berries or cordial. Red berries, like lingonberries or raspberries, are most often used.

If you're using cordial, then make it up with an equal quantity of cordial syrup and water mixed; it should be stronger than if you were going to drink it.

Preparation and cooking time: 30 minutes
Serves: 6 for dessert

1 litre/34 fl oz (4¼ cups) strong cordial
  (made with an equal amount of water)

good pinch of salt
8 tablespoons fine semolina

Fill your sink with a generous amount of ice in cold water.

Combine the cordial and salt in a pot and bring to the boil over a medium heat. Add the semolina, whisking hard to prevent lumps forming. Simmer for about 5 minutes, whisking all the time, until the porridge has thickened.

Transfer the pot to the ice-filled sink and stir until it has cooled down. When the porridge is completely cold, tip into the bowl of a stand mixer and whisk until very fluffy. Serve immediately.

WITH FRESH BERRIES (VARIATION)

Instead of making the porridge with cordial you can make it with fresh red berries.

Preparation and cooking time: 15 minutes
Serves: 6 for dessert

500 g/1 lb 2 oz red berries
120 g/4 oz (½ cup plus 2 tablespoons) sugar
a pinch of salt
8 tablespoons fine semolina

Follow the recipe method above, but in place of the cordial, combine 500 ml/17 fl oz (2 cups plus 1 tablespoon) water with the berries, sugar and salt in a large pan. Bring to the boil over a medium heat, then whisk in the semolina and simmer for about 5 minutes.

Chill the porridge and whisk in the stand mixer, as described above.

ROLLED RYE FLAKE PORRIDGE

Rågflingegröt (Sweden)

Enjoy hot, with some pieces of dried fruit, jam (page 690) or sugar and cold milk.

A lot of people like to add a half-tablespoon of flax seeds per portion to this porridge to make it even richer in dietary fibre.

Preparation and cooking time: 15 minutes
Serves: 4

120 g/4 oz (1¼ cups) rolled rye flakes
1 teaspoon salt
2 tablespoons flax seeds (linseeds), optional

Put the rye flakes and salt in a pot with the flax seeds (if using) and 1 litre/34 fl oz (4¼ cups) water. Bring to the boil over a medium heat, stirring constantly. Lower the heat and continue simmering for another 10 minutes, or until the flakes are cooked and the right texture is achieved. If you are using flax seeds, you might have to add just a bit more water towards the end to adjust the texture.

RYE FLOUR PORRIDGE

Ruispuuro (Finland)
Rågmjölsgröt (Sweden)

I used to really hate this porridge when I was growing up: its gluey texture, its strong grain flavour, everything about it! Those who love it though, usually eat it with cold milk, Sugared Lingonberries (page 692), Apple Compote (page 700) or sugar, or possibly with a knob of butter melting in it.

Preparation and cooking time: 15 minutes
Serves: 4

1 teaspoon salt
180 g/6½ oz (1½ cups) coarse rye flour

Pour 1 litre/34 fl oz (4¼ cups) water into a large pan, add the salt and bring to the boil. Add the flour a little at a time, whisking briskly. It is extremely important to whisk the flour into the water rather than stirring it, as any lumps that form now will remain in the porridge until you eat it.

When all the flour has been added, simmer, stirring occasionally, or until the porridge has thickened and tastes of cooked grains and cereal.

BARLEY FLOUR PORRIDGE

Kornmjölsgröt (Sweden)

Serve hot with cold milk, jam (page 690), Apple Compote (page 700) or sugar.

Preparation and cooking time: 15 minutes
Serves: 4

1 teaspoon salt
160 g/5½ oz (1 cup) barley flour

To serve, your choice of:
cold milk
sugar
jam (page 690)
Apple Compote (page 700)

Pour 1 litre/34 fl oz (4¼ cups) water into a large pan, add the salt and bring to the boil. Add the flour a little at a time, whisking briskly. It is extremely important to whisk properly at this stage, as any lumps that form now will remain in the porridge until you eat it.

When all the flour has been added, simmer until the porridge has thickened and tastes of cooked grains and cereal.

FINNISH POTATO PEARL PORRIDGE

Helmipuuro (Finland)

Helmi is actually the brand under which a particular granulated potato starch is manufactured and sold in Finland. But it is so closely linked to the dish that it has given its name to it. Serve hot with sugar, ground cassia cinnamon and cold milk.

Preparation and cooking time: 20 minutes
Serves: 4

800 ml/28 fl oz (3¼ cups) milk
100 g/3½ oz (1 cup) Helmi potato
   pearls
good pinch of salt
1 tablespoon butter

Pour the milk into a pot and bring to a simmer. Whisk the potato pearls into the hot milk, then add some salt. Simmer for 10 minutes over a medium heat, stirring from time to time. Add the butter, cover the pot and leave it to sit for 5 minutes before serving.

DANISH BARLEY PORRIDGE WITH APPLE AND RAISINS

Vandgrød (Denmark)

This used to be everyday food served at any time for any meal in simpler homes. I like it for breakfast.

Serve it piping hot with cold milk and honey or sugar, to taste.

Preparation and cooking time: 1 hour
Serves: 4

200 g/7 oz (1 cup) pearl barley
good pinch of salt
1 handful raisins
2 apples, coarsely chopped or cut into
   wedges, peeled or not, as you prefer

Put the barley and salt in a pot and add 1 litre/34 fl oz (4¼ cups) water. Bring to the boil, then simmer over a medium heat for about 5 minutes, stirring continuously. Lower the heat, cover the pan and simmer very gently for 45 minutes, stirring from time to time. Add the raisins and apples during the last 10 minutes of cooking. Adjust the texture if necessary with a little more water if it is too firm for your liking.

NORWEGIAN SOUR CREAM PORRIDGE

Rømmegrøt (Norway)

Rømmegrøt is a wheat flour-based porridge made with a Norwegian sour cream called *rømme*. It is considered a dish for special occasions and is often served with the butterfat that renders out during the cooking process, as well as a sprinkling of sugar and some cinnamon. Traditionally, *rømmegrøt* can also be served with Norwegian cured meats called *spekemat* (like Norwegian Cured and Aged Leg of Mutton, page 348) or with raisins. The best *rømme* is called *Seterrømme* and comes from small mountain farms called *seter*.

Preparation and cooking time: 30 minutes
Serves: 4

500 ml/17 fl oz (2 cups plus 1 tablespoon)
   rømme
120 g/4 oz (¾ cup plus 1 tablespoon)
   plain (all-purpose) flour
500 ml/17 fl oz (2 cups plus 1 tablespoon)
   full-fat milk
salt, to taste

Put the sour cream in a pot and bring to the boil over a medium heat, stirring continuously. Lower the heat and simmer for about 5 minutes.

Sift the flour into a bowl and then whisk it straight into the warm sour cream. Whisk vigorously to avoid lumps forming.

Continue to simmer until the fat begins to split and render out of the porridge. Spoon enough of this from the porridge to top with later and set aside.

Add the milk and salt and simmer for about 10 more minutes. Serve immediately, with the rendered butterfat either on top of the porridge in the pan or spooned over each portion on the plate.

ICELANDIC SKYR AND PORRIDGE MIX

Hræringur (Iceland)

Hræringur is usually a mix of hot or cold porridge made from rolled oats (page 470) and *Skyr* (page 72), but can also contain other sources of starch, like barley (opposite page), rice (page 466) or rye (page 467), or some Icelandic moss (page 134).

It is commonly served with milk and/or Icelandic Liver Sausage (page 424) or Icelandic blood sausage.

Preparation and cooking time: 5 minutes

equal amounts hot or cold porridge, made
   from rolled oats, barley or rice, and Skyr
   (page 72)

Mix the porridge and skyr together.

ROLLED OAT PORRIDGE

Havregrøt (Norway)
Kaurapuuro (Finland)
Havregrød (Denmark)
Havregrynsgröt (Sweden)

I would say that this is probably one of the most common breakfasts eaten in Sweden. Enjoy hot with cold milk, sugar or Sugared Lingonberries (page 692).

Preparation and cooking time: 15 minutes
Serves: 4

160 g/5½ oz (1¾ cups plus 2 tablespoons)
  rolled oats
1 teaspoon salt

Put the oats and salt in a pot and add 1 litre/ 34 fl oz (4¼ cups) water. Bring to the boil over a medium heat, stirring constantly. Lower the heat and continue simmering for 10 minutes, or until the oats are cooked and the right texture is achieved.

For image see opposite page

TOASTED DRY OAT PORRIDGE

Nävgröt (Sweden)

This dish comes from the central Swedish region of Värmland and it is made from a particular flour made from toasted oat kernels, called *skrädmjöl*.

This is not quite a porridge as the texture is dry and when eaten, it would more often be broken up in pieces to be dipped in fat from Fried Salt Pork (page 302) and Sugared Lingonberries (page 692) than eaten with a spoon.

Preparation and cooking time: 30 minutes
Serves: 4

1 teaspoon salt
250 g/8 oz *skrädmjöl* flour or toasted oatmeal
400 g/14 oz Fried Salt Pork (page 302)

Pour 300 ml/10½ fl oz (1¼ cups) water into a large frying pan or skillet. Add the salt and bring to the boil. Tip in the flour, all at once. Don't stir, but instead, press down on the flour with a large wooden spoon to ensure it sinks into the water evenly. Cover the pan and remove it from the heat. Leave it to sit next to the stove until all the water has been absorbed into the flour.

Meanwhile, fry the salt pork slices according to the instructions on page 302.

Break the porridge up into pieces and serve with the slices of pork and rendered fat on top.

For image see opposite page

Clockwise from top left: Danish Rye Bread and Beer Soup (page 474); Rolled Oat Porridge (page 470); Sweet-and-Sour Prune and Rice Soup (page 473); Rice Porridge (page 466); Toasted Dry Oat Porridge (page 470)

PAJALA PORRIDGE

Pajalagröt (Sweden)

A porridge is especially good for your stomach; I doubt you will find many other foodstuffs with the same amount of dietary fibre in them. Pajala is a small town in the very north of Sweden, just on the border with Finland.

Serve *pajalagröt* hot, with cold milk.

Preparation and cooking time: 15 minutes
Soaking time: overnight
Serves: 4

30 g/1 oz (3 tablespoons) flax seeds (linseeds)
35 g/1¼ oz (¼ cup) raisins
10 dried apricots
10 pitted prunes
20 g/¾ oz (2 tablespoons) rye bran
1 teaspoon salt
100 g/3½ oz (1 cup) rolled oats

Combine all the ingredients, except for the oats in a large mixing bowl. Pour in about 700 ml/24 fl oz (3 cups) cold water and leave in the refrigerator overnight to soak.

The next day, transfer the mixture to a pot. Add the oats and bring to the boil over a medium heat. Simmer for 5 minutes, stirring from time to time. If the porridge is very thick, adjust the consistency with a bit more water.

FINNISH OVEN PORRIDGE / OVEN PUDDING

Uunipuuro (Finland)

This oven porridge is essentially a mix of barley and milk, or rice and milk, which is baked for an extended time in the oven so that it reduces down, and some of the starch breaks down into sugars and the mix becomes rather sweet. *Uuni puuro* is served with milk and/or sugar, cassia cinnamon, berries or jam, or Soup of Dried Fruits (page 696). I have also seen recipes that have raisins or whole prunes incorporated into the actual porridge.

Preparation and cooking time: 1¾ hours
Serves: 4

200 g/7 oz (1 cup) pearl barley or
   short-grain rice
1.3 litres/43 fl oz (5¼ cups) milk
1 teaspoon salt
butter, for greasing

Preheat the oven to 150°C/300°F/Gas Mark 2.

Mix all of the ingredients in a lightly buttered ovenproof dish and cook for about 1½ hours.

RYE SOURDOUGH, POTATO AND PEA SOUP FROM VIROLAHTI

Hapanvelli (Finland)

Serve this thick South Eastern Finnish soup with a knob of butter and some cold milk.

You will need to soak the split peas in plenty of water overnight before preparing the soup.

Preparation and cooking time: 1½ hours
Soaking time: overnight
Serves: 4

130 g/4½ oz (⅔ cup) dried yellow split peas,
   soaked overnight
300 g/11 oz potatoes, peeled and coarsely
   chopped into small pieces
300 ml/10 fl oz (1¼) rye sourdough starter
pinch of salt

Drain the split peas. Place in a pot with 800 ml/28 fl oz (3¼ cups) water and bring to the boil over medium heat. Lower the heat and simmer for 10 minutes. Add the potatoes and continue to cook, stirring frequently, to stop them sticking to the bottom of the pan and burning.

When the potato is almost done after around 20 minutes, add the sourdough and simmer for another 30 minutes, stirring from time to time. Season with salt before serving.

SWEET-AND-SOUR PRUNE AND RICE SOUP FROM TRONDHEIM

Trondheimssuppe (Norway)

Serve hot with a dollop of whipped cream or *Rømme* sour cream.

Make up the cordial to taste, as if you were going to drink it.

Preparation and cooking time: 45 minutes
Serves: 4

50 g/2 oz (¼ cup) white short-grain rice
1 litre/34 fl oz (4¼ cups) Raspberry Cordial
  (pages 692–3)
20 g/¾ oz (2 tablespoons) plain
  (all-purpose) flour
200 ml/7 fl oz (¾ cup plus 1 tablespoon)
  milk
pinch of salt
1 handful pitted prunes or raisins

Combine the rice and cordial in a pot and bring to the boil over a medium heat. Simmer for about 15 minutes, stirring frequently to prevent it sticking to the bottom of the pot.

In a separate bowl, mix the flour and milk, then add to the simmering sweet soup. Simmer for another 15 minutes, stirring from time to time, then season with salt. Stir in the prunes or raisins just before serving.

For image see page 471

FINNISH BEER SOUP

Kaljakeitto (Finland)

Serve *Kaljakeitto* hot with some croutons sprinkled on top.

Preparation and cooking time: 20 minutes
Serves: 4

750 ml/25 fl oz (3 cups) milk
3 tablespoons plain (all-purpose) flour

750 ml/25 fl oz (3 cups) *Kotikalja* beer
  (page 721)
4 tablespoons brown sugar
½ teaspoon ground ginger
1 cassia cinnamon stick and/or a
  few cloves (optional)
salt, to taste

Mix the milk and the flour in a pan and bring to a simmer over a medium heat. Stir continuously to avoid lumps forming or the mix sticking to the bottom of the pan.

In a pot, mix the beer with the sugar and spices and bring to the boil. Carefully pour the boiling mixture through a sieve straight onto the thickened milk. Stir to combine, add a little salt and serve immediately.

DANISH RYE BREAD
AND BEER SOUP

Øllebrød (Denmark)

This sweet and malty soup is one of the most iconic Danish dishes. Traditional recipes are often seasoned with citrus fruits like lemon or orange and it is often served with some cold milk or a dollop of whipped cream. *Øllebrød* is made from dried scraps of dried Danish Rye Bread (page 504) and *Hvidtøl* beer (page 716). Almost all of the more recent recipes I have read state that bread without rye kernels should be used, and some even say that the finished soup should be passed through a strainer to make it very smooth. Older recipes seem to make less fuss of which type of Danish rye bread is used and how smooth and velvety the end result really is. I imagine this is because this is a recipe that developed from necessity, as a cunning way of using bread scraps, because you had to, into something that people do today because they like it. *Øllebrød* is also available in instant-mix preparations.

Preparation and cooking time: 20 minutes
Soaking time: 10 minutes
Serves: 4

350 g/12 oz Danish Rye Bread
   (page 504) scraps, cut into 1 cm/½ inch
   dice and dried
1 strip orange or lemon zest
2 bottles, about 660 ml/22½ fl oz (2⅔ cups),
   Hvidtøl beer (page 716)
1 cassia cinnamon stick
juice of ½ orange or ¼ lemon
80 g/2¾ oz (⅓ cup) sugar

Place the dried bread and the citrus rind in a pot and pour on the beer and 500 ml/17 fl oz (2 cups plus 1 tablespoon) water. Leave to soak for 10 minutes, then bring to a simmer over a medium heat. Stir regularly with a whisk to gradually break down the structure of the bread during the cooking process. Cook for about 10 minutes, then add the citrus juice and the sugar. Whisk the *øllebrød* until smooth and shiny before serving.

For image see page 471

SWEDISH BEER SOUP

Ölsupa (Sweden)

This was historically (up until a hundred years ago) a very common food, not only in Sweden but in other parts of the Nordic region too. Today not so much. I think it is a bit of a pity. I kind of like this soup; it is sweet and rich, but strangely balanced by the bitterness in the beer.

In a more fancy setting, beer soup would be further enriched by adding egg yolks to the hot soup just before serving. If you do so, add 4 yolks to the recipe, but remember that you can't reheat it again after the eggs have gone in.

Preparation and cooking time: 15–20 minutes
Serves: 4

500 ml/17 fl oz (2 cups plus 1 tablespoon)
   milk
2 tablespoons plain (all-purpose) flour
1 teaspoon ground ginger
200 ml/7 fl oz (¾ cup plus 1 tablespoon)
   Sweet Small Beer (*Svagdricka*, page 719)
1 tablespoon golden syrup
good pinch of salt
4 egg yolks (optional)

Whisk the milk, flour and ginger in a pot. Bring to the boil, continuing to whisk. Simmer for a few minutes, then add the remaining ingredients. Simmer for a few more minutes, whisking all the time. The soup is done when it no longer tastes of raw starch. Take off the heat, add the egg yolks, if using, and stir briefly with a whisk until fully incorporated. Serve the soup frothing and piping hot.

Clockwise from top: Hawaiian, béarnaise sauce, Ham, Cabbage Salad (page 96), garlic sauce, Kebab, Calzone

PIZZA IN THE NORDIC REGION

What makes a dish part of national or regional food culture? The simple answer to that is, of course, when people start consuming it somewhere in a region. That would, however, more or less mean that we have no specific regional food culture left in the world as pretty much everything can now be had almost everywhere. You can eat a decent piece of sushi in London, great Indian food in New York and a pretty good open-faced Danish *smørrebrød* (page 522) sandwich in Tokyo.

I think that a dish really becomes part of a food culture when it has been established long enough to have become a part of people's everyday lives, when it isn't a curiosity anymore, and when it has started to adapt to its environment, sometimes changing from the original, becoming a new and unique occurrence.

We eat a lot of pizza in parts of the Nordics, especially in Norway, Sweden and Finland, and pizza is by most people considered a quintessentially Italian food.

If we look at its origins, there is no evidence that the first flattened bread dough with cheese on it was baked in an oven somewhere around Naples. There is plenty of proof that this had been done there for a long time, yes, but we are talking about the very first one. As a matter of fact, it's even more probable that the momentous event didn't happen around Naples. It would stand to reason that any country having a tradition of making flatbreads in wood-fired ovens at the same time as having a tradition of cheese-making could be the coincidental and unacknowledged birthplace of the mother of all pizzas. The northern parts of the Nordic mainland regions have an extensive history of both those food items and it seem logical to me that at some point, somewhere, someone sprinkled some cheese on one of those breads before it went into the oven.

Why didn't it stick then? Why didn't pizza develop to what it is today here instead of in Italy? Why isn't pizza known as a quintessentially Nordic food? I don't know and I think that it is safe to say that, regardless of how it is viewed today, the true historical origins of flatbread with cheese on it is purely speculative.

An historical fact, though, is that the first Italian-style pizza served in Sweden was done so in the city of Västerås at the Asea staff canteen in 1947. On the menu of a restaurant open to the public, it first featured in 1968 at place in Stockholm called Östergök. The first real pizzeria, Pizzeria Piazza Opera was launched the following year. In Finland the first pizzeria opened in 1961 and was called Restaurant Giovanni.

Regardless of the origin of thinly rolled-out bread dough with cheese on it, these events mark the start of the conquering of the Nordics by Italian-style thin-crust pizza in some form or another.

After the late 1960s, the spread of the pizza gospel proved an unstoppable movement and the interesting thing is that it has evolved since. The original has been tweaked, not only to suit the produce in the Nordic region, but also to fit the preferences of those baking and eating it.

Today you can find a pizzeria in almost every Swedish village. Most of them are not run by Italians or ethnic Swedes, but rather by immigrants predominantly from Turkey, the Balkans or from the Middle East. This has obviously also influenced the evolution of the Nordic pizza; nowhere else is one of the standard fixtures of the pizzeria menu a kebab pizza, at least as far as I know.

The availability of it and the fact that the pizza has been adapted to suit the local palate has led to it becoming one of the most popular foods altogether, further pushing the development of it into becoming a regional speciality at the same time as it has removed itself further from its Italian roots.

In the Nordic region a pizza is almost always served with a plate of Cabbage Salad (page 96) on the side. Different sauces to dip your slice in is very common, anything from hot sauce to garlic yogurt to Bearnaise is considered normal. A Nordic pizza can be topped with anything from the classic Italian toppings to Falu Sausage (page 416) or banana, peanuts and curry powder, or, as previously mentioned, kebab meat. A Nordic pizza does not have real mozzarella on it, it should be made using a grated yellow, hard cheese.

In Sweden and Finland, the pizza culture is very much carried by small pizzerias and in Norway much more so by the processed food industry. Over the last thirty years, several brands of frozen home-made pizza have shaped the Norwegian way of consuming flatbreads with cheese on them. In Norway, frozen pizza consumption per capita is somewhere close to 3.5 kg (7 lb) per year, about ten times as much as that of its neighbouring countries. As a consequence, the Norwegian pizza culture is considerably less diverse and adapted to local circumstances than what you would find in Finland or Sweden.

In Denmark, pizza just isn't quite as common as it is further north, and what's there is closer to its Italian origins than to a unique regional speciality. I imagine that this difference in development could be attributed at least in some part to the fact that Denmark is much more urbanized than the other parts of the Nordic region. A large part of the Danish population will have easy access to a bigger variety of everyday restaurants and take-out places. My theory is that they will, therefore, also consume from them in a more varied way. The motivation for pizza culture to evolve into something new simply hasn't been big enough. In a city there is always going to be more space to stay the same (some would perhaps use the word 'authentic'), as long as enough people like what you do. In the countryside, you might have to change what you offer to suit those living close by because there aren't enough of them to be picky. At the same time, those living in the countryside most often have little else to choose from – it becomes a symbiotic relationship of mutual development.

For image see page 475

Previous page: Thermally active area, south of Lake Mývatn, Iceland, May 2013. The site is considered a communal area and each family in the neighbouring village has their own hole in the ground in which they will bake Icelandic Rye Bread (page 503).

As I walk through the door, the rainy and cold streets of Helsinki turn into a humid but warm and comforting haze. In the little pastry shop on Hesperiankatu Street it feels as though time has stood still, at least since the early Sixties, judging from the decor. Bare-breasted girls adorn the walls in a graphic mural and some benches toward one side of the room are made from dark wood and positioned closed to each other, a bit like in a Scandinavian ski cabin.

Most of the remaining, unfurnished space is being occupied by a dense queue of Finns, dressed in outer garments to various degrees soaked by the outside drizzle. The line ends, or perhaps rather begins, at a glass counter filled with traditional Karelian pastries (page 519). Everyone is patiently and quietly waiting for his or her turn. The air feels electric with equal parts eager anticipation and mild annoyance over the queue and the unexpected logistical hindrance in everyone's lunch break that it poses. No one really seems to feel much like talking and the only sounds audible, besides those from the chatty lady by the cash register asking the queuing people what they would like to have in Finnish, are some low voices coming from a room I presume to be the kitchen. They come out slightly garbled by the sharp rasping of a radio, also somewhere in the back. The cheery, old-fashioned Finnish folk tunes are, judging by the quality of the sound, straining the little radio's only speaker to its limit and when a, to me, previously unknown singer takes a particularly high note, the music turns into a scraping buzz for a few seconds before returning to normal again.

The scent of the room is a curious mix of caramelizing dough, cinnamon, braising meats, butter, cooking cabbage and sweat from Karelian ladies working heavy rye-based doughs by hand. It is the smell of old and rough Finland, not the sleek Alvar Alto-designed, functionalist version. It is a smell that seems etched into the space by the passing of decades during which it has been occupied by Pirkko, her sister and before that their mother who bought it in 1964. Long from now, if Hopia bakery turns into a boutique for other commodities than food, perhaps clothing, I suspect it to be a complicated transition – food culture this deep, and the scent that comes with it, is not something that can be hidden simply by a new coat of paint.

As I walk past the line of people, I can feel the gaze of their eyes and their thoughts stinging my neck. Who is this interloper? Who does he think he is, sneaking past the queue like that? No one says anything.

At the doorway to the kitchen I find a former cabinetmaker turned baker's assistant, who greets me and ushers me through to the kitchen. It is small and cramped and what space isn't occupied by ovens, kitchen utensils and two worn, wooden work counters is effectively filled out by the two sisters baking. They are in their late sixties or perhaps early seventies. Thick forearms, indicating a lifetime of kneading, and a low centre of gravity, indicating a passion for ingesting baked goods, characterize their appearance. When we talk through her kitchen, she translating my questions from English and the sisters' answers from Finnish, the pride in their work is tangible. They are doing what they learnt from their mother growing up, which was in turn what she learnt back in the eastern Finnish province of Karelia when she grew up. This is culture, not just running a place to feed people.

Pirkko uses the palm of her hand with force, shaping lumps of grey, rye-based dough into thin discs. The base of

Karjalanpiirakka, or Karelian pastries, looks almost as stiff as pasta dough and smells freshly acidic as it is being worked against the wooden surface. The rounds are placed in a pile and covered, so as not to dry, while resting before they are distributed over the whole work counter again. Each round gets either a dollop of soft, coarse and buttery mash potato or rice porridge spread over most of its surface. When all the discs have been spread, Pirkko crimps them by squeezing the edges together, her hands moving so fast that actually understanding the action making the crimp is impossible. To my back Pirkko's sister is making cinnamon rolls and in the room next to us, a timer buzzes to tell the former cabinetmaker that it is time to take out the first cooked batch of *Karjalanpiirakka*. I walk over there and watch her deftly flipping the pastries, gently touching their belly with her bare fingers. Like a veterinarian touching the belly of a hamster in search of some unknown ailment, she judges whether they are cooked or not. The ones that aren't go back into the oven and the others gets spread out on a sheet of baking (parchment) paper placed on a windowsill. Light spilling in through the frosted windows highlights the crimps and texture of the pastries – it looks like an imaginary autumn (fall) landscape.

Just after cooking, the *piirakka* get a generous basting with clarified butter. The former cabinetmaker explains to me that it has taken the better part of the six months she has been working at Hopia to learn how to judge the cooking of the *piirakka*. She also tells me that many customers who come here make a detour from all over Helsinki for what are considered to be the best Karelian pastries available.

I exit the kitchen, a freshly baked pastry and a slab of minced meat lihalevy on a plate, to sit down at one of the free tables in the shop. The benches that the customers sit on are placed so tightly that if you were seated back to back, your bodies would in fact be touching and acting like a sort of human backrest, turning every customer into a part of the furnishing. As I bite through the crispy and yet oddly chewy crust of my *piirakka* to reach the succulent and buttery potato filling, a woman asks if she can sit down at the opposite side of my table. The rest of the tables are occupied and I don't mind. She is in her late fifties and her name turns out to be Hannela. She tells me that she is a teacher in mathematics and that she comes here often, very often. We chat for a few minutes before we both run out of pleasantly shallow things to say, and I return to my book and she to her lunch.

After a few minutes my concentration is broken by a soft sound of pleasure and I glance up at Hannela over the brim of my cup. Her eyes involuntarily closed from deep enjoyment, she is savouring the deliciousness in front of her, enjoying every bite viscerally.

When she opens them our eyes meet for a brief moment, I feel awkward – staring at a woman eating, what is that about?

I sense that she feels as awkward as I do, moaning in a crowded café over some layers of dough with cabbage tucked between them is probably not socially acceptable even here, below the unblinking eyes of the bare-breasted lady depicted in the mural.

Previous page: Finnish lady preparing Karelian Pasties (page 519) in a Helsinki bakery, October 2013.

Opposite: Karelian Pasties (page 519) just brushed with melted butter in a Helsinki bakery, October 2013.

Previous page: My mum and aunt being filmed for an American television production while baking traditional flatbreads. Do note the particular patterns on the rolling pins, the ridged one to roll the very sticky dough out really thin with lots of flour and the knobbed one to prevent it from blowing up into a pita pocket when being baked. Also note the dazed expression of the producer to the left.

Opposite: Icelandic Rye Bread (page 503) in a bucket, ready to be lowered into a hole in the hot ground of a thermally active area, south of Lake Mývatn, Iceland, May 2013.

Following page: Schønnemann restaurant, smørebrød (page 522) Copenhagen, August 2014. A good example of Danish hygge (page 524).

GOLDEN SYRUP LOAF

Sirapslimpa (Sweden)

Enjoy sliced and buttered with hard cheese and a glass of ice-cold chocolate milk on the side. At least that's how I ate it as a kid – although it was the commercially made kind, rather than homemade, just like the one in the photo on page 517.

The flavourings may vary: it often contains fennel, aniseed and/or caraway, but sometimes no spices at all.

Preparation and cooking time: 1 hour,
  plus cooling time
Rising time: 1½–2 hours
Makes: 2 loaves

500 ml/17 fl oz (2 cups plus 1 tablespoon)
  milk
50 g/2 oz (3½ tablespoons) butter,
  plus extra to grease the loaf pans,
  if using
150 g/5 oz (½ cup) golden syrup,
  plus extra for brushing
25 g/1 oz (1½ tablespoons) fresh yeast
450 g/1 lb (3⅓ cups) strong bread
  flour
350 g/12 oz (2½ cups) Swedish rye/
  wheat bread flour (*rågsikt*) or
  210 g/7 oz (1½ cups) bread flour, and
  140 g/4¾ oz (1 cup plus 1 tablespoon)
  rye flour
15 g/½ oz salt
1 tablespoon fennel seeds, crushed
1 tablespoon aniseeds, crushed
1 tablespoon caraway seeds, crushed

Combine the milk, butter and golden syrup in a pan and heat gently until the butter and syrup melt. Remove from the heat and leave to cool to room temperature.

Dissolve the yeast in the milk and butter mixture. Pour the liquid into the bowl of a stand mixer fitted with the dough hook. Add the rest of the ingredients and knead at medium speed until shiny, smooth and very elastic. It should take a good 10 minutes. Cover the bowl with a clean dish cloth and leave the dough at room temperature for about 1½ hours, or until it has doubled in size.

Line 2 baking sheets with baking (parchment) paper or butter two 23 x 13 x 8 cm/9 x 5 x 3 inch loaf pans. Tip the dough onto a lightly floured work counter and divide it in two. Shape into 2 loaves and lift onto the baking sheet or place into the pans. Cover the loaves and leave for another 30 minutes, or until they double in size again.

Meanwhile, preheat the oven to 175°C/345°F/ Gas Mark 4.

Bake the loaves until they are quite dark. Remove from the oven and, while they are still hot, brush the top surface of the loaves with syrup. Leave to cool on wire racks. If you used loaf pans, turn them out of the pans before brushing them with the syrup.

For image see page 517

BUTTERMILK LOAF

Piimälimppu (Finland)
Kärnmjölkslimpa (Sweden)

Prepare and bake exactly as in the Golden Syrup Loaf recipe (see left) but substitute the milk with buttermilk or another liquid cultured milk product and omit the brushing with golden syrup after the baking.

POMERANS LOAF

Pomeranslimpa (Sweden)

Prepare and bake exactly as in the Golden Syrup Loaf recipe (see left) but substitute the fennel, aniseed and/or caraway seeds with a good chunk of dried bitter orange peel, ground to a powder. Add it to the pan when you are heating the milk, butter and syrup.

FINNISH SWEET-AND-SOUR LOAF

Setsuuri / Sötsur limpa (Finland)
Setsuuri / Sötsur limpa (Sweden)

This iconic Finish loaf originates from the area around the city of Åbo but is today found almost everywhere in the country. It is also found, from time to time, in Swedish bakeries having been brought here by Finns living here. If you search the internet or look this recipe up in other printed media you will find a huge variation in style and content. The recipe below is to be considered a basic recipe and the important characteristics of the Finnish sweet-and-sour loaf, regardless of the recipe, are the following: a balanced but pronounced sweet and sourness, most often from using cultured milk and a generous amount of golden syrup in the dough; a pronounced note of sweet spices, most commonly caraway and aniseed but quite often also bitter orange peel; and a dark and shiny exterior from being brushed with syrupy water. It can sometimes be a little sticky to the touch.

The Finnish Christmas loaf, called *Jullimpa / Joululimppu*, is made by adding a couple of handfuls of raisins to the recipe below.

Preparation and cooking time: 1½ hours
Rising time: 1–2 hours
Makes: 2 loaves

50 g/2 oz yeast
500 ml/17 fl oz (2 cups plus 1 tablespoon)
  cultured milk, at room temperature
250 g/9 oz (¾ cup) golden syrup
1 tablespoon salt
½ tablespoon aniseed, ground
½ tablespoon caraway seeds, ground
½ tablespoon dried bitter orange peel,
  ground
420 g/14¾ oz (3 cups plus 1 tablespoon)
  strong wheat flour
400 g/14 oz (3 cups plus 1 tablespoon)
  rye flour, sifted

For the syrupy water
2 tablespoons golden syrup

Dissolve the yeast in the cultured milk in the bowl of a stand mixer fitted with the dough hook. Add the syrup, salt, spices and orange peel. Add the two flours and work for about 10 minutes, or until smooth and shiny. Cover the bowl with a clean dish cloth and leave to rise at room temperature for 30 minutes to 1 hour, or until it has doubled in size.

Line 1–2 baking sheets with baking (parchment) paper.

Shape the leavened dough into 2 loaves on a lightly floured work counter. Transfer them to the prepared baking sheets, cover and again leave to rise for 30 minutes to 1 hour, or until they double in size.

Preheat the oven to 175°C/345°F/Gas Mark 4.

To make the syrupy water, mix the golden syrup with 100 ml/3½ fl oz (⅓ cup plus 1 tablespoon) water in a bowl until thoroughly combined.

Bake the loaves in the oven for about 1 hour or until done. After 20 minutes, open the door of the oven and brush the surface of the loaves with syrupy water. Repeat after 35 minutes and again after 50 minutes. When the loaves are taken out of the oven and are still hot, brush them one last time with the syrupy water and allow them to cool completely before cutting into them.

WORT LOAF

Vörtbröd (Sweden)

This dark loaf sweetened with wort (the liquid from which beer is brewed) and flavoured with plenty of sweet spices is considered essential by many southern Swedes at Christmas dinner and it is the bread of choice for dipping in ham broth (page 436).

To make this loaf, you need a wort for making a beer at 8% alcohol, as a weaker wort won't be sweet enough and you will need to sweeten it with some malt extract (mixed in a little water).

Some people add raisins to their wort loaf; I am not a huge fan of this, but feel free to add them to the recipe if you like. If so, add a good handful towards the end of the kneading process so that they don't break up too much but get fully incorporated.

Preparation and cooking time: 2 hours
Rising time: 25–45 minutes
Makes: 4 loaves

1 litre/34 fl oz (4¼ cups) strong,
   dark brewer's wort, plus 50 ml/2 fl oz
   (3½ tablespoons) extra for brushing
   the loaves
100 g/3½ oz (7 tablespoons) butter
200 g/7 oz (⅔ cup) golden syrup
40 g/1½ oz (2 tablespoons) salt
1 tablespoon ground fennel seeds
½ tablespoon ground aniseeds
½ tablespoon grated bitter orange peel
½ tablespoon ground cloves
½ tablespoon ground cardamom
½ tablespoon grated dried ginger
25 g/1 oz yeast
2 kg/4½ lb (14¾ cups) Swedish rye/wheat
   bread flour (*rågsikt*, sifted or
   1.2 kg/2½ lb (8¾ cups plus 1 tablespoon)
   bread flour, and 800 g/1¾ lb (3 cups plus
   2 tablespoons) rye flour
500 g/1 lb 2 oz (3⅔ cups) strong wheat flour

Combine the wort, butter, golden syrup, salt and spices in a large pot and warm over a low heat until hand hot. Add the yeast to the mixture and pour it into the bowl of a stand mixer fitted with the dough hook. Add both the flours and start to knead the dough at a low speed until everything is incorporated. Increase the speed to medium and work the dough until it is smooth, shiny and elastic. It should take 5–10 minutes, depending on how powerful your mixer is.

Cover the bowl with a clean dish cloth and leave the dough at warm room temperature to double in size. It should be relatively quick, 15–25 minutes, as the dough at this stage is fairly warm and the yeast is very active.

Line 2 baking sheets with baking (parchment) paper. Place the dough on a lightly floured work counter and divide it in 4 equal pieces. Shape each piece into an elongated loaf and arrange them in pairs on the prepared baking sheets. Cover with a clean dish cloth and leave to prove for another 20 minutes, or until doubled in size again.

Meanwhile, preheat the oven to 200°C/400°F/ Gas Mark 6.

Bake for 40 minutes. During the last 10 minutes of the baking, open the oven and lightly brush the surface of the loaves with the extra wort. Repeat this at least twice to produce a dark, shiny surface.

Allow the loaves to cool completely on wire racks before slicing.

PLAIN WHEAT LOAF

Loff (Norway)
Vehnäleipä / Ranskanleipä (Finland)
Franskbrød (Denmark)
Vitt bröd / Franskbröd (Sweden)

Preparation and cooking time: 2 hours
Makes: 2 free-form loaves or 3 loaves made
   in loaf pans

500 ml/17 fl oz (2 cups plus 1 tablespoon)
   water or milk
50 g/2 oz yeast
2 teaspoons salt
50 g/2 oz (½ stick) butter, at room
   temperature
750 g/1 lb 10 oz (5½ cups) strong wheat flour

Pour the liquid into the bowl of a stand mixer fitted with the dough hook and dissolve the yeast into it. Add the salt, butter and flour. Work everything together for 10–12 minutes at a rather high speed until very shiny and elastic.

Cover the bowl with a clean dish cloth and leave the dough to rise for about 35 minutes, or until it has doubled in size.

Line 2 baking sheets with baking (parchment) paper or butter three 23 x 13 x 8 cm/9 x 5 x 3 inch loaf pans.

Cut the dough in half if you are making free-form loaves or into 3 if you are fitting it into loaf pans. Shape them nicely and then, if you are making free-form loaves, place each one on a prepared baking sheet, If, however, you are baking your dough in loaf pans, place them in the buttered pans.

Cover the shaped dough again and leave for another 20 minutes, or until they double in size again.

Preheat the oven to 200°C/400°F/Gas Mark 6.

Bake the loaves for 20–25 minutes, or until cooked through and nicely golden. Leave the bread to cool completely on a wire rack before you cut into them.

and Norrköping, the three cities in which Jewish immigrants were first allowed to settle and to construct synagogues, following an order from parliament and the Swedish king on May 27th 1782.

Preparation and cooking time: 1½ hours
Makes: 2 loaves

1 quantity Plain Wheat Loaf dough
  (see opposite page), in which half of the
  water has been substituted with milk
1 egg
2 tablespoons milk
30 g/1 oz (3 tablespoons) poppy seeds

Make the wheat loaf according to the instructions opposite, substituting half of the water with milk.

Preheat the oven to 200°C/400°F/Gas Mark 6 and line 2 baking sheets with baking (parchment) paper.

Whisk the egg and milk together to make an egg wash. Brush the leavened loaf lightly with the egg wash then sprinkle with a dense layer of poppy seeds. Bake the shaped dough for 20–25 minutes or until cooked through and nicely golden. Remove from the baking sheet and cool on a wire rack.

WHEAT LOAF WITH POPPY SEEDS

Barkis / Bergis (Sweden)

In Sweden, *barkis* (from Stockholm) or *bergis* (from Gothenburg) refers to a loaf of white milk-bread that is covered in poppy seeds before being baked. The bread has its roots in the traditional Jewish bread, challah, eaten on the Sabbath, and the word itself comes from the Yiddish word, *berakhot*. The Swedified version does not contain the eggs of the original, nor has it the traditional braided appearance.

White loaf with poppy seeds is available over the whole country as a commercially baked product, but is not commonly referred to as *barkis* or *bergis* outside Stockholm, Gothenburg

STONE GROUND WHEAT BREADS
FROM ÅLAND

Hemvete (Finland)
Hemvete (Sweden)

If you ask someone who grew up in Åland or someone who has spent a lot of time there, perhaps visiting relatives, to name an item of food off the top of their head, there's a pretty good chance that they will mention *hemvete*.

The name, which is a combination of the Swedish words for 'home' and 'wheat', refers to the use of stoneground whole-wheat flour. Historically this flour was ground at home, on each separate farm. Today, special *hemvete* flour is sold commercially for baking these soft, rather thick flat cakes of bread. It is essentially a stoneground, whole-grain wheat flour with a fairly uniform texture.

Preparation and cooking time: 2 hours
Makes: 3 breads

500 ml/17 fl oz (2 cups plus 1 tablespoon)
    milk (or use water or a mixture of both)
50 g/2 oz (3½ tablespoons) butter
10 g/¼ oz (2 teaspoons) fresh yeast
600 g/1 lb 5 oz (4 cups plus 1 tablespoon)
    stone ground, whole-grain wheat flour
15 g/½ oz (1 tablespoon) salt

Heat the milk or water in a pan over low heat and stir in the butter to melt it. Remove from the heat and leave to cool to room temperature.

Dissolve the yeast into your chosen liquid and butter mixture. Pour the liquid into the bowl of a stand mixer fitted with the dough hook. Add the flour and salt and knead at medium speed until shiny, smooth and elastic. It should take about 10 minutes. And the dough should come away from the edge of the bowl when it's done.

Cover the bowl with a clean dish cloth, and leave the dough at room temperature to double in size.

Line 1 or 2 baking sheets, depending on the size of your oven, with baking (parchment) paper.

Tip the dough onto a lightly floured work counter and divide it into 3 equal pieces. Be careful not to incorporate more flour into the dough. Shape each piece into a rough ball and then, with a lightly floured rolling pin, roll them into rounds, about 1.5 cm/¾ inch thick and 16.5 cm/6½ inches wide. Transfer the cakes to the prepared baking sheets, cover and leave at room temperature until almost doubled in thickness.

Preheat the oven to 225°C/435°F/Gas Mark 7.

Prick the cakes with a fork and bake until dark golden in colour. It will take about 15 minutes, depending your oven. Transfer to wire racks and leave to cool.

TEA BUNS

Teboller (Denmark)
Tekakor (Sweden)

I love these hot from the oven with some butter, honey or marmalade and a thick slice of mature cheese. Some people like a bit of cardamom in their tea buns, I am one of those people. Add 2 teaspoons crushed cardamom seeds with the milk if you want to.

Preparation and cooking time: 1 hour
Makes: 15–20 tea buns

600 ml/20 fl oz (2½ cups) milk
2 teaspoons crushed cardamom seeds
    (optional)
50 g/2 oz yeast
1 egg
800 g/1¾ lb (5¾ cups plus 2 tablespoons)
    strong wheat flour
80 g/3 oz (¾ cup plus 1 tablespoon) rolled oats
4 tablespoons sugar
3 teaspoons salt

Mix the milk and yeast in the bowl of a stand mixer fitted with the dough hook and stir until the yeast has dissolved. Add the remaining ingredients and knead the dough for 5–10 minutes, or until shiny and elastic. Cover the bowl with a clean dish cloth and leave to rise for about 30 minutes, or until it has doubled in size.

Line 2 baking sheets with baking (parchment) paper.

Tip the dough onto a lightly floured work counter and roll to a thickness of 1.5 cm/¾ inch. Using a cookie cutter, cut out 15–20 circles of about 1 cm/½ inch in diameter. Transfer the dough circles to the prepared baking sheets, prick them with a fork and cover with a clean dish cloth. Leave to rise for another 20–30 minutes, or until doubled in size.

Preheat the oven to 250°C/480°F/Gas Mark 9.

Bake the circles for 8–10 minutes, or until golden. Eat them when they are fresh as breads like these don't store very well.

For image see page 517

GRAHAM BUNS

Grahamsboller (Denmark)
Grahamsbulle (Sweden)

These buns are made with graham flour, an unbleached wholegrain wheat flour where the wheat endosperm (the core of the grain) is ground finely, then mixed after the grinding with the bran and germ, which are ground separately and a bit more coarsely.

Enjoy them still warm with butter, marmalade and mature hard cheese.

Preparation and cooking time: 30 minutes
Rising time: 1 hour
Makes: 20 buns

500 ml/17 fl oz (2 cups plus 1 tablespoon) milk or water (or a mixture of both)
50 g/2 oz (3½ tablespoons) butter
25 g/1 oz fresh yeast
3 tablespoons sugar
300 g/11 oz (2¼ cup) strong wheat flour
500 g/1 lb 2 oz (3½ cups plus 1 tablespoon) graham flour
15 g/½ oz (2½ teaspoons) salt

Heat the milk or water in a pan over a low heat and stir in the butter to melt it. Remove from the heat and leave to cool to room temperature.

Dissolve the yeast in the liquid in the bowl of a stand mixer fitted with the dough hook. Add the flours and salt. Knead at medium speed until the dough is smooth and shiny, which will take about 10 minutes.

Cover the bowl with a clean dish cloth and leave the dough at room temperature for about 30 minutes, or until it has doubled in size.

Line 2 baking sheets with baking (parchment) paper.

Tip the dough onto a floured work counter and divide it into 20 equal pieces. Roll them into smooth buns and transfer to the prepared baking sheets. Cover with a clean dish cloth and leave at room temperature for another 30 minutes.

Preheat the oven to 225°C/435°F/Gas Mark 7.

Bake the buns until dark golden brown. Transfer to wire racks and leave to cool slightly.

ICELANDIC POTATO BREAD

Kartöflubrauð (Iceland)

Preparation and cooking time: 1¼ hours
Rising time: 2 hours
Makes: 1 loaf

10 g/¼ oz (2 teaspoons) yeast
250 ml/8 fl oz (1 cup) milk, lukewarm
400 g/14 oz floury potatoes, boiled, peeled,
    pushed through a ricer and cooled to
    room temperature
500 g/1 lb 2 oz (3⅔ cups) strong bread flour
2 teaspoons salt

For the egg wash
1 egg
50 ml/2 fl oz (3½ tablespoons) milk

Dissolve the yeast in the milk in a large mixing bowl. Add all the other ingredients and work the dough until shiny and smooth. Leave to rise for about an hour, or until doubled in size.

Tip the dough onto a lightly floured work counter and shape into an oval. Lift into a 23 x 13 x 8 cm/ 9 x 5 x 3 inch loaf pan and leave to rise again for an hour, or until it has doubled in size.

Meanwhile, preheat the oven to 180°C/350°F/Gas Mark 4.

Whisk the egg with the milk to make an egg wash. Brush the loaf lightly with the egg mixture and bake for about 45 minutes, or until done. Leave for a few minutes before turning the loaf out of the pan and leaving it to rest on a wire rack.

SCANIAN RYE BREAD

Kavring (Denmark)
Kavring (Sweden)

Kavring is a dense bread made from partially scalded rye and fermented over two days. In my mind it is flavoured mainly with caraway and aniseed, but in many recipes fennel and bitter orange peel are also added.

Sugar colouring is optional, but it is often added to make the bread dark brown – and some recipes can also contain Chinese mushroom soy sauce. Personally I don't like this, but if you want a darker and more savoury bread then go ahead and try it.

I often see recipes for *kavring* that contain bicarbonate of soda (baking soda), buttermilk, seeds, grains and all kinds of different things. These are probably all delicious breads in their own right, but they are not *kavring*.

I like *kavring* with some butter and a nice topping such as cured salmon, some charcuterie or a strong hard cheese. *Kavring* is also great lightly buttered as a little accompaniment for oysters on the half shell.

In Norway, up until very recently, *kavring* always referred to rusks, the one we call *skorpor* in Sweden (Crisp Rolls/Rusks, page 573). However, more recently cultural diffusion between the countries has led to confusion in the matter. If you do an internet search today on Norwegian *kavring* recipes, 85 per cent wil still be rusks whilst 15 per cent will show the recipe for a bread like the Swedish one.

You can reduce the recipe to make 1 or 2 loaves, but *kavring* stores really well, for up to 2 weeks in a paper bag and almost indefinitely in the freezer.

Preparation and resting: 3 days
Cooking time: 1 hour
Makes: 3 loaves

butter, to grease

Day 1
600 ml/20 fl oz (2½ cups) water
360 g/12 oz (3 cups) fine rye flour
30 g/1¼ oz (1½ tablespoons) salt
1 tablespoon caraway seeds
1 tablespoon aniseeds

Day 2
250 g/9 oz (2 cups) strong white bread flour,
    plus extra for the pans
600 g/1 lb 5 oz (4½ cups) Swedish rye/
    wheat bread flour (*rågsikt*) or
    360 g/12¼ oz (2⅔ cups) strong wheat flour
    and 240 g/8¾ oz (2 cups) rye flour
350 g/12 oz (3 cups) fine rye flour

200 g/7 oz (¾ cup plus 1 tablespoon) golden
  syrup
25 g/1 oz yeast

Day 1: Bring the water to the boil in a large pan.
Combine the rye flour, salt and seeds in a large
heatproof mixing bowl, then pour on the boiling
water and stir until smooth. Leave overnight at
room temperature. Do not cover the bowl, as you
want the lactobacillus in your room to infect the
dough, together with whatever life is present in
the flour.

Day 2: Transfer the dough to the bowl of a stand
mixer fitted with the dough hook. Add all the ingredients (reserving 2 handfuls of the rye flour for
later) and 350 ml/12 fl oz (1½ cups) of cold water. Knead the dough at a medium speed for about
15 minutes or until smooth, shiny and elastic.

Cover the bowl with a clean dish cloth and leave
the dough at room temperature to double in size.
It can take anything from 30 minutes to 2 hours.

Preheat the oven to 175°C/345°F/Gas Mark 4.
Butter and flour three 21 x 11 x 6 cm/8½ x 4½ x 2½
inch loaf pans.

Flour a work counter with the reserved rye flour
and tip out the risen dough. Divide into 3 equal
pieces and shape into loaves. Lift them into the
prepared pans and leave to prove a final time, until
they reach 1.5 cm/⅝ inch below the top of the pan.

Place the pans on a baking sheet and cover each
with a piece of baking (parchment) paper. Place
another baking sheet on top and weight with
something heavy and heatproof. This is important
for producing the characteristic brick shape and
density this bread is recognized for.

Bake for about 1 hour or so. The loaves will still be
slightly sticky inside and they need to be taken out
of the pans and rested on wire racks for another
24 hours before slicing and eating.

ICELANDIC RYE BREAD

Rúgbrauð / Hverabrauð / þrumari (Iceland)

In Iceland the rye loaf is usually quite dense, leavened with bicarbonate of soda (baking soda) and
rather sweet, almost like cake. It is not baked in
the oven but rather steamed, either in a geothermal area or sometimes in the oven. Historically
a sort of wooden vessel was used but today more
commonly a simple bucket with lid. Sites for baking bread can be found around hot springs close
to villages in the Icelandic countryside. They function a bit like communal spaces and every family
will have a hole in the ground in which they bake
their bread. It is funny walking over the steaming
ground, criss-crossing between holes covered by
ramshackle lids, the smell of sweet bread mingling
with the sulphurous scent of volcanic activity.

This recipe comes from Gudrun Einarsdottir who
helped me out with a lot of the Icelandic content
for this book. It was originally her grandmother's.

Rúgbrauð means rye bread, *hverabrauð* refers
specifically to bread baked next to hot springs and
þrumari, 'thunder bread', refers to the effects from
eating any bread containing a lot of dietary fibres.

Preparation and cooking time: 13 hours
Makes: 1 loaf

460 g/1 lb 1 oz (3½ cups) rye flour
260 g/9¼ oz (2 cups plus 2 tablespoons)
  plain (all-purpose) flour
1 litre/34 fl oz (4¼ cups) cultured milk
400 g/14 oz golden syrup
3 teaspoons salt
3 teaspoons bicarbonate of soda (baking
  soda)

Line a 3 litre/5¼ UK pint (12¾ cup) vessel, pot or
bucket with a lid with baking (parchment) paper.

Mix everything together until fully combined and
transfer to the prepared vessel. If you do not have
access to a suitable geothermal area, place the
vessel – with the lid on – in the oven at 90°C/195°F
overnight or for 12 hours. Let the bread cool down
completely before cutting into it.

If you do have a geothermal area close by, place
the dough-filled vessel in the ground and cover it
to start baking and proceed as described above.

DANISH RYE BREAD

Rugbrød (Denmark)

I love Danish rye bread, it is probably the tastiest bread I know. It can be found made either from finely ground flour and is then called *rugbrød uden kerner*, or with a coarser mix of grains containing a lot of whole kernels. This version is called *rugbrød med kerner*. It is a dense bread with little or no sweetening added. It is made without the addition of any fats and it is leavened slowly. It is also baked slowly and for a long time, sometimes up to 24 hours. It is quite common though to make the dough with either buttermilk or cultured milk. The longer you bake bread like this, the darker the interior will be, even if the temperature is rather low. It is good to let the rye bread sit for another 24 hours after they are baked before cutting in to them so they can set properly.

Rugbrød provides the base of most Open-faced Danish Sandwiches (page 522).

Preparation and cooking time: 5 days
Makes: 3 loaves

Step 1
10 g/¼ oz yeast
200 ml/7 fl oz (¾ cup plus 1 tablespoon)
    buttermilk or cultured milk, at
    room temperature
150 g/5 oz (1 cup plus 2 tablespoons)
    coarse rye flour
1 teaspoon salt

Step 2
500 ml/17 fl oz (2 cus plus 1 tablespoon)
    buttermilk or cultured milk
2 tablespoons salt
500 g/1 lb 2 oz (2½ cups) rye kernels
1 kg/2¼ lb (8 cups) coarse rye flour

Step 3
500 g/1 lb 2 oz (2½ cups) rye kernels

Step 1: Dissolve the yeast in the buttermilk or cultured milk in a bowl, add the remaining ingredients, mix well and leave to sit, covered, for 72 hours at room temperature.

Step 2: Transfer the now fermented and freshly acidic smelling dough from step 1 to a large bowl. Add the ingredients for step 2 and 1 litre/34 fl oz (4¼ cups) water and mix well with your hands or a wooden spoon. Cover and leave to sit for another 24 hours at room temperature.

Step 3: Place the rye kernels from step 3 in a new bowl and pour 500 ml/17 fl oz (2 cups plus 1 tablespoon) boiling water over them. Leave to steep for 45 minutes.

Meanwhile, butter 3 23 x 13 x 8 cm/9 x 5 x 3 inch loaf pans.

Add the step 3 mixture to the dough from step 2 and mix well. Transfer to the prepared loaf pans and cover with clingfilm (plastic wrap). Leaving to rise a bit for 3 hours at room temperature.

Preheat the oven to 150°C/300°F/Gas Mark 2.

Bake for about 3 hours. Cover with aluminium foil after the first 1½ hours so that the top does not colour too much. Unmould and allow to cool on wire racks.

For image see page 517

FINNISH RYE BREAD

Ruisleipä (Finland)

Finnish rye bread, *hapanleipä*, differs from the Scandinavian rye breads in several ways. The first is that it is often made solely from un-sifted, coarse rye flour, whilst in most other Nordic countries rye breads are usually based on a cereal mix, perhaps using some fine rye as a base flour, some whole rye kernels for texture and perhaps a bit of wheat flour to provide gluten. *Hapanleipä* is also most often baked as a flatter cake rather than as a loaf or in a tin, and the cakes are often prepared with a hole in the middle to hang them on a pole under the ceiling for storage.

Finnish rye bread is often quite sour from a lengthy fermentation process and is almost never seasoned with anything more than salt. More recent recipes often contain a bit of wheat flour and sometimes even spices or golden syrup. I prefer the older-style, all-rye versions, with their fresh sourdough acidity and dense texture.

To sour properly, the flour should be organic and untreated. I prefer to add some yeast to the first starter to ensure proper balance (and correct leavening) between the lactobacillus and yeast cells. If you prepare this recipe in a space where you bake often, the yeast cells floating around in the air will be of the right kind and probably plentiful enough to make it work anyhow, so you can omit the added yeast if you want.

Preparation and resting time: 4 days
Cooking time: 45–60 minutes
Makes: 8 cakes

Day 1
120 g/4 oz (¾ cup plus 2 tablespoons) coarse
    rye flour
5 g/⅛ oz fresh yeast

Day 2
220 g/7¾ oz (1⅔ cups) coarse rye flour

Day 3
330 g/11½ oz (2½ cups) coarse rye flour
10 g/¼ oz (2 teaspoons) salt

Day 1: Mix 175 ml/6 fl oz (¾ cups) water with the rye flour and yeast in a large bowl. Leave overnight at room temperature. Do not cover the bowl, as you want the lactobacillus in your room to work on the dough, together with what's present in the flour.

Day 2: Add the flour and another 330 ml/11 fl oz (1¼ cups plus 2 tablespoons) water and more flour and mix well. Cover and leave overnight again.

Day 3: Check the starter dough to make sure that you have plenty of active fermentation. Is it frothing? Taste it to make sure you have lactobacillus in there, creating lactic acid. Does it taste fresh and acidic? If the answer to both these questions is yes, then proceed with the recipe.

To finish the dough, add the salt and the rest of the flour and transfer to the bowl of a stand mixer fitted with the dough hook. Knead for quite some time. It might take up to 30 minutes on medium

speed, depending on the efficiency of your mixer. The dough should be sticky and dense, but shiny-looking.

Cover the bowl with a clean dish cloth and leave the dough at room temperature to double in size. The time it takes will depend on several factors: the raw materials used in the dough, the level of activity in the starter, the temperature of the room and so on.

Line 2 baking sheets with baking (parchment) paper.

With wet hands transfer the dough to a floured work counter and divide it into 8 equal pieces. Shape them into round cakes, then poke a hole in the middle of each cake and expand the hole to a diameter of about 4.5 cm/1¾ inches. Still with wet hands, smooth the surface of each cake – it should look silky. Dust the cakes lightly with flour and transfer them to the prepared baking sheets. Cover with a clean dish cloth and leave to rise. It can take a couple of hours and they should be almost but not quite doubled in size when ready to bake.

Preheat the oven to 200°C/400°F/Gas Mark 6.

Prick the cakes with a fork before baking. It will take longer than you think, I would guess about 1 hour and, since the cakes are already a dark colour, using colour to indicate doneness is dangerous. I prefer to cook until the cakes have a core temperature of about 96°C/205°F. When the cakes are done, wrap them immediately in clean cloths and leave them to the next day to cool and slowly soften, before cutting into them.

For image see page 517

PINE BARK (*PINUS SYLVESTRIS*)

In all parts of the Nordic region, in times of famine and poor harvest people have padded out their cereals with other things to make them last longer (page 132). In those regions where pine trees are abundant, pine bark flour has often been the material of choice. Especially in Finland, breads baked with pine bark had a strong tradition and historically have been eaten on a regular basis, not just when grains were not plentiful enough to last through the winter.

If you are interested in baking pine bark bread, the first step is to chop down a pine tree in early spring. You then need to strip away the inedible outer bark, and harvest the light-green inner bark – the phloem – from the wood by scraping it off with a knife or another sharp instrument. The outer bark is discarded, the wood is chopped up and dried into firewood and the strips of phloem are hung up to dry somewhere warm (some people also lightly toast their phloem).

When completely dry, the phloem is ground and sifted into a fine flour, which is mixed with cereal grain flour in proportions of roughly a quarter to a third. The result will contain about 80 calories per 100 g/3½ oz, compared with wheat flour, which contains well over 300 calories per 100 g/3½ oz.

FINNISH RYE AND PINE BARK BREAD

Pettuleipä (Finland)

I quite like the slightly bitter and almost spicy flavour of this bread, and I do think that it suits the Finnish style of rye bread especially well. If you want, you can substitute up to a third of the amount of flour in any bread recipe with pine bark flour to see what happens.

For this particular recipe, I think that the easiest way to add the pine flour in the correct quantity is to weigh out 1.5 kg/3¼ lb (11½ cups) coarse rye flour and 500 g/1 lb 2 oz pine bark flour. Mix them together very thoroughly and then use this mixture in the recipe below.

In some health food stores pine bark flour is available for purchase.

Preparation and resting time: 4 days
Cooking time: 45–60 minutes
Makes: 2 cakes

Day 1
120 g/4 oz (¾ cup plus 2 tablespoons) mixed
    rye and pine bark flour
5 g/⅛ oz fresh yeast

Day 2
220 g/7¾ oz (1⅔ cups) mixed rye and pine
    bark flour

Day 3
330 g/4 oz (2½ cups) mixed rye and pine
    bark flour
10 g/¼ oz (2 teaspoons) salt

Day 1: Mix 175 ml/6 fl oz (¾ cup) water with the rye and pine bark flour and yeast in a big bowl. Leave overnight at room temperature. Do not cover the bowl, as you want the lactobacillus in your room to work on the dough, together with what's present in the flour.

Day 2: Add the flour and another 330 ml/11 fl oz (1¼ cups plus 2 tablespoons) water and more flour and mix well. Cover and leave overnight again.

Day 3: Check the starter dough to make sure that you have plenty of active fermentation. Is it frothing? Taste it to make sure you have lactobacilli in there, creating lactic acid. Does it taste fresh and acidic? If the answer to both these questions is yes, then proceed with the recipe.

To finish the dough, add the salt and the rest of the flour and transfer to the bowl of a stand mixer fitted with the dough hook. Knead for some time. It might take up to 30 minutes on medium speed, depending on the efficiency of your mixer. The dough should be sticky and dense, but shiny-looking.

Cover the bowl with a clean dish cloth and leave the dough at room temperature to double in size. The time it takes will depend on several factors: the raw materials used in the dough, the level of activity in the starter, the temperature of the room and so on.

Line 2 baking sheets with baking (parchment) paper.

With wet hands transfer the dough to a floured work counter and divide it into 2 equal pieces. Shape them into round cakes, then poke a hole in the middle of each cake and expand the hole to a diameter of about 4.5 cm/1¾ inches. Still with wet hands, smooth the surface of each cake – it should look silky. Dust the cakes lightly with flour and transfer them to the prepared baking sheets. Cover with a clean dish cloth and leave to rise. It can take a couple of hours and they should be almost but not quite doubled in size when ready to bake.

Preheat the oven to 200°C/400°F/Gas Mark 6.

Prick the cakes with a fork before baking. It will take longer than you think, I would guess about 1 hour and, since the cakes are already a dark colour, using colour to indicate doneness is dangerous. I prefer to cook until the cakes have a core temperature of about 96°C/205°F. When the cakes are done, wrap them immediately in clean cloths and leave them to the next day to cool and slowly soften, before cutting into them.

UPPLANDIC RYE BREAD

Upplandskubb (Sweden)

This recipe from the eastern province of Sweden that includes Stockholm, Uppland, is not often seen anymore, but deserves to be, simply because it is both unique and delicious.

This recipe has its origins in the kitchens of the 1920s where many people didn't yet have access to an oven suitable for baking in. The original versions had the bread steamed in a smaller pot, placed in a bigger pot with some water at the bottom, which was covered with a lid and put straight on the stovetop rather than in an oven. This technique vaguely resembles the one used for the rye breads of Iceland (see pages 478–9), which are commonly baked in the island's thermal springs. More recent recipes for *upplandskubb* place the pot containing the bread dough in a water bath, which is in turn placed in an oven to be baked.

Preparation time: 7 hours
Makes: 1 loaf

50 g/2 oz yeast
15 g/½ oz (1 tablespoon) salt
210 g/7¼ oz (⅔ cup) golden syrup
350 g/12 oz (3 cups) fine rye flour
300 g/11 oz (2¼ cups) strong wheat flour
butter, to grease
flour, to dust

Combine all of the ingredients, except for the 2 flours, with 300 ml/10½ oz (1¼ cups) cold water in the bowl of a stand mixer and mix together well. Add the flours and knead for about 10 minutes, or until the dough is smooth and shiny.

Butter a 3-litre/5-UK-pint (ovenproof) pot and dust lightly with flour. Put the dough in the pot, cover with a clean dish cloth and leave it at room temperature for about 30 minutes, or until it doubles in size.

If you want to cook it in the oven, while the dough is rising, preheat the oven to 200°C/400°F/Gas Mark 6. If you are steaming it on the stove, a medium boil is required to generate enough steam. Remember to refill the water from time to time.

If steamed on the stove. Place a pot big enough to hold the smaller pot containing the bread on the stove. Add water to a depth of about 3 cm/1 inch. Place an up-side-down cup or something to distance the bread pot from the bottom of the one containing the water at the bottom. Place the one containing the bread on top of that and put the lid on both.

Bring to a simmer and cook until steamed though, which will take a couple of hours.

Turn it out of the pot and place it on a wire rack to cool.

ICELANDIC UNLEAVENED RYE FLATBREADS

Flatkaka / Flatbrauð (Iceland)

These flatbreads were traditionally cooked directly on hot stones, later on the flat top of a cast-iron stove and today most often in a cast-iron frying pan or skillet.

Commercially available *flatbrauð* usually contain wheat flour in addition to the rye of more authentic recipes. Most often the rye flour used in *flatbrauð* are scalded with boiling water to improve the texture.

Flatbrauð is often buttered and served as the bottom of a sandwich or as a side to a main dish like Icelandic Cold-smoked and Aged Mutton (*Hangikjöt*, page 345).

Preparation and cooking time: 45 minutes
Makes: about 10 cakes, depending on size

550 g/1 lb 4 oz (4 cups plus 2 tablespoons)
  fine rye flour, plus extra for dusting
10 g/¼ oz (2 teaspoons) salt

Mix the flour and salt together in a large mixing bowl. Pour on 300 ml/10½ fl oz (1¼ cups) boiling water and mix it in thoroughly. Start with a wooden spoon and then use your hands. It should take at least 10 minutes; the dough shouldn't be too stiff but it will always be quite sticky.

Tip the dough out onto a lightly floured work counter. Roll it out to about 3–10 mm/⅛–½ inches thick then cut into circles using a large ring cutter or cut around a round template, like a plate, with a sharp knife.

Preheat a dry griddle, cast-iron frying pan (skillet) or electric hotplate to medium.

Prick the cakes with a fork and fry them on both sides until they are quite dark in places. Stack the cakes into a pile, as they are done, so they don't dry out.

RYE AND GRAHAM BREADS FROM ÅLAND / BLACK BREAD

Saaristolaisleipä / Skärgårdslimpa (Finland)
Svartbröd (Sweden)

This dense and flavourful round loaf of rye and graham flours is a traditional speciality from the islands of Åland, located in the Baltic Sea between Sweden and Finland. It is prepared over several days, the amylase enzymes in the malt breaking down the starch into sugars that ferment and ultimately make the dough quite acidic from the activity of both lactobacillus and a little acetobacter.

Sometimes the Åland bread is started with a Finnish cultured milk called *surmjölk*, and at other times, with water. The recipe below uses water and I do think that is the more traditional way. If you want to try using cultured milk, you will have to omit the scalding stage of the dough on the first day, as you can't boil the milk without curdling it.

The baking of the bread is divided into two stages: the raw dough is first baked in the same way as any other bread, and it is then tightly wrapped in foil for a secondary longer bake at a lower temperature for an extended time. This causes the starches and sugars to caramelize throughout the bread, creating a very characteristic flavour and appearance. Today you simply set the oven to the desired temperature, but in the old days I would assume that this technique was executed by leaving the loaves in the slowly cooling brick oven overnight, after the baking was done and the fires had gone out.

Preparation and resting time: 2 days
Baking time: 6½ hours
Makes: 4 loaves

Day 1
First mix
100 g/3½ oz (¾ cup) ground rye malt
200 g/7 oz (1½ cups) coarse rye flour

Second mix
100 g/3½ oz (¾ cup) ground rye malt
200 g/7 oz (1½ cups) coarse rye flour

Third mix
50 g/2 oz (¾ cup) ground rye malt
200 g/7 oz (1½ cups) coarse rye flour

Last addition
25 g/1 oz yeast

Day 2
600 g/1 lb 5 oz (4½ cups) graham flour, plus
   extra to dust
250 g/9 oz (¾ cups) golden syrup
20 g/¾ oz (1 tablespoon) salt

To brush the baked breads
2 tablespoons golden syrup
100 ml/3½ fl oz (⅓ cup plus 1 tablespoon)
   hot strong coffee

Day 1: Make the starter dough. In a large pot, heat
400 ml/14 fl oz (1⅔ cups) water to 40°C/105°F. Pour
into a large mixing bowl with the first mix ingredients and stir everything together until smooth.

Tip on the second mix ingredients, then cover the
bowl and leave it to rest in a warm spot for about
20 minutes.

Pour on 400 ml/14 fl oz (1⅔ cups) boiling water
and stir again until the mixture is smooth. Top
with the third mix ingredients, then cover again
and rest in a warm spot for another 20 minutes.

Pour on another 400 ml/14 fl oz (1⅔ cups) boiling
water and mix until smooth. Cover and rest in a
warm spot for a further 20 minutes.

Dissolve the yeast in 50 ml/2 fl oz (3 tablespoons)
water and add to the dough. Mix in thoroughly,
then cover and leave at room temperature to ferment overnight.

Day 2: Transfer the starter dough to the bowl of
a stand mixer fitted with the dough hook. Add
the graham flour, syrup and salt and knead at a
medium speed for around 10 minutes, or until it is
smooth, shiny and elastic.

Cover the bowl and leave the dough at room temperature to double in size.

Line 2 baking sheets with baking (parchment) paper. Tip the dough onto a floured work counter
and divide it into 4 equal pieces. Shape each into a
rough ball and then roll them into round flat cakes,
about 1.5 cm/¾ inch thick. Transfer the cakes to
the prepared baking sheets, cover and leave to rest

at room temperature until it has almost doubled in
thickness.

Meanwhile, preheat the oven to 225°C/435°F/Gas
Mark 7.

Bake for about 20 minutes, or until done. While
the loaves are baking, mix the syrup with the hot
coffee. Take the loaves out of the oven and brush
them quite liberally all over with the coffee syrup.
Stack them in pairs, with the top sides together,
and wrap tightly in aluminium foil or lightly moistened paper towels.

Lower the oven temperature to 110°C/225°F/Gas
Mark ½. Return the wrapped loaves to the oven and
bake for 6 hours. You will see when you take them
out that they have darkened considerably. This is
normal and is what gives this bread its special flavour and appearance. Leave to cool on wire racks.

SOFT WHEAT AND RYE CAKES / HÖNÖ CAKES

Hönökaka (Sweden)

These slightly thicker, quite sweet flatbreads are named after Hönö Island just outside of Gothenburg on the Swedish west coast.

Hönökaka are usually sold in halves and are a traditional form of bread baked by the families of the fishermen in the region. Historically, they were, like many other flatbreads, baked with a hole in the middle so that they could be hung up to dry. Now they are mostly consumed fresh and soft as a sandwich. Today most *hönökaka* sold is baked commercially and it can be a bit of a challenge to find a good quality version to buy. The chances of finding authentic examples will be best around big family holidays, like Christmas, when people sell them in open-air markets and fairs.

Hönökaka are traditionally baked in a wood-fired, arched brick oven at a very high temperature. A pizza oven – if you have one – is ideal for this, but otherwise you can bake them on a heavy baking sheet in an oven set to the highest temperature.

Preparation and cooking time: 1½ hours
Rising time: 1 hour
Makes: 5 cakes

500 ml/17 fl oz (2 cups plus 1 tablespoon)
  milk
50 g/2 oz (3½ tablespoons) butter
70 g/2¾ oz (3 tablespoons) golden syrup
25 g/1 oz yeast
220 g/7¾ oz (1¾ cups) rye and wheat
  flour mix (*rågsikt*) or 130 g/4½ oz
  (1 cup) strong wheat flour and 90 g/
  3¼ oz (⅔ cup) rye flour, plus extra to dust
550 g/1 lb 4 oz (4 cups plus 1 tablespoon)
  strong wheat flour
15 g/½ oz (1 tablespoon) salt

Combine the milk, butter and golden syrup in a pan and heat gently until the butter and syrup melt. Leave to cool to body temperature.

Dissolve the yeast in the milk and pour it into the bowl of a stand mixer fitted with the dough hook and add the flours and the salt. Knead at medium speed for about 10 minutes, or until smooth and shiny. It will always be quite sticky.

Cover the bowl with a clean dish cloth and leave at room temperature for 20-30 minutes, until the doubled in size.

Tip the dough out onto a floured work counter and divide it into 5 equal pieces. Shape them into even-sized balls and leave to rest for another 25 minutes.

Heat a pizza oven or preheat your kitchen oven to 250°C/480°F/Gas Mark 9 (or to its highest temperature) and preheat a heavy baking sheet.

Flour the work counter generously and roll each dough ball into a round cake, about 1 cm/½ inch thick. Finish the rolling with a knobbed rolling pin then brush off any excess flour.

Use a peel (pizza shovel) to lift the *hönökaka* into the pizza oven and bake until golden. Otherwise, bake on the baking sheet in a normal oven.

PEA FLOUR FLATBREAD

Ärtbröd (Sweden)

Big parts of the Nordic region are marginal climates for growing certain grains – especially wheat, essential to bake most breads. During years of poor crop growth people everywhere have found many ways of bulking out their precious cereals with other things to make them last longer. Adding dried and ground peas and beans to the dough has been quite common in many places, and in old recipes I have found that sometimes more than half the amount of flour made from grains was substituted with that of peas. The variety of pea that was used varied greatly depending on which was traditionally grown in the different regions. Today however, most recipes use flour ground from ordinary yellow split peas.

These flatbreads can be baked either as thin rounds of about 5 mm/¼ inch thickness or thicker ones of about 1.5 cm/¾ inch. They are generally baked in a wood-fired, arched brick oven and the thicker the bread, the lower the temperature should be. A thick flatbread would preferably be cooked without actual flames but, rather, on the residual heat of the bricks themselves – perhaps after baking other, thinner flatbreads.

Some recipes contain extra seasonings like fennel seeds, aniseed, and/or caraway but I prefer it plain. It is also a funny thing how the dough, which initially tastes bitter from the raw pea flour, transforms during cooking to a buttery yellow sweetness that is quite special.

Pea breads are usually eaten fresh and soft on the day of baking, but I imagine that, historically, they were probably also dried and stored like most other breads of this type.

Preparation and cooking time: 45 minutes
Rising time: 1 hour
Makes: 5 large thin or 5 small thick flatbreads

350 ml/12 fl oz (1½ cups) milk
50 g/2 oz (3½ tablespoons) butter
10 g/¼ oz yeast
75 g/2¾ oz (½ cup) pea flour
450 g/1 lb (3⅓ cups) strong wheat flour,
   plus extra to dust
2 teaspoons salt
1 tablespoon sugar

Gently heat the milk and butter in a pan until the butter melts. Leave to cool to body temperature.

Dissolve the yeast in the milk and butter. Tip into the bowl of a stand mixer fitted with a dough hook, together with the rest of the liquid, the flours, salt and sugar. Knead at medium speed for about 30 minutes, or until smooth and very sticky. Cover the bowl with a clean dish cloth and leave the dough at room temperature for about an hour, or until it doubles in size.

Heat a pizza oven or preheat your kitchen oven to 250°C/480°F/Gas Mark 9 (or to its highest temperature) and preheat a heavy baking sheet.

Tip the dough onto a floured work counter and divide into 5 equal pieces. Shape into even-sized balls and roll each one out to a thin or thick flatbread, depending on your preference. Finish the rolling with a knobbed rolling pin (see illustration).

Use a peel (pizza shovel) to lift the flatbread into the pizza oven and bake until golden. Otherwise, bake on the baking sheet in a normal oven.

GRIDDLED RYE BREADS FILLED WITH SEMOLINA OR RICE PORRIDGE

Sultsina (Finland)

These Finnish stuffed flatbreads are a bit similar to the Karelian Pasties (page 519), except they are fried on a griddle before being filled and rolled up, instead of being stuffed and baked. They are either made with a semolina or rice porridge filling.

Preparation and cooking time: 1 hour
Makes: 20 breads

1 quantity Rye Dough (page 519)
1 quantity Rice Porridge Filling (page 519)
   or 1 quantity Wheat Semolina Porridge
   with Milk (page 466)
salted butter, melted, to brush

Divide the dough into 20 balls and roll them into thin circles, as described in the recipe.

Preheat a dry griddle, cast-iron frying pan (skillet) or electric hotplate. Fry the flatbreads on both sides until lightly coloured.

When all the flatbreads are cooked, brush them on one side with some salted butter and spread your choice of filling across the centre before rolling them up into little tubes. Brush them all over lightly with a little more butter and let them sit a bit at room temperature before you serve them.

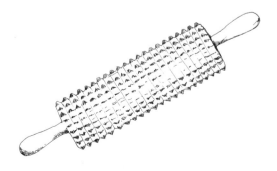

FLATBREAD FROM HARDANGER

Krotekake | Hardangerkake (Norway)

In the Norwegian region of Hardanger, this thin flatbread – which can be both dry and crisp or fresh and soft – is known as *krotekake*. In other parts of Norway it is called *Hardangerkake*, bread from Hardanger. Traditionally this flatbread was cooked in a wood-fired, arched brick oven and was therefore not turned over during the baking. Today, however, most people cook *krotekake* on a flat electric hotplate (see illustration, page 515), which means that you need to cook it on each side separately.

Some recipes for *krotekake* combine wheat flour with rye flour, while others use a mixture of wheat, rye and barley flour, or even wheat and barley flour.

Krotekake are rolled out first with a smooth rolling pin and then with a disked and knobbed one, which is rolled away from you; then once straight across the first pattern of dimples – creating a pattern of small squares.

Krotekake is often eaten buttered and sugared. If it has been dried, to preserve it, it is sometimes moistened a bit before eating.

Preparation and cooking time: 1 hour
Rising time: 2 hours
Makes: 15 flatbreads

10 g/¼ oz (2 teaspoons) fresh yeast
500 g/1 lb 2 oz (4 cups plus 1 tablespoon)
    fine rye flour, plus extra for dusting
140 g/5 oz (1 cup) wholemeal
    (whole-wheat) flour
1 teaspoon salt

Dissolve the yeast in 400 ml/14 fl oz (1⅔ cups) water the bowl of a stand mixer fitted with a dough hook and add the flours and the salt. Knead at medium speed until smooth and shiny, which will take about 10 minutes.

Cover the bowl, and leave the dough at room temperature to double in size. It should take 2 hours.

Tip the dough out onto a floured work counter and divide it into 15 equal pieces. Shape each piece into a round ball, keeping them covered with a clean dish cloth while you work, so they don't dry out. You can be generous with the flour on your work counter, as you will brush it off later.

Roll each dough ball into a round, flat cake, 30–35 cm/12–14 inches in diameter. Use the special *hardanger* roller (see illustration below) to create the cross-hatch pattern on the surface of each flatbread.

Preheat a dry griddle, cast-iron frying pan (skillet) or electric hotplate. Or, if you have an old-fashioned wood-fired arched brick oven, then use this.

Brush any excess flour off the flatbreads (as this will burn) and fry them on both sides until golden around the edges. Stack the flatbreads in a pile, as they are done, weighting it with a wooden board to avoid excessive curling.

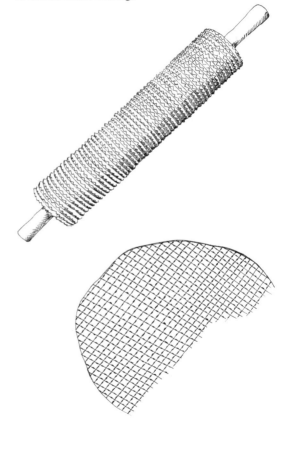

NORWEGIAN CRISP FLATBREAD

Flatbrød (Norway)

This flatbread used to be one of the true staples of Norwegian food culture and is still widely consumed. It is different from most other Nordic flatbreads as it is unleavened and because it is baked on a flat top griddle rather than in the oven, much like Norwegian *lefse*. Historically the electric hot plate was a hot stone, later it was a wood-fired cast-iron one and today it is most often electric.

The contents vary greatly and is often a mix between whole-grain wheat and other grains like barley or oat, or potatoes, and in some parts of the country ground split peas. Allow for 50% plain (all-purpose) flour to ensure an easier rolling out process for those unaccustomed to making *flatbrød*. Barley flour is good for rolling the cakes out in.

Historically, as with many other dry or crisp flatbreads in the Nordic region, Norwegian *flatbrød* was not baked very often but rather a couple of times a year and in large quantities. As it contains no fat and is dry it can be stored almost indefinitely in the right conditions.

Other *knäckebröd*-style crisp flatbread, which were historically more common in Sweden and Finland, are different from the Norwegian ones as they are most often leavened and baked in an oven.

Preparation and cooking time: 2 hours
Resting time: overnight
Makes: 10–20 flatbreads depending on the
  size of your griddle

650 g/1 lb 7 oz a mix of flours as
  described above
2 teaspoon salt
couple of handfuls of barley flour to roll the
  breads out in

Place the flours and salt in the bowl of a stand mixer fitted with a dough hook.

Bring 700 ml/24 fl oz (3 cups) water to a boil and pour it over the flour. Work the hot mixture in the stand mixer for about 10 minutes, or until firm. Wrap the dough in clingfilm (plastic wrap) and place it in the refrigerator overnight to rest.

Cut the dough into 10–20 equal-sized pieces and flatten each piece out as much as you can with your hands. Stack the dough discs to prevent them from drying out and cover the stack with some clingfilm as you are working.

Spread a layer of barley flour onto your work counter and start rolling one of the pre-flattened discs out. Ensure that it doesn't stick to the counter and keep it floured at all times. It should be very thin, barely millimetres in thickness. When you are satisfied with the thickness of the bread, carefully brush off the excess flour with a soft brush. This is important to make sure they cook well. Continue with the remaining pieces of dough.

Preheat a large, round electric hotplate (see illustration, page 515) or flat top griddle to medium.

Transfer a dough disc to the griddle. Place the side that was facing up when you were rolling it, face down on the hot griddle. As the flatbread is cooking, brush away any excess flour from the side now facing upwards. Once it is beginning to colour on the first side, flip it over. It doesn't have to cook until dry on the griddle. Place the cooked bread in a stack and weight it down with something flat and heavy to keep it straight. Continue with the remaining discs of dough.

ICELANDIC LEAF BREAD

Laufabrauð (Iceland)

Essential to many family's preparations for Christmas and often served with the Christmas dinner dishes, *Hangilaeri* (page 345) and *Jólarjúpa* (page 286), these flat, deep-fried and richly decorated breads are something made by the whole family together, as a sort of social event just before the holidays. Originating in northern Iceland, the custom of making *laufabrauð* is now widely spread throughout the whole island. These days ready-made *laufabrauð* dough can be bought in Icelandic supermarkets.

The intricate patterns are cut either with a small knife or with a special brass roller called *laufabrauðsjárn* (see illustration right). You will also need a deep, wide pot for frying the leaf breads. It should be wide enough that they can lie flat. The traditional fat of choice for the frying would be rendered sheep's tallow, but any kind of suitable fat or oil can be used.

Preparation and cooking time: at least an
  entire afternoon, depending on how many
  people are involved in the preparation
Makes: about 40 leaf breads

1 kg/2¼ lb (8½ cups) plain (all-purpose) flour
40 g/1½ oz (3 tablespoons) sugar
1 teaspoon baking powder
1 teaspoon salt
40 g/1½ oz (3 tablespoons) butter
500 ml/17 fl oz (2 cups plus 1 tablespoon)
  milk, lukewarm
neutral oil, for deep-frying

Mix all the dry ingredients together in a large bowl. Melt the butter in the warm milk. Make a little well in the middle of the flour mixture, then pour in the liquid and start stirring it in, as though you were making a traditional Italian pasta dough. Use your hand to stir the liquid so that more and more of the flour gets caught up in motion and incorporated into the dough. Continue working until all the flour is absorbed. The resulting dough should be rather firm and completely smooth.

Divide the dough in half, shape the pieces into logs then wrap them in clingfilm (plastic wrap) or a clean, damp dish cloth. Leave to rest for about 30 minutes.

Heat the oil in a deep, wide pot to 190–200°C/375–400°F.

Because the dough dries out so fast, at this stage you need to be working with several other people. Cut a thin slice of dough and roll it out to a very, very thin disc, 15–20 cm/6–8 inches in diameter; it should be almost see-through. As soon as the dough is rolled out, hand it over to the next person for decoration (see illustrations below), who hands it over to yet another person for frying.

The cooking itself takes only seconds, and the result should be a very pale, golden colour. As soon as they are fried, the breads can be pressed between 2 flat surfaces for a short while to make them completely flat, although this is only necessary for aesthetic reasons. Once you are happy, leave them on wire racks to cool down and crisp up.

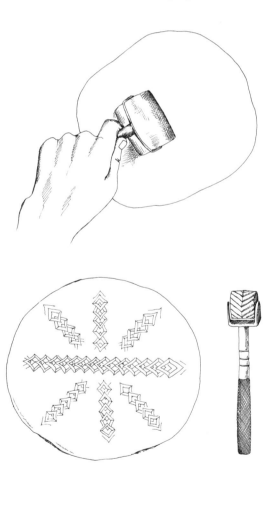

NORWEGIAN THIN CRISPBREAD BAKED FROM POTATO AND OATMEAL

Skjenning (Norway)

The name of this very thin, crisp flatbread, often served with the Norwegian Mutton and Meatball Soup from Trøndelag (page 354), comes from the Norwegian word for 'shiny'. This, in its turn, refers to the shiny surface of the bread that is brushed with milk and sugar after cooking.

Even though it is today made in other parts of the country (as the recipe has spread with people moving around), *skjenning* comes from a region called Innherred, located around the inner parts of the Trondheim fjord. If the *skjenning* is produced for sale it has to contain potatoes and oats from the Innherred region or it cannot bear the name *skjenning* as it has legal status as a protected regional speciality.

Preparation and cooking time: 1 hour
Makes: 40 crispbreads

500 g/1 lb 2 oz floury potatoes, boiled, peeled, pushed through a ricer and cooled to room temperature
250 g/9 oz (2 cups) fine oatmeal (or a mix of oatmeal and barley flour), plus extra to dust
2 tablespoons sugar
200 ml/7 fl oz (¾ cup plus 1 tablespoon) milk

Put the potato in a large mixing bowl. Add the oatmeal gradually, working until you have a smooth and elastic dough which is quite firm. How much oatmeal you need to add depends on the potato. It varies a lot, and the quantity stated in the recipe should serve as a rough guideline.

Preheat a large, round electric hotplate (see illustration right) or griddle.

Divide the dough into 5 equal portions. On a floured work counter, roll the first ball out thinly to the size of the hotplate. Finish the rolling with a knobbed rolling pin (see illustration, page 511) so that it doesn't fluff up into a balloon when heated. Brush off any excess flour.

Cook the *skjenning* cake over medium heat on one side only until the side facing the heat is a light golden colour.

Mix the sugar into the milk thoroughly. Brush one-fifth of the sweetened milk on the uncooked side of the *skjenning*, then remove from the heat.

Repeat with the remaining four dough balls. Once the *skjenning* have all cooled and are dry to the touch, trim the edges neatly and cut each one into 8 triangular pieces (see illustration below). Stack and weight them, to ensure they do not curl up as they cool and dry. They should be pressed until completely dry and crisp.

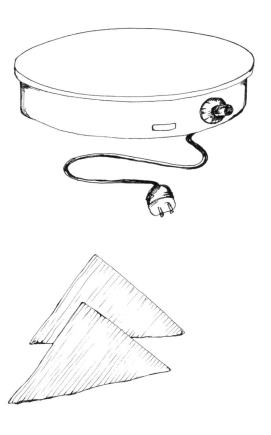

RYE CRISPBREAD

Knekkbreyð (Faroe Islands)
Hrökkbrauð (Iceland)
Knekkebrød (Norway)
Näkkilepa (Finland)
Knækbrød (Denmark)
Knackerbrod (Sweden)

These leavened flatbreads are baked in an oven unlike the uniquely Norwegian Crisp Flatbread (page 513), which is not. They are common all over the Nordic region and in many other parts of the world to which they are being exported. Their origins lie in Sweden and Finland where they have been baked more or less in their current form for about 500 years. In Sweden archaeologists have found evidence of flatbreads being made as early as the sixth century, those however were baked on hot stones. Since the early nineteenth century, when wood-fired baking ovens started to become more common on many farms, the dried crispbread with its characteristic hole in the middle became really common. Before the invention of the iron stove, baking was something people out on the farms did perhaps twice a year. Once in autumn (fall) after the harvest and once in spring when the winter stores had run out. The hole in the middle was simply there to facilitate the hanging and handling of the breads on long wooden poles, which would rest between the rafters of the farmhouse itself or those of a dedicated storage house.

Today very few people bake these kinds of breads themselves but rather buy them readymade. A meal with pickled herring that doesn't include darkly toasted rye sourdough crispbread, good salty butter and mature cheese is for many, including myself, unthinkable.

Apart from when trying this recipe, I can barely remember a time when I made this myself but I thought it would be interesting to include it anyway. Not only because it is very tasty but also because it explains the method behind a very important part of Nordic food culture even though it isn't practised any more.

It is a bit awkward to bake these in an ordinary domestic oven but it works ok. If you have access to a wood-fired bread oven or a pizza oven, that works the best.

Preparation and cooking time: 3 hours
Second baking: overnight (optional)
Makes: about 20 crispbreads

500 ml/17 fl oz (2 cups plus 1 tablespoon)
  milk
50 g/2 oz yeast
330 g/11½ oz (2½ cups) coarse rye flour, plus
  extra for sprinkling
400 g/14 oz (3 cups) strong wheat flour, plus
  extra to dust
2 teaspoons aniseed, crushed

Pour the milk into the bowl of a stand mixer fitted with the dough hook, add the yeast and stir until dissolved. Add the remaining ingredients and knead at medium speed until it doesn't stick much to the edges of the bowl any more. It will take at least 10 minutes but can take longer. Leave the dough to rise for 30 minutes.

Tip the dough out onto a floured work counter and divide into 15–20 equal-sized pieces, shape them with a floured hand into round buns and leave them to rise for another 20 minutes.

Preheat the oven to 225°C/435°F/Gas Mark 8. Line a baking sheet with baking (parchment) paper and place in the oven to heat up.

Sprinkle a good handful of rye flour onto a work counter and place a bun onto it. Roll the bun out into a round of at least 20 cm/8 inches in diameter and finish by rolling over it with a knobbed rolling pin. Continue with the remaining buns.

Place each round on the preheated baking sheet and bake for about 5 minutes. They don't have to stay in the oven until they are crisp as they will dry afterwards. Let them cool on wire racks until completely crisp before eating them.

Tip: I like toasted crispbread, which means that you put them in the oven for a second baking and drying after they have all been baked the first time. To do this, reduce the oven temperature to 100°C/200°F/Gas Mark ¼, stack all of the crispbreads in a pile and place them in the oven on a wire rack overnight. They will darken considerably and dry completely.

For image see opposite page

Clockwise from top left: Wheat Buns (page 524); Finnish Rye Bread (page 504); Tea Buns (page 500); Danish Rye Bread (page 504); Rye Crispbread (page 516); store-bought Golden Syrup Loaf (page 496)

517 Recipes / Breads and savoury pastries

SANDWICH TORTE / SAVOURY LAYER CAKE

Brauðterta (Iceland)
Voileipäkakku (Finland)
Smörgåstårta (Sweden)

A man named Gunnar Sjödahl is claimed to have invented the sandwich torte while working at Wedemarks coffeehouse in the Swedish city of Östersund, incidentally also the city where I grew up. Even though it was only popularized as late as the mid-1960s, this oddity of a dish has become a modern classic. Often served at occasions like weddings, funerals, birthdays and other festivities when a lot of people are to be fed in a practical way, it is usually consumed with beer and Aquavit (page 712) on the side.

The sandwich torte is made up of layers of white bread (instead of cake) and savoury fillings such as seasoned mayonnaises and the like (instead of pastry cream). The stack of bread and fillings is then covered with a mix of mayonnaise and crème fraîche or mayonnaise and whipped cream – much like a cream torte is covered in whipped cream.

This savoury layer cake can be topped with almost anything and wild combinations like salmon, meatballs, grapes, shrimp, cucumbers, pineapple, cheese, preserved mandarin wedges and ham are more common than they are uncommon.

However surreal it might sound, if you make it from proper bread, put some effort into the seasoning, and use tasty combinations of toppings, all of which are great in quality, then it is basically just a tasty, giant sandwich – which is easily cut into pieces and conveniently feeds a huge number of people. Highly recommended.

The recipe below is for a seafood torte, but feel free (and get excited) to add or subtract anything, seafood or not.

Preparation time: 30 minutes
Serves: 20 for lunch

2 loaves good white bread
400 g/14 oz (1⅔ cups) cream cheese
35 g/1½ oz (¾ cup) finely snipped chives
1 quantity Mayonnaise (page 674)

500 ml/17 fl oz (2 cups plus 1 tablespoon)
   cream
salt and white pepper, to taste

For the topping
500 g/1 lb 2 oz cold-smoked salmon
   or Gravlax (page 216), thinly sliced
500 g/1 lb 2 oz cooked shrimp
   (baby shrimp), peeled
grated horseradish, to taste

To garnish
dill fronds
2 lemons, cut into 20 wedges

Cut the bread into 1.5 cm/¾ inch slices and trim off the crusts.

Combine the cream cheese, chives and half the mayonnaise in a mixing bowl and season well with salt and pepper.

You will be making 4 layers, so divide the slices into 4 even sets. Lay out the first set of bread slices on a serving platter in a rectangle and spread with one-third of the cream cheese mixture. Continue layering with more slices of bread and filling until you have all 4 layers with 3 layers of filling. Make sure you get nice straight edges on the assembled stack of bread – it should look neat, not just like a pile of bread.

Whip the cream to stiff peaks and mix it with the remaining mayonnaise. Season well with salt and pepper. Spread the mayo cream all over the torte, covering the top and all the sides neatly. You could even pipe on some decorations with a piping bag if you want to.

Arrange the salmon, shrimp and horseradish daintily on top of the cake and, if you want, around its edges. Finish with the dill fronds, horseradish and the lemon wedges, arrange them in a way that seem pleasing to you.

FOLDED FLATBREAD SANDWICH

Klämma, Stut (Sweden)

A *klämma* or *stut* is any sandwich made from Swedish soft flatbreads folded around some kind of topping. It could be charcuterie, a Sweet Reduced Whey Spread (page 72), or even Sour Herring (page 172), potatoes, onion and sour cream.

KARELIAN PASTIES

Karjalanpiirakat (Finland)

This iconic savoury pasty comes from Karelia, a region in eastern Finland that is shared between Russia and Finland. A very thin rye crust envelops a filling made either from rice porridge or buttery mashed potatoes. If potatoes are used the pasty is simply called Potato Pasty – or *perunapiirakka*. *Karjalanpiirakat* are often served with Finnish Egg Butter (page 655).

Preparation and cooking time: 2 hours
Makes: 25 pasties

For rice porridge filling
250 g/9 oz (1¼ cups) short-grain rice
1 teaspoon salt
1 litre/34 fl oz (4¼ cups) milk
50 g/2 oz (3½ tablespoons) butter

For mashed potato filling
1 quantity Mashed Potatoes (page 118)

For the rye dough
280 g/10 oz (2¼ cups) fine rye flour, plus
   extra to dust
1 teaspoon salt
50 g/2 oz (3½ tablespoons) melted butter,
   for brushing

To prepare the rice porridge filling, put the rice and salt in a large pan and add 500 ml/17 fl oz (2 cups plus 1 tablespoon) water. Bring to a boil over a medium heat, stirring constantly. Lower the heat and stir in the milk. Continue simmering for a further 35 minutes, stirring every now and then. You don't want to break up the grains of rice too

much. If the porridge becomes too thick before the rice has softened, adjust the consistency with a bit more milk. Add the butter in the last 5 minutes of the simmering time. When the porridge is done, stir the butter into it until fully incorporated.

Regardless of whether you are making potato filling or rice filling, it should be cooled to room temperature before you make the pasties.

To make the rye dough, combine the rye flour and salt in a bowl and pour in 200 ml/7 fl oz (¾ cup plus 1 tablespoon) cold water. Work the ingredients together until you have a stiff, but smooth, dough. Shape into 2 logs and cover them with a clean, damp dish cloth to prevent them from drying out as you work.

Cut a little piece of dough from the log and shape it into a ball. Dust your work counter generously with fine rye flour and roll the dough ball out to a very thin circle of 12–14 cm/4½–5½ inches in diameter. Continue with the remaining dough. Place the completed circles in a stack and cover them with a clean, damp dish cloth as you work, to prevent them from drying out.

Preheat the oven to 250°C/480°F/Gas Mark 9 and line a baking sheet with baking (parchment) paper.

Place a couple of tablespoons of filling onto each dough circle, then fold the edges in towards the middle and crimp them tightly so the whole pasty forms an oval. Push the crimps down a little into the filling so that they don't stand up into the air too much; this will prevent them from burning in the oven.

Arrange the pasties on the prepared sheet and bake them for 5–10 minutes; they should be lightly golden. Take them out of the oven and brush them generously with the melted butter straight away.

For image see page 489

OPEN-FACED LINGONBERRY AND POTATO PASTIES

Rönttönen (Finland)

These pasties, just barely sweeter than the Karelian Pasties (page 519) which are considered savoury food, are often enjoyed with coffee as a snack.

Preparation and cooking time: 1½ hours
Resting time: 4 hours
Makes: 20 pasties

1 quantity Rye Dough (page 519)

For the filling
300 g/10½ oz floury potatoes
50 g/2 oz (½ cup) rye flour, plus extra to dust
100 g/3½ oz (½ cup) lingonberries
3 teaspoons sugar
pinch salt

Boil the potatoes in salted water until tender. Drain and mash them well, then stir in the remaining filling ingredients. Flatten the now pink mash.

Cover the pot and set it aside in a warm place for 4 hours. During this time the residual heat causes a kind of malting process to occur, where some of the starch is converted into sugar and makes the mash taste sweeter. In Finnish this process is called *imellyttäminen*.

When ready to make the pasties, preheat the oven to 250°C/480°F/Gas Mark 9 and line a baking sheet with baking (parchment) paper.

Break off a small piece of the rye dough and shape it into a ball. Dust your work counter generously with fine rye flour and roll the dough ball out to a very thin circle of 12–14 cm/4½–5½ inches in diameter. Continue with the remaining dough. Place the completed circles in a stack and cover them with a clean, damp dish cloth as you work, to prevent them from drying out.

Place a couple of tablespoons of filling onto each dough circle, then fold the edges in towards the middle and crimp them tightly so the whole pasty forms a round. Push the crimps down a little into the filling so that they don't stand up into the air too much; this prevents them burning in the oven.

Arrange the pasties on the prepared sheet and bake them for 5–10 minutes; they should be lightly golden. Take them out of the oven and brush them generously with the melted butter straight away.

NORWEGIAN MINCED MEAT AND CHEESE GRILLED SANDWICH

Snadderloff (Norway)

Ok, so this recipe might seem a bit crazy, but this is the way it is supposed to be, and yes, the Chinese (napa) cabbage goes in there with the dressing before it is all cooked.

This is a dish that can be found in quite a few Norwegian roadside diners but which people also cook in their homes. Let's call it 'modern Norwegian comfort food' – the kind of thing a couple of 17 years olds would make themselves and eat in front of the television when their parents are out.

Preparation and cooking time: 20 minutes
Serves: 4

2 baguettes, cut in half
a couple of handfuls of shredded Chinese
    (napa) cabbage
store-bought hamburger dressing,
    to taste
butter, for frying
600 g/1 lb 5 oz minced (ground) beef
200 g/7 oz (1⅔ cups) grated cheese
salt and pepper, to taste

Slice the 4 pieces of baguette lengthwise through the top but not all the way through to the bottom. Place a layer of Chinese (napa) cabbage in the bottom of each slit and follow that with a layer of hamburger dressing. Set aside.

Melt some butter in a frying pan over medium heat, add the beef, season with salt and pepper, and fry until cooked through. Preheat the grill (broiler) to 225°C/435°F/Gas Mark 8.

Spread the fried beef out on top of the dressing and finish with a good layer of cheese. Grill (broil) the sandwiches for about 5 minutes, or until golden.

SAMI SOFT FLATBREAD

Gaahkoeh / Gáhkku (Sami)
Glödkaka (Sweden)

These rather thick, soft flatbreads where tradi- tionally baked by the semi Nomadic Sami families of the Nordic region and they where a common source of starch, eaten with a hot main meal. As you could add the water on site where you were camping, you only really had to bring the dry in- gredients – very practical in the old days. Today they are leavened with commercial yeast and are often quite fluffy. Historically I assume that they where leavened much like breads where tradition- ally, namely by naturally occurring strains of yeast during a much slower fermentation that gave a denser and less sweet bread.

They are still common but today, more so spread with butter and topped with something to make an open faced sandwich. *Gaahkoeh* would tradition- ally be baked on a flat stone heated by fire, on a piece of sheet metal, or in a cast iron frying pan.

Preparation and cooking time: 1 hour
Makes: 20 cakes

50 g/2 oz yeast
1 litre/34 fl oz (4¼ cups) water or reindeer
  broth
70 g/2¾ oz (3½ tablespoons) golden
  syrup
1½ teaspoons salt
50 ml/1¾ oz (3⅓ tablespoons) oil or
  rendered reindeer fat
800 g/1¾ lb (6⅔ cups) plain (all-purpose)
  flour, plus extra to dust
500 g/1 lb 2 oz (4 cups plus 2 tablespoons)
  fine rye flour

Dissolve the yeast in 1 litre/34 fl oz (4¼ cups) wa- ter or broth in a large bowl. Mix in all the remain- ing ingredients to form a sticky dough. Leave to rise for about 45 minutes.

Divide the dough into 20 equal balls. On a floured work counter roll out each dough ball into a small flat cake.

Cook the cakes over medium heat in a dry frying pan until golden on both sides.

NORWEGIAN GRIDDLED SOFT POTATO FLATBREAD

Potetlefse / Potetlompe / Mjukbrød (Norway)

This Norwegian potato flatbread is popular- ly rolled around a hot dog with different fillings. They are also very tasty hot from the hotplate lightly buttered and sprinkled with some sugar as a sweet snack. Another way of serving it is togeth- er with Norwegian Fermented Trout (page 175).

The name depends a little on who you ask but a general consensus is that *potetlompe* is the smaller and slightly thicker version I have described in the method below. If it is called *mjukbrød* it is general- ly rolled out into a larger and much thinner cake, as thin a1.5mm. If you want to make the rolled out version you wont be able to lift it on to the hot plate by hand, you will have to roll them up on a special stick (see image, page 449) before rolling them out again onto the hot surface itself to cook them. *Mjukbrød* can in some part of Norway also be something much more similar to Swedish Soft Flatbreads (page 527), but cooked on the electric hot plate rather than in the oven.

Preparation and cooking time: 1 hour
Makes 10 cakes

1 kg/2¼ lb potatoes, boiled, peeled and
  cooled to room temperature
1 teaspoon salt
200 g/7 oz (1¾ cups) plain (all-purpose) flour

Pass the potatoes together with the salt though a meat mincer (grinder) on the fine plate setting. Transfer to a bowl, add the flour, and work with your hands until firm but smooth in texture.

Preheat a large, round electric hotplate (see illus- tration right) or griddle, if using.

On a floured work counter, divide the dough into 10 pieces and press each one out with a floured hand to a round 3 mm/⅛ inch thick and 15–18 cm/6–8 inches in diameter. Prick with a fork all over and fry on the hotplate or in a large, dry fry- ing pan over medium heat. Cook until golden on both sides. Stack them as they finish and cover with a clean dish cloth so that they don't dry out too much while cooling.

OPEN-FACED DANISH SANDWICHES

Smørebrød (Denmark)

All over the Nordic region sandwiches are considered important. They consist of a bread of some sort with something tasty on top or in-between layers. In the north and in harsher climates flatbreads, often made with at least some quantity of barley in them, are common. Further south, and in slightly milder climates, rye-based loaves often act as the bread base of choice. In Denmark, with its rich agriculture and its cultural connections to Europe, the open-faced sandwich has evolved not only into a lavish art form but also a completely indispensible part of Danish eating habits. The Danish open-faced sandwich called *smørebrød* is mostly considered a lunch dish and is often enjoyed in restaurants serving pretty much only that. It is commonly served with a beer on the side and a glass of Aquavit (page 714). Every time I go to Copenhagen I will have lunch at Schønnemann, a modern-day Danish institution where these often-mistreated sandwiches are executed to absolute perfection.

Below is a selection of very well-known *smørebrød* with illustrations and a short step-by-step on how to put them together. A general tip is that for most Danish open-faced sandwiches there should be enough toppings to completely obscure the bread, also they are often really large. I always go to Schønnemann with the ambition of eating five of them, but end up only getting through three.

I am not going to provide quantities and a normal recipe for these sandwiches – it seems so overly on the nose. I will however try my best to explain how to put them together and why. They all start with a slice of Danish rye bread.

Dyrlægens natmad means 'the veterinarian's midnight snack'. Spread the bread with butter or lard and a thick slice of coarsely ground liver pate. Continue with slices of cold Brined and Boiled Eye of Round (page 436) – enough to completely cover the pate. Cut some jellied beef stock in stripes of about 2 cm/¾ inch in width and place a couple of them over the meat. Top with some raw red onion rings and some cress. The onion is a more recent addition to this recipe, which originates from Oskar Davidsen's *smørebrød* restaurant during the 1920s, however it is the way most people will have it today.

Røget ål med røræg means smoked eel and scrambled eggs. Butter a slice of rye bread and place two large pieces of smoked eel fillet (at room temperature) on top. The fish fillets should cover the bread entirely and almost create a square when placed next to each other. Cover the seam between the two pieces of eel with some great, lukewarm scrambled egg and sprinkle the whole dish with finely cut chives.

Rullepølse means rolled headcheese. Spread the rye bread with lard and cover the surface with slices of Spiced Meat Roll (page 432). Place a strip of jellied beef broth, 2 cm/¾ inch in width, across the top of the sandwich and top with raw red onion rings.

Tatar is made with beef tartar. Spread a slice of rye bread with butter or lard, cover the whole top with a flat layer of finely cut or ground beef so that it covers even the edges of the bread. Season well with salt and black pepper and top with a raw egg yolk, raw red onion rings and grated horseradish.

Stjerneskud means 'shooting star'. This *smørebrød* is one of the few that is not made with rye bread but rather with buttered toast. Place a fillet of steamed white fish like plaice or something similar, so that it covers one half of the toast. Place another piece of fish, which has been breaded and fried, parallel to the first one so that they together cover the whole piece of toast. Place some Mayonnaise (page 674) along the seam between the two pieces of fish and top with shrimp (baby shrimp), Quick Pickled Cucumber (page 658) and lumpfish roe. Serve with a lemon wedge on the side.

Sol over Gudhjem means 'sun over Gudhjem'. Gudjem is a village on the Baltic island of Bornholm. Spread a slice of rye bread with butter or lard and place two fillets of smoked herring on top so that they pretty much cover the whole piece of bread. Place a raw egg yolk on top of the herring and top with finely cut chives and pieces of radish.

For image see page 229

Clockwise from top left: Sol over Gudhjem; Rullepølse; Røget ål med røræg; Dyrlægens natmad; Tartar; Stjerneskud

WHEAT BUNS

Boller (Norway)
Sämpylä / Semla (Finland)
Boller (Denmark)
Källarfranska (Sweden)

Variations of these simple little buns exist throughout the whole Nordic region and they resemble each other quite closely form country to country. They are often baked in people's homes and consumed rather quickly, split in two and turned into sandwiches. Before baking, they can be brushed with egg wash or milk and/or sprinkled with sesame or poppy seeds. They can also be left just as they are. They do not store particularly well.

They can be sweet to various degrees. This particular recipe, not so much. For a sweeter version refer to the Sweet Wheat Bun Dough recipe on page 538.

Preparation and cooking time: 1 hour
Makes: 20 buns

50 g/2 oz yeast
500 ml/17 fl oz (2 cups plus 1 tablespoon) water or milk, at room temperature
50 ml/1¾ fl oz (3½ tablespoons) rapeseed (canola) oil
2 teaspoons salt
2 tablespoons sugar
825 g/1 lb 13 oz (6⅓ cups) plain (all-purpose) flour

Line 2 baking sheets with baking (parchment) paper.

Dissolve the yeast in the water or milk in the bowl of a stand mixer. Add the remaining ingredients and work for about 5 minutes on medium speed.

On a lightly floured work counter split the dough half and roll it out into 2 logs. Cut each log into 10 pieces and shape into round buns with your hands. Place the buns onto the prepared baking sheets and cover with clean dish cloths. Allow to rise for about 40 minutes or until doubled in size.

Preheat the oven to 200°C/400°F/Gas Mark 6.

Bake the buns for about 10 minutes. The buns should colour but not too much. Leave them to cool covered with clean dish cloths – you don't want a dry crust to form.

For image see page 517

HYGGE, THE DANISH WAY

The Nordic region can be divided in two rough cultural sub-regions based on something as old as the way the ancient kingdoms of Scandinavia split the geography between them. Roughly speaking there is a Danish-influenced part including the country itself, the Faroe Islands, Iceland and Greenland. Then there is a Swedish-influenced part including itself and Finland. Norway has not really been fully independent for more than 110 years and before that belonged first to the Danes between 1523–1814 and was then in union with Sweden until 1905, Norway has very clear traces of both Danish and Swedish influence on top of its own distinctive culture.

Denmark is in most ways unmistakably Nordic, but still also unmistakably continental. I think that Denmark is often looked upon perhaps with a bit of secret envy by the other Nordic countries. It is the slightly unkept, very free-spirited neighbour in the south, who doesn't conform but still seems to do really well. For me Denmark is a country where people seem to – at least superficially – enjoy life a bit of a more frivolously than the rest of us. It is perfectly fine to drink a couple of shots of Aquavit (page 714) for lunch now and then; to have a slice of rye bread with a layer of fatty Liver Pâté (page 440) so thick that you leave teeth marks in it when you have taken a bite; it is fine to enjoy a smoke and to have a very pleasant time without feeling guilty about it. I think this manifests itself very clearly when having a meal in a Danish high-end restaurant. You know, the type of venue that, regardless of where it is located in the world, often runs the risk of stumbling over its own ambition, tumbling down into a deep void of awkward dining room quietness, but which in Copenhagen most often has roughly the same atmosphere as that of a high school party, in an entirely good and extremely pleasant way.

This carefree and convivial approach to life manifests itself in a mood between people, an atmosphere described in Danish as *hygge*.

MEAT PASTIES

Lihapiirakka (Finland)

The Finnish pasty culture is more complex than what first meets the eye and it can at times be very confusing. One thing, which is the same everywhere, can be called different names in different parts of the country, whilst other things, which are not the same at all, can share the same name depending on where they are being made and eaten. The name *lihapiirakka* for example, is deceptively simple, meaning 'meat pasty', but actually it contains a universe of variation enveloped in different dough-based casings. If you go to a Helsinki street-food stall and ask for it, you will be served a small deep-fried pasty made from a wheat-based dough and filled with meat, rice and onion. This fast-food pasty, sometimes abbreviated to *lihis*, is also commonly sliced open and filled with less traditional trimmings like ham, fried eggs, cheese, mustard, ketchup, chopped cucumbers and garlic and is then called *atomipiirakka* (yes, it means 'atomic pasty'). This is mostly considered a drunken nighttime treat. However, if you go to a bakery or a café in the same city and you ask for the same thing, a *lihapiirakka*, you will most likely be served something completely different. The filling based on meat, rice and onion might be the same but the exterior will not be. Rather than the individual deep-fried pastry of the street stall, the bakery version consists of two large sheets of puff pastry with the filling inbetween them. The resulting pie, which is not even always called *lihapiirakka*, but sometimes also *lihalevy*, meaning 'meat disc', is cut into suitable pieces before being served on a plate.

To further complicate this already complex structure of Finnish pasties, a savoury version of the east Finnish *lörtsy* can also be referred to as a *lihapiirakka* in that part of Finland. However, if you ask for a *lörtsy* with meat filling in the same street-food stall in Helsinki where you were just served a *lihapiirakka*, they are going to shake their heads at you. Even though the *lörtsy*, which is to-day most commonly made with apples, was up until the 1980s very much a meat-only pasty and is still indeed deep fried just like *lihis* are today.

The recipe on page 526 is for the puff pastry version of *lihapiirakka*. I think the deep-fried one is best enjoyed on site at a Helsinki street corner with milk drunk straight from the carton.

A *lihapiirakka* can also be a more elongated oven-baked pastry similar to the Russian *coulibiac*. I have also supplied a recipe for that version on page 526.

Sometimes the oven-baked versions of these meat pasties contain chopped Hard-boiled Eggs (page 53). I have marked this as optional in the relevant recipes, but I quite like it myself.

FINNISH MEAT PASTY MADE WITH PUFF PASTRY

Lihapiirakka (Finland)

Preparation and cooking time: 1 hour
Serves: 4, with a couple of pieces to spare for
* lunch another day*

2 x 30 x 40 cm/11½–15¾ inch sheets of puff
  pastry, 5–8 mm/¼–½ inch in thickness

For the filling
600 g/1 lb 5 oz minced (ground) beef
2 onions, finely chopped
½ quantity rice porridge filling from
  Karelian Pasties (page 519), cooled to
  room temperature
4 Hard-boiled Eggs (page 53), finely
  chopped (optional)
salt and pepper, to taste
butter, to fry and grease

For the egg wash
1 egg
50 ml/2 fl oz (3½ tablespoons) milk

Lightly butter a 30 x 40 cm/11½–15¾ inch sheet
pan and place one of the puff pastry sheets on it.

Melt some butter in a frying pan and lightly brown
the minced (ground) beef and fry the onion until
soft and translucent. Transfer the warm beef and
onion to a bowl and add the cooled down porridge
and the chopped egg if you are using it. Mix and
season well before spreading the filling out onto
the puff pastry in the sheet pan. Place the other
sheet of pastry onto the meat mixture.

Preheat the oven to 200°C/400°F/Gas Mark 6.

Whisk the egg and milk together. Brush the top
sheet of pastry lightly with the egg wash, cook in
the oven for about 30 minutes, or until golden and
cooked through. Let the *lihalevy* cool down a little
before cutting into it.

ELONGATED LOAF LIKE FINNISH MEAT PASTY

Lihalevy (Finland)

Preparation and cooking time: 2½ hours
Serves: 4, with a couple of pieces to spare for
* lunch another day*

1 quantity meat filling from Finnish Meat
  Pasty made with Puff Pastry (see left)

For the dough
500 ml/17 fl oz (2 cups plus 1 tablespoon) milk
50 g/2 oz yeast
750 g/1 lb 10 oz (6¼ cups) plain (all-
  purpose) flour
150 g/5 oz (1¼ sticks) butter, cold and cut
  into cubes
2 teaspoons salt

For the egg wash
1 egg
50 ml/2 fl oz (3½ tablespoons) milk

To make the dough, pour the milk into the bowl
of a food processor with the blade attached. Add
the yeast and stir to dissolve it in the liquid. Add
the remaining ingredients to the bowl and knead
on full speed until it has combined and is smooth.
Cover and leave the dough to rise at room temperature for about 1 hour or, until doubled in size.

Preheat the oven to 200°C/400°F/Gas Mark 6 and
line a baking sheet with baking (parchment) paper.

Divide the dough into 2 pieces and roll them out
into to 2 rectangles, about 15 x 40 cm/6 x 15¾
inches each. Place one of the rectangles on the prepared baking sheet and spread the filling in a neat
line in the middle of it leaving a 3 cm/1¼ inch border around the whole pastry with no filling on it.

Whisk the egg and milk together. Brush the
3 cm/1¼ inch edge of dough with a little egg wash
and place the other layer of dough on top of
everything. Crimp the edges to seal the filling inside. Sometimes the edges are folded in underneath
the pasty; other times the crimp is left so that it can
be seen. I prefer to leave it out. Brush the top of
the pastry lightly with egg wash and bake it in the
oven for 20–30 minutes, or until golden.

SWEDISH SOFT OR HARD FLATBREADS

Mjukbröd / Tunnbröd (Sweden)

These flatbreads are really important childhood memories for me. When you bake them and fire up the big wood-fired flatbread oven, the whole extended family will seize the opportunity to come and bake together. Baking flatbreads like these is not something we do often, perhaps twice a year, once before Christmas and once in the spring. I remember at my grandparents' farm, especially before Christmas, vast quantities were made. Up to a couple of hundred cakes each of soft and hard flatbreads in a day. When you are a kid the first task for which you assume responsibility is to start sweeping the excess flour off the rolled out cakes before they go into the oven. This is an important task as excess flour will easily burn and turn black in the superheated oven. The task reserved for the most seasoned veteran is the baking, often done by an older lady who has, over the years, gotten accustomed to the heat of the oven, which can reach over 400°C/750°F degrees. In a very hot oven, during full production, the baking of a single bread takes only about 25–40 seconds.

The difference between soft and hard flatbreads in Sweden is simply that the soft ones, which where historically meant to be eaten fresh as a treat after baking, are a bit thicker, while the hard ones are left to dry and stored for eating later.

Preparation and cooking time: 2 hours
Rising time: 2 hours
Makes: 15 soft or 25 hard flatbreads

750 ml/25 fl oz (3 cups) milk
250 g/9 oz (2¼ sticks) butter
280 g/10 oz (¾ cup plus 1 tablespoon) golden syrup
1 tablespoon ground aniseed
1 tablespoon ground fennel seed
½ tablespoon ground coriander seed
2 teaspoons baker's ammonia
1 tablespoon salt
1.75 kg/3 lb 13½ oz (12¾ cups) strong wheat flour

For the first dough
25 g/1 oz yeast
750 ml/25 fl oz (3 cups) milk

750 g/1 lb 10 oz (5½ cups) Swedish rye/wheat bread flour (*rågsikt*)

Dissolve the yeast in the milk for the first dough in a bowl, add the rye and strong wheat flour and mix until smooth and very sticky. I usually do the mixing at this point with my hand or with a big wooden spoon but it works fine using a stand mixer too. Cover with a clean dish cloth and leave the first dough somewhere warm (20–24°C/68–75°F) to rise for about an hour, or until doubled in size.

Combine the milk and butter in a pan and heat until 35°C/95°F, or until the butter has melted. Add the syrup and the spices to the milk and pour the mix into the bowl containing the first dough. Mix until combined then add the remaining flour, baker's ammonia and salt together. Work the dough for about 10 minutes by hand or 5 in a stand mixer. It should be very sticky and quite loose. Cover with a clean dish cloth and leave to rise for about 45 minutes, or until again doubled in size.

Tip the dough onto a floured work counter and divide it into 15–25 equal pieces, depending on whether you are making soft or hard flatbreads. Shape them into equal balls and leave to rest for another 25 minutes.

Heat a pizza oven to as high as it goes or preheat your kitchen oven to 250°C/500°F/Gas Mark 9 (or to its highest temperature) and preheat a heavy baking sheet.

Flour the work counter generously and roll each dough ball into a round flatbread, around 3 mm/⅛ using a ridged rolling pin if you are making soft ones, and as thin as possible if you are making hard ones. Finish the rolling with a knobbed rolling pin (see illustration, page 511) then brush off any excess flour with a soft brush.

Use a baker's peel (pizza shovel) to lift the flatbread into the pizza oven and bake until bubbly and just beginning to blacken around the edges. Otherwise, bake on the preheated baking sheet in a normal oven.

Fold and bag immediately when they have cooled down if you are making soft flatbreads or leave them out on a wire rack to dry if you are making hard ones.

PASTRIES, BISCUITS AND SWEETS

Previous page: Atlantic Ocean, April 2013.

The importance of fika

The word *fika* simply means a break for a snack in between meals; most often it includes coffee and sometimes a *fika* can mean only a cup of coffee.

It is a Swedish institution and something that goes on in every Swedish home and in every Swedish workplace. It is a cherished time to spend with friends, colleagues or just on your own. Its existence in the workplace has been heavily debated from time to time in collective agreement negotiations but it has always remained in place.

The typical *fika* would be a cup of coffee, possibly with milk for those who are into that, served with a sweet cookie, cake or bun on the side. It can also be an open-faced sandwich served with coffee, almost like a light lunch.

Fika is typically done quite a few times during a normal day and is probably one of the reasons why Swedes, just after the Finns and just before Danes, are at the very top of the world's coffee consumption per capita, in 2014 beaten only by the Dutch.

My generation, 1980s and onwards, still love our *fika* but we have rationalized it a bit and adapted it to the fact that everyone's workdays aren't as similar as they used to be. I would typically *fika* two times a day and, to illustrate the difference, I will share the meal schedule of my father from when I grew up. I believe he is very representative of his generation and the Swedes in general.

06:00–06:15 Pre breakfast *fika* in solitude:
Bun and coffee.

07:00–07:30 Breakfast with the kids:
Porridge, or cultured milk and cereal, coffee.

10:00–10:15 *Fika* with colleagues:
Bun, cake or cookie and coffee.

12:00–13:00 Lunch:
Warm food followed by coffee and maybe some cake.

14:15–14:30 *Fika* with colleagues:
Bun, cake or cookie and coffee.

17:30–18:30 Dinner with the family:
Warm food followed by coffee.

21:00–21:30 *Kvällsfika* with the family:
Sandwiches and tea, possibly some cake or a bun.

To have this many meals per day might seem odd today but historically, the further north you lived in the world, the more you had to produce during summer and the time of light to keep you alive in winter. A sixteen-hour day of manual labour was nothing particularly unusual in summer. With passing time and inventions like industrial food production evening out the access to food around the year, and electrical light evening out the difference between day and night, our need for that much food in parts of the year has diminished. The number of calories has probably decreased significantly whilst the number of meals culturally considered normal has remained higher than those in cultures further south. The difference is even visible within Sweden as a country. My family, coming from the north, would not think of not having *kvällsfika* before ending the day. My wife, who comes from the very south of the country, thought we were insane when she first moved up, she also thought we were quite insane to eat dinner at 5.30 in the afternoon. Historically, in the very south of Scandinavia, it is not unlikely that dinner would mark the end of the farmer's work day as it would grow dark in the evening also in summer. In the north, people probably preferred a slightly earlier dinner, almost like a second, very late lunch allowing them to go outside and work another six to eight hours afterwards before finishing their day, also making it necessary to eat another meal before going to bed.

Previous page: Man thinking about something and interior of traditional north Swedish mountain farm house, Summer 2014.

Opposite: Godarad, Faroe Islands, early May 2012.

SWEET WHEAT BUN DOUGH,
BASE RECIPE

This recipe is a bit richer than most classic recipes. My wife uses it, and I am a bit unclear on exactly where it came from originally. Tove is very good at baking; she has a natural feel for it, and most of her recipes have evolved from classics, to emphasize the particular characteristics that she likes (and that I do too, for that matter).

If you are making rusks, this recipe is just a bit too much; lower the butter content to 100 g/3½ oz (⅓ cup) and the sugar to 75 g/2¾ oz (⅓ cup).

Preparation and cooking time: 1½ hours

320 ml/11 fl oz (1¼ cups plus 1 tablespoon) milk
150 g/5 oz (1 stick plus 2 tablespoons) butter
1 tablespoon cardamom (optional)
50 g/2 oz yeast
1 egg
125 g/4½ oz (½ cup plus 2 tablespoons) sugar
1 teaspoon salt
750 g/1 lb 10 oz (5 cups) strong wheat flour, plus extra for dusting

Combine the milk, butter and any spices (if using) in a small pan and heat until the butter has melted. Leave to cool down to just above room temperature and dissolve the yeast into the milk.

Transfer the mix to the bowl of a stand mixer fitted with the dough hook, add the egg, sugar, salt and flour and knead for about 10 minutes or until very smooth, shiny and elastic. The dough shouldn't adhere to the sides of the bowl as it's being worked.

Cover the bowl and leave to rise for 20–40 minutes, or until doubled in size (it will depend on the temperature in your kitchen).

Tip the dough out onto a lightly floured work counter and knead briefly. Roll into whatever shape your recipe calls for, then transfer to a baking sheet lined with baking (parchment) paper.

Cover and leave to rise until almost doubled in size; around 75% is fine for this rise. The time will again vary, but will generally be a little shorter and 15–20 minutes should be about right.

When ready to bake, follow the instructions for each particular recipe. Cool on wire racks.

CINNAMON BUNS

Snúður (Iceland)
Korvapuustit (Finland)
Kanelsnegl (Denmark)
Kanelbullar (Sweden)

These are sticky cinnamon buns, plain and simple. Enjoy with a big glass of cold milk or a cup of coffee.

In Sweden, cinnamon buns are often sprinkled with some pearl sugar before being baked, and in Norway and Denmark they are often decorated with icing – plain or chocolate (page 679) – after they have cooled down.

I think it is really important to bake these buns in little individual paper cases, otherwise the filling has a tendency to leak out onto the baking sheet and burn, instead of soaking into the bun itself.

If you have any leftovers, cut them in half and turn them into rusks according to the instructions on page 573.

Preparation and cooking time: 1½ hours
Makes: 20 buns

1 quantity Sweet Wheat Bun Dough (see left) made with 1 tablespoon ground cardamom seeds

For the filling
200 g/7 oz (1¾ sticks) very soft butter
2 tablespoons ground cassia cinnamon
100 g/3½ oz (½ cup) sugar

For the egg wash
1 egg
50 ml/2 fl oz (3 tablespoons) milk

To decorate
pearl sugar (optional)
White Icing (page 679) or Chocolate Icing
    (page 679), optional

Follow the instructions on the opposite page for making the sweet wheat bun dough, flavoured with cardamom. After the second rise, roll the dough out on a lightly floured work counter to 60 x 40 cm/24 x 16 inches.

Use a fishslice (spatula) to spread on an even layer of the very soft butter. Leave a 4 cm/1½ inch clear border along the long edge that is furthest away from you. Sprinkle the cinnamon and sugar all over the butter. Roll the dough up into a tight log, starting at the long edge closest to you and working away. Finish so that the unbuttered edge is underneath.

With a very sharp knife, cut the log into 20 slices. Lift each slice into a paper case and transfer to baking sheets. Cover the buns with a clean dish cloth and leave to rise for about 25 minutes, or until they are doubled in size.

Preheat the oven to 200°C/400°F/Gas Mark 6.

Whisk the egg and milk together to make an egg wash. Brush the buns very lightly with the egg wash and sprinkle with pearl sugar, if using. Bake for 10–12 minutes, or until golden, then remove from the oven and cool on wire racks. (Sneak a bun just for yourself, as soon as they are cool enough to handle.) Once the buns are completely cold, decorate with icing, if using.

FAROESE CINNAMON BUNS

Sniglar (Faroe Islands)

Preparation and cooking time: 30 minutes
Makes: 20 buns

100 g/3½ oz (7 tablespoons) butter
150 g/5 oz (¾ cup) sugar
2 eggs
500 g/1 lb 2 oz (4 cups plus 2 tablespoons)
    weak (soft) wheat flour

4 teaspoons baking powder
150 ml/5 fl oz (⅔ cup) milk
For the filling
200 g/7 oz (1¾ sticks) very soft butter
2 tablespoons ground cassia cinnamon
100 g/3½ oz (½ cup) sugar

For the egg wash
1 egg
50 ml/2 ½ fl oz (3 tablespoons) milk

Preheat the oven to 180°C/350°F/Gas Mark 4.

Combine the butter and sugar in the bowl of a stand mixer and beat together until pale. Add the eggs, one by one, until fully incorporated. Sift over the flour and baking powder and mix together at medium speed. With the motor running, pour in the milk, a little at a time.

Use a fishslice (spatula) to spread on an even layer of the very soft butter. Leave a 4 cm/1½ inch clear border along the long edge that is furthest away from you. Sprinkle the cinnamon and sugar all over the butter. Roll the dough up into a tight log, starting at the long edge closest to you and working away. Finish so that the unbuttered edge is underneath.

With a very sharp knife, cut the log into 20 slices. Lift each slice into a paper case and transfer to baking sheets.

Whisk the egg and milk together and brush the buns very lightly with the egg wash.

Bake the buns for 8–10 minutes, or until a light golden brown, then remove from the oven and cool on wire racks before eating.

BUTTER BUNS

Voipullat (Finland)
Smørboller (Denmark)
Smörbullar (Sweden)

My grandmother used to bake these little buns of pure deliciousness. Some people make them with cardamom in the dough, like many other Scandinavian sweet buns leavened with yeast. I don't think that this is appropriate. For me, this bun is all about the sweetness and flavour of dairy. I tend to use a little vanilla sugar in the filling, though, as this rather emphasizes the flavour of the butter itself.

Some recipes indicate that the seam of the bun should face downwards in the paper cup, and others that it should face upwards. I prefer the latter, for no other reason than my grandmother did it that way and it feels better. Seam down produces a smoother bun and the seam up a more irregular-shaped one.

Preparation and cooking time: 2 hours
Rising times: 50–70 minutes
Makes: 20 buns

1 quantity Sweet Wheat Bun Dough (page 538), omitting cardamom from the recipe

For the filling
150 g/5 oz (1 stick plus 3 tablespoons) butter, at room temperature
200 g/7 oz (1 cup) sugar
1 teaspoon vanilla sugar

For the egg wash
1 egg
2 tablespoons milk

To make the sweet wheat bun dough, follow the instructions on page 538.

While the dough is rising (for the first time), prepare the filling by stirring all the ingredients together in a medium bowl.

After the dough has risen, divide it into 20 equal portions and shape them into round buns. With a sharp pair of scissors, cut a cross into each bun from directly above; it should go more than halfway into the dough. Place a good spoonful of filling into the middle of each cross-cut. Use the 4 flaps that formed from the cut to enclose the filling by folding them up and over it, with some overlap.

Place each bun in a paper cupcake case, seam side up, then sit them on a baking sheet. Cover with a clean dish cloth and leave to rise for 30 minutes.

Preheat the oven to 225°C/435°F/Gas Mark 8.

Whisk the egg and milk to make an egg wash. Brush the buns lightly, then bake until golden.

Allow the buns to cool to temperature before tasting them. It is very tempting to bite into a bun when they come straight out of the oven, but at this stage the filling has roughly the same temperature as volcanic lava.

DANISH DOUGHNUTS

Munker (Norway)
Æbleskiver (Denmark)
Berlinermunkar / Danska munkar (Sweden)

The name of these doughnuts in Danish translates to 'apple slices' and refers to their origin as slices of apple that were coated in batter and fried. The *æbleskiver* of today, though, very rarely contain any apple. They are fluffy, somewhat pancake-like balls fried in an *æbleskiver* pan, sometimes sprinkled with icing (confectioners') sugar, sometimes with ordinary sugar and sometimes not sprinkled with anything at all.

Danish doughnuts are usually served with some jam to dip them in, and they are an important part of Danish Christmas traditions, often served alongside Mulled Wine (page 716).

Some recipes include grated lemon zest for flavour; if you add that, do so into the warmed milk.

Preparation and cooking time: 1 hour
Rising time: 25 minutes
Makes: 20 doughnuts

100 g/3½ oz (7 tablespoons) butter, plus extra for frying
250 ml/9 fl oz (1 cup) milk

grated zest of 1 lemon (optional)

2 tablespoons sugar

pinch of salt

25 g/1 oz yeast

250 g/9 oz (2¼ cups) plain (all-purpose)
  flour

3 eggs

sugar or icing (confectioners') sugar, for
  sprinkling (optional)

Put the butter in a small pan and melt over low heat. Add the milk and heat to 37°C/98.6°F. Add the lemon zest (if using), sugar, salt and yeast to the warm mixture and stir to dissolve. Sift over the flour, then mix in with a very sturdy whisk to form a thick and very sticky batter, stir in the eggs. Cover the bowl and leave the batter to rise for 25 minutes.

Place a buttered *æbleskiver* pan over a medium heat and spoon in dollops of batter. Fry until a deep golden brown, then flip the doughnuts over and cook on the other side.

SHROVE TUESDAY CELEBRATIONS IN THE NORDIC COUNTRIES

Even though most Nordic people of today don't actively practise religion, and certainly don't fast during Lent, Shrove Tuesday (the last day before Lent begins) is often celebrated by having a special pastry.

In Sweden, Norway and Finland, a bun flavoured with cardamom and filled with almond paste (Sweden) or almond paste or jam (Finland), and topped with whipped cream is eaten. And in Denmark and Iceland, another type of bun, more resembling a filled and glazed Danish (page 540) is eaten. There is a lot of crossover in names and traditions on the Shrove Tuesday bun between the countries, so one thing can mean something else when you cross a border, or not.

An example is in southern Sweden where the traditional Swedish Shrove Tuesday pastry, *semla* is referred to as a *fastlagsbulle*, very similar to the Danish *fastelavnsbolle*, which is frankly, a completely different pastry altogether, even if it is

eaten the same day of the year. If you happen to ask for a *semla* in Finland though, you'll be given a plain bun, more intended to be spread with butter and turned into a sandwich.

Each year, at least in Sweden, the Shrove Tuesday buns become available in bakeries a bit earlier. As I am sitting here writing, a new year has just started a few days ago and the first buns are already being sold in my local supermarket; Shrove Tuesday is still months away. Don't get me wrong, I love this rich pastry as much as most other Swedes do, but I think it takes away from the specialness of it to have it all the time. I eat one (or maybe two) a year and even though I might on occasion also go for one after Shrove Tuesday, I at least restrict myself to that week.

The practice of filling a bun with something rich for Shrove Tuesday is very old; people have been doing it at least since the Middle Ages, even though their buns probably didn't look and taste much like the ones we eat today. The cream was added sometime during the sixteenth century (but not whipped), while almonds were obviously not used before people started importing them, around the same time. Cardamom might have been used in very wealthy homes during the seventeenth and early eighteenth centuries but it didn't become a standard Shrove Tuesday bun flavouring in Sweden, Norway and Finland until after industrialization, when imported spices became more readily available and more accessibly priced. The whipped cream, which today is what in many ways signifies the bun in several countries, wasn't added until the early twentieth century.

SHROVE TUESDAY SWEET BUNS

All around the Nordic region people still practice the tradition of eating special sweet buns before the fasting diet of the Lent period begins – even though few people continue on with the actual fasting! Historically *semla* – as they are generally known – were only eaten on Shrove Tuesday, but nowadays the window for eating them is beginning earlier and earlier in the year.

SWEET SHROVE TUESDAY BUNS FROM NORWAY, SWEDEN AND FINLAND (VERSION 1)

Fastlavnsbolle (Norway)
Laskiaispulla (Finland)
Semla / Fettisdagsbulle/ Fastlagsbulle (Sweden)

If you want to go Finnish-style, substitute the almond paste filling with a good spoonful of strawberry jam or raspberry jam (page 690).

Preparation and cooking time: 2 hours, plus cooling time
Makes: 12 buns

1 quantity Sweet Wheat Bun Dough (page 538), flavoured with cardamom
300 ml/10½ fl oz (1¼ cups) cream, whipped
icing (confectioners') sugar, for dusting

For the filling
100 g/3½ oz almond paste, grated on the coarse side of a box grater
50 ml/2 fl oz (3½ tablespoons) milk

Preheat the oven to 200°C/400°F/Gas Mark 6.

Follow the method on page 538 for making sweet wheat buns. Shape them into 12 balls.

Bake for 10–12 minutes, or until golden, then remove from the oven and cool on wire racks.

When the buns have cooled cut off the very top, either in a circular piece making a round lid or with 3 incisions making a triangular one. With your fingers, dig a little of the bread out of the interior of the bun to make a small cavity, which you can fill with the filling.

Mix the bread that you have dug out of the buns with the almond paste and milk. It should be quite smooth and sticky. Spoon a little of this filling back into the buns and top with a dollop of whipped cream – or pipe it on, if you're feeling fancy. Put the round or triangular hats back on top of the cream and dust with icing (confectioners') sugar before serving.

SWEET SHROVE TUESDAY BUNS FROM DENMARK AND ICELAND (VERSION 2)

Fastelavnsbolle (Iceland)
Fastelavnsbolle (Denmark)

This Shrove Tuesday bun can be made in various ways. It can be a kind of Danish Pastry (page 550), which has the top cut off before being filled with cream and/or jam or Vanilla Pastry Cream (page 680). Alternatively, as below, it is made with a Sweet Wheat Bun Dough and filled with Vanilla Pastry Cream (page 680) or, more traditionally, a White Sugar Pastry Filling (page 680).

Preparation and cooking time: 2 hours
Makes: 12 buns

½ quantity Sweet Wheat Bun Dough (page 538), enriched with 1 egg

For the filling
1 quantity White Sugar Pastry Filling (page 680) or 1 quantity Vanilla Pastry Cream (page 680)
1 quantity Chocolate Icing (page 679)

Follow the method on page 538 for making the sweet wheat bun dough, adding the egg to the cooled milk and butter mixture before you add the flour.

Divide the dough in half and roll each portion out on a lightly floured work counter. You need to create 2 rectangles about 1 cm/½ inch in thickness. Use a 6 cm/2½ inch cookie cutter to mark 12 bun outlines on one piece of the dough. Place a spoonful of filling into the centre of each outline, then sit the second layer of dough on top. Make sure that the edges are nicely sealed and that not too much air is trapped inside before cutting them all the way through with the cutter, creating a sort of ravioli of dough with filling inside.

Line a baking sheet with baking (parchment) paper. Transfer the buns to the baking sheet and cover with a clean dish cloth.

Leave the buns to rise and then bake, as instructed in the recipe opposite. After baking, leave the buns to cool on a wire rack. Glaze with chocolate icing before serving.

SWEET SHROVE TUESDAY BUNS IN MILK (VERSION 3)

Hetvägg (Sweden)

In Sweden, some people like to eat their annual Shrove Tuesday bun in a bowl of hot milk, which makes it into more of a dessert, called *hetvägg*. In English this translates to 'hot wall', although it has nothing at all to do with walls. It actually derives from the old north German word *hetwegge* – from *het*, meaning 'hot' and *wegge*, meaning a 'wedge' shape. Originally, the dessert could include any kind of bread that was formed into a double wedge. The connection to Shrove Tuesday – and to a specific use of wheat flour bread – wasn't made until the eighteenth century, when the practice merged with the existing tradition of eating rich, filled sweet buns on the last day before Lent began.

Up until the cream was added in the early years of the twentieth century and what was a dish turned into an individual pastry, this was the prevailing way of consuming the Shrove Tuesday bun, simply because it made a dry, stale bread into something soft, rich and tasty. As baking and food production became more efficient and refrigeration made it possible to store foods for longer, the need to soak a dry bread in warm milk diminished and the fresh bun with its almond filling and whipped cream topping became the standard.

In several books dating from around 1920, I have found references to soaking the now modernized *semla* in warm milk in the way that was done to the old creamless dry type many years earlier. I think this could have been a case of caring for the traditional ways more than an actual unbroken tradition slowly evolving, as it quite frankly doesn't make sense to soak perfectly fresh and already soft bread in hot milk as it does with a dry one, which was the reason for the soaking in the first place.

Even today I have curiously observed that kind of backwards behaviour among those defending this way of eating their *semla*. Those who eat it in milk seem to rather often be people who look at themselves as a sort of defender of the traditional way, the real way or simply the way that is better than other peoples' ways just because it isn't the same as what everyone else is doing. The same men or women who write a sternly worded letter (not an email) to the newspaper after spotting a spelling error on page 11 or who shudder at the thought of wearing a brown belt with their trousers (pants) for dinner after 6.00 p.m.

I do think (and hope) that they all actually like the soggy swollen bread and the melting cream, even if I don't. But their claim that it is the traditional way is simply faulty as the soaking practice – it seems to me – pretty much dies out, as it wasn't needed any more, before being picked up again a couple of decades later and just applied to an entirely updated Shrove Tuesday bun, which is objectively and by a majority of people seen as more tasty left as it is. An act probably committed by the same people, then as those keeping it today, the defenders of a slightly more proper way, even if it doesn't make sense.

But after all, it is great that we are all different even in this case.

SAINT LUCY'S DAY SAFFRON BUNS

Lussebulle | Saffransbröd | Lussekatt
  (Norway)
Luciapulla (Finland)
Lussekatter (Sweden)

This sweet saffron wheat dough is rolled out into many shapes, all having different names. The most common version – and the one favoured by industry, I guess for its simplicity – is the *julgalt*, or 'Christmas boar'. This is often wrongly named *lussekatt*, or 'Saint Lucy's Cat', which is, as you can plainly see below, a completely different shape.

Serve saffron buns with a cup of coffee as a snack, or why not with your Mulled Wine (page 718)? Oh, and these buns can go insanely dry: do eat them the same day they are baked or place in plastic bags and freeze if you need to store them.

You'll need to start this recipe the night before, as the saffron needs sufficient infusing time to develop an intense colour.

Preparation and cooking time: 2 hours
Infusing time: overnight
Makes: 20 julgalt, 10 lussekatt, or 2–5 more
  elaborate buns, depending on size

1 g/0.03 oz strands saffron
1 tablespoon vodka
1 quantity Sweet Wheat Bun Dough
  (page 538)
1 handful raisins

For the egg wash
1 egg
50 ml/2 fl oz (3½ tablespoons) milk

Grind the saffron threads to a powder and add them to the vodka. Leave overnight to infuse.

Add the saffron liquid to the milk when making the sweet wheat bun dough and leave to rise, as instructed.

Line 2 baking sheets with baking (parchment) paper.

On a lightly floured work counter, divide the dough into as many pieces as you need for the shape of rolls you want to make (see illustration right).

Shape as required and place on the prepared baking sheets. Push the raisins into the dough where indicated in the illustrations, then cover the buns and leave to rise until doubled in size. Before baking, you may have to push the raisins back into the dough with a cocktail stick (toothpick); sometimes they can pop out during the rising.

Preheat the oven to 225°C/435°F/Gas Mark 8.

Whisk the egg and milk together to make an egg wash and brush the buns lightly all over. Bake until nicely golden. Do not overcook them, or they will be the driest things you have ever eaten. The cooking time will depend on what size and shape you have made but should be between 8 and 15 minutes.

Types of bun shapes, from top left to bottom right: *gullvagn, julvagn, lussekatt, lussekatt, pojke, lilja, julgalt,* and *julkuse*.

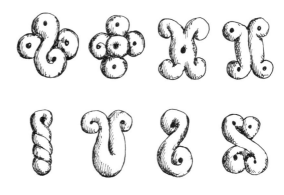

SWEET PRETZELS

Nordic-style pretzels are generally known as *kringles*, and come in many guises – both sweet and savoury (page 568). There are many variations on the sweet pretzel theme: some are filled and others not, some are shaped into a pretzel knot and others into more of a circular shape. Most sweet pretzels are made from a Sweet Wheat Bun Dough (page 538) but can sometimes be made from Danish Pastry (page 550).

In Denmark and the Faroe Islands, filled sweet pretzels are often served at birthdays, when they are known as *fødselsdagskringle* in Denmark and *föðingardagskringla* on the Faroe Islands, both meaning 'birthday pretzel'.

DANISH SWEET PRETZEL

Gerkringla (Faroe Islands)
Kringle (Denmark)

This large pretzel is usually filled with a White Sugar Pastry Filling (page 680) – either plain, or with the addition of a good handful of raisins. I have also seen some recipes that include orange zest or candied orange peel for added flavouring.

It is often sprinkled with flaked or chopped almonds and/or pearl sugar for decoration or sometimes it can be drizzled with White Icing (page 679).

Large sweet pretzels are often served a bit like a torte, on a serving plate, to be cut by a host or by the eater into suitably sized servings.

Preparation and cooking time: 1 hour
Rising time: 30–40 minutes
Makes: 1 large pretzel, enough for
  10–12 pieces

For the dough
50 g/2 oz fresh yeast
50 ml/2 fl oz (3½ tablespoons) milk
2 eggs
100 g/3½ oz (½ cup) sugar
pinch of salt
1 teaspoon finely ground cardamom seeds
200 g/7 oz (1¾ sticks) butter, cubed
350 g/12 oz (2½ cups plus 1 tablespoon)
  strong wheat flour, plus extra for dusting

For the filling
1 quantity White Sugar Pastry Filling
  (page 680)
1 good handful raisins (optional)

For the topping
1 egg

50 ml/2 fl oz (3½ tablespoons) milk
flaked or chopped almonds and/or pearl
  sugar, to decorate
White Icing (page 679), optional

In the bowl of a stand mixer fitted with the paddle attachment, mix the yeast to a paste with the milk. Add the eggs, sugar, salt, cardamom and butter to the mixture. Sift in the flour and work until fully combined and smooth.

Line a baking sheet with baking (parchment) paper.

Roll the dough out on a lightly floured work counter to a 15 x 50 cm/6 x 20 inch rectangle. Spread the filling thickly along the centre of the rectangle, leaving a 2.5 cm/1 inch margin at each end. Brush the long edges lightly with water, then bring them up and over the filling to enclose it completely. Allow about 2 cm/¾ inch of overlap to ensure the filling doesn't ooze out of the pretzel while it bakes. You should end up with a long, fat log.

Lift the log onto the prepared baking sheet. You can then leave it as a log shape or bring the ends together to form a circle or form into the traditional knot shape. If you choose the last option, then taper the ends a little, so the knot isn't too thick.

Cover with a clean dish cloth and leave to rise for 30–40 minutes. Preheat the oven to 175°C/345°F/ Gas Mark 4.

Whisk the egg and milk together to make an egg-wash and brush the pretzel lightly all over. Scatter on your choice of topping. Some people now use a pair of scissors to cut decorative patterns in the dough – sometimes all the way down to the filling – others leave the pretzel intact. If you do cut all the way down to the filling, then some will ooze out during the baking and caramelize, which can be quite delicious. Do beware of cutting the sides of the pretzel, as all the filling will drain out.

Bake until the pretzel is golden in colour. Leave to cool on a wire rack, it should take about 30 minutes.

SWEDISH SUGARED SWEET PRETZELS

Sockerkringlor (Sweden)

After baking, these individual pretzels are brushed with melted butter and then rolled in sugar to coat them completely. They are leavened with both yeast and baking powder (or in some recipes, with yeast and baker's ammonia), which gives them a very particular texture. The dough has diced butter worked into it, similar to a French brioche, which remains emulsified during the kneading. This is different to most Swedish sweet buns, where the butter is melted before being added to the dough.

Some recipes are plain, while others are flavoured with cardamom or vanilla; I prefer cardamom.

Preparation and cooking time: 1 hour
Rising time: 50–60 minutes
Makes: 20 pretzels

250 ml/8 fl oz (1 cup) milk
50 g/2 oz fresh yeast
4 eggs
100 g/3½ oz (½ cup) sugar
pinch of salt
2 tablespoons baking powder
1 kg/2½ lb (7½ cups) strong wheat flour,
   plus extra to dust
2 teaspoons finely ground cardamom seeds
   or 2 teaspoons vanilla sugar (optional)
250 g/8 oz (1 cup) cold butter, cut into
   1 cm/½ inch dice

For the filling
100 g/3½ oz (7 tablespoons) butter,
   at room temperature

To coat
50 g/2 oz (3½ tablespoons) butter, melted
sugar, to coat the pretzels

Dissolve the yeast into the milk in the bowl of a stand mixer fitted with the dough hook. Add the eggs, sugar, salt, baking powder, flour and flavourings, if using. Knead for a few minutes before adding the butter. Knead at a medium speed until the butter is completely incorporated and the dough is smooth and shiny.

Cover the bowl and leave to rise for 25–30 minutes, until doubled in size.

While the dough is rising, line a baking sheet with baking (parchment) paper.

Roll the dough out on a lightly floured work counter to a 35 x 55 cm/14 x 22 inch rectangle. Brush half of the rectangle along its length with some butter. Fold the buttered half over the other half to form a thicker rectangle. Slice this into 20 short strips (of dough sandwiched with butter), which will each become a pretzel.

Pick up a strip and twist along its length. Form into the traditional knot shape and place on the prepared baking sheet. Repeat with the remaining dough strips. Cover with a clean dish cloth and leave to rise for 30 minutes.

While the pretzels are rising, preheat the oven to 225°C/435°F/Gas Mark 8.

Bake until the pretzels are pale gold in colour. Brush with melted butter while they are still warm, then roll them in sugar to coat completely. Leave to cool on a wire rack.

NORWEGIAN CHRISTMAS BREAD

Julekake (Norway)

Julekake is a sort of sweet and rich wheat bread, leavened with yeast. It is flavoured with cardamom and often filled with dried and candied fruits. *Julekake* is traditionally served for Christmas with different toppings, which can be either sweet or savoury. I have also seen a few recipes flavoured with saffron, a bit like the Swedish Saint Lucy's Day Saffron Buns (page 544).

Preparation time: 45 minutes
Rising time: 50 minutes
Cooking time: 30–40 minutes
Makes: 2 loaves

150 g/5 oz (1 stick plus 3 tablespoons) butter
500 ml/17 fl oz (2 cups plus 1 tablespoon) milk
50 g/2 oz yeast

650 g/1 lb 7 oz (4½ cups) strong wheat flour,
  plus extra for dusting
140 g/5 oz (⅔ cup) sugar
½ teaspoon salt
2 teaspoons ground cardamom
150 g/5 oz (1¼ cups) raisins or other dried or
  candied fruits

For the egg wash
1 egg
1 tablespoon milk

Melt the butter slowly in a medium pan. Pour in the milk and warm very gently to a temperature of about 37°C/98.6°F. Add the yeast and stir to dissolve.

Pour the mixture into the bowl of a stand mixer fitted with the dough attachment, then add the flour, sugar and salt. Knead until the dough is shiny and smooth and comes away from the sides of the bowl.

Cover the bowl and leave to rise at room temperature until almost doubled in size. It will take about 30 minutes.

Line 2 baking sheets lined with baking (parchment) paper.

Place the dough on a lightly floured work counter and add the dried fruits. Work the dough by hand until the fruits are evenly incorporated. Divide the dough into 2 equal pieces and shape into large round buns. Place them on the prepared baking sheets. Cover with a clean dish cloth and leave again to double in size, about 20 minutes.

Preheat the oven to 175°C/345°F/Gas Mark 4.

Whisk the egg and milk together. Brush the buns lightly with the egg wash and bake for 30–40 minutes. They should have a nice golden colour to them when ready.

CRULLERS

Kleynur (Faroe Islands)
Kleina (Iceland)
Fattigmann (Norway)
Klejner (Denmark)
Klenäter (Sweden)

Crullers are deep-fried, knot-shaped pastries popular all over the Nordic region, but perhaps especially in southern Sweden and Denmark. For many people, they are an essential part of the Christmas celebrations. They have been baked at least since the sixteenth century in Sweden and the name itself comes from the Swedish word for a precious object, *klenod*.

Crullers are often flavoured with Cognac, lemon juice, *Ättika* vinegar (page 656) or in some cases, cardamom. They were traditionally fried in a mixture of lard and tallow called *Flottyr* (page 654) and in Iceland, in sheep's tallow. Today crullers are most often fried in some kind of flavourless, vegetable-based fat, suitable for deep-frying.

After cooking, the individual pastries are sometimes covered in icing (confectioner's) sugar, plain sugar or cinnamon sugar and served on their own with coffee, as a snack, or with whipped cream and jam (page 690) as a dessert. The latter is more common in Sweden. In the other Nordic countries crullers are usually just eaten on their own, and the crullers themselves are most often flavoured with cardamom.

These pastries can be unleavened or leavened with baking powder, baking soda or baker's ammonia. Older recipes are often unleavened or can even be leavened with yeast. I have included recipes for both unleavened and leavened crullers.

UNLEAVENED CRULLERS
(VERSION 1)

Preparation and cooking time: 1 hour
Resting time: 1 hour
Makes: 40 crullers

50 g/2 oz (3½ tablespoons) butter,
 at room temperature
4 tablespoons icing (confectioners')
 sugar
4 egg yolks
150 g/5 oz (1¼ cups) weak (soft)
 wheat flour, plus extra for dusting
neutral/flavourless fat or oil, for deep-frying

Your choice from the following flavourings
1 tablespoon Cognac and grated zest of
 1 lemon
1 tablespoon lemon juice and grated zest
 of 1 lemon
1 tablespoon *Ättika* (12%) vinegar
 (page 656,) and/or 1 teaspoon finely
 ground cardamom seeds

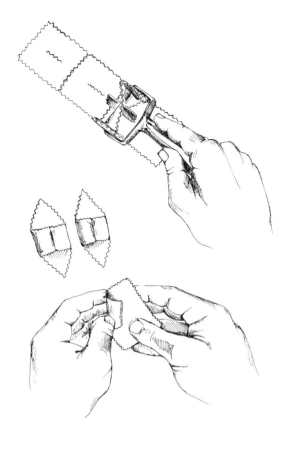

Beat the butter and sugar in a mixing bowl until white. Add the egg yolks, one at a time. Stir in
your choice of flavouring, then sift the flour into the
bowl. Work the dough with your hand until fully
combined and smooth.

Shape the dough into a ball, wrap in clingfilm
(plastic wrap) and refrigerate for at least 1 hour.

Roll the dough out on a lightly floured work counter to a thickness of about 3 mm/⅛ inch. Use a special cruller cutter (or a sharp knife) to cut the dough
into 40 strips, each about 3 x 10 cm/1¼ x 4 inches. If you are not using the cruller cutter you also
have to make a slit along the length of each strip.
The specialized cutter not only portions the dough
perfectly, but it also makes this incision for you.

Form each strip into the traditional cruller shape
by pulling the ends over and through the slit,
creating a sort of inside-out knot.

Heat the fat in a medium pan or deep-fryer to
180°C/350°F. Deep-fry the crullers until golden on
both sides. Remove the crullers from the oil and
leave to cool for a few minutes on a wire rack or
paper towels to absorb any excess oil.

LEAVENED CRULLERS
(VERSION 2)

Preparation and cooking time: 1 hour
Resting time: 1 hour
Makes: 40 crullers

40 g/1½ oz (3 tablespoons) butter, at room
 temperature
75 g/2½ oz (⅓ cup) sugar
1 egg
50 ml/2 fl oz (3½ tablespoons) cultured milk
 (page 719)
250 g/8 oz (2 cups plus 1 tablespoon) weak
 (soft) wheat flour, plus extra for dusting
1 teaspoon baker's ammonia
1 teaspoon baking powder
neutral/flavourless fat or oil, for deep-frying

Flavourings
1 tablespoon Cognac and grated zest of

1 lemon, or 1 tablespoon lemon juice and
grated zest of 1 lemon, or 1 tablespoon
Ättika (%) vinegar (page 656) and/or
1 teaspoon finely ground cardamom seeds

Follow the method described opposite, for unleavened crullers. Add the cultured milk to the mixture
after adding the egg. Sift the baker's ammonia and
baking powder into the bowl with the flour.

BROWN SUGAR YEAST CAKE FROM FUNEN ISLAND

Brunsviger (Denmark)

This recipe is originally from the central Danish
island of Funen – or *Fyn* in Danish – but these
days *brunsviger* are found all around the country.
Brunsviger cake is often flavoured with ground
cassia cinnamon and served lukewarm for breakfast. In Funen, slices of *brunsviger* are sometimes
served as a sandwich topping on buttered Danish
breakfast buns or *rundstykker*, in which case the
sugared side of the cake should be placed directly
onto the buttered side of the bread.

Preparation and cooking time: 1 hour
Rising time: 20–40 minutes
Makes: 15 portions

25 g/1 oz yeast
250 ml/8 fl oz (1 cup) milk
120 g/4 oz (1 stick) butter, at room
  temperature, plus extra to grease
2 tablespoons sugar
1 teaspoon salt
2 eggs
500 g/1 lb 2 oz (4 cups plus 2 tablespoons)
  weak (soft) wheat flour

For the brown sugar pastry topping
150 g/5 oz (1 stick plus 3 tablespoons) butter,
  at room temperature
250 g/8 oz (1⅓ cups) soft brown sugar
2 tablespoons ground cassia cinnamon

Pour the milk into the bowl of a stand mixer,
fitted with the dough hook, dissolve the yeast in
the milk, then add all the remaining ingredients.

Knead at a medium speed until smooth and shiny,
which can take 8–12 minutes depending on the
efficiency of the machine you use.

Butter a 25 x 30 cm/10 x 12 inch baking sheet.
Spread the sticky dough out onto the prepared
sheet and leave to rise until doubled in size.

Meanwhile, preheat the oven to 200°C/400°F/Gas
Mark 6.

To make the topping, combine all the ingredients
in a small pot and heat gently until it is all melted
and shiny looking.

Wet your hands and press your fingers down into
the dough to make little indentations where pud-
dles of the melted topping can form. Pour the
topping evenly over the dough and bake until
the surface is golden and bubbly and the cake is
cooked through.

Let the cake cool a little in the pan. Cut into 15
portions and serve while still warm.

DANISH PASTRY

Vinarbreyð (Faroe Islands)
Vínarbrauð (Iceland)
Wienerleipä (Finland)
Basser | Wienerbrød (Denmark)
Wienerbröd (Sweden)

The Danish Pastry, or 'Danish', is actually only called this in the English-speaking world. In the Nordic countries it is know as Viennese bread and in most Germanic countries it is often called something that relates to the city of Copenhagen. The dough used for making Danish pastries is based on the Viennoise dough, which is a leavened type of puff pastry containing eggs. There are conflicting stories of exactly how and when the Danish was invented, but they all agree on one thing: the origins of this pastry, now intimately connected to Denmark, and especially to Copenhagen, are in Austria. It was brought to the Nordic region about 130–150 years ago and since then it has been adapted to suit the Nordic taste, becoming a bit sweeter and a bit richer than the original.

When you make Danish pastries it is an advantage to do it in a cool environment and with cool equipment: a chilled stone or marble work counter in a refrigerated space would be ideal, but opening your kitchen window on a chilly autumn (fall) morning shortly before you start also works. It is also a good idea to refrigerate equipment like rolling pins and knives, before starting. If you work really quickly, none of these precautions are necessary. But if not, they will buy you some extra time before the butter melts as you work it, turning your ambitious baking project into something that needs to be disposed in your compost bin, rather than baked in your oven.

Preparation and resting time: 2 hours
Makes: enough for 20 pastries

500 ml/17 fl oz (2 cups plus 1 tablespoon)
  cold milk
25 g/1 oz yeast
40 g/1½ oz (¼ cup) sugar
4 eggs
1 teaspoon salt
1.2 kg/2½ lb (9 cups) strong wheat flour, plus
  extra for dusting
1 kg/2¼ lb (9 sticks) butter, cut into 1 cm/½
  inch thick slices

Combine the milk, yeast, sugar, eggs, salt and flour in the bowl of a stand mixer fitted with the dough attachment. Mix at medium speed until the dough is smooth and shiny. Cover the bowl and place in the refrigerator to rest for an hour.

Roll the dough out on a lightly floured work counter to a 60 x 45 cm/24 x 18 inch rectangle. Place the cold sliced butter onto the half of the rectangle closest to you, leaving a 3 cm/1¼ inch edge of dough around the buttered part. Fold the butterless half of dough towards you over the butter and crimp the edges together using the spare 3 cm/ 1¼ inch.

The 45 cm/18 inch seam should now point towards you, if not then correct that. Roll the dough out evenly to a thickness of 2 cm/¾ inch. Roll in one direction only and maintain the width of the rectangle at 45 cm/18 inches.

Now imagine the rectangle being made up of 3 smaller rectangles beginning closest to you, and fold the closest imaginary rectangle away from you so that it covers the second one. Subsequently fold the third imaginary rectangle towards you so that it covers both the previous ones and makes 3 layers of dough. Again, turn the dough so that its short side faces you.

Once again, roll the dough out evenly to a thickness of 2 cm/¾ inch. This time you can roll in both directions, but try not to exceed the dimensions of the first rectangle (60 x 45 cm/24 x 18 inches).

Repeat the folding in thirds, turning and rolling process twice more. If the butter seems to be melting at any stage, then place it in the refrigerator to chill again before you resume rolling.

Once you've rolled the pastry out to a rectangle for the third time, cover it with a clean dish cloth and refrigerate for 30 minutes to rest before proceeding with any of the following pastries.

SPANDAUER

Preparation and cooking time: 30 minutes
Rising time: 20 minutes
Makes: 20 pastries

1 quantity Danish Pastry (page 550)
1 tablespoon Vanilla Pastry Cream (page
  680) or raspberry jam (page 690)
1 quantity White Icing (page 679)

Preheat the oven to 225°C/435°F/Gas Mark 8. Line 2 baking sheets with baking (parchment) paper.

Roll the dough out into a rectangle of about 1 cm/½ inch in thickness and cut it into 20 x 12 cm/ 4 inch squares, spoon the pastry cream or jam on to each square, fold the corners in towards the middle and squeeze them together.

Transfer to the prepared baking sheets and leave for another 20 minutes to rise.

Bake for about 12 minutes or until golden, transfer to wire racks and allow to cool a bit. Decorate with icing.

ROSENBRØD

Whether there should be Danish dough at the base of a *rosenbrød* seems to be a matter of some debate in Denmark. It can also be a simple leavened, slightly shortened yeast dough rolled into the same shape as I am about to describe here. Anyhow, this text is about different shapes of Danish. To use Danish dough to make *rosenbrød* seems to be largely a Sjælland thing. Sjælland is the island on which Copenhagen is located.

Preparation and cooking time: 30 minutes,
  plus cooling time
Rising time: 20 minutes
Makes: 20 pastries

1 quantity Danish Pastry (page 550)
1 quantity White Icing (page 679), flavoured
  with 2 drops rosewater

Preheat the oven to 200°C/400°F/Gas Mark 6. Line 2 baking sheets with baking (parchment) paper.

Roll the dough out into 2 rectangles of about 20 x 50 cm/7¾ x 11¾ inches. Transfer to the prepared baking sheets, leave to rise for about 20 minutes.

Bake for 12–15 minutes, or until golden, and leave on the baking sheets to cool.

Glaze the entire top surface of the baked dough with rosewater white icing, leaving an edge of 2.5 mm/⅛ inch around the pastry without glaze. Cut straight across into 4 x 20 cm/1½ x 7¾ inch strips.

SNEGLE

Preparation and cooking time: 30 minutes
Rising time: 45 minutes
Makes: 20 pastries

1 quantity Danish Pastry (page 550)
1 quantity Danish, dark, butter and sugar
  pastry filling (page 680), flavoured with
  2 teaspoons ground cinnamon
1 quantity Chocolate Icing (page 679)

Preheat the oven to 200°C/400°F/Gas Mark 6. Line 2 baking sheets with baking (parchment) paper.

Roll the dough out into a rectangle about 5 mm/ ¼ inch in thickness.

Spread the filling onto the rolled out dough and roll it tightly together into a log. Refrigerate.

Once chilled, cut the roll into 20 x 3 cm/1¼ inch slices, place the slices on the prepared baking sheets and leave them to come to room temperature and rise a bit – it will take about 45 minutes.

Bake for about 12 minutes or until golden. Leave to cool on the baking sheets before transferring to wire racks. Decorate with chocolate icing.

HANEKAM

Preparation and cooking time: 30 minutes
Rising time: 20 minutes
Makes: 20 pastries

1 quantity Danish Pastry (page 550)
1 quantity White Sugar Pastry Filling
    (page 680)
1 egg
50 ml/2 fl oz (3½ tablespoons) milk pearl
    sugar or flaked almonds, for sprinkling

Preheat the oven to 225°C/435°F/Gas Mark 8. Line 2 baking sheets with baking (parchment) paper.

Cut the dough in half and roll it out into 2 rectangles about 5 mm/¼ inch in thickness. Cut with a sharp knife into 10 x 10 cm/4 x 4 inch squares.

Place a tablespoonful of filling across the middle of each square and fold it once so that it turns into a 5 x 10 cm/2 x 4 inch rectangle. Press the edges firmly together and cut 5 slashes so that it resembles a cocks comb.

Place the *hanekam* on the prepared baking sheets and allow to rise for about 20 minutes.

Whisk the egg and milk together to make an egg wash and brush the dough. Sprinkle with pearl sugar or flaked almonds.

Bake for 12 minutes or until golden. Allow to cool on the baking sheets.

BIRKES

Preparation and cooking time: 30 minutes
Rising time: 20 minutes
Makes: 20 pastries

1 quantity Danish Pastry (page 550)
1 egg
50 ml/2 fl oz (3½ tablespoons) milk
poppy seeds, to coat

Preheat the oven to 225°C/435°F/Gas Mark 8. Line 2 baking sheets with baking (parchment) paper.

Cut the dough in half and roll it out into 2 rectangles about 5 mm/¼ inch in thickness and 20 cm/7¾ inches in width and about 40–50 cm/15–19½ inches in length. Fold a third of the width towards the middle and continue folding it one more time so that you get a sort of flat roll 40–50 cm/15–19½ inches in length. Cut each roll into 10 slices.

Whisk the egg and milk together to make an egg wash and brush the top of the slices lightly.

Invert onto a plate of poppy seeds and then place them poppy-seed side up on the prepared baking sheets. Allow to rise for 20 minutes.

Bake for 12 minutes or until golden. Allow to cool on the baking sheets.

BORGMESTERSTANG

Preparation and cooking time: 30 minutes
Rising time: 20 minutes
Makes: 2 pastries/loaves

1 quantity Danish Pastry (page 550)

For the filling
200 g/7 oz almond paste
2 egg whites
75 g/2¾ oz (⅓ cup plus 1 tablespoon) sugar
1 egg
50 ml/2 fl oz (3½ tablespoons) milk
chopped almonds, for sprinkling

Line 2 baking sheets with baking (parchment) paper.

To make the filling, mix the almond paste, egg whites and sugar in a bowl.

Divide the dough in half and roll it out into 2 rectangles about 5 mm/¼ inch in thickness and 20 cm/7¾ inches in width. Cut each rectangle into 3 long strips and pipe a string of filling along the length of each strip. Fold each strip over the filling and press the edges firmly to seal them. Braid 3 filled and sealed strips to make a loaf. Repeat with the remaining 3 strips to make the second loaf.

Place them on the prepared baking sheets and leave them to rise for 20 minutes.

Preheat the oven to 225°C/435°F/Gas Mark 8.

Whisk the egg and milk together to make an egg wash and brush the dough. Sprinkle with chopped almonds.

Bake for about 20 minutes or until golden. Leave to cool on the baking sheets before attempting to move.

TREKANT

Preparation and cooking time: 30 minutes
Rising time: 20 minutes
Makes: 20 pastries

1 quantity Danish Pastry (page 550)

For the filling
100 g/3½ oz almond paste
100 g/3½ oz (7 tablespoons) butter
100 g/3½ oz (½ cup) sugar

Preheat the oven to 225°C/435°F/Gas Mark 8. Line 2 baking sheets with baking (parchment) paper.

To make the filling, mix the almond paste, butter and sugar to a paste in a bowl.

Divide the dough in half and roll it out into 2 rectangles about 5 mm/¼ inches in thickness. Cut with a sharp knife into 10 x 10 cm/4 x 4 inch squares.

Place a tablespoonful of the paste in the middle of each square. Fold the dough once across the filling diagonally and press the edges firmly together to seal.

Place the *trekant* on the prepared baking sheets and allow to rise for about 20 minutes.

Bake for 12 minutes or until golden. Allow to cool on the baking sheets.

JULEBOLLE

Preparation and cooking time: 30 minutes
Rising time: 20 minutes
Makes: 20 pastries

1 quantity Danish Pastry (page 550)
1 quantity White Icing (page 679) or
  Chocolate Icing (page 679)

For the filling
100 g/3½ oz almond paste
100 g/3½ oz (7 tablespoons) butter
100 g/3½ oz (½ cup) sugar

Preheat the oven to 225°C/435°F/Gas Mark 8. Line 2 baking sheets with baking (parchment) paper.

To make the filling, mix the almond paste, butter and sugar to a paste in a bowl.

Roll the dough out into a rectangle about 1 cm/ ½ inch in thickness and cut it into 20 x 12 cm/4¾ inch squares.

Place a tablespoonful of the paste onto each square, fold the corners in towards the middle and squeeze them together to seal. Invert and transfer to the prepared baking sheets so that the seam faces downwards and leave for 20 minutes to rise.

Bake for about 12 minutes or until golden, transfer to wire racks and allow to cool a bit. Decorate with white or chocolate icing.

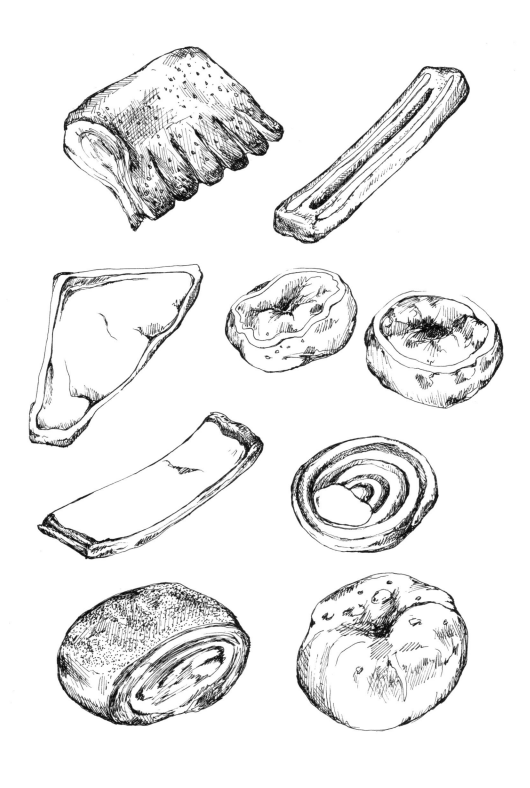

Clockwise from top left: Hanekam (page 552), Borgmesterstang (page 552), Spanduer (page 551), Snegle (page 551), Julebolle (page 553), Birkes (page 552), Rosenbrød (page 551), Trekant (page 553)

DOUGHNUTS

Smultringer (Norway)
Munkki (Finland)
Munkar (Sweden)

I like to fry doughnuts in *flottyr* (page 654), which is a mixture of lard and tallow, but any neutral, vegetable-based fat or oil is also fine.

Preparation and cooking time: 2 hours
Rising time: 1 hour
Makes: 30 doughnuts

20 g/¾ oz fresh yeast
150 ml/5 fl oz (⅔ cup) cold milk
150 g/5 oz (¾ cup) sugar
2 eggs
600 g/1 lb 5 oz (4⅓ cups plus 1 tablespoon)
  strong wheat flour, plus extra for dusting
1 teaspoon salt
125 g/4½ oz (1 stick plus 1 tablespoon)
  butter, at room temperature
vegetable-based fat or oil, for deep-frying
sugar, for coating

Mix the milk and yeast in the bowl of a stand mixer fitted with the dough hook and add the sugar, eggs, flour and salt. Knead for a few minutes before adding the butter. Knead until the dough is smooth and shiny.

Cover the bowl and leave to rise for about 30 minutes, until doubled in size.

Roll the dough out on a lightly floured work counter to a thickness of 1–1½ cm/½–¾ inch. Cut into 30 circles with a pastry (cookie) cutter, then leave to rise for 20–30 minutes.

Heat the oil in a medium pan or deep-fat fryer to 180°C/350°F. Deep-fry the doughnuts in batches, making sure they don't stick together. Turn them around in the oil a couple of times and cook until golden. Remove the doughnuts from the oil and leave to rest for a few minutes on a wire rack placed over paper towels, so any excess oil can run off.

Roll the doughnuts in sugar to coat and serve while still warm.

ROSETTES

Rosettebakkels (Norway)
Struvor (Sweden)

Rosettes are star-shaped, deep-fried pastries commonly served around Christmas. They are traditionally made with a special *struvor* iron, which is first preheated in hot oil before being dipped into batter and returned to the hot oil. As it fries in the hot oil, the pastry falls away from the iron in a pretty shape.

Preparation and cooking time: 40 minutes
Resting time: 20 minutes
Makes: 10 rosettes

130 g/4½ oz (1 cup plus 1 tablespoon)
  weak (soft) wheat flour
100 ml/3½ fl oz (⅓ cup plus 1 tablespoon)
  milk
100 ml/3½ fl oz (⅓ cup plus 1 tablespoon)
  cream
1 egg
1 tablespoon sugar
fat or oil, for deep-frying (most people use
  coconut oil)
sugar or icing (confectioners') sugar,
  to serve (optional)

Whisk all the ingredients together (except the cooking oil) to make a smooth batter. Leave to rest for about 20 minutes.

Heat the oil in a deep pan to 180°C/350°F. Keep the batter close to the stove top. Preheat the *struvor* iron in the hot oil. Dip it into the batter briefly, then return to the oil straight away. After a few seconds the rosette will loosen on the iron and you can shake it off into the oil. Repeat with more batter.

Deep-fry the rosettes for a couple of minutes, turning them around in the oil so they colour evenly. Remove from the oil and rest briefly on paper towels to absorb any excess oil.

Either leave plain or dust the rosettes with sugar while warm and serve at room temperature.

ICELANDIC DEEP-FRIED DOUGHNUT BALLS (LOVE BALLS)

Ástarpungar (Iceland)

Preparation and cooking time: 30 minutes
Makes: 20 doughnut balls

2 eggs
85 g/3 oz (⅓ cup plus 2 tablespoons) sugar
250 g/8 oz (2 cups) plain (all-purpose) flour
2 teaspoons baking powder
pinch of salt
125 ml/4 fl oz (½ cup) milk
1 teaspoon ground cardamom, vanilla sugar
   or grated lemon zest
100 g/3½ oz (¾ cup) raisins
neutral oil, for deep-frying

Whisk the eggs and sugar together until fluffy and light. Sift the flour, baking powder and salt together onto the mix, then add the milk and the flavourings of your choice. Stir vigorously so that no lumps remain. Add the raisins and mix.

Heat the oil for deep-frying the balls in a deep, heavy pan or deep-fat fryer to 180°C/350°F.

Use 2 spoons to shape the batter into little balls, then carefully drop them straight into the hot oil. The balls should be about the size of a ping-pong ball; they will inflate further when cooked. You can cook about 4 doughnuts at the same time, but make sure that they don't stick to each other. Turn them around in the oil a couple of times and cook until golden. Remove the doughnuts from the oil and leave to rest for a few minutes on paper towels to absorb any excess oil. Eat while still lukewarm.

FINNISH MAY DAY FUNNEL CAKES

Tippaleipä / Struvor (Finland)
Struvor (Sweden)

These funnel cakes are most often dusted with icing (confectioners') sugar after they are deep-fried and then enjoyed with a glass of *Sima* (page 720) for the Finnish May Day celebrations.

Old recipes use a combination of lard and tallow (*flottyr*, page 654) but most new ones use some kind of vegetable-based cooking fat or oil instead.

Some people have their *Tippaleipä* dusted with plain icing (confectioners') sugar, some with icing sugar mixed with vanilla sugar and others with cinnamon sugar.

Preparation and cooking time: 30–45 minutes
Makes: 10 cakes

3 eggs
1 tablespoon sugar
good pinch of salt
grated zest of 1 lemon
150 ml/5 fl oz (⅔ cup) milk
350 g/12 oz (3 cups) weak (soft)
   wheat flour
2 teaspoons baking powder
fat or oil, for deep-frying

Whisk the eggs with the sugar until pale and creamy. Add the salt (the batter should be quite salty for a pastry), lemon zest and milk and stir until fully incorporated. Sift the flour and baking powder together into the bowl and mix again until smooth.

Heat the oil in a deep, medium pot to 180°C/350°F.

Spoon the batter into a piping bag fitted with a 3 mm/⅛ inch nozzle. (If you want to go all traditional, you can pour the batter through a funnel, but this way is about a thousand times easier.)

Pipe the batter into the hot oil, working in a swirling motion. You are aiming to create intersecting concentric rings, about 8 cm/3¼ inches at the bottom, and building up to create a tall, bird's nest shape.

Deep-fry for a few minutes, flipping the cakes over once in the oil, until they are golden brown all over. Drain on a wire rack, then transfer to a baking sheet lined with paper towels to remove excess fat. Repeat with the remaining batter.

Let the cakes cool slightly. Dust with icing (confectioners') sugar, either plain, or mixed with your choice of flavoured sugar, to taste.

FINNISH STICKS

Finsk breud (Faroe Islands)
Finskbrød (Denmark)
Finska pinnar (Sweden)

This iconic Swedish shortbread called *finsk pinne*, is a kind of enigma. My guy in Finland, Kenneth Nars, assures me that it does not exist over there and that there is no other pastry similar to it which the name could refer to. As a matter of fact, I have not been able to find out why it is called what it is called. Anyhow, it is one of Sweden's most loved classic biscuits (cookies), delicately flavoured with bitter almonds.

Preparation and cooking time: 30 minutes
Resting time: 1 hour
Makes: about 25 sticks

3 bitter almonds, finely grated
100 g/3½ oz (7 tablespoons) butter, soft
50 g/2 oz (¼ cup) sugar
150 g/5 oz (1¼ cups) weak (soft) wheat flour
1 egg
50 ml/2 fl oz (3½ tablespoons) milk
25 g/1 oz sweet almonds, coarsely chopped
1 tablespoon pearl sugar

Combine the bitter almonds, butter, sugar and flour in the bowl of a food processor fitted with the knife attachment. Blitz until just combined and then shape the dough into a ball, wrap it in clingfilm (plastic wrap) and refrigerate for 1 hour.

Preheat the oven to 175°C/345°F/Gas Mark 4 and line a baking sheet with baking (parchment) paper.

Roll out the dough into 2 logs about 2 cm/¾ inch in thickness.

Whisk the egg and milk together. Brush each log lightly with the egg wash and sprinkle with pearl sugar and chopped almonds. Cut the logs into 5 cm/2 inch pieces and transfer them to the prepared baking sheet. Bake for 10–12 minutes. They shouldn't colour too much.

Let the sticks cool down on the sheet before trying to pick them up, as they are fragile when warm.

For image see page 559

COCONUT PYRAMIDS

Kokostoppe (Denmark)
Kokostoppar (Sweden)

These pastries don't have to be shaped like pyramids, I just like them that way. It works just as well to simply spoon them out onto the paper in rough piles before cooking them.

Preparation and cooking time: 45 minutes
Makes: about 20 pyramids

2 eggs
90 g/3¼ oz (⅓ cup plus 3 tablespoons) sugar
200 g/7 oz (2⅔ cups) coconut flakes
good pinch of salt
75 g/2¾ oz (5 tablespoons) butter, melted
    and allowed to cool to room temperature

Preheat the oven to 175°C/345°F/Gas Mark 4 and line a baking sheet with baking (parchment) paper.

Put the eggs and sugar in a bowl and whisk until mixed. Add the coconut flakes, salt and the butter and stir until fully combined. Let the batter sit for 20 minutes so that the coconut can absorb a bit of moisture and swell, this makes shaping the pyramids considerably easier.

Spoon 20 piles of the mixture onto the prepared baking sheet and shape them into pyramid shapes using your hands or a spatula. Bake for 10–15 minutes. They should be golden on the edges of the pyramid but blonde on the flat sides. Coconut pyramids go dry if overcooked.

For image see page 559

DREAMS

Drömmar (Sweden)

These Swedish biscuits (cookies) are called 'dreams' and they have a very fragile and unique texture achieved by the addition of baker's ammonia. A leavening agent the non-Swedish chefs working at my restaurant usually refer to as 'piss salt' because of how it smells when the cookies are being baked. The good thing is that the nightclub urinal touch given by the baker's ammonia vents off in a matter of minutes when the cookies are cooling down.

Preparation and cooking time: 20 minutes
Makes: about 20 biscuits

100 g/3½ oz (7 tablespoons) butter, soft
90 g/3¼ oz (⅓ cup plus ½ tablespoon) sugar
1 teaspoon vanilla sugar
160 g/5½ oz (1⅓ cups) weak (soft) wheat flour
½ teaspoon baker's ammonia
small pinch of salt

Preheat the oven to 175°C/345°F/Gas Mark 4 and line a baking sheet with baking (parchment) paper.

Beat the butter, sugar and vanilla sugar until light in colour. Add the flour and baker's ammonia by sifting them together into the bowl and beat again, this time until fully combined but not longer.

Shape the dough into 20 little balls and place them on the prepared baking sheet. Bake for about 15 minutes. The biscuits (cookies) should have no, or very little, colouration and they should break up slightly during the cooking. Do not touch the cookies until they have completely cooled down as they are very fragile when still warm.

For image see opposite page

SLIGHTLY CHEWY CARAMEL SHORTBREADS

Kolakakor / kolasnittar (Sweden)

Preparation and cooking time: 30 minutes
Makes: about 20 shortbreads

100 g/3½ oz (7 tablespoons) butter, soft
90 g/3¼ oz (⅓ cup plus 1 tablespoon) sugar
50 g/2 oz (2 tablespoons) golden syrup
150 g/5 oz (1¼ cups) weak (soft) wheat flour
½ teaspoon bicarbonate of soda (baking soda)
1 teaspoon ground ginger
good pinch of salt

Preheat the oven to 175°C/345°F/Gas Mark 4 and line 2 baking sheets with baking (parchment) paper.

Beat the butter, sugar and syrup together in a bowl until light in colour. Add the flour, bicarbonate of soda (baking soda) and ginger by sifting them together, into the bowl. Beat again until fully combined.

Shape the dough into 2 logs a bit shorter than the width of your baking sheet. Place the logs on the prepared baking sheets and bake for about 15 minutes or until golden. The logs will float out considerably during the cooking.

Let the logs cool down a little, but before they go hard and crisp take them off the baking sheets and onto a chopping (cutting) board. Cut straight across in ribbons about 3 cm/1¼ inch in width and leave to cool completely.

For image see opposite page

Clockwise from top: Coconut Pyramids (page 557); Dreams (page 558); Rolled Tuiles (page 570); Scanian Thick and Chewy Gingersnaps (page 562); Chocolate Oatmeal Balls (page 575); Slightly Chewy Caramel Shortbreads (page 558); Douglas' Shortbread Biscuits (page 560); Finnish Sticks (page 557)

DOUGLAS' SHORTBREAD BISCUITS

Dogges Syltkakor (Sweden)

One of the first chefs to be employed at Fäviken was Douglas, who started making these biscuits (cookies) from an old recipe given to him by his grandmother. When Douglas left us to take on another challenge we continued baking the biscuits. There is always a batch on the go somewhere at Fäviken. They are served daily after breakfast or as a snack during the day.

Preparation and cooking time: 30 minutes
Makes: 20 biscuits

500 g/1 lb 2 oz (4 cups plus 2 tablespoons)
   plain (all-purpose) flour
1 tablespoon baking powder
220 g/7¾ oz (1 cup plus 2 tablespoons) sugar
300 g/11 oz (2½ sticks plus 1 tablespoon)
   butter, at room temperature
2 eggs, at room temperature
your choice of jam, I like raspberry and
   cloudberry best (page 690)

Preheat the oven to 200°C/400°F/Gas Mark 6 and line a baking sheet with baking (parchment) paper.

Knead all the dry ingredients together with the butter until well mixed.

Lightly beat the eggs, add them to the mixture and work until smooth, taking care not to overwork the dough.

Immediately shape the dough into 20 little balls with your hands and place on the prepared baking sheet. Make an indentation in each one with your finger and fill the indentation with jam. Bake in the oven for about 10 minutes, or until golden brown. Eat them as soon as soon as they are cool enough, to enjoy them at their best.

For image see page 559

BITTER ALMOND SHORT BUNS

Mandelkubb (Sweden)

These little buns, flavoured with bitter almond oil or grated bitter almonds, are leavened with baker's ammonia. They should have a short texture as is typical for most other pastries leavened with ammonia. They must be consumed pretty much the same day they are baked because they dry out and go stale very quickly.

Let the buns cool down completely on a wire rack before eating them or storing them so that the ammonia can vent off properly. Otherwise they can have a very unpleasant odour.

Preparation and cooking time: 40 minutes
Makes: 15–20 buns

450 g/1 lb (3¾ cups) weak (soft) wheat flour
150 g/5 oz (⅔ cup) sugar
2 teaspoons baker's ammonia
6 bitter almonds, very finely grated
   (or use bitter almond oil, as instructed
   on the bottle)
150 g/5 oz (1 stick plus 3 tablespoons) butter,
   roughly chopped, at room temperature
150 ml/5 fl oz (⅔ cup) milk
1 egg
pearl sugar and/or chopped almonds,
   to decorate

Preheat the oven to 200°C/400°F/Gas Mark 6 and line 2 baking sheets with baking (parchment) paper.

Sift the flour, sugar and baker's ammonia together into a large bowl, then add the bitter almonds or bitter almond oil. Add the butter and mix with your hands to a crumbly texture.

In a separate bowl, mix the milk with the egg and add to the bowl containing the dry ingredients. Mix with your hands until you get a smooth dough, but do not overwork it.

On a lightly floured work counter, roll the dough out to a cylinder about 50 cm/20 inches in length and then cut into 15–20 equal pieces. Shape each piece into a roughly square, slightly flattened bun. Press one side of each bun into a pile of pearl sugar and/or chopped almonds and arrange, that side up, on the prepared baking sheets. Leave enough space between them as they will expand a bit.

Bake until they are a light golden colour; they shouldn't get too much colour.

DANISH GLAZED RASPBERRY SQUARES

Hindbærsnitter (Denmark)

For this popular pastry, a layer of firm-set raspberry jam is spread between two layers of shortcrust pastry (basic pie dough) and topped with quite a thick layer of icing (frosting). *Hindbærsnitter* are often decorated with multi-coloured sprinkles and I have even seen them in some Copenhagen pastry shops being scattered with liberal amounts of freeze-dried raspberries. Some recipes also indicate that decorating *hindbærsnitter* with fresh raspberries is a good idea, but I imagine that this would only make the icing wet and the berries would wilt. I prefer them with no additional decoration on top of the icing.

Preparation and cooking time: 40 minutes
Resting time: 1 hour
Makes: 12 squares

For the shortcrust pastry (basic pie dough)
220 g/7¾ oz (2 sticks) cold salted butter, cut into small cubes
350 g/12 oz (3 cups) weak (soft) wheat flour, plus extra for dusting
155 g/5½ oz (1¼ cups) icing (confectioners') sugar
1 teaspoon vanilla sugar
1 egg
265 g/9¼ oz (¾ cup plus 1 tablespoon) firm-set raspberry jam (page 690) or marmalade
1 quantity White Icing (page 679)

Pulse the butter, flour and sugars in a food processor until it looks like sand. Add the egg and pulse just until it is completely incorporated, but no longer. Shape the dough into a ball and wrap it tightly in clingfilm (plastic wrap). Leave to rest in the refrigerator for a minimum of 1 hour.

Preheat the oven to 175°C/345°F/Gas Mark 4.

Unwrap the dough and divide it into 2 equal portions. Place each portion on a sheet of baking (parchment) paper and roll it out to a 30 x 40 cm/12 x 16 inch rectangle. Lift onto baking sheets and bake until a light golden colour.

Remove the cooked pastry layers from the oven and leave to cool down a little. Spread one pastry layer with raspberry jam, then lift the other layer on top. Press gently and leave to cool completely.

Top with a thick layer of icing and leave it to set completely before cutting into 12 squares.

GRAHAM FLOUR CRACKERS

Grahamskex (Sweden)

Preparation and cooking time: 30 minutes
Makes: 40 crackers

400 g/14 oz (3 cups plus 1 tablespoon) graham flour, plus extra for dusting
2 teaspoons baking powder
120 g/4 oz (1 stick) butter, cold and cut into 1-cm cubes
150 ml/5 fl oz (⅔ cup) cream
pinch sea salt

Preheat the oven to 225°C/435°F/Gas Mark 6 and line a baking sheet with baking (parchment) paper.

Combine all of the dry ingredients and the butter in a food processor and process to the consistency of coarse sand. Add the cream and process until just combined.

Tip the dough out onto a lightly floured work counter and roll it out to about 3 mm/¼ inch thickness. These crackers don't rise very much. Prick the dough over its surface and cut into the desired shapes. Circles look nice, but are a bit wasteful as I find re-rolling the dough scraps doesn't produce a great result. I prefer to cut rough squares instead.

Arrange the crackers on the prepared baking sheet and bake for 5–8 minutes, depending on the thickness of the crackers, until they are lightly golden. Transfer to wire racks to harden and cool.

ALMOND TART SHELLS

Mandelmussla (Sweden)

These delicate tart shells, flavoured with some bitter almond, are usually baked in small individual *mandelmussla* pans with a fluted edge. They are often served with a bowl of whipped cream and some berries or jam (page 690) on the side. To me they are an essential part of the sweet selection of the Swedish Christmas dinner.

You could substitute the almonds in the recipe – which in my method you grind yourself – for homemade ground almonds, but it is a bit like using sawdust instead of lovely fragrant almonds and, which quite frankly seems unnecessary since grinding almonds isn't very difficult or laborious.

If you are unable to find the special *mandelmussla* pans, then use any mini, fluted tart pans.

Preparation and cooking time: 1 hour
Resting time: 20 minutes or, preferably,
*   overnight*
Makes: 20 shells

65 g/2½ oz (⅓ cup plus 2 tablespoons)
    almonds, blanched, peeled and dried
65 g/2½ oz (⅓ cup) sugar
110 g/3¾ oz (7 tablespoons) butter, at room
    temperature, plus extra to grease
1 egg
275 g/9¾ oz (1¾ cups) soft (weak) wheat
    flour, plus extra for dusting
2 bitter almonds

Grind the almonds finely in a mortar with a pestle or in a spice grinder.

Combine the sugar and butter in the bowl of a stand mixer and beat until pale and creamy. Add the egg to the mix and beat until well combined. Add the ground almonds, then sift the flour directly into the bowl. Use a microplane or fine grater to grate the bitter almonds straight into the mixture, then mix until fully combined, but not for any longer.

Shape the dough into a ball and wrap it in clingfilm (plastic wrap). Place in the refrigerator to rest for a minimum of 20 minutes, but preferably overnight.

Preheat the oven to 175°C/345°F/Gas Mark 4 and lightly butter the *mandelmussla* pans.

Unwrap the dough and roll it into a long log and cut it into 20 equal pieces. Roll each piece into a ball and place one in each buttered pan. Press the dough in evenly with your fingers, making sure you press it into all of the fluted edges.

Bake until just golden. Leave the shells for a few minutes before taking them out of the pans.

SCANIAN THICK AND CHEWY GINGERSNAPS

Skåne pepparkaka (Sweden)

I love these gingersnaps spread with salty butter and mature hard cheese, for a snack with coffee on the side.

They should be chewy, and for them to remain so, you need to store them in an airtight container.

Preparation and cooking time: 1½ hours
Resting time: 2 days
Makes: about 25 gingersnaps

80 g/3 oz (⅓ cup) sugar
210 g/7¼ oz (⅔ cup) golden syrup or
    molasses
75 g/2¾ oz (5 tablespoons) butter
1 teaspoon ground ginger
1 teaspoon ground cloves
1 teaspoon ground cinnamon
50 ml/2 fl oz (3½ tablespoons) milk

1 egg
1 teaspoon baker's ammonia
1 teaspoon baking powder
400 g/14 oz (3¼ cups) weak (soft) wheat
  flour, plus extra for dusting
a good of pinch salt

Combine the sugar, golden syrup or molasses, but-ter, salt and spices in a pan and melt over a medi-um heat, stirring continuously. Remove from the heat and add the milk to the mixture. Stir contin-uously until it cools almost to room temperature. Add the egg and mix until fully incorporated.

Transfer the mixture to the bowl of a stand mixer. Sift the flour and leavening agents together into the bowl and beat until properly combined, but not for any longer. Tip the dough out of the bowl and wrap it in clingfilm (plastic wrap). Refrigerate for 48 hours.

Preheat the oven to 200°C/400°F/Gas Mark 6 and line several baking sheets with baking (parch-ment) paper.

Unwrap the chilled dough and place it on a lightly floured work counter. Shape into a long log and cut into 25 slices. Shape each slice into a little ball, then place on the prepared baking sheets, flatten-ing them gently with the palm of your hand.

Bake the gingersnaps for 12–15 minutes, until they are cooked, but not dry. Once they start to brown a little around the edges they are generally done. Leave to cool on the baking sheet before moving.

For image see page 559

PEPPERNUTS

Peppernøtter (Norway)
Pebernødder (Denmark)
Pepparnötter (Sweden)

These little biscuits (cookies) are commonly eaten in several parts of the Nordic region. The flavour-ing differs a little from recipe to recipe, but nothing consistent to a single country. They are actually one of the very few recipes that seem to be quite similar everywhere.

The spices that are used in different combinations and proportions are ground ginger, cardamom, black pepper, cloves and cinnamon. There is also some variety to how the biscuits are leavened from one recipe to another. Some use baker's ammonia, others use bicarbonate of soda (baking soda) and yet others use baking powder.

Preparation and cooking time: 1 hour
Resting time: overnight
Makes: about 100 peppernuts

125 g/4½ oz (1 stick) butter
80 g/3 oz (⅓ cup) sugar
100 g/3½ fl oz (⅓ cup) golden syrup
2 teaspoons ground cinnamon
2 teaspoons ground cloves
2 teaspoons ground ginger
2 teaspoons ground cardamom seeds
1 teaspoon ground black peppercorns
1 teaspoon bicarbonate of soda
  (baking soda)
250 g/9 oz (2¼ cups) weak (soft) wheat flour
pinch of salt

Combine the butter and sugar in the bowl of a stand mixer and beat until pale and creamy. Add the golden syrup and beat until fully incorporat-ed. Sift the dry ingredients together into the bowl. Work until the mixture is just combined and forms a smooth dough, but not for any longer. Cover the bowl and refrigerate overnight.

Preheat the oven to 175°C/345°F/Gas Mark 4 and line several baking sheets with baking (parch-ment) paper.

Remove the dough from the refrigerator and shape into balls, the size of a large, unshelled hazelnut. Arrange them on the prepared sheets, leaving some space between them to allow for spreading as they cook.

Bake for 10 minutes, or until golden, then leave to cool on the baking sheets before moving. Once completely cold, store the peppernuts in an air-tight container.

GINGERBREAD

Piparkökur (Iceland)
Pepperkaker (Norway)
Piparkakut (Finland)
Brunkager (Denmark)
Pepparkakor (Sweden)

There can be no Nordic Christmas without gingerbread and almost everyone I know bakes at least a couple of batches during the month of December.

Most of them buy their gingerbread dough from the supermarket, which is a pity as it is quite simple to make it yourself. There are some differences between the countries; one of them is which leavening agent we use. In Denmark most of the recipes I have found use potash, which is potassium carbonate. (Potash was also used elsewhere in the old days but today you can hardly find it in food stores – at least not in Sweden.) In Sweden and Finland almost every recipe I found uses bicarbonate of soda (baking soda), while in Norway some recipes use bicarbonate of soda and others use baking powder.

I would assume that the resulting differences between the finished gingerbread would be minute. All of the chemicals mentioned above function the same way, and I think that the only real difference is that they are alkaline to different degrees. Potash is the strongest, baking powder the weakest and bicarbonate of soda somewhere in the middle. In general terms, a more alkaline leavening agent gives a shorter texture to the gingerbread.

The recipe below is my grandma's. It uses bicarbonate of soda, but you can use potash if you want. I have tried and it is almost exactly the same.

The way the dough is fashioned into gingerbreads also differs a bit from country to country. The Danes like to shape theirs into a log, before chilling it and cutting it into thin slices that are subsequently baked. This works really well when you add almonds and pistachios to your gingerbread, also a Danish thing. The dough is stiff enough to cut without disturbing the nuts, and it creates a really pretty mosaic effect. The other option, which is more common in Sweden and in other places too, sometimes also in Denmark, is to roll the dough out and use a cookie cutter to create shapes before baking them.

It is also quite common to decorate your home at Christmas with large gingerbreads decorated with icing (page 679), hanging in the windows from red silk ribbons, spreading their aroma from room to room. Gingerbreads started becoming associated with Christmas around the nineteenth century. Before that they were eaten all year around by those fancy enough to afford the excessive amounts of expensive spices required.

Oh, and a weird thing: we all put ginger in our gingerbreads, but we don't call them gingerbreads; we call them pepper cakes – and we don't put any pepper in them. The only ones that come close to this are the Danes, who add some allspice. In Sweden we stopped putting pepper in our *pepparkakor* in the early part of the nineteenth century, although the reason for this is a bit of a mystery.

Preparation and cooking time: 1½ hours
Resting time: 2 days
Makes: enough for a traditional, Nordic
family gingerbread free-for-all – including a
small gingerbread house/enough gingerbread
to decorate a fairly large house and feed a
small family. There is no point in making
any less.

350 g/12 oz (1¾ cups) sugar
280 g/10 oz (¾ cup plus 2 tablespoons) golden syrup
200 ml/7 fl oz (¾ cup plus 1 tablespoon) milk
250 g/9 oz (2 sticks) butter, cut into 2 cm/¾ inch cubes
2 teaspoons salt
1 tablespoon ground cloves
1 tablespoon ground cardamom seeds
2 tablespoons ground cassia cinnamon
1 tablespoon ground ginger
1 tablespoon ground allspice (for a Danish version)
300 g/11 oz whole blanched almonds and 100 g/3½ oz pistachios (for a Danish version)
1 tablespoon bicarbonate of soda (baking soda), or use potash, for a Danish version
1 kg/2¼ lb (8½ cups) weak (soft) wheat flour, plus extra for dusting

Combine the sugar, golden syrup and milk in a pan. Bring it to the boil, then remove the pan from the heat and leave it to cool down a little.

Place the butter, salt and the spices in a bowl and pour on the still warm (but not hot) syrup. Stir until all the butter has melted and the mixture has cooled down to room temperature. If you are making a Danish version, this is when you add the nuts.

Sift the flour and bicarbonate of soda (baking soda) together into the bowl and mix everything together with your hands until fully combined. Shape into a tight lump and wrap in clingfilm (plastic wrap). Leave the dough to rest in the refrigerator for 48 hours before using it.

For gingerbread rounds, unwrap the rested dough (which will be rather stiff) and divide into equal-sized portions. Roll each piece into a log and cut them into 3 mm/⅛ inch slices – or thicker, if you prefer. If you have added nuts to the dough you will need a really sharp knife to cut them neatly.

Alternatively, for gingerbread shapes, unwrap the rested dough (which will be rather stiff) and divide into workable portions. Roll each one out on a very lightly floured work counter (too much flour will make them dry). Cut them into the desired shapes with a knife or a cookie cutter (I like them shaped like little pigs).

To bake the gingerbread, preheat the oven to 200°C/400°F/Gas Mark 6 and line several baking sheets with baking (parchment) paper.

Arrange the gingerbreads on the baking sheets and bake for no longer than 5 minutes. Remove from the oven and leave to cool on the baking sheets. Time them carefully as it is very easy to burn them at the edges, which I hate. It doesn't matter if they are a little bit soft in the middle as they harden while they cool down.

GLAZED INDIVIDUAL ALMOND TARTS

Mazarin (Denmark)
Mazarin (Sweden)

These are best made in oval, disposable aluminium cups called *mazarin* cups but can be made in any other little moulds that seem suitable.

Preparation and cooking time: 45 minutes
Makes: 10 tarts

For the dough
100 g/3½ (7 tablespoons) butter, cold and diced, plus extra to grease
40 g/1½ oz (3 tablespoons) sugar
1 egg
200 g/7 oz weak (soft) wheat flour

For the filling
200 g/7 oz almond paste, grated on the coarse side of a box grater
100 g/3½ oz (7 tablespoons) butter, at room temperature
pinch of salt
2 eggs

To decorate
½ quantity White Icing (page 679)

Preheat the oven to 150°C/300°F/Gas Mark 2 and butter 10 cups or moulds.

Place all of the ingredients for the dough in a food processor and blitz until just combined.

On a work counter, shape the dough into a loaf and divide that into 10 equal pieces. With your fingers press the dough out in the prepared moulds so that they get an even thickness.

To make the filling, mix the almond paste, butter and salt in a bowl until smooth and creamy. Mix in the eggs one by one until fully incorporated. Spoon the filling into the dough-lined moulds. The filling should reach about three quarters of the way to the top.

Bake the almond tarts for about 10 minutes or until lightly golden and set. Leave to cool before glazing with white icing.

For image see page 609

ALMOND BISCUITS

Mandelbiskvier (Sweden)

These are great as a little snack with coffee or, more commonly, as sweet croutons in sweet soups (pages 694–700).

Preparation and cooking time: 30 minutes
Makes: 80–150 biscuits, depending on size

275 g/9¾ oz almond paste, at room
  temperature
1 egg white

Preheat the oven to 175°C/345°F/Gas Mark 4. Line a baking sheet with baking (parchment) paper.

Grate the almond paste on the coarse side of a box grater. Mix with the egg white with a stiff whisk until there are no lumps remaining and it is a smooth but firm batter.

Scrape the batter into a piping bag fitted with a round nozzle and pipe little 2 cm/¾ inch mounds onto the prepared baking sheet. Bake until golden. Leave the biscuits to cool down on the baking sheet.

For image see page 697

CHOCOLATE GLAZED, CHOCOLATE BUTTERCREAM ALMOND BISCUITS

Biskvier (Sweden)

Substitute the buttercream of this coffee-shop classic with a simple chocolate ganache to make Sarah Bernhardt pastries/biscuits (cookies), named after the French early twentieth-century film actress. In this recipe I have specified that you simply melt the chocolate. This works fine but if you want the chocolate to be all shiny looking and brittle in texture, as it would be in a pastry shop, you will have to do something called tempering. I am not going to describe exactly how that is done as it is a rather complex process.

Preparation and cooking time: 1 hour
Makes: 12 biscuits

1 quantity Almond Biscuit batter
  (see left)
1 quantity Chocolate Buttercream
  (page 679)
200 g/7 oz dark (bittersweet) chocolate,
  melted

Preheat the oven to 175°C/345°F/Gas Mark 4 and line a baking sheet with baking (parchment) paper.

Using a piping bag fitted with a round nozzle, make little rounds of the biscuit batter on the prepared baking sheet. To make it easier to create rounds I like to draw circles on the backside of the semi-translucent paper using round as a template.

Bake the biscuits until they are light golden. They should still be a little soft in the middle. Leave the biscuits to cool down on the baking sheet.

When the biscuits have cooled down, take them off the baking sheet and spread buttercream on what was the side facing downwards on the baking sheet. The buttercream should be shaped into a pointy mound with a palette knife. Glaze the top by quickly dipping it in the melted chocolate. Remember that the chocolate coating needs to be done swiftly for the buttercream not to melt. Leave to set for a bit before serving.

JEWISH BISCUITS

Jødekakur (Iceland)
Jødekakor (Norway)
Jødekager (Denmark)
Judebröd (Sweden)

Among the many traditional recipes of Nordic cooking that have been given racist names in the past (Chocolate Oatmeal Balls, page 575 and Peppermint and Chocolate Pastilles, page 577, to name two), I think this is a misunderstood biscuit (cookie), falsely accused of anti-Semitism by those not understanding its past. The name, which is *judebröd*, literally translating to 'Jew bread', simply refers to the origin of this particular pastry, brought to Scandinavia by Sephardic Jews emigrating from Spain and Portugal during the seventeenth century. Since then the recipe has been Scandified, and what was a biscuit fattened with olive oil and sweetened with honey is now more of a shortbread, containing butter and brown sugar.

Judebröd are flavoured with cinnamon and cardamom and many people, especially in Norway, Denmark and Sweden, have them around Christmas. In Sweden, the *judebröd* dough is rolled out into a sheet and then cut into either half-moons or circles before being decorated. In Denmark it is more often rolled into a fat log, which is then chilled and cut into slices. In Sweden, *judebröd* are garnished either with pearl sugar or ordinary sugar mixed with chopped almonds and ground cinnamon. In Denmark, ordinary sugar mixed with ground cinnamon seems to be the prevalent topping. Some recipes contain white sugar rather than brown. Do as you like; I prefer brown.

Preparation and cooking time: 1 hour
Makes: 20 biscuits

200 g/7 oz (1¾ sticks) butter, cut into cubes
250 g/9 oz (1¼ cups) brown sugar
1 teaspoon cardamom seeds, finely crushed
1 teaspoon ground cassia cinnamon
2 eggs
1 teaspoon baker's ammonia
380 g/13½ oz (3 cups plus 1 tablespoon) weak (soft) wheat flour
pearl sugar, cane sugar, chopped almonds and/or ground cinnamon, to decorate

Place the butter, sugar, spices and eggs in the bowl of a food processor. Sift the flour and baker's ammonia together into the bowl. Process until just combined, then tip out the dough and shape it into a ball (for Swedish *judebröd*) or a log (for Danish *judebröd*). Wrap in clingfilm (plastic wrap) and refrigerate for at least 30 minutes.

Preheat the oven to 200°C/400°F/Gas Mark 6. Line 2 baking sheets with baking (parchment) paper.

Roll out the ball of dough on a lightly floured work counter and cut into your preferred shapes, or cut the log into thick slices. Brush the surface of the biscuits very lightly with water and decorate with your choice of topping.

Lift the *judebröd* onto the prepared baking sheets

and bake until lightly golden. Remove from the oven and leave to cool on the baking sheets.

BERLIN CROWNS / EGG PRETZELS

Berlinerkranser (Norway)
Berlinerkransar/Äggkringlor (Sweden)

This classic Scandinavian-style pretzel gets its very short texture and rich flavour from quite a bit of egg yolk – both hard-boiled and raw – in the batter.

Preparation and cooking time: 30 minutes
Resting time: 30 minutes
Makes: 20 crowns

2 hard-boiled egg yolks
3 egg yolks
125 g/4½ oz (⅔ cup) sugar
250 g/9 oz (2¼ sticks) butter, at room temperature
300 g/11 oz (2½ cups) weak (soft) wheat flour
1 tablespoon milk
pearl sugar, to decorate

Press the hard-boiled egg yolks through a sieve into a large bowl and mix with 2 of the raw yolks and the sugar. Whisk until smooth and creamy.

Add the butter and flour alternately, little by little, working it into a thick batter with your hand. Shape it into a rough ball, then wrap it in clingfilm (plastic wrap) and place in the refrigerator to rest for 30 minutes.

Preheat the oven to 200°C/400°F/Gas Mark 6. Line 2 baking sheets with baking (parchment) paper.

Unwrap the dough and divide it into 2 rolls, cut them into smaller pieces and shape each piece into a smaller roll 12–14 cm/4½–5½ inches in length. Place them onto the prepared baking sheets in the shape of circles with the ends visibly overlapping.

Whisk the remaining egg yolk with the milk and brush lightly onto each pretzel. Sprinkle with a little pearl sugar and bake until golden. Leave the pretzels to cool on the sheet before moving them.

MERINGUE

Pikekyss (Norway)
Marenki (Finland)
Marengs kys (Denmark)
Maräng (Sweden)

This is a good base recipe for meringue, although the baking temperature and cooking time vary, depending on what you are trying to achieve.

If you want to make snowy-white meringues, then bake them at 110°C/225°F/Gas Mark ½. If you prefer them golden, then bake them at 140°C/275°F/Gas Mark 1 first, until they have the colour you want, then lower the temperature to 110°C/225°F/Gas Mark ½ to finish. The cooking time depends on how dry you want your meringues to be. Sometimes a chewy meringue is pretty delicious, but sometimes you want them to be bone-dry, which will take overnight.

As egg sizes vary so much, it is best to weigh out the correct amount of egg whites for this recipe. Also, I prefer to use egg whites that have been standing, uncovered, in a bowl for a few days so that they have dried out a bit. This makes the meringue much more stable.

Preparation time: 10 minutes
Cooking time: 1–15 hours depending on what
  you are going to do with it and the size of
  the meringue

160 g/5½ oz egg whites
200 g/7 oz (1 cup) sugar

Preheat the oven to 110°C/225°F/Gas Mark ½ and line several baking sheets with baking (parchment) paper.

Place the egg whites in the bowl of a stand mixer (or a large stainless steel mixing bowl) and start whisking them slowly until they begin to foam. Add the sugar, little by little, making sure you leave enough time between each addition for the sugar crystals to dissolve completely. For meringue perfection, it is important not to hurry too much, or to whisk too quickly, or to add the sugar too fast, as this will result in more of a runny fluff, with less of the velvety, brilliant, shiny quality that really good meringue has.

After you have added about half of the sugar – let's say it takes you about 5 minutes – you can start whisking at a faster speed and adding the sugar at a slightly faster pace. When all the sugar has been added, lower the speed again and keep whisking the meringue slowly until all the sugar crystals have dissolved and the meringue looks like fresh white paint, in both brilliance and shine. It should be very stiff.

Pipe, spoon or otherwise shape the stiff meringue straight onto the prepared baking sheets in whatever shape or form you feel like, or the recipe you are making calls for.

A small meringue, the size of a walnut, will cook in about an hour and a really big thick one, the size of a grapefruit might not really fully cook at all but always remain a little chewy inside.

Place the meringue in the oven and if you have a fan (convection) one, turn the fan off, otherwise your meringue will blow around as it dries up and lightens.

Cook until the meringue is as dry or chewy you want it to be. Store in airtight containers.

KROKAN CAKE

Krokaani (Finland)
Krokan (Sweden)

Krokan is a traditional pastry sometimes served at weddings in Sweden. It resembles the Almond Wreath Cake (page 604) common in other Nordic countries in the sense that it is based on almond paste with the addition of egg white, and in the way that it is assembled in tiers to sometimes quite imposing heights. However, the Swedish *krokan* is piped out into bows that are glued together with melted sugar rather than the round wreaths of the Almond Wreath Cake, which are stacked on top of each other in a more compact way. The Swedish ones are also baked until dry as opposed to the ones in other countries, which have a moist centre. A *krokan* usually has three tiers whilst an Almond Wreath Cake usually has more.

Today the *krokan* is on the brink of extinction since more international style wedding cakes have pushed it out of fashion.

If you are to venture into the world of *krokan* baking you will need more guidance than I have space to give in this book but I have included a recipe on the batter below anyhow so that you can understand at least the proportions and basic technique of making them.

Preparation and cooking time: a very
* long time*
Makes: enough for a wedding of 50 guests

5 kg/11 lb almond paste
10 egg whites
350 g/12 oz (1¾ cups) sugar

Preheat the oven to 150°C/300°F/Gas Mark 2.

Mix the almond paste and egg whites together in a large bowl to obtain a smooth but stiff batter. Transfer the batter to a piping bag fitted with a star nozzle and pipe it out onto a sheet of baking (parchment) paper. Step-by-step designs for *krokans* can be found on the internet to be printed and used as templates for the piping. The best way of using them is to print them on ordinary paper and place that under the baking paper onto which you pipe the batter.

Bake all the parts until golden and quite dry. Leave them to cool down.

To melt the sugar, carefully heat it over a medium heat in a suitable pot and do not stir until all the sugar has melted and started to caramelize. If you stir it, mixing melted and non-melted sugar, it tends to form lumps, which are difficult to melt. When the sugar has started browning and smells of caramel, quickly dip the bottom of the pan in some cold water to stop the cooking process.

Use the melted sugar to 'glue' the *krokan* parts together. As you assemble the *krokan*, if the sugar cools down and stiffens, simply reheat it a bit.

ROLLED TUILES

Sometimes, like once or twice a year, I drive down to Östersund, the city closest to where we live, to record some radio. The show in which I am from time to time invited to participate is called *Meny*, and it is broadcast on Swedish Radio 1. Radio one, or P1, is proper grown-up radio, with music for grown-ups and subjects for grown-ups. I always used to think that it was a radio station dull like nothing else, but then, one day, just before I turned thirty, I realized that it is in fact genius.

Meny is one of the most popular shows on the station and it is one of those shows where a panel of guests chat along with a very convivial and pleasant host, where listeners can call in with questions about this and that concerning food and where general advice on cooking and entertaining is given.

Each time I have participated, exactly four days after the broadcast, with absolute accuracy, a small box wrapped in brown paper arrives at my restaurant, Fäviken. The box weighs almost nothing and you can see that someone, probably an older person, has put effort and care into wrapping it up before sending it. The brown paper creased and folded around the box with sharp corners, a piece of string tied around the edges and no tape to hold anything in place. The address and my name are always written in the same corner with ballpoint pen, in a very neat and very small longhand, a simple card rests between the brown paper and the box inside, thanking me for a nice broadcast, still in the same neat and hard-to-read longhand. The contents of the actual box are also the same every time. Ten *rullrån*, rolled tuiles, just like the ones my grandmother used to make when I was growing up. *Rullrån* is one of those cookies that almost no one makes any more, they are kind of tedious to produce. I don't know who is sending them to me and from where, but it always makes me happy to see that someone still puts the time and effort into making these delicious pastries.

The first time I didn't dare eat them at once since I didn't know who had sent them, but I couldn't bear throwing them in the bin either. They sat there for quite some time in their box until I nibbled a bit of one, waiting almost an afternoon, anxiously pacing around the house, thinking that

I might die soon. The day after, I ate a whole one and then on the third day I served them to my family for dessert, with whipped cream and some Sugared Cloudberries (page 692).

Whoever you are, sending me the rolled tuiles after listening to me on the radio, thank you so much. They are really tasty and I especially like that you fry them in salted butter, it makes all the difference.

Preparation and cooking time: 1 hour
Makes: about 30 tuiles

120 g/4 oz (½ cup plus 2 tablespoons) sugar
100 g/3½ oz (7 tablespoons) butter, melted
small pinch of salt
215 g/7½ oz (1¾ cups plus 1 tablespoon)
  weak (soft) wheat flour
soft butter, for brushing

Stir the sugar into the melted butter with the salt. Sift in the flour and combine. Add 300 ml/10½ fl oz (1¼ cups) water, stir and let the batter sit for 20 minutes.

Heat the tuile iron (page 559) over a medium heat. When it is hot brush it lightly with some soft butter and add a good spoonful of batter. Close the iron and turn it around. Cook until the tuile is golden in colour on both sides, then remove it from the iron and wrap it around a suitable cylindrical stick to shape it. They will cool and harden rather quickly.

For image see page 559

NORWEGIAN WAFERS

Krumkaker (Norway)
Rullrån (Sweden)

Thin *krumkaker* wafers are often filled with Norwegian Cloudberry Cream (page 639), whipped cream or other fillings. Depending on what you roll it around, it can be used for different things. The traditional formats for a *krumkaker* wafer are a cone, a straight tube, around 1.5 cm/¾ inch in diameter or an open shell, which looks a little like a taco shell.

The wafers should be cooked on a special *krum-kaker* iron.

Preparation and cooking time: 1½ hours
Resting time: at least 30 minutes, but
  preferably overnight
Makes: 25 wafers

3 eggs
150 g/5 oz (¾ cup) sugar
150 g/5 oz (1¼ cups) weak (soft) wheat flour
150 g/5 oz (1 stick plus 3 tablespoons) salted
  butter, melted, but not too hot, plus extra
  for the iron
Norwegian Cloudberry Cream (page 639) or
  whipped cream, to fill

Beat the eggs and sugar together until creamy. Sift on the flour and mix it in evenly. Add the melted butter and 50–100 ml/2–3½ fl oz (¼–½ cup) water, until the texture looks like a thick pancake batter. Leave the batter to rest in the refrigerator for at least 30 minutes, but preferably overnight.

Grease a *krumkaker* iron with butter and heat to a medium temperature. Add a tablespoonful of batter to the iron and press it together immediately. If you are using an electric iron, cook it until the wafer has a light amber colour. If you are using a stovetop model, flip it over immediately after pressing, so that you get the wafer evenly browned.

When the wafers are cooked, remove them from the iron and, while they are still hot, shape them around something suitable to create a cone or shell. Leave each wafer to firm up while the next wafer is cooking in the iron, then remove from the mould and transfer it to a wire rack for further cooling, just before the next wafer is ready.

Once completely cool, fill the wafers with your chosen cream.

ALMOND WAFERS

Mandelflarn (Sweden)

Serve these straight, as a sweet snack (*fika*, coffee break, page 531) with coffee or bend them over something round, while warm, into a little taco-style shell and fill with Lingonberry Cream (page 638), or something else tasty, and serve as a dessert.

These wafers are not particularly biscuit- (cookie-) like but rather like a thin sheet of buttery caramel with almonds in it.

Preparation and cooking time: 30 minutes
Makes: 12 wafers

75 g/2¾ oz (¾ cup) chopped almonds
60 g/2¼ oz (4 tablespoons) butter
85 g/3 oz (⅓ cup plus 2 tablespoons) sugar
1 tablespoon plain (all-purpose) flour
65 ml/2 fl oz (¼ cup) milk
pinch of salt

Preheat the oven to 175°C/345°F/Gas Mark 4 and line a baking sheet with baking (parchment) paper.

Mix all of the ingredients, except the lingonberry cream, together in a small pan and bring them to a simmer over a medium heat. Transfer the mixture to a bowl and leave for a few minutes to cool down and firm up a little.

Spoon dollops of the mixture onto the prepared baking sheet. Space them widely apart, not more than 4 per baking sheet as they will spread out a lot. Bake until they have flattened out in the heat and turned golden.

If you want to keep the wafers flat, then leave them to cool down on the sheet. To bend them, leave for a few minutes on the baking sheet so that they cool just a little but are still pliable, then pick them up with a palette knife or an offset spatula and place them on an appropriately shaped object. Leave them there until they have cooled down completely and are crisp before filling with lingonberry cream.

FAROESE WAFERS

Góðaráð (Faroe Islands)

Góðaráð means 'good advice' in Faroese, or 'tasty wafers'. It's a very witty name for a pastry. As with other wafers, you need a wafer iron (electric or stovetop) to make them. Serve with berries or jam (page 690) on the side, as a dessert or as a snack with coffee.

Preparation and cooking time: 30 minutes
Makes: about 20 wafers, depending on the size
  of your wafer iron

220 g/7¾ oz (2 sticks) butter, plus extra to
  grease
400 ml/14 fl oz (1⅔ cups) milk or water
3 eggs
220 g/7¾ oz (1 cup plus 2 tablespoons) sugar
200 g/7 oz (1¼ cups) potato starch
200 g/7 oz (1⅔ cups) weak (soft) wheat flour
1 tablespoon vanilla sugar

Combine the butter and milk or water in a pan and heat until the butter has melted. Leave to cool to room temperature.

Whisk the eggs and sugar together until pale and creamy, then add the cooled butter and milk/water mixture and stir until smooth. Sift the potato starch, flour and the vanilla sugar together into the liquid and whisk gently until fully incorporated.

Heat the wafer iron to a medium temperature. Grease lightly, then add a spoonful of batter to the iron and press it together immediately. If you are using an electric iron, cook it until the wafer has a light amber colour. If you are using a stovetop model, flip it over immediately after pressing, so that you get the wafer evenly browned.

When the wafers are cooked, remove them from the iron and transfer to a wire rack to cool.

NORWEGIAN SWEET PRESSED CARDAMOM AND VANILLA WAFERS

Goro (Norway)

To make these traditional Norwegian buttery biscuits (cookies) with cardamom and vanilla you need a *goro* iron to cook them in.

Preparation and cooking time: 2 hours
Resting time: minimum 2 hours, or preferably
  overnight
Makes: around 20 wafers, depending on the
  size of your goro iron

300 g/11 oz (2½ sticks) chilled butter, cut
  into 1 cm/½ inch pieces
500 g/1 lb 2 oz (4 cups plus 2 tablespoons)
  soft (weak) wheat flour, plus extra for
  dusting
1 teaspoon cardamom seeds, finely ground
1 vanilla bean, split and seeds scraped
175 ml/6 fl oz (¾ cup) cream
120 g/4¼ oz sugar
1 egg

Put the butter, flour, ground cardamom and vanilla seeds into the bowl of a food processor. Process to the texture of coarse sand.

Whisk the cream to soft peaks. Beat the sugar with the egg. Add the cream and egg mixture to the food processor and pulse until just combined. Do not overwork the dough. Wrap in clingfilm (plastic wrap) and leave to rest in the refrigerator for at least 2 hours. I prefer to leave it overnight because it makes it easier to roll out.

Roll the cold dough out on a lightly floured work counter to about 4 mm/⅛ inch. Cut into the desired shapes, then transfer to the *goro* iron and cook over a medium heat. The iron should be brushed lightly with butter for each new biscuit. The biscuits should be of a light golden tone when ready. Leave to cool on a wire rack.

Tip: Draw the size and shape of your *goro* iron onto a sheet of baking (parchment) paper, and cut it out with a pair of sharp scissors. Use that as a template when cutting the dough into suitable shapes for cooking.

CRISP ROLLS / RUSKS

Kavringer (Norway)
Korput (Finland)
Tvebakker (Denmark)
Skorpor (Sweden)

I love these with some salty butter and a slice of mature cheese. It's the perfect thing to nibble on in the afternoon with a cup of coffee next to it.

Preparation and cooking time: 1½ hours
Drying time: overnight
Makes: 40 rolls

1 quantity Sweet Wheat Bun Dough
  (page 538), flavoured with cardamom

For the egg wash
1 egg
1 tablespoon milk

Preheat the oven to 225°C/420°F/Gas Mark 7 and line a baking sheet with baking (parchment) paper.

Roll the leavened dough into 2 logs and place them on the prepared baking sheet. Proceed to leaven, brush with eggwash and bake for about 15 minutes until golden.

When still warm but not hot from the oven, cut each log horizontally in half along its whole length. Cut each half log into suitable pieces, perhaps 3 cm/1¼ inch wide. Place the pieces, cut-side-up on a baking sheet and put them in the oven again at 150°C/300°F/Gas Mark 2. Keep them in there until they take on a light golden colour, about 45 minutes, then turn the oven off and keep the door open just a bit by inserting a spoon or something in there. Leave the rusks in the oven overnight to dry and crisp up.

ALMOND RUSKS

Mandelskorpor (Sweden)

Preparation and cooking time: 30 minutes,
  plus cooling and drying time
Makes: 30–36 rusks

120 g/4 oz (1 stick) butter, at room
  temperature
200 g/7 oz (1 cup) sugar
2 eggs
100 g/3½ oz (⅔ cup) whole almonds
  (skins on), finely chopped
325 g/11¾ oz (2½ cups) soft (weak) wheat
  flour, plus extra for dusting
1 teaspoon baking powder

Preheat the oven to 225°C/435°F/Gas Mark 7. Line a baking sheet with baking (parchment) paper.

Combine the butter and sugar in the bowl of a stand mixer and beat until pale and fluffy. Add the eggs, one at a time, making sure each is fully incorporated before you add the next.

Add the chopped almonds, then sift the flour and baking powder together into the bowl. Mix everything together gently until smooth and sticky but be careful not to overwork the dough.

Transfer the dough to a lightly floured work counter. Divide into 3 equal pieces, shape them into long logs and lift onto the prepared baking sheet.

Bake until light golden in colour.

Leave the baked logs to cool on the baking sheet, then use a serrated knife to slice each log into 10–12 rusks. Leave to dry out completely on a wire rack. If you want them golden all over, then toast them in a hot oven for a few minutes.

SWEET RUSKS TO SERVE WITH
SWEET SOUPS

Sukkerkavringer (Norway)
Kammarjunkere (Denmark)
Sockerskorpor (Sweden)

These sweet and crisp rusks are usually flavoured with vanilla, lemon or cardamom and served a bit like croutons with sweet fruit soups (pages 694–700) and other sweet soups like Cold Buttermilk Soup (page 74). Add cardamom with the dry ingredients, and lemon or vanilla with the egg and cream.

Preparation and cooking time: 1 hour plus
   time to dry completely
Makes: 40 rusks

250 g/9 oz (2 cups plus 2 tablespoons) weak
   (soft) wheat flour, plus extra for dusting
1 tablespoon baking powder
75 g/2¾ oz (⅓ cup) sugar
good pinch of salt
100 g/3½ oz (7 tablespoons) butter, soft
1 egg
50 ml/2 fl oz (3½ tablespoons) cream

Preheat the oven to 200°C/400°C/Gas Mark 6 and line a baking sheet with baking (parchment) paper.

Sift all the dry ingredients together into the bowl of a standmixer. Add the butter and beat until fully incorporated; the mix will look sort of gravelly and a bit dry. Add the egg and the cream to the mixture and work it again until fully incorporated.

Tip the dough out onto your floured work counter and divide into 2 equal portions. Roll each into a log, about 3 cm/1¼ inches in diameter. Cut each log into 10 slices and use your hands to shape them into balls. Place the balls onto the prepared baking sheet and bake until golden.

Remove the baked rusks from the oven and split each one in half, a bit like a hamburger bun is split using a fork and pulling, rather than a knife. Place them back onto the baking sheet, cut side up. Lower the oven temperature to 150°C/300°F/Gas Mark 2. Bake the rusks until lightly golden on the cut surface. Turn off the oven and leave the rusks inside until the oven is cold and the rusks are crisp.

SWEET SATURDAY

I vividly remember how special Saturdays felt when I was a kid growing up in Sweden. The excitement of going to bed Friday night, knowing that tomorrow, after breakfast, riding shotgun in the Volvo 245 station wagon which was blue, we were going to the shop to get that week's ration of sweets (candy).

The smells, the colours and the feeling of unlimited possibility were heaven. Faced with the wall of plastic boxes in which you were (under strict parental supervision of course) allowed to pick a few sweets into a little white paper bag with multi-sized pastel-coloured, overlapping circles on the front, this was truly the highlight of the week.

Why, you ask yourself, do the Swedes restrict most of their sweet eating to one day a week?

It all started with a mid-twentieth century wish by the social democrat government to improve the dental hygiene of the country's citizens. Many different reforms were put in place, among them a generous public dental-care system, compulsory fluoride rinsing at schools and other sensible stuff like that.

However, in addition to more balanced proceedings like making people brush their teeth, from 1945–1955, one of the most scandalous and abusive medical experiments on humans ever to take place in a western democracy was carried out on the south Swedish Vipeholm institution for the mentally ill. To study the actions of tooth decay a group of at least 1000 people was needed, preferably in a controlled environment for an extended period of time. These requirements were met by by mental institutions of the time, where patients were often locked up for life.

The ill were fed large amounts of particularly sticky toffee over extended periods of time to encourage the formation of caries and to study the long-term effects of carbohydrates on dental hygiene. Of course at the price of terrible pain and loss of quality of life for those participating without consent.

It was soon concluded that carbs weren't good for your teeth and that if you concentrated the intake of, for example, sweets to once a week, it would probably be better for you.

The information was rolled out to the eager citizens of my home country, who listened to the injunctions of their beloved government, and started eating sweets mostly on Saturdays.

This has led us to present times where most of us do have really good teeth, probably not because of the sweet Saturday though, as we also eat the most candy per person and year in the whole world, a good 18 kg/40 lb on average.

Prepare a plate with a generous layer of your choice of coating.

Divide the chocolate mixture into 20 equal-sized portions and roll into balls with your hands. Let them drop directly into your desired coating and roll them around to coat evenly.

Wash your hands so they are clean. This way you will not get smudgy brown pearl sugar on the coconut flakes as you transfer the finished chocolate balls to a serving plate.

For image see page 559

CHOCOLATE OATMEAL BALLS

Havregrynskugler (Denmark)
Chokladbollar (Sweden)

I must have made these *chokladbollar* a thousand times when growing up, as I am sure many Swedes and other Nordics have.

Some people like their chocolate balls rolled in pearl sugar; myself, I prefer coconut flakes. Some recipes contain strong coffee, which I think is silly, since it makes the texture much less fantastic. The extra water content melts the sugar so that you lose that little crunchy feeling and it makes the rolled oats swell and lose their texture. If you want the coffee flavour, then add a tablespoon of instant coffee powder to this recipe; it works much better.

Preparation time: 15 minutes
Makes: 20 balls

200 g/7 oz (1¾ sticks) butter, at room
  temperature
175 g/6 oz (¾ cup) sugar
2 tablespoons vanilla sugar
6 tablespoons cocoa powder
pinch of salt
210 g/7½ oz (1⅔ cups) rolled oats
pearl sugar or coconut flakes, to coat

Combine the butter, sugar, vanilla sugar, cocoa powder and salt in a large bowl and work with your hands until well combined. Add the oats and continue working until they are just combined.

CHOCOLATE COOKIE CRUMB BALLS FLAVOURED WITH ARRACK

Arraksbollar (Sweden)

These are similar to the Chocolate Oatmeal Balls on page 575, but flavoured with *arrack* (see Swedish Punsch on page 717) and coated with chocolate sprinkles, instead of sugar or coconut.

Preparation time: 20 minutes
Makes: 20 balls

chocolate sprinkles, to coat
100 g/3½ oz (7 tablespoons) butter, at
 room temperature
85 g/3 oz (⅓ cup plus 1 tablespoon) sugar
3 tablespoons cocoa powder
arrack, to taste
300 g/11 oz (2½ cups) biscuit (cookie) crumbs

Prepare a plate with a generous layer of chocolate sprinkles.

Combine the butter, sugar, vanilla sugar, cocoa powder and *arrack* in a large bowl and work with your hands until well combined. Add the biscuit (cookie) crumbs and continue working until they are just combined.

Divide the chocolate mixture into 20 equal portions and roll into balls with your hands. Let the balls drop directly into the sprinkles and roll them around to coat evenly.

STRIPED PEPPERMINT STICKS

Polkagrisar (Sweden)

Polkagrisar are Swedish candy sticks flavoured with quite a bit of peppermint oil. These red-and-white canes are claimed to have been invented by Amalia Eriksson, a Swedish woman, in 1859. However, red-and-white canes were made in other parts of Europe during the same period of time, and all-white ones flavoured with peppermint had been produced much earlier, so talking about her inventing them is perhaps a bit of an exaggeration. Where her inspiration came from is not document-

ed, but she was surely the first person to make these particular sweets (candies) in her home town of Gränna, which is now very famous for them and receives in excess of one million visitors a year, who go there mostly to see the many sweet (candy) shops and buy themselves a few *polkagrisar*.

To make this recipe it is essential to have a work counter made from marble or some other heavy stone. This, to first cool the melted sugar and then to keep it from cooling too much so that it becomes hard before you are done working it.

As always, when handling boiling sugar syrup, it's important to work very carefully and to wear gloves to avoid burns.

1kg is quite a bit of candy but it is very difficult to make less as the sugar will cool down to quickly as you handle it if the amount is any smaller. They keep well though so make the full recipe, eat what you want and give the rest away to some friends.

Preparation and cooking time: 1 hour
Makes: 1 kg/2¼ lb

neutral oil, for the work counter
1 kg/2¼ lb (5 cups) sugar
1 tablespoon *Ättika* (12%) vinegar
 (page 656)
25 drops peppermint oil
red food colouring

Lightly oil your marble work counter, a couple of stainless steel spatulas and a baking sheet.

Put the sugar into a heavy-bottomed pot and pour in 400 ml/14 fl oz (1⅔ cups) water. Bring to the boil, then continue boiling until the mixture reaches the 'hard crack' stage on a sugar thermometer (150°C/300°F). If you don't have a thermometer, you can test the consistency by spooning a drop of it into a cup of cold water. After a few seconds, when it has cooled, you will be able to judge the final texture. At the hard crack stage it should form brittle threads that snap easily.

Taking care not to get hot sugar onto your skin, carefully pour the hot syrup directly onto the work counter, keeping about 100 ml/3½ fl oz (6 tablespoons) back in the pan. Add red food colouring to this smaller amount and keep it warm over a very low heat while you work the remaining sugar.

Add the drops of peppermint oil to the mass of hot sugar on your counter. Use the oiled spatulas to fold the edges in to the centre. Repeat this folding and, as soon as it has cooled enough to touch, use your hands to work it. Start stretching the candy out into lengths, and then folding it back over on itself to incorporate air. As you work it, it will start to stiffen and turn white. At this point, roll it out to a long rope, about 4 cm/1½ inches in diameter. Set aside.

Scrape the red-tinted syrup onto the work counter and work it in the same way until it stiffens a little. Roll it out to the same length as the uncoloured white piece, although the red piece will be much thinner.

Press the red piece on top of the white piece and pull the whole thing out to a long, even rope, about 80 cm/31½ inches. Twist the rope slightly, and fold it in half on top of itself. Stretch it out again, then roll it on the work counter until it is as thin as you want it to be. Use oiled scissors to cut it into sticks or snip into small lozenges (see illustrations below). Transfer to the prepared baking sheet to cool and harden. Store them in an airtight container, as they will go sticky if allowed to get moist.

AMMONIUM CHLORIDE LIQUORICE

Ammonium chloride liquorice, or salty liquorice, is a type of sweet (candy) common in the Nordic region, Holland and Germany. It is particularly popular in Finland where it is called *salmiakki* and in Sweden where it is called *salmiak*. The name *salmiak* comes from the old Latin name for ammonium chloride – *sal ammoniacus* – which has also given name to ammonia and ammonium. It is not known how long liquorice has been flavoured with ammonium chloride but it has been produced industrially at least since the 1930s. It is also a key ingredient in Salty Liquorice Vodka (page 715). These types of sweets are said to be an acquired taste and many people who are not accustomed to the flavour from when they were kids never seem to learn to like it much.

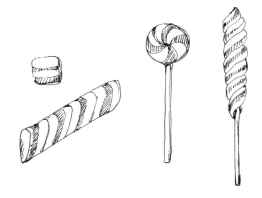

PEPPERMINT AND CHOCOLATE PASTILLES

Mintkyssar (Sweden)

These little pastilles are often made for Christmas and served with coffee after the actual meal.

Preparation time: 15 minutes
Drying time: minimum 4 hours, preferably
  overnight
Makes: 40 pastilles

1 egg white
220 g/7¾ oz (1 cup) icing (confectioners')
  sugar
peppermint oil, to taste
50 g/2 oz very good quality dark (semisweet)
  chocolate

Line 2 baking sheets with baking (parchment) paper.

Whisk the egg white to soft peaks. Sift in the icing (confectioners') sugar and add peppermint oil to taste. Stir until thoroughly combined. Spoon the mixture into a disposable piping bag and cut the tip to a suitable size.

Pipe neat flat discs of the mixture onto the prepared baking sheets. Leave them at room temperature to dry. It will take at least 4 hours, but it's best to leave them overnight.

Place the chocolate in a heatproof bowl and set over a pan of simmering water to melt, stirring constantly. Don't allow the bowl to touch the water as it will turn grainy. Once the chocolate has melted, transfer it to a disposable piping bag and pipe a generous dot of chocolate on top of each pastille. Leave the chocolate to set before serving.

SWEDISH CHRISTMAS TOFFEE

Knäck (Sweden)

Knäck is the Swedish word for 'break', and I assume that it refers to the texture of the finished sweet. Personally I like my *knäck* a bit chewy and so I cook it for a slightly shorter time. *Knäck* is always poured hot into small paper moulds and left to set in them. For those people preferring a very sticky texture, the paper won't let go of the toffee when cool so they will have to put the whole thing into their mouth, paper and all, to release the sweet from its packaging.

Most recipes will include a couple of tablespoons of chopped almonds, others include some breadcrumbs – and some include both. While I have never understood the breadcrumbs, I do like the almonds. *Knäck* is considered essential during the Christmas weeks by most Swedish families.

It is easy to make this toffee if you have a good thermometer, but perfectly possible without. 122°C/252°F makes a soft but not sticky toffee, a temperature below this will give sticky toffee; 125°C/257°F makes a firm toffee, and temperatures above will produce a hard result.

Preparation and cooking time: 1 hour, plus
  setting time
Makes: 45–60 pieces, depending on how long
  you boil it and how big the paper cups are

200 ml/7 fl oz (¾ cup plus 1 tablespoon)
  cream
170 g/5¾ oz (¾ cup plus 1 tablespoon) sugar
280 g/10 oz (¾ cup plus 1 tablespoon) golden
  syrup
2 tablespoons salted butter
2 tablespoons finely chopped almonds and/
  or breadcrumbs (optional)

Mix all of the ingredients, except for the almonds and/or breadcrumbs, in a heavy pan. I like to use a cast-iron frying pan or skillet for this. Bring to a simmer over a medium heat, stirring with a wooden spoon from time to time. Continue cooking until the desired temperature – indicating the temperature your *knäck* will have – is reached. It will take 30–40 minutes.

If you don't have a thermometer you can test the consistency of the *knäck* mix – and thereby judge if it is done cooking – by spooning a drop of it into a cup of cold water. After a few seconds, when the toffee has cooled, you will be able to judge the final texture.

As soon as it is ready, add the almonds and/or breadcrumbs to the caramel and spoon it into the moulds to set.

CAKES AND TORTES

Chapter title page: Night sky, Iceland, May 2013.

Previous page: Interior from Café Ekberg, Helsinki, Finland, Autumn 2013.

Opposite: Interior of an historical house on the Faroe Islands, April 2013. This house was built almost a thousand years ago in Norway, disassembled, moved to its current location and then put together again.

NORDIC SPONGE CAKES

We love sponge cakes in the Nordic region; they are baked and eaten in several different ways and are used in many of the traditional layer cakes (page 598).

There is a great deal of cultural cake crossover between the various Nordic countries and the ingredients and flavourings of the most popular sponge cakes are almost identical. However there are some regional differences. In Sweden, for example, the most widely made sponge is called *sockerkaka*, which literally means 'sugar cake', while in Denmark it is called *sandkage*, 'sand cake' (see opposite page) and the main difference is in the method. In the Swedish cake the butter is melted with milk and added to whisked eggs and sugar; the dry ingredients are then sifted into the wet ingredients. In the Danish version, butter and sugar are creamed together, and the eggs are incorporated before adding the dry ingredients. This method keeps the butter emulsified all through the preparation of the batter. In general terms, the Danish way gives a slightly shorter, crumblier cake whereas the Swedish one gives a firmer, spongier result. Anyhow, I am probably splitting hairs here. A cake is a cake, and most people can't tell one from another one except by their level of deliciousness – which has nothing to do with the technicalities described above.

You can flavour your sponge with a couple of teaspoons of good vanilla sugar, the grated zest of a lemon or anything else you feel is appropriate. If using a dry flavouring, it is best to add it with the flour and baking powder. If it is wet enough to stick to your sifter, just add it to the batter at the very end.

The recipes below are suitable for a 24-cm/9½-inch round cake pan or a regular 23 x 13 x 8 cm/9 x 5 x 3 inch loaf pan.

If you are making a layer cake with any of the following sponge recipes, then leave it to cool down in the pan, rather than on a wire rack. This makes the crust softer, and it will be easier to slice horizontally into layers. With the Danish sponge cake, it's important to invert the pan onto the wire rack, so the butter content can even out within the cake. Leave the pan over it as a little cover.

BASIC SPONGE CAKE

Sukkerkake (Norway)
Sokerikakku (Finland)
Sukkerkage (Denmark)
Sockerkaka (Sweden)

Almost all books on traditional Nordic cooking and baking have at least three recipes for this type of cake or some similar cakes, and at least one for a special, light-and-airy version that is meant to be extra-suitable for layer cakes. The recipe here is the richest one and the one I like the most. When I was growing up this would have been labelled as 'fine' or 'moist' sponge cake. I never understood why there should be a need for a sponge cake that wasn't 'fine' or 'moist'…

If you want a lemony cake, measure out the juice and use it to replace the same amount of milk. But only add the lemon juice after the dry ingredients have already been incorporated into the batter.

Preparation and cooking time: 1 hour
Makes: 8 pieces

250 g/9 oz (2¼ sticks) butter, plus
    extra to grease
breadcrumbs, to coat
100 ml/3½ fl oz (⅓ cup plus 1 tablespoon)
    milk
4 eggs
350 g/12 oz (1¾ cups) sugar
320 g/11¼ oz (2⅔ cups) weak (soft)
    wheat flour
2 teaspoons baking powder
2 teaspoons vanilla sugar and/or grated
    zest of 1 lemon (optional)

Preheat the oven to 175°C/345°F/Gas Mark 4. Butter a 24-cm/9½-inch cake pan and coat with breadcrumbs.

Combine the butter and milk in a small pan and heat until the butter has melted. Leave to cool down to room temperature.

Whisk the eggs with the sugar until light and fluffy. Add the butter and milk mixture and mix in thoroughly. Sift the dry ingredients into the bowl, adding the dry flavourings, if using, and whisk in gently. Add lemon zest or juice last.

Scrape the batter into the prepared cake pan, smooth the surface and bake for about 40 minutes, or until cooked through. When the cake is done, it should have shrunk slightly from the sides of the pan and a toothpick inserted into the centre of the cake should come out clean.

If you like crisp edges, then unmould the cake onto a wire rack and leave it to cool completely. If you prefer soft edges, leave the cake in the pan to cool.

For image see page 609

DANISH SPONGE CAKE

Sandkage (Denmark)

It is easier to keep the butter emulsified through the whole process if the butter and eggs are at roughly the same temperature, so take them both out of the refrigerator at the same time. This batter is dry enough to take the juice of a whole lemon if you want, however to make a really lemony cake you may want to add even more lemon juice, in which case you might have to increase the cooking time a bit.

Some older recipes state that you place this cake in a cold oven that is set to 175°C/345°F/Gas Mark 4. This was probably perfect in the early days of electric ovens, but today they heat up really quickly and I think this technique produces too dark a colour. I have described my method below, but if you want to try the old-fashioned way – or if you have a really old oven – then proceed as described above.

Preparation and cooking time: 1 hour
* 15 minutes (or a bit longer if you bake it in*
* a loaf pan)*
Makes: 8 pieces

350 g/12 oz (3 sticks) butter, at room
  temperature, plus extra to grease
breadcrumbs, to coat
350 g/12 oz (1¾ cups) sugar
5 eggs, at room temperature
350 g/12 oz (3 cups) weak (soft) wheat flour
1 teaspoon baking powder
2 teaspoons vanilla sugar and/or grated zest
  of 1 lemon (optional)

Preheat the oven to 150°C/300°F/Gas Mark 2. Butter a 24-cm/9½-inch cake pan or a 23 x 13 x 8 cm/ 9 x 5 x 3 inch loaf pan and coat with breadcrumbs.

Combine the butter and sugar in the bowl of a stand mixer and beat at medium speed until pale and fluffy. Add the eggs, one at a time, making sure each is fully incorporated before you add the next.

Sift the dry ingredients together into the bowl and mix in gently until just combined. The batter should be quite stiff.

Scrape the batter into the prepared cake pan and smooth the surface. Bake for about 1 hour, or until cooked through. When the cake is done, it should have shrunk slightly from the sides of the pan and a toothpick inserted into the centre of the cake should come out clean. Leave in the pan for 10 minutes before inverting it onto a wire rack. Leave to cool upside down on the wire rack so that the butter doesn't all end up in the bottom part of the cake.

LIGHT SPONGE CAKE FOR LAYER CAKES

Tårtbotten (Sweden)

I've included this 'light' sponge cake recipe just as a formality. But just so that you know, I would never bake it and would definitely never use it in one of my own layer cakes.

Preparation and cooking time: 1 hour
Makes: 8 pieces

butter, to grease
breadcrumbs, to coat
4 eggs
180 g/6½ oz (¾ cup) sugar
65 g/2½ oz (½ cup) weak (soft) wheat
    flour
75 g/2¾ oz (¼ cup plus 3 tablespoons)
    potato starch
1 teaspoon baking powder
2 teaspoons vanilla sugar and/or grated zest
    of 1 lemon (optional)

Preheat the oven to 175°C/345°F/Gas Mark 4. Butter a 24-cm/9½-inch cake pan and coat with breadcrumbs.

Whisk the eggs with the sugar until light and fluffy. Sift the dry ingredients together into the bowl and whisk in gently.

Scrape the batter into the prepared cake pan and smooth the surface. Bake for about 30 minutes, or until cooked through. When the cake is done, it should have shrunk slightly from the sides of the pan and a toothpick inserted into the centre of the cake should come out clean. Leave to cool in the pan.

ALMOND SPONGE CAKE

Mandelkage (Denmark)
Mandelkaka (Sweden)

This is a recipe for a very delicious, very dense and very fantastic almond sponge cake. I usually just refer to it as, 'the cake'. Eat a slice with your afternoon coffee or at any other time of the day.

I like to have quite a bit of acidity in it as it easily becomes too sweet. Sometimes I use lemon and sometimes I use *Ättika* (12%) vinegar (page 656). I usually don't add zest to this as I prefer the taste of almond without it but feel free to add some if you like.

And yes, I know, the recipe looks a bit insane but it should really be like this, it will almost fill the loaf pan but it won't rise as much as ordinary cake.

Preparation and cooking time: 1½ hours,
* plus cooling time*
Makes: 8 pieces

200 g/7 oz (1¾ sticks) butter, soft, plus
    extra to grease
breadcrumbs, to coat
170 g/6 oz (¾ cup plus 2 tablespoons)
    sugar
200 g/7 oz almond paste, grated on the
    coarse side of a box grater
2 tablespoons *Ättika* (12%) vinegar
    (page 656) or lemon juice
5 eggs
130 g/4½ oz (1 cup plus 1 tablespoon)
    weak (soft) wheat flour
1 teaspoon baking powder
a good pinch salt

Preheat the oven to 150°C/300°F/Gas Mark 2. Butter a 23 x 13 x 8 cm/9 x 5 x 3 inch loaf pan and coat with breadcrumbs.

Place the butter, sugar, almond paste and vinegar or lemon juice in the bowl of a stand mixer. Mix until smooth and a little lighter in colour – the mix should be really stiff. Add the eggs one at a time and mix until fully incorporated. Sift the flour, baking powder and salt into the bowl. Work a bit more in the stand mixer. The flour should be mixed in well and the batter should be smooth, but do not overwork it. Pour the batter into the prepared loaf pan and bake in the oven for 1 hour.

When it is done, place the cake upside down onto a wire rack to cool. This is a very important step. By inverting the cake the fat from the butter and almonds will be given the possibility to spread evenly in it. If you leave it as it was baked to cool it will be very greasy at the bottom and too dry at the top. After a few minutes remove the pan and let the cake cool to room temperature still upside down, before cutting into it.

GLAZED ORANGE SPONGE CAKE WITH CANDIED ORANGE PEEL / AMBROSIA CAKE

Ambrosiakaka (Sweden)

Preparation and cooking time: 1 hour
Makes: 8 pieces

250 g/9 oz (2¼ sticks) butter, plus extra
  to grease
breadcrumbs, to coat
100 ml/3½ fl oz (⅓ cup plus 1 tablespoon)
  milk
4 eggs
350 g/12 oz (1⅔ cups) sugar
320 g/11¼ oz (2⅔ cups) weak (soft)
  wheat flour
2 teaspoons baking powder
grated zest and juice of 1 orange
50 g/2 oz (⅓ cup) candied orange peel,
  finely diced
chopped pistachios, to sprinkle (optional)

For the icing
240 g/8½ oz (2 cups)
  icing (confectioner's) sugar
2 tablespoons fresh orange juice, possibly
  a little more

Preheat the oven to 175°C/345°F/Gas Mark 4. Butter a 24-cm/9½-inch cake pan and coat with breadcrumbs.

Combine the butter and milk in a small pan and heat until the butter has melted. Leave to cool down to room temperature.

Whisk the eggs with the sugar until light and fluffy. Add the butter and milk mixture and mix in thoroughly.

Sift the dry ingredients together into the bowl and mix until fully incorporated but not longer. Mix the orange zest and juice into the batter.

Scrape the batter into the prepared cake pan and smooth the surface. Bake for about 40 minutes, or until cooked through. When the cake is done, it should have shrunk slightly from the sides of the pan and a toothpick inserted into the centre of the cake should come out clean.

If you like crisp edges, then unmould the cake onto a wire rack and leave it to cool completely. If you prefer soft edges, leave the cake in the pan to cool.

Mix the icing (confectioner's) sugar with the fresh orange juice in a bowl and spread onto the cold cake. Before the icing sets, sprinkle on the diced orange peel and pistachios, if using.

POTATO STARCH SPONGE CAKE / SAND CAKE

Sandkaka (Sweden)

This cake prepared with no flour is not, as the name might imply, in any way dry. Maybe the name, 'sand cake', refers to the rather crumbly texture of moist sand. *Sandkaka* is often flavoured with a good dash of Cognac.

Preparation and cooking time: 1 hour
Standing time: overnight
Makes: 8 pieces

200 g/7 oz (1¾ sticks) butter, at room
  temperature, plus extra to grease
breadcrumbs, to coat
200 g/7 oz (1 cup plus 1 tablespoon)
  potato starch
2 teaspoons baking powder
1 teaspoon vanilla sugar
3 eggs
225 g/8 oz (1 cup plus 2 tablespoons)
  sugar
3 tablespoons Cognac

Preheat the oven to 175°C/345°F/Gas Mark 4. Butter a 24-cm/9½-inch cake pan and coat with breadcrumbs.

Combine the butter with the potato starch, baking powder and vanilla sugar in the fitted bowl of a stand mixer with the paddle attachment and beat at medium speed until light in colour.

In a separate bowl whisk the eggs with the sugar until light and fluffy, then add the Cognac. Add the eggs to the butter mixture, little by little, with the motor on low.

Scrape the batter into the prepared cake pan and smooth the surface. Bake for about 40 minutes, or until cooked through. When the cake is done, it should have shrunk slightly from the sides of the pan and a toothpick inserted into the centre of the cake should come out clean.

Turn the cake out of the pan and let it cool down on a wire rack. Put the pan back on the cake as a kind of lid and let it stand overnight before cutting into it.

TIGER CAKE

Tigerkake (Norway)
Marmorkage (Denmark)
Tigerkaka (Sweden)

Almost all over the Nordic region, a plain sponge cake marbled with chocolate sponge is referred to as a 'tiger' cake.

Preparation and cooking time: 1 hour
Makes: 1 loaf cake

250 g/9 oz (2¼ sticks) butter, plus extra
  to grease
breadcrumbs, to coat
100 ml/3½ fl oz (⅓ cup plus 1 tablespoon) milk
4 eggs
350 g/12 oz (1⅔ cups) sugar
320 g/11¼ oz (2⅔ cups) weak (soft)
  wheat flour
2 teaspoons baking powder
2 tablespoons cocoa powder

Preheat the oven to 175°C/345°F/Gas Mark 4. Butter a 23 x 13 x 8 cm/9 x 5 x 3 inch loaf pan and coat with breadcrumbs.

Combine the butter and milk in a small pan and heat until the butter has melted. Leave to cool down to room temperature.

Whisk the eggs with the sugar until light and fluffy. Add the butter and milk mixture and mix in thoroughly.

Sift the dry ingredients together into the bowl and whisk in gently.

Scrape half of the batter into the prepared loaf pan. Sift the cocoa powder into the remaining batter and mix it in thoroughly. Scrape this chocolate batter into the loaf pan, then use the end of a wooden spoon to swirl the two batters together.

Bake for about 40 minutes, or until cooked through. When the cake is done, it should have shrunk slightly from the sides of the pan and a toothpick inserted into the centre of the cake should come out clean.

If you like crisp edges, then unmould the cake onto a wire rack and leave it to cool completely. If you prefer soft edges, leave the cake in the pan to cool. Remove from the pan and serve.

For image see page 609

ALL EGG-WHITE SPONGE / SILVER CAKE

Silverkaka (Sweden)

I never really liked this cake much growing up, but I think it has a place in the book, partially because it is quite common – especially in older cookbooks and with my grandparents' generation – and because it is a good way of using up leftover egg whites.

Remember that the egg whites must be completely clean and contain no egg yolk, otherwise they won't whisk properly.

Preparation and cooking time: 1 hour
Makes: 8 pieces

100 g/3½ oz (7 tablespoons) butter, at room
   temperature, plus extra to grease
breadcrumbs, to coat
160 g/5¼ oz (¾ cup plus 1 tablespoon) sugar
225 g/8 oz (1¾ cups) weak (soft) wheat flour
2 teaspoons baking powder
1 tablespoon vanilla sugar and/or grated zest
   of 1 lemon
100 ml/3½ fl oz (⅓ cup plus 1 tablespoon) milk
100 ml/3½ fl oz (⅓ cup plus 1 tablespoon)
   egg whites (3–4 depending on size)

Preheat the oven to 175°C/345°F/Gas Mark 4. Butter a 24-cm/9½-inch cake pan and coat with breadcrumbs.

Combine the butter and sugar in the bowl of a stand mixer fitted with the paddle attachment and beat at medium speed until white and fluffy.

Sift the flour and baking powder together into the bowl, and mix until fully incorporated, but the mixture should be quite dry. Add the vanilla sugar or lemon zest and the milk and mix until smooth.

In a separate, perfectly clean bowl, whisk the egg whites to a stiff foam, then fold them into the batter. Pour the batter into the prepared pan, smooth the surface and bake for about 40 minutes until the cake is golden and cooked through. When the cake is done, it should have shrunk slightly from the sides of the pan and a toothpick inserted into the centre of the cake should come out clean.

Turn the cake out of the pan and leave to cool on a wire rack before cutting into it.

CHOCOLATE AND COCONUT GLAZED CHOCOLATE SPONGE CAKE

Mokkabitar i Skuffu (Faroe Islands)
Skúffukaka (Iceland)
Chokolade drømmekage (Denmark)
Kärleksmums (Sweden)

This cake can be made in an ordinary cake or loaf pan, but it is also often made in a sheet pan and cut into small square pieces after glazing.

If you are intending to make it in a full sized sheet pan, a double quantity of the cake batter will be sufficient. If you choose this format the cake will, and should be, slightly thinner, perhaps 4 cm/1½ inches thick when baked, and you will have to reduce the baking time to 25–30 minutes rather than the 40 minutes mentioned below. The same way of verifying the 'doneness' of the cake can be used though.

Regardless of whether you make a single batch in an ordinary pan or a double batch in a sheet pan, the cake should be left in the pan until cool and glazed before being removed as otherwise the glaze will run off. Plus, the sheet-pan size won't lift easily in one piece.

Preparation and cooking time: 1 hour
Makes: 8 pieces

For the cake batter
250 g/9 oz (2¼ sticks) butter, plus extra
   to grease
breadcrumbs, to coat
100 ml/3½ fl oz (⅓ cup plus 1 tablespoon)
   milk
4 eggs
350 g/12 oz (1¾ cups) sugar
320 g/11¼ oz (2⅔ cups) weak (soft)
   wheat flour
2 teaspoons baking powder
30 g/1 oz (⅓ cup) cocoa powder

To decorate
Chocolate Icing (page 679)
1 good handful coconut flakes, to sprinkle

Preheat the oven to 175°C/345°F/Gas Mark 4. Butter a 24-cm/9½-inch cake pan and coat with breadcrumbs.

Combine the butter and milk in a small pan and heat until the butter has melted. Leave to cool down to room temperature.

Whisk the eggs with the sugar until light and fluffy. Add the butter and milk mixture and mix in thoroughly.

Sift the dry ingredients together into the bowl and whisk everything in gently.

Scrape the batter into the prepared cake pan and smooth the surface. Bake for about 40 minutes, or until cooked through. When the cake is done, it should have shrunk slightly from the sides of the pan and a toothpick inserted into the centre of the cake should come out clean. Remove from the oven and leave to cool.

Make the chocolate icing and spread it onto the cooled cake. Before the icing sets, sprinkle generously with coconut flakes.

For image see page 609

CHOCOLATE, COFFEE AND COCONUT GLAZED CHOCOLATE SPONGE CAKE (VARIATION 1)

Mokkabitar i skuffu (Faroe Islands)
Mockabitar (Sweden)

Follow the recipe above but when you are making the icing, substitute water in the recipe with the same amount of cold, strong coffee.

MAJ'S SPRING BITES (VARIATION 2)

Majs vårbitar (Sweden)

Follow the recipe for Chocolate and Coconut Glazed Chocolate Sponge Cake (see left), making the cake in a sheet pan, but replace the cocoa powder in the sponge cake batter with 2 teaspoons of vanilla sugar instead.

FAROESE GREEN ALMOND SPONGE CAKE

Grønakaka (Faroe Islands)

Follow the recipe for Chocolate and Coconut Glazed Chocolate Sponge Cake (see opposite page) but omit the cocoa powder in the sponge cake batter and skip the coconut topping. Instead add 2 teaspoons of almond extract and 1 tablespoon of green food colouring to the cake batter.

SPONGE CAKE GLAZED IN ALMONDS AND CARAMEL / TOSCA CAKE

Toscakakku (Finland)
Toscakaka (Sweden)

This is a Swedish *fika* (coffee break, page 531) favourite that uses a slightly denser sponge cake recipe than the basic recipe on page 586. The quantities below are just enough to bake the cake (which shouldn't be too high) in a 24-cm/9½-inch round cake pan.

Preparation and cooking time: 1 hour, plus cooling time
Makes: 8 pieces

100 g/3½ oz (7 tablespoons) butter,
  plus extra to grease
breadcrumbs, to coat
75 ml/2½ fl oz (⅓ cup) milk
2 eggs
150 g/5 oz (¾ cup) sugar
125 g/4½ oz (1 cup) weak (soft) wheat flour
1 teaspoon baking powder

For the glaze
100 g/3½ oz (7 tablespoons) butter
85 g/3 oz (⅓ cup) sugar
2 tablespoons weak (soft) wheat flour
2 tablespoons milk
100 g/3½ oz (1 cup) flaked almonds

Preheat the oven to 175°C/345°F/Gas Mark 4. Butter a 24 cm/9½ inch loose-bottomed cake pan and coat with breadcrumbs.

Combine the butter and milk in a pan and heat until the butter has melted. Leave to cool down to room temperature.

Whisk the eggs with the sugar in a large bowl until light and fluffy. Add the cooled butter and milk mixture and mix in thoroughly.

Sift the dry ingredients together into the bowl and mix in gently.

Scrape the batter into the prepared cake pan, smooth the surface and bake for about 20 minutes.

While the cake is baking, prepare the glaze. Combine all the ingredients in a pan and heat gently over low heat until the mixture simmers and thickens a bit. It doesn't take long, a few minutes should be enough. Pour the glaze over the cake without really taking it out of the oven, rather just open the door and pour it onto the cake before putting the cake back to finish baking for another 15–20 minutes. There is no need to spread the glaze as that will happen automatically in the oven. When ready it should be deeply golden.

Leave the cake to cool in the pan, then turn it out of the pan before serving.

GINGERBREAD CAKE

Brun formakaka (Faroe Islands)
Mjuk pepparkaka (Sweden)

Most recipes for this cake contain some kind of cultured dairy product like *filmjölk*, *gräddfil* or yogurt, and most recipes are leavened with bicarbonate of soda (baking soda).

In Sweden it is quite common to add Sugared Lingonberries (page 692) and on the Faroe Islands, a couple of handfuls of raisins are often added to the batter.

In some more recent recipes cardamom is used in addition to the spices in this recipe but as much as I (like most Swedes) love cardamom, I can't see what good it does in this recipe.

Preparation time: 20 minutes, plus
 cooling time
Cooking time: 50 minutes
Makes: 8 pieces

100 g/3½ oz (7 tablespoons) butter, plus
  extra to grease
breadcrumbs, to coat
2 eggs
180 g/6½ oz (¾ cup) sugar
150 ml/5 fl oz (⅔ cup) cultured milk
  or cream
180 g/6½ oz (1¼ cups) weak (soft) wheat
  flour
2 teaspoons bicarbonate of soda
  (baking soda)
1 teaspoon ground cassia cinnamon
1 teaspoon ground ginger
1 teaspoon ground cloves
100 ml/3½ fl oz (⅓ cup plus 1 tablespoon)
  Sugared Lingonberries (page 692) or
  a few handfuls of raisins

Preheat the oven to 175°C/345°F/Gas Mark 4. Butter a 23 x 13 x 8 cm/9 x 5 x 3 inch loaf pan and coat with breadcrumbs.

Melt the butter, then leave to cool down to room temperature.

Whisk the eggs and the sugar in a large bowl until light and fluffy, then add the cultured dairy of your choice. Sift the dry ingredients together into the bowl and whisk everything together gently. Add the melted butter and the lingonberries or raisins and mix in gently but evenly. The batter will be fairly stiff.

Scrape the batter into the prepared loaf pan, smooth the surface and bake for about 50 minutes, or until the cake has shrunk slightly from the sides of the pan and a toothpick inserted into the centre of it comes out clean. If the surface browns too much during the cooking, then open the oven door very carefully and cover the cake with aluminium foil.

Turn the cake out of the pan and leave to cool on a wire rack before cutting into it.

SPICED HONEY CAKE

Honningkake (Norway)

Sometimes this cake is served plain and sometimes it is glazed with dark chocolate and sprinkled with flaked almonds.

Preparation and cooking time: 1 hour
Makes: 8 pieces

butter, to grease
breadcrumbs, to coat
4 eggs, yolks and whites separated
250 g/9 oz (1¼ cups) sugar
250 g/9 oz (1 cup plus 2 tablespoons) honey
100 g/3½ oz (7 tablespoons) butter, melted
  and cooled
½ teaspoon ground cloves
½ teaspoon ground ginger
½ teaspoon ground black pepper
250 g/9 oz (2 cups plus 1 tablespoon) weak
  (soft) wheat flour
1 teaspoon baking powder
pinch of salt

Preheat the oven to 150°C/300°F/Gas Mark 2. Butter a 21 x 11 x 6 cm/8½ x 4½ x 2½ inch loaf pan and coat with breadcrumbs.

Whisk the egg yolks and sugar in a bowl until pale and creamy. Add the honey, melted butter and spices to the egg mixture. Sift the dry ingredients together into the bowl and mix in thoroughly.

Whisk the egg whites to soft peaks, then fold them into the cake batter. Scrape the batter into the prepared loaf pan and smooth the surface.

Bake the cake for about 50 minutes, or until golden and cooked through. Turn the cake out of the loaf pan and leave to cool on a wire rack before icing, if you like.

For image see page 609

POTATO AND ALMOND CAKE/ 'THE CROWNS' CAKE

Kronans kaka (Sweden)

This dense, flourless cake is baked with cold, cooked potatoes and almonds and has a name which implies that it has its origins within the Swedish army, which historically, as in all monarchies, belonged to the king. I haven't been able to figure out if this is true, but the first recipe for it was published in a cookery book called *Hemmets Kokbok* in 1903. Many recipes state that it should be served with a lemon sauce. I don't know if this is the original way but I prefer it just as it is, alongside a cup of coffee in the afternoon.

The original recipe calls for 100 g/3½ oz (⅔ cup) whole almonds to be finely ground, but in this version I substitute almond flour (ground almonds) instead. Flavour with a couple of finely grated bitter almonds or some bitter almond oil for a more pronounced almond flavour if you prefer that.

Preparation and cooking time: 1 hour
Makes: 8 pieces

2 floury potatoes
75 g/2¾ oz (5 tablespoons) butter at room
  temperature, plus extra to grease
breadcrumbs, to coat
125 g/4½ oz (⅔ cup) sugar
2 eggs

2 bitter almonds, very finely grated (or
  use a drop of bitter almond oil)
110 g/3¾ oz (1 cup plus 2 tablespoons)
  almond flour (ground almonds)

Boil the potatoes until just tender. Drain and allow them to cool, then peel them and grate on the coarse side of a box grater.

Preheat the oven to 175°C/345°F/Gas Mark 4. Butter a 23 x 13 x 8 cm/9 x 5 x 3 inch loaf pan and coat with breadcrumbs.

Combine the butter and sugar in the bowl of a stand mixer fitted with the paddle attachment and beat at medium speed until pale and fluffy. Add the eggs, one at a time, making sure each is fully incorporated before you add the next.

Add the flavouring, followed by the grated potatoes and the almond flour.

Scrape the batter into the prepared loaf pan and smooth the surface. Bake for about 40 minutes, or until golden and cooked through. When the cake is done, it should have shrunk slightly from the sides of the pan and a toothpick inserted into the centre of the cake should come out clean. It should be quite dense. Leave to cool, then either turn out or serve it straight from the pan.

SWEDISH GOOEY CHOCOLATE CAKE

Kladdkaka (Sweden)

Kladdkaka is a relatively recent addition to Swedish cake culture. Its origins are a bit unclear and the accounts on where it came from are as colourful as they are conflicting. One thing is certain though: there was no *kladdkaka* before the mid 1970s. One can also assume without going out too much on a limb that the unleavened, very gooey and soft cake of today is the result of naturally occurring cake evolution. Someone had a really good recipe for chocolate cake, perhaps a brownie one, or why not something more central European in style? The same person, in the heat of the moment, forgets to add baking powder only to realize his or her mistake halfway through the cooking process. They then remove the undercooked cake from the oven and they are astounded by its deliciousness. Those character traits that were liked with the first failed cake have then, through generations of cakes, been reinforced, whilst those that weren't liked have been changed to improve it. On a timeline we can see that the *kladdkaka* of today contains less flour than the one twenty years ago, meaning that even if it isn't technically cooked it won't taste starchy. We can see that the cakes of yesteryear are made from soft butter creamed with the other ingredients like any other cake, whilst those of today are most often made from melted butter effectively making sure as little air as possible is incorporated into the cake, making it even gooier.

Kladdkaka only exists in Sweden and during its brief existence it has gained an enormous following. It is actually the most common recipe search from Swedish websites. If you type it into your internet search engine you will get well over 650,000 hits.

There are as many conflicting ideas on how to eat this cake as there are recipes for it. Some like it warm with ice cream, some like it at room temperature with nothing, and I like it as my wife – whose recipe this is – will tell you to eat it: cold from the fridge with whipped cream on the side.

Preparation and cooking time: 30 minutes
Makes: 8 pieces

butter, to grease
breadcrumbs, to coat
200 g/7 oz (1 cup) sugar
a good pinch salt
40 g/1½ (5¼ tablespoons) cocoa powder
1 tablespoon vanilla sugar
150 g/5 oz (1 stick plus 1½ tablespoons) butter, melted and cooled
2 eggs
125 g/4 oz (1 cup) weak (soft) wheat flour

Preheat the oven to 175°C/345°F/Gas Mark 4. Butter a 24-cm/9½-inch springform cake pan and coat with breadcrumbs.

Add the sugar, salt, cocoa and vanilla sugar to the cooled, melted butter and mix in the bowl of a stand mixer fitted with the paddle attachment until no lumps remain. Add the eggs one at a time and mix until fully incorporated. Add the flour by sifting it into the butter mixture and incorporate it fully but do not overwork it.

Pour the batter into the prepared cake pan and bake in the oven. In my oven it is perfect after exactly 13 minutes on an egg timer. This cake requires a delicate balance of liquid and dry. It should barely set in the oven and form a sort of skin. It should be very wobbly when warm.

For image see page 609

CURRANT CAKE

Korintkake (Norway)
Korintkaka (Sweden)

Preparation and cooking time: 1 hour
Makes: 8 pieces

breadcrumbs, to coat
200 g/7 oz (1¾ sticks) butter, at room temperature, plus extra to grease
200 g/7 oz (1 cup) sugar
4 eggs
2 teaspoons baking powder
250 g/9 oz (2 cups plus 1 tablespoon) weak (soft) wheat flour
125 g/4½ oz (¾ cup plus 2 tablespoons) currants (Corinthian raisins)

freshly ground cardamom seeds or bitter
  almond oil, to flavour
pinch of salt

Preheat the oven to 180°C/350°F/Gas Mark 4.
Butter a 23 x 13 x 8 cm/9 x 5 x 3 inch loaf pan and
coat with breadcrumbs.

Combine the butter and sugar in a mixing bowl and
whisk together until pale and fluffy. Add the eggs,
one at a time, and mix until thoroughly combined.

Sift the dry ingredients together into the bowl and
beat in thoroughly. Mix in the currants, together
with the flavourings, if using.

Scrape the batter into the prepared loaf pan and
smooth the surface. Bake the cake for about 40
minutes, or until cooked through.

Sift the flour and baking powder together into the
bowl and then mix until smooth but not for longer.
The batter will be fairly stiff.

Scrape the batter into the prepared loaf pan and
sprinkle the surface with plenty of pearl sugar. Bake for about 40 minutes, or until cooked
through. When the cake is done, it should have
shrunk slightly from the sides of the pan and a
toothpick inserted into the centre of the cake
should come out clean.

Unmould the cake and leave to cool on a wire
rack before serving.

CARDAMOM CAKE

Kardemummakaka (Sweden)

Preparation and cooking time: 1 hour
Makes: 8 pieces

125 g/4½ oz (1 stick) butter at room
  temperature, plus extra to grease
breadcrumbs, to coat
1 tablespoon cardamom seeds (not the whole
  pod), ground with a pestle and mortar
225 g/8 oz (1 cup plus 2 tablespoons) sugar
1 egg
200 ml/7 fl oz (¾ cup plus 1 tablespoon) sour
  cream
400 g/14 oz (3¼ cups) weak (soft) wheat flour
2 teaspoons baking powder
pearl sugar, to decorate

Preheat the oven to 175°C/345°F/Gas Mark 4.
Butter a 24-cm/9½-inch cake pan or a regular
23 x 13 x 8 cm/9 x 5 x 3 inch loaf pan and coat with
breadcrumbs.

Combine the butter, ground cardamom and sugar
in the bowl of a stand mixer fitted with the paddle
attachment and beat together well. Add the egg and
incorporate fully before adding the sour cream.

APPLE CAKE

Eplakaka (Iceland)
Æblekage (Denmark)
Äppelkaka (Sweden)

For this popular cake you can use either the Basic Sponge Cake (page 586) or the Almond Sponge Cake (page 588) recipe as a base. I like to use nicely acidic apples – something like a Granny Smith is ideal.

Serve with whipped cream or Vanilla Pastry Cream (page 680).

Preparation and cooking time: 1 hour
  10 minutes
Makes: 8 pieces

250 g/9 oz (2¼ sticks) butter, plus
  extra to grease
breadcrumbs, to coat
100 ml/3½ fl oz (⅓ cup plus 1 tablespoon) milk
4 eggs
350 g/12 oz (1¾ cups) sugar, plus extra
  for the apples
320 g/11¼ oz (2⅔ cups) weak (soft)
  wheat flour
2 teaspoons baking powder
8 acidic apples, peeled, cored and cut
  into wedges
½ teaspoon ground cinnamon (optional)

Preheat the oven to 175°C/345°F/Gas Mark 4. Butter a 24-cm/9½-inch cake pan and coat with breadcrumbs.

Combine the butter and milk in a small pan and heat until the butter has melted. Leave to cool down to room temperature.

Whisk the eggs with the sugar until light and fluffy. Add the butter and milk mixture and mix in thoroughly.

Sift the dry ingredients together into the bowl and whisk gently. Scrape the batter into the prepared cake pan and smooth the surface.

Toss the apple wedges with a little sugar and cinnamon, if using. Press them into the cake batter, one at a time, so they are evenly distributed.

Bake for about 50 minutes, or until cooked through. When the cake is done, it should have shrunk slightly from the sides of the pan and a toothpick inserted into the centre of the cake should come out clean.

Unmould the cake or serve it from the pan, whichever you prefer, and serve it warm or at room temperature.

LAYER CAKES

Lagkaka (Faroe Islands)
Bløtkage (Norway)
Lagkage (Denmark)
Tårta (Sweden)

Layer cakes and tortes are common pretty much all over the Nordic region. Almost every pastry shop will have a good selection and you will find one in most homes when someone is having a birthday party or just feels like a good *fika* (coffee break, page 531). It ranges from a couple of layers of sponge (page 586), some vanilla custard, berries and whipped cream, to very elaborate wedding cakes and other creations that most often feel like they are not made for eating. I can't imagine a Midsummer without a simple layer cake served with Strawberries and Cream (page 625) or a birthday without Princess Torte (page 599). On the next few pages is a small selection of layered cakes and tortes, although the variety is endless and it kind of merits a book of its own.

GREEN MARZIPAN LAYER CAKE/ PRINCESS TORTE

Prinsesstårta (Sweden)

First documented in the iconic Swedish cookbook, *Prinsessornas Kokbok* (*The Princesses Cookbook*), with the name 'Green Torte', my favourite layer cake is thought to have been invented by the author, legendary cookery writer Jenny Åkerström. She was also a teacher of the three Danish princesses, Margaretha, Märtha and Astrid, and the recipe name was later changed to reflect its popularity with the three girls.

The original version of the cake consists of three layers of airy sponge sandwiched with plenty of thick vanilla pastry cream that has been lightened with whipped cream. It should be dome-shaped, covered in a smooth layer of green marzipan and dusted with powdered sugar. Most Princess Tortes you see today just have a layer of raspberry jam between the two bottom layers and a thicker layer of the vanilla pastry cream on top of the final layer of cake to compensate. I refuse to believe that Swedish pastry chefs don't know that this is technically incorrect. I think that it is simply that most people – including traditionalists like myself – agree that the modern version is vastly superior, and so they don't bother 'bitching' about it. There is also a version of this cake, called *operatårta*, that uses pink marzipan (which has always contained jam) but who wants to eat something that looks like an old lady's hat? (I do myself from time to time actually.)

Since I have already admitted to preferring the sacrilegious jam version of *prinsesstårta*, I might as well also confess to not really liking the sort of airy, dry 'styrofoam' sponge used for the original either. I prefer to use a heavier cake; the kind that is normally eaten in its own right, rather than just as part of a torte. The recipe for *sockerkaka* (see page 586) is perfect and you just need to bake it in a round 24-cm/9½-inch springform cake pan instead of a loaf pan.

Preparation and cooking time: 2 hours
Makes: 8 pieces

1 quantity Vanilla Pastry Cream
  (see page 680)
4 leaves gelatine
2 tablespoons sugar
400 ml/14 fl oz (1⅔ cups) cream
1 circle of *Sockerkaka* (page 586)
  or *Tårtbotten* (page 588)
raspberry jam (page 690) or a
  good quality purchased raspberry jam
  (optional, but not quite traditional)
350 g/12 oz green marzipan
icing (confectioner's) sugar, for dusting
1 pink marzipan rose, to decorate (optional)

Follow the instructions on page 680 to make the vanilla cream. While it is still hot, add the gelatine leaves, then leave it to cool.

Meanwhile, add the sugar to the cream and whip it to soft peaks.

Once the vanilla cream has cooled and thickened, whisk briskly to loosen it up a bit, then gently, but thoroughly, fold in the whipped cream. It should be smooth, velvety and thick.

Slice the cake into 3 horizontal layers. Spread either a layer of jam or a quarter of the vanilla cream onto the bottom layer. Place another layer of cake on top and spread on another quarter of the vanilla cream. Finish with the third layer of cake and use the remaining vanilla cream to coat the sides evenly and create a perfectly smooth dome on top of the cake. This cream dome should be almost shamefully thick.

Roll out the marzipan thinly so that it is large enough to more than cover the cake. Lift it on carefully and use your hands to stretch and smooth it over the dome and down the sides, trying to avoid creases. Trim the bottom edge of any excess marzipan with a sharp knife. Just before serving, dust the surface with some icing (confectioner's) sugar and decorate with the pink marzipan rose, if using.

STRAWBERRY LAYER CAKE

Jordgubbsgräddtårta (Sweden)

This cake, which for many Swedes is an integral part of their midsummer meal, is very simple to make. A round sponge cake (page 586) is cut into two or more layers, fillings like jam (page 690) or fresh berries stirred with sugar, crushed banana, and/or Vanilla Pasrty Cream (page 680) are spread on each layer before the cake is assembled, covered with whipped cream and decorated with plenty of whole strawberries.

It is integral for the success of the cake to have a really good and tasty sponge. I like one that is a bit heavier than those commonly used for layer cakes. I also prefer the simplest possible version: two layers of sponge with one layer of strawberries stirred with sugar in between. Use plenty of berries so that their juices can further moisten the cake itself.

Preparation and cooking time: 1 hour, plus cooling time
Macerating time: 10 minutes
Makes: 8 pieces

250 g/9 oz (2¼ sticks) butter, plus extra to grease
breadcrumbs, to coat
100 ml/3½ fl oz (⅓ cup plus 1 tablespoon) milk
4 eggs
350 g/12 oz (1⅔ cups) sugar
320 g/11¼ oz (2⅔ cups) weak (soft) wheat flour
2 teaspoons baking powder

For the filling
500 g/1 lb 2 oz strawberries
sugar, to taste
500 ml/17 fl oz (2 cups plus 1 tablespoon) cream

Preheat the oven to 175°C/345°F/Gas Mark 4. Butter a 24-cm/9½-inch cake pan and coat with breadcrumbs.

Combine the butter and milk in a small pan and heat until the butter has melted. Leave to cool down to room temperature.

Whisk the eggs with the sugar until light and fluffy. Add the butter and milk mixture and mix in thoroughly. Sift the dry ingredients together into the bowl and whisk in gently.

Scrape the batter into the prepared cake pan and smooth the surface. Bake for about 40 minutes, or until cooked through. When the cake is done, it should have shrunk slightly from the sides of the pan and a toothpick inserted into the centre of the cake should come out clean. Leave the cake in the pan to cool.

To prepare the filling, roughly chop the strawberries, reserving about 20 nice ones for the top of the cake. Stir them with some sugar and leave to macerate for about 10 minutes, or until the sugar has dissolved.

Meanwhile, whip the cream to soft peaks in a bowl.

Use a sharp serrated knife to split the cold sponge cake in half horizontally. Spoon the sugared strawberries onto one half of the sponge cake. Place the other half of the sponge cake carefully on top. Spread an even layer of whipped cream over the sides and top of the cake and decorate with the reserved whole strawberries.

ALMOND AND BUTTER EGG-CREAM TORTE/OSCAR II'S TORTE

Oscar IIs tårta / Oscarstårta / Kung Oscars tårta (Sweden)

This cake is named after the very popular King Oscar of Sweden, who ruled the country between 1872–1907 and you'll find it in every traditional coffee house or pastry shop in Sweden. It is made from 4 layers of almond meringue, sandwiched together with a rich, yolky buttercream filling, and it is at its tastiest the day after it is assembled.

The exterior of the torte should also be spread with buttercream and then covered in toasted flaked almonds. Today, some people simply take layers of the almond meringue and spread on some creamy filling, making it just like any old vacherin-style torte. But this is not right! You shouldn't be able to see the meringue until you cut into the torte. And the cream should be stiff enough to make the sides of the torte straight and smooth before you apply the almond flakes.

Preparation and cooking time: 2 hours
Resting time: overnight
Makes: 8 pieces

5 egg whites
180 g/6½ oz (1½ cups) icing
   (confectioner's) sugar
150 g/5 oz (1½ cups) ground almonds
toasted almond flakes, to decorate

For the buttercream
170 g/6 oz (¾ cup plus 2 tablespoons) sugar
8 egg yolks
500 g/1 lb 2 oz (4½ sticks) butter, cut
   into cubes

Preheat the oven to 125°C/240°F/Gas Mark 1 and line 2 baking sheets with baking (parchment) paper.

To make the meringue, place the egg whites in the spotlessly clean bowl of a stand mixer and whisk at medium speed until they begin to foam and thicken. Add the sugar, little by little, and continue whisking until you have a stiff meringue. Fold the ground almonds in gently.

Spread or pipe the almond meringue onto the baking (parchment) paper to create 4 x 22 cm/ 8½ inch discs. The easiest way to do this is to draw a perfect round circle on an extra piece of paper. Place this underneath the parchment as you pipe, to act as a template.

Bake the meringue discs for about 15 minutes, or until set and very lightly coloured. Leave them to cool a bit before you remove them from the parchment and transfer them to wire racks to cool completely.

To make the buttercream, combine the sugar with 200 ml/7 fl oz (¾ cup plus 1 tablespoon) water in a small pan and bring to the boil. Heat over a medium heat until it reaches 112°C/240°F on a thermometer.

Meanwhile place the egg yolks in a large mixing bowl. When the sugar syrup reaches the correct temperature, drizzle it into the egg yolks slowly and steadily, whisking vigorously as you do. Be careful not to pour too quickly or whisk too slowly as the yolks might curdle.

Place the butter in the bowl of a stand mixer fitted with the paddle attachment. Beat at a medium speed and slowly add the cooling sugar and egg mixture. Be sure not to add it too quickly as this will melt the butter and split the emulsion.

As soon as the egg mixture has all been incorporated into the butter, turn off the motor. The buttercream should be shiny, thick, yellow and smooth.

Spread a layer of buttercream onto each almond meringue and stack them neatly on top of each other. Spread an even layer of buttercream over the sides and top of the torte, smoothing it neatly. Finish by sprinkling the sides and the top with plenty of toasted almond flakes.

ICELANDIC LAYER CAKE

Randalín (Iceland)

Icelandic layer cakes are often, but not exclusively, eaten around Christmas. They are usually made up of 4 layers of soft shortbread with filling in-between each layer. If the shortbread is white, then jam is used – often rhubarb jam (page 690) – and if it is brown from cocoa, a plain Buttercream (page 679) is common. *Randalín* means, 'the striped one', and refers to the striped appearance of the cake when it is cut.

Another version of layer cake, using white shortbread and Prune Compote (page 701), is called *vínarterta*. This version has become very popular among North Americans with Icelandic roots and the American recipes often use more layers than are seen in Iceland – 6–8 sheets of cake are not uncommon. The North American versions are also sometimes glazed with icing (frosting).

Some *randalín* recipes indicate that the dough should be rolled out, much like a conventional shortcrust pastry (basic pie dough), whilst others are much less firm and need to be spread out with a spatula directly onto a sheet of baking (parchment) paper. I have included a recipe for each version. To make chocolate layer cake, add 2 tablespoons of cocoa powder to either shortbread recipe.

Some recipes, especially older ones, are leavened with baker's ammonia, which will give an even shorter texture than baking powder, but which might also add a slight scent of nightclub urinal if overdosed.

Regardless of which filling you decide to use, you will need about 300 ml/10½ fl oz (1¼ cups) of it for the amount of shortbread in the recipes below.

SPREAD ONTO BAKING PAPER (VERSION 1)

Preparation and cooking time: 1 hour
Standing time: 3 hours
Makes: 1 x 4-layer cake, 10 slices

100 g/3½ oz (7 tablespoons) butter, soft
125 g/4½ oz (⅔ cup) sugar
2 eggs
360 g/12¾ oz (3 cups) weak (soft) wheat flour
1 teaspoon baking powder
150 ml/5 fl oz (⅔ cup) cold milk
300 g/10½ oz (1¼ cups) jam (page 690)

Preheat the oven to 200°C/400°F/Gas Mark 6. Line 2 baking sheets with baking (parchment) paper.

Combine the butter and sugar in the bowl of a stand mixer fitted with the paddle attachment and beat until white and fluffy. Decrease the speed and add the eggs, one at a time. Whisk at medium speed between each addition, until fully incorporated.

Sift the flour and baking powder together into the bowl, and mix until the flour is fully incorporated, but not any longer. Finally, add the milk and whisk in until fully incorporated but not longer.

Spread the batter onto the prepared baking sheets, forming rectangles of roughly 30 x 40 cm/12 x 16 inches.

Bake for about 10 minutes, or until lightly golden in colour. Remove from the oven and leave to cool.

Cut each large rectangle in half lengthways, to make 4 small rectangles of 15 x 40 cm/6 x 16 inches. Spread 3 of the shortbread layers with a thick layer of jam – it shouldn't be much thinner than the pastry itself – then stack them on top of each other. Top with the final shortbread layer. Cover the cake with clingfilm (plastic wrap) and leave for a few hours. Before serving, use a sharp serrated knife to trim the edges to neaten them and to reveal the striped layers.

ROLLED OUT (VERSION 2)

Preparation and cooking time: 1 hour
Resting time: 1 hour
Standing time: 3 hours
Makes: 1 x 4-layer cake, 10 slices

225 g/8 oz (2 sticks) butter, soft
220 g/7¾ oz (1 cup) sugar
2 eggs

450 g/1 lb (3¾ cups) weak (soft) wheat flour
1 teaspoon baking powder
100 ml/3½ fl oz (⅓ cup plus 1 tablespoon)
  cold milk
300 g/10½ oz (1¼ cups) jam (page 690)

Preheat the oven to 175°C/345°F/Gas Mark 4. Line
2 baking sheets with baking (parchment) paper.

Combine the butter and sugar in the bowl of a
stand mixer fitted with the paddle attachment and
beat until white and fluffy. Decrease the speed and
add the eggs, one at a time. Whisk at medium speed
between each addition, until fully incorporated.

Sift the flour and baking powder together into the
bowl, and mix until the flour is fully incorporated, but not any longer. Finally, add the milk and
whisk in briefly.

Shape the dough into a ball and wrap tightly
with clingfilm (plastic wrap) before resting in the
refrigerator for at least 1 hour.

Place the dough on a lightly floured work counter
and divide it into either 2 or 4 pieces. You'll need
2 for a rectangular cake and 4 if you are making a
round one.

For the rectangular version, roll the 2 pieces out
into rectangles of about 30 x 40 cm/12 x 16 inches
and transfer to the prepared baking sheets. For a
round cake, roll the 4 pieces out to 20 cm/8 inch
circles.

Bake for 15–30 minutes, or until lightly golden.
Remove from the oven and leave to cool.

For a rectangular cake, cut each large rectangle
in half lengthways, to make 4 small rectangles of
15 x 40 cm/6 x 16 inches.

Whether rectangular or round, spread 3 of the shortbread layers with a thick layer of jam – it shouldn't
be much thinner than the pastry itself – then stack
them on top of each other. Top with the final
shortbread layer. Cover the cake with clingfilm
(plastic wrap) and leave for a few hours.

For a rectangular cake, before serving, use a sharp
serrated knife to trim the edges to neaten them and
to reveal the striped layers.

PANCAKE TORTE

Pannkakstårta (Sweden)

Serve for dessert or as a sweet snack on a Sunday
afternoon. Top with fresh berries, if they are in
season.

Preparation and cooking time: 10 minutes
Makes: 8 pieces

500 ml/17 fl oz (2 cups plus 1 tablespoon)
  cream
8 cold leftover Thin Pancakes (page 450)
200 g/7 oz (⅔ cup) jam of your choice (I like
  raspberry or blueberry jam, page 690)
fresh berries, to serve (optional)

In a mixing bowl, whip the cream to soft peaks.

Spread 7 of the cold pancakes with a layer of jam
followed by a layer of the cream, then stack them
in a pile. Top with the final pancake, spread with
a layer of cream only. Finish with fresh berries, if
you are using them.

For image see page 453

SWEDISH ALMOND MERINGUE TORTE

Brittatårta / Pinocchiotårta (Sweden)

My grandmother used to make this torte quite often for birthdays and other torte-friendly occasions; I never really liked it. When I was served it growing up, the browned sticky meringue on sponge and the darkly toasted almond flakes always tasted a bit like defeat. Perhaps more child-friendly pastries, like Strawberry Layer Cake (page 600) or Princess Torte (page 599), were on my mind. Today I have learned to tolerate this very popular classic, to an extent where I can look in the eye someone who baked it and served it to me, politely thank them and smile, without my true feelings for this otiose cake shining through.

The recipe below is just for the cake and meringue part of the torte as you can really use anything you like for the filling. Most people would use whipped cream and berries or fruit but it's your choice. You are only limited by your own sense of adventure, daring or shame. I've seen everything in there, from mashed banana to Skittles with vanilla cream or liquorice-flavoured yogurt. My childhood *brittatårta* usually used the more restrained combination of whipped cream, raspberries and kiwi fruit.

Preparation and cooking time: 2 hours
Serves: 10–12 people

For the cake
100 g/3½ oz (7 tablespoons) butter
100 g/3½ oz (½ cup) sugar
5 egg yolks
50 ml/2 fl oz (3½ tablespoons) milk
pinch of salt
125 g/4½ oz (1 cup) weak (soft) wheat flour
2 teaspoons baking powder

For the meringue
5 egg whites
160 g/5½ oz (¾ cup) sugar
100 g/3½ oz (1 cup) flaked almonds

Preheat the oven to 150°C/300°F/Gas Mark 2 and line a baking sheet with baking (parchment) paper.

To make the cake, combine the butter and sugar in the bowl of a stand mixer fitted with the paddle attachment. Mix until pale and creamy. With the motor on low, add the egg yolks, one at a time, until they are all fully incorporated. Mix in the milk and the salt. Sift in the flour and the baking powder and mix until smooth.

To make the meringue, place the egg whites in another large bowl and whisk at medium speed until they begin to foam and thicken. Add the sugar, little by little, and continue whisking until you have a stiff meringue.

Spread the cake batter out onto the prepared baking sheet. Spread the meringue on top of the batter and sprinkle on the flaked almonds.

Bake for 25–35 minutes. When it is ready, both the meringue and the almonds should be a nice amber colour. Leave to cool completely.

To assemble, cut the torte in half evenly. Spread one section with whipped cream and your choice of other filling ingredients. Sit the other piece on top and transfer carefully to a serving platter.

ALMOND WREATH CAKE

Kransekage (Denmark)
Kransekake (Norway)

A festive pastry served at celebrations like weddings, baptisms, Christmas and New Year's Eve. The cake consists of a number of rings baked from ground almonds, sugar and egg whites, stacked on top of each other, with each new layer being a slightly smaller diameter than the previous one. Each layer is decorated with icing before the next is put in place, the icing acting like a sort of glue. Some people want their almond wreath cake crisper and therefore cook it for longer, while most people that I have spoken to prefer it to be firm to the touch, but soft and a bit chewy in the middle.

To serve the cake, take individual rings out of the stack and break or cut them into suitable pieces. I have been told that the proper way of doing this is to always remove the bottom ring first, so that the top part of the cake remains intact and pretty for as long as possible. This is tricky and I think that your genome might have to be of Danish or

Norwegian descent for you to have the skills to do this without the whole thing toppling over. Sometimes a bottle of wine or some other surprise is hidden inside the cake.

Most Danish recipes are based on readymade marzipan whilst most Norwegian recipes are based on almonds, which are blanched, dried and ground before being mixed with sugar and egg whites. The two methods produce the same result since marzipan itself is made from ground almonds and sugar. I think that this cultural difference in preparation, which is still evident in today's recipes, comes from the fact that in Denmark, marzipan has been more readily available thanks to Odense Marzipan, a big and old manufacturer of almond-based sweets.

The only clear benefit and difference that I can see in making the marzipan yourself is that you can decide whether or not to blanch the almonds and you can vary the degree to which the almonds are ground. To leave some or all of the skins will give a darker cake and grinding the almonds less finely will give a coarser texture.

Preparation and cooking time: 30 minutes
Serves: 10

250 g/9 oz (1¼ cups) sugar
2 egg whites
500 g/1 lb 2 oz marzipan (buy it or make it yourself, if you prefer), at room temperature
pinch of salt
1 quantity White Icing (page 679)

Mix the sugar with the egg whites in a bowl until light and fluffy.

Grate the marzipan on the coarse side of a box grater to make it easier to mix.

Combine all the ingredients, except the icing, in a large mixing bowl and work them together with a sturdy whisk or wooden spoon until you have a smooth batter.

Draw the circles you need onto baking (parchment) paper, and then place it on a baking sheet. Measure each circle with a tape measure.

Preheat the oven to 220°C/425°F/Gas Mark 7.

Roll the batter into logs of varying lengths, according to your measurements and then shape each log into rings and fit them into the circles you have drawn out on the paper. Alternatively you can use a special *kransekage* mould which gives you more precise rings and allows you to skip the measuring and drawing out of circles on paper (see illustrations below).

Bake the rings until pale gold.

Leave to cool for a while on a wire rack before piping the icing onto the rings and layering them up into a cone shape.

MERINGUE LAYER CAKE

Marengslagkage (Faroe Islands)
Marengslagkage (Denmark)
Marängtårta (Sweden)

This layer cake is made up from 3–4 discs of meringue, each around 25–30 cm/10–12 inches in diameter, stacked on top of each other with lightly sweetened, whipped cream and fresh berries or jam (page 690), in between and also on the top layer to decorate. Sometimes the cake is also drizzled with Chocolate Sauce (page 677) and/or has chocolate grated over it.

Preparation time: 3 hours
Makes: 8 pieces

160 g/5½ oz egg whites
200 g/7 oz (1 cup) sugar

Preheat the oven to 110°C/225°F/Gas Mark ½. Line 2 baking sheets with baking (parchment) paper.

Place the egg whites in the spotlessly clean bowl of a stand mixer (or a large stainless steel mixing bowl) and start whisking them slowly until they begin to foam. Add the sugar, little by little, making sure you leave enough time between each addition for the sugar crystals to dissolve completely. For meringue perfection, it is important not to hurry too much, or to whisk too quickly, or to add the sugar too fast, as this will result in a more of a runny fluff, with less of the velvety, brilliant, shiny quality that really good meringue has.

After you have added about half of the sugar – lets say it takes you about 5 minutes – you can start whisking at a faster speed and adding the sugar at a slightly faster pace. When all the sugar has been added, lower the speed again and keep whisking the meringue until all the sugar crystals have dissolved and the meringue looks like fresh white paint, in both brilliance and shine. It should be very stiff.

Spread or pipe the meringue onto the baking (parchment) paper to create 3–4 x 25–30 cm/10–12 inch discs. The easiest way to do this is to draw a perfect round circle on an extra piece of paper. Place this underneath the parchment as you pipe, to act as a template.

Bake the meringue discs for about 45 minutes. Turn off the oven and leave the meringues in there with the oven door slightly open. Allow them to cool and dry completely before you remove them from the paper. It will take a couple of hours a bit depending on how humid your climate is.

To assemble, spread the discs of meringue with whipped cream and your choice of berries or jam. Sit them on top of each other and transfer carefully to a serving platter. Finally, top with more berries and sprinkle with grated chocolate or chocolate sauce, if you want to.

CHOCOLATE BISCUIT CAKE

Hjalskaka (Faroe Islands)
Radiokaka (Sweden)

I remember both eating and making this cake as a kid. There is something quite special about the way the coconut fat melts at a low temperature, and in a different way to anything else, when you eat it. The cake is made from cocoa powder, which has, in the manufacturing process, had all the cocoa fat removed. That fat is then substituted with a totally different fat. It's a bit strange, but in a way, it is a sort of reconstructed chocolate.

In Swedish it is called *radiokaka*, or 'radio cake'. There are different stories as to why, but I believe it is simply because when you slice it, it sort of looks like an old-fashioned radio. Some people like to scatter multi-coloured sprinkles over the top, but I have never been a huge fan of that.

Use plain sweet biscuits (cookies) like Rich Tea or Marie biscuits.

Preparation and setting time: 1½ hours
Makes: 1 loaf cake

250 g/9 oz coconut fat (pressed
  cocnut oil)
2 eggs
250 g/9 oz (2 cups) icing (confectioner's) sugar
50 g/2 oz (½ cup plus 1 tablespoon)
  cocoa powder
pinch of salt

1 packet of sweet biscuits (cookies) or
  crackers

Line a 23 x 13 x 8 cm/9 x 5 x 3 inch loaf pan with
baking (parchment) paper.

Melt the coconut fat carefully in a pan over low
heat, then let it cool down to just above room
temperature.

Beat the eggs with the sugar until pale and fluffy.
Sift over the cocoa powder and fold it in. Drizzle
in the coconut fat, a little at a time, stirring continuously. Make sure you fully incorporate each
addition until you add more; it's a bit like making
a mayonnaise.

Spoon a layer of cocoa mixture into the prepared
loaf pan, then arrange a layer of biscuits (cookies)
or crackers on top. Continue layering the cocoa
mixture with biscuits until you run out. Refrigerate until the cake has completely set.

To serve, turn the cake out of the mould and cut
into slices with a sharp knife.

ROLLED TORTE / ROULADE

Rullukaka (Faroe Islands)
Rullekaka (Norway)
Kääretorttu (Finland)
Roulade (Denmark)
Rulltårta (Sweden)

This is a very versatile cake that can be filled with
plain Buttercream (page 679), Chocolate Buttercream (page 679) or your favourite jam (page 690).
I have even seen a couple of recipes from the Faroe
Islands where it is filled with Prune Compote (page
701) or with mashed banana. You can also flavour
the cake itself with grated lemon zest or vanilla
sugar if you want.

Preparation and cooking time: 35 minutes
Makes: 8 pieces

3 eggs
100 g/3½ oz (½ cup) sugar, plus extra
  for sprinkling

pinch of salt
55 ml/1¾ fl oz (¼ cup) milk
130 g/4½ oz (1 cup plus 1 tablespoon) weak
  (soft) wheat flour
1 teaspoon baking powder

Preheat the oven to 225°C/435°F/Gas Mark 7 and
line a baking sheet with baking (parchment) paper.

Whisk the eggs with the sugar until pale and fluffy,
then add the salt and milk. Sift the flour and baking powder straight into the bowl and stir until
fully combined.

Spread the mixture out on the prepared baking
sheet to form a neat 30 x 40 cm/12 x 16 inch rectangle. Bake for 5–7 minutes, or until the surface
is golden. Be careful that it doesn't burn. The
cake can look a little weird while baking, going all
bubbly and uneven, but it will flatten out when it
is taken out of the oven.

While the cake is baking, place a fresh sheet of
baking (parchment) paper on the work counter and
sprinkle it with a generous amount of sugar; it is
important that the whole surface of the paper is
evenly covered.

When the cake comes out of the oven, give it 10
seconds or so for any bubbles to subside before
turning it out onto the bed of sugar. Leave it for
2 minutes, then lightly brush the parchment which
is stuck to the bottom of the cake (now on top)
with some cold water and cover with a clean,
damp dish cloth. When the cake is just cool, remove
the dish cloth and carefully peel the paper away
from the cake.

Spread the cold cake with your choice of filling
and roll it up. I think that the easiest way to do
this is to lift the sugared paper it is resting on
upwards with one hand, while at the same time
using the other hand to ensure an even roll.
Arrange the torte on a serving platter so the seam
is underneath and leave it for a couple of minutes
to firm up before slicing.

For image see page 609

CHOCOLATE ROLLED TORTE / ROULADE

Brun rullukaka (Faroe Islands)
Chokolade roulade (Denmark)
Chokladrulltårta med smörkräm /
Drömtårta (Sweden)

Some people make rolled tortes like this with a mix of potato starch and weak (soft) wheat flour to make it more pliable for the rolling, I don't like the texture that brings, but if you want, you can just substitute half of the plain flour with potato starch – or even all of it, if you want to make the torte gluten free.

Preparation and cooking time: 45 minutes
Makes: 8 pieces

3 eggs
100 g/3½ oz (½ cup) sugar, plus extra
   for sprinkling
pinch of salt
60 g/2¼ oz (½ cup) weak (soft) wheat flour
2 tablespoons cocoa powder
1 teaspoon baking powder
1 quantity Buttercream (page 679)

Preheat the oven to 225°C/435°F/Gas Mark 7 and line a baking sheet with baking (parchment) paper.

Whisk the eggs with the sugar until pale and fluffy, then add the salt. Sift the flour, cocoa powder and baking powder straight into the bowl and stir until fully combined.

Spread the mixture out on the prepared baking sheet to form a neat 30 x 40 cm/12 x 16 inch rectangle. Bake for 7–10 minutes, or until the surface is golden. Be careful that it doesn't burn. The cake can look a little weird while baking, going all bubbly and uneven, but it will flatten out when it is taken out of the oven.

While the cake is baking, place a fresh sheet of baking (parchment) paper on the work counter and sprinkle it with a generous amount of sugar; it is important that the whole surface of the paper is evenly covered.

When the cake comes out of the oven, give it about 10 seconds or so for any bubbles to subside before turning it out onto the bed of sugar. Leave it for

2 minutes, then lightly brush the paper which is stuck to the bottom of the cake (now on top) with some cold water and cover with a clean, damp dish cloth. When the cake is just cool, remove the dish cloth and carefully peel the paper away from the cake.

Spread the buttercream onto the cold cake and roll it up. I think that the easiest way to do this is to lift the sugared paper it is resting on upwards with one hand, while at the same time using the other hand to ensure an even roll. Arrange the torte on a serving platter so the seam is underneath and leave it for a couple of minutes to firm up before slicing.

For image see page 609

Clockwise from top left: Rolled Torte/Roulade (page 607); Chocolate Rolled Torte/Roulade (page 608); Spiced Honey Cake (page 594); Chocolate and Coconut Glazed Chocolate Sponge Cake (page 592); Tiger Cake (page 590); Swedish Gooey Chocolate Cake (page 596); Basic Sponge Cake (page 586); Glazed Individual Almond Tarts (page 565)

FAROESE BROWN ROULADE

Brun rullukaku (Faroe Islands)

Preparation and cooking time: 35 minutes
Makes: 1 roulade

3 eggs
100 g/3½ oz (½ cup) brown sugar, plus
    extra for sprinkling
pinch of salt
55 ml/1¾ fl oz (¼ cup) milk
130 g/4½ oz (1 cup plus 1 tablespoon) weak
    (soft) wheat flour
1 teaspoon baking powder
1 teaspoon ground cinnamon
1 teaspoon ground cardamom

For the filling
150 g/5 oz (¾ cup) butter, at room
    temperature
150 g/5 oz (1¼ cups) icing (confectioners')
    sugar
1 egg yolk

Preheat the oven to 225°C/435°F/Gas Mark 7 and line a baking sheet with baking (parchment) paper.

Whisk the eggs with the sugar until pale and fluffy, then add the salt and the milk. Sift the flour, baking powder and spices straight into the bowl and stir until fully combined.

Spread the mixture out on the prepared baking sheet to form a neat 30 x 40 cm/12 x 16 inch rectangle. Bake for 5–7 minutes, or until the surface is golden. Be careful that it doesn't burn. The cake can look a little weird while baking, going all bubbly and uneven, but it will flatten out when it is taken out of the oven.

While the cake is baking, place a fresh sheet of baking (parchment) paper on the work counter and sprinkle it generously with sugar; it is important that the surface of the paper is evenly covered.

When the cake comes out of the oven, give it 10 seconds or so for any bubbles to subside before turning it out onto the bed of sugar. Leave it for 2 minutes, then lightly brush the parchment which is stuck to the bottom of the cake (now on top) with some cold water and cover with a clean, damp dish cloth.

When the cake is just cool, remove the dish cloth and carefully peel the paper away from the cake.

To make the filling, beat the butter and icing (confectioners') sugar in a small bowl. Add the egg yolk and whisk together.

Spread the cold cake with the filling and roll it up. I think that the easiest way to do this is to lift the sugared paper it is resting on upwards with one hand, while at the same time using the other hand to ensure an even roll. Arrange the roulade on a serving platter so the seam is underneath and then leave it for a couple of minutes to firm up before slicing.

SCANIAN FESTIVE CAKE BAKED ON A SKEWER

Spettekaka (Sweden)

Spettekaka is traditionally eaten at special occasions like weddings, as a dessert with strong coffee served alongside it, or sometimes with vanilla ice cream, and occasionally with some fortified wine.

Spettekaka means 'skewer cake' or 'spit cake' because it is made by applying a ribbon of batter (made from eggs, potato starch and sugar) onto a horizontal wooden skewer that rotates slowly next to a heat source – traditionally a wood fire. It takes several hours of constant work to cook a medium-size cake, as it needs to dry out slowly without colouring. Today there are only a few bakeries left where *spettekaka* are still made by hand over an open flame. Very few people actually have the skill and equipment to make this in their homes.

Once cooked, the cake is glazed with icing (frosting). The colour of the icing and the visual texture of the cake – depending on how you layer the ribbon of batter – differs from region to region. The cake is traditionally cut with the blade from a very fine-toothed hacksaw and it is considered better to have very straight and precise cuts with no breakage. *Spettekaka* is cut into cube-shaped blocks and the top of the cake should be left standing for as long as possible, while pieces are carved away around it.

Spettekaka is a very dry cake and needs to be consumed straight after cooking or preserved in an airtight bag.

HAZELNUT AND MANDARIN ROLLED TORTE/BUDAPEST ROLL

Budapestrulle / Budapeststubbe (Sweden)

This torte was invented in the southern Swedish town of Vetlanda during the first half of the twentieth century, by pastry chef Ingvar Strid. It is one of the more iconic and widespread recipes that you find in classic-style Swedish pastry shops and it is said that it was somehow inspired by the Austrian/Hungarian Esterházy Torte. I myself fail to see the resemblance, or any other link, apart from in the name and its reference to the Hungarian capital. Originally decorated with canned mandarin segments, these days the 'Budapest roll' can be served with many other types of fruit and berries.

The *Budapestrulle* doesn't contain any flour and most old recipes use potato starch. Quite a few more recent versions include some instant flan or custard powder and even though this feels a bit strange, I tend to like these recipes better.

Preparation and cooking time: 45 minutes
Serves: 10

6 egg whites
200 g/7 oz (1 cup) sugar
100 g/3½ oz (⅔ cup) hazelnuts
  (not blanched), finely chopped
50 g/2 oz (3 tablespoons) instant flan
  or custard powder
400 ml/14 fl oz (1⅔ cups) cream
300–400 g/11–14 oz canned mandarin
  segments, drained
100 g/3½ oz dark (semisweet) chocolate
  (optional)

Preheat the oven to 175°C/345°F/Gas Mark 4 and line a baking sheet with baking (parchment) paper.

Place the egg whites in the spotlessly clean bowl of a stand mixer and whisk at medium speed until they begin to foam and thicken. Add the sugar, little by little, and continue whisking until you have a stiff meringue. Add the chopped hazelnuts and the flan powder together to the meringue and stir until just incorporated.

Spread the meringue out on the prepared baking sheet to form a neat 30 x 40 cm/12 x 16 inch rectangle. Bake for about 15–20 minutes.

While the meringue is baking, place a fresh sheet of baking (parchment) paper on the work counter. When the meringue comes out of the oven, turn it onto the baking (parchment) paper and carefully peel away the paper that is stuck to the bottom of the meringue (now on top). Leave on the counter to cool completely.

Whip the cream to soft peaks and spread it evenly over the meringue. Scatter most of the mandarin segments on top of the cream, but keep some for decoration. Roll up the meringue carefully, then place on a serving platter so the seam is underneath and leave it for 10 minutes or so to firm up.

Decorate the rolled torte in a 1950s-pastry-shop way with the reserved mandarin segments and melted dark (semisweet) chocolate piped from a disposable piping bag in a pattern of your liking, if you wish.

If you are using chocolate to decorate the torte, break it into chunks, put it in a heatproof bowl and microwave at half power. Heat it for 30 seconds, then stop to stir and repeat until just melted. Transfer it to a piping bag and pipe onto the torte.

FINNISH ALMOND AND RUM TORTES

Runebergintorttu (Finland)
Runebergstårta / Fredrika tårta (Sweden)

These little almond cakes are named after the Finnish national poet, Johan Ludvig Runeberg (1804–1877), who reputedly ate one for breakfast every day, with a glass of *punsch* (page 717) on the side. Today *runebergintorttu* can be bought pretty much all year around in Finland, but it is especially popular on and around the 5th of February, which is the commemorative Runeberg Day.

Some people serve the tortes as they are, glazed with white icing (pink is just not right) and topped with a spoonful of raspberry jam. Others prefer to soak them in a light sugar syrup flavoured with rum, Arrack Flavoured Liqueur (page 717) or another liqueur. The soaked version is sometimes called *Fredrika tårta*, after Mr Runeberg's wife.

Ideally, you should use special deep Runeberg pans for these tortes or other individual pans of a similar size.

Preparation and cooking time: 2 hours
Makes: 10 tortes

150 g/5 oz (1½ sticks) butter, soft, plus extra
   to grease
130 g/4½ oz (⅔ cup) sugar
2 eggs
100 ml/3½ fl oz (⅓ cup plus 1 tablespoon)
   cream
60 g/2¼ oz (½ cup) ground almonds
75 g/2¾ oz (¾ cup) biscuit (cookie) crumbs,
   or sweet breadcrumbs from stale brioche
   or another sweet bread
90 g/3¼ oz (¾ cup) weak (soft) wheat flour,
   plus extra for the pans
1½ teaspoons baking powder
100 ml/3½ fl oz (⅓ cup plus 1 tablespoon)
   sugar syrup flavoured with Arrack
   Flavoured Liqueur (page 717) or
   rum (optional)

To decorate
raspberry jam (page 690)
White Icing (page 679)

Preheat the oven to 200°C/400°F/Gas Mark 6. Butter and flour the Runeberg pans.

Combine the butter and sugar in the bowl of a stand mixer and beat until pale and creamy. Add the eggs one at a time. Add the cream and mix until just incorporated. Add the ground almonds and the biscuit (cookie) crumbs, then sift the flour and baking powder directly into the bowl. Mix until fully combined.

Spoon the cake batter into the prepared pans and bake for about 15 minutes. Turn the cakes out of their pans and leave them on a wire rack to cool. If you want to soak the tortes, then do so in the liqueur or rum-flavoured syrup while they are still warm. Otherwise leave the tortes to cool completely before decorating.

Top each torte neatly with a blob of raspberry jam, then pipe a circle of white icing around the jam (see illustration below).

DESSERTS

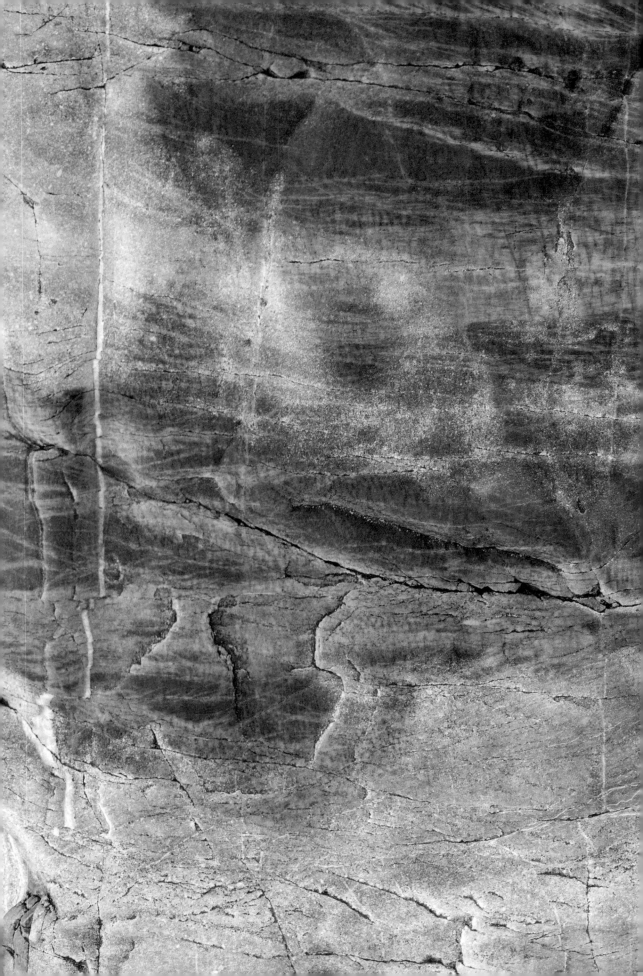

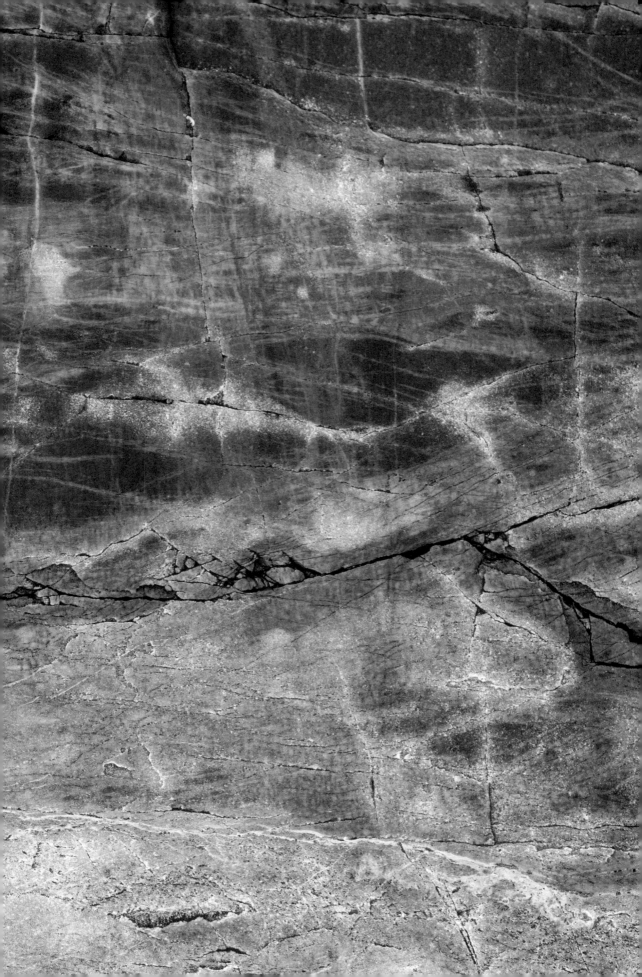

Previous page: A really beautiful stone surface by the Norwegian coast. Unfortunately, I have forgotten exactly where I photographed it, but it was in Norway, May 2014.

Opposite: Interior of a traditional stone cellar next to a Swedish mountain farm. The cellar is used for keeping milk. Note the cover of spruce on the floor, changed weekly to keep the cellar clean and smelling nice, Jämtland, Summer 2014.

SWEDISH CURD CAKES

Ostkaka (Sweden)

Desserts based on fresh curds are commonly eaten year round at festive occasions, and in some parts of Sweden they are considered more or less essential for holidays like Christmas and Easter.

The best-known examples of Swedish curd cakes come from the central region of Småland and from the eastern region of Hälsingland. The Småland version is richer and more grainy and is always flavoured with bitter almonds. It is most often served lukewarm with whipped cream and berries or jam (page 690). The Hälsingland version is smoother and denser, not flavoured with bitter almonds and is often cut in thick slices to be reheated in a frying pan or skillet, or in the oven with a bit of cream. It is usually served with Cordial Soup (page 694) or cloudberry jam (page 690) and whipped cream. In most cases curd cake from Hälsingland, as opposed to the one from Småland, contains no eggs or sugar.

The leftover whey from making curd cakes can be used to make, for example, reduced whey cheeses like Brown Cheese (page 72).

For image see page 71

CURD CAKE FROM SMÅLAND

Småländsk ostkaka (Sweden)

Traditionally, curd cakes in Småland are served starting from the middle of the pan and working outwards to the edges in widening circles. The reason for this is debated, but one theory is that in the old days, when much ovenware was made from tinned copper, the centre, which was potentially less exposed to the toxic heavy metals, was offered to more prominent eaters and guests, while the edges of the cake, which had been in direct contact with the metal itself, were given to workers and people considered less important. Another theory states that it was because the browned crusty parts were just considered less

fine than the creamy pale centre, and this is the reason for the serving etiquette.

It is hard to make this recipe in smaller quantities, so freeze leftover curd cake, it stores for many months in the freezer.

Preparation time: 1 ½ –2 hours
Cooking time: 1 hour
Makes: 2 cakes, each serving 6–8

3 litres/5 UK pints (12½ cups) full-
fat (whole), unpasteurized and
unhomogenized milk
50 g/2 oz (⅓ cup plus 1 tablespoon) weak
(soft) wheat flour
1 tablespoon liquid rennet
butter, to grease
3 eggs
50 g/2 oz (¼ cup) sugar
40 g/1½ oz (⅓ cup plus 2 tablespoons)
ground almonds
300 ml/10½ fl oz (1¼ cups) cream
2 bitter almonds or a little bitter almond or
almond extract

Pour the milk into a large pot, then sift in the flour and whisk vigorously to make sure that no lumps form. Heat the milk slowly over a low heat to 35°C/95°F. Add the liquid rennet and immediately mix well. Cover the pot with a lid and leave it beside the stove to set and curdle. It will take 30 minutes, or possibly a bit longer. If you touch the surface of the curd it should leave a distinct milky-white film on your finger.

Cut the curds with a big whisk. You only want to break the mixture up into coarse chunks at this stage, so don't make the pieces too small. Cover the pan again and leave for another 30 minutes or so. You will see that the curds start to sink in the increasing amount of liquid as they release more whey.

Use a colander to transfer the curds into a sieve lined with muslin (cheesecloth) and leave them for another 30 minutes.

Preheat the oven to 175°C/345°F/Gas Mark 4 and butter an oven proof dish of about 20 cm in diameter.

Whisk the eggs and sugar in a mixing bowl. Add the ground almonds and the cream, then use a microplane or fine grater to grate in the bitter almonds and mix everything together gently. Add this mixture to the curds in a big bowl and incorporate fully without breaking the curds up too much.

Pour the batter into the prepared cake pan, but don't fill it more than three-quarters full. Bake for about 1 hour, or until the cake has set and the surface is golden. If it seems to be getting too dark, but isn't yet completely set, cover with a sheet of aluminium foil and continue baking.

CURD CAKE FROM HÄLSINGLAND

Hälsingeostkaka (Sweden)

As with the previous recipe, it is hard to make in smaller quantities, so freeze leftover curd cake, it stores for many months in the freezer.

Preparation time: 2¼ hours
Cooking time: 1 hour
Reheating time: 10 minutes
Makes: 1 cake, serving 8–10

5 litres/10½ UK pints (20 cups) full-
  fat (whole), unpasteurized and
  unhomogenized milk
65 g/2½ oz (⅓ cup plus 2 tablespoons)
  weak (soft) wheat flour
1 tablespoon liquid rennet
butter, to grease
200 ml/7 fl oz (¾ cup plus 1 tablespoon)
  cream

Pour the milk into a heavy pot and heat it slowly over a low heat to 35°C/95°F. Sift in the flour and whisk vigorously to make sure that no lumps form. Add the liquid rennet and immediately mix well. Cover and set aside for 30 minutes or so for the milk to set and curdle.

Use a knife to cut a cross in the curd to form 4 large wedge-shaped chunks. Cover and leave for another 30 minutes or so for the curds to release more whey.

Use a colander to transfer the curds to a sieve lined with muslin (cheesecloth) and leave for about 1 hour.

Preheat the oven to 220°C/425°F/Gas Mark 7 and butter a 23 x 13 x 8 cm/9 x 5 x 3 inch loaf pan.

Transfer the curds into the prepared loaf pan and bake for about 1 hour, or until the cake has set and the surface is golden.

Remove the cake from the oven and allow it to cool in the pan. Transfer to the refrigerator and leave to chill completely.

To serve, preheat the oven to 250°C/480°F/ Gas Mark 9. Turn the curd cake out of the pan and cut into 1 cm/½ inch thick slices. Place the slices in an ovenproof dish, pour on the cream and bake in the oven until just golden brown.

STRAWBERRIES AND CREAM

Jordbær med fløde (Denmark)
Jordgubbar med grädde (Sweden)

The further north you go in the world, the more people cherish the short moments where an abundance of summer fruit is available to them.

Few things are so instinctively delicious as strawberries and dairy. I like to eat my strawberries in a big bowl. They should never have been refrigerated; something odd happens to their vibrant aroma when they are chilled. I pour equal parts of cream and milk over them and then add a couple of spoons of sugar. I like the sugar, not because the berries aren't sweet and tasty, but because of its crunch between my teeth when I eat it. Some people eat their strawberries like me, but with only cream or only milk, and others want them with whipped cream.

RICE PUDDING

Risgrynspudding (Sweden)

Serve warm with Cordial Soup (page 694), or a spoonful of a jam you like (page 690) and some whipped cream.

Preparation and cooking time: 40 minutes
Serves: 4

2 tablespoons sugar
1 egg
½ quantity Rice Porridge (page 466)

Preheat the oven to 200°C/400°F/Gas Mark 6.

Stir in the sugar and egg to the rice porridge. Pour the batter into an ovenproof dish to a depth of about 4 cm/1½ inches and bake for about 30 minutes until golden and fluffy.

For image see opposite page

RICE PUDDING FOR DESSERT

Risalamande (Denmark)
Riskrem (Norway)
Ris ala Malta (Sweden)

To have cold, sweetened rice porridge mixed with whipped cream started to be more common with the Danish upper class around the beginning of the twentieth century and the Danish name for the dish, *risalamande*, comes from the French *riz à l'amande* – rice with almonds – which is, indeed, how it is served in Denmark. The Swedish name, *ris ala Malta*, is presumed to derive from the Danish name, rather than having anything to do with the island of Malta, and it changes the dish even further from the original French one, also dropping the almond content in the process. In Sweden and Norway this dessert is often served with Cordial Soup (page 694) or with Berry Compote (page 701).

Preparation time: 10 minutes
Serves: 4

400 ml/14 fl oz (1⅔ cups) cream
½ quantity chilled Rice Porridge (page 466)
sugar, to taste

Whip the cream to soft peaks.

Sweeten the porridge to taste – it should be quite sweet – then stir in about half of the cream so it is fully incorporated. Gently fold in the rest of the cream and serve.

Clockwise from top: Sweet Cherry Sauce (page 677); cream; Rice Pudding (page 626); Cordial Soup (page 694); Danish Almond Rice Pudding (page 628)

DANISH ALMOND RICE PUDDING

Risalamande (Denmark)

Sometimes, in addition to the chopped almonds, this dish is flavoured with a bit of bitter almond extract and/or some vanilla. It is most often served with a Sweet Cherry Sauce (page 677). The hiding of a whole almond in the Christmas Rice Porridge common in other Nordic countries is in Denmark practised with this Almond Rice Pudding. The person who gets the almond receives a small present called *mandelgave* (almond gift), often a marzipan pig.

Preparation time: 10 minutes
Serves: 4

400 ml/14 fl oz (1⅔ cups) cream
½ quantity chilled Rice Porridge (page 466)
sugar, to taste
few drops bitter almond extract (optional)
vanilla sugar, to taste or ½ vanilla bean, scraped (optional)
1 large handful blanched almonds, coarsely chopped

Whip the cream to soft peaks.

Sweeten the porridge to taste – it should be quite sweet – then add your choice of flavourings. Stir in about half of the cream so it is fully incorporated, then add the chopped almonds, fold them in with the rest of the cream and serve.

RICE PUDDING WITH ORANGE

Apelsinris (Sweden)

This dessert is sometimes also decorated with a sprinkling of toasted almond flakes or some grated chocolate. When I was growing up, canned mandarin segments were often used, which gave the dish a very particular flavour.

Preparation time: 15 minutes
Serves: 4

400 ml/14 fl oz (1⅔ cups) cream

½ quantity chilled Rice Porridge (page 466)
sugar, to taste
vanilla sugar, to taste, or ½ vanilla bean, scraped (optional)
4 oranges
grated zest of an orange (optional)
toasted almond flakes or grated chocolate (optional)

Whip the cream to soft peaks.

Sweeten the porridge to taste – it should be quite sweet – then add the vanilla sugar or seeds, if using.

Use a knife to peel the oranges. Slice the segments out of their skin casings, making sure there's no trace of pith or membrane (see illustrations below). Set aside.

Stir in half the whipped cream so it is fully incorporated, then add half the orange segments and fold them in with the rest of the cream. Top with the remaining orange segments (supremes) and sprinkle on a little grated zest, if using.

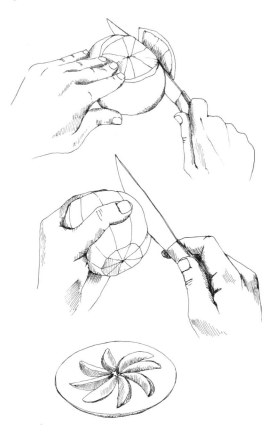

SEMOLINA PUDDING

Mannagrynspudding (Sweden)

Serve lukewarm with whipped cream and jam (page 690) or Cordial Soup (page 694).

Preparation and cooking time:
 40 minutes
Serves: 4

1 litre/34 fl oz (4¼ cups) milk
1 teaspoon salt
70 g/2½ oz (⅓ cup plus 2 tablespoons)
  wheat semolina
2 tablespoons sugar
2 bitter almonds, grated, or some
  bitter almond or almond essence
  if you can't find them
1 egg

Preheat the oven to 200°C/400°F/Gas Mark 6.

Combine the milk and salt in a pan and bring to the boil over a medium heat. As soon as it boils, whisk in the semolina, making sure that no lumps form, then simmer for about 5 minutes.

Leave the semolina mixture to cool for a few minutes before stirring in the sugar, bitter almonds and egg. Pour the batter into an ovenproof dish to a depth of about 4 cm/1½ inches and bake for about 30 minutes until nicely golden and fluffy.

MERINGUES, CREAM AND CHOCOLATE SAUCE

Marängsviss / Hovdessert (Sweden)

This dish has been documented as a festive dessert in Sweden since the late nineteenth century. Its name, *marängsviss*, comes from the French name for a meringue cooked over a bain marie (water bath), *meringue Suisse* (Swiss meringue) – although today it has nothing to do with that type of meringue.

Marängsviss is traditionally served as is, but in more recent recipes often with banana or other fruit and ice cream. If served with almond flakes and fresh berries the dish is called *hovdessert*, which means 'dessert for the royal court'.

Preparation time: 10 minutes
Serves: 4

300 ml/10½ fl oz (1¼ cups) cream
½ quantity Meringue (page 568), baked dry
  in small pieces or a larger piece, crushed
1 quantity Chocolate Sauce (page 677)

In a large bowl, whip the cream to soft peaks.

To assemble the dessert, layer the meringues and cream on a serving platter in a mound and drizzle generously with chocolate sauce.

SCANIAN APPLE PIE

Skånsk äppelkaka (Sweden)

This dessert might be one of the most delicious apple pies ever invented, traditionally served after a goose dinner on St Martin's Day (page 273) in the southern Swedish region of Skåne, with thick vanilla custard on the side.

Scanian apple pie is made with crumbs from a particular kind of dark rye bread called *Kavring* (page 502), which are slowly fried with butter and sugar to make the crust, before it is filled with Apple Compote (page 700).

Preparation and cooking time: 1 hour,
  plus cooling time
Makes: 8 pieces

For the crust
150 g/5 oz (1⅜ sticks) butter
150 g/5 oz (¾ cup) sugar
750 ml/7½ oz (3 cups) fresh
  breadcrumbs from a *Kavring*
  loaf (page 502)
pinch of salt

For the filling
500 g/17 oz (2 cups plus 1 tablespoon)
  Apple Compote (page 700) or about half
  a batch

Preheat the oven to 150°C/300°F/Gas Mark 2.

Melt the butter and the sugar in a cast-iron frying pan with an ovenproof handle. When the butter has melted, but before it starts to brown, add the breadcrumbs to the pan. Continue cooking over a medium heat, stirring from time to time, until the mixture caramelizes a deep brown and smells, tastes and looks fantastic.

Set aside a third of the mix. Use a spoon to press the remaining caramelized crumbs into the bottom and sides of the pan to form a shell. Pour in the apple compote and finish by sprinkling the reserved caramelized crumbs over the top in a thick layer to seal the apple in from all directions. Make sure that the top layer is solid and has no gaps before putting the pie into the oven. Bake for about 35 minutes, or until it is all warmed through, but not boiling inside.

Take the pie out of the oven and leave it to cool down to room temperature. By this point it will be completely stuck to the inside of the pan.

Just before serving, heat the pie over a medium heat until the sugar adhering to the pan melts and the pie comes loose. Invert the pie onto a serving platter. You have only got a few minutes to get the pie out of the pan before the whole thing starts to warm up and soften, which makes it impossible.

FINNISH FUDGE PIE

Tjinuskipaj (Sweden)

This is a very popular birthday cake in Finland and it is fantastic with some whipped cream on the side and some tart berries, like lingonberies.

Although the pie itself is quick to assemble, re-member that the Fudge Sauce for the filling takes up to 3 hours to make (page 678) and you also need to allow a good half hour for it to set.

Preparation time: 3 hours
Setting time: 30 minutes
Makes: 8 pieces

1 prebaked Pie Crust (page 637)
1 double quantity Finnish Fudge Caramel
  Sauce (page 678)

Make the Finnish fudge sauce following the recipe on page 678, but boiled for longer, until thicker. A temperature of about 120°C/250°F on a thermometer results in a creamy filling that is thick enough to cut.

Pour the hot fudge sauce into the prebaked pie crust and leave it at room temperature to cool and set before serving with whipped cream and berries.

CRUMBLE, BASE RECIPE

Smulpaj (Sweden)

Few things are as tasty as a good crumble. I like recipes containing some rolled oats; I like the way they caramelize. Serve a crumble warm or at room temperature, by itself or with a dollop of whipped cream or some vanilla cream.

Sometimes people cook a crumble at a slightly too high temperature, making the topping itself brown quickly and cook, but leaving the filling undercooked – or even semi-raw. This is not very tasty. I suggest a temperature of 175°C/345°F/ Gas Mark 4 and at least 35 minutes of baking time is essential.

Use with any soft fruits like raspberries, blueberries, gooseberries or similar. It also works really well with any fruit that softens with cooking like rhubarb or apples. The amount of sugar depends on how acidic the fruit and how sweet you like your pie to be. I usually add about 100 g/3½ oz to 500 g/17 oz of fruits ready for the oven. The amount of startch you need to add really depends on how watery your fruit is. For an apple I don't add any potato or cornstartch at all, whilst for blueberries I might add a tablespoon to the quantity mentioned above.

Preparation and cooking time: 45 minutes
Resting time: 10 minutes
Serves: 6–8

For the crumble topping
150 g/5 oz (1⅜ sticks) cold butter, cut into
    1 cm/½ inch cubes
120 g/4 oz (1 cup) plain (all-purpose)
    flour
60 g/2¼ oz (½ cup) rolled oats
150 g/5 oz (⅔ cup) sugar
good pinch of salt

Place all the ingredients for the crumble topping in a large mixing bowl. Work with your hands until the butter starts to warm up a little and mix with the other ingredients. The overall texture should be rather granular, but there shouldn't be too many lumps of pure butter in the final crumble.

Preheat the oven to 175°C/345°F/Gas Mark 4.

Mix your choice of fruit or berries with sugar and spices. Spread over the bottom of an ovenproof dish in an even layer.

Sprinkle the crumble mix over the fruit in an even layer and bake for about 35 minutes, or until the crumble is golden and the fruit is bubbling and cooked through.

Let the crumble sit for a good 10 minutes before serving.

APPLE CRUMBLE

Äppelsmulpaj (Sweden)

Add a dash of lemon juice to the apple and sugar mix if you feel that the apples lack in acidity. Also add ground cassia cinnamon if you like it.

Preparation and cooking time: 45 minutes
Resting time: 10 minutes
Serves: 6–8

1 quantity Crumble, Base Recipe (see left)

For the filling
6 cooking apples, peeled, cored and
    coarsely chopped
sugar, to taste
dash of lemon juice, to taste (optional)
ground cassia cinnamon, to taste (optional)

Preheat the oven to 175°C/345°F/ Gas Mark 4.

Mix the apples with sugar, to taste, and lemon juice and cinnamon to taste, if using. Spread over the bottom of an ovenproof dish.

Sprinkle the crumble topping over the fruit in an even layer and bake for about 35 minutes, or until the crumble is golden and the fruit is bubbling and cooked through.

Let the crumble sit for a good 10 minutes before serving.

RAW EGGS AND SUGAR

Eggedosis (Norway)
Söt äggröra (Sweden)

This simple dessert or sweet snack is something I have really only seen in Sweden and Norway, but it is possible that it exists also in the other Nordic countries. When I was growing up, my sister and I used to get a coffee cup, each containing two yolks and two teaspoons of sugar, plus the actual spoon. Then you had to beat the mixture in the cup with the spoon until it was just right. I liked it to be pretty fluffy but still having little grains of undissolved sugar that crunched between my teeth when I ate it.

Sometimes this preparation is served with fresh berries or some jam. It can also be dusted with cocoa powder. I have never been a fan of the berry or cocoa variations, but prefer my eggs and sugar in a more ascetic and pure fashion, straight up.

The relationship between the egg white and egg yolk depends on how fluffy/rich you want it to be: the more egg white you use the lighter the result, and vice versa with the egg yolk. The more white you add, the more sugar you'll also need, since the volume increases with the amount of white.

Preparation and cooking time: 5 minutes
Serves: 4

8 egg yolks
3 egg whites
5½ tablespoons sugar

Whisk the egg yolks, egg whites and sugar together in a bowl until fluffy and serve immediately.

DANISH APPLE TRIFLE

Gammeldags æblekage (Denmark)

The Danish name for this dessert means 'old-fashioned apple cake', although I would say that it is more of a trifle, with its layers of apple compote, cream and sweet crumbs. Sometimes the compote is flavoured with vanilla and sometimes the finished dessert is dusted with cinnamon.

Preparation and cooking time: 30 minutes,
* plus cooling time*
Serves: 4

50 g/2 oz (3½ tablespoons) butter
150 g/5 oz (1⅔ cups) breadcrumbs
100 g/3½ oz (½ cup) sugar
pinch of salt
50 g/2 oz Almond Biscuits (page 566),
  crushed into little pieces
300 ml/10½ fl oz (1¼ cups) cream
1 quantity Apple Compote (page 700),
  cold

Melt the butter in a pan over a medium heat and add the breadcrumbs, 80 g/3 oz (⅓ cup) of the sugar and salt. Toss in the pan and fry until the mixture starts to smell delicious and looks as if it is caramelizing. Stir in the crushed biscuits (cookies), then tip onto a plate and leave for about 30 minutes to cool down to room temperature.

While the crumbs are cooling, whip the cream to soft peaks with the remaining sugar.

In a large glass bowl (or in 4 individual small bowls), create layers of the apple compote and the sweet crumbs – as many or as few layers as you like. Finish with a thick layer of cream.

NORWEGIAN LAYERED APPLE DESSERT

Tilslørte bondepiker (Norway)

The name in Norwegian, *Tilslørte bondepiker*, means 'veiled peasant girls' and this dessert was at its most popular before ice cream became common. It is most often made with Apple Compote (page 700) today, but in older recipes other orchard fruits, like pears and plums, seem to have been used.

Preparation and cooking time: 20 minutes,
* plus cooling time*
Serves: 4

3 tablespoons butter
3 tablespoons sugar
good pinch of salt
6 tablespoons breadcrumbs or rusk crumbs
1 teaspoon ground cassia cinnamon
400 g/14 oz (1⅔ cups) Apple Compote
  (page 700)
400 ml/14 fl oz (1⅔ cups) cream

Heat the butter, sugar and and a pinch of salt in a pan over a medium heat. When the sugar has dissolved and the mixture is golden, add the breadcrumbs and the cinnamon and salt. Continue cooking, stirring from time to time, until the mixture caramelizes to a deep brown and smells delicious. Tip out onto a baking tray to cool a little.

Meanwhile, in a medium bowl, whip the cream to soft peaks.

Serve in a bowl or 4 individual glasses. Spoon in layers of the apple compote, the cream and the caramelized breadcrumbs, finishing with a layer of cream.

Preparation and cooking time: 1 hour
Serves: 10

1 quantity Rice Porridge (page 466), cold
butter, to grease
3 eggs
400 ml/14 fl oz (1⅔ cups) milk
2 tablespoons sugar
1 g/0.04 oz saffron threads
1 handful almonds, finely chopped

Preheat the oven to 200°C/400°F/Gas Mark 6. Butter an ovenproof dish.

Put the cold rice porridge into a large mixing bowl. In a separate bowl, mix the eggs with the milk, then pour into the porridge, together with the remaining ingredients. Mix until thoroughly combined, then pour the batter into the prepared dish, to a depth of about 3 cm/1¼ inches. Bake until golden.

RICE AND SAFFRON OVEN PANCAKE FROM GOTLAND

Gotländsk saffrans-pannkaka /
Gotlandspannkaka (Sweden)

Oven pancakes have been commonly served as dessert on the island of Gotland for many hundreds of years. Traditionally made on Christmas Day after with leftover rice porridge from Christmas Eve, this dessert was also served on other big occasions, like weddings.

Gotlandspannkaka as we see it today though was developed during the second half of the nineteenth century, when people added the rice, the saffron and the sugar to the pre-existing recipes. It was considered a very festive dessert for those who could afford it, due to the price of both sugar and saffron.

Gotlandspannkaka is traditionally served with whipped cream and dewberry jam (page 690).

FINNISH RYE MALT PUDDING

Mämmi / Memma (Finland)
Memma (Sweden)

Mämmi is traditionally eaten in Finland for dessert during Easter. It is, as with many other Finnish casseroles, both savoury and sweet, based on the breakdown of starch into sugars by amylase enzymes in the malt. *Mämmi* was traditionally baked and distributed in baskets made from birch bark, called *rivor*, but today it is almost always sold in cardboard boxes, often with a birch pattern printed on them. *Mämmi* is often served with cream and sugar, but in many homes also with vanilla ice cream, a more modern pairing.

Preparation and cooking time: 6 hours
Serves: 4 generous portions, with a bit
 to spare

2 strips dried bitter orange peel
400 g/14 oz (3 cups plus 1 tablespoon)
 coarse rye flour
150 g/5 oz (1 cup plus 1 tablespoon) ground
 rye malt
1 teaspoon salt
140 g/4¾ oz (⅓ cup plus 1 tablespoon)
 golden syrup

Pour 2 litres/3½ UK pints (8¼ cups) water into a heavy-bottomed pot. Add the strips of orange peel and heat to 60°C/140°F. Add the flour and the malt and mix well. Keep the temperature as close as possible to 60°C/140°F for about 3 hours, while the enzymes in the malt work on the starch in the rye flour. Don't allow it to get any hotter, as this would destroy the enzymes. Just for fun, taste the mixture just after you have added the flour and then once again at the end of the 3 hours. I always find the difference in sweetness quite fascinating.

Preheat the oven to 175°C/345°F/Gas Mark 4.

Now, add the salt and the golden syrup to the mixture and bring to the boil while stirring. Be careful not to let it stick to the bottom of the pot and burn. Simmer for 10 minutes over a medium heat before pouring into an ovenproof dish. Do not fill it all the way to the top since the *mämmi* will expand a bit in the oven. Cook for 3 hours and stir every 15 minutes during the first half of the cooking time. Eat hot, or leave covered in a cool place for a few days before serving.

SEMOLINA OVEN PANCAKE
FROM ÅLAND

Ahvenanmaan pannukakku (Finland)
Ålandspannkaka (Sweden)

This dessert is often served lukewarm with Prune Compote (page 701) and whipped cream.

Preparation and cooking time: 1 hour, plus
 cooling time
Serves: 10

1 litre/34 fl oz (4¼ cups) milk
1 teaspoon salt
70 g/2¾ oz (⅓ cup plus 2 tablespoons)
 wheat semolina
45 g/1¾ oz (⅓ cup) weak (soft) wheat flour
1 teaspoon cardamom seeds, crushed
2 eggs
75 g/2¾ oz (⅓ cup) sugar

Preheat the oven to 200°C/400°F/Gas Mark 6.

Combine the milk and salt in a pot and bring to the boil over a medium heat. As soon as it boils, whisk in the semolina, making sure that no lumps form, then simmer for about 5 minutes, until thickened. Remove the pot from the heat and leave it to cool down to room temperature, stirring occasionally. I like to place a sheet of clingfilm (plastic wrap) on the surface of the batter as it cools to prevent a thick skin from forming.

Once the batter has cooled, fold in the flour and cardamom.

In a separate bowl, whisk the eggs and sugar together until pale and creamy, then fold them into the batter too. Pour the batter into an ovenproof dish to a depth of about 3 cm/1¼ inches. Bake for 35–40 minutes, until the pancake is golden and fully set.

For image see opposite page

Clockwise from top: Semolina Oven Pancake from Åland (page 634);
Prune Compote (page 701); whipped cream

FINNISH QUARK PUDDING

Pasha (Finland)

This rich dessert is traditionally served for Easter in Finland and in some of the other Baltic countries. It is also part of Russian Orthodox Easter traditions from where it originates. The name *pasha* refers to the Russian word *Пасха* meaning Easter. On the side of the pudding itself the Cyrillic letters 'ХВ' are often inscribed, being short for *Христос воскресе* (*Hristos voskrese*), Christ is risen.

Pasha is usually made in a traditional mould, which allows the mixture to drain and firm up. You'll also need some clean muslin (cheesecloth) to line the mould.

Serve *pasha* just as it is or with some fresh fruit or candied cherries on the side.

Preparation time: 20 minutes
Draining: at least 24 hours
Serves: 20

2 egg yolks
270 g/9½ oz (1⅓ cups) sugar
100 g/3½ oz (7 tablespoons) butter, melted and cooled
100 g/3½ oz (⅓ cup plus 2 tablespoons) *smetana* or sour cream
750 g/1 lb 10 oz (3 cups plus 2 tablespoons) quark
100 g/3½ oz (½ cup) coarsely chopped candied cherries
50 g/2 oz (⅓ cup) coarsely chopped raisins
50 g/2 oz (⅓ cup) coarsely chopped candied citrus peel
50 g/2 oz (⅓ cup) blanched, skinned and coarsely chopped almonds

Line a *pasha* mould with a layer of muslin (cheesecloth).

Combine the egg yolks and sugar in the bowl of a stand mixer and whisk until white and creamy. Add the cooled melted butter and incorporate fully. Add the *smetana* or sour cream and quark and mix in well.

Add the dried fruit, citrus peel and almonds and mix them into the *pasha* thoroughly.

Pour the batter into the prepared mould, set it on a shallow tray or baking sheet to collect the liquid, and leave it to drain in a cool place for at least 24 hours.

When ready to serve, invert the mould onto a serving platter and carefully remove the muslin.

DANISH BERRY DESSERT WITH CREAM

Rødgrød med fløde (Denmark)

A Berry Compote (page 701) thickened with a little bit of potato starch and served warm or cold, with a generous drizzle of cream, is one of the most iconic and common Danish desserts.

Preparation and cooking time: 20 minutes
Serves: 4

500–700 g/1 lb 2 oz–1 lb 8½ oz (3–4 cups) raspberries, blueberries or strawberries, rinsed, cut and hulled if necessary
sugar, to taste
2–3 tablespoons potato starch
cream, to serve

Put three-quarters of the berries in a large pan and pour in 500 ml/17 fl oz (2 cups plus 1 tablespoon) water. Bring to a simmer over a medium heat, then stir in sugar, to taste.

In a small bowl, mix the potato starch with a couple of tablespoons of water. Stir it into the compote and return to a simmer for a couple of minutes. Add the rest of the berries, then remove the pan from the heat.

For image see page 697

BLUEBERRY AND SOUR CREAM PIE

Mustikkapiirakka (Finland)

When you search for *mustikkapiirakka* on the internet, or ask Finnish people what it is, it seems that most consider it to be this. It comprises a piecrust which is not precooked, but rather baked together with its filling – usually blueberries and a simple kind of sour cream custard. I have seen this kind of dish many times in other Nordic countries – we even make one in my own family with raspberries – but they all seem to be quite recent inventions in comparison with the Finnish one. Perhaps Finland is the origin of this fantastic pie?

Preparation time and cooking time: 50–60 minutes
Resting time: 10 minutes
Makes: 8 pieces

For the pie crust
250 g/9 oz (2 sticks) soft butter, plus extra to grease
160 g/5½ oz (¾ cup plus 1 tablespoon) sugar
2 eggs
260 g/9¼ oz (2 cups plus 2 tablespoons) weak (soft) wheat flour, plus extra for dusting
2 teaspoons baking powder
pinch of salt

For the filling
400 g/14 oz (1⅔ cups) full-fat sour cream or crème fraîche
2 eggs
100 g/3½ oz (½ cup) sugar
300 g/11 oz (2 cups) blueberries or bilberries, fresh or frozen

Preheat the oven to 200°C/400°F/Gas Mark 6. Butter a 24cm/9½ inch springform cake pan and dust with flour.

To make the pie crust, combine the butter, sugar and salt in the bowl of a stand mixer. Beat until white and fluffy, then, with the motor on low, add the eggs, one at a time. Sift over the flour and baking powder and mix until fully incorporated, but for no longer.

With lightly floured hands, press the mixture into the prepared pan, making sure it reaches fairly high up the sides. The crust on this pie should not be too thin.

In another bowl, stir the sour cream or crème fraîche, eggs and sugar together until smooth.

Pour the mixture into the unbaked crust, then sprinkle in the blueberries or bilberies. Bake for 30–40 minutes, or until the filling is set and lightly golden.

Once the pie is done, leave it in the pan for about 10 minutes before releasing it, which makes it much easier to separate the pie from the pan itself. But don't leave it for much longer than 10 minutes, as this can make the crust soggy and it won't have the proper crunch.

BLUEBERRY PIE

Blåbärspaj (Sweden)

This classic Nordic blueberry pie may be served warm or cold, on its own or with vanilla custard, whipped cream or ice cream.

Preparation and cooking time:
  1–1¼ hours
Setting time: 1 hour
Makes: 8 pieces

For the pie crust
150 g/5 oz (1⅜ sticks) butter, melted and cooled down, plus extra to grease
180 g/6¼ oz (¾ cup) sugar
360 g/12¾ oz (3 cups) weak (soft) wheat flour, plus extra for dusting
2 teaspoons baking powder
pinch of salt

For the filling
700 g/1 lb 8½ oz (4½ cups) blueberries or bilberries, fresh or frozen
5 tablespoons potato starch
sugar, to taste

Preheat the oven to 150°C/300°F/Gas Mark 2. Butter a 24 cm/9½ inch springform cake pan and dust with flour.

To make the pie crust, mix the melted butter, sugar and salt in a mixing bowl. Sift on the flour and baking powder and mix until fully incorporated.

With lightly floured hands, press the mixture into the prepared pan, making sure it reaches all the way up the sides.

In another bowl, mix the berries with the potato starch and sugar, then tip into the unbaked crust.

Bake for at least 45 minutes, or until the crust is nicely golden. It is important that the potato starch is allowed to cook properly so the pie doesn't end up too runny and taste starchy. Leave to set for at least 1 hour after you take it out of the oven.

GRIDDLED SWEET NORWEGIAN FLATBREADS

Tynnlefse (Norway)

This is a thin and slightly sweet Norwegian griddled flatbread, which is spread with a kind of buttercream filling before being folded or rolled up and cut into pieces.

Tynnlefse is often served after a meal or as a sweet snack with coffee on the side.

This type of filled flatbread freezes really well with the filling inside so do keep some in the freezer if you can't eat it all at once.

Preparation and cooking time: 1 hour
Rising time: 40 minutes
Makes: 6 flatbreads, each enough
  for 6 pieces

For the dough
5 g/⅛ oz yeast
250 ml/8 fl oz (1 cup) cultured milk
50 g/2 oz (3½ tablespoons) butter
50 g/2 oz (¼ cup) sugar
350 g/12 oz (3 cups) plain (all-purpose) flour
½ teaspoon baking powder
½ teaspoon baker's ammonia

For the filling
125 g/4 oz (1 stick) butter, at room temperature
125 g/4 oz (½ cup plus 2 tablespoons) sugar
75 ml/21/2 fl oz (⅓ cup) cream
a pinch of salt

Melt the butter and allow to cool a bit.

Dissolve the yeast into the cultured milk, add the butter and the sugar and stir well with a large wooden spoon. Add the flour, baking powder and baker's ammonia together into the bowl. With you hands, work together to a firm but smooth dough, cover with a clean dish cloth and leave for 40 minutes to leaven.

Divide into 6 pieces and roll them out on a work counter to a round cake about 3 mm/¼ inch in thickness. Bake on an iron flat top griddle over a medium heat until golden. Flip over and cook the other side until golden. Stack the cooked flatbreads and cover them up so that they don't dry while you make the filling.

Stir all of the ingredients for the filling together until creamy and white.

Place a flatbread on the work counter in front of you and brush it on both sides, evenly with a very light coating of water. This is to save it from cracking when you fold it later. Spread an even layer of the filling onto the flatbread and fold 2 of the edges opposite to each other so they meet in the middle. Fold it once more and press down firmly. Repeat with all the remaining flatbreads.

Before serving cut each flatbread into 6 pieces of a convenient size to pick up and eat.

NORWEGIAN LIGHT LINGONBERRY MOUSSE

Trollkrem (Norway)

A very traditional Norwegian dessert, this extremely light and refreshing mousse is often served as it is, with a few fresh lingonberries sprinkled on top, or with an option of vanilla custard.

Preparation time: 5 minutes
Serves: 4

200 g/7 oz (¾ cup plus 1½ tablespoons) lingonberries, fresh or frozen and defrosted, plus extra to serve
85 g/3 oz (⅓ cup plus 2 tablespoons) sugar
1 egg white

Use an electric whisk or a stand mixer to whisk all the ingredients together until thick and creamy.

NORWEGIAN CLOUDBERRY CREAM

Multekrem (Norway)

In Norway *multekrem* is often eaten at Christmas and served with either Norwegian Wafers (page 571) or Almond Wreath Cake (page 604) as a dessert.

Preparation and cooking time: 5 minutes
Serves: 4

400 ml/14 fl oz (1⅔ cups) double (heavy) cream
200 g/7 oz (¾ cup plus 1 tablespoon) cloudberry jam (page 690)

Whip the cream to soft peaks in a bowl.

Carefully fold the jam into the cream with a rubber spatula. Some people like it to be completely mixed in, but I like it when there are some streaks of jam and pure cream still in the mixture.

This dessert is best served when it has just been folded, rather than being left to sit in the refrigerator.

LINGONBERRY CREAM

Lingongrädde (Sweden)

Whipped cream mixed with Sugared Lingonberries (page 692) can be served with pancakes (pages 450–4) or waffles (pages 455–7) or as an accompaniment to Gingerbread Cake (page 594).

Preparation and cooking time: 10 minutes
Serves: 4 as a condiment or dessert

150 ml/5 fl oz (⅔ cup) cream
150 ml/5 fl oz (⅔ cup) Sugared Lingonberries (page 692)

Whip the cream to stiff peaks in a bowl and then fold in the sugared lingonberries.

BASICS AND CONDIMENTS

Previous page: Melting glacier and volcanic ash, Iceland, Spring 2013.

Opposite: Whale seasoning, north Norway, Spring 2014.

Previous page: Corrugated steel rooftop with beautiful bits and pieces lying on it, photographed in an Icelandic harbour May 2013. Behind and above me hundreds of kilos of rotten shark are hung up to dry.

Opposite: Lady separating milk and cream in her kitchen, Iceland, early May 2013.

STOCKS

Stocks (broths) are very important: they make up the base of sauces and soups but can also be delicious served just as they are. They can be made from meat, poultry, fish, seafood and vegetables. They should really taste of what they are made of.

Most often the proteins are in some way cooked before the liquid is added. I would even go as far as saying that I don't think any raw meat should ever go into an ordinary stock. It will create unnecessary cloudiness because the proteins leak out into the liquid and coagulate there, creating small particles that can be difficult to strain away.

The way you prepare the ingredients before adding any liquid is the simplest method of controlling the stock's colour and flavour profile. If you are making a light stock with no colouration, simply blanch the meat once in boiling water to coagulate the proteins. For a darker stock, slowly brown the meat and/or bones in a 150°C/300°F/Gas Mark 2 oven, or in a large pot over a medium heat. The darker the protein is allowed to become, the darker the resulting stock will be. The important thing for a clear and balanced stock is to cook the meat thoroughly, regardless of what it is, before adding the liquid.

You can also roast vegetables for additional colour or if you want the flavour profile, but there is no need to cook them from a perspective of the clouding of the stock, as they will not affect the clarity of the stock in the way that raw meat does. However one of the worst things I know is an overly sweet stock. This often comes from excessive addition of vegetables, poor choice of vegetables and adding them too early in the cooking process. I tend to add my vegetables towards the very end, so that they are perfectly cooked (I mean the way they would be if you were to serve them) when the stock is just ready to be strained. Overcooked, mushy vegetables will make your stock taste like overcooked, mushy vegetables, and most often will also turn it cloudy since they break down into fine particles as they cook.

Also, there is no point whatsoever in adding too much water to not enough aromatics and meat. You will just have to boil that away in the end to get the right level of concentration for the stock. The more you boil it after the meat and the aromatics have given what they can, the less good it will be. There is a point when everything in the stockpot has given all it can to the surrounding liquid, and cooking beyond this point will possibly dissolve more gelatine and some flavour compounds that don't really evaporate easily, but from that point on, every minute of additional cooking will cost the broth complexity through loss of aroma. All the aroma you sense in a kitchen where a stock is being made is actually aroma leaving the stock, i.e. not flavouring it any more.

This is also the case with excessive reduction. It's better to use less water from the start and reduce less after the solids are taken out. If your stock isn't good in the beginning it's not going to be any good after being reduced either. Some additional reduction can be beneficial, but only do it until your stock tastes really nice and balanced, and then stop. If you want it thicker when you make a sauce, for example, add a little bit of starch rather than boiling out every molecule of volatile aroma out of it.

As a general principle, when I make stocks I prepare all the ingredients ahead of time, varying their preparation to match the broth I want to make. I brown the meat/bones to the degree I want and cut all the vegetables to the appropriate size, so that I can add everything at the right time for it all to be perfectly cooked.

If you are making a gelatinous oxtail stock, for example, you know that it's going to take hours for those pieces of tail to give what they have to the liquid in terms of flavour and texture. Start with just the tail and the water, and when perhaps 45 minutes remain of the total cooking time, add your vegetables, cut in big pieces, to the stockpot.

If you are making a light beef broth, one that shouldn't be gelatinous and that needs to be crystal clear straight from the stockpot, perhaps cut pieces of lean beef in dices of 1 cm/½ inch dice to slowly brown and cook them with some butter in the pot itself, adding vegetables cut to the same size towards the very end of the browning, barely adding enough water to cover. Bring it to a gentle simmer and then just let it steep off the heat for 30 minutes or so before straining it – like a kind of meat tea.

Fish and shellfish generally lend their flavour very quickly. I sometimes actually do add the raw meat and shells to the broth and use them almost like the clarifying raft of a consommé at the same time as the broth is being made. If you are making a light stock of langoustine or fish, perhaps just blitz the heads and shells with the vegetables in a food processor, transfer the goo to a pot with a tiny amount of water and bring to a slow simmer, the proteins solidifying and creating a fine network of pieces of meat and vegetable, a bit like a sponge, through which the liquid is filtered and flavoured at the same time. No cooking time of more than 20 minutes will ever be necessary for a broth like this one.

If you are making a stock from fish, in which you want to add gelatine – perhaps a stock of turbot – feel free to roast the bones and head a bit if you want it dark. Otherwise just cook them as if you were poaching pieces of fish the same size in the liquid of the stock. They are much more fragile than pieces of mammals like beef or pig, and any handling, excessive boiling or just too lengthy cooking will only break them up and not really produce any more flavour.

Throughout the whole process of cooking a stock, any fat floating to the top should be strained away as it appears, if you don't want it there of course. If the stock is to be reduced, all of it needs to go away; otherwise it will emulsify into the liquid, making it cloudy. The same goes if you want to store it, as it goes rancid quickly and therefore shortens the life span of the rest of the liquid. If I am making a little broth for a clear soup, I don't mind some pearls of fat floating around on top of it. However, this is a matter of personal preference, and if you are keeping some fat, do be careful not to boil the liquid.

When you strain a stock, do not pour it from the pot through a sieve. It will just push unwanted solids through the mesh, making them really difficult to remove later. Ladle the stock slowly into your sieve, little by little, never more than one ladleful in the strainer, letting it pour slowly along one side of the mesh, rather than dumping it straight into the middle of the sieve. When you have strained away the solids, leave the stock undisturbed for 30–60 minutes. You'll be surprised how many particles sink down to the bottom of the pot.

Again, ladle or carefully siphon the broth from the top and down into a chinois (conical strainer) lined with a layer of muslin (cheesecloth). Leave any cloudy, yucky mud at the bottom. Don't be cheap about this; discard a little too much rather than risk clouding your precious stock.

Now either use the stock straight away or chill immediately for storage. Stocks freeze really well and providing you've skimmed away any fat, they will keep for a really long time. Freeze small cups of stock, rather than one big container, so that you can use it conveniently when you need it; instead of defrosting a 5-litre/10½-UK-pint bucket when you need just a spoon. At home I do this in ice cube bags.

When you prepare any stock or broth, the choice of pan or stockpot is very important. It should not be too big – the meat and aromatics should just fit in it. When you add the water, it should just barely cover the rest of the stuff.

Do not cook the shit out of your produce just because you want to extract more flavour from it. It is a bad and dated practice. Most products give their best flavour to the stock when they are just perfectly cooked. A carrot should be cooked like a carrot you would serve as a side, not until it dissolves. A piece of oxtail should be braised until just tender but not until falling off the bone; a bunch of langoustine shells just until the proteins coagulate – as if you were frying a piece of its tail in a pan.

The more sweet vegetables you add, the sweeter the stock. The longer you cook them, the sweeter the stock. I use between roughly a third of vegetables to the volume of meat, to none at all. It all depends on what kind of flavour you want.

In the stock recipes, I have described what kinds of vegetables and meats I would normally use. The exact recipe though, has to depend on what you are going to use your stock for and what you have to hand in terms of produce.

All the recipes overleaf will give about 500 ml/ 18 fl oz (2 cups plus 1 tablespoon) of finished stock and can be prepared in both a light and dark version.

VEGETABLE STOCK

Vegetable stocks are the most difficult to make. Even a poorly made chicken stock can sometimes be useful when making delicious things. A poorly made vegetable stock is a bit like dishwater and you can't reduce it to make it taste better because most of the flavour profile consists of aromatics, which evaporate.

The key is to size the vegetables correctly and to add each one at the right moment. When you strain and chill the vegetable stock they should all be perfectly cooked – as if you were going to serve them for eating – and not overcooked.

For a good all-round kind of vegetable stock, I like parsnip, carrot, a bit of turnip, celery stalk, leek, a fresh perfectly ripe tomato and possibly some parsley stalks. Perhaps start with the parsnip, which will take a good while to cook depending on size and age, and the way you cut it, and finish with the tomato cut into pieces, which more or less just sits in the stock pot for a minute before you strain it all.

If I am making a vegetable-specific stock, let's say a carrot stock, to make it taste very complex of carrot, I would first make a stock of only carrot, then when just done, I would strain it over another equal amount of raw carrot, grated, and steep them for just a few minutes, giving the liquid the soft sweetness of the cooked vegetable and the fresh aroma of the raw one.

Remember not to make the selection too sweet, containing only vegetables like carrot, parsnip and onion, but select a balance.

Vegetable stocks should not be kept, but made fresh when you need them.

Preparation time: 20 minutes
Cooking time: 5–45 minutes

1.5 kg/3¼ lb mixed vegetables

Follow the general principles above and on page 648 for preparing, cooking, straining and storing your stock.

FISH STOCK

With fish, I usually use celery, leek or shallot and a bit of carrot.

Preparation time: 20 minutes
Cooking time: up to 1 hour

1 kg/2¼ lb fish bones, heads and trimmings, rinsed and cleaned
up to 300 g/10½ oz mixed vegetables

Follow the general principles on page 648 for preparing, cooking, straining and storing your stock.

CHICKEN STOCK

Use raw chicken carcasses or meaty bones, purchased specially for making your stock or use leftovers from a previously roasted or cooked bird.

With chicken, I usually use carrot, celery and leek.

Preparation time: 20 minutes
Cooking time: about 1 hour

1 kg/2¼ lb chicken meat and bones
300 g/10½ oz mixed vegetables

Follow the general principles on page 648 for preparing, cooking, straining and storing your stock.

MEAT STOCK

If you use a lot of bones and cartilage in your stock, it will become more gelatinous than if you use mostly meat, and it will also take a bit longer for the meat to give up its flavour and texture to the liquid. A gelatinous stock can be desirable if you are making, for example, a sauce that relies on the texture of the stock itself to thicken the sauce itself. I am not overly fond of this kind of demi-glace sauce, however, and I prefer stocks that are made from meat or meat and just a bit of bone. I would rather thicken my sauce with a little bit of starch.

I usually use carrot, celery and leek when I'm making classic Nordic-style dishes, such as clear soups. Feel free to add a little swede or turnip as well.

Preparation time: 30 minutes
Cooking time: 1– 3 hours

1.5 kg/3¼ lb meat and bones or 1 kg/2¼ lb
  if using mainly meat
up to 500 g/1 lb 2 oz mixed vegetables
butter, to fry (if you are browning your meat
  and bones)

Follow the general principles on page 648 for preparing, cooking, straining and storing your stock.

BEURRE MANIÉ

Beurre manié is a paste of wheat flour and butter, kneaded together into a smooth paste, which is used to thicken warm sauces. It is very easy to use and it rarely gives lumps if properly prepared, as the fat keeps all of the flour particles separated.

To use beurre manié, simply spoon a bit of it into simmering liquid and whisk to dissolve. Continue cooking for a couple of minutes until the liquid has thickened and no longer tastes of flour.

Preparation time: 5 minutes
Makes: enough to thicken 500 ml/17 fl oz
  (2 cups plus 1 tablespoon) of liquid

25 g/1 oz (1¾ tablespoons) butter, soft
25 g/1 oz (3 tablespoons) plain (all-purpose)
  flour

Work the butter and flour together in a bowl until fully combined and smooth.

ROUX

The word roux is French and means 'reddish'. In cooking, it refers to a mixture of butter and flour that is used to thicken warm sauces and soups. Roux are divided into: white (briefly cooked), blonde

(cooked a little longer) and brown (cooked thoroughly). It is not possible to give precise cooking times as you can only really check the progress of the roux by looking at it.

Preparation and cooking time: 10–20 minutes,
  depending on which colour roux you want
Makes: enough to thicken about 500 ml/
  18 fl oz (2 cups plus 1 tablespoon) of liquid

25 g/1 oz (1¾ tablespoons) butter
25 g/1 oz (3 tablespoons) plain (all-purpose)
  flour

Melt the butter in a pan over a medium heat. As soon as it stops foaming, sift in the flour, stirring constantly to prevent lumps forming. Continue cooking over a medium heat, still stirring, until the desired colour is achieved. When it is just right, transfer the hot roux to a cold container to immediately stop the cooking process.

VELOUTÉ

Velouté is usually made from light, unroasted stock (broth) of some kind simply thickened with blonde Roux (page 651). However the technique itself is very versatile and lends itself to many different preparations with all kinds of stocks, broths and cooking liquids giving different results. Cream can also be added to make a simple creamy sauce tasting of whatever base you made it from and whatever seasoning you decide to finish it with. I like to make my velouté not too thick, but if you want it thicker than this, just increase the amount of flour in the roux a bit or boil the velouté for a bit longer to reduce it.

If you are making a creamy velouté, substitute 150 ml/5 fl oz (⅔ cup) of the base liquid with cream but do not add it until everything else has simmered for about 5 minutes. If you add all the liquid at once there is a chance that the cream will curdle if the base is a cooking liquid containing some acidity rather than just a pure stock.

Preparation time: 15 minutes
Makes: about 500 ml/17 fl oz (2 cups plus
  1 tablespoon)

1 quantity Roux (page 651)
550 ml/18 fl oz (2½ cups) stock, broth or
  cooking liquid depending on how you are
  going to use the velouté
salt and pepper, to taste

Heat the liquid in a pot until simmering and keep the roux in the pot in which it was made. The pot used to make the roux needs to be large enough to eventually hold all of the liquid.

Add the liquid to the pot with the roux while whisking briskly so that no lumps form. Place the pot on the stove over medium heat and bring to a simmer, stirring once in a while. Cook for 10 minutes or until the liquid has thickened and no longer tastes of flour. Season according to the recipe in which the velouté is included.

MUSTARDS

Mustards are common in the Nordic region, both as condiments but also as components in dishes. Most often they contain equal, or almost equal, parts brown and yellow mustard seeds, which distinguishes them from mustards in other parts of the world that often contain less brown seeds and in some cases none at all. A large amount of brown seeds equals a more aromatic mustard and a larger amount of yellow seeds would mean one with a more direct, horseradish-like sting. Many Nordic mustards are also seasoned with different spices and sweetened to some degree.

Seasoning can be dried, ground ginger, peppers, cloves and other sweet spices. None of the following recipes contain any seasoning aside of the mustard itself and some salt, but feel free to add some ground spices if you want to.

A good amount of spices for the following recipes would be:

5 g/⅛ oz ground, dried ginger
10 black peppercorns, finely ground
4 cloves, finely ground

Some mustards are boiled; others are ground raw. Generally a mustard in which the seeds have been boiled will be smoother and more homogenous.

ORDINARY, STRONG MUSTARD

Preparation and cooking time: 30 minutes
Sitting time: overnight
Makes: about 200 ml/7 fl oz (¾ cup plus
  1 tablespoon)

50 g/2 oz yellow mustard seeds
25 g/1 oz brown mustards seeds
2 tablespoons mustard powder
2 tablespoons sugar
2 teaspoons salt
50 ml/1¾ fl oz (3 tablespoons) neutral
  cooking oil

Combine the mustard seeds and 150 ml/5 fl oz (⅔ cup) water in a small pot and bring to a boil.

Simmer for about 5–10 minutes, or until the seeds have absorbed most of the water and gone a bit soft. Transfer the seeds to a blender and add all of the remaining ingredients and any additional seasoning. Blend until smooth, then transfer to a suitable sterilized glass jar, seal and leave overnight to sit.

SWEET-AND-STRONG MUSTARD

Sötstark senap (Sweden)

So, this is a really unusual mustard for those who are not from a north Scandinavian part of the world. It is very sweet and we love it on everything salty. Especially on hot dogs. Some recipes for this have cream in them instead of water. I have never been a fan of this but please go ahead and try it if you want – the method remains exactly the same.

Preparation and cooking time: 30 minutes
Sitting time: at least overnight
Makes: about 300 ml/10½ fl oz (1¼ cups)

120 g/4 oz (½ cup plus 2 tablespoons)
  sugar
40 g/1½ oz (¼ cup) plain (all-purpose)
  flour
2 teaspoons salt
1 tablespoon *Ättika* (12%) vinegar
  (page 656)
25 g/1 oz (3 tablespoons) yellow mustard
  seeds, ground very fine
25 g/1 oz (3 tablespoons) brown mustard
  seeds, ground very fine

Mix everything except the mustard seeds in a small pot with 250 ml/8 fl oz (1 cup) water and bring to a simmer while stirring. Cook for 5 minutes.

Pour the hot mixture into a stand mixer, add the mustard seeds and any other seasoning and mix on full speed for a few minutes. Transfer to a sterilized glass jar, seal, and refrigerate at least overnight.

SCANIAN MUSTARD

Skånsk senap (Sweden)

Scanian mustard is a coarse and sweet mustard from the south Swedish region of Skåne. It goes really well with thick slices of ham, for example Swedish Christmas Ham (page 438).

Preparation and cooking time: 10 minutes
Sitting time: at least overnight
Makes: about 200 ml/7 fl oz (¾ cup plus
  1 tablespoon)

100 ml/ 3½ fl oz (⅓ cup plus 1 tablespoon)
  yellow mustard seeds
100 ml/3½ fl oz (⅓ cup plus 1 tablespoon)
  brown mustard seeds
2 tablespoons *Ättika* (12%) vinegar
  (page 656)
3 tablespoons sugar, brown or white
2 tablespoons salt

Combine all the ingredients plus any seasoning in a mortar and pestle and work until most of the seeds are cracked but not finely ground. Add some water to give it a thick, creamy texture. Transfer to a sterilized glass jar, seal, and let the mustard sit overnight. Adjust the texture again with water if necessary. The resulting mustard should be quite thick but not dry.

For image see page 349

BOILED RICE

I like my rice without any salt at all in it, but feel free to add salt if you want; most people in the Nordic countries will also do so.

You wouldn't think that rice is part of the traditional Nordic diet but we eat about as much rice as any other western region does and it has been served in different preparations for as long as there has been a trade between Asia and Europe.

The general principle for boiled rice is to use 2 parts water to 1 parts rice, by volume.

Preparation and cooking time: 30 minutes
Serves: 4

3 cups long-grain, white rice
6 cups cold water

Wash the rice thoroughly in a sieve, keeping the water running until it is clear of any starchy cloudiness. Drain it well.

Place the rice in a pot with the water and bring to the boil over medium heat. Cover the pot tightly with a lid. Remove from the heat and leave next to the stove until the water has been absorbed into the rice. Use a fork to fluff up the rice and serve.

RENDERED ANIMAL FATS

Flottyr (Sweden)

I think this mix is one of the very best for rich-tasting, crisp and delicious deep-fried pastries. It is not very common today, but if you have the opportunity, do make some and freeze it in a bag, ready to defrost and use when you need it.

Preparation and cooking time: 1 hour
Makes: 2 kg | 4¼ lb rendered fat

1.5 kg/3¼ lb leaf pork lard, coarsely broken into chunks
1.5 kg/3¼ lb beef suet (kidney fat), coarsely broken into chunks

Bring 200 ml/7 fl oz (¾ cup plus 1 tablespoon) water to a boil in a pot big enough to hold all the fat. Add the fat to the water and cover the pot with a lid. Simmer carefully for about 30 minutes. When all the fat looks translucent and has warmed through properly, strain it through an ordinary sieve and then through muslin (cheesecloth) or a chinois (conical) strainer. Remember to keep the fat warm as you strain it so that it doesn't solidify.

Cool completely then transfer to a bag or a lidded container and freeze until you need it.

EGG ROLL

Äggrulle (Sweden)

This is a classic side with poached white fish, such as pike-perch (page 170), Browned Butter (page 662) and horseradish. Sometimes cold boiled prawns (shrimp) are served alongside the fish.

The egg roll can be prepared several days in advance and stored in the refrigerator to be taken out and sliced for serving.

Preparation and cooking time: 10 minutes,
* plus cooling time*
Chilling time: at least 2 hours
Resting time: 30 minutes before serving
Serves: 4, as a condiment

100 g/3½ oz (7 tablespoons) butter
4 Hard-boiled Eggs (page 53), at room
  temperature
salt and white pepper, to taste

Melt the butter in a small pan, then leave to cool to room temperature.

Shell and chop the hard-boiled eggs into 5 mm/ ¼ inch dice.

Mix the butter and eggs together. The yolks should break up and turn creamy with the butter, while the whites should remain in dice. Season well with salt and pepper. Scrape the mixture onto a sheet of greaseproof paper and shape roughly into a fat log, about 6 cm/2½ inches in diameter. Roll up neatly in the paper, fix with some tape and twist the ends tightly. Refrigerate for at least 2 hours to set firm.

To serve, remove the egg roll from the fridge at least 30 minutes before serving so it reaches room temperature. Unwrap the butter from the paper and cut into 4 thick slices, like little hockey pucks.

FINNISH EGG BUTTER

Munavoi (Finland)

A very popular spread or topping for Karelian Pasties (page 519).

Preparation and cooking time: 5 minutes
Makes: enough for 8 pasties

2 Hard-boiled Eggs (page 53), unshelled and chilled
2 tablespoons butter, at room temperature
salt, to taste

Shell the eggs, then chop them coarsely and place in a small mixing bowl. Add the butter and work gently with a spoon until creamy but not completely smooth. Season with salt, if necessary.

DILL BUTTER

Dildsmør (Denmark)
Dillsmör (Sweden)

There are two ways of making this condiment. Either you just chop the dill with a knife as fine as you want, or you mix it all in a blender. The latter way might be a bit difficult depending on the size of your blender, and you might have to make double the recipe for it to mix properly. Mixing in a blender will give a slightly more 'restaurant' looking green butter, whilst the hand-chopped result looks more like it did at my grandmother's house when I was growing up.

Either serve the butter fresh and soft in a bowl with a spoon on the side or roll it up in grease-proof paper and chill it so that you can cut it in slices. Dill butter doesn't really keep that long but should be fine for a day or two before it goes all military in colour.

Preparation and cooking time: 5 minutes
Serves: 4, as a condiment

1 big bunch dill, fronds picked
120 g/4 oz (8 tablespoons) butter, at room temperature
salt and white pepper, to taste

If making by hand, chop the dill fronds as finely as you like with a very sharp knife. Chop the stalks finely too, if using. Transfer all the dill to a mixing bowl with the butter and use a wooden spoon or spatula to beat together well. Season liberally – it is a condiment, after all.

Alternatively, combine double quantities of all the ingredients (but leave out the stalks) in a blender and blend to an even consistency.

If not eating straight away, shape the dill butter into a log and roll in greaseproof paper. Twist and secure the ends. Chill in the refrigerator and serve in slices.

PARSLEY BUTTER

Persillesmør (Denmark)
Persiljesmör (Sweden)

Preparation and cooking time: 5 minutes
Serves: 4, as a condiment

1 big bunch parsley, leaves picked (stalks optional)
120 g/4 oz (8 tablespoons) butter, at room temperature
salt and white pepper, to taste

Follow the recipe for Dill Butter (see left) but substitute the dill with parsley.

PICKLING IN VINEGAR

This basic method of pickling is used all over the world, but especially in Sweden and elsewhere in Scandinavia. No matter what we want to pickle, it is done in much the same way: by lowering the osmotic pressure in the cells of that ingredient with salt, then adding a vinegar-and-sugar solution which, due to the low osmotic pressure, penetrates the ingredient easily.

This method preserves things in two different ways. The first is that less water is less available for bacterial growth because of the salt and sugar. Second – and most important – is that the pH level creates a very acidic environment, which is something microorganisms do not like. A typical pickling liquid in Sweden has a pH level of 3.1 and not many things can survive in that.

Typically, Swedish pickles are preserved in a mixture called *1-2-3 lag* (1-2-3 Pickling Liquor, opposite page), which is one part Ättika vinegar (page 656), two parts sugar and three parts water. This mixture is the base for nearly all Swedish pickles, and is used with different flavourings to preserve everything from beetroot (beets) and gherkins to herring. It can be used for both raw and cooked products and also as a flavouring in itself.

To add to their shelf life, many vinegar pickles can also be pasteurized or canned, although I do not like to do this. I think pickling is enough as it is and I don't particularly like the texture of pasteurized pickles.

PICKLING IN BRINE

This is a very good technique for preserving root vegetables and cucumbers.

Thoroughly clean and rinse your choice of vegetables and peel them if you want. Cut them into pieces, or leave them whole, and put into a sterilized glass jar that is sitting on a weighing scale. When the jar is full and tightly packed, top up with un-chlorinated water and add salt at 2.5% of the total weight. Ensure you leave a 1 cm/½ inch head space and close the lid.

Leave the jar at room temperature (20°C/68°F) for a week or so. During that period of time, loosen the lid every day to relieve the pressure building up in the jar. Check the pH level regularly with litmus paper or a digital pH meter and once it reaches the correct level of around pH 3.3, place in a cool dark space (a cellar is ideal), where it will keep for more than a year.

PICKLING IN SALT

This is a technique I often use with berries that contain a lot of juice, or where a compact texture is desirable.

Thoroughly clean and rinse the berries. Put into a sterilized glass jar that is sitting on a weighing scale. When the jar is full and tightly packed add salt at 2.5% of the total weight and close the lid. Invert the jar a few times so that the salt is evenly distributed in the jar.

Leave the jar at room temperature (20°C/68°F) for a week or so, and turn the jar every day so the salt and the liquid extracted from the berries are evenly distributed. If this is not done properly, the top layers will rot.

Check the pH level regularly with litmus paper or a digital pH meter and once it reaches the correct level of around pH 3.3, place in a cool dark space (such as a cellar), where it will keep for more than a year.

ÄTTIKA

Ättika is a solution of acetic acid in water used as vinegar in the Nordic region. It is most often produced by oxidization of wood alcohol or as a by-product from the paper industry. This crystal-clear vinegar is sold in several concentrations of acetic acid that are suitable for different purposes.

Solutions of acetic acid in water similar to this are available in most countries under different names, – often something along the lines of 'distilled white vinegar' or just 'white vinegar'. In Central Europe it is mostly used for cleaning and is sometimes found around the cleaning supplies.

Below are the Swedish names of the different strengths available here.

Absolut ren ättika 24% is not suitable for consuming before diluting with water, but it is space-saving, in comparison to lower concentrations. It can also be used to polish windows and remove calcium stains on hard surfaces like stainless steel work counters and sinks. If your room smells of smoke or is musty it is said that *Ättika* in a saucer left overnight absorbs the smell. If there is any actual absorption taking place or if it is the smell of the vinegar itself rather covers any previous smell is perhaps a debatable fact.

Ättika / Ättiksprit 12% is what is used in recipes if *Ättika* is mentioned and no other concentration is specified. Equal parts *absolut ren Ättika* 24% and clean water makes *Ättika / Ättiksprit* 12%.

Inläggningsättika 6% can be used straight from the bottle to make unsweetened quick pickles and as a seasoning in cooking. It has a similar concentration of acetic acid (sourness) as vinegar made from wine. One quarter *absolut ren Ättika* 24% and three-quarters water or equal parts *Ättika / Ättiksprit* 12% and water makes *Inläggningsättika* 6%.

Matättika 3% is used mainly as a seasoning in finished dishes or as a condiment. It can be used, for example, on a salad or on a piece of fried fish instead of a squeeze of lemon. One eighth *absolut ren ättika* and seven-eighths of water or a quarter of *Ättika / Ättiksprit* and three-quarters of water makes *Matättika* 3%.

1-2-3 PICKLING LIQUOR

1-2-3 Lag (Sweden)

As a largely non grape-growing region, most Scandinavian pickling has traditionally been done with vinegars produced from other sources of alcohol than wine. This recipe, using *Ättika* vinegar (see opposite), is the base of almost all Swedish-style pickling, from herring to gherkins and beetroot (beet). This sweet-and-sour pickling liquor, which is also common in the other Nordic countries, is very versatile and there is almost no end to the different ways of seasoning and using it in your kitchen.

The name *1-2-3 lag* refers to the amount by volume of each ingredient used. Myself, for the most part I actually make a *1-2-2 lag*, using one part less of water to produce a liquor with a bit more bite.

Preparation and cooking time: 10 minutes
Makes: enough to pickle about 5 kg/11 lb
of ingredients

3 litres/5 UK pints (12⅔ cups) water
2 litres/3½ UK pints (8½ cups) sugar
1 litre/34 fl oz (4¼ cups) *Ättika* (12%)
vinegar (opposite page)

Combine the water with the sugar in a pot big enough to also accommodate the vinegar. Bring to a boil and stir until all the sugar has dissolved into the water. Stir the vinegar into the sugar syrup then cool before using.

Tip: The pickling liquor from fresh-tasting, mild pickles such as gherkins, can be drizzled over salads like a dressing.

QUICK PICKLED CUCUMBER

Ättiksgurka (Sweden)

This sweet-and-sour pickle is most often flavoured with dill-flowers, blackcurrant leaves, mace, white peppercorns and mustard. Use a wholegrain mustard, not one that has been ground, which would make a very cloudy pickle. If you can't find a wholegrain mustard, you can use yellow and brown mustard seeds.

Both whole cucumbers and cucumber slices can be pickled, however I tend to prefer whole ones. If you need slices, you might as well slice them when you are going to serve them. Both special pickling cucumbers and ordinary summer cucumbers can be used here, but the texture of a variety particularly suited for pickling is generally better.

In old recipes, the cucumbers are often brined first and then pickled in a saltless pickling syrup. I have tried this method and can't seem to find any upside to doing this. I prefer to add salt to the syrup so you know exactly what level of salt you will have in the finished product, ensuring consistency in flavour and texture.

In this recipe the hot pickling syrup is poured over the cucumbers, which helps in the preservation of them, but which is also necessary to produce the correct texture and flavour. In many old recipes the pickling syrup was drained off after one week and boiled once more before being poured back onto the cucumbers. I assume that this was to further extend the shelf-life of the finished pickle, but I can't really see that it is necessary; they keep for at least six months anyhow.

Some people add benzoic acid to their finished pickle, but I don't think this is necessary.

Preparation and cooking time: 30 minutes
Pickling time: 1 week
Makes: 1 large pickle jar

1 kg/2¼ lb small pickling cucumbers,
  carefully brushed and rinsed
large bunch of dill-flowers and/or
  blackcurrant leaves

For the pickling liquor

350 ml/12 fl oz (1½ cups) *Ättika* (12%)
  vinegar (page 656)
350 g/12 oz (1⅔ cup) sugar
50 g/2 oz (⅓ cup) salt
15 white peppercorns
2 mace flowers
1 tablespoon wholegrain mustard (or use
  ½ tablespoon each of yellow and brown
  mustard seeds)

Sterilize a large glass pickle jar.

Place the cucumbers (whole or sliced) in the jar, layering them with the dill flowers and/or blackcurrant leaves.

Put the pickling liquor ingredients in a large pot and add 500 ml/17 fl oz (2 cups plus 1 tablespoon) water. Bring to a boil then pour it immediately over the cucumbers, leaving a 1 cm (½ inch) head space.

Seal the jar straight away and store in a cool, dark place for at least 1 week before using.

For images see pages 269, 357

QUICK PICKLED FRESH CUCUMBER

Agurkesalat (Denmark)
Pressgurka (Sweden)

For me, one of the strongest and most vivid childhood memories of summer was my grandmother's refrigerator in late July/early August. The whole bottom section was occupied by a big plastic bowl, brimming over with bright green slices of fragrant and crunchy cucumber. The fresh and clean scent spread into her kitchen with little puffs of cool air each time the door was opened.

In this recipe, slices of cucumber are salted first, the salt drawing out water from its cellular structure, creating a lower osmotic pressure in the cucumber when the pickling liquor is added, resulting in the pickling liquor more or less being sucked into the cucumber slices. As the slices absorb the sweet-and-sour liquor, they plump up a bit again from being shrivelled by the salting and they gain a very particular soft kind of crunch.

Some people peel their cucumbers for this recipe. I don't and never understand why. I like the slight bitterness from the skin, plus it makes a more pretty pickle.

Preparation time: 30 minutes
Pickling time: 2 hours
Makes: enough to last 1 week, which is how
long it will keep if refrigerated

1 kg/2¼ lb cucumbers, rinsed
2 tablespoons fine salt
1 quantity 1-2-3 Pickling Liquor (page 657),
    cooled to fridge temperature

Slice the cucumbers into 2 mm/¹⁄₁₆ inch thick slices on a mandoline or with a sharp knife.

Put the slices in a large mixing bowl with the salt and toss them around thoroughly. Leave to cure for about 15 minutes.

With your hand, gently press the salted slices down towards the bottom of the bowl and, securing them with your hand, pour off the water that has been drawn out by the salt.

Pour in enough pickling syrup to completely cover the slices then transfer the bowl to the refrigerator. Leave them for 2 hours before eating.

The cucumber slices will keep in the pickling liquor stored the refrigerator for about a week. They will be bright green to start with and remain like that for perhaps a day. The colour will gradually change to a military kind of khaki. This colour change doesn't mean the cucumber is bad, but it tends to lose its texture after about a week – not that they are likely to last that long.

For image see page 375

FRESHLY BRINED, UNFERMENTED
CUCUMBER PICKLES

Färsksaltad gurka (Sweden)

This is simply the Brined Cucumber (page 660) in an unfermented stage, meant to be consumed straight away rather than being stored for winter.

Readymade cucumbers like these are often available for purchase in food markets in late summer and early autumn (fall).

For this recipe you can use ordinary slicing cucumbers or pickling cucumbers as opposed to pickling cucumbers only for the fermented version. If fermented, slicing cucumbers tend to go a bit slimy.

The unfermented brined cucumbers are best consumed within a week of making, but should keep if properly made and refrigerated for up to a month.

Preparation and cooking time: 30 minutes
Resting time: 24 hours
Makes: 1 large pickling jar

1 quantity Brined Cucumbers (page 660)

Prepare the brine and sterilize the pickle jar. Add the cucumbers and aromatics to the jar and pour in the brine.

Instead of leaving them in a warm place for 2 days (to encourage fermentation), seal the jar straight away and refrigerate for 24 hours before eating.

BRINED CUCUMBERS

Suolakurkku (Finland)
Saltgurka (Sweden)

This type of preserved cucumber relies on quite high levels of salt to counteract microbial spoilage. Recipes for home use often have a bit of Ättika vinegar (page 656) added to lower the pH-level. However, this will happen naturally, as lactobacillus (which can still live in rather high levels of salt), convert sugars in the cucumber itself to lactic acid, further enhancing its flavour at the same time as it protects it from going bad. Some recipes also include an addition of sugar, to speed up the growth of lactobacillus. I haven't really found this necessary either and I prefer my cucumbers to be brined without sugar or vinegar.

Brined cucumbers are most often seasoned with dill flowers, blackcurrant leaves, cherry leaves, horseradish or a mixture of two or more.

If properly prepared and stored somewhere cool and dark, brined cucumbers can keep for at least a year. If you intend to keep them for a long time and are anxious of mould growing in the jar, then add a bit of benzoic acid to the finished pickle. I, however, have never felt the need for this and I would rather eat my cucumbers untainted by preservatives and throw out the occasional jar that would grow mouldy after half a year or so.

Preparation and cooking time: 30 minutes
Pickling time: 1 month
Makes: 1 large pickle jar

1 kg/2¼ lb small pickling cucumbers,
  carefully brushed and rinsed
75 g/2¾ oz (½ cup) salt (preferably sea salt
  with no added iodine)
big handful of your choice of aromatics

Combine 1 litre/34 fl oz (4¼ cups) water and the salt in a large pot. Bring to a boil and stir to dissolve the salt. Remove from the heat and leave to cool down.

While the brine solution is cooling, sterilize a large glass pickle jar.

Place the cucumbers in the jar, layering them with the aromatics. Pour on the brine, making sure everything is completely covered. You can weight the cucumbers down if you want with a small plate or something heavy as long as it sterilized before.

Cover the jar with a small plate or a layer of muslin (cheesecloth), just to prevent anything from dropping down into it. Place the jar somewhere quite warm (ideally 25°C/77°F) for about 2 days, to allow the fermentation to start. You may see the liquid foam a bit, which is fine. After 2 days, seal the jar and store in a cool, dark place for at least a month before using.

For image see page 403

PICKLED BEETROOT

Syltet rødbeder (Denmark)
Inlagda rödbetor (Sweden)

A common accompaniment to many classic winter dishes, these pickled beetroot (beets) can be flavoured with whatever sweet spices you like. I tend to use some black and white peppercorns, a couple of cloves, a piece of fresh ginger and maybe a bay leaf. Don't add too much though, and don't crush or grind the spices; put them in whole, together with the beetroot.

When you are making the Pickling Liquor (page 657), season it with plenty of salt. Remember that this is a condiment – it should be well seasoned – so don't be shy of the saltiness. And since the beets are already cooked, you can use the pickling liquor warm; you don't have to wait for it to cool down before pouring it onto the vegetables.

Beetroots pickled this way will keep for at least one year if prepared properly and stored somewhere cool and dark.

Preparation and cooking time: 30 minutes
Pickling time: 1 week
Makes: 1–2 large pickle jars

1 kg/2¼ lb red beetroot (beets)
1 quantity 1-2-3 Pickling Liquor (page 657)
your choice of aromatics
salt, to taste

Follow the method on page 115 for boiling the beetroot (beets). Then peel and cut into wedges or slices. Leave the beetroot whole if they are small.

Prepare the pickling liquor following the instructions on page 657.

While the pickling liquor is boiling, sterilize 1 or 2 large glass pickle jars.

Add the beetroot and your choice of aromatics to the jars. Don't worry about mixing them about too much as time will take care of that. Pour on the pickling liquor, leaving 1 cm/½ inch head space. Seal the jars and store in a cool, dark place for at least a week before using.

For images see pages 203, 357 and 403

FAROESE PICKLED TURNIPS

Súltadar røtur (Faroe Islands)

This sweet-and-sour pickle is commonly served as a condiment with Faroese traditional dishes.

The flavourings for *súltadar røtur* varies with the recipes, but can consist of fresh ginger, bay leaf, peppercorns, cloves and or cassia cinnamon sticks.

Pickles like these, if properly prepared, keep for many months if stored in a cool and dark space.

Preparation and cooking time: 1 hour
Pickling time: 2–3 days
Makes: about 1 kg/2¼ lb

1 kg/2¼ lb turnips, peeled and cut into slices
   or wedges
500 ml/17 fl oz (2 cups plus 1 tablespoon)
   Ättika (6%) vinegar (page 656)
500 g/1 lb 2 oz (2½ cups) sugar
your choice of aromatics: bay leaves,
   peppercorns, cloves, cassia cinnamon sticks
   or slices of fresh ginger

Place all of the ingredients in a pot and pour in 500 ml/17 fl oz (2 cups) water. Bring to a simmer then cook until just tender but not soft.

Spoon into some sterilized glass jars leaving a 1 cm (½ inch) head space, cover, seal and let cool to room temperature. Store in a cool dark place for 2–3 days before eating.

QUICK PICKLED PURSLANE STALKS

Sylted portulakk (Norway)

The leafy parts of the purslane plant are traditionally served sautéed or cooked in a similar way to spinach, and the thicker stalks are used for pickling, to be served as a tangy condiment to dishes like Fish Soup from Bergen (page 237). It is also possible to pickle the purslane leaves, but they require less cooking than the stalks. They can be added to the stalks during the last two minutes of their cooking time for a good result.

I have seen recipes that use brown sugar or regular white sugar. Use the one you prefer yourself.

Preparation and cooking time: 20 minutes
Serves: 4

500 ml/17 fl oz (2 cups plus 1 tablespoon)
   Eddik (7%) vinegar
750 g/1 lb 10 oz (3¼ cups) brown or
   white sugar
1 cassia cinnamon stick
5 cloves
1 kg/2¼ lb purslane stalks, cleaned
   and rinsed

Combine the vinegar, sugar and spices in a pot and bring to the boil. Add the purslane stalks and cook for 5 minutes or so, or until just tender.

Transfer the hot stalks to sterilized glass jars. Bring the liquid in the pan to a boil again, then pour it over the stalks, put the lids on the jars and leave to cool down slowly before storing in a cool dark place. Eat within 2 weeks.

BROWNED BUTTER

Brynt smör (Sweden)

Browned butter is an excellent sauce with fish. A piece of perfectly poached white fish, a couple of good spoons of the hot, brown and nutty butter with a wedge of lemon on the side is probably one of the most delicious things there is.

Use only salted butter for this, it will be much more tasty.

Clarified or browned butter will be about 75% the volume or weight of whole butter. I think that about 50 g/2 oz (3½ tablespoons) per person is a good amount if used as a sauce for a main course.

Put the butter a heavy-bottomed pan and melt it over a medium heat. As the butter melts, whisk it continuously to ensure it browns evenly. Whisking also keeps the milk solids that form during the browning process, small. As the butter cooks it will start foaming and then, as the water evaporates, the colour will start to darken and the foam will subside.

Once the solids have turned a medium-dark brown (like the exterior of a good cake) and the foaming has stopped, the butter should smell of lovely toasting hazelnuts. Pour it straight away into a clean pan, to stop the cooking process and avoid burning. Continue whisking the butter off the heat for another minute then serve it immediately.

BASIC FISH SAUCE

This sauce acts as a base for many recipes throughout this book, adapting to different dishes depending on the flavourings.

If you have more stock (broth) to hand than the recipe calls for, reduce until you have the desired quantity, which will make your sauce even more packed with flavour and aroma. If using a cooking liquid that has previously been used to prepare a main dish, just be careful that it doesn't become too salty.

This base recipe contains no seasoning because the sauce is most often used in a recipe that will say

how to finish it. If you want to use it in a recipe of your own, just add salt to taste and your sauce is finished. Remember that a sauce like this will never be better than the base it is made from, so only use great, tasty stocks and cooking liquids.

Preparation and cooking time: 20 minutes
Makes: 400–500 ml/14–17 fl oz (1⅔–2 cups
plus 1 tablespoon) of finished sauce, enough
for 4 people with a main course

30 g/1¼ oz (2 tablespoons) butter
20 g/¾ oz (2 tablespoons) plain (all-purpose) flour
100 ml/3½ fl oz (⅓ cup plus 1 tablespoon) cream
200 ml/7 fl oz (¾ cup plus 1 tablespoon) fish stock or cooking liquid
100 ml/3½ fl oz (⅓ cup plus 1 tablespoon) milk

Melt the butter in a pot and add the flour while whisking. Brown the mixture lightly over a medium heat and, when the desired level of caramelization is achieved, add the liquids, little by little, whisking hard to avoid lumps forming. I usually start with the cream, as I find it the easiest way to achieve a smooth result.

NORWEGIAN BUTTER AND PARSLEY SAUCE / SANDEFJORD SAUCE

Sandefjordsmør (Norway)
Sandefjordsmör (Sweden)

An emulsion of cream, butter and lemon juice flavoured with chopped parsley, this sauce works very well with simple fish dishes.

Remember that butter emulsions like this don't really reheat well, so be careful if you want to make it warmer before serving.

Preparation and cooking time: 10 minutes
Serves: 4

50 ml/2 fl oz (3½ tablespoons) cream
200 g/7 oz (1½ sticks) butter, cold and cut into 1 cm/½ inch cubes
juice 1 lemon

bunch parsley, leaves finely chopped
salt and white pepper, to taste

Pour the cream into a small pot and bring to a boil over a medium heat. Add the butter, a few cubes at a time, whisking all the time.

When half the butter has been added, take the pan off the heat and, still whisking, add the lemon juice.

Gradually whisk in the rest of the butter, then season with salt and pepper before adding the parsley. Serve straight away.

BASIC CREAM SAUCE

Flødesovs (Denmark)
Gräddsås (Sweden)

Preparation and cooking time: 20 minutes
Makes: about 500 ml/17 fl oz (2 cups plus 1 tablespoon)

1 quantity Roux (page 651)
400 ml/14 fl oz (1⅔ cups) stock, broth or
 cooking liquid depending on how
 you are going to use the sauce
150 ml/5 fl oz (⅔ cup) cream
salt and pepper, to taste
Seasoning according the recipe in which the
 cream sauce is included

Heat the liquid in one pot until simmering and keep the roux in the pot it is made in. The pot used to make the roux needs to be large enough to eventually hold all of the liquid.

Add the liquid to the pot with the roux while whisking briskly so that no lumps form. Place the pot over a medium heat and bring to a simmer stirring once in a while. After 5 minutes pour in the cream. Cook for about 10 minutes or until the liquid has thickened and no longer tastes of flour. Season according to the recipe in which you are going to use the sauce.

For images see pages 269 and 375

ONION CREAM SAUCE

Löksås (Sweden)

Often served with slices of Fried Salt Pork (page 302), this sauce should be quite sweet from the onions and a pinch of sugar.

Preparation and cooking time: 30 minutes
Serves: 4

25 g/1 oz (1¾ tablespoons) butter
4 onions, diced or finely sliced
1 tablespoon weak (soft) wheat flour
200 ml/7 fl oz (¾ cup plus 1 tablespoon)
 cream
200 ml/7 fl oz (¾ cup plus 1 tablespoon) milk
pinch of sugar, or to taste
salt and white pepper, to taste

Melt the butter in a pot over medium heat. Add the onions and fry them until they are soft but not coloured. Add the flour and stir for a few minutes. Add the cream, whisking so that no lumps form. Whisk in the milk and bring to a boil. Reduce the heat to low and simmer until it reaches the consistency you want. Season with sugar, salt and pepper to taste.

For image see page 107

BROWN ONION CREAM SAUCE

Brynt löksås (Sweden)

It is less classic, but I actually prefer this brown, a bit more savoury version of the onion cream sauce.

Preparation and cooking time: 30–40 minutes
Serves: 4

25 g/1 oz (1¾ tablespoons) butter
4 onions, diced or finely sliced
1 tablespoon weak (soft) wheat flour
200 ml/7 fl oz (¾ cup plus 1 tablespoon) cream
200 ml/7 fl oz (¾ cup plus 1 tablespoon) milk
1 tablespoon Chinese mushroom soy sauce
pinch of sugar, or to taste
salt and white pepper, to taste

Melt the butter in a pan over medium heat. Add the onions and fry them until they caramelize deeply. Stir frequently to ensure they colour evenly.

Add the flour and stir for a few minutes. Add the cream, whisking so that no lumps form. Whisk in the milk and bring to a boil. Reduce the heat to low and whisk in the soy sauce, then simmer until it reaches the consistency you want. Season with sugar, salt and pepper to taste.

SWEET-AND-STRONG MUSTARD SAUCE FOR CURED FISH

Gravlaxsås / Hovmästarsås (Sweden)

This sauce will be seen on many Nordic tables throughout the year and it is the classic condiment to have with, for example, Gravlax (page 216). It can be finished with some chopped dill and is then called *Hovmästarsås*, 'sauce maître d'hotel' after the practice of the front of house manager who used to finish the sauce in front of the guests in the dining room. This sauce is emulsified but not like a mayonnaise which is really thick and homogenous as it contains egg, but rather like a failing mayo that's almost about to split.

I tend to prefer it without the dill and with a bit of barely crushed mustard seed in there instead. Some Chinese mushroom soy sauce and/or a dash of cold, strong coffee are added to some recipes but not many. If you want to add one of these, substitute half of the vinegar with it.

Preparation time: 15 minutes
Makes: 200 ml/7 fl oz (¾ cup plus 1 tablespoon)

3 tablespoons mustard
3 tablespoons sugar (I like brown sugar but white is probably more common)
2 tablespoons vinegar, red or white wine for a milder acidity and *Ättika* (12%) vinegar (page 656) for a bit more edge
150 ml/5 fl oz (⅔ cup) neutral oil
salt and white pepper, to taste
bunch dill, chopped, or 1 tablespoon mustard seeds, crushed (optional)

Put the mustard, sugar and vinegar into a bowl and stir for a bit until the sugar has almost completely dissolved. Season well with salt and pepper. (You can add these components after adding the oil but it is always better to add them here to avoid any risk of breaking the emulsion.)

Add the oil little by little, stirring continuously until it is all incorporated and the mixture has thickened. Add the dill or mustard seed, if you are using it.

MUSTARD CREAM SAUCE

Sennepssaus (Norway)
Sennepssovs (Denmark)
Senapssås (Sweden)

This sauce is often served with boiled cod.

Use a strong smooth mustard – or one with grains if you want – but not a sweet mustard.

Preparation and cooking time: 10 minutes
Serves: 4

1 quantity creamy Béchamel Sauce (page 666)

1 tablespoon strong mustard
salt and white pepper to taste

Make the cream sauce following the instructions on page 663. Once it reaches the desired consistency, stir in the mustard. Season to taste with salt and pepper.

For image see page 667

CURRY CREAM SAUCE

Karrysovs (Denmark)
Currysås (Sweden)

The Nordic curry sauce, which is a very common and popular thing in almost all of the countries, is served with everything from chicken or beef, to boiled fulmar eggs on the Faroe Islands (page 291). It is really only a cream sauce that is flavoured with a very mild kind of yellow curry powder. Not a fancy one, the supermarket variety – containing plenty of turmeric, some coriander, cumin, fenugreek and cardamom – will give the right aroma.

Preparation and cooking time: 10 minutes
Serves: 4

25 g/1 oz (1¾ tablespoons) butter
2 tablespoons curry powder
1 tablespoon plain (all-purpose) flour
200 ml/7 fl oz (¾ cup plus 1 tablespoon) cream
200 ml/7 fl oz (¾ cup plus 1 tablespoon) milk
salt and pepper, to taste

Melt the butter in a pot over medium heat. Add the spices and stir for a minute to warm through. Add the flour and stir for a few minutes. Add the cream, whisking so that no lumps form. Whisk in the milk and bring to a boil. Reduce the heat to low and simmer until it reaches the consistency you want. Season with salt and pepper to taste.

DANISH-STYLE CURRY CREAM SAUCE (VARIATION)

In some Danish recipes the curry powder is fried in butter with chopped onions and diced apple.

Preparation and cooking time: 20 minutes
Serves: 4

25 g/1 oz (1¾ tablespoons) butter
2 tablespoons curry powder
1 onion, finely chopped
1 apple, peeled, cored and finely chopped
1 tablespoon plain (all-purpose) flour
200 ml/7 fl oz (¾ cup plus 1 tablespoon) cream
200 ml/7 fl oz (¾ cup plus 1 tablespoon) milk
salt and pepper, to taste

Melt the butter in a pot over a medium heat. Add the curry powder, onion and apple and fry until the onion is soft but not coloured. Add the flour and stir for a few minutes. Add the cream, whisking so that no lumps form. Whisk in the milk and bring to a boil. Reduce the heat to low and simmer until it reaches the consistency you want. Season with salt and pepper to taste.

BÉCHAMEL SAUCE

Preparation and cooking time: 30 minutes
Serves: 4

50 g/2 oz (3½ tablespoons) butter
25 g/1 oz (3 tablespoons plus 1 teaspoon)
  plain (all-purpose) flour
500 ml/17 fl oz (2 cups plus 1 tablespoon)
  milk
salt and white pepper, to taste
freshly grated nutmeg (optional)

Melt the butter in a small pot over a medium heat. Remove the pot from the heat and whisk in the flour. Return the pot over a medium heat, gradually whisk in all the milk, making sure the sauce is smooth between each addition. Season with salt. Lower the heat, cover the pot and simmer gently, stirring occasionally, for about 20 minutes. The sauce should be thick enough to coat the back of a spoon and not run off. Season with more salt if necessary, then add pepper and nutmeg, if using. If the sauce is too thick, add a little more milk. If it is too runny, simmer for a bit longer.

For image see opposite page and page 391

UPPSTÚF

Uppstúf is a Béchamel Sauce (see above), seasoned with nutmeg and sometimes a spoon or two of sugar. Commonly served with Icelandic dishes like *Hangilæri* (page 345).

NORWEGIAN WARM SAUCE

Duppe (Norway)

Duppe is a Norwegian sauce based on béchamel. It is made and flavoured differently in almost every part of the country, and it is served with a number of different dishes, which each call for slightly different ingredients. I have included in the following recipes the two most common versions I have come across.

DUPPE TO SERVE WITH FRIED SALT PORK (VERSION 1)

This sauce is prepared with the dripping from a pan of fried salt pork. Sometimes onions are added, and sometimes herbs like parsley or chives are added to finish it. Most of the time, though, it is just the plain sauce.

You can make either a light or a darker version of this sauce by varying how much you brown the flour in the fat before adding the milk.

Preparation and cooking time: 25 minutes
Serves: 4

50–75 ml/2–2½ fl oz pork dripping, from
  frying the salt pork
25 g/1 oz (3 tablespoons plus 1 teaspoon)
  plain (all-purpose) flour
500 ml/17 fl oz (2 cups plus 1 tablespoon)
  milk
salt and white pepper, to taste

Melt the dripping in a pot over medium heat. Add the flour, whisking continuously to ensure it browns evenly. If you want a light sauce, then it should only be barely browned; for a dark sauce, cook until it is deeply amber.

Still over medium heat, gradually add the milk, whisking to ensure the sauce is smooth between each addition. Season with salt and pepper, but remember that the dripping is already quite salty. Lower the heat, cover the pot and simmer gently for about 20 minutes, stirring occasionally. The sauce should be thick enough to coat the back of a spoon and not run off. Season with more salt (if necessary) and with pepper. If the sauce is too thick, add a little more milk. If it is too runny, simmer for a bit longer.

Clockwise from top left: grated horseradish; allspice; Lutefisk (page 230) with Boiled Potatoes (page 117); Mustard Cream Sauce (page 664); Swedish mustard; Norwegian Mashed Peas with dried peas (page 137); Green Peas (page 136); bacon; Béchamel Sauce (page 666); Brown Cheese (page 72); Lutefisk (page 230) on flatbread

DUPPE TO SERVE WITH DUMPLINGS (VERSION 2)

This version of *duppe* is prepared with Brown Cheese (page 72), making it rather sweet in that lactic kind of way and it is most commonly served with Norwegian Potato Dumplings (page 462). Some recipes I have come across also add vinegar, which makes them a bit sweet-and-sour and I like those versions a lot. If you do decide to have a bit of vinegar in there, you need to add it towards the very end, when the sauce is practically done and you have to whisk it in quickly to prevent it from curdling the sauce.

Preparation and cooking time: 20 minutes
Serves: 4

500 ml/17 fl oz (2 cups plus 1 tablespoon) milk
50 g/2 oz (3½ tablespoons) butter
20 g/¾ oz plain (all-purpose) flour
125 g/4½ oz Brown Cheese (page 72), grated
  (either cow or goat is fine)
3 tablespoons sugar
2 tablespoons *Ättika* (12%) vinegar,
  (page 656), optional
salt, to taste

Heat the milk in a pot and stir in the butter to melt it. Leave to cool to room temperature.

Put the flour in a small pot, add around a fifth of the cool milk and whisk until no lumps remain. Whisk in the rest of the milk, set the pot over a medium heat and bring to a simmer. Add the cheese and sugar to the pan and let them melt, stirring continuously.

Season with salt and add a little more milk if the sauce is too thick. If using vinegar, whisk it in briskly, just before serving.

MUSHROOM SAUCE

Svampesovs (Denmark)
Svampsås (Sweden)

A lot of people like the very savoury flavour and dark colour of Chinese Mushroom soy sauce in this recipe. I am not a big fan; I think that mushrooms fried in butter with shallots are savoury enough as it is.

Use any kind of mushrooms that you like, but make sure that they are of a very good quality and not too wet from rain or someone trying to rinse them. If they are wet a lot of that weight will disappear as you cook them so increase Otherwise increase the quantity to 300 g/11 oz and fry them for longer. Cut very large mushrooms into suitable pieces depending on what you like.

Preparation and cooking time: 30 minutes
Serves: 4

25 g/1 oz (1¾ tablespoons) butter
1 shallot, finely chopped
200 g/7 oz mushrooms (girolles, yellowfoot
  chanterelles or porcini)
1 tablespoon weak (soft) wheat flour
200 ml/7 fl oz (¾ cup plus 1 tablespoon) cream
200 ml/7 fl oz (¾ cup plus 1 tablespoon) milk
1 tablespoon Chinese mushroom soy sauce
  (optional)
salt and white pepper, to taste

Melt the butter in a pot over medium heat. Add the shallot and mushrooms and fry until everything is well browned and most of the liquid has evaporated.

Add the flour and stir for a few minutes. Add the cream, whisking so that no lumps form. Whisk in the milk and bring to a boil. Reduce the heat to low and whisk in the soy sauce, if using, then simmer until it reaches the consistency you want. Season with salt and pepper to taste.

HORSERADISH SAUCE

Peberrodssovs (Denmark)
Pepparrotssås (Sweden)

Often served with braised beef cuts like breast or shoulder, this sauce should have a proper 'bite' from the horseradish. In Sweden it is sometimes made sweet-and-sour with vinegar and sugar, something I like a lot.

Make the Velouté (page 652) with 550 ml/18 fl oz (2½ cups) of the cooking liquid from whatever meat you are serving the sauce with.

Preparation and cooking time: 30 minutes
Serves: 4

1 quantity Velouté (page 652)
12 cm/4¾ inch piece fresh horseradish,
  peeled and finely grated on a box grater
salt and white pepper, to taste

Prepare the velouté, following the instructions on page 652.

Return to a simmer over a medium heat. Adjust the seasoning if necessary. Add the grated horseradish, stir well and leave to infuse in the sauce for no more than 30 seconds. Strain the sauce into a clean pot and serve immediately.

SWEET-AND-SOUR HORSERADISH SAUCE (VARIATION)

For a sweet-and-sour version of this sauce, when you make the Velouté (page 652), add 2 table-spoons *Ättika* (12%) vinegar along with the braising liquid. Just before adding the horseradish to the sauce, stir in 3 tablespoons sugar and season with salt and pepper. Finish the sauce by infusing the grated horseradish, as described above. Strain the sauce into a clean pot and serve immediately.

SWEET-AND-SOUR CURRANT SAUCE

Korintsås (Sweden)

Korintsås is a sweet-and-sour sauce traditionally served with Herring Balls (page 200), or in some recipes with salmon.

Preparation and cooking time: 30 minutes
Serves: 4

large handful currants (Corinthian raisins)
25 g/1 oz (1¾ tablespoons) butter

1 tablespoon weak (soft) wheat flour
200 ml/7 fl oz (¾ cup plus 1 tablespoon) Fish
  Stock (page 650)
4 tablespoons golden syrup
3 tablespoons *Ättika* (12%) vinegar
  (page 656)
2 teaspoons Chinese mushroom soy sauce
salt and white pepper, to taste

Put the currants into a pot with 200 ml/7 fl oz (¾ cup plus 1 tablespoon) water, bring to a simmer over a medium heat, then simmer until soft. Strain, reserving both the currants and the cooking juice separately.

Melt the butter in another pot over a medium heat. Add the flour and brown it lightly, whisking constantly. Take the pot off the heat and add the still-warm currant liquid, followed by the fish stock (broth). Bring to a simmer, then add the golden syrup, vinegar and soy sauce. You might have to adjust the amount of syrup and vinegar depending on the sweetness of the currants. The sauce should be distinctly sweet and sour and have a proper vinegar bite.

Season with salt and pepper and add the currants just before serving so that they don't break up too much while you stir the sauce.

SWEET-AND-SOUR DILL SAUCE

Dildsovs (Denmark)
Dillsås (Sweden)

This popular sauce is often served in Sweden with braised veal or lamb. It needs to have a proper sweet-and-sour feeling to it. There should be a good amount of dill in this sauce, not just a few sad fronds floating around. Add the dill at the end; it goes the colour of khaki very quickly because of the acidity and heat. I also like to cut the dill stalks finely and add them for crunch.

Make the Velouté (page 652) using the braising liquid from whichever meat dish you want to serve the sauce with.

Preparation and cooking time: 30 minutes
Serves: 4

1 quantity Velouté (page 652)
3 tablespoons *Ättika* (12%) vinegar
  (page 656)
3 tablespoons sugar, or more to taste
1 big bunch dill, fronds picked, stalks finely
  chopped
salt and white pepper, to taste

Prepare the velouté, following the instructions on page 652, adding the vinegar along with the meat braising liquid.

Return to a simmer and add sugar, salt and pepper until you are happy with the sweet-and-sour balance. Add the dill just before serving.

EGG SAUCE FOR FISH

Munakastike (Finland)
Äggsås (Sweden)

I grew up eating this sauce with poached cod, and in Finland it is often served as part of the dish *Hauki kera muna kastike* (page 165), which is a classic pike recipe.

The sauce is made with a creamy velouté prepared from fish stock – maybe from the bones of what-ever fish you are cooking. Some people finish the sauce with snipped chives, others with parsley, yet others with no herbs at all. I like parsley.

Preparation and cooking time: 20 minutes
Serves: 4

1 quantity creamy Velouté (page 652)
3 cold Hard-boiled Eggs (page 53), peeled,
  shelled and cut into 1 cm/½ inch cubes
1 bunch chives or parsley, chopped
  (optional)
salt and white pepper, to taste

Follow the recipe for the creamy velouté on page 652.

Add the chopped eggs to the hot sauce and stir a little so that the yolks start to dissolve and thicken the sauce a bit more. Season with salt and pepper and add the herbs, if you are using them.

FAROESE SWEET-AND-SOUR SAUCE

Súrsøt sós (Faroe Islands)

Preparation and cooking time: 20 minutes
Serves: 4

400 ml/14 fl oz (1⅔ cups) Beef or Fish Stock
  (page 650)
3 tablespoons sugar, or more to taste
white vinegar, to taste
salt and white pepper, to taste
1 quantity Roux (page 651), optional

Bring the stock (broth) to a simmer in a large pot over medium heat. Stir in the sugar, then add enough vinegar to give the sauce a distinct sweet-and-sour flavour. Season with salt and pepper to taste.

If you like a thicker sauce, then thicken with roux.

PARSLEY SAUCE

Persillesovs (Denmark)
Persiljesås (Swweden)

In this sauce I would skip the nutmeg in the béchamel and go large on white pepper but that's of course up to you.

Preparation and cooking time: 30 minutes
Serves: 4

50 g/2 oz (3½ tablespoons) butter
25 g/1 oz (3 tablespoons plus 1 teaspoon)
  plain (all-purpose) flour
250 ml/8 fl oz (1 cup) milk
250 ml/8 fl oz (1 cup) cream
salt and white pepper, to taste
freshly grated nutmeg, to taste (optional)
1 large bunch parsley, leaves chopped and
  stalks, finely chopped

Melt the butter in a small pot over a medium heat. Remove the pot from the heat and whisk in the flour. Still over medium heat, gradually whisk in all the milk and cream, making sure the sauce is smooth between each addition. Season with salt. Lower the heat, cover the pot and simmer gently, stirring occasionally, for about 20 minutes.

The sauce should be thick enough to coat the back of a spoon and not run off. Season with more salt if necessary, then add pepper and nutmeg, if using. I like this sauce to have a noticeable, nose-tingling sting of white pepper. If the sauce is too thick, add a little more milk. If it is too runny, simmer for a bit longer.

Stir in the parsley just before serving the sauce.

BROWN GRAVY

Brun Sovs (Denmark)
Brunsäs (Sweden)

Brown gravy is served with common Nordic dishes made from minced (ground) meats like Danish Minced Beef Patty with Onions (page 374) or meatballs. At its most basic brown gravy is a dark broth, stock or cooking liquid from the dish it is served with, or a combination of them. It's thickened with Roux (page 651) and then seasoned simply with salt and pepper. Brown gravy is often coloured really dark with gravy browning. Sometimes, especially in Sweden, Chinese mushroom soy sauce is added for colour and additional savouriness.

If you make, for example, minced (ground) meat patties that are fried in a pan, when you are done frying them, deglaze the pan with the stock you are later going to make the sauce with.

If you are making a creamy gravy, substitute 150 ml/5 fl oz (⅔ cup) of the base liquid with cream but do not add it until everything else has simmered for about 5 minutes. If you all the liquid at once there is a chance the cream will curdle if the base is not just a pure stock but a cooking liquid containing some acidity.

Preparation and cooking time: 15 minutes
Makes: about 500 ml/17 fl oz (2 cups plus
  1 tablespoon), or 4 portions

500 ml/17 fl oz (2 cups plus 1 tablespoon)
  tasty broth, stock or cooking liquid, or a
  combination of them
1 quantity Roux, dark (page 651)
salt and pepper, to taste
gravy browning or Chinese mushroom soy
  sauce, to taste

Heat the liquid in a pot until simmering and keep the roux in the pot in which it was made. The pot used to make the roux needs to be large enough to eventually hold all of the liquid.

Pour the liquid gradually into the pot with the roux while whisking briskly so that no lumps form. Place the pot on the stove over medium heat and bring to a simmer, stirring once in a while. Cook for 10 minutes or until the liquid has thickened and no longer tastes of flour. Season to taste with salt and pepper and colour with gravy browning or Chinese soy sauce.

For images see pages 275 and 305

GOLDEN SYRUP GRAVY

Sirapsky (Sweden)

Golden syrup gravy is served with Pork Mince and Rice Cabbage Rolls (page 308) and it should be sweet and salty. Gravy browning and/or Chinese mushroom soy sauce is often added for colour and additional savouriness. Combine all of the liquid that leaks out of the cabbage rolls during the cooking process with some good stock or broth and use this to make the sauce.

Preparation time: 15 minutes
Makes: about 500 ml/17 fl oz (2 cups plus
1 tablespoon), or 4 portions

500 ml/17 fl oz (2 cups plus 1 tablespoon)
  cooking liquid from Pork Mince and
  Rice Cabbage Rolls (page 308) and
  stock or broth
1 quantity Roux, dark (page 651)
70 g/2½ oz (3 tablespoons) golden syrup
salt and white pepper, to taste
gravy browning and or Chinese mushroom
  soy sauce, to taste

Heat the liquid in a pot until simmering and keep the roux in the pot in which it was made. The pot used to make the roux needs to be large enough to eventually hold all of the liquid.

Pour the liquid gradually into the pot with the roux while whisking briskly so that no lumps form. Place the pot on the stove over medium heat and bring to a simmer, stirring once in a while. Cook for 10 minutes or until the liquid has thickened and no longer tastes of flour. Add the syrup, season to taste with salt and pepper and colour with gravy browning or Chinese soy sauce.

CURED COD'S ROE SPREAD

Kaviar (Norway)
Smörgåskaviar (Sweden)

This mix of cured (and often cold-smoked) cod's roe, mixed with potatoes, tomato paste and some oil is eaten in all of the Scandinavian countries and in Finland. In Sweden, *smörgåskaviar* is considered by a broad majority of people to be an absolute essential when eating eggs. It is extremely savoury, due to the curing process, and people who are not used to eating it (read non-Scandis) are often hard to win over.

Very few people make *smörgåskaviar* themselves. It is usually bought in aluminium tubes, a bit like old-fashioned toothpaste tubes. But I thought it would be interesting to see how it is actually done; it is also more delicious to do it yourself.

Oh, and if you have it for breakfast, under no circumstances should you drink orange juice just before eating *smörgåskaviar*. It is one of the least successful combinations of food and beverage known to mankind.

Preparation and cooking time: 1½ hours
Makes: 1.5 kg/3¼ lb

500 ml/17 fl oz (2 cups plus 1 tablespoon)
  cured, cold-smoked cod's roe
500 g/1 lb 2 oz potatoes, boiled, peeled and
  riced and cooled
50 g/2 oz (¼ cup) tomato paste
50 g/2 oz (¼ cup) sugar
250 ml/8 fl oz (1 cup) neutral oil

Push the cod's roe through a fine-mesh sieve to separate the membranes.

Combine all of the ingredients, except for the oil, in the bowl of a stand mixer, and add 100 ml/3½ fl oz (⅓ cup plus 1 tablespoon) water. Drizzle in the oil, a little at a time, as the mixture is being combined as if you were making Mayonnaise (page 674). Make sure the oil is fully incorporated between each new addition.

Distribute between sterilized glass jars, then seal and refrigerate them. The spread will keep for at least a month in the fridge.

For image see opposite page

Top to bottom: Bleak Roe (page 179); trout roe; Cured Cod's Roe Spread (page 672); white fish roe

CURED COD'S ROE CREAM SAUCE

Kaviarsås (Sweden)

Serve with poached white fish.

Preparation and cooking time: 20 minutes
Serves: 4

1 quantity Basic Cream Sauce (page 663)
2 teaspoons Swedish Cured Cod's Roe
  Spread (page 672)
3½ tablespoons finely snipped chives
salt and white pepper, to taste

Make the cream sauce following the instructions on page 663. Once it reaches the desired consistency, stir in the cod's roe spread and chives. Season to taste with salt and pepper, but remember that the spread itself is very salty.

MAYONNAISE

Majoneesi (Finland)
Mayonnaise (Denmark)
Majonäs (Sweden)

I hate mayo that is not thick enough; it should be stiff! If not, it goes very liquid from dilution as soon as it comes in contact with any type of moist food you are eating or mixing it with. Add more oil if it isn't really thick. If you are using it in a sauce that has more liquids in it, or a salad, it could be on the verge of splitting from containing a lot of oil when you mix it with the remaining ingredients. The water content in the thing you are mxing the mayo with will make it perfect as it dilutes it a bit.

Preparation time: 20 minutes
Serves: 4

2 egg yolks
1 tablespoon Dijon mustard
2 tablespoons white vinegar
250 ml/8 fl oz (1 cup) neutral oil
salt and white pepper, to taste

Put the egg yolks in a bowl. Whisk in the mustard and vinegar then season with a pinch of salt and a little white pepper. Add the oil, a drop at a time, beating slowly but constantly, until no oil remains and the mayo is nice and thick. Season to taste.

DILL MAYONNAISE

Dildmayonnaise (Denmark)
Dillmajonäs (Sweden)

If you want a restauranty-looking, bright green mayo, mix the oil and dill in a blender and make the mayo with that oil, rather than a neutral one.

Green mayo with loads of dill kick to it is pretty looking and nice, but I tend to prefer the more grandmotherly – and vastly more delicate – method of just mixing picked dill tips and cut dill stalks into a delicious mayonnaise.

Preparation and cooking time: 5 minutes
Serves: 4

1 good handful dill
1 quantity Mayonnaise (see left)
white vinegar, to taste
salt and white pepper, to taste

Pick the dill into small fronds and chop the stalks finely. Transfer to a bowl with the mayonnaise and mix together well. Taste and add extra vinegar, salt and pepper, if need be.

NOBIS SAUCE

Nobissås (Sweden)

This sauce was created by Swedish chef Werner Vögeli when he worked at the iconic Stockholm restaurant, Operakällaren. It is great with roasted meats, chicken and fish – actually almost anything and everything. It is also great to use as a salad dressing; imagine a bit like you would use the creamy dressing for a Caesar salad – I like to use the Nobis sauce to dress some just steamed kale, cooled down to slightly above body temperature. Not traditional but damned good.

Preparation and cooking time: 10 minutes
Serves: 4

1 egg
1 teaspoon Dijon mustard
2 teaspoons white wine vinegar
1 small clove garlic, finely grated
150 ml/5 fl oz (⅔ cup) neutral oil
2 tablespoons finely snipped chives
salt and white pepper, to taste

Put the egg in a small pan of water and bring to the boil over medium heat. Cook for exactly 3 minutes, and cool under running water.

Crack the egg open with a spoon and scrape the contents into a mixing bowl. Add the mustard, vinegar and garlic and whisk it a bit to break the egg up. Add the oil little by little, whisking the whole time. Add the chives and finish by seasoning with plenty of salt and pepper.

CURED COD'S ROE SPREAD CREAM

Kaviargrädde (Sweden)

Often seen as a little dollop on halved, hard-boiled eggs for Easter dinner in Sweden, this spread is also great on a piece of Rye Crispbread (page 516). It is also used in dishes like Ann-Charlotte's Kipper Casserole (page 211). Some people add dill to the spread; I don't.

Preparation and cooking time: 10 minutes
*Serves: 4, as a spread for bread, or enough to
   top 10 hard-boiled egg halves*

150 ml/5 fl oz (⅔ cup) cream
2 tablespoons Cured Cod's Roe Spread (page 672)
finely chopped dill, to taste (optional)
5 Hard-boiled Eggs (page 53), halved or Rye
   Crispbread (page 516) to serve

Pour the cream into a mixing bowl. Stir the cured cod's roe spread into the cream and start whisking it slowly and carefully. It thickens a lot faster than pure cream, so don't over-whisk or it may split. Fold in the chopped dill, if using, or sprinkle it onto the finished cream.

COLD HORSERADISH SAUCE

Kall pepparrotssås (Sweden)

Preparation and cooking time: 10 minutes
Serves: 4

½ quantity Mayonnaise (opposite page)
100 ml/3½ fl oz (⅓ cup) sour cream
10 cm/4 inch piece fresh horseradish, peeled
   and finely grated on a box grater
a little splash of *Ättika* (12%) vinegar (page
   656), to taste
salt and white pepper, to taste

Combine all the ingredients in a mixing bowl and stir together well. Taste and adjust the balance of seasoning to taste. It should be quite acidic – and strong enough to burn your nose, in a pleasant way.

TARTARE SAUCE

Remember that mayonnaise used for sauces like this needs to be really thick and all the wet ingredients need to be quite dry, otherwise the sauce is not going to be thick enough, don't add too little oil when you make it.

Preparation and cooking time: 10 minutes
Serves: 4

1 quantity Mayonnaise (page 674)
1 shallot, finely chopped
2 Brined or Pickled Cucumbers (page
   656–60), cut into very small dice
1 good handful herbs, chopped (parsley,
   chervil, chives and tarragon are all good)
1 tablespoon finely chopped capers
Dijon mustard, to taste
salt and white pepper, to taste

Spoon the mayonnaise into a mixing bowl. Add the remaining ingredients and stir everything together thoroughly. Taste the sauce and make sure it is seasoned really well. Remember that it is a condiment, so it needs to be really flavourful.

HARD-BOILED EGG AND CREAM SAUCE

Skarpsås (Sweden)

This classic Swedish sauce is great with fish dishes or cold cuts of meat. Some people flavour it with dill while others like it with finely snipped chives or just as it is, plain. Regardless of which, it's important that it is well seasoned. It is a condiment, and it needs to be both salty and acidic enough.

Preparation and cooking time: 15 minutes
Serves: 4

2 Hard-boiled Eggs (page 53)
2 raw egg yolks
1 tablespoon strong mustard
3 teaspoons sugar
4 tablespoons white wine vinegar
200 ml/7 fl oz (¾ cup plus 1 tablespoon) cream
dill or chives, finely chopped (optional)
salt and white pepper, to taste

Press the shelled hard-boiled eggs through a sieve into a mixing bowl. Add the egg yolks, mustard, sugar and vinegar and mix everything together well.

Whisk the cream to soft peaks. Fold into the sauce, then add the herbs (if using) and season well.

VINAIGRETTE

Use a neutral-flavoured oil (like sunflower oil) if you like it or a more flavourful one like olive oil if you prefer that.

Preparation time: 5 minutes
Makes: 150 ml/5 fl oz (⅔ cup)

3 tablespoons white wine vinegar
6 tablespoons oil
Dijon mustard, to taste (optional)
salt and white or black pepper, to taste

Whisk all the ingredients together in a bowl. If you are using mustard, it will emulsify and thicken it a little bit.

CITRONETTE

Add the grated zest of the lemon also, if you want a more aromatic citronette.

Preparation time: 5 minutes
Makes: about 150 ml/5 fl oz (⅔ cup)

50 ml/2½ fl oz (3½ tablespoons) lemon juice (about 1 lemon)
90 ml/3 fl oz (6 tablespoons) neutral oil
Dijon mustard, to taste (optional)
salt and white or black pepper, to taste

Whisk all the ingredients together in a bowl. If you are using mustard, it will emulsify and thicken it a little bit.

BERRY SAUCE

Saftsås (Sweden)

This sauce is made from a concentrated cordial you boiled up in summer. It is often served cold with Rice Pudding (page 626) but is also delicious with other desserts, like ice cream.

Preparation and cooking time: 5 minutes
Serves: 4

100 ml/3½ fl oz (⅓ cup plus 1 tablespoon) concentrated cordial (blackcurrant and raspberry are my favourites)
1 tablespoon potato starch
Rice Pudding (page 626), to serve

Combine the cordial and potato starch in a pan with 200 ml/7 fl oz (¾ cup plus 1 tablespoon) water. Mix until there are no lumps, then bring to a simmer and cook for 2 minutes. Remove from the heat and allow to cool completely before chilling in the refrigerator.

SWEET CHERRY SAUCE

Kirsebærsauce (Denmark)

This is the most common condiment for Danish Almond Rice Pudding (page 628), served at Christmas time.

Most of the recipes I have seen seem to use a ready-bought cherry jam that is diluted with water and thickened with some starch. Quite a few recipes use a little alcohol towards the end. It can be cherry wine, rum, pretty much anything it seems. Add that if you want to.

Serve your cherry sauce warm or cold.

Preparation and cooking time: 15 minutes
Serves: 4

250 g/9 oz cherries, fresh or frozen, pitted
80 g/3 oz (⅓ cup) sugar
cherry wine, rum, or your choice of alcohol,
　to taste
1 tablespoon potato starch
Danish Almond Rice Pudding (page 628),
　to serve

Combine the cherries, sugar and alcohol, in a small pot. Add 200 ml/7 fl oz (¾ cup plus 1 tablespoon) water, bring to a simmer and cook until the cherries are tender. Mix the potato starch with a little water and pour into the pot, stirring constantly. Return to a simmer and cook for another 2–3 minutes.

Add the alcohol, if using, just before serving the sauce.

For image see page 627

CHOCOLATE SAUCE

Preparation and cooking time: 10 minutes
Serves: 4, generously

100 ml/3½ fl oz (⅓ cup plus 1 tablespoon)
　cream
100 g/3½ oz (7 tablespoons) butter
40 g/1½ oz (⅓ cup) cocoa powder
140 g/5 oz (⅓ cup plus 2 tablespoons) golden
　syrup
85 g/3 oz (⅓ cup) sugar
good pinch salt

Combine all the ingredients in a pot and bring to a boil over a medium heat. Simmer until it reaches the consistency you want.

FINNISH FUDGE / CARAMEL SAUCE

Kinuski (Finland)
Karamelsovs (Denmark)
Kinuski (Sweden)

Kinuski is different from other fudge and caramel sauces made in the Nordic countries in the sense that a great part of its flavour profile comes from the aroma of caramelizing lactose – much like French *confiture de lait* or the Latin American *dulce de leche*. The name comes from the Russian word *мянучки* (*tyanuchki*). *Kinuski* was brought to Finland, (commercially, at least), by Karl Fazer, the founder of Fazer, one of Finland's largest producers of processed food and sweets (candy).

In Sweden, where the sauce is also popular, a great deal of confusion exists about what to put in a *kinuski*. Many recipes use butter, which is unthinkable in Finland, and quite a few are also flavoured with dried and ground ginger. These recipes produce a very tasty caramel sauce but not a true *kinuski*.

Finnish recipes vary a bit in the sense that the balance between cream and milk can differ from all milk to all cream – and everything in between. The more cream, the richer the sauce and the more milk, the stronger the flavour of caramelized lactose.

A slow cooking is essential for a proper caramelization, so even though you could achieve the proper colour in a much shorter time, it is essential to let it take its time for a great flavour.

Kinuski is often poured hot over frozen tart berries (like lingonberries) as a dessert. Sometimes ice cream is served on the side.

Preparation and cooking time: 3 hours
Serves: 4

250 g/9 oz (1¼ cups) sugar
250 ml/8 fl oz (1 cup) milk or cream,
  or a mixture of both

Combine the sugar and milk or cream in a pot and heat gently over a low heat. Keep at a low simmer, stirring frequently, until the sauce thickens to a nice consistency, is a good amber in colour and tastes of deeply caramelized dairy. Be prepared for this to take a good 2½–3 hours. If it gets too thick you can add a little more milk towards the end.

If you are uncertain of the correct consistency, it should reach a thick, but still runny sauce at about 105–107°C/220–225°F on a thermometer.

POACHED APPLES STUFFED WITH JAM

Súreplasúlta (Faroe Islands)

Often filled with jam made from rhubarb or berries (page 690), this is served as a condiment with various Faroese dishes.

Preparation and cooking time: 30 minutes
Serves: 4

2 apples, peeled, halved and cored
100 g/3½ oz (½ cup) sugar
4 teaspoons jam (page 690), to serve

Place the apple halves in a pot. Add the sugar and 500 ml/17 fl oz (2 cups plus 1 tablespoon) water and bring to a very low simmer over a medium heat. Move the pot to the side of the stove and leave to rest for about 20 minutes.

Carefully lift the apple halves out of the pot with a slotted spoon and place them, cut side up, on a serving platter. Place a spoonful of jam onto each apple where the core used to be.

BUTTERCREAM

Flavour your buttercream with vanilla or grated lemon zest, according to taste.

Preparation time: 10 minutes
Makes: 400 g/14 oz (1½ cups)

175 g/6 oz (¾ cup) butter, soft
200 g/7 oz (1½ cups) icing (confectioners') sugar
seeds and scrapings of 1 vanilla pod or the grated zest of 1 lemon
1 egg yolk

Beat the butter with the icing (confectioners') sugar and your choice of flavouring until smooth, pale and creamy white. Add the egg yolk and mix until just combined.

CHOCOLATE BUTTERCREAM

Chokladsmörkräm (Sweden)

Preparation and cooking time: 20 minutes
Makes: 400 g/14 oz (1½ cups)

75 g/2¾ oz dark chocolate, coarsely broken into pieces
125 g/4½ oz (1 stick plus 1 tablespoon) butter, at room temperature
160 g/5⅔ oz (1¼ cups) icing (confectioners') sugar
1 egg yolk
2 teaspoons vanilla sugar

Place the chocolate in a heatproof bowl and set over a pot of simmering water to melt. Don't allow the bowl to touch the water. Once the chocolate has melted, stir briefly to ensure no lumps of unmelted chocolate remain.

Combine the butter, icing sugar, egg yolk and vanilla sugar in a medium bowl and mix well until pale and fluffy.

Add the melted chocolate, little by little. It is important not to add it too quickly or to use too hot chocolate, as it will melt the butter and split the emulsion.

WHITE ICING

Glasur (Denmark)
Glasyr (Sweden)

In most Nordic pastries the icing tends to be a bit less firm than in other parts of the world. If using a piping bag, only use a round nozzle because the icing simply won't hold any other shape. In most cases, though, a spoon is a better way to apply the icing. If you are making more elaborate decorations or need very thin lines, such as for gingerbread houses and the like, you will need a slightly thicker and more creamy icing. In this case just substitute the water for an egg white and beat the icing until thick.

Preparation time: 5 minutes
Makes: 300 g/11 oz (1 cup)

240 g/8½ oz (2 cups) icing (confectioners') sugar

Place the icing (confectioners') sugar in a bowl and mix with 2 tablespoons water (possibly a little more). Use immediately.

CHOCOLATE ICING

Chokoladeglasur (Denmark)
Chokladglasyr (Sweden)

Preparation time: 5 minutes
Makes: 300 g/11 oz (1 cup)

240 g/8½ oz (2 cups) icing (confectioners') sugar
2 tablespoons cocoa powder

Place the icing (confectioners') sugar and cocoa powder in a bowl and mix with 2 tablespoons water (possibly a little more). Use immediately.

DANISH PASTRY FILLINGS

Remonce (Denmark)

This French-sounding pastry filling is actually a Danish invention used in many classic baked goods. The brown sugar version is used for Brown Sugar Yeast Cake (page 549) and might contain cassia cinnamon for flavouring. The white sugar version is used for many Danish pastries (page 550) and sometimes contains a bit of egg white. The recipe I use doesn't and seems to work just fine anyhow.

BROWN SUGAR PASTRY FILLING
(VERSION 1)

Mørk remonce (Denmark)

Preparation and cooking time: 10 minutes
Makes: about 375 g/13 oz (1½ cups)

150 g/5 oz (1⅜ sticks) butter, at room
  temperature
250 g/9 oz (1⅓ cups) soft brown sugar
2 tablespoons ground cassia cinnamon
  (optional)

Cream the butter and sugar (and cinnamon, if using) together just before using.

For Brown Sugar Yeast Cake, combine all the ingredients in a small pot and heat gently until they have melted and dissolved to a smooth, shiny consistency.

WHITE SUGAR PASTRY FILLING
(VERSION 2)

Lys remonce (Denmark)

Preparation time: 10 minutes
Makes: about 375 g/13 oz (1½ cups)

125 g/4½ oz (1⅛ sticks) butter, at room
  temperature
125 g/4½ oz (½ cup) sugar
125 g/4½ oz almond paste, grated on the
  coarse side of a box grater

Cream the butter, sugar and almond paste together just before using.

VANILLA PASTRY CREAM

This is a good and versatile recipe for vanilla pastry cream. This is a really thick basic recipe and if you are going to use it on its own, for example with a pie for dessert, whisk 300 ml/10 fl oz (1¼ cups) cream and fold into the custard base just before serving. If you are using it as part of a pastry like the Green Marzipan Layer Cake (page 599), use the base recipe below and add only those things to it specified in the recipe in which it is used.

Preparation time: 30 minutes
Makes: about 500 ml/17 fl oz (2 cups plus
  1 tablespoon)

5 egg yolks
100 g sugar
2 tablespoons cornflour (cornstarch)
250 ml/8 fl oz (1 cup) milk
250 ml/8 fl oz (1 cup) cream
1–2 vanilla pods, split open

Mix the egg yolks, sugar and cornflour (cornstarch) in a bowl and whisk until the sugar has dissolved and everything has turned a bit thicker and lighter.

Pour the milk and cream into a pot, add the vanilla pods and bring to a simmer over medium heat. Remove the pot from the heat and pour a third of the hot milk mixture into the bowl containing the eggs. Whisk so that the eggs don't curdle, then pour everything back into the pot, mixing it with the remaining milk mixture. Stir vigorously until fully combined and place the pot back onto the heat. Stir all the time using a stiff whisk until the cream has thickened, then continue to cook slowly for another 5 minutes, stirring all the time.

Remove the pot from the heat and continue stirring for another couple of minutes, then transfer the very thick pastry cream to a bowl and remove the vanilla pods. Leave to cool to room temperature then transfer to the fridge. Cool to fridge temperature before using or store refrigerated until you need it.

Before you use the pastry cream, you have to stir the cold and very firm cream with a stiff whisk to loosen it up and to make it smooth again. This can be quite tough but you can use a stand mixer if necessary.

JAMS, CORDIALS AND SWEET SOUPS

Previous page: Old barn in a little bit of snow, telephone lines, Jämtland, Sweden, early winter 2014

In a part of the world where vitamin C and many other nutrients can be very scarce during a large part of the year, you can just imagine the effect on the culture of eating and cooking that industrialization of sugar production and the discovery of pasteurization have had.

Before sugar was available in larger cheap quantities and before we could heat a closed jar to kill off the microbes in the product within, preservation of fruit was very difficult and probably not practised much.

It is easy to imagine that people have been eating berries in large quantities all year around since forever, but that is simply not the case. Up until the two factors mentioned above and the time of modern transportation, the joy of eating fruits and berries was largely and with few exceptions a pleasure enjoyed during the short blink of time in summer when these products were naturally ripe and good to eat and before they spoiled.

I think that this might be one important reason among others as to why the preparation of berries and fruit during late summer is still such a beloved and cherished part of Nordic cooking, even though most of us could probably, and do actually, get most of our nutritional needs covered by imported crops through the dark parts of the year.

How we like to eat today is so much more coloured by how we had to eat before than people realize.

Opposite: Interior of north Swedish mountain farm house, Summer 2014.

Opposite: Fjord, Norway, Spring 2014

JAM

Making jam is one of the best ways of preserving fruits. What preserves a jam and keeps it from spoiling is, firstly, that you kill off many unwanted bacteria and microbes with the actual cooking process and that you are able to keep them out by the way you store it. The sugar in jam also reduces the amount of bacteria available to microbes – making it difficult for them to live and multiply, even if they are present in the jam despite the cooking.

A lot of people today see jam as being too sweet and unhealthy. I think this is a real misconception. Jam needs to be a bit sweet in order to keep and to best preserve the character of the fruit used. Yes it contains a lot of sugar but then eat less of it. When you do eat it though, eat a proper homemade one, full of flavour from a distant summer.

When people try to cut down on the amount of sugar in jam, most of the time they have to boil the jam longer to make it set and behave the way they want. This only really means that less fruit makes less jam and the end result is as sweet as if you had added more sugar to start with because you boil away more liquid. As the liquid boils, so do a lot of the aromatics that you want to keep within the jam itself.

To me the actual setting of the jam is relatively unimportant; some jams set easily and others don't. All fruits and berries contain different amount of pectin, and that's just how it is. I focus on how to preserve as much as possible of the flavour, colour and vibrancy of the fruit itself, rather than trying to obtain a thick, marmalade-like texture.

To set jams made from fruit containing very little natural pectin, the usual solution is to add refined pectin to the mixture. I don't do this. If you are using fruit such as raspberries, which do not set naturally, leave it soft and runny; it will be delicious anyway. The amount of sugar in old recipes, though, is sometimes crazily high and will leave fruits lacking in acid, overwhelmingly sweet.

In the old days, when people didn't understand hygiene as well as we do today, sugar was a way of ensuring that their jam didn't go bad. Today it's a bit unnecessary. Carefully following the cooking process described below and by either pasteurizing or sterilizing the finished jars (if you use glass ones) the jam keeps for a really long time anyhow. If you don't want to pasteurize your jam because it seems difficult, don't. Instead, freeze it in suitable containers and take them out one by one as you need them.

A lot of people like to add benzoic acid to keep their jams from going mouldy. I think this is really unnecessary; properly made, it doesn't most of the time.

Lastly, do not cook the jam for too long. Often I see recipes where we are told to cook the jam until it reaches a certain temperature, indicating that it is concentrated enough to set. For every minute longer than necessary that you cook your fruit, the more freshness and primary aroma they will lose. I prefer a jam which tastes vibrantly from the fruit its made but a bit runny before one that is cooked for too long and dull tasting but set.

Choose perfectly ripe, soft fruit with a good amount of acidity in it.

Preparation and cooking time: depends on the size of jars used
Makes: about 1.5 kg/3¼ lb jam

1 kg/2¼ lb soft fruit (such as raspberries, blueberries, cherries or really almost any other soft fruit)
650 g/1 lb 7 oz (3¼ cups) sugar

Place the fruit in a large pot and add a few spoonfuls of the sugar. Leave it to sit until the sugar has dissolved and started to extract the juice from the fruit.

Once a layer of sweet fruit juice has formed in the bottom of the pot, bring it to the boil over gentle heat. Stir it carefully from time to time to ensure that it doesn't burn at the bottom.

When the fruit is perfectly cooked (soft but not completely disintegrated), add the remaining sugar and bring to the boil once more. Skim off any froth that accumulates on the surface during this stage of the cooking.

Preheat a steam oven to 100°C/212°F/Gas Mark ½ and place a thermometer in the centre of the oven. Sterilize equal-sized glass jars and their lids.

Wearing oven gloves, carefully ladle the jam into hot sterilized jars, leaving a 1 cm (½ inch) head space. Screw on the lids loosely, but don't seal the jars tightly. Place the filled jars on a baking sheet and put it in the oven. They will be properly pasteurized when the temperature in the jam reaches 90°C (195°F) and is then maintained at that level for 10 minutes. Check the temperature using a digital thermometer before putting on the lid.

Remove from the oven and seal the lids tightly (wearing oven gloves) and leave them to cool. Store somewhere cool and dark.

For image see page 71

JELLIES

Jellies are cooked fruit juices set with the naturally occurring pectin in them. High pectin fruits, like apples, rowan berries, redcurrants and blackcurrants, are most suitable – unless you want to add refined pectin. If you do, you can use any fruit you like and make it set. Do use a portion of under-ripe fruit in the mix when making a jelly, something that often makes the setting part easier. Pour a spoon of jelly onto a chilled plate and check if it sets when it cools down. If not, then cook the jelly for a bit longer. If your jelly doesn't seem to want to set at all, or if you are using fruits low in natural pectin, follow the instructions on a packet of refined fruit pectin.

I never add benzoic acid or other preservatives to my jellies. I think it is quite unnecessary as jellies are naturally very high in sugar and keep well in any case if you pour the very hot syrup into a sterilized glass jar – or even better, if you pasteurize the jars after filling them (see above).

How much juice any given fruit renders is difficult to say, and I have chosen to write this recipe in a way that accommodates this.

Cut any larger, tougher fruits into small pieces first, then weigh and place in a pot. Add 100 ml/3½ fl oz (⅓ cup plus 1 tablespoon) water for every 1 kg/2¼ lb of fruit. Bring to a slow boil and cook for about 30 minutes, or until the fruits are completely soft. It will take a little time and you shouldn't rush the process. You need a combination of heat and time to dissolve the pectin into the juice of the fruit, which is essential for it to set.

Ladle the cooked fruit into a sieve (strainer) lined with muslin (cheesecloth) set over a large container. Leave to sit for a good 30 minutes so that as much juice as possible can drain from the fruit by gravity alone. Once again, do not rush.

Discard the pulp. Measure the juice and pour it into a new pot. Weigh out 750 g/1 lb 10 oz (3¾ cups) sugar for every litre of juice. Bring the juice to the boil and add the sugar. Return to the boil. With high pectin fruits the jelly will set almost immediately after this first boil but sometimes you have to continue simmering for a bit longer, testing every 5 minutes or so to check if it will set.

Sterilize glass jars and their lids. If pasteurizing, preheat a steam oven to 100°C/200°F/Gas Mark ½ and then place a thermometer in the centre of the oven.

Carefully ladle the hot liquid jelly into the sterilized jars, leaving a 1 cm (½ inch) head space. If you are not pasteurizing, screw on the lids on tightly and store the jars somewhere cool and dark. Otherwise, screw on the lids loosely, place the filled jars on a baking sheet and put it in the oven. They will be properly pasteurized when the temperature in the jelly reaches 90°C (195°F) and is then maintained at that level for 10 minutes.

Remove from the oven and seal the lids tightly (wearing oven gloves) and leave them to cool. Store somewhere cool and dark.

SUGARED LINGONBERRIES

Rårörda lingon (Sweden)

Lingonberries contain a lot of naturally occurring benzoic acid, something that industry adds to many preserves and jams to help them keep. The levels are so high that lingonberries just don't go bad. Thanks to this, there is really no point in boiling them into jam and bottling them; you can just add some sugar for flavour and they will keep in a fairly clean jar at the back of your fridge for years. You can use fresh or frozen berries. It makes no difference to the end result.

Especially in northern Scandinavia and Finland, we eat sugared lingonberries on so many things, sweet and savoury. They all seem to benefit from a good scoop of sweet and astringent ruby loveliness.

Preparation and cooking time: 5 minutes
Resting time: at least overnight
Makes: 650–700 g/1 lb 7 oz–1 lb 8½ oz

500 g/1 lb 2 oz (5 cups) lingonberries
150–200 g/5–7 oz (⅔–¾ cup) sugar

Place the lingonberries and sugar in a large bowl and mix with a spoon. Keep the bowl at room temperature and stir from time to time, until the sugar has dissolved. It should take a while for this to happen, at least overnight. Refrigerate when done.

For images see pages 307, 375, 397 and 459

SUGARED CLOUDBERRIES

Rårörda Hjortron (Sweden)

You can use fresh or frozen berries, it makes no difference to the end result.

Preparation time: 5 minutes
Resting time: overnight
Makes: 650–700 g/1 lb 7 oz–1 lb 8½ oz

500 g/1 lb 2 oz (5 cups) cloudberries
150–200 g/5–7 oz (¾–1 cup) sugar

Put the berries and sugar in a bowl and stir with a spoon. Keep the bowl at room temperature and stir from time to time, until the sugar has dissolved. It shouldn't take longer than overnight. Refrigerate when done.

For image see page 453

TO MAKE CORDIALS

Mehu (Finland)
Saftevand (Denmark)
Saft (Sweden)

Making cordials is one of the best ways of preserve the abundance of high quality fruits from summer. They have been an important source of vitamins and flavour through the dark Nordic winter season.

You can make your cordials either in a pot on the stove, straining the juice through muslin (cheesecloth), or you can make it in a steam juicer. A steam juicer is very simple to work with and makes very little mess, but produces a less concentrated product than making it in a pot. This is because in recipes where the sugar is added into the steamer along with the berries, the dry sugar will absorb a lot of the steam, diluting the syrup more than necessary.

Myself, I like to combine the two methods, making the juice in a steamer but boiling it in pot with sugar. I just think straining the cooked berries the old-fashioned way is unnecessarily messy, and I prefer the convenience of the steam juicer. However, in recipes where the sugar is added into the steamer with the berries, the dry sugar will absorb a lot of the steam, diluting the syrup more than necessary. My way is a little less messy than the more traditional way and it produces a more concentrated result than using the steam juicer alone does.

A lot of people add preservatives to their syrups; I think this is quite unnecessary. Make sure you maintain a good standard of hygiene throughout the preparation process, do not lower the amount of sugar and store your cordials in the refrigerator, and you are going to be fine. Alternatively, pasteurize the filled bottles. If you do this you will be able to keep them at room temperature for a really long time.

Oh, and ideally use only glass bottles. You can use plastic jars or bottles, but then it is better to freeze them for storage.

The glass bottles should be really clean and both them and the corks or caps are best boiled – or steamed if you have a steam oven – just before bottling, so that the bottles are still hot when the syrup goes into them. This is good because it kills most microbes, but also prevents the glass from shattering due to big temperature differences.

The recipes below work with more or less all kinds of soft berries and fruits. The yield can vary by about 500 ml/17 fl oz (2 cups), depending on the variety and quality of the berries used.

You will need 500 g/1 lb 2 oz (2½ cups) sugar per litre/34 fl oz (4¼ cups) of fruit juice.

For this quantity of berries, about 1.25 kg/ 2 lb 12 oz (6¼ cups) is about right.

Preparation and cooking time: 1½ hours
Makes: about 3 litres/5 UK pints (12½ cups) cordial

3 kg/6¾ lb soft fruits or berries
sugar

IN A POT ON THE STOVE (VERSION 1)

Bring 500 ml/17 fl oz (2 cups plus 1 tablespoon) water to the boil in a pot which is large enough to accommodate all of the berries. Once the water boils, add the berries and cover with a lid. Boil for 10–15 minutes until the berries look cooked and shrivelled. While they are boiling, stir once or twice so that the fruit cooks evenly. Don't stir more than this, however, as you don't want to crush the fruit unnecessarily; it will make the straining process slower and harder if there are a lot of small particles floating around in the juice.

Ladle into a large sieve or strainer, lined with muslin (cheesecloth) set over a large container, and leave the juices to drain through by gravity alone for 1 hour.

Meanwhile, clean the pot. Once the cooked berries have drained, measure the resulting juice and return it to the pot. Weigh out the required amount of sugar (see above) and add it to the pot. Bring to the boil, then lower the heat and simmer for 5 minutes, skimming the surface thoroughly every now and then.

Carefully transfer to hot sterilized bottles using a ladle and a funnel. Seal the bottles and leave to cool.

IN A STEAM JUICER (VERSION 2)

Put the fruit and 1.25 kg/2 lb 12 oz (6¼ cups) sugar into the fruit compartment of your steam juicer. Fill the bottom section with water. Assemble the steamer by sitting the fruit compartment on top of the part that collects the juice and position them both on top of the bottom section. Put on the lid and make sure that the hose that drains from the juice reservoir is clamped off.

Turn the heat up to medium and wait for steam to form. It's important to ensure that there is always water in the bottom section during the steaming process. Steam for about 45 minutes, or until the berries have cooked and released their juice.

Carefully unclamp the hose and drain the fruit syrup straight into hot sterilized bottles. Seal the bottles and leave to cool.

MAGNUS'S WAY (VERSION 3)

Follow the instructions for steaming, but don't add any sugar to the berries. Once they've yielded all their juice, instead of bottling it, measure it out, then transfer it to a large pot.

Weigh out the required amount of sugar (see page 693) and add it to the pot. Bring to the boil, then lower the heat and simmer for 5 minutes, skimming the surface thoroughly every now and then.

Now comes the clever part; instead of fiddling with a ladle and funnel, disassemble your steam juicer and pour the syrup into the juice reservoir. Now you can carefully unclamp the hose and drain the fruit syrup straight into hot sterilized bottles. Seal the bottles and leave to cool.

CORDIAL SOUP

Saftsuppe (Denmark)
Saftsuppe (Norway)
Mehukeitto (Finland)
Saftsoppa (Sweden)

Cordial soups are often served as warm or cold snacks or as dessert. I remember growing up, that when we went for an outing with school, my parents often packed a thermos of warm cordial soup in my backpack.

Cordial soups can be accompanied by things like Almond Biscuits (page 566), Sweet Rusks (page 574), whipped cream or ice cream, pieces of fruit or berries, or even cottage cheese. Sometimes cordial soups are themselves served as a condiment with Rice Porridge (page 466) or Rice Pudding (page 626).

In Norway, a variation of this soup is made with rolled oats or pearl barley (see right).

Any cordial can be used, but the ones made from red fruits are preferred.

Preparation and cooking time:
 10 minutes
Makes: 1 litre/34 fl oz (4¼ cups)

1 litre/34 fl oz (4¼ cups) cordial, made
    with water to the level of sweetness and
    concentration desired
2 tablespoons potato starch
sugar, to taste

Mix all the ingredients together in a pot and bring to the boil over medium heat. Once it boils, pour through a sieve (strainer) to remove any lumps of starch from the finished soup.

For image see page 627

CORDIAL SOUP WITH OATS
OR BARLEY

Saftsuppe med havregryn / bygg (Norway)

Preparation and cooking time: 10 minutes
Makes: 1 litre/34 fl oz (4¼ cups)

1 litre/34 fl oz (4¼ cups) cordial, made
    with water to the level of sweetness and
    concentration desired
100 g/3½ oz (1 cup plus 3 tablespoons)
    rolled oats or (½ cup) pearl barley
sugar, to taste

Mix all the ingredients together in a pot and bring to the boil over medium heat. Simmer for a few minutes until the grains are soft and the soup has thickened.

SWEET BLUEBERRY OR BILBERRY SOUP

Blåbærsuppe (Norway)
Mustikkakeittoa (Finland)
Blåbærsuppe (Denmark)
Blåbärssoppa (Sweden)

Blueberry soup is very commonly drunk in the wintertime from a thermos when you are out skiing. You can either leave the broken, cooked berries as they are in the soup (which I do), mix it with an immersion blender after the cooking stage, or strain them out altogether.

Bilberry soup can be served as a snack, or it could be served with some Almond Biscuits (page 566) and a dollop of whipped cream for dessert.

Preparation and cooking time: 20 minutes
Serves: 4

750 g/1 lb 10 oz (5 cups) blueberries
  or bilberries, fresh or frozen
80 g/3 oz (⅓ cup plus 1 tablespoon) sugar,
  plus extra to taste
2 tablespoons potato starch

Place the berries in a large pot with the sugar and pour in 750 ml/25 fl oz (3 cups) water. Bring to a simmer over medium heat and cook for 5 minutes.

In a small bowl, mix the potato starch with a couple of tablespoons of cold water, then stir it into the soup. Return to the boil and cook until it thickens, then taste and adjust the sweetness to your liking with a little sugar.

For image see page 697

CHERRY SOUP

Körsbärssoppa / Spottsoppa (Sweden)

Use either sweet or sour cherries, whichever you prefer, and vary the amount of sugar according to taste and type of fruit used. If you leave the pit in the cherries through cooking, the soup is called *spottsoppa* in Swedish, which refers to the fact that you would have to spit out the pits when you eat the soup later. I like this because it gives a nice bitter almond kind of aroma to the soup. Serve it warm or cold with whipped cream and/or Sweet Rusks (page 574).

Some people like to add a piece of cassia cinnamon, a couple of cardamom pods or a piece of vanilla pod to their soup.

Preparation and cooking time: 20 minutes
Serves: 4

750 g/1 lb 10 oz (5 cups) fresh cherries
80 g/3 oz (⅓ cup plus 1 tablespoon) sugar,
  plus extra to taste
1 cassia cinnamon stick, 1–2 cardamom
  pods or a vanilla bean (optional)
2 tablespoons potato starch

Pit the cherries if you wish, then put them in a large pot with the sugar and your choice of flavourings. Add 750 ml/25 fl oz (3 cups) water, then bring to a simmer over medium heat and cook for about 5 minutes.

In a small bowl, mix the potato starch with a couple of tablespoons of cold water, then stir it into the soup. Return to the boil, then taste and adjust the sweetness to your liking with a little sugar.

ROSEHIP SOUP

Nyponsoppa (Sweden)

I remember, growing up, having this soup – which is very commonly prepared in Sweden from a mix bought in supermarkets – with ice cream and almond biscuits as a snack in the afternoon. I think that almost no one actually makes it themselves from real fruit, which is a pity. It is much more delicious.

The soup can be made from both fresh or dried rosehips but I actually prefer dried ones because I find it is easier to get the right concentration to it. If you happen to have fresh rosehips available, just use twice the amount as dried. Skip the soaking part of the method, discard any leafy/twiggy parts before cooking them, but leave the seeds in. Start with a bit less water to make sure the soup doesn't taste too diluted in the end.

Preparation and cooking time:
  20–40 minutes
Soaking time: overnight
Serves: 4

400 g/14 oz (5 cups) dried rosehips
sugar, to taste
squeeze of lemon juice (optional)
1–2 tablespoons potato starch (optional)

Soak the dried rosehips overnight in 1 litre/34 fl oz (4¼ cups) water.

Transfer the rosehips and their soaking liquid to a pot. Bring to a simmer and cook until tender.

Use an immersion blender to purée the soup, or use a sturdy whisk to break up the rosehips. You won't be able to crush the seeds, at least not without breaking your blender. Push the mixture through a fine sieve back into the cleaned-out pot and discard the skins and seeds.

Taste the soup and add sugar to taste and lemon juice if you want a bit of extra freshness. Bring to the boil over medium heat and adjust the thickness of the soup, if you need to, by adding some potato starch mixed with a few tablespoons of cold water.

For image see page opposite

SOUP OF DRIED FRUITS

Mehukeitto (Finland)
Frugt Suppe (Denmark)
Fruktsoppa (Sweden)

Serve warm or cold as a dessert or a snack in between meals. Flavour with a stick of cassia cinnamon, some vanilla, cardamom or grated lemon zest if you want to.

Preparation and cooking time: 20 minutes
Soaking time: at least 3 hours, but preferably
  overnight
Serves: 4

250 g/9 oz (1¼ cups) mixed dried fruit
  (choose from dried apple, raisins, prunes,
  apricot or any other dried fruit)
1 cassia cinnamon stick, 1–2 vanilla beans,
  2–3 cardamom pods, or the grated zest of
  a lemon (optional)
sugar, to taste
1 tablespoon potato starch
juice of 1 lemon juice, to taste

Soak the dried fruit in 1 litre/34 fl oz (4¼ cups) water for at least 3 hours, but preferably overnight. If any of the fruits have swollen into dimensions too large to eat in one piece, then cut them into smaller pieces and return them to the soaking liquid.

Transfer the fruit and soaking liquid to a large pot and add your choice of spiced flavourings as they will need to simmer with the fruit for a bit. Taste and adjust the sweetness to your liking with a little sugar. Bring everything to a simmer over medium heat and cook for about 5 minutes.

In a small bowl, mix the potato starch with a couple of tablespoons of cold water, then stir it into the fruit soup. Return to the boil and cook until it thickens, then add lemon juice and the grated lemon zest, if using, to taste.

For image see page opposite

Clockwise from top: Berry Compote (raspberry), page 701; Danish Berry Dessert with Cream (page 636); Almond Biscuits (page 566); Sweet Blueberry Soup (page 694); Rosehip Soup with Cream (page 696); Soup of Dried Fruits (page 696)

APPLE SOUP

Æblesuppe (Denmark)
Äppelsoppa (Sweden)

Serve warm or cold as a dessert or a snack. Some recipes I have read include a piece of cassia cinnamon stick or some vanilla beans as flavourings.

Preparation and cooking time: 30 minutes
Serves: 4

4 crisp apples with plenty of acidity, peeled, halved and cored
1 litre/34 fl oz (4¼ cups) fresh apple juice
80 g/3 oz (⅔ cup) raisins
1 cassia cinnamon stick or 1–2 vanilla beans (optional)
sugar, to taste
2 tablespoons potato starch
lemon juice, to taste

Cut each apple half into about 6 thin wedges.

Combine the apple juice and raisins in a large pot and add your choice of cinnamon stick or vanilla beans, if using. Bring to the boil, then taste and adjust the sweetness to your liking with a little sugar.

Add the apple wedges to the pan and simmer for about 15 minutes, or until they start to soften.

In a small bowl, mix the potato starch with a couple of tablespoons of cold water, then stir it into the apple soup. Return to the boil, then taste again and adjust the sweet-sour balance with more sugar or lemon juice, to taste.

RHUBARB SOUP

Rabarbersuppe (Denmark)
Rabarbersoppa (Sweden)

Enjoy warm or cold for dessert or as a light snack with a dollop of whipped cream or vanilla ice cream and a handful of Almond Biscuits (page 566) or some Sweet Rusks (page 574).

Preparation and cooking time: 20 minutes
Serves: 4

500 g/1 lb 2 oz (4–6 sticks) rhubarb, chopped
sugar, to taste
2–3 tablespoons potato starch

Bring 700 ml/24 fl oz (3 cups) water to the boil in a pot over a medium heat. Add the rhubarb and cook until it is tender, then stir in sugar, to taste. How much the rhubarb will break down depends on how young and tender the sticks are to begin with.

In a small bowl, mix the potato starch with a couple of tablespoons of cold water. Stir it into the soup and return to a simmer. Take off the heat. Serve warm or leave to cool completely.

GOOSEBERRY SOUP

Stikkelsbærsuppe (Denmark)
Krusbärssoppa (Sweden)

Enjoy warm or cold for dessert or as a light snack with a dollop of whipped cream or vanilla ice cream and a handful of Almond Biscuits (page 566) or some Sweet Rusks (page 574).

Preparation and cooking time: 20 minutes
Serves: 4

680 g/1 lb 8 oz (4¼ cups) fresh gooseberries
sugar, to taste
2–3 tablespoons potato starch

Bring 500 ml/17 fl oz (2 cups plus 1 tablespoon) of water to the boil in a pot over a medium heat. Add the gooseberries and cook until they are soft. They should not be raw, but rather, they should burst open a little and be warm all the way through.

Stir in the sugar. You will need more if the gooseberries are tart and less if they are sweet and ripe.

In a small bowl, mix the potato starch with a couple of tablespoons of water. Stir it into the soup and return to a simmer. Take off the heat and serve immediately or leave to cool for later.

PRUNE SOUP

Luumukiisseli (Finland)
Sveskesuppe (Denmark)
Katrinplommonkräm / Sviskonkräm
  (Sweden)

Prune Compote (page 701) – the classic condiment to Finnish desserts like Semolina Oven Pancakes from Åland (page 634) – can be diluted with more water to a soup-like consistency and served as a sweet soup, warm or cold, perhaps with a dollop of cream.

SAGO PEARLS

Sago pearls are small (3 mm/⅛ inch) round grains made from starch derived from the Southeast Asian true sago palm tree (*Metroxylon sagu*). Sago pearls have been important and widely used in the Nordic countries since the mid-eighteenth century. The traditional use was to thicken mainly sweet soups like Yellow Sago Pearl Soup (see right), Red Sago Pearl Soup (page 700) and Sago Pearl Milk Soup (page 700). Today most of the recipes that used sago pearls instead use tapioca pearls, which are more commonly found in grocery stores.

Sago pearls are naturally white, but may also be coloured in many different shades.

SWEET SAGO PEARL SOUPS

Sagosuppe (Denmark)
Sagogrynssoppa (Sweden)

Not seen very often these days, sweet soups thickened with sago pearls used to be commonly served as a popular snack in the afternoon or as a dessert. They can be served warm or cold and they often have raisins or prunes mixed into them just before serving.

I like to cook my sago pearls so that they are still a little bit uncooked in the centre. This makes them look kind of like little frogs eggs and provides a bit more texture than if you boil them all soft.

YELLOW SAGO PEARL SOUP

Gul sagosuppe (Denmark)

Preparation and cooking time: 20 minutes
Makes: about 1 litre/34 fl oz (4¼ cups)

50 g/2 oz (½ cup) sago pearls
4 egg yolks
100 g/3½ oz (½ cup) sugar
juice and finely grated zest of 1 lemon
2 tablespoons good dark rum
1 handful raisins or prunes

Pour 1 litre/34 fl oz (4¼ cups) water into a large pot and bring to the boil. Add the sago pearls while whisking, so that they don't stick together. Boil for 5–7 minutes, or until the grains are cooked, but still a little firm in the centre.

While the sago pearls are cooking, whisk the egg yolks with the sugar until white and fluffy. Add the lemon juice and zest and the rum to the egg mixture and mix well. Pour in the hot sago and cooking liquid which will have thickened a little, then add the raisins or prunes to the soup and serve.

RED SAGO PEARL SOUP

Rød sagosuppe (Denmark)

Preparation and cooking time: 20 minutes
Makes: about 1 litre/34 fl oz (4¼ cups)

1 litre/34 fl oz (4¼ cups) raspberry cordial,
  made with water to the level of sweetness
  and concentration desired
50 g/2 oz (½ cup) sago pearls
1 handful raisins or prunes

Pour the raspberry cordial into a pot and bring to
the boil. Add the sago pearls while whisking, so
they don't stick together. Boil for 5–7 minutes, or
until the grains are cooked, but still a little firm in
the centre. Add the raisins or prunes and serve.

SAGO PEARL MILK SOUP

Sagovælling (Denmark)
Sagovälling (Sweden)

In Sweden this recipe in older books is prepared
with a piece of vanilla bean to flavour the milk
and is served with sugar. In Denmark it is cooked
without the vanilla and served with ground cassia
cinnamon and sugar, which you sprinkle on top
to taste when it is served.

Preparation and cooking time: 20 minutes
Makes: about 1 litre/34 fl oz (4¼ cups)

1 litre/34 fl oz (4¼ cups) milk
1 teaspoon sugar, plus extra
  to serve
a small pinch salt
80 g/3 oz (¾ cup) sago pearls
⅓ vanilla bean (optional)

Combine the milk, sugar and salt in a large pot,
add the piece of vanilla bean, if using, and bring
to the boil. Add the sago pearls while whisking, so
that they don't stick together. Boil for 5–7 minutes,
or until the grains are cooked, but still a little firm
in the centre. Serve immediately, sprinkled with
extra sugar and cassia cinnamon, if using.

RHUBARB COMPOTE

Rabarberkompot (Denmark)
Rabarberkräm (Sweden)

Serve warm or cold for dessert, or as a light meal
with cold milk and some sugar sprinkled on top.

Preparation and cooking time: 20 minutes
Serves: 4

530 g/1 lb 3 oz rhubarb, chopped
sugar, to taste
2–3 tablespoons potato starch

Bring 500 ml/17 fl oz (2 cups plus 1 tablespoon)
water to the boil in a pot over a medium heat. Add
the rhubarb and cook for 10 minutes, or until tender. Stir in the sugar.

In a small bowl, mix the potato starch with a couple
of tablespoons of water. Stir it into the compote
and return to a simmer. Remove from the heat and
serve immediately or leave to cool for later.

APPLE COMPOTE

Æblekompot (Denmark)
Äppelkräm (Sweden)

A classic dessert served warm or cold, often in a
bowl with milk or cream poured over it. Can be
flavoured with cassia cinnamon, cardamom pods
or grated lemon zest. The sweet and sour balance
is important. If your apples are not tart enough,
add a dash of lemon juice towards the end.

Preparation and cooking time: 20 minutes
Serves: 4

500 g/1⅛ lb peeled, cored and diced tart apples
90 g/3¼ oz (⅓ cup plus 1 tablespoon) sugar
2 tablespoons potato starch
cassia cinnamon stick, lemon zest and juice,
  or lightly crushed cardamom seeds,
  to taste (optional)

Combine the apples, sugar and your choice of
spice flavourings in a large pot. Spices will need

to simmer for a bit with the fruit. Pour in 500 ml/ 17 fl oz/(2 cups plus 1 tablespoon) water, bring to the boil and then reduce the heat. Simmer until the apples begin to soften all the way through.

In a small bowl, mix the potato starch with a couple of tablespoons of cold water. Stir it into the compote and bring to the boil once again. Adjust the balance of sweetness and acidity and add any more fragile seasoning like the lemon zest.

PRUNE COMPOTE

Luumukiisseli (Finland)
Sveskekompot (Denmark)
Katrinplommonkräm / Sviskonkräm
  (Sweden)

This compote is the classic condiment for the Semolina Oven Pancake from Åland (page 634).

Preparation and cooking time: 20 minutes
Makes: 400 ml/14 fl oz (1⅔ cups)

150 g/5 oz (⅔ cup) pitted prunes
1 tablespoon sugar
1 tablespoon potato starch

Put the prunes and the sugar in a pot and pour in 300 ml/10½ fl oz (1¼ cups) water. Bring it to a simmer over a medium heat, then cook for about 5 minutes, or until the prunes are soft.

In a small bowl, mix the potato starch with a few tablespoons of cold water. Whisk it into the compote, then bring it back to a simmer and cook until it thickens. Some of the prunes will break up and others will remain in one piece.

GOOSEBERRY COMPOTE

Stikkelsbærkompot (Denmark)
Krusbärskräm (Sweden)

Serve warm or cold for dessert, or as a light meal with cold milk and perhaps a sprinkle of sugar.

Preparation and cooking time: 20 minutes
Serves: 4

500–700 g/1 lb 2 oz–1½ lb fresh gooseberries
sugar, to taste (more if the berries are tart
  and less if they are sweet and ripe)
2–3 tablespoons potato starch

Bring 500 ml/17 fl oz (2 cups plus 1 tablespoon) of water to the boil in a pot over a medium heat. Add the gooseberries and cook until they are done. They should not be raw, but rather, they should burst open a little and be warm all the way through. Stir in the sugar.

In a small bowl, mix the potato starch with a couple of tablespoons of cold water. Stir it into the compote and return to a simmer. Take off the heat and serve immediately or leave to cool for later.

BERRY COMPOTE

Bærkompot (Denmark)
Bärkräm (Sweden)

Serve warm or cold in a bowl for dessert, or as a light meal with cold milk poured over it and perhaps some sugar sprinkled on top.

Preparation and cooking time: 20 minutes
Serves: 4

500–700 g/1 lb 2 oz–1½ lb raspberries,
  blueberries or strawberries, rinsed
  and hulled if necessary
sugar, to taste
2–3 tablespoons potato starch

Put three-quarters of the berries in a large pot and pour in 500 ml/17 fl oz (2 cups plus 1 tablespoon) of water. Bring to a simmer over a medium heat, then stir in the sugar.

In a small bowl, mix the potato starch with a couple of tablespoons of cold water. Stir it into the compote and return to a simmer. Add the rest of the berries, then take off the heat.

For image see page 697

DRINKS

Previous page: Electrical substation, north Norway, end of Winter 2014.

Alcoholic drinks in the Nordic region

The Nordic region has no significant viticulture today, and no historical production of wine either. People have, like in all parts of the world, used what they had at hand also when making alcoholic drinks.

All of the Nordic countries except Denmark and the Faroe Islands are considered belonging to the so-called 'vodka belt', a region spanning a large part of the northernmost parts of the northern hemisphere. The vodka belt is defined as a region where distilled spirits have historically been the dominant part of alcohol culture.

The raw material of choice for making beer is malted barley and, for distilled spirits, also other grains and rarely potatoes, something more common in the Baltics and further east.

Denmark also has a tradition of distilled spirits but not the same drink-half-a-bottle-of-raw-alcohol-as-a-thirst-quencher-thing. But rather more balanced, as part of a central European drinking culture where you drink less at a time but a bit more often. Historically and also today the Danes have had a larger proportion of their total alcohol consumption coming from beer, more like the culture of neighbouring Germany.

The way alcohol is consumed in the Nordic region has changed a lot over the past twenty years or so, becoming more like the rest of the western world and less like it was before. We have moved away from drinking almost exclusively hard liquor and beer and more towards a mix of different drinks, with wine and beer in domination.

Historically, the northern Nordic countries were places where almost no alcohol was consumed during the weekdays, and then, during the weekends, everything was consumed at once. To drink during the week would have been a sign of extremely poor character or even alcohol abuse. This is really the polar opposite of the more central European way, where drinking a glass of wine or a beer now and then is something no one raises an eyebrow about whilst if they saw a group of people in a public area drinking themselves unconscious on a Saturday, that would be considered most peculiar and probably rather shameful.

The destructive way of consuming alcohol in the Nordics has in most parts of the region, at different times, been addressed by both Church and state. Church on moral grounds like elsewhere and state from the mixed stance of trying to help its drunken citizens while at the same time, making big money on alcohol tax. In the Faroe Islands, Finland, Sweden, Norway and Iceland, the sale of alcohol has long been monopolized, and at times people were given a ration, the size of the allowance depending on factors like, sex, age, income and position in society.

There have also been times of prohibition in most of the countries belonging to the vodka belt; on Iceland, for example, beer was forbidden up until 1989.

The Faroe Islands, which historically have had some of the strictest alcohol laws in the whole world, where sale of alcohol was more or less forbidden until 1992 and what little alcohol there was being sold before that was rationed, has now also got six state-owned stores for the distribution of alcoholic beverages.

Opposite: A bottle of Jaffa orange soda, the preferred beverage with grilled lampreys (page 176) unless they are served with the distilled neutral spirit Koskenkorva (page 731).

Following page: Dancing and drinking, Thorshavn, a Friday night in early May 2012.

Opposite page: Red cottages, Vega Archipelago, Norway, Spring 2014.

DISTILLED NEUTRAL SPIRIT IN THE NORDIC COUNTRIES

Brennivín (Faroe Islands)
Brennevin (Norway)
(Palo)Viina (Finland)
Brændevin (Denmark)
Brännvin (Sweden)

Vodka is Russian and even though neutral, distilled spirits from the Nordics are usually called so, especially when they are exported, this name is a novelty, not much used for domestic Nordic products until maybe fifty or sixty years ago.

These spirits, which are made from potato, grains and historically also cellulose, usually contain between 30% and 40% alcohol by volume. The practice of making drinkable alcohol from cellulose was eventually abandoned because it is less energy efficient than other methods, and today it is forbidden within the European Union, which allows only agricultural products to be used for this purpose.

Distilled spirits have been produced in the region since the fifteenth century and have mostly, with the exception of short times of national prohibition laws in some countries, been a big part of the drinking culture in a part of the world that produces no wine because of its climate.

The distilled neutral spirits are either consumed as they are, in cocktails or flavoured in different ways, for example in Aquavit (see below).

AQUAVIT

Akvavitt (Faroe Islands)
Ákvavíti (Iceland)
Akevitt (Norway)
Akvaviiti (Finland)
Akvavit (Denmark)
Akvavit (Sweden)

The name aquavit derives, like many other liquors, from the Latin phrase, *aqua vitae*, 'water of life'. Aquavit is a neutral spirit most often distilled from potato or grains, which have been flavoured before bottling. It is mainly produced in Scandinavia, and has been since the sixteenth century.

Many people, even those from the Nordic countries, tend to confuse aquavit and the Danish/Swedish term 'schnapps'. However, snaps is not the name for an actual beverage but, rather, the more general word for a small shot of liquor drunk from a special schnapps glass. Aquavit can be served as a snaps – and often is – but a snaps doesn't necessarily have to be aquavit, it could really be any hard liquor.

To classify as an aquavit the alcoholic strength needs to be above 37.5% alcohol by volume and the beverage needs to contain either caraway or dill, aside from whatever else it might have been flavoured with. There are hundreds of flavourings of aquavit, below is a list of a few commercially available, emblematic and popular ones:

Lysholms Linie Aquavit (Norway): caraway seeds, dill, bitter orange, fennel, plenty of oak
Løitens Export Aquavit (Norway): caraway seeds, aniseed, fennel, orange rind, plenty of oak
Aalborg Jubilaeums Akvavit (Denmark): dill flowers, coriander seed and very light oak
Rød Aalborg | Aalbord Taffel Akvavit (Denmark): caraway is completely dominant in both aroma and flavour, strong at 45% alcohol by volume
OP, Andersson (Sweden): caraway seeds, aniseed, fennel, very light oak
Skåne Akvavit (Sweden): caraway seeds, aniseed, fennel

Aquavit is drunk with many traditional meals all over the Nordic region and is considered especially important for festive occasions like Christmas, Easter and Midsummer. Few things cut though the fatty and salty foods that make up a lot of the traditional Scandinavian food culture.

MARSHALL MANNERHEIM'S AQUAVIT

Marskin ryyppy (Finland)

Marshall Mannerheim (1867–1951), Finnish war hero and later President, was a lover of fine foods and has had considerable influence on Finnish food culture. One of the recipes that he is associated with is *Marskin ryyppy* – the Marshall's shot or drink. The blend itself was invented by Ragnar Grönvall, his aide, when he was asked by the Marshall to do something about the flavour of the bad quality vodka that was part of the army rations.

Marskin ryyppy should be served ice-cold in a stemmed schnapps glass poured so full that the level of the beverage itself is above the actual rim of the glass, only surface tension preventing it from spilling. It is supposed to be picked up and drunk in one mouthful without spilling and this tradition is said to come from the Chevalier Guard.

Preparation time: 10 minutes
Makes: 1 litre/34 fl oz (4¼ cups)

500 ml/17 fl oz (2 cups plus 1 tablespoon)
   Extra Aquavit
500 ml/17 fl oz (2 cups plus 1 tablespoon)
   Finnish table liquor, Pöytäviina or vodka
4 teaspoons Noilly Prat vermouth
2 teaspoons gin

Mix all of the ingredients together. Done!

SALTY LIQUORICE VODKA

Salmiakkikossu / Salmari (Finland)

This mix of Viina and salty liquorice (page 577) is as emblematic of Finland as anything. Made from Koskenkorva Viina, the most commonly consumed distilled spirit in Finland and a brand of salty liquorice called *Tyrkisk Peber* ('Turkish pepper'), it is even available from Finland's state monopoly liquor stores as a pre-mixed cocktail called *Salmiakkikossu*.

It is unclear when the practice of producing this drink started, but it seems to have been first made sometime during the 1980s or 1990s in Finland and has spread to the salty liquorice-loving countries of the Nordics since, using whatever ammonium chloride-laced sweets (candies) are preferred locally.

I remember during high school that some people (never myself, obviously) took a three-quarter full bottle of vodka, added the salty liquorice to it, put the cork on again and then ran the sealed bottle through a dishwasher, the heat quickly melting the sweets, fusing them into the liquor. For the recipe below I suggest that you *don't* do that unless you are *really* in a hurry.

Preparation time: 10 minutes
Macerating time: 1 week
Makes: about 1 litre/34 fl oz (4¼ cups)

700 ml/23 fl oz (2¾ cups) neutral grain spirit,
   about 40% alcohol by volume
250 g/9 oz salty liquorice sweets (candies),
   such as *Tyrkisk Peber* or *Ga-Jol*

Mix the ingredients together in a sterilized glass bottle or lidded jar. Seal tightly and leave at room temperature for a week, or until the sweets have dissolved. Agitate the jar from time to time to speed up the process. Serve very cold in shot glasses.

GAMMEL DANSK

Gammel Dansk (Denmark)

One of the most iconic Danish beverages of today is actually not really that old. In 1964 work started on the development of the bittersweet herbal liquor that was eventually launched in 1967. *Gammel Dansk* is drunk on many different occasions and also at breakfast, especially with Danish pastries.

The bottle reads '*Gør godt om morgenen, efter dagens dont, under jagten, på fisketuren eller som aperitif*'. This means something like, 'Good for you in the morning, after a day of toil, when you are hunting or fishing, or as an aperitif'.

Gammel Dansk is flavoured with twenty-nine different botanicals of which star anise, Seville orange, cinnamon, angelica and gentian are the most recognizable. A select few people at the company producing the beverage know the full recipe.

SWEDISH CHRISTMAS COCKTAIL

Mumma (Sweden)

At its simplest and most original, this beverage consists of only porter beer (dark beer), a sweet fortified wine (like port or Madeira) and a Swedish soft drink (soda) called *sockerdricka*. Today, most recipes for *mumma* also contain gin and some of them contain cardamom and different citrus flavourings as well. *Mumma* is a popular drink to have with Christmas dinner.

Make sure that the serving jug (pitcher), glasses and all the ingredients are ice cold when you start; it will foam like nothing you have ever seen otherwise.

Preparation time: 10 minutes
Makes: 1 litre/34 fl oz (4¼ cups)

500 ml/17 fl oz (2 cups plus 1 tablespoon)
    porter beer, chilled
330 ml/11 fl oz (1⅓ cups) *sockerdricka* or
    another lemonade, chilled
100 ml/3½ fl oz (⅓ cup plus 1 tablespoon)
    sweet Madeira, chilled
50 ml/2 fl oz (3½ tablespoons) gin, chilled
1 lemon
pinch of finely ground cardamom,
    to serve

Carefully pour all the liquids into a large chilled jug (pitcher). Grate the lemon zest on top and stir very gently.

To serve, pour into chilled serving glasses and add a pinch of cardamom to the foam. It's in no way traditional, but I also like to keep the lemon to hand so that anyone who wants to can add a squeeze of the juice to their own glass. I think this is delicious.

MOONSHINE

Landi (Iceland)
Hjemmebrent (Norway)
Pontikka (Finland)
Hjemmebrændt (Denmark)
Hembrännt (Sweden)

The Nordic region – especially in the big farming countries of Scandinavia and Finland – has historically had a big tradition of making illegal hard liquors at home. It used to be a real problem for governments, with people producing large quantities for sale and often of questionable quality. This practice has been reinforced by very high alcohol taxes and the state monopolization of alcoholic beverages. The connection can really be seen in the difference between, for example, Denmark which has low taxes, no monopoly and a very small tradition of home distilling and Sweden, which has both high taxes and a state monopoly and which up until about twenty years ago, had a huge level of illegal alcohol production.

When I was growing up, it was a matter of pride for the distiller to produce the strongest and cleanest brew possible, and many people built very elaborate miniature distilling machines, such as reflux stills – normally only seen in big industry – which could produce industrial-grade strength and quality spirits.

Even though taxes have gone down and many people bring in cheaper alcohol from within the European Union, home distilling is still quite common, especially in the north. Today, most people that still brew do it for themselves and, it seems to me, mostly for fun. The raw materials used can range from sugar and water to a mash made from potato or grains.

FINNISH CUT BRANDY

Jaloviina (Finland)
Ädelbrännvin (Sweden)

Jaloviina is a popular Finnish beverage made from imported brandy, grain spirits and possibly a little caramelized sugar for colour and to round it off a bit. The more brandy the final product contains, the less sugar will generally be added.

Jaloviina is produced in four grades:

0 Stars, very little brandy
1 Star, 33% brandy
2 Stars, 50% brandy
3 Stars, 75% brandy

JALOVIINA AND PUNSCH COCKTAIL

Kullager (Finland, Sweden)

Kullager means 'ball bearing', and this classic drink consists of equal parts *jaloviina* (page 716) and *punsch* (see below). Mix the well-chilled spirits together and pour into a highball glass with a couple of ice cubes just before serving.

SWEDISH PUNSCH

Punsch is a sweet liqueur based on arrack, an alcoholic beverage made from rice or molasses and the sap from coconut flowers, fermented into a mash, which is then distilled.

Arrack should not be mistaken for arak, the traditional anise seed-flavoured drink from countries like Lebanon, Iraq, Syria, Jordan, Palestine, Israel, Turkey and Iran.

Most of the arrack used in *punsch* is imported from Indonesia and is called Batavia Arrack, after the old Dutch name for Jakarta, which was the capital of the Dutch East Indies.

Punsch consists of arrack, black tea, sugar, lemon and water. It should have an alcohol strength of about 25% alcohol by volume and it can, but doesn't have to, be aged in oak barrels.

During the time *punsch* was popularized it was drunk warm, like strong alcohols in general, a practice that has lived on until today. *Punsch* is either served heated to just above body temperature or served ice cold. The drink is most commonly served in a little mug or cup with a handle, even though a suitable glass is in my opinion more enjoyable for cold punsch.

Punsch is pretty much only enjoyed in Sweden and in Finland and in addition to being an absolutely essential beverage with Split Pea Soup (page 140), it is also commonly drunk in academic and student culture.

The commercially available punsch of today is very sweet and, comparing it to older recipes, it seems safe to say that it has grown sweeter and blander in seasoning from both tea and citrus.

Punsch was introduced to the Swedish palate during the first half of the eighteenth century when arrack was for the first time imported by the Swedish East Indian Company – that time the base alcohol came from Java.

It is difficult to give a good recipe for *punsch*, because different teas are tannic to different degrees and lemons too are not all the same. The recipe below can serve as a guideline but you have to taste it yourself and decide if it tastes good. Remember that it is not a cocktail, it is a liqueur, it needs to have some concentration to it.

When I make *punsch* I want it to be sweet, but with fresh acidity and a good mouth-drying, tannic feeling from the tea.

ARRACK FLAVOURED LIQUEUR

Punssi (Finland)
Punsch (Sweden)

Preparation time: 10 minutes
Sitting and maturing time: 4 weeks
Makes: about 2 litres/3½ UK pints (8¼ cups)

1 litre/34 fl oz (4¼ cups) battavia arrack
500 ml/17 fl oz (2 cups plus 1 tablespoon)
   black tea, so strong that it would cure your
   tongue if you tried to drink it
juice of 6 lemons
250 g/9 oz (1¼ cups) sugar or 400 g/14 oz
   (1¼ cups plus 1 tablespoon) honey, or
   a mix of 150 g/5 oz (¾ cup) sugar and
   200 g/7 oz (⅔ cup plus 1 tablespoon) honey

Mix all of the ingredients together in a bowl, add the sugar and/or honey last and add until you are satisfied with the taste. Remember that it is a liqueur, not a cocktail, so it should be sweet. Strain and transfer to sterilized bottles. Place the bottles somewhere cool and dark to rest for a month or so before consuming. The resting will make the liquid clearer in appearance and more balanced in flavour.

PEOPLE'S BEER / FOLKÖL, A UNIQUELY SWEDISH BEER

Folköl (Sweden)

In Sweden, beer is divided into three taxation categories, each with different sales and consumption rules: light beer, beer and strong beer. Light beer, or *lättöl*, falls below 2.25% alcohol by volume, and strong beer, or *starköl*, is any malt beverage over 3.5% alcohol by volume. Between these two thresholds, practically wedged in between the boundaries of soda and real beer, a special product called *folköl* – people's beer – exists. Strong enough to get you drunk (if barely), but not strong enough to be sold only at the state monopoly chain of liquor stores (*Systembolaget*). Malt beverages containing less than 3.5% alcohol by volume are considered foodstuffs, and therefore they can be sold at ordinary food stores – although only to people over eighteen years of age.

Folköl is generally consumed by those people who want to have a beer with their food or just by itself on a weekday but don't want to drink too much alcohol. But it's also bought by those who want to get drunk but who can't get access to stronger alcohol – mainly those underage, or those who have turned eighteen but are not yet twenty so they can't go to the *Systembolaget*, which funnily enough has an age limit of twenty, even though at eighteen you are allowed to consume any alcoholic beverage in your own home or in a bar.

This particular beer has been shaped into what it is because of the alcohol policy of a country and the way its population consumes alcohol but, incidentally, a lager-style *folköl*, served icy cold, might be one of the most refreshing beverages ever produced by man.

HVIDTØL

Hvidtøl (Denmark)

Hvidtøl is a traditional Danish beverage, which is usually produced with an alcohol content of less than 2% abv. Historically it has been very popular and commonly drunk all year round. Today it is mostly drunk around Christmas, especially with the rice pudding called *Risalamande* (page 626). *Hvidtøl* means 'white beer', but it is actually a very dark beverage. The name comes from the time when malt dried in kilns started to replace the older method of production, which was to dry it over an open fire, a technique that produced a smoky malt and therefore a smoky-tasting beer. *Hvidtøl* is quite sweet from unfermented sugars and it resembles Swedish *Svagdricka* (page 719) a little in that aspect. *Hvidtøl* is also used in a very old Danish dish called *Øllebrød* (page 474). Today *Hvidtøl* can also be completely free of alcohol and more of a malt soda.

MULLED WINE

Glögi (Finland)
Gløgg (Denmark)
Glögg (Sweden)

The Nordic names for this warm and sweet Christmas drink come from the word *glödga*, meaning 'to heat'. The tradition of serving spiced hot wine dates back to Roman times and has been popular in the Nordic countries at least since the early seventeenth century. By the mid-nineteenth century it has been possible to buy bottles of pre-flavoured wine to heat. It is available today in countless variations made from different wines with different flavourings and also in non-alcoholic versions.

Mulled wine in the Nordics is generally drunk from special handled cups or glasses that hold between 50–75 ml/2–2¼ fl oz of liquid. Common accompaniments to mulled wine are raisins and blanched almonds, which are spooned into the cups by each drinker.

In Norway, Finland and Sweden the drink is often served at Christmas as a sort of snack with Scanian Thick and Chewy Gingersnaps (page 562) and in Sweden and some parts of Finland also with Saint Lucy's Day Saffron Buns (page 544). In Denmark *gløgg* can also be paired with *Æbleskiver* (page 540). Mulled wine can also be part of the traditional Christmas dinner – either served before as an aperitif or to go with the dessert.

There are as I mentioned countless versions of this mulled wine but I have included two: one that I like, which is fresher in acidity than the most common ones, and one that is based on a blackcurrant cordial (page 692) and therefore free of alcohol.

MAGNUS'S GLÖGG (VERSION 1)

Many old recipes for mulled wine in the Nordic state that you are supposed to make a kind of essence from the aromatics and hard liquor that you then add to the sweetened wine. I prefer to mix everything together and keep it in a glass jar rather than a bottle, aromatics macerating in the wine itself before being strained as you pour the *glögg* into a pot to heat and drink it.

Choose a young red wine, not too tannic and not too oaky. I like to use a not-too expensive Burgundy or another pinot noir of that style. For the brandy, do not use a too-oaky one, but rather a young fruity kind. Often a simpler and cheaper one from the bottom range of the brands is perfect.

Preparation and cooking time: 30 minutes
Macerating time: at least a week
Makes: 1 litre/34 fl oz (4½ cups)

750 ml/25 fl oz (3 cups) young red wine
1 knob fresh ginger
1 vanilla bean
5 cardamom pods
20 cloves
2 cassia cinnamon sticks
10 black peppercorns
1 orange, sliced (rind and all)
1 lemon, sliced (rind and all)
100 ml/3½ fl oz (⅓ cup plus 1 tablespoon)
   sweet Madeira
150 g/5 oz (¾ cup) sugar
a dash of Cognac or Calvados
3 tablespoons honey, or to taste

Combine all of the ingredients, except the honey, in a sterilized, lidded glass jar. Seal tightly and leave to macerate for at least a week. Agitate the jar from time to time so that the sugar doesn't just sit at the bottom but dissolves into the wine.

When you are ready to drink the wine, strain it through a fine-mesh sieve straight into a pot. You don't have to use it all at once; you can strain just the amount you need and leave the rest to continue macerating. If the spices become too strong, then add a splash more red wine as you heat it, and perhaps some extra sugar.

Heat the wine gently, adding honey until you think it is sweet enough.

ALCOHOL-FREE GLÖGG (VERSION 2)

To make a *glögg* without alcohol, some people just boil one that had alcohol in it. I don't much like this as it completely destroys the aromas of the beverage. I prefer to make one from a blackcurrant cordial (page 692) instead.

Follow the recipe for Magnus's Glögg (see left), but substitute the total amount of alcohol 850 ml/29 fl oz (3⅓ cups plus 1 tablespoon) with a strong mix of Blackcurrant Cordial and water.

Since it contains no alcohol, it is possible for the mixture to start fermenting if you are unlucky. Also cordial isn't quite as effective at drawing flavour out of the spices.

To ensure a good result, bring the cordial to the boil with the sugar, then carefully pour the boiling liquid onto the aromatics in a heatproof sterilized glass jar. Cover with a lid, seal tightly and leave to macerate for around 3 days. Strain through a fine-mesh sieve and freeze if you are not going to use it straight away.

When ready to serve, heat the *glögg* gently, adding honey until you think it is sweet enough.

COFFEE AND HARD LIQUOR

Karsk (Norway)
Kask (Sweden)

Kask is a drink made from a long, strong, hot coffee and hard liquor. Either vodka or Moonshine (page 716) would traditionally be used and perhaps, if served in a restaurant or bar, other spirits like Cognac or whisky would come into question.

For the proper balance of alcohol and coffee, place a coin in a white coffee cup. Add coffee until the coin is no longer visible, then add liquor until you can see the coin once again. The above guideline is a traditional one and the one I was taught. Technically it is ridiculous though, since no two kinds of cups or coins will give the same relationship between coffee and liquor. The depth, diameter and the angle of the cup's sides all create different lighting at the bottom of the cup, not to mention the variation of intensity from whatever light is available where you are mixing.

Anyhow, equal parts of coffee and liquor give the drink the proper bite to warm you when it's chilly outside. Make sure the coffee is piping hot so it doesn't cool too much when you add the liquor.

FINNISH MAY DAY BREW

Sima (Finland)
Finskt Valborgsmjöd (Sweden)

This beverage, which has its origin somewhere in the mead family of drinks and which was, in the past, made from honey, is today most often made from white and/or brown sugar and water. *Sima* is flavoured with lemon and is drunk before all the sugar has been consumed by the yeast cells and turned into alcohol. It should be fresh and fruity tasting, with a light sparkle. It is predominantly drunk on *Vappu,* the Finnish May Day, and is often served alongside the traditional Finnish May Day Funnel Cakes (page 556), which are also an integral part of many Finns' 1st of May routines.

The slightly odd-looking addition of 5 raisins is actually very clever. They will ferment alongside the brew itself and puff up like little balloons with CO_2. When they float up to the surface, the *sima* is ready to drink.

Sima should be consumed within a week of being made and if you keep it too long or at too warm a temperature, beware of the risk of bottles exploding due to a continuous build-up in CO_2 pressure from the on-going fermentation.

This recipe has been adapted from one for 10 litres/21 UK pints (10½ quarts), divided by ten, hence the very tiny and difficult-to-measure-accurately looking amount of yeast. It will still be fine if it differs fractionally either way.

If you like the flavour of honey, then add 2–3 tablespoons honey to the recipe and reduce the amount of sugar to 80 g/3 oz (⅓ cup plus 1 tablespoon).

Preparation and cooking time: 15 minutes,
  plus cooling time
Fermenting time: about 4 days
Makes: 1 litre/34 fl oz (4¼ cups)

100 g/3½ oz (½ cup) brown sugar
  (or use half brown and half white
  sugar)
juice and grated zest of 1 lemon
5 raisins
1 g/0.03 oz yeast

Put the sugar into a large pot and add 800 ml/28 fl oz (3¼ cups) water. Bring to the boil, then remove from the heat and leave to cool down to room temperature.

Add the lemon juice and zest and the raisins. Dissolve the yeast in a tablespoon of the liquid, then whisk it into the water; as with anything that is going to ferment, some initial aeration is good to get things started.

Pour into an appropriate sterilized container, cover and leave at room temperature for 24 hours. Ideally, use a dedicated fermentation vessel that has a special airlock valve.

Stir the *sima,* then decant into sterilized bottles. Seal tightly and leave for another 24 hours at room temperature. Refrigerate for at least 2 more days before consuming.

GOTLANDIAN JUNIPER AND HONEY BEER

Gotlandsdrikku (Sweden)

This is a very ancient form of beer from the Swedish island of Gotland in the Baltic Sea. It is related to the Finnish beer, *sahti* (see right), in the sense that it dates back to a time before hops were grown in the Nordics and has stayed hopless.

Gotlandsdrikku is brewed from malt, water and honey or sugar. The sugar obviously being quite a recent addition, not older than the access to cheap sugar, which began during the twentieth century. Original recipes were definitely based on locally produced honey from the island. The flavouring of *Gotlandsdrikku* can vary between juniper (much like *sahti*) and bog myrtle, commonly used in Sweden to flavour Aquavit (page 714).

Gotlandsdrikku is semi-sweet and can contain anything between 5% and 15% of alcohol by volume. It is best consumed fresh and should not be stored for more than two weeks.

SWEET SMALL BEER

Svagdricka (Sweden)

Sweet or semisweet, low-alcohol malt beverages have been consumed all over Europe since the Middle Ages as an everyday drink.

In the Nordics it was and usually still is brewed to about 2% alcohol by volume and is most of the time produced with the addition of hops or juniper. In Sweden sweet small beer is often sweetened with the artificial sweetener, saccharin.

Sales of sweet small beer have declined dramatically, partly because now, as opposed to during the Middle Ages, most people have access to drinkable water. After industrialization and the introduction of commercially branded soft drinks and sodas, during the twentieth century, sales of sweet small beer further decreased.

FINNISH JUNIPER BEER

Sahti (Finland)

Sahti is a very old type of beer, still common in Finland. It is made from a mixture of light and dark malts and it contains no hops. Instead it is flavoured with juniper berries. *Sahti* is brewed with baker's yeast rather than brewer's yeast and therefore has a high content of isoamyl acetate, giving it a distinctive character of banana or artificial, almost candy-like fruit.

After the mashing, the beer is strained through a trough-shaped wooden strainer called a *kuurna*. This strainer is usually built from a hollowed-out log of about 2.5 metres/8 feet in length (see illustration below). The log is placed so that one end is a little bit lower than the other end. The lower half, which has a drainage hole, is then lined with juniper branches. The mash, still containing all the grains, is poured into the top end and on its way, pouring from one end to the other, the brew is simultaneously filtered and flavoured by the juniper branches.

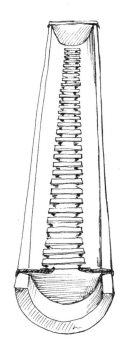

SUGAR WINE / SUGAR MASH

Kilju (Finland)
Mäsk (Sweden)

Generally considered the cheapest way of getting drunk, this variety of homebrew, which is also usually used when distilling *pontikka*, or Swedish *hembrännt* Moonshine (page 714), is not commonly consumed as it is. Often associated with underage drinking and heavy drinkers who can't afford other alcohol, it is still a part of the Scandinavian drinking culture and deserves a place in this book.

Properly made, mash like this contains around 15% alcohol by volume. It has a crystal-clear appearance and very little flavour except that of the ethanol itself. Often, though, when you see mash being consumed it is clouded by yeast deposits that have not been properly racked off or filtered away and it generally has a very funky aroma from poor production hygiene.

In Finland it is forbidden to ferment sugar wine from only sugar and water and therefore a few token raisins or slices of orange are often added to the mix straight into the fermentation vessel. If consumed, sugar wine is commonly mixed with orange juice or another fruit juice.

Preparation time: 30 minutes, plus cooling
Fermentation time: 2 weeks
Makes: 10 litres/21 UK pints
  (10½ quarts)

2 kg/4½ lb (10 cups) sugar
50 g/2 oz brewer's yeast
raisins or slices of orange (optional)

Mix the sugar with 9 litres/19 UK pints (9½ quarts) water in a large pot and bring it to the boil over a high heat. Carefully pour the piping hot liquid into a suitable, scrupulously clean container, cover with a lid and leave it to cool to room temperature. Ideally, use a dedicated fermentation vessel that has a special airlock valve.

From this point on the liquid is very susceptible to unwanted microorganisms, so don't touch it with your hands or use non-sterile equipment. Wear rubber gloves, boil all utensils before using and try to keep the lid on as much as is possible.

Dissolve the yeast in a few tablespoons of the liquid, then add it to the rest of the liquid and whisk in well. Cover the container again and leave to ferment at room temperature until it stops bubbling. , It can take anything from 5–10 days.

Transfer the container to a chest freezer and chill the whole thing to 0°C/32°F – it won't actually freeze because of the alcohol content – which makes the yeast fall to the bottom of the container as a sediment leaving a clear, clean liquid above.

With the aid of a hose, carefully transfer the sugar wine to sterilized glass bottles, taking care not to disturb the yeast sediment. Cover with lids and seal. Sugar wine doesn't benefit from aging so drink it when fresh and store it in the refrigerator.

MILK AS A DRINK IN THE NORDIC COUNTRIES

Dairy is a very prominent part of Nordic food culture, especially in the Scandinavian countries and Finland. The island nations, which have more complicated circumstances for farming, have a slightly less dairy-centric history.

Milk has been drunk as long as people have lived in the Nordics, but the extreme quantities enjoyed during the twentieth century and up until today are a relatively new occurrence.

Historically, milk from cows, sheep and goats was a great way of converting the summer sun into storable goods. Even though people surely drank milk, there was simply less of it available than there is today because farming was less efficient, hygiene was poorer and modern transportation not yet been invented, meaning that fresh milk was only available to those who had animals of their own.

After the industrial revolution, with more efficient farming methods, pasteurization, refrigeration, efficient transportation and other modernities, milk became a bigger part of people's everyday intake of food. For many, it even became the preferred choice of beverage to accompany food – something very uncommon in other parts of the world. This development was actively supported by the government and by farmers' associations, like the Swedish *Mjölkpropagandan* – a lobbying organisation for dairy producers formed in 1924.

Today, all the Scandinavian countries and Finland are found at the top of those consuming the most dairy products in the world. Finland is the undisputed number one, clocking in at an astonishing 361 kg/795 lbs of milk consumed per inhabitant per year (latest complete data). By comparison, the Americans, who landed in sixteenth place, also quite high, consumed a mere 253 kg/557 lbs in the same year.

I love to pour myself a big glass of ice-cold milk to drink with a helping of salt pork and lingonberries.

SWEDISH MALT SODA

Must / Julmust / Påskmust (Sweden)

This Swedish spiced malt soda was introduced to the country in 1910 and has since become an indispensable institution for festive occasions such as Easter and Christmas, when it is sold under the names *julmust* (meaning Christmas must) and *påskmust* (meaning Easter must). Coca-Cola, which is, like most other parts of the world, very popular here, experiences a drop in sales every December of about 50%, attributed to the sales of *julmust*.

The word *must* derives from the Latin *vinum mustum*, meaning 'young wine', or fresh (unfermented) grape juice and the original recipe was invented by the Roberts family as a non-alcoholic alternative to beer. Today, even though many brands of the beverage exist, they all buy their raw materials from the Roberts company, based in the mid-Swedish town of Örebro where only three people know the actual recipe.

Each brewer is allowed to decide for themselves on the concentration of raw material in relation to water and how much sugar to add – something which gives every brand a unique flavour.

Julmust is an excellent match with the salty foods of a traditional Swedish Christmas.

FINNISH SEMISWEET FERMENTED RYE MALT DRINK

Kotikalja / Kalja / Vaarinkalja (Finland)

One of several Finnish homebrews, like *sima* (page 718) and *sahti* (page 719). *Kalja* is today most often made from a mix of sugar and liquid rye malt, water and yeast. These products can be purchased pre-packaged and prepared in Finland. This recipe has a more traditional approach, where ground rye malt is used instead. *Kalja* is not left to ferment dry but is rather drunk in mid-fermentation, semisweet and lightly sparkling within only a few days. Because almost none of the sugar has been consumed by the yeast by the time you drink it, it will be very low in alcohol. In most of the recipes I have seen *kalja* is unflavoured. However, a few juniper berries in the brew is not entirely uncommon, hops though are very rarely used.

Preparation and cooking time: 20 minutes,
  plus cooling time
Fermentation time: at least overnight
Makes: just over 1 litre/34 fl oz (4¼ cups)

130 g/4½ oz (⅔ cup) sugar
200 g/7 oz (1⅓ cups plus 1 tablespoon)
  ground rye malt
¼ tablespoon yeast

Pour 3 litres/5 UK pints (12½ cups) water into a large pot and bring to the boil. Dissolve the sugar in the boiling water. Remove the pot from the heat, add the malt, then leave the mixture to cool down to about 35°C/95°F. Add the yeast, mix well, then pour into a glass demijohn, or another suitable fermentation vessel.

Leave overnight at room temperature and decant into sterilized bottles on the second day. Store in the fridge from then on and consume within a few days. If CO_2 build-up from the fermentation becomes too great, the bottles could explode, so don't keep them in the fridge too long, without venting out excess pressure from time to time.

GLOSSARY

ALDER WOOD

A type of wood from the birch family often used for smoking and planking, the technique of directly roasting fish and game on hardwood in a way that preserves moisture. It has a light flavour that works well with poultry and fish, particularly whitefish (page 172).

ARRACK

An alcoholic spirit distilled from sugar cane, rice, molasses or the sap of coconut or date palms. Produced in India, Sri Lanka and Java, Arrack is used in Sweden for pastries, confectionaries, and most commonly, a liqueur called *punsch* (page 717), which is similar to *grogg*. Can be found in specialty stores or ordered online.

AUKS

Auks (*Alcidae*) are a family of birds that live on the open seas and only go ashore to breed. This is where the populations on the northern Nordic islands and coastal regions hunt the birds themselves and also, in some places, collect their eggs. In Iceland, the auks or *svartfugl* (black birds) are commonly eaten even today. And each spring their eggs are an eagerly awaited delicacy, picked from the steep cliffs of the northern part of the island by people whose families have had the right to forage for eggs on particular sites for many generations. On the Faroe Islands, these same types of eggs used to be a very common and important trade commodity, especially for those living on the outer islands. Today, partly because of the declining number of all seabirds, like the auks, and partly because of the great personal risk it involves to climb the cliffs, no one there collects eggs commercially. In some parts of Iceland and in the Faroe Islands people still net puffins, which are also a member of the auk family. This is described in more detail in the section on puffins (pages 279–281).

The three most commonly eaten birds of the auk family in the Nordic region are the razorbill (*Alca torda*), the common guillemot or common murre (*Uria aalge*) and the Atlantic puffin (*Fratercula arctica*).

All of these birds subsist on a diet of sea life, from which they take flavour. They taste to me a little like fatty fish, like mackerel or herring, when cooked. In most traditional recipes they are braised, often with sweet things, but in more recent recipes they are also fried pink. In many recipes it is said that they should marinate in different things overnight – milk, beer, berry juices, etc. – to draw the fishy flavour out of the bird. I say, embrace that glorious fishy flavour instead of trying to mask it, or eat another type of bird instead.

BAKER'S AMMONIA

Also known as ammonium carbonate. A classic leavener and an ancestor of modern baking powder that was originally made from the ground antlers of reindeer. It leads to a crispier bake and has a pungent smell during cooking, which dissipates.

BAKER'S PEEL

A flat, shovel-like tool made from wood and used to slide bread or pizza into an oven.

BARLEY FLOUR

A non-wheat, low-fat flour made from grinding whole barley. Can sometimes be substituted with other non-wheat flours, like cornmeal, buckwheat or rice flour.

BENZOIC ACID

A colourless and crystalline acid that, when combined with sodium hydroxide, creates the sodium benzoate used as a food preservative. Benzoic acid occurs naturally in fruits and berries like prunes, plums, cranberries and cloudberries.

BITTER ALMONDS

A rarely commercialised type of almond that is slightly broader and shorter than the common sweet almond and contains about 50% of the fixed oil that occurs in sweet almonds. These can be poisonous if consumed in large quantities and are banned in the US, despite the believed health benefits of its oil in small quantities. Though they have slightly less flavour, almond and bitter almond extract can be used as substitutes.

BLACKCURRANT LEAVES

A leaf of the blackcurrant shrub. With sweet, earthy notes, the leaves are sometimes used to flavour pickles like Brined Cucumbers (page 660) and help keep them crunchy.

BLEAK ROE

Also known as *kalix löjrom* caviar. A Swedish delicacy of roe from the bleak, a freshwater whitefish, that is harvested during the autumn (fall) spawning season in northern Sweden. Most commonly served with crème fraîche, diced red onion and chives, a slice of lemon, a dill sprig, and toasted bread, as on page 179.

BOG MYRTLE

Also known as sweet gale. Its foliage releases a sweet resinous scent, and its slightly bitter properties made it a common additive to early Scandanavian beers. Bog myrtle beers are still brewed on the west coast of Norway, and the shrub is likewise still widely used in Sweden to flavour Aquavit (page 714).

BREWER'S YEAST

Used to brew beer, this yeast is made from a one-celled fungus. It can also be used for nutritional supplements, as it is a rich source of vitamins and minerals. Yeast extract or nutritional yeast may be used as a substitute.

TO BROWN

To cook food briefly over high heat so that it turns brown, often to enhance flavour or texture.

BROWN BEANS

A rare type of bean cultivated solely on Öland Island and often used in the preparation of Swedish brown bean stew, which is typically served with fried bacon (page 141).

BRUN FARIN

Also known as soft brown sugar or light brown sugar. Often used to make cakes or pastries like the Brown Sugar Yeast Cake (page 549).

BUTTERFAT

The natural fatty constituent of cows' milk and the chief component of butter. Milk and cream are often sold according to the amount of butterfat they contain. Full-fat (whole) milk usually has around 3.5%, whipped cream can have between 30% and 35%, and double (heavy) cream contains at least 36%. Too little butterfat will leave a dish watery and too much will leave it greasy and sticky.

CARTOUCHE

A round piece of baking (parchment) paper that covers the surface of a stock, soup or sauce to prevent the liquid from evaporating or forming a skin as it cooks.

CASINGS

A material that encloses the filling of a sausage. Natural casings are made from the intestines of animals, like pigs and cows, whereas artificial casings are mostly made from processed collagen. Natural casings must be soaked in fresh water (20–30°C/68–86°F) before using. Soak sheep casings for at least 45 minutes, pig casings for at least 2 hours or overnight, and cow casings for at least 12 hours or overnight.

CASSIA CINNAMON

Also known as Saigon cinnamon. An evergreen tree whose bark can be used in stick or ground form to provide a spicy-warm flavour to confectionery, desserts, pastries and meat. It is thicker and coarser than classic cinnamon, which can serve as a substitute if used in a smaller amount than that for which the recipe calls.

CAUL FAT

A lacy, fatty membrane that encases the internal organs of animals like cows, sheep and pigs (the most common type of caul fat). Often used for wrapping pâtés or sausages, it comes in sheets and can be bought from most butchers.

CHEESE MOULD

A container in which freshly made cheese is put to set. It consolidates the curds and gives finished cheese its desired shape.

CHERRY LEAVES

A leaf from the cherry tree that can be eaten when salted and pickled (which gives it a salty-sour taste) but is poisonous when eaten raw. Sometimes used to flavour Brined Cucumbers (page 660).

CHINESE MUSHROOM SOY SAUCE

A dark soy sauce that is infused with either dried straw mushrooms or dried Chinese black mushrooms. It can serve as a table condiment and be used to add an earthy flavour to dishes (particularly red meats).

CHINOIS

A cone-shaped metal strainer with a very fine mesh used for straining custards, purées, stocks, sauces and items that need to have a very smooth texture or very clear appearance.

CLOUDBERRIES

A type of amber-coloured wild berry native to the Arctic and subarctic regions of the North Temperate Zone. They are rich in Vitamin C and have a particular place of honour in Swedish cooking. Raspberries make good substitutes, though they are stronger in flavour.

COCONUT FAT

An oil extracted by grating and pressing the flesh of mature coconuts. It is liquid at room temperature, does not taste overpoweringly of coconut, and can be used as a healthy replacement for butter or olive oil.

COD CHEEK

A medallion of boneless flesh found either side of the codfish jaw. Often high in taste and fat, they are most similar to scallops with respect to cooking properties.

COD TONGUE

A gelatinous piece of flesh from the throat of the codfish (not actually the tongue). Often served fried, the flavour and texture falls somewhere between a cod fillet and a whole soft-shell clam.

TO COLD-SMOKE

A process of flavouring or preserving food by exposing it to wood smoke at a low temperature, thus preventing it from cooking and helping to retain moisture. This process uses the naturally occurring compounds in smoke to extend further the food's shelf life. Cold smoked-foods are often cooked before eating. (For more information, see page 416.)

COLOSTRUM

A form of milk produced by the mammary glands of mammals in late pregnancy and the few days after giving birth.

CULTURED DAIRY

A type of dairy food that has been fermented with lactic acid bacteria in order to increase the shelf life of the product while simultaneously enhancing the taste and improving the digestibility of the milk. Yogurt and sour cream are the two most common cultured dairy foods.

CURED COD'S ROE

Cod eggs that have been salted and preserved, either by brining or dry salting. Bright and salty, the roe is traditionally sliced thinly or ground and sprinkled on top of dishes for added flavour and texture. See image on page 672.

TO DEGLAZE

To add liquid like stock to a pan to loosen and dissolve brown food particles that are stuck to its bottom. These particles have lots of deep flavour and can be used to season sauces, gravies, and soups.

DEHYDRATOR

A device that preserves raw food by drying it at a low temperature. This process is especially helpful for fresh foods like mushrooms (page 126), as dehydration increases lifespan while decreasing volume for easier storage.

DILL FLOWERS

An umbrella-shaped compound flower composed of many tiny blossoms that has a stronger flavour than the dill seeds. It retains its shape and colour well when added to jars of pickles.

DRIED BITTER ORANGE PEEL

An ingredient consisting of the dehydrated peel of bitter oranges, such as the Seville variety. Its mild and slightly savoury citrus flavour makes it especially good for marinades and baking. Orange or mandarin zest work as close substitutes.

DRIED ROSEHIPS

A dried version of the cherry-sized fruit of the rose bush left behind after the bloom has died. One of the most concentrated sources of Vitamin C available, dried rosehips are citrusy and sour and often used to flavour jelly, jam, soup, oil, and tea.

ELECTRIC HOTPLATE

A portable electric cooker on which food can be cooked directly. Used especially for making flatbreads. See illustration on page 515.

FARINSOCKER

A brown sugar consisting of sugar crystals and dark brown cane sugar syrup, *farinsocker* is less refined than plain white sugar and has a slightly spicy taste that lends itself well to baking and marinades.

FERMENTATION VESSEL

A special sterilized, airlocked container in which sugars and yeasts can ferment without attracting unwanted organisms. These vessels come in plastic, stainless steel, and glass and are often used for home brewing wines and malt beverages, like Sugar Wine (page 722) or the Finnish May Day Brew (page 720).

FILMJÖLK

A Nordic cultured dairy product made from soured milk. Similar to yogurt, but produced at a lower temperature and using different bacteria and cultures, it has a different taste and texture. It is the modern version of the traditional product *surmjölk* and can be found in some cake or cheese recipes.

FLOUR

Try to use good-quality flour, as this is the foundation of most of your baking. When a recipe calls for 'weak (soft) wheat flour', if you are in the UK use plain flour plus cornflour, which lowers the protein content of the flour and subsequently provides the tenderness necessary for a good cake. If you are based in the US, use good-quality unbleached flour, which has a more natural pale cream colour, rather than bleached flour, which is very white and has been treated with chemicals. For 'weak (soft) wheat flour' use unbleached cake flour.

By contrast, strong wheat flour (strong bread flour in the UK and US) provides a high protein content that gives plenty of structure to bread doughs. Rye flour – used for making a variety of grain products – can vary in density (fine or coarse), but also in colour (light, medium, or dark), depending upon its intended use and the amount of bran in the flour. Flours can vary in water content, so if your dough or batter seems dry after following the recipe exactly, you can always add a tiny bit more liquid.

GINGER, DRIED

A tangy, spicy form of ginger that is stronger than the fresh root and can be candied for use in desserts or powdered for use in stews, casseroles and other dishes. Known for its beneficial affects on stomach ailments. Allspice, cinnamon, mace or nutmeg can be used as substitutes.

GOLDEN SYRUP

Also known as light treacle (light molasses). Similar in appearance to honey and often used as a substitute sweetener when honey is unavailable, golden syrup is sweeter in taste than dark treacle (molasses).

GORO BISCUIT IRON

A cooking appliance consisting of two hinged metal plates moulded to create the sophisticated patterns found on goro biscuits (page 572). The modern versions can sit atop a stove to cook.

GRÄDDFIL

A dairy product made from cream with added lactic acid bacteria, which gives a thickened, slightly sour result. Less sour than yogurt, the closest substitute is sour cream, though some sour creams can have a fat content close to 18%, whereas *gräddfil* has 12% fat.

GRAHAM FLOUR

A type of unbleached and unrefined whole-wheat flour in which the components (bran, germ and endosperm) are ground separately, which creates a coarse-textured flour with a good shelf-life.

GROUND RYE MALT

A coarse flour made from whole dried germinated rye grains. Containing a strong, but not overly aggressive, malty and bitter flavour, this type of rye produces breads and beers that pair well with sausages and meats. Standard rye would work as a substitute.

GROUND ELDER LEAVES

A common woodland plant that is popular in Sweden. The leaves smell and taste mildly like carrot with a slightly nuttier undertone. Best eaten in the springtime, before the flowers grow and the leaves become too bitter. Avoid eating once the plant has flowered.

HARDANGER ROLLER

A rolling pin made of knobbed disks that create a pattern of dimples or small squares on dough. Used to make the Flatbread from Hardanger (page 512).

HELMI POTATO PEARLS

A gluten-free brand of instant mashed potato made primarily from potato starch. Can be used to give porridges or pastries a moist, soft texture.

HEMVETE FLOUR

Flour used for making *hemvete*, a black bread with rye, coffee and caraway seeds, made in the Finnish region of Åland.

HERBAMARE®

A combination of organic herbs, vegetables and sea salt (celery, leek, watercress, onions, chives, parsley, lovage, garlic, basil, marjoram, rosemary, thyme, and kelp) that adds flavour in cooking or serves as a table salt replacement.

JUNIPER BERRY

A female seed cone produced by the various species of junipers. It is not a true berry but a cone with unusually fleshy and merged scales, which give it a berry-like appearance. It is spicy and aromatic, can be used fresh or dried and provides the main flavouring for gin and some Finnish beers.

KNOBBED ROLLING PIN

A traditionally styled pin used to roll out dough. See illustration on page 511.

KOSKENKORVA VIINA

A clear spirit drink that is similar to vodka, produced in western Finland and made from high purity ethanol that is diluted with spring water and a small amount of sugar.

KRANSEKAGE MOULD

A circular mould with ring-shaped cavities and used to bake *Kransekake*, a traditional Danish and Norwegian confection usually eaten on special occasions. See illustration on page 605.

LAUFABRAUÐSJÁRN

A rolling tool used to create the leaf-like, geometric patterns on a traditional kind of Icelandic Leaf Bread (page 514) eaten in the Christmas season.

LEAF LARD

The highest grade of lard (pig fat), obtained from the soft fat around the kidneys and inside the loin. It has a high smoke point and little pork flavour, making it ideal for frying and baking.

LINGONBERRY

A bright red berry, similar to the cranberry, and also known as the cowberry. Appears on small evergreen shrubs and can be used as a preservative or as an ingredient in its own right.

LITMUS PAPER

Paper used to indicate the acidity or alkalinity of a substance.

LYE

A strong alkaline liquor rich in potassium carbonate extracted from wood ashes. Food-grade lye can be used for tenderising, curing or adding colour and texture. Highly corrosive, so take extra care when using and do not allow to come into contact with skin.

MALTING (*IMELLYTTÄMINEN*)

To convert the starch of cereal kernels into sugar via the process of steeping, germination and drying.

MANDOLINE

A kitchen tool with adjustable blades for thinly slicing vegetables and other food.

MARROWFAT PEAS

A mature green pea that has been allowed to dry out naturally in the field, rather than be harvested while still young.

MESSMÖR

Whey butter produced when cream is separated from curds during cheese-making. With a firm texture and a slightly cheesy and acidic flavour, whey butter is typically oilier, less shiny, and lower in fat than commercial butters.

MYSA

Liquid whey manufactured and sold in Iceland. While this whey can be used to add freshness to game recipe, such as the Icelandic Christmas Grouse (page 286), it can also be collected as a natural by-product when making Skyr (page 73).

NETTLES

A herbaceous flowering plant whose stinging quality is neutralised when cooked.

PASHA MOULD

A wooden pyramid-shaped mould that is lined with muslin (cheesecloth) and used to let the mixture set in the process of making Pasha (a traditional Finnish dessert served for Easter, page 636).

PALE

A specific Norwegian categorization by size, of saithe (*Pollachius virens*). Specimens of saithe weighing more than 3 kg (6¾ lb) are referred to as *sej*; the really small ones are called *mort*, or *pale-mort*; and everything in between is called *pale*. *Pale* saithe is essential for making the broth in a traditional Fish Soup from Bergen (page 237).

PEA FLOUR

A flour that is milled from yellow split peas that have been roasted, dried and ground. Used to make Pea Flour Flatbread (page 510), this type of flour harkens back to the time when dried legumes or pulses would be added to a dough to change its consistency.

PEARL SUGAR

A type of sugar made from large blocks that have been crushed and broken up into rock salt-sized granules. It has a high melting point, resulting in granules that stay crunchy without crystallizing.

PIG'S PLUCK

The lungs, heart and liver of a pig.

PILOT WHALE BLUBBER

A layer beneath the skin of a pilot whale where the fat is stored. Also see SPIK.

PILOT WHALE MEAT

An important food source in the Faroe Islands. The hunted whale meat is salted or dried for eating all year round.

PIZZA OVEN

An oven consisting of a baking chamber made of fireproof brick, concrete, stone or clay and that is traditionally wood-fired.

PLÄTTJÄRN PAN

A frying pan or skillet with round indentations used to make mini-crepes.

PORK BACK FAT

A cut of hard fat taken from under the skin of a pig's back. It is typically used in sausages and can be cured as a delicacy in its own right Like most animal fats, it has a high smoking point, so it is good for frying.

POTASH

The common name for various potassium-containing compounds that are found in seawater, and can be mined or manufactured. Its ability to temper mild toxins makes it ideal for soaking very bitter substances, like Icelandic Moss (page 132), prior to cooking to increase digestibility.

PURSLANE

A shrub that grows on salt marshes, with salty-tasting leaves. Compared to other edible plants, it contains the highest amount of omega-3 fats and 10 to 20 times more melatonin.

RÅGSIKT FLOUR

A mix of sifted bread flour (60%) and rye flour (40%) found in Sweden. Often used to make thick, somewhat dense breads, such as the Golden Syrup Loaf (page 496) or Scaniana Rye Breads (page 502).

RÅGSIKTSKAKA

A traditionally round Swedish bread made from wheat and rye flour.

RÆSTUR FISKUR

A Faroese delicacy of fermented mature fish.

RENNET

A complex of enzymes produced in the stomachs of calves, lambs or goats that causes proteins in milk to form a curd. It is used in the production of most cheeses and can be found in both tablet and liquid forms as well as in animal and vegetable forms.

RIVOR (BIRCH BARK)

A type of bark previously used to weave the baskets in which Finnish Rye Malt Pudding (page 634) would be distributed. Today these puddings are almost always sold in cardboard boxes.

ROCK PTARIGAN (*LAGOPUS MUTA*)

A medium-sized variety of grouse most often found in countries north of the Arctic Circle.

ROLLED RYE FLAKES

The hulled kernels of rye grains that are roasted, steamed and rolled into flakes.

RØMME

A Norwegian heavy sour cream usually containing about 20% fat in industrial production and 35% fat in the artisanal/traditional type called *seter-rømme*. It can be substituted with crème fraîche or other soured cream products with similar fat contents. rømme is used as both a condiment, as with Norwegian Waffles (page 456), and as a main component in dishes like Norwegian Sour Cream Porridge (page 468).

ROSEROOT LEAVES

Small grey-green leaves of the roseroot plant. Juicy and fibrous in texture and high in vitamins A and C, they add a slightly bitter flavour to dishes. Can be eaten cooked or raw.

ROWAN BERRIES

A bitter, red fruit of the rowan tree that is poisonous to humans when raw but can be eaten when cooked. High in pectin, the berries work well as a jelly (page 691).

RYE BRAN

The hard outer layers of the rye cereal grain.

RYE FLOUR

A powder made by grinding rye cereal grains. Can be fine or coarse.

SAITHE

A versatile saltwater white fish with firm flesh that carries flavour well, and is often salted or smoked. Also known as coley (UK) and pollock (US).

SALT PORK

A cut from the belly or side of the pig that has been salt-cured, but not smoked, and is often blanched before use to extract some of the salt.

SAMBAL OELEK

A bright red, raw chili paste, originally from Indonesia, with a sharp-sweet taste. Used to add a depth of spice to stews, like Falu Sausage Stroganoff (page 418).

SANDALWOOD, GROUND

An aromatic flavouring made from the ground wood of the Santalum tree. Its most typical culinary use is in *ansjovis*, the Swedish dish of cured sprats as well as spiced herring. Also referred to as sandalwood dust or powder.

SHEEP'S STOMACH

A form of offal sometimes used as casing (see CASING) or as an ingredient in its own right, such as tripe.

SKRÄDMJÖL

A flour of Finnish origin, now made in the Swedish province of Värmland from roasted oat kernels.

SLAKED LIME

A colourless crystal or white powder most commonly used for clarifying, binding and pickling. Also known as calcium hydroxide. Unprotected exposure can cause chemical burns so take extreme care when using and do not allow to come into contact with skin.

SMETANA

A central and Eastern European dairy product made from soured double (heavy) cream. It is favoured in cooking as it typically has a high fat content, which prevents it from splitting when heated.

TO SMOKE

To expose cured meat or fish products to smoke from burning or smoldering material for the purposes of preserving them and increasing their palatability by adding flavour. (For more information, see page 416.)

SMOKER

A chamber in which meats, vegetables and other ingredients are smoked. Can be used for slow-cooking, barbecuing, roasting and hot/cold smoking.

SOCKERDRICKA

A Swedish soft drink first produced in the 1800s. It was traditionally brewed and flavoured with ginger, whereas modern versions are made with carbonated water and fruit flavourings that make the beverage similar to *Fruktsoda* (the Swedish equivalent to Sprite or 7Up).

SODIUM SILICATE

Also known as water glass. A preserving agent that can be used to keep eggs, such as those from a northern fulmar (page 290), fresh for months.

SPEKEMAT

A generic term for Norwegian salted and dried meats made from mutton or pork.

SPELT

An ancient species of wheat with an inedible outer husk, and a nutrient-rich bran and grain.

SPIK (WHALE BLUBBER)

A layer beneath the skin of a whale where its fat is stored. Also see PILOT WHALE BLUBBER.

SPRAT

A small, oil-rich, herring-like fish found in the North East Atlantic, Adriatic and Mediterranean seas.

STEAM OVEN

An oven that boils water from an inbuilt reservoir to create a cloud of steam within the oven chamber, which helps achieve crisp crusts and prevents nutrients from being leeched from vegetables. In some cases, using a covered steamer basket over simmering water will achieve the same effect.

TO STERILISE A GLASS JAR

Heat the oven to 130°C/266°F and wash the jar and lid in hot, soapy water. Place the jar and lid on a baking sheet and place in the oven until it dries completely. Remove from the oven and fill while the jar is still hot. Do not fill hot jars with cold food, as this may cause them to shatter.

STRUVOR IRON

A cooking appliance with a long metal rod and decorative shapes that attach to one end used to make traditional Scandinavian biscuits like Rosettes (page 555).

SÚPUJURTIR

A special mixture of dried vegetables and herbs, including carrots, celery and lovage, that is most typically used in soups (for example, the Icelandic Meat Soup on page 346).

SUET

A cooking fat made from beef or mutton that is obtained from the area around the kidney and loins. Its high smoke point and ability to add texture and moisture without adding a strong meaty flavour makes it ideal for frying and pastry making.

SURMJÖLK

A traditional Nordic dairy product made from soured milk. Similar in character to runny yogurt. Also see FILMJÖLK

SWEDISH RYE FLOUR

See RÅGSIKT FLOUR.

THERMOMETER

A thermometer used to measure the temperature of a cooking sugar solution and which can read extremely high temperatures (usually up to 200°C/400°F).

TYRKISK PEBER

A hot, peppery and salty hard liquorice sweet that was created in Denmark in the 1970s. Sometimes crushed and added to vodka to make a liquorice liqueur (page 713).

UNPASTEURISED MILK

A fresh milk that has not been pasteurised (heated to 72°C/161°F) or homogenised. Many believe that it tastes better and is more nutritious than homogenised milk, but distribution is carefully regulated as it has the potential to contain harmful bacteria.

WEAK (SOFT) WHEAT FLOUR

See FLOUR

WORT

A sweet liquid drained from the brewing process of mashing grain with water, which is then fermented to make beer and whiskey.

YMER

A Danish dairy product that resembles *filmjölk* and is made by fermenting milk before draining its whey, resulting in a higher content of solids, but a relatively low fat content of about 4%.

ÅLAGILLE

An annual Swedish feast that takes place between August and November. Traditionally held in an eel shed on the seafront, where various types of cooked eel are eaten.

DIRECTORY

Many of the special ingredients and equipment that you will need for the recipes are widely available in markets, grocery stores and supermarkets in major cities.

If they are not available near you, here is a list of selected online suppliers specializing in Nordic ingredients, utensils and cookware.

UNITED KINGDOM

www.scandikitchen.co.uk
Stocks an array of edible goods, including flours, sweets, alcohol and fresh yogurt from Scandinavian brands.

www.danishfooddirect.co.uk
Specializes in Danish products, particularly seafood, meats and cheese. Ships its fresh and packaged food items internationally.

www.totallyswedish.com
Sells everything Swedish from biscuits (cookies) to fishballs. Also offers classic pantry basics like *filmjölk* and golden syrup.

UNITED STATES

www.ingebretsens.com
Stocks a wide selection of specialist Nordic cooking equipment, including rosette cutters, *lefse* rolling pins (also used to make flatbread), and *kransekake* rings.

www.scandinavianfoodstore.com
Stocks fresh meats and seafood (like *fenalår*, *flaeskesteg*, *lutefisk* and smoked cod) as well as jams, candy and biscuits (cookies) from Norway, Sweden, Denmark and Finland. Also carries traditional waffle irons and *krumkake* irons.

www.lefsetime.com
Offers a large selection of Nordic cookery equipment and a limited selection of pantry items.

www.kingarthurflour.com
Stocks many of the specialty flours, grains and hard-to-find yeasts used in Nordic recipes. Mostly ships to North America, but offers international shipping.

www.scandinavian-south.com/cookware
Carries Nordic sweets, licorice, crispbreads, biscuits (cookies) and baking mixes.

www.lindensweden.com
A wholesaler that carries some specialty Nordic baking equipment, like the *lefse* rolling pin.

AUSTRALIA

www.swedishgoodies.com.au
Stocks a mix of Nordic ingredients, confectionary, snacks and pantry basics as well as canned items like herring, crispbreads, biscuits (cookies) and mushrooms.

INTERNATIONAL

www.ikea.com
The food market offers fresh and packaged Swedish goods like lingonberry jam, Scandinavian ginger biscuits and *matjes* herring.

INDEX

RECIPE NOTES

Butter should always be unsalted, unless otherwise specified.

All herbs are fresh, unless otherwise specified.

Eggs and individual vegetables and fruits, such as onions and apples, are assumed to be medium, unless otherwise specified.

All sugar is white caster (superfine) sugar and all brown sugar is cane or demerara unless otherwise specified.

All cream is 36–40% fat heavy whipping cream unless otherwise specified.

All milk is full-fat (whole) at 3% fat, homogenized and lightly pasteurized, unless otherwise specified.

All yeast is fresh, unless otherwise specified.

All salt is fine sea salt, unless otherwise specified.

Breadcrumbs are always dried, unless otherwise specified.

Cooking times are for guidance only, as individual ovens vary. If using a fan (convection) oven, follow the manufacturer's instructions concerning oven temperatures.

Exercise a high level of caution when following recipes involving any potentially hazardous activity, including the use of high temperatures, open flames, slaked lime, and when deep-frying. In particular, when deep-frying, add food carefully to avoid splashing, wear long sleeves, and never leave the pan unattended.

Some recipes include raw or very lightly cooked eggs, meat, or fish, and fermented products. These should be avoided by the elderly, infants, pregnant women, convalescents, and anyone with an impaired immune system.

Exercise caution when making fermented products, ensuring all equipment is spotlessly clean, and seek expert advice if in any doubt.

When no quantity is specified, for example of oils, salts, and herbs used for finishing dishes or for deep-frying, quantities are discretionary and flexible.

All herbs, shoots, flowers and leaves should be picked fresh from a clean source. Exercise caution when foraging for ingredients; any foraged ingredients should only be eaten if an expert has deemed them safe to eat.

Both metric and imperial measures are used in this book. Follow one set of measurements throughout, not a mixture, as they are not interchangeable.

All spoon and cup measurements are level, unless otherwise stated. 1 teaspoon = 5 ml; 1 tablespoon = 15 ml.

Australian standard tablespoons are 20 ml, so Australian readers are advised to use 3 teaspoons in place of 1 tablespoon when measuring small quantities.

Phaidon Press Limited
Regent's Wharf
All Saints Street
London N1 9PA

Phaidon Press Inc.
65 Bleecker Street
New York, NY 10012
www.phaidon.com

First published 2015
Reprinted 2016 (twice)
© 2015 Phaidon Press Limited
ISBN 978 0 7148 6872 1

A CIP catalogue record for this book
is available from the British Library.

Commissioning Editor: Emilia Terragni
Project Editor: Sophie Hodgkin
Production Controller: Amanda Mackie

Designed by Henrik Nygren Design
Photography by Magnus Nilsson
and Erik Olsson (recipes only)
Illustrations by Samantha Dion Baker

The publisher would like to thank Jane Ellis,
Lena Hall, Cindi Kruth, Laura Nicholl, Alysha
Owen, Lucy Rushbrooke, Jo Skullbacka, Ellie
Smith, Simon Wallhult and Kate Wanwimolruk
for their contributions to the book.

Printed in Italy